WHY WE FOUGHT

Film & History

The Film & History series is devoted to creative scholarly works that focus on how feature films and documentaries represent and interpret history. Books in the series explore the significant impact of motion pictures on our society and analyze films from a historical perspective. One goal of the series is to demonstrate how historical inquiry has been reinvigorated by the increased scholarly interest in the intersection of film and history. The Film & History series includes both established and emerging scholars and covers a diverse array of films.

Series Editors

Peter C. Rollins and John E. O'Connor

WHY WE FOUGHT

America's Wars in
Film and History

*Edited by Peter C. Rollins
and John E. O'Connor*

THE UNIVERSITY PRESS OF KENTUCKY

"The Great War Viewed from the 1920s: *The Big Parade*," by
Michael T. Isenberg, originally appeared in the journal
Film & History and is reprinted in this volume by permission.

Editorial and Sales Offices: The University Press of Kentucky
663 South Limestone Street, Lexington, Kentucky 40508-4008
www.kentuckypress.com

08 09 10 11 12   5 4 3 2 1

Library of Congress Cataloging-in-Publication Data

Why we fought : America's wars in film and history /
edited by Peter C. Rollins and John E. O'Connor.
    p.   cm.
Includes bibliographical references and index.
ISBN 978-0-8131-2493-3 (hardcover : alk. paper)
ISBN 978-0-8131-9191-1 (pbk. : alk. paper)
1. War films—History and criticism. 2. United States—History,
Military. I. Rollins, Peter C. II. O'Connor, John E.
PN1995.9.W3W53 2008
791.43'6581—dc22
                              2008006082

To the memory of those who served their country during America's wars—both at the battlefront and on the home front

CONTENTS

Robert Fyne

FOREWORD

American audiences have always enjoyed flag-waving war movies. They cheered when U.S. forces ran up San Juan Hill in the silent short *Tearing Down the Spanish Flag* (1898), hooted when Union troops attacked Confederate forces in *The Birth of a Nation* (1915), and whistled when Charlie Chaplin single-handedly captured the kaiser in *Shoulder Arms* (1918).

When the industry moved to balmy Southern California, the Hollywood moving picture became the country's most popular form of entertainment. Why wouldn't it? Using elaborate sound equipment, sophisticated sets, well-known writers, and established actors, these photodramas radiated with appeal. But the war film caught the nation's particular attention. With their strong patriotic messages, frontal attacks, and hand-to-hand fighting, these titles highlighted important victories and recalled glorious moments from recent history. Soon they also became instruments of learning. Moviegoers came to better understand the reasons for past confrontations and comprehend how battles were fought and won.

Always in favor, this genre—despite its ups and downs, changing ideologies, and blatant revisionism—appealed to young men yearning for the adventures they had never realized or, conversely, to U.S. veterans recalling moments of triumph. Why not? Isn't the motion picture industry called the dream factory?

Often criticized and frequently praised, Hollywood's war dramas offered moving evidence that the republic would prevail. When the farmers of the Mohawk Valley were attacked, Henry Fonda stepped forward. Remember Audie Murphy's foray into the Confederate lines? And don't forget Gary

Cooper, who captured scores of Germans in the Great War. Give Spencer Tracy some credit too. What about his Tokyo bombing raid? Say a prayer for William Holden, whose Korean War death validated America's anticommunist determination. Stand up and cheer for Mel Gibson, who brought his men home from Vietnam.

With all its glories and tragedies, its triumphs and mistakes, the Hollywood war film remains a prominent fixture in the nation's moviegoing experience. In his *Born on the Fourth of July* memoir, Ron Kovic admits that, as an impressionable teenager, watching John Wayne blasting Japanese pillboxes in *Sands of Iwo Jima* inspired him to join the Marine Corps and volunteer for action. One can only speculate how many other young men were similarly influenced by combat motion pictures. For a broader public, these feature films also instill pride, inspiration, loyalty, and respect; they foster an enduring sense of patriotism and provide humble reminders of the high cost of freedom. Not only do these screenplays mirror a nation's past, but they also offer tangible evidence of the ways millions of Americans have become devoted, as was General Douglas MacArthur, to "duty, honor, and country."

ACKNOWLEDGMENTS

Deborah Carmichael of *Film & History* was regularly involved in bringing this project to completion and deserves the highest praise for her professionalism. Her diligence on behalf of the 2005 conference "War in Film & History," from which these chapters emerged, assured a strong start for this project. (See conference information at www.uwosh.edu/filmandhistory/.)

Debbie Olson was a diligent reader of manuscripts, taking up the task when the editors found themselves too close to the materials.

Leslie Fife contributed document design skills to shape the final manuscript into a usable text. Everyone in the popular culture movement owes a debt of gratitude to this conscientious and diligent colleague, especially in her role as program chair for the national meetings of the Popular Culture Association and the American Culture Association.

Susan Rollins provided fruit snacks and offered Internet advice.

The editors are grateful to Paul Fleming for his knowledge of the military and its representation in documentary and feature film media.

As with our six previous books, most of the illustrations contained herein are from our personal collections of press kits and photos acquired in more than thirty years of film research in the United States, Great Britain, and Europe. The Imperial War Museum, the Library of Congress, the U.S. National Archives, the Museum of Modern Art's Film Stills Archive, the UCLA Film and Television Archive, the Margaret Herrick Library of the Academy of Motion Picture Arts and Sciences, and the Museum of Broadcasting were all indispensable contributors to our research, and we thank the staffs of these institutions for their help. Some materials were supplied by veterans of the

Gulf and Iraq wars. Also forthcoming were the Film Archive, the Edmon Low Library, Special Collections; KERA-TV, Dallas; the Marine Corps Museum; the Marine Corps Film Archive; the U.S. Army Historical Division; the U.S. Air Force Historical Division; the Swarthmore College Peace Collection; and the City Museum of Göttingen, Germany. Photofest of New York City and the George Grube Advertising Company of Oklahoma City provided images and press kits. Other stills and DVD covers are reproduced courtesy of Autumn Productions, Orion Pictures Corporation, 20th Century-Fox, Universal, Greenhouse Pictures/Subdivision Productions, Lions Gate, United Artists, Guerrilla News Network, HBO, Discovery Channel, NBC, and CNN.

John E. O'Connor and Peter C. Rollins

INTRODUCTION

Military conflicts have influenced American society and reshaped the lives of Americans in complex and subtle ways. Although public documents, legislative debates, and battlefield statistics may be the best sources for understanding some of the more traditional historical issues such as war aims, strategies, and logistical successes and failures, evidence from popular culture may show more clearly how wars can liberate and also corrupt nations morally, just as they can bankrupt them financially. On a more profound level, it can help us see how nations can be born and—like soldiers at the front—die in wars. Moreover, what Carl von Clausewitz describes as "the continuation of diplomacy by other means" (6) also involves the continuation of all sorts of other human concerns and interrelationships under pressures induced by war. *Why We Fought: America's Wars in Film and History* explores how motion pictures have influenced, reflected, and interpreted the American experience of war.

War, like other critical life situations, really does bring out the best and the worst in people. And the exigencies of war provide defining moments in people's lives. These universal principles were identified in the literature of the ancients and still surface in today's headlines. On an individual level, war places people in frightening situations they must face on their own, yet it also lays the foundation for friendships and support networks stronger than any other. Subtle yet powerful evidence of such relationships is found in the letters written home by members of the armed forces and in the images created by battlefield artists—as well as in popular films (Chenoweth).

Unfortunately, war encourages soldiers (and civilians) to dehumanize and demonize their enemies to make them easier to eliminate, but ironically, when warriors on opposing sides of a conflict are faced with similarly perilous situations, it initiates the preconditions for comradeship that few noncombatants can comprehend. Surely brothers in arms, even allied soldiers of different na-

Library of Congress

During America's wars, public art—which includes motion pictures—strives to foster national cohesion.

tional backgrounds, are wont to forget the prejudices they might have harbored before putting on the uniform and find, to their surprise, a fellowship where they least expected it. For example, the famous "Christmas exchange" on the battlefields of France (25 December 1914) is remembered for such a mutuality between armies engaged in deadly conflict—before and after the event. And if, on the battlefield, denying the existence of any God seems too absolute, there are surely very few atheists in foxholes. We have seen in letters, poetry, and video that the daily confrontation with mortality—in the trenches of World War I, on the landing beaches in the Pacific during World War II, out on patrol in Vietnam, or after an improvised explosive device incident in Iraq—can strip away superficial concerns, revealing human beings' stark need for God.

Some have argued that literature has been particularly successful in elucidating such perennial themes, but motion pictures have sometimes been even more poignant. Consider Erich Maria Remarque's novel *All Quiet on the Western Front* (1929) or Ambrose Bierce's short story "An Occurrence at Owl Creek Bridge" (1874). In both cases, it can be argued that the cinematic adaptations are even more forceful than the works of literature from which they were adapted. The first is a 1930 feature film spelling out the horrors

The motion picture version of *All Quiet on the Western Front* reached the world with its antiwar message.

of trench warfare in World War I from the perspective of youthful members of the German infantry (see chapter 8). The second is a very famous, short French film, *La rivière du hibou* (1962), about the experience of a Civil War–era Alabama farmer hanged on a bridge by Union soldiers and the desperate—yet futile—fantasies of survival that may have gone through his mind at the split second of his execution. There is an interesting contrast here to yet another war film that enhances its dramatic effect by drawing out time, *The Longest Day* (1962), which focuses on the first twenty-four hours of the 1944 Allied landing at Normandy, chronicling the critical period for both the invading Allies and the German defenders (see chapter 14).

Films about war often highlight cosmic ironies: for example, the feature film *The Victors* (1963) portrays a group of American GIs in World War II France who do not appear particularly victorious; indeed, they are the pathetic victims of an unfeeling command hierarchy—in this case, the U.S. Army, which decided that, as late as January 1945, executions for cowardice were still appropriate. In addition to political documentaries, feature films and television programs have questioned the wisdom of war. Some use black humor to satirize the very idea of war in the nuclear age, such as *Dr. Strangelove; or, How I Learned to Stop Worrying and Love the Bomb* (1964), a classic that, as the years go by, seems to become more outrageously entertaining. Films such as *Mr. Roberts* (1955) and *M*A*S*H* (1970) create humorous situations even in the midst of suffering. Some Hollywood warriors have been devoted to keeping themselves completely out of danger, such as Lieutenant Commander Charles Madison (James Garner) in *The Americanization of Emily* (1964), who does everything possible to keep himself safe in England rather than become a D-day statistic. And then there is Captain Yossarian (Alan Arkin) in the Mike Nichols adaptation of Joseph Heller's memorable *Catch-22* (1970), a World War II story that never would have cleared the Office of War Information during the conflict. A comic twist occurs in *Hail the Conquering Hero* (1944), in which Eddie Bracken, playing an American common man with the unlikely but unquestionably patriotic name Woodrow Lafayette Pershing Truesmith, is mistakenly given a combat hero's welcome on his return home, although, through no fault of his own, he was declared physically unfit and never saw service at all.

Why We Fought takes on more than a score of period feature films and some major documentaries along the lines of film scholarship developed over the last thirty years. Since the nineteenth century's professionalization of historical scholarship, most people's image of historical research has involved a sequestered university professor huddled over a dusty box of papers or squinting into a microfilm reader. In the public mind, at least, the more distant the events and the more explicit and more traditional the documentation, the more acceptable the interpretation. Yet, looking back from our own highly visual era, we notice that the oldest evidence of human experience is not in written manuscripts at all but in the iconic forms of cave paintings and physical artifacts left behind by ancient civilizations.

As scholars in the last three decades have broadened the types of questions that interest them—to include what is now called "popular memory"—they have turned to different kinds of evidence, such as motion pictures and television. Like the archaeologists studying images on cave walls, the work of popular culture scholars involves a different language and demands a different sensibility. They ask, Who were the filmmakers, and what influenced them to adopt the approaches they took? Who were the audiences for whom these films were originally produced, and what contemporary frames of reference influenced how those audiences made sense of the films they saw?

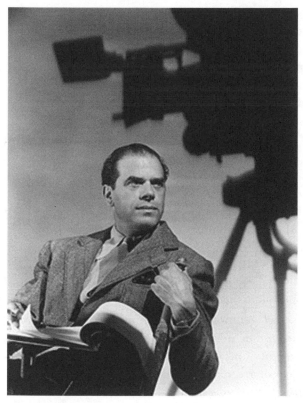

Museum of Modern Art/Film Stills Archive

Frank Capra: American spokesman.

After first studying a film's content, considering the accuracy of the information presented and the factors that may have influenced its production and reception, the second phase of historical analysis demands studying the film in the context of one or more of the four following frameworks for historical analysis, established not by the film itself but by the type of historical inquiry being undertaken (O'Connor):

Framework 1. A moving-image document as a representation of history. Does it tell a historical story? This might be any documentary or feature film that interprets a historical period or event.

Framework 2. A moving-image document as evidence for social or cultural history. Does a film made for a mass audience evoke the social or cultural values of the audience to which the producers were trying to appeal?

Framework 3. A moving-image document as evidence for historical fact. Does the film provide actual footage of a historical event as it took place in front of the camera?

Framework 4. A moving-image document as evidence for the history of film and television. Although historians' talents have been particularly valuable in urging the study of the paper trail (such as the studio archives or papers of the principals in the production process), there are also specific questions to be asked about the films themselves, dealing, for example, with the development of technology and the evolution of film style.

In relation to each of these four analytical frameworks, the information learned about content, production, and reception might have different meanings. A wartime propaganda documentary such as one of the films in Frank Capra's *Why We Fight* series, for example, would hardly be reliable as unbiased reporting from the front, but it could certainly be productive for the study of social and cultural values: the camera angles and characterizations chosen, even the manipulation of images (editing), offer insight into the way the filmmaker hoped to influence viewers. Knowing the role that government played in censoring newsreels, one would be loath to use such films as factual records of actual battlefield events, but when the records of the censoring agency, or even the edited scripts of the newsreel commentaries, are available, intriguing work can be done on the history of public information—and misinformation.

Most war films are representations of history—they tell a historical story about war or about individuals or groups of people, affirming, in the process, values, morals, and identities. Sometimes such films deal with recent history, such as the battle drama *Wake Island* (released 1 September 1942), a fact-based fictionalized account of U.S. marines valiantly defending a Pacific outpost immediately after the Japanese attack on Pearl Harbor. (Japanese planes attacked Wake Island on 8 December 1941, and the garrison surrendered on 23 December after killing some seven hundred Japanese adversaries and sinking four destroyers.) In life, as well as in the film, Wake Island was a microcosm of American determination and teamwork. On other occasions, despite the differences in weapons and tactics, producers have reached back into history to remark on the commonalities of war throughout the ages. Peter Watkins's *Battle of Culloden* (1965) contrasts the soldiers of the strictly disciplined and well-equipped British army with the poorly armed and discouraged Scots in April 1746 during the final Jacobite rising. The film is shocking in the verisimilitude of its hand-to-hand combat, and it is also thought provoking when one considers the different style of combat American soldiers were experiencing in 1965 in the jungles and rice paddies of Southeast Asia.

As should be expected, Hollywood films representing past American wars have often been influenced by events going on at the time of their production. Producers at 20th Century-Fox argued all the way to the top of the studio

The main title was rendered in needlepoint for antique effect.

hierarchy in the late 1930s that making a film about the American Revolution while the Germans were threatening Europe would not compromise Americans' resolve to support Great Britain—as long as the film cast American Loyalists and their Indian allies as the enemies, rather than British regulars. The project went forward, and John Ford's *Drums Along the Mohawk* became a prime release of 1939 (see chapter 1).

Similarly, when Warner Bros. sought access to federal lands and cavalry horses for *They Died With Their Boots On* in early 1941, the studio pointed out to the War Department that "all possible consideration was given to the construction of a story which would have the best effect upon public morale in these present days of national crisis." It went on to suggest that "through the life of the hero [General Custer, played by Errol Flynn, eulogized for the sake of a new war effort], we have endeavored to show the real meaning of . . . what an officer is, what his standards and obligations are; what a regiment is and why it is something more than six hundred trained men." The film was scheduled for release, the studio observed, "at the moment when thousands of youths are being trained for commissions, and when hundreds of new and tradition-less units are being formed. If we can inspire these to some appreciation of a great officer and a great regiment in their own service, we shall have accomplished our mission" (MacKensie). To be sure, it is unusual to find such forthright statements of the motives of the moguls of the motion picture business. After all, the mission of the Hollywood studios has more often been oriented toward the bottom line than the recruiting line. But there should be no question that, thoughtfully approached, film—and its cousin, television—can become a valuable tool for understanding the gestalt of historical eras.

THE EIGHTEENTH AND NINETEENTH CENTURIES: REVOLUTION, CONQUEST, AND UNION

The American Revolution

This book opens with the American Revolution (1776–1783). Hollywood has made films about America's wars before Lexington and Concord—struggles in which the colonists fought beside the British against the French or the Spanish or the Indians allied with one or another of them—but the first conflict for which we can posit a national war effort was the War for Independence. John E. O'Connor discusses briefly a few of the earliest productions about the Revolution dating back to 1911, including the first feature film to deal with the subject, D. W. Griffith's *America* (1924). After providing this cinematic background, O'Connor concentrates on two major films about the Revolutionary War produced decades apart. Although *Drums Along the Mohawk* (1939) and *The Patriot* (2000) both deal with rural farming communities during the eighteenth century rather than the revolutionary centers of Boston, New York, and Philadelphia, they both also reflect contemporary concerns—in the first case, an impending war with Germany, and in the second case, the recent memory of America's traumatic debacle in Vietnam. Each historical interpretation opens a portal into its own time.

The producers of *Drums Along the Mohawk* at 20th Century-Fox, who hoped to profit from the success of Walter Edmunds's best-selling novel (1936), were sensitive about the English market; there were concerns that the film might be read as an attack on the Atlantic Alliance. Proponents argued that Edmunds's story would finesse this problem, because the aggression against the colonists in the Mohawk Valley was launched by Loyalists and Indians rather than British regulars or Hessians.

Studio heads were also concerned about earning back their investment, because the production was so expensive—driven by the costs of extensive set construction and shooting on location, not to mention the economics of filming in the new, complicated Technicolor process. When requesting assistance from

Columbia Pictures

Benjamin Martin (Mel Gibson) is finally aroused to the colonial cause after his family is attacked in *The Patriot.*

Washington to gain access to locations, they argued that the film would support the national interest by helping to prepare the public for the approaching war in Europe. The rationale of the producers comes through clearly in the detailed interoffice memos in the studio's extensive archives. *Drums Along the Mohawk* can also be understood in the context of evolving historical scholarship during the 1930s, which, in the histories of Samuel Eliot Morrison and Perry Miller, was rebounding to a more patriotic view after more than a decade of debunking by Charles Beard and such sardonic pundits as H. L. Mencken.

Director Roland Emmerich's *The Patriot* was produced under very different conditions. By the end of the twentieth century, the major studios no longer dominated the film industry; more and more films, like *The Patriot,* were the outcome of ad hoc collaborations among independent screenwriters, producers, and directors. *The Patriot* reflected both the state of scholarship on Revolutionary America and the world situation at the time of the film's production—as had *Drums Along the Mohawk* some sixty years before. As in the earlier film, the protagonist is a backcountry farmer inclined toward colonial separation but driven to support the war less by ideology than by personal motives—specifically, the callous murder of one of his seven children and the destruction of his home by the British. At a time when memories of America's role in Vietnam were still vivid in the public mind, *The Patriot* reawakened smoldering emotions. O'Connor explores both the historiographical and the cinematic interpretations.

The Mexican-American War

America's next war, the War of 1812, has attracted little attention from Hollywood. Films addressing it have focused on a few naval engagements plus Andrew Jackson's heroic leadership against the British during the Battle of New Orleans (1815). (See, for example, the two versions of *The Buccaneer*, made in 1938 and 1958.) It seems that the nation saw nothing heroic in a war fought principally through an embargo, a passive strategy at best and one deeply resented in states dependent on nautical trade. At the Hartford Convention in 1814, for example, New Englanders suffering from the naval embargo agitated for secession from a Union dominated by Virginians.

The next two chapters march forward to consider the defense of the Alamo in 1836 and the Mexican-American War of 1846–1848. Although the dramatic siege of the Alamo by Santa Anna's Mexican army was, in fact, part of an earlier war for Texan independence, it marked the onset of a continuing conflict between the United States and its southern neighbor. In the end, Texas was admitted to the United States in 1845, and the Treaty of Guadalupe Hidalgo in 1848 brought under U.S. control what are now west Texas, New Mexico, Arizona, and California. Frank Thompson's "Reprinting the Legend: The Alamo on Film" concentrates on the pivotal 1836 battle for the stronghold (now located in downtown San Antonio). For many, the brief—and unsuccessful—defense is a symbol of American grit and determination in the tradition of *Wake Island*. Thompson's role as historical consultant for the most recent treatment of the event, *The Alamo* (2004), adds an intriguing dimension to his discussion. Having spent time on the movie set, he has insightful observations, for example, on Billy Bob Thornton's characterization of Davy Crockett. Thompson credits the film with seeking to "embrace the emotional truth of the moment [of Crockett's death] while respecting the historical truth," although he admits that we do not know exactly how Crockett died. Thompson himself plays a state legislator in one contentious scene of John Lee Hancock's epic.

The "manifest destiny" extolled by such newspapers as the *Democratic Review* and by southern expansionists exploited the momentum of the Texas revolution, of which the Alamo was just one early episode. In 1998 KERA-TV of Dallas, Texas, broadcast a serious, in-depth television history of the Mexican-American War—calling the series *The U.S.-Mexican War (1846–1848)* and thereby implying the United States' aggression in the conflict. James Yates engaged in original research and found the writers, producers, and directors at KERA very cooperative. The war is little remembered in the United States; in contrast, *la intervención norteamericana* is a lively and sensitive issue in Mexico among both ordinary citizens and scholars. Funded by the National Endowment for the Humanities (NEH), the series was designed for broadcast by the Public Broadcasting Service (PBS) and was obliged to consider multiple perspectives. In four hours of television, the KERA production team blended narration, historical drawings, reenactments, and interviews to bring a distant conflict to life with both significant drama and thoughtful interpretation. Yates finds the resulting production to be a success for public television and for the cause of historical understanding, although he identifies some of the pitfalls of producing a visual history for television. His helpful comparison of the PBS series and feature films about the Mexican-American War complements the analysis provided by Thompson in the previous chapter.

The Civil War

The signal example of writing history on film in the last twenty years is the television series *The Civil War* (1990), an epic produced and directed by Ken Burns. Gary R. Edgerton takes on the daunting task of evaluating the sixteen-hour television series. Rather than adopting a single, dominant interpretation of the war, Burns tried "to embrace . . . a variety of viewpoints." As Edgerton explains, Burns accomplished this cinematic goal by weaving together four types of scenes: narrative descriptions, emotional chapters, "telegrams" (contemporary reactions to or observations about the evolving narrative in the words of a variety of individuals, such as Southern diarist Mary Chesnut and Northern lawyer George Templeton Strong), and editing clusters (montages of corroborating and conflicting observations that create "a collage of multiple viewpoints"). In this way, Edgerton believes, Burns bridges the divide between popular and professional history—clearly, a significant achievement. *The Civil War* was funded by the NEH and, more than any other such venture, made friends for public support of the arts on Capitol Hill and along Main Street America.

The second contribution on the American Civil War comes from Robert M. Myers, who argues that *Cold Mountain* (2003) attempts to "justify secession and account for the military defeat of the South." This Lost Cause approach began as early as the 1870s, promoting three ideas: "that the South fought for states' rights, not slavery"; that Robert E. Lee was "a military genius and a perfect embodiment of the Southern gentleman"; and that, "despite the heroism of the individual Confederate soldier, the North's overwhelming resources and numbers eventually forced the South to succumb." Myers places both the novel (1997) and the film version of *Cold Mountain* in the context of this popular paradigm, which he argues also holds true for the two best-known cinematic treatments of the war: *The Birth of a Nation* (1915) and *Gone with the Wind* (1939). He argues that although the source of the story, Charles Frazier's novel *Cold Mountain,* was steeped in the Lost Cause tradition, the subsequent adaptation of the screenplay by Englishman Anthony Minghella may have been additionally influenced by contemporary antiwar concerns.

The Twentieth Century: Total War

World War I

After the Civil War, U.S. military actions involved subduing American Indian populations on the western frontier, followed by the Spanish-American War in Cuba and the Philippines. Unlike these "splendid little wars," America's experience in World War I was fortuitously timed to mesh with Hollywood's growing capacity to reach millions of viewers. While Michael T. Isenberg concedes that war films were not particularly popular in the years immediately following World War I, he discounts the traditional wisdom that Americans in the 1920s rejected war and were overly embittered by the experience of World War I. The coming together of a talented trio set *The Big Parade* (1925) apart as the most memorable war film of the 1920s. King Vidor, Irving Thalberg, and Laurence Stallings were responsible for the film, which ran in New York's Astor Theater for ninety-six weeks, bringing in a total of $1.5 million. Although the soldiers in *The Big Parade* "yearn for the blessings of peace," Isenberg explains, they also demonstrate that "the doughboy is a committed civilian who, when aroused, becomes a dominant warrior." Two years later, William A. Wellman's *Wings* (1927) added momentum to this view by rendering World War I as a noble adventure in the skies over France.

The second contribution on the World War I era addresses images and documents often passed over by film scholars. James Latham explains that hundreds of advertisements were created to promote films to local exhibitors, who were "encouraged to see themselves not simply as merchants but as actively serving both their local communities and the country." Latham focuses on film advertisements that touted new technologies that could make a difference in combat—the machine gun, the submarine, the tank, the airplane. He discusses a series of such advertisements and how they helped shape wartime public opinion both directly and indirectly. He concludes that the promotion of war-related films "conveyed cultural meanings of patriotism and national identity, as well as reasons why the country was at war and why the public should participate." Reinforcing the messages of the films, "advertisements functioned to rally support for the war effort" and showed "how film could portray the leaders, heroes, villains, and victims of the war in ways that furthered national interests." Latham's chapter should remind scholars that film studies need to consider more than just the viewing experience.

Interim and Isolationism

World War I generated its share of heroes, but it also shocked America and the rest of the world with the costs—human and financial—of modern conflicts. The 1920s saw enlightened but ultimately unsuccessful efforts by international agencies to outlaw war. Three chapters deal with this interim period (1918–1941). David Imhoof devotes attention to the meaning of World War I films as they were viewed by the local audience of Göttingen, Germany. He concludes that, "like other cultural activities in Germany, local moviegoing in the interwar period aided the process of Nazification as much as national and international political events did." Göttingen had a smaller working class than most of its neighboring industrial cities, which may help explain its tendency toward conservatism on cultural as well as political issues. In the end, through a careful reading of the local newspapers, Imhoof is able to trace the local reception of two films: *Westfront 1918* (1930), the first German sound film about the war, and Hollywood's *All Quiet on the Western Front* (1930) in its German dubbed version. Although most reviewers approved of the realism and general antiwar orientation of *Westfront 1918*, *All Quiet on the Western Front* was met with "raucous protests" in the streets of Berlin and "direct appeals from politicians in Saxony, Brunswick, Thuringia, Württemberg, and Bavaria [that] eventually convinced the Appellate Censorship Board to reconsider the approval of the film." In the end, each of these films created a "popular platform for talking about politics."

John Whiteclay Chambers II studies the relationship between Hollywood and the isolationist debate in the United States between 1930 and 1941. He divides the movement into three distinct parts: a peace movement—internationalist, not isolationist—that advocated nonviolent methods; an isolationist movement, opposed to U.S. intervention overseas but willing to support military defense of the Western Hemisphere; and an anti-interventionist movement comprising participants from both the political Left and Right who were opposed to U.S. entry into World War II. In various ways, all three "tried to shape members' attitudes and actions toward motion pictures, the film industry, and U.S. foreign policy." Chambers joins others in finding Lewis Milestone's *All Quiet on the Western Front* to be a touchstone for antiwar ideology, noting its rerelease in 1934 and the release of an augmented version in 1939, by which time the nation's aversion to war had led to the production of other "disillusionist" films such as *Cavalcade* (1933) and Paramount's *The President Vanishes* (1935), in which the chief executive goes into hiding rather than make decisions that might lead to war. At first, peace organizations spoke out against films that promoted war but then decided to sponsor special nontheatrical screenings of films that supported international peace. Most noteworthy was Francis Skillman Onderdonk's Peace Films Caravan, which, during the early 1930s, sponsored antiwar screenings in local churches and clubs in several states. The outbreak of the Spanish Civil War in 1936 and German rearmament and aggression after 1938 had an obvious impact. By 1939, Chambers notes, "new antiwar films became increasingly rare." Soon thereafter, Hollywood began distributing features such as *The Fighting 69th* (1940) and *Sergeant York* (1941), which were clearly "preparedness" productions designed to nudge a quiescent American public toward intervention.

Cynthia J. Miller studies *Hitler, Beast of Berlin* (1939) as a film that, rather than whispering words of fear in the ears of American moviegoers, "screamed . . . mocked, shocked, and menaced in defiance of the Third Reich." It was "one of the first to openly cast the Nazi regime in a villainous light." But, ready for distribution after a production schedule of less than a week, *Hitler, Beast of Berlin* ran into opposition from the Production Code Administration because it was deemed inflammatory and prowar. In response, the Producers Distribution Corporation and filmmaker Ben Judell agreed to a number of edits and even dropped Hitler's name from the title in several distribution markets. The central characters are members of a small underground group in Germany resisting the growing Nazi "beast." The film opens with scenes of storm troopers parading through small towns to the "reluctant salutes" of townspeople. The plot also introduces concentration camps, venues of physical and psychological torture. It is little wonder that the film was advertised as "a wail of anguish from a nation in chains." As Miller points out, the film is of special interest today because it maximizes the melodramatic techniques of the B movies and noir films of the day—both in the production and in its zany advertising stunts. No trick was missed for attracting public attention and selling a message.

World War II

Although President Woodrow Wilson proclaimed World War I to be "the war to end all wars," the technological developments in the decades following the conflict raised the costs of World War II by astronomic proportions—especially for civilian populations, the ultimate targets of total war. In the first of four chapters on World War II, Ian S. Scott studies Frank Capra and Robert Riskin and their documentary films supporting America's war effort. Although the two men had worked together previously in a string of successful commercial projects, including *Mr. Deeds Goes to Town* (1936), *Lost Horizon* (1937), and *You Can't Take It with You* (1938), in their greatest contributions to the war effort—documentaries made for the U.S. government—they functioned independently. Scott describes Capra's *Why We Fight* series of films as narrative history imbued with "a strong Christian ethos." Scott sees Riskin's documentary work for the Overseas Branch of the Office of War Information, the *Projections of America* series, as more of "a quiet affirmation of life in America, of accomplishment, and, indeed, of social attainment and cultural appreciation." The quiet films of the Riskin team deserve more study and acknowledgment, since a number of them fulfill one of the primary goals established by John Grierson, father of the documentary: "to make peace as exciting as war."

Obviously, the Hollywood studios continued to provide a product that would please audiences, and there were numerous opportunities as they advanced the war effort. Yet the postwar era posed problems of its own: How would a mobilized nation—deprived of consumer goods during the war years—return to a market economy? And what about the psychological stress of veterans as they made the transition from the military, where life was structured, scheduled, and controlled by direct and clear orders? Could young men who had battled America's enemies settle down to civilian "chaos"?

Filmmakers did not ignore the plight of those who would later be described as "the greatest generation." One of the classic works of the postwar era, director William Wyler's *The Best Years of Our Lives* (1946), follows three veterans back to their hometown in the American heartland—tracing their attempts to get in step with a peacetime economy. Frank J. Wetta and Martin A. Novelli consider Wyler's film along with other selected film portrayals. Contrary to writers such as Paul Fussell and Michael C. C. Adams, who dismiss such productions as misrepresenting the impact of war on veterans, Wetta and Novelli argue that a mature "realism" in the post–World War II film justifiably includes stories of adjustment and creative reintegration. In *The Best Years,* each of three former servicemen must overcome challenges, but each emerges as an adjusted and constructive member of society: one rejects his drinking habit, an unfortunate "hangover" from military life; another experiences divorce but discovers a rejuvenating relationship; and a physically handicapped sailor finds acceptance from his family and learns to adapt to his new limitations. No single solution in the film is perfect for all, but these three stories argue that despair and anger are not the only options for those tested in the fires of combat. In this regard, the subject of *Pride of the Marines* (1945), Joe Schmid (John Garfield), loses his sight but finds ways to succeed back home. As actor Garfield said of his character, "I found him the kind of kid we like to think of as the wholesome American type—brave, determined, resourceful, fun loving, but not without some of the faults that are American, too" (Nott 156). Schmid is a human being, not an irreparably wounded soul. Likewise, Tom Rath (Gregory Peck) in *The Man in the Gray Flannel Suit* (1956) comes home with problems but finds happiness with his loving wife (Jennifer Jones) and growing son.

Although film is a popular medium, it has not been employed sufficiently to tell the story of ordinary people during times of crisis. In her chapter on both the novel and film versions of *From Here to Eternity,* J. E. Smyth believes that author James Jones produced his book and Fred Zinnemann the award-winning feature film to bring the unofficial—yet significant—history of America's "Good War" to the public. Indeed, it is Smyth's contention that Jones devoted much of his career to validating the perspective of "the hairy, swiftly aging, fighting lower class soldier" in World War II. An uncompromisingly proletarian writer in the tradition of Theodore Dreiser, Jones felt contempt for the officer corps and, by extension, for America's Establishment—including historians, whom he decried as members of the upper classes writing *for* the upper classes. Although permission was granted for filming at the Schofield Barracks in Hawaii, the film's undermining of authority did not sit well with the Department of Defense. Basing her chapter on a study of the literary original, studio documents such as correspondence and scripts, and the film itself, Smyth concludes that James Jones's vision of the U.S. Army prior to the attack on Pearl Harbor was more than a personal statement; it was an ambitious attempt to revise the image of the American military. When *From Here to Eternity* reached theaters in the fall of 1953, it was a harbinger of an entirely new Hollywood paradigm for the war film, one that would reach its apogee during the post-Vietnam era.

Robert Brent Toplin, who is responsible for the fourth contribution on World War II, brings his own considerable experience as both filmmaker and historian. Both *The Longest Day* (1962) and *Saving Private Ryan* (1998) address the Allied invasion of France in 1944, an accomplishment that represented one of America's finest efforts for the Allied cause, even though some ten thousand U.S. troops were killed in this invasion to liberate Europe. As Toplin demon-

National Archives

Berlin: a divided city in a divided world.

strates, in addition to the obvious historical questions, each film can be read as a comment on issues that were relevant at the time of its production. In the 1960s, for example, the German military commanders of 1944 were presented in a relatively benign way because the nations of the West were relying on the Federal Republic of Germany as a Cold War ally in holding the line against the Soviet Union. As a result, in *The Longest Day,* leaders of the German military elite "seem confused, fumbling . . . sometimes comic. . . . [and] not enthusiastic about Nazi policies." By 1998, after years of disillusionment with Vietnam and scores of films that questioned the necessity of war, Steven Spielberg's *Saving Private Ryan* reminds audiences that "some battles are worth fighting" and that the men who fight them "deserve to be honored."

COLD WAR AND INSURGENCY

The Cold War

The firestorm over Dresden and the mushroom clouds over Hiroshima and Nagasaki raised the stakes of military conflict so high that most world powers seemed to abandon plans for conventional warfare; then the threat of annihilation was escalated after the first H-bomb tests in the mid-1950s. The result

David Winter

Marine platoon commanders in Vietnam were often very young.

was a Cold War of challenges and containment. In Asia, victory of the insurgent communists in China created yet another world power and set the stage first for a war in Korea (1950–1953) and later for extended "low-intensity" conflicts over several decades in Vietnam, Laos, and Cambodia—what Nikita Khrushchev, in his famous "secret speech" of 1956, dubbed "wars of national liberation."

Immediately after World War II, the city of Berlin became a compact microcosm of Cold War confrontation—a polity dramatizing the tensions of a divided Germany and a larger divided Europe and, ultimately, a polarized world. Thomas W. Maulucci Jr. surveys films that portray "the morally ambiguous human landscape and the still fluid and uncertain political situation of postwar Germany." These "rubble films," as Maulucci calls them, "stress the need for a clean break with the past." Representing a "door in the Iron Curtain" (because it was embedded in East Germany), Berlin became a meeting place for East and West. Maulucci compares Berlin films from the West, particularly Billy Wilder's American production *One, Two, Three* (1961), with an East German documentary that "premiered exactly one year to the day after construction began on the Berlin Wall." Until it came down in 1989, the infamous barrier was a metaphor for world divisions as well as a physical obstacle that thwarted freedom seekers. As the author concludes, "Cold War Berlin continues to fascinate filmmakers and moviegoers who themselves remain divided about life in Germany since reunification [in 1990]."

Susan A. George explains how, from the mid-1940s through most of the 1950s, "shaken by the trial of the 'Hollywood Ten' and the communist blacklists that put more than three hundred directors, technicians, writers, and actors out of work," a mood of fear and anxiety took root in Hollywood. But Robert Wise's *The Day the Earth Stood Still* (1951) was different. Through inventive manipulation of generic conventions, this now-classic science fiction film "opens a space for emergent ideologies" and "offers a different worldview." As George demonstrates, films of this period tend to show women locked in as homemakers in traditional families rather than as accomplished professionals; they are basically "high-heeled, well-dressed damsels . . . who represent traditional American notions of hearth, home, and family." In contrast, in *The Day the Earth Stood Still,* it is a woman (Helen Benson, played by Patricia Neal) who "disrupts dominant ideologies" by rejecting her suitor's proposal of marriage and protecting Klaatu (Michael Rennie), the alien invader who announces his goal of promoting world peace.

The Vietnam Conflict

Turning to the war in Vietnam, Peter C. Rollins addresses what he sees as a significant tendency toward bias in most histories, novels, films, and television productions about the war. After surveying several memoirs, collections of GI letters, and oral histories about the war, he observes that "war viewed from a foxhole shows vivid pyrotechnics, but the view is often as narrow as it is intense." Vietnam as portrayed on television has been equally problematic. Rollins underscores difficulties with the thirteen-episode WGBH series *Vietnam: A Television History* (1983) and compares it with two rebuttal documentary productions: *Television's Vietnam: The Real Story* (1985) and *Television's Vietnam: The Impact of Media* (1986). Finally, he surveys a series of Hollywood films about the Vietnam conflict, explaining how they reflect the opinions Americans had about Vietnam and how important it is to ensure that students have "the tools to identify opinion and point of view as they consider the meaning of our longest war."

The "gritty realism" of Oliver Stone's *Platoon* (1986) is what interests Lawrence W. Lichty and Raymond L. Carroll, although they also examine three earlier films about Vietnam: *The Green Berets* (1968), *The Boys in Company C* (1978), and Francis Ford Coppola's *Apocalypse Now* (1979). *Platoon* accompanies Chris Taylor (Charlie Sheen) as he arrives for a tour of duty in Vietnam, just as Stone had done as a soldier twenty years earlier. Lieutenant Wolfe (Mark Moses) leads his unit into an area where all the confusion—and much of the distress—of service in Vietnam becomes evident. This first part of the film presents what Lichty and Carroll call "the 'small war' fought by the ordinary grunt." But as the story goes on, it presents some troubling questions. For example, "when the bad soldier kills the good soldier, and young Taylor must avenge the act, how are we to think about heroes or murderers?" *Platoon* raises other provocative questions, too, about the "madness of war" and Taylor's corruption by it. Subsequent to the release of *Platoon*, Stone's actual company commander, Robert Hemphill, wrote a brief history of his infantry unit entitled *Platoon: Bravo Company*, in which he details an alternative history of the filmmaker's experience, one more in keeping with the honored traditions of the U.S. Army and its citizen-soldiers.

The final contribution on Vietnam takes a longer view. William S. Bushnell studies the vision of two screenwriters, working almost fifty years apart, and their different takes on Graham Greene's 1955 novel *The Quiet American*. Bushnell describes the literary base as "part political thriller, part romance, and part detective story set in exotic French Indochina in 1952." Joseph Mankiewicz was responsible for the first screenplay, filmed in 1958, which enraged Greene because of its "reworking of his novel." The second version, which reached screens in 2002, was by Australian writer-director Phillip Noyce and "devotes more interest to the character relationships and the introspective quality of Greene's text." Taken together, the two films yield insight into America's experience in Indochina and the ways films can inform history; as is so often the case, each reflects the preoccupations and prejudices of its own time. The 1958 version upholds a staunch Cold War vision of America's rightful defense of South Vietnam; in contrast, informed by the "Vietnam syndrome," the 2002 rendering is more in the spirit of the British novelist's skeptical interpretation. Bushnell concludes that Noyce achieved a cautionary tale with the prescience of the original.

THE TWENTY-FIRST CENTURY: TERRORISM AND ASYMMETRICAL CONFLICTS

Lawrence Suid has devoted a research career and two respected volumes to studying the Pentagon's involvement in helping Hollywood producers make better war-related films—films that, by virtue of "getting the history right," also protect and defend the reputation of the armed forces. Using the methods pioneered by Suid, John Shelton Lawrence and John G. McGarrahan focus on *Black Hawk Down* (2001), a classic example of a film that the Pentagon wanted made. In December 1992, during Operation Restore Hope, President Bill Clinton sent twenty thousand U.S. marines to bring law and order to Somalia and its capital, Mogadishu, in the wake of a short but violent civil war. In June 1993, after a system for distributing humanitarian aid had been set up and a United

U.S. Army

Rebel forces in Somalia had firepower.

Nations multinational peacekeeping force had been established, U.S. troops were reduced to twelve hundred, but some of the remaining American forces were responsible for a July 1993 raid that set the stage for violent conflict and humiliating losses. Eventually, by March 1994, there was a complete (and some believe ignominious) withdrawal of American troops from a nation in chaos. In the end, despite the involvement of Pentagon consultants hoping for a positive "spin," *Black Hawk Down* presents a story of confusion, ill preparedness, and command failure. Some observers have suggested that the film fits very comfortably into the Vietnam War film formula rather than a new, heroic mold.

More recently, there have been attempts to reconfigure the war film. In his chapter, Jeffrey Chown surveys a wide selection of films that have emerged from Operation Iraqi Freedom. The baseline for comparison is the famous Vietnam-era documentary *Hearts and Minds* (1974) by Peter Davis. Chown sees Davis's Academy Award–winning film as a template of dramatic devices and editorial techniques that Michael Moore used in his own widely seen documentary *Fahrenheit 9/11* (2004). In a survey of documentary productions, Chown believes that *Baghdad E.R.* (2006) is the film on Iraq with "the most graphic shock value," as it depicts wounded American soldiers being brought in off the line. Yet he concludes that this film—presented in the style of television's *E.R.*—is less critical of the war than might be expected. Proposing a "Vietnam template," Chown also compares *The Anderson Platoon* (1967) and *Occupation: Dreamland* (2005), the latter of which traces the experiences of a squad in Iraq, and he comments on the influence of lightweight video cameras in the hands of combatants. As the war has evolved, so have the cinematic treatments. Although the new war genre cannot be defined with exactitude, this early survey of recent documentaries lays the groundwork for a critical exploration. In a style fulfilling many of Chown's predictions, Brian De Palma's *Redacted* (2007) blends documentary footage with acted sequences to track the destructive impact of prolonged combat.

Some of the earliest documentaries and feature films concerning the Iraq war focus on the narrative of Pfc. Jessica Lynch, who was captured by fedayeen after her convoy made a disastrously wrong turn and was ambushed near Nasariyah. Since the Puritan-era revelations of Mary Rowlandson in 1682, Americans have been fascinated with stories of captivity and have found lessons in them about national character and identity. Stacy Takacs devotes a chapter to examining some of the treatments of Lynch's ordeal, delineating how gender issues become enmeshed with political rhetoric. Motion picture formulas apply as well: Jessica Lynch was a "damsel in distress" who embodied the values of America's homeland. (It is interesting to note how many war films posit their protagonists from the Appalachians, assuming that such a locale confers special heartland values and an innocent, politically unsophisticated character. To name only a few, consider Benjamin Martin in *The Patriot,* Davy Crockett in *The Alamo,* Inman in *Cold Mountain,* the Henry Clark family in Riskin's World War II documentary *Valley of the Tennessee,* the protagonist of *Sergeant York,* the Gary Cooper character in *Friendly Persuasion,* and, of course, Robert E. Lee Prewitt in *From Here to Eternity.*) The filmmakers who rushed their Jessica Lynch documentaries and features to the screen in 2003 must have been surprised to tune in to C-SPAN in late April 2007 and find the subject of their films testifying before a congressional committee and rejecting her heroic status: "I am still confused as to why they chose to lie and try to make me a legend when the real heroics of my fellow soldiers that day were legendary." (Notably, Lynch did not offer to return the fees she received for her story from filmmakers and the networks.) Looking at the record of Hollywood's wars and American mythmaking, it comes as no surprise that the details of her story were woven into a national fable; the resulting films are a combination of generic and historical necessity.

National Archives

Hitting the Pentagon, a symbol of U.S. military might.

The recent mobilization of political and screen resources commenced, of course, after the terrorist attacks on symbolic sites in New York and Washington on 11 September 2001. Those watching NBC's *Today Show* at 8:45 A.M. were told that the first collision into the South Tower of the World Trade Center was probably an accident. Then, while "experts" speculated for Katie Couric and recalled the 1945 collision of a B-25 bomber into the Empire State Building, the nation watched as, at 9:03, a second plane smashed directly into the North Tower of that icon of American capitalism. Within forty minutes, a Boeing 757, acting as a flying bomb, hit a recently reinforced section of the Pentagon just across the river from the National Mall, killing the 64 people aboard the aircraft and some 125 workers in an edifice that has been a symbol of the American military since World War II. Some twenty-seven minutes later, a heroic group of Americans confronted their hijackers over Pennsylvania, thwarting a third aerial attack on a Beltway target—either the Capitol or the White House.

The world gasped as it watched in real time and was then overwhelmed by seemingly endless rewinds and reruns of the horrific events of what became known as 9/11. James Kendrick considers the news and documentary renderings of these events and two feature films: Oliver Stone's *World Trade Center* (2006), which focuses on the heroism of Americans on that tragic day in the nation's history; and Paul Greengrass's *United 93* (2006), a tense narrative of the flight that went down in Shanksville, Pennsylvania. Kendrick discusses how news programs and documentaries presented the events of that fateful day and then compares them with the feature film renderings. Many people thought that the films came too soon after the event, but given the recycling of the actual images on television at every opportunity, Kendrick questions why there would be any sensitivity remaining. Both feature films examined "are built around themes of heroism and resilience." In the case of *United 93*, the "hero" is a group of ordinary Americans who stand up to the challenge of terrorism. In *World Trade Center,* one central figure—in the Hollywood war film tradition—takes the lead in asserting "the refusal of the United States to back down in the face of aggression." As marine staff sergeant Dave Karnes, actor Michael Shannon "becomes a ready metaphor for the undaunted American spirit in the face of catastrophe." (After 9/11, the real Dave Karnes gave up his career as an investment counselor and went back on active duty as a U.S. marine, eventually serving two tours of duty in Iraq.)

The collection concludes with both a filmography and a bibliography assembled by John Shelton Lawrence. Previous books have shown that listing the films considered in a chronological sequence helps readers grasp the evolution of the genre and see the relationships among the various productions. Lawrence lists those films focused on by the contributors to this volume, as well as other films that have received significant public recognition. Considering the rich tradition of commentary, the authors could not be comprehensive in citing every important book in their chapters; therefore, the bibliography extends the chapter references and offers a guide—organized by war era—for future investigation. These resources provide excellent launch points for researchers.

THE FILM AND HISTORY APPROACH

Why We Fought takes a "film and history" approach, based on a commitment to studying both the historical and the communications issues of the artistic medium of motion pictures. Other methods exist, and each has value. The following thematic rubrics, discussed in detail below, stress the interests and commitments of film and history scholars who treat wartime motion pictures or motion pictures about war as historical documents and apply the same methods of analysis that would be directed toward texts in any archive—verbal or visual (see more at www.uwosh.edu/filmandhistory/):

1. War films must be studied in their historical contexts.
2. War films are propaganda vehicles.
3. Censorship and sponsorship influence war films.
4. War films constitute a genre of their own.
5. War films should be studied with caution.

Historical Contexts

Every war film is made within a cultural milieu that either dictates its approach or more subtly influences its construction in ways that are often not perceived by the filmmakers themselves. Anyone "reading" a cinematic text about war must take into account the zeitgeist of the period in which it was made. For example, most scholarship about the 1920s agrees with F. Scott Fitzgerald's famous lament that it was a decade the younger generation found empty of heroic opportunities, with "all Gods dead, all wars fought, all faith in mankind shaken" (Fitzgerald 185). Yet Michael T. Isenberg discovered that there was a heroic way of remembering World War I and that King Vidor's *The Big Parade* (1925) documents an important alternative historical memory—yes, there was suffering, but heroism and national maturation were fostered by the "Great War." Many years later, during the controversy over Vietnam, Vidor felt obliged to apologize to Hollywood peers for the film's (unintended) positive vision.

In the case of Oliver Stone's *Platoon* (1986), it is important that the film was not made until after the Watergate scandal of 1972–1974. Indeed, during an interview with *Playboy* magazine, the iconoclastic director admitted that it was Watergate-related revelations that inspired the script—not Stone's experience as a U.S. Army rifleman in Vietnam during 1967–1968. This detail about the creative environment should inspire scholars to rethink their evaluation of the film and to consider how it *uses* Vietnam as a vehicle to explore Stone's views on the culture crisis of the 1970s. In this context, Charles Reich's *The Greening of America* may be more relevant to decoding the messages of the film than any military or diplomatic history. Such a reading would certainly exonerate the film of the volleys of criticism launched by Vietnam veterans who were angered by its many misrepresentations (see chapter 17).

Any study of America's war films in context must consider where the pendulum is located as it swings between isolationism and interventionism, for the American national mood keeps shifting—seemingly by decade. With respect to these moods, motion pictures often impact viewers by reinforcing their established mind-sets—so much so that, in some cases, the antiwar film of one generation becomes the recruiting poster of the next. This unexpected

As you have seen, on September 1st., 1939, the German armies, without warning, blitzed into Poland. The Nazi bid to smash the world into slavery was on.

U.S. Signal Corps

Why We Fight spoke in simple terms that everyone could understand.

reversal is confirmed by the fascination engendered by a DVD of *Apocalypse Now* among the marines in *Jarhead* (2005) who are participating in the first Gulf War.

Propaganda

Sometime prior to World War I, governments decided that motion pictures could serve as psychological weapons. During the period of strict neutrality, prior to the American declaration of war in 1916, motion picture producers were asked to avoid partisanship. Indeed, antiwar efforts by such leading filmmakers as D. W. Griffith were released to a public that was not willing to become involved in a war that, by 1916, had already consumed hundreds of thousands of lives in combat. (The Battle of the Somme in 1916 alone inflicted some 300,000 battle deaths.) Productions such as Thomas Ince's *Civilization* (1916) played to isolationist audiences receptive to messages from the Prince of Peace. Once America was committed to war, however, such films were quashed, and in a prominent case, film producer Robert Goldstein was imprisoned for sedition (see chapter 1).

After hostilities began, even Griffith produced his quota of films denigrating the German "Hun" and depicting damsels in distress, most notably in

Hearts of the World (1918), starring Lillian Gish. Never lax in his zeal, Griffith made "war-front" documentaries with British troops going "over the top" in such manageable geographical settings as Scotland. No one noticed this falsification at the time, and the footage is still used repeatedly in television documentaries and on covers of "historical" publications. Apparently, the images proved to be too convincing to be rejected, long after their fraudulent nature had been exposed.

For World War II, the peace movement derived considerable support from the dramatic success of director Lewis Milestone's *All Quiet on the Western Front*, a film so powerful in its antiwar statement that its star, Lew Ayres, converted to pacifism and refused military service even after Pearl Harbor. (He did *not* refuse to serve in the medical corps and was highly decorated for his combat bravery as a frontline medic in the Pacific.) Chapter 8 reveals that there were other uses for the film—uses by audiences. In Göttingen, Germany, *All Quiet* became a Rorschach test around which citizens, unions, and elites defined their attitudes toward the military disaster behind them.

And just as there are different kinds of propaganda, there are countervailing efforts designed to swim against the stream and contradict the official portrayal of the military—films such as *From Here to Eternity* (1953). In his epic 1951 novel, James Jones vowed to reveal the "untold story" of the working-class members of the American military, a story that—according to Jones—had been left out of the history books because history is written by the elite for the elite. Both the novel and the film portray an antiheroic military rife with indecency, brutality, and corruption—a portrait that never would have been permitted during the war it portrayed. Part of the permissiveness stemmed from the distance from the war, and part from Hollywood's discovery that its cooperation with the government during World War II had led not to continued support but to congressional probes, blacklisting, and a crushing Supreme Court decision that abolished the studio system. It seems clear, in retrospect, that the frustration of a limited war in Korea further undermined America's trust in the military. Newsreels (accurately) showed Americans outgunned and overpowered in the early days of the struggle, to the point that the U.S. Army was backed into a defensive perimeter around Pusan, Korea, during the late summer of 1950. Here was a context ripe for negative portrayals.

The Vietnam War saw very few government-sponsored films in support of the struggle, in part because President Lyndon B. Johnson and Secretary of State Dean Rusk believed that a World War II–style public information campaign would make it difficult to wage a limited war. The government-produced *Why Vietnam?* (1965) included speeches by President Johnson and diplomats

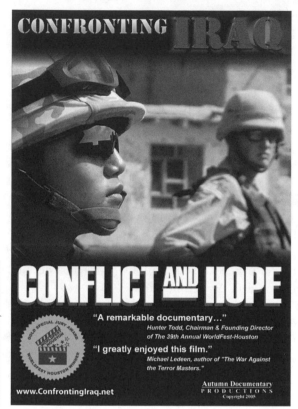

Some rebuttals of *Fahrenheit 9/11* reached American theaters.

laying out a rationale for the struggle, but the preponderant response by theatergoers was negative. Later, PBS would release its own ambitious chronicle of the struggle, *Vietnam: A Television History,* a thirteen-part series critiqued by answer films from Accuracy in Media (see chapter 17).

The war in Iraq inspired documentaries such as the very popular *Fahrenheit 9/11,* in which Michael Moore emulates the style and themes of Peter Davis's anti-Vietnam classic. Moore's analysis, in turn, was answered by such films as Roger Aronoff's *Confronting Iraq: Conflict and Hope* (2005), a feature that showcases historians, cultural critics, and diplomats who argue that the war is a viable strategy but requires political will to succeed.

It is safe to say that *all* war films have political implications, even when they appear to avoid didacticism. There is not a single film considered in this collection that does not carry lessons about American society, domestic issues, or foreign policy. When all else fails, such films can be used to examine the nature of America's national character. For example, *The Best Years of Our Lives* and *The Man in the Gray Flannel Suit* make no explicit attempt to buttress any

U.S. troops fire a missile at a fortified position.

view of World War II, yet both consider the nature of America's fighting men and their resilience as they confront the new challenges of the marketplace in the postwar era. Not political in any way, but also preoccupied with the issue of character, is *Jarhead* (2005). The narrative follows a small group of marines from boot camp through Operation Desert Storm and then back home; the film has a "destruction of innocents" message, which should not be surprising since the screenplay was written by former marine William Broyles, a Vietnam veteran. What makes the film so interesting is its avoidance of political commentary; what it does deliver is a bleak message of what it means to be a marine (according to Broyles). The final scene gives a mixed judgment, but the overall story is one of indoctrination and discipline, which are irrelevant to a world that needs peacemakers.

Finally, the documentaries examined in chapter 21 seem more interested in grandstanding or memorializing than in delivering a political message. The proliferation of technologies has created an entirely novel production context, leaving behind the days when messages were dispensed to a passive audience by governments, defense departments, and oligopolistic television networks. In the new context, even photos taken for personal use can prime political debate. In a noteworthy example, the "humorous" photographs of Lyndy England and Charles Graner touched off the Abu Ghraib scandal. Members of the 372nd

Military Police Company never realized that their e-mails would become political bombshells. England and Graner may have found it "cool" to torment the prisoners under their supervision, but the world thought otherwise—and so did the army, which sentenced both to prison terms (England for three years and Graner for ten years). Yet political statement was the last thing the two pranksters had in mind as they "built" human pyramids, humiliated naked prisoners, and mocked the dead and dying in their charge.

Censorship and Sponsorship

The federal government found ways to control film content during both world wars because, as iterated in *Why We Fought,* motion pictures were important weapons. Though it is easy to scoff at this effort to control public exhibitions, it is also important to consider the observation of David Welch: "In all political systems policy must be explained, the public must be convinced of the efficacy of governmental decisions (or at least remain quiescent), and rational discussion is not always the most useful means of achieving this, particularly in an age of mass society" (xviii).

During the 1930s, President Franklin D. Roosevelt tapped the power of radio to reach millions of Americans with his message of a "New Deal." When war came to America, Roosevelt—an avid movie buff—and General George C. Marshall, his chief of staff, saw the importance of motion pictures in stimulating the national will. An obvious corollary was that control of overall movie content was essential so that the messages would have the desired cumulative effect. Likewise, through much of World War II, radar antennas were erased from still photographs released to the public because it was assumed that the enemy was better off not knowing about this advance in tracking—a special advantage for naval operations under the cover of night.

Sometime in 1943 it was decided that the public had lost enthusiasm for the struggle and needed to be made aware of the sacrifices being made at the front. From that time on, bodies of American soldiers were shown floating in the surf at Tarawa and other Pacific beachheads. *Life* magazine explained its publication of such images as follows: "The love of peace has no meaning or stamina unless it is based on a knowledge of war's terror. . . . Dead men have indeed died in vain if live men refuse to look at them" (Roeder 34). The goals were to persuade civilians to donate to the war-bond drives and to subdue the strong demand for consumer goods that was building against restrictions on purchases.

Scripts for Hollywood films were vetted closely during both world wars, and guidelines were provided to the studios. The studios normally cooperated with the government in these requests, although there was some tension before the United States entered World War II and was still claiming "neutrality," a condition that came to an end at 0800 (Hawaiian time) on Sunday, 7 December 1941. A number of studies discuss the studios' wartime commercial concerns, including the availability of raw materials for film stock, but it can be assumed that the studios were behind the war effort. In fact, most of the Hollywood moguls were ahead of the public when it came to supporting intervention. Their European backgrounds and business contacts kept them up-to-date about the "progress" of totalitarianism in Italy, Germany, and the Soviet Union.

More significant was the notion of sponsorship and partnership between the studios and the government. War films, in search of verisimilitude, needed costumes, locales, equipment, and the guidance of military professionals. Although it was (and still is) fairly easy to acquire the advice of retired military personnel interested in serving as consultants, it was very expensive to procure the machines and personnel of war. Here, cooperation with the Department of War (1942–1947) and later the Department of Defense would continue to be essential to the bottom line.

Some examples are worth mentioning. In making *The Big Parade* several years after World War I, director King Vidor had the full support of the U.S. Army (see chapter 6). An assistant director was sent to Killeen, Texas, to film large bodies of troops and trucks advancing toward the front as part of the "big parade." The scenes must have taken a full day to complete, but the assistant director came back with footage that Vidor rejected as unusable for aesthetic reasons. Vidor then traveled to Fort Hood, where the scenes were reshot, once more with army assistance; this second effort provided the epic mass and rhythm sought by the Hollywood artist. For its part, the army believed that it was improving its image with the postwar public.

Some fifty-four years later, Francis Ford Coppola discovered that the Department of Defense was unwilling to provide the helicopters and troops he needed for *Apocalypse Now*. The media liaison office concluded that the adaptation of Joseph Conrad's novella to a Vietnam setting—and its ending with a statement about "the horror"—would reflect negatively on the armed forces of the United States and on national policy. Coppola's epic encountered all kinds of equipment, weather, and budgetary problems in addition to a lack of cooperation by the government, but it finally recouped its investment. The film is now considered one of the great American war productions—at least by film critics.

During World War I, World War II, and the Cold War, the armed forces cooperated with many filmmakers out of self-interest. Frank Capra's *Tunisian*

Victory (1944), a film about the North African campaign, was filmed in New Mexico with an armored unit still undergoing combat training. Because the early battles in Africa had gone badly for the Americans, it was very much to the army's benefit to have a heroic rendering. Therefore, track vehicles, fuel, and troops were supplied in abundance. (It is inexplicable that Capra would later deny his use of reenactments for any of his wartime productions.) In a more complex twist during the Cold War, director Edward Dymytrk brought to the military a project proposal designed to bring Herman Wouk's *The Caine Mutiny* to the screen. Dymytrk, who had been imprisoned as one of the "Hollywood Ten," was using this film as a vehicle to work his way back into the movie business after being what was called a "friendly witness" for the House Committee on Un-American Activities. The tiresome introduction to the film is an unabashed commercial advertisement for the U.S. Navy, stressing the impressiveness of its ships as well as the humor and humanity of the sailors who man them: music, lighting, and color reveal an impressive nautical environment where it is fun to serve. The navy was clearly happy to cooperate with the project, and the director was working very hard to prove his loyalty, making it difficult for the Department of Defense to turn down such a sanguine propagandist.

A classic survey of the interactions between Hollywood and the Pentagon can be found in Lawrence Suid's *Guts & Glory: The Making of the American Military Image in Film.* As Suid notes, he is concerned with "the irony of filmmakers' claims that they make only anti-war movies while continuing to portray combat as exciting and as the place where boys become men, where men become heroes, and even role models to the next generation"(xii). Suid notes in his preface that motion picture hagiography contributed to the unseemly ease with which Americans permitted an escalation of the war in Vietnam. No one interested in understanding the impact of governmental support and sponsorship can ignore this work of truly original scholarship.

The War Film Genre

The study of popular culture and motion pictures is accepted by scholars in the twenty-first century, but many have forgotten how it all got started. Back in 1970, a pioneering work by John Cawelti entitled *The Six-Gun Mystique* was published by Ray Browne of the Popular Press—published so hurriedly that Browne neglected to stake a copyright claim for the volume. Cawelti's fundamental argument is that the popular arts employ and embellish formulas that are worked and reworked over time and that the study of the popular arts must focus on these core motifs and their evolution, because the popular arts reflect the concerns of the times in which they are produced. According to Cawelti, "formula . . . is cultural; it represents the way in which a particular culture has embodied both mythical archetypes and its own preoccupations in narrative form" (30). Obviously, his book focuses on the Western film, but he later examined the detective and mystery genres, and his many readers were inspired to apply the notion to other literary and motion picture genres as well.

One such scholar is Jeanine Basinger, whose book *The World War II Combat Film* is to the war film genre what Suid's *Guts & Glory* is to the issue of sponsorship. With a very empirical style, Basinger defines and then explores the characteristics of the combat film, tracing its evolution over time from 7 December 1941 until January 1945. An update provides a chronology of war films up to 2003. The overview identifies the genre's "introductory stage" (7 December 1941 to 31 December 1943), consisting of such films as *Wake Island* and *Flying Tigers,* films that vilify the enemy while linking the conflict back to earlier embattled moments in America's history. Next, an "emergence of a basic definition" of genre fundamentals occurred (1943), when productions such as *Bataan* and *Air Force* introduced the formula of the "international platoon" that included American regional, class, and ethnic types working together as part of a cohesive fighting team. Finally, during a "repeat of the definition" (1 January 1944 to 31 December 1945), films stressed the sacrifice of servicemen in such dark stories as *Objective Burma* and *They Were Expendable.* Later evolutionary variations are also examined, including *Battleground* and *The Story of GI Joe.* About *Battleground,* Basinger suggests that "it was a pure combat movie that celebrated, finally with the full audience, the fact that we won the war and could dare to be proud of it. It healed, united, and entertained" (147). About *The Story of GI Joe,* she concludes that the film "announces itself as celebratory of the American common man, a democratic look at the forces who fought for democracy" (129). In *Why We Fought,* these two popular films are studied for their commentary on the much debated topic of "Hollywood realism" (see chapter 12).

Basinger is a true popular culture scholar, in that her study unapologetically explores the combat genre as art form. With empathy for the efforts of Hollywood, she observes, "World War II films were not intentionally unrealistic. In the most cynical terms, that was not good business. Instead, working within the limitations of censorship, wartime materiel restrictions, 'good taste,' and propaganda, they accepted their task as one in which they were to entertain the audience but also gain acceptance by coming close to the experiences they were living through outside the theater" (256). Basinger's book should be mandatory reading as part of any investigation of Hollywood's war films. Her respect for the popular arts allows her to examine the details of the formula in a way that yields insights that would likely be missed by the traditional scholar.

U.S. Signal Corps

Epic images of struggle on that "longest day" of 6 June 1944. Here, British troops go ashore, bringing their three-speed Raleighs with them.

Caution

War as a theme has attracted a number of independent filmmakers who, though perhaps free of some of the commercial motives driving the major studios, may still be in the grips of an ideology. Many of these people, lacking training in history themselves, tend to grasp a single source—usually an easily illustrated visual one—and make it their only source or become overly committed to the ideas of their historical and military consultants. Thus, the fact that a motion picture or television study of war has been made outside the studio system does not guarantee a truly balanced perspective; in fact, the reverse may be true.

Visual literacy is certainly a goal to strive for in our media environment. This is especially so when it comes to Hollywood's wars, where government support and studio budgets have often produced overwhelming experiences. Films such as *The Longest Day* (see chapter 14) are of such epic proportions that their very scope can be humbling. Throughout the D-day film, the technique of parallel action—used for the first time by D. W. Griffith in *The Birth of a Nation* (1915)—starts with developments on the Allied side of the war and then cuts to the German forces and their preparations; the implied omniscience of such editing can deprive theater audiences of critical capacity. In *Patton* (1970), actor George C. Scott is built into a demigod through low angle shots, telephoto lens manipulation, editing, music, and mise-en-scène from the grandiloquent opening (in which Patton addresses his imagined troops) to one of the most powerful montages in the history of the war film. During the Battle of the Bulge sequence of the film, "Patton's Prayer" combines poetry, music, and *lack of sound* to evoke a warrior's ecstatic vision of conflict and victory. Director Carl Foreman's *The Victors* (1963) contains an execution sequence visualized against a sound track in which Frank Sinatra sings, "Have yourself a merry little Christmas," an audio track that directly conflicts with the grim story in a definitive example of "film irony." As Cynthia Miller points out in chapter 10, newsreel footage was inserted into *Hitler, Beast of Berlin* to blur the line between what the audience knew was real and what was fiction (viewers often lacked the visual literacy to discern the distinction). Those who have been taught how motion pictures communicate will both appreciate such artistic touches and be aware of their intentions. The editors of this volume believe in this approach—for all visual experiences—and have expressed concern over the years that those who are not ready to decode such messages will become the unwitting victims of them. In the case of war films, the ramifications could be disastrous.

Viewers forget how much thought and planning go into a film production. In many cases, production files are available for inspection, and these paper trails reveal the contending goals and varied production techniques explored by filmmakers. Often, the Motion Picture Code Administration forced script rethinking and changes; even more often, there were exchanges among writers, producers, and directors about the core issues in the films. From *Drums Along the Mohawk* to *Saving Private Ryan, Why We Fought* has attempted to show how much can be learned about the final released film by examining such documentation.

The Internet provides a new portal, a gateway with unprecedented opportunities for researchers. Increasingly, documents about films are available at dedicated Web sites. Press kits, correspondence, trailers, interviews, and scripts are coming online, as are details about the lives of creative personalities in the film business. List-servs such as those on H-NET invite scholars to post queries and to engage in public discussions of research problems and opportunities. When the editors of *Why We Fought* began their own study of film back in the 1970s, it took a major effort to find important reviews, essays, and opinions.

U.S. Army

An allied soldier in Iraq prepares for evening.

Today, such readily available resources as the Internet Movie Data Base (IMDB) provide "external reviews," details of plot, and even exact locations where films were produced; through Project MUSE and other academic assistance available via university libraries, major journals around the globe can be searched. Finally, documentary and feature films themselves are coming online to be viewed or downloaded. And when all else fails, there is Netflix.

What will be needed in the future, of course, is a means to filter the proliferating information from war films and to interpret the origins, messages, and impacts of such information. This collection consolidates much of what is now known and points to future "after-action reports" about Hollywood's wars. As we study these films, it is important that we remember the men and women of our armed forces who, when called to serve, risked their lives—and sometimes surrendered them. Hollywood's wars project images of real events for which they sometimes provide insight and sometimes obscure; either way, the wars *and the films* deserve the attention of responsible citizens.

The task is not easy: King Vidor, director of *The Big Parade*, concluded production of his epic with a sense of satisfaction that he had made an antiwar film. How could he have been so wrong? After the release of his first Vietnam film in 1986, Oliver Stone was surprised that *Platoon* was not accepted by all as "Vietnam as it really was." *Time* magazine ran a cover story to that effect, but members of Stone's unit and countless other combat veterans were outraged about what they saw as a gross misrepresentation of their service and sacrifice. Why would a veteran so demean his comrades? Similarly, director Eric Zwick's very popular *Glory* (1989) cannot be understood without examining the foregrounding of racial issues in the 1980s; the film valorizes the significant contribution of freedmen to the Union army during the Civil War, an additional 10 percent of manpower that, according to the film, made the difference between victory and defeat for the North. This story of the fighting 54th from Massachusetts was no secret, but it took an era of affirmative action to consider it important enough to become a major motion picture. That Clint Eastwood's 2006 feature about Iwo Jima, *Flags of Our Fathers* (2006), would be followed almost immediately by his motion picture from the Japanese perspective, *Letters from Iwo Jima* (2006), is a reflection of the current rapport between the two former adversaries. The objective of *Why We Fought: America's Wars in Film and History* is to map out such connections and to identify avenues of approach for future researchers.

WORKS CITED

Adams, Michael C. C. *The Best War Ever: America and World War II*. Baltimore: Johns Hopkins UP, 1994.

Basinger, Jeanine. *The World War II Combat Film: Anatomy of a Genre*. 1986. Middletown, Conn.: Wesleyan UP, 2003.

Cawelti, John. *The Six-Gun Mystique*. Bowling Green, Ohio: Popular Press, 1970.

Chenoweth, H. Avery. *Art of War: Eyewitness U.S. Combat Art from the Revolution through the Twentieth Century*. New York: Friedman/Fairfax, 2002.

Clausewitz, Carl von. *On War*. Trans. Michael Eliot Howard and Peter Paret. Princeton, N.J.: Princeton UP, 1976.

Confronting Iraq: Conflict and Hope. Dir. Roger Aronoff. Autumn Documentary Productions, 2004. <www.confrontingiraq.net>.

Fitzgerald, F. Scott. *This Side of Paradise*. 1920. New York: Modern Library, 2001.

Fussell, Paul. *Wartime: Understanding and Behavior in the Second World War*. New York: Oxford UP, 1989.

Hemphill, Robert. *Platoon: Bravo Company*. Foreword by Joseph L. Galloway. Fredericksburg, Va.: Sergeant Kirkland's, 1998.

MacKensie, Aeneas. Memorandum to Hal Wallis. 13 May 1941. Warner Bros. Collection, U of Southern California, Los Angeles.

Nott, Robert. *He Ran All the Way*. New York: Limelight Editions, 2004.

O'Connor, John E. *Image as Artifact: The Historical Analysis of Film and Television*. Malabar, Fla.: Robert E. Krieger, 1990.

Reich, Charles. *The Greening of America*. New York: Random House, 1970.

La rivière du hibou. Dir. Robert Enrico. Filmartic, 1962.

Roeder, George H. *The Censored War: American Visual Experience during World War Two*. New Haven, Conn.: Yale UP, 1993.

Rollins, Peter C. *Television's Vietnam: The Impact of Media.* Accuracy in Media, 1986. Rereleased on DVD in 2007.

———. *Television's Vietnam: The Real Story.* Accuracy in Media, 1985. Rereleased on DVD in 2007.

Suid, Lawrence. *Guts & Glory: The Making of the American Military Image in Film.* Rev. ed. Lexington: UP of Kentucky, 2002.

Welch, David. "Introduction: Propaganda in Historical Perspective." *Propaganda and Mass Persuasion: A Historical Encyclopedia, 1500 to the Present.* Ed. Nicholas Cull, David Culbert, and David Welch. Santa Barbara, Calif.: ABC-CLIO, 2003.

Part I

The Eighteenth and Nineteenth Centuries
Revolution, Conquest, and Union

THE AMERICAN REVOLUTION ON THE SCREEN

Drums Along the Mohawk and The Patriot

Hollywood productions about the American past have been relatively common over the century-long history of motion pictures—especially if one counts all the representations of the western frontier and all the films about American wars. In this context it is somewhat surprising that there have been so few thoughtful productions about the period of the American Revolution (1763–1789). The truly memorable films dealing with the nation's founding can easily be counted on two hands, with a few fingers left over.

After all, the only feature-length film that focuses on the councils of the Revolution, *1776* (1972), is a musical. A few of the earliest silent productions, most too short to qualify as feature films, did deal with aspects of the Revolution. Consider *The Pride of Lexington* (1911), *Washington at Valley Forge* (1914), and *The Spirit of '76* (1917). The last of these was a two-hour film that landed its producer, Robert Goldstein, in prison, charged with producing a film "designed to arouse antagonism, hatred, [and] enmity between the American people and the people of Great Britain at a time when the defendant well knew that the government of Great Britain . . . was an ally of the United States in prosecution of war against . . . Germany" (Slide 207–11). Perhaps, twenty years later, the producers of *Drums Along the Mohawk* (1939) were aware of Goldstein's troubles when they decided to portray America's eighteenth-century enemy differently. Sixty years later still, producers of *The Patriot* (2000) were more sensitive to the issues raised by foreign invaders in an agricultural countryside after decades of debate and protest about America's role in Vietnam.

The earliest well-known feature film to focus on the Revolution was D. W. Griffith's *America* (1924), a sweeping representation of the main events of the Revolution from the Boston Tea Party to Yorktown, with special care taken in the re-creation of such locations as Independence Hall in Philadelphia.

The scope of Griffith's epic was surely influenced by his previous productions about major American military conflicts, such as *The Birth of a Nation* (1915) and *Hearts of the World* (1918). Like these two films, made when World War I was in the headlines, several of Hollywood's small collection of Revolutionary War–era films seem to have been influenced by the world situation at the time of their production. Although the European conflict was over by the time of *America*'s release, and, presumably, a generation of American doughboys had proved the amity that now existed between the two nations, the film was initially banned in Britain, despite Griffith's traveling there to make a personal appeal. Perhaps because of the difficulties Griffith faced in distributing his film in Britain, added to what people knew of Goldstein's troubles, there was a tendency in future productions to have American Tories rather than Englishmen play a central role and to allow Native Americans to take the blame for most atrocities (Glancy 523–45).

Another of the handful of notable films about the Revolution, *Drums Along the Mohawk,* was released in 1939 as war clouds gathered again over Europe and Americans began to worry about their possible role in a second world war. John Ford's film was based on Walter Edmunds's popular 1936 novel about farming settlers in upstate New York defending themselves against Indian raids and later marching off to do their part in the larger conflict.[1] As had been the case before World War I, it was clear that were America to be drawn into the European conflict, Britain would be its ally. This certainly occurred to at least some of the decision makers at 20th Century-Fox when they decided to make an American Revolution film in which it would barely be noticed that the British were the enemy. Domestic audiences were crucial, but a production such as *Drums* could also expect European bookings. In normal times, had the British enemy been featured, it might have been considered innocuous, but in 1939, as one interoffice memo took pains to explain, "the international situation is so delicately balanced, that the powers to be in England weigh feathers and might find the picture injudicious."[2]

In the same way that 1939 audiences might have been influenced in their reception of *Drums,* viewers of *The Patriot* in 2000 may have responded to Benjamin Martin's (Mel Gibson) original hesitancy to fight, followed by his seemingly uncontrollable outbursts of violence on the battlefield, with thoughts of America's recent extended experience in Vietnam, as well as to the potential for war looming in the Middle East. In addition, there were worldwide terror threats that were soon to become very present even in downtown New York City.

Drums Along the Mohawk and *The Patriot* are interesting because they both deal with the Revolution as it impacted not the famous leaders of the move-

Drums Along the Mohawk
portrays a young rural family
under attack.

ment in Philadelphia and Boston but ordinary people, young families living
in western New York and in the Carolina backcountry and being driven to support a war that they did not start, or necessarily want, but one that nonetheless
reached out to engage them.

Historical spectacles about America were hardly a new genre in 1939, but
they did enjoy a spurt of popularity that year.[3] Why did Hollywood producers
choose this time to deal with the American past? Why did audiences respond
so well, choosing *Drums Along the Mohawk*, for example, as one of their favorite
movies of the 1939–1940 season? The answers to these questions lay buried
deep in the changing national consciousness as the Great Depression drew to
a close and involvement in another world war loomed on the horizon.

Even at the end of the decade, the vast majority of the American people
were still caught up in the malaise of the 1930s. Many suffered from a psychological depression brought on by the harsh economic realities of everyday life.

Columbia Pictures

Mel Gibson stars as farmer Benjamin Martin in *The Patriot*.

The Americans who had grown up in the freewheeling 1920s and felt that they had every reason to look forward to success in life were forced to reshape their images of America and of themselves. For some it was a trauma they would carry for the rest of their lives.

As Europe turned toward fascism to confront its economic crisis, American disillusionment and despair increased. Dreams of democracy and individual success may have seemed unrealistic to many people living in a crisis-ridden world. In this climate of tension and insecurity, panaceas became more appealing: Huey Long proposed to "Share Our Wealth," Father Charles Coughlin promised to expose those who conspired to betray America's economic interests, and Francis Townsend explained that pensions for the elderly would prime the economic pump by boosting consumer spending. When FDR sought to defuse such movements by co-opting some of their suggestions in his proposals for a social security program and a progressive income tax, a storm of indignation arose from those who still held dear the conservative gospel of rugged individualism that supporters of Herbert Hoover had believed so fervently a decade before. Even supporters of the New Deal were unsure where the new, seemingly uncharted course would take the nation. People felt the need to reassure themselves that traditional American ideals were still alive and that the United States would not follow Europe headlong into radical antidemocratic experiments. This thirst for reassurance reached a new intensity in 1939 and 1940 as friends and allies overseas were caught up in another total war that threatened, like the last one, to drag in the United States.

One manifestation of this concern of the 1930s was the passion for rediscovering the roots of America's national heritage. During the 1920s, an era marked by extraordinary confidence in America, the trend in historical writing had been toward debunking the legends of the founding fathers and adopting a more cynical attitude toward the ideals for which they had supposedly stood: James Truslow Adams condemned seventeenth-century Puritans for being repressed autocrats, and Charles Beard accused the authors of the U.S. Constitution of being concerned with pecuniary gain rather than the public good. In his three-volume biography of George Washington, Rupert Hughes pulled the legendary general off his pedestal and tried to set the record straight with regard to all those supposed patriots in the struggle for independence: "The fact [was] that the generation of Americans that coincided with the Revolution, was far from being the supremely virtuous race its descendants have been pleased to pretend. . . . A few soldiers, a few statesmen, a few devoted men did all the work, suffered all the hardships, and saved the country in spite of itself, while the majority ran away or kept aloof, grew fat and looked on" (691, 694). The time was ripe for rebuilding the reputations of America's founders.

The task began in 1930 with Samuel Eliot Morison's respectful new look at seventeenth-century New Englanders and was continued by Clifford Shipton, Perry Miller, and others. An interesting index of popular history can be found in the guides prepared in the 1930s by the Works Progress Administration, including historical surveys of every state and major city in the nation. By cataloging the historic sites that related to the experiences of ordinary Americans, as well as the homes of the great and the famous, the guides helped to restore a recognition that ordinary people as well as their leaders made history. By the late 1930s, a significant body of literature sought to reaffirm the virtues of American heroes and to resurrect their positive images. Even radicals and communists who before had devoted their efforts to pointing out the flaws in American society now turned to highlighting the traditional American values that united people of diverse backgrounds in opposition to fascism—thus American leftists who went off to Spain in 1936 and 1937 to struggle against Franco and Hitler called themselves the Abraham Lincoln Brigade.

DRUMS ALONG THE MOHAWK

Published in 1936, Walter Edmunds's *Drums Along the Mohawk* is a pastoral novel. A man builds a home for himself in the wilderness, then marries a pretty young girl and takes her to live with him there. They farm the land in an idyllic setting and survive with the rest of their agrarian community of simple folk. Their greatest challenge comes in the form of repeated savage attacks by Indian "destructives" who remain loyal to the British and threaten frontier settlements during the war for independence.

The novel owed its popularity to more than its romantic interest, its bucolic setting, and its excitement and suspense. Edmunds so revered the historical facts that he indicated in a foreword which of the characters were fictional and which real and almost apologetically pointed out where a few stories of actual persons had been altered for dramatic emphasis. Moreover, he acknowledged his debt to specific historians, encouraged interested readers to study further, and recommended primary as well as secondary sources for the period. Edmunds also noted that the characters in the book were moved by some of the same types of concerns that preoccupied Americans in the 1930s. The challenges of everyday life on the colonial frontier were complicated by the military struggle for independence, in which neither Continental troops nor state militia could be relied on to defend tiny settlements on the fringe of civilization, and in which the hopes and dreams of ordinary people were shattered as families were terrorized and homesteads destroyed. Now the Depression had shattered hopes and dreams too, and, as in revolutionary days, it seemed as though the solutions that were proposed from above sometimes made things worse. As Edmunds explains in his foreword, "These people of the [Mohawk] valley were confronted by a reckless Congress and ebullient finance, with their inevitable repercussions of poverty and practical starvation. The steps followed with automatic regularity. The applications for relief, the failure of relief, and then the final realization that a man must stand up to live" (xi). Here was the relevant and comforting (if only implied) message of the book: through reliance on their inner strength and traditional American ideals, twentieth-century Americans could live to prosper and to dream again about the future just as the colonists had. The public responded so well to the book that it seemed only a matter of time before it would be put to the screen.

Indeed, Darryl F. Zanuck had purchased the movie rights to the book in 1936, even before it went into circulation. The book's sales moved slowly at first, but in the first month of 1937, there were five printings of ten thousand copies each, and *Drums* became a best seller. Still, Zanuck described himself as "not terrifically enthused" about the project, and when several other companies made offers, he considered disposing of the property (memorandum). Only the continuing popularity of the book (it went into thirty-one printings by 1939) encouraged him to stick with the uplifting story. He personally supervised revision after revision of the screenplay in a process that eventually involved William Faulkner (who tried to simplify the story in a short narrative treatment dated 15 March 1938), Sonya Levein (who wrote two dialogue treatments and a first-draft continuity script with shots, angles, and cuts spelled out in detail), and Lamar Trotti (who polished Levein's work, made more changes to satisfy Zanuck, and completed the shooting script in May 1939). At every stage, Zanuck maintained close contact with the writers, dictating detailed conference notes on several editions of the screenplay in which he specified places to tighten the story and techniques to heighten the drama.

To Levein's first-draft continuity script of 2 December 1938, Zanuck responded,

> In the first place, let us get it understood that we do not want to make a picture portraying the revolution in the Mohawk Valley. We want to tell a story about a pioneer boy who took a city girl to the Mohawk Valley to live and we must tell the story of what happened to them—their ups and downs, their trials and tribulations—the same as it was told about the Chinese couple in *The Good Earth* [1937]. In *The Good Earth* the producers wisely discarded chapter after chapter of the book and concentrated on the personal story and on one spectacular trick with the locusts. We must follow this example. We have in the script practically all of the necessary ingredients to accomplish this but now they are dissipated and lost in a rambling jumble of historical and revolutionary data.

After giving another writer three months to work on the project, the producer was again dissatisfied, especially with the still complicated plot development. Zanuck's reactions on 11 March 1939, as written up by one of his assistants, ran to eleven pages, but a few sentences carry the gist of his feelings:

> We must not let ourselves be bound by the contents of the book—but simply retain the *spirit* of the book. We must concentrate our drama, tighten what plot we have and make it more forceful—so that we build and build to a sustaining sock climax where we let everything go with a bang. So as long as we capture the general line, the characters, the period—we can and should forget the book. Mr. Zanuck could not be emphatic enough in bringing home the fact that we are in the business to *Give A Show*—that our first job is to *Make Entertainment*.

Zanuck was happier with the "final" script of 24 April, but he and John Ford, who had been chosen to direct the picture, still found seven pages of corrections

Gil and Lana Martin (Henry Fonda and Claudette Colbert) share an idyllic moment in the Mohawk Valley.

to suggest. All through the writing process, Zanuck looked to Julian Johnson, chief story editor for the studio, for insight and reassurance. As Johnson observed to him some weeks later in a memorandum dated 31 July: "I think the thing that gave us the fine script we shot was, as much as anything else, your own constant revision and elimination, revision and elimination, every time a new treatment showed its head. The shooting final was a triumph of *perspiration* as well as *inspiration*."

Historian Edward Countryman has argued that, as a result of such pressure, the script transformed an essentially historical novel into a "mythic" story driven by the characters in "one isolated community." In the process the writers "transformed the social history of the Revolution. . . . By de-revolutionizing the Revolution, even as it reconstructs it, the film has helped to rob Americans of an appreciation of their past. Its social meaning cannot be grasped without reference to this other, pseudo-revolutionary, de-politicizing part of its content" (89). Screenwriters also altered some significant aspects of the plot and the characterizations presented in the novel. For example, the scene that contributes the dramatic high point of the film never actually happened, either in history or in the novel. The settlers were forced into the fort and, from there, did witness the burning of several of their homes, but this came earlier in the story. The eventual victory was more of an anticlimax, as the overall defeat of the British, culminating at Yorktown, Virginia, meant that they would no longer be promoting the Indians' attacks on the settlers. The main characters, Lana and Gil Martin, also underwent transformation during the adaptation. Edmunds had been much more sensitive to the plight of the pioneer woman and portrayed her inner strength. In the film she does grow into a stronger character, but the script gives her none of the depth and complexity possessed by Edmunds's heroine. The simplification of her role early in the film was dictated by Zanuck, who feared that otherwise viewers would not see how far she had developed by the end of the story (conference notes, 5 Apr. 1939). Gil's character was polished for the film. Early in the novel he takes part in the burglarizing of the house of a suspected Loyalist, and later he joins a party of Americans that deliberately seeks vengeance against a Tory settlement by setting fire to homes and raping the defenseless women there. In each of these two cases, Gil's participation is only halfhearted, and he is plagued by second thoughts, but even with those qualifications, the film's Gil Martin could not take part in such atrocities. Neither the Motion Picture Production Code nor the patriotic tone of the film would permit it.

In their final form, the plot, characters, and dramatic elements of *Drums Along the Mohawk* seemed tailor-made for the special talents of John Ford. Ford's skills as a director were well known, but they had resulted in only a few memorable films: *Iron Horse* (1924), *The Informer* (1935), and *Hurricane* (1938). There was also a series of Ford films with Will Rogers culminating with *Steamboat Round the Bend* (1935)—films that focused on cherished American values. It was in 1939 that Ford began to turn out hit after hit with *Young Mr. Lincoln*, *Stagecoach* (his first Western since the introduction of sound), *Drums Along the Mohawk*, and finally *The Grapes of Wrath* (1940). Each of these, like his 1941 classic *How Green Was My Valley*, gave him the opportunity to develop characters based on common people. Ford's best films shared with those of Frank Capra a populist view of American society. Although Capra's plot situations were usually comedies, in contrast to Ford's popular dramas, both men had a special talent for portraying ordinary people who struggle to preserve significant human values challenged by forces far more powerful than themselves.

Drums Along the Mohawk offered Ford a rare opportunity. Here he could depict an idyllic, early-American agrarian community in more explicit terms than in any of his other films. That this idealized lifestyle was menaced by barbarous Indians who would not hesitate to rape and torture innocent victims served to accentuate the virtuous qualities of the God-fearing settlers. In

Tory leader Caldwell (John Carradine), rather than British regulars, is the villain of *Drums Along the Mohawk.*

dramatizing the life of New York's Mohawk Valley in the 1770s, the film strikes a careful balance between the individualism and the mutual interdependence that typify the frontier ideal. It is punctuated by scenes that celebrate the simple agrarian life: weddings, births, and harvests, and a scene in which neighbors come seemingly from miles around to help Gil Martin (Henry Fonda) clear his land. The frontier people are outgoing and friendly. Some are comical, such as Christian Real (Eddie Collins), who forgets to respond to his own name while calling roll for militia muster, and the Scots-Irish parson (Arthur Shields) who works an advertisement for a local dry goods store into his Sunday sermon. Gil's bride, Lana (Claudette Colbert), raised in a comfortable home in Albany, is heartbroken at the first glimpse of his cabin on the fringe of the wilderness and terrified at the sight of Blue Back, an Indian who turns out to be peaceful and friendly. She demands that Gil take her back home. But soon the beauty of the surroundings, the sense of accomplishment in seeing their own farm take shape, and the feeling of belonging to the open and congenial community of settlers bring her to love their simple life. Ford paints this picture in such appealing terms that the audience understands perfectly when she prays, "Please, God, let it go on like this forever." Unfortunately, the American Revolution disturbs their serenity.

Thanks to Zanuck and his screenwriters, the story that reached the screen is a fine example of movie drama with three carefully paced climaxes, increasing in intensity until the final climax of the film. Shortly after the crops are harvested, the colonists meet their first challenge as bloodthirsty Indians come whooping through the woods and, under the direction of a Tory leader named Caldwell (John Carradine), destroy the Martins' farm, sending the settlers scurrying to the nearby fort to keep the women and children safe. When Gil returns from chasing the Indians, he finds his house burned to the ground and his wife barely surviving the miscarriage of their first child. Gil is disheartened by their bad luck, and now it is Lana's turn to sustain the pioneering couple. They go to work for a wealthy widow, Mrs. McKlennar (Edna May Oliver), and begin planning their family once more. But, as if on cue, a second crisis arises. It is reported that Indians and Loyalists are gathering at the head of the valley in preparation for a major attack, and the militia marches off to meet them. This time we do not see the Indians themselves, but we do see the human cost of their "war fever" as the men are pictured, weak and wounded, straggling back from Oriskany. In a daze, Gil explains that the militia force was ambushed and nearly wiped out, but they rallied and finally sent the Indians running. As Gil sleeps off the exhaustion of battle, General Nicholas Herkimer (Roger Imhof) lies outside in Mrs. McKlennar's parlor, dying at the hands of a young doctor performing his first amputation.

For a year after the Battle of Oriskany, the Martins and their infant son live happily with Mrs. McKlennar, hoping someday to rebuild their cabin. Then, on the day after they have celebrated a bumper crop, a party of hostile Indians sets fire to the McKlennar house and lays waste to the neighboring farms. The terrified colonists, huddled at the fort at German Flats, find themselves besieged by an overwhelming force. The plot becomes more active as the situation at the fort becomes more desperate. The colonists are outnumbered by their attackers, and the women take weapons and join the men on the walls. Mrs. McKlennar is the first to be hit. She takes an arrow in the chest and dies. Things look bleak. Ammunition is getting dangerously low. In desperation, Joe Boleo (played by Francis Ford, the director's brother) resolves to escape and run to Fort Dayton for aid. Unfortunately, Boleo is captured by the Indians, who tie him atop a wagon loaded with hay and, in full view of the fortress, set the wagon aflame. To spare him from being burned alive, the parson shoots Boleo. It is left to Gil to make another try. Assuring Lana that he can outrun any "redskin," he lowers himself through a portal in the fort wall and takes off, with three Indians close at his heels.

Gil's escape is the most memorable action sequence of the film, as Ford drags out the chase for almost five minutes. It is worth noting that this is another example of the screenwriters' "adjusting" historical facts to improve the film's plot. The actual run, as described in Edmunds's book and as noted above, came earlier in the conflict and was made by a man named Adam Helmer (played by Ward Bond in the film). It was made *to* the fort at German Flats, not away from it. Furthermore, Helmer's warning, instead of bringing Continental reinforcements, frightened the colonists and their militia into hiding within the walls of the fort. As portrayed in the novel, this was one of dozens of confrontations with the "destructives," none of which was truly conclusive. In the film's version of the run, it becomes the dramatic turning point. The sun comes up a vivid orange in the background as Gil finally leaves his pursuers gasping behind. In the next shot, the main force of Indians is seen breaching the fort walls, and Lana, the woman who had cowered in fear at her first encounter with the harmless Blue Back, is bravely shooting one of the intruders at point-blank range. As Zanuck wanted it, alerted by Gil, the Continental reinforcements arrive just in time to rout the savages and save the day. Fortunately, the fight will not recur. In the last scene, an officer arrives with the news that General Washington's troops have defeated Cornwallis at Yorktown in the final battle of the Revolutionary War. But thanks to the pencil of fiction wielded by Zanuck's writers, in 20th Century-Fox's version of the war, the farmers of the valley have enjoyed their own victory at German Flats before the news of Yorktown arrives.

From the outset it was obvious that, because of the sets and locations required, *Drums* would be a very expensive picture to make. The greatest problems were logistical. The open spaces called for in the script required shooting on location. Any thought of shooting in the Mohawk Valley itself was quickly rejected because industrialization had transformed almost every inch of the landscape. Moreover, Zanuck's decision to film in Technicolor led him to search for special atmospheric conditions to maximize the quality of the photography. They finally chose a high plateau in the Wasatch Range of the Rocky Mountains, near Cedar City, Utah, where the lack of haze in the morning allowed vast distances to be photographed with perfect clarity, and beautiful cloud formations appeared on schedule every afternoon to accent the panoramic views (*Drums* press book).

As with its previous historical films, 20th Century-Fox was scrupulous about details. The studio claimed to have searched all over Hollywood for Iroquois Indians to play in the film. They could find only two, however, and one of them

Columbia Pictures

Benjamin Martin (Mel Gibson), a member of the South Carolina
Assembly.

was thought to be too short and fat. The other was a seventy-two-year-old man
named Chief Big Tree who was purported to have posed for the buffalo nickel.
He was given the role of Blue Back, a friendly but rather dull-witted native
who has been Christianized and now fights on the side of the colonists. Great
attention was also given to the uniforms the men would wear and the weapons
they would use. In a paean to its enterprising agents abroad, the studio boasted
that the flintlock muskets employed had been purchased in Africa, where their
anachronistic ineffectiveness had been proved in Ethiopia's failed attempt to
ward off Mussolini's modernized army in 1935 (*Drums* press book).

THE PATRIOT

Both the world situation and the nature of movie production were rather different in 2000 than they were in 1939. The two world wars were buried safely
in the history books, and the cold war seemed to be over as well. To be sure,
there were new tensions in the world, ones more colored by religious extremism, terror, and the world supply of oil. Americans still worried about being
drawn into foreign wars, but the conflicts seemed more likely to take place in
the Middle East, and the enemy was more likely to be driven by a commitment

to Islamic fundamentalism than to the tenets of Hitler or Marx. Daily reports of street bombings came from Jerusalem and Tel Aviv, and it seemed that diplomats might be unsafe almost anywhere in the world. At the same time, the movie studios were becoming things of the past. No longer did giant studios maintain sound stages, stables of writers, costume departments, and contract players ready to adapt themselves to whatever new project came along. Instead, financial backers, producers, directors, and on-screen personalities might form ad hoc relationships for a few pictures at a time.

The Patriot was the outcome of one of these collaborations. While working together on the World War II drama *Saving Private Ryan* in 1996, screenwriter Robert Rodat and producer Mark Gordon had the idea of making a film about the American Revolution. They found the story of South Carolina planter Benjamin Martin particularly appealing because it was "the story of a man who has conflicting responsibilities to the then developing nation and to his family." The main character has to deal with "obligations that are in direct conflict." As the pieces came together for *The Patriot,* the team continued to work together on *Stargate* (1994), *Independence Day* (1996), and *Godzilla* (1998) (Fritz and Aberly 14).

The production of *The Patriot* was undertaken by Columbia Pictures and Sony Pictures Entertainment, but the day-to-day work was put in the hands of director Roland Emmerich and producer Dean Devlin through their independent production company, Centropolis Entertainment. In a preproduction boot camp, as they called it, they prepared their cast with training in the arts of horsemanship and eighteenth-century warfare. In the end, the sixty-three principal actors were supported by ninety-five stuntmen, four hundred extras, and four hundred more reenactors familiar with re-creating battle scenes of two centuries before. Whereas 20th Century-Fox had been able to utilize its many in-house resources to research and acquire or produce what it needed in terms of props and costumes for *Drums,* the Centropolis group enlisted the Smithsonian Institution both to assist with research and to provide some of the items required. The goal, as explained by associate producer Diane McNeff, was to achieve a "subtle accuracy" in which viewers weren't necessarily aware of the work that had been done because "everything looks perfectly believable." The filming was done in South Carolina, where some major construction was called for. The entire town of Pembroke was rebuilt, as were the ruins of Cowpens and Benjamin Martin's plantation, where we first meet the characters (Fritz and Aberly 14).

As the film begins, we hear Benjamin Martin's voice before we see him. It's an inner voice expressing concern about his problems with self-control: "I have long feared that my sins will come to revisit me and the cost is more

Columbia Pictures

British regulars torch the Martin homestead.

than I can bear." We soon learn that the sins he regrets relate to his tendencies toward violence, which expressed themselves in his conduct during the French and Indian War. Yet our first sight of him is a picture of domesticity. His wife having died recently, he is raising his seven children on his own. His efforts at homemaking extend to his trying, without much success, to craft a spindle-backed chair. Part of his problem is his short temper, which leads easily to frustration and to a woodworking project gone awry.

Although he lives in the countryside, Martin is a community leader who travels to the capital at Charleston to sit in the colonial assembly as it votes for independence. We see and hear the debate on the issues of taxation and imperial control, but the factors that really matter to Martin and at least some of his neighbors are more personal. Martin wants to avoid fighting and thus protect his family, as well as escape having to face his insecurity about his own penchant for violence. But when his eldest son, Gabriel (Heath Ledger), enlists and British regulars arrive in his neighborhood, Benjamin is driven to pick up his weapons and go off to fight. Harking back to his experience in the Indian wars, with his musket he carries another symbolic weapon of choice, a tomahawk, which he wields expertly. In some ways Gibson's character seems to be a reprise of his role as a crazed Scottish freedom fighter against the British in *Braveheart* (1995). In other ways, particularly in its revenge scenario, the film is reminiscent of *Lethal Weapon* (1987), in which Gibson plays an "ordinary man driven to manic despair and crazed violence by circumstances out of his control" (Glancy 532).

The ultimate challenge that drives Benjamin into the conflict is the defense of his family. His son Gabriel has already been in the fight for some months. He is identified as a dispatch rider for the American army, is captured on a visit to his father's plantation by a particularly boorish British officer named Tavington (Jason Isaacs), and is taken off for military trial and expected execution (a punishment that we learn is inappropriate for a lowly dispatch rider). In the confrontation, Tavington (a character based on Banastre Tarleton, leader of the Green Dragoons in South Carolina during 1780) shoots one of Benjamin's younger sons dead for trying to defend Gabriel and orders that the house be put to the torch. Benjamin's first action in support of the larger cause is the ambush of the small party that is taking Gabriel away and achieving his escape. Thereafter, Benjamin becomes the bane of the British regulars and their Tory supporters by leading a ragtag but very effective local militia made up of his neighbors and former fellows in arms. Before they can identify him, the British refer to Martin as the "Ghost" because of his capacity to attack by surprise and then disappear.

In this way the plot seems to resemble most closely the career of Francis Marion, the South Carolina revolutionary known to the British as the "Swamp Fox" because of his consistent ability to attack and then retreat to hide in the protection of nearby swamps. Aspects of two other revolutionary leaders are also reflected in Martin's character. Daniel Morgan of Hunterdon County, New Jersey, accompanied Benedict Arnold in his assault on Quebec and fought at Saratoga. Later in the war he led troops seeking to slow the advance of Lord Cornwallis in the South, culminating in the victory at Cowpens in January 1781. A third source for Martin's achievements was the life of Thomas Sumpter, a Virginia-born officer who earned the nickname "Carolina Gamecock" for his fighting against the British there (Fritz and Aberly 28).

After the British defeat at Saratoga (1777) and other losses in the North, and with the formal entry of the French as an ally of the colonists, the British adopted a "southern strategy." They took Savannah and resisted an American assault there. Subsequently they besieged Charlestown (an attack that is portrayed in the film). Then in 1780 and 1781 the war became centered in the Carolinas, with the British, led by Cornwallis, enjoying the considerable assistance of Loyalists there. *The Patriot* follows the struggle of the colonists' militia forces in resisting the British as they fight their way north through the Carolinas: there is the British defeat at Cowpens, the bloody confrontation at Guilford Courthouse, and the final cornering of the British at Yorktown, where they are forced to surrender. (For the fullest and most recent treatment of these events, see John Ferling's *Almost a Miracle: The American Victory in the War of Independence,* especially his chapter "The Pivotal Southern War.") Along the way Martin satisfies his thirst for revenge, killing Tavington (his younger son's shooter) in a face-to-face confrontation.

We also observe two love stories—Benjamin's growing affinity for his widowed sister-in-law (Joely Richardson) and Gabriel's feelings for Anne Howard (Lisa Brenner), who is smitten with Gabriel when she hears him stir the community to fight. Anne marries Gabriel in a seaside ceremony but then dies in the most vicious of the British attacks on local citizens: the British board up and set fire to a church full of worshippers. This is perhaps the most questionable event portrayed in the film. Producer Devlin claims, "We tried to keep all the events in the film real to the events that happened in the American Revolution. They may not have happened in the same way or in the same place, but the spirit of everything in the film can be drawn from real events all throughout the American Revolution" (quoted in Fritz and Aberly 18). The immolation of religious people in a house of worship certainly seems more twentieth than eighteenth century—and more Nazi than British—in spirit. But it may have rung true to most viewers of the 2000 film as they matched the film's acts of terror with what they read in daily newspapers.[4]

There are touching moments, too, in the film, such as the relationship that develops between Martin and revolutionary officer Colonel Burwell (Chris Cooper), one of Martin's previous fellows-in-arms who comes to appreciate even more the guerrilla fighters led by his old friend. And a few interesting symbols are used. Benjamin gives Gabriel a star amulet as a remembrance of his mother. He passes it to Anne as a symbol of their love and commitment to each other, only to find it later in the ashes of the church. As a symbol of the indestructibility of Gabriel and Anne's love, the amulet survives the fire. In contrast, as the military engagements progress and Benjamin needs lead for musket balls, we see him on several occasions melting down the toy soldiers he kept in remembrance of his younger son, who was killed by the British in the first confrontation at their home. The toy soldiers are melted to form shot to kill real soldiers.

Both *Drums Along the Mohawk* and *The Patriot* were widely reviewed at the time of their release. Critic Louella Parsons called *Drums* "unexcelled entertainment." Most reviewers were impressed with the action scenes, such as the

Indian attacks and Gil's dash for reinforcements. Almost all liked Fonda and Colbert. Several also noted approval for Arthur Shields and Edna May Oliver, especially for the scene in which she browbeats two Indians who have just set her house on fire into carrying her and her bed through the flames to safety (see *New York Times* 2 Nov. 1939; *Variety* 9 Nov. 1939; *New York World Telegram* 4 Nov. 1939). Movie critic Herbert Cohn, who saw the film at the Roxy Theater in Manhattan (along with a stage show featuring "Bobby May, the juggling jester"), was more perceptive than some of the better-known reviewers. He noted that the film needed "dramatic tightening" and more "fluidity of plot" (*Brooklyn Daily Eagle* 4 Nov. 1939). *Time* magazine (20 Nov. 1939) predicted that the film would appeal to "fans who like their warpaint thick, their war whoops bloodcurdling, and their arson Technicolored." Moviegoers who responded to questionnaires in twenty-six newspapers across the country ranked *Drums* their thirteenth favorite film of the year (*Film Daily Yearbook* 1941), and the studio was pleased enough with the profits to rerelease the film in 1947 for another successful run.

Reviewers of *The Patriot* were also generally pleased with what they saw. (Some were concerned about the images of youngsters using guns, but it was a revolution, after all.) By 2000, even prestigious historical journals were reviewing films, and here there was more dissatisfaction. The reviewer for the *Journal of American History,* for example, expressed concern about an interview with Mel Gibson indicating that the filmmakers had "taken license with history to make it more compelling" and noted the film's "almost complete omission of the Loyalists. . . . Though Loyalist provincial and militia units constituted one-half of the British army in the South, the film portrays only one Loyalist soldier" (St. George 1146). In Britain, according to one analyst, "critics discussed the film in a dismissive manner rather than a condemnatory one" (Glancy 536). FreeRepublic.com, an online conservative news forum, reported that British prime minister Tony Blair "demanded an apology from Mel Gibson for 'Anti-British' Sentiments in *The Patriot*" (Shamaya). And there was a flurry of gripes from viewers who noted mistakes, especially in the film's editing and continuity.[5]

The study of the evolution of these two productions, and the comparison of the two films that eventually reached the screen, suggests a few generalizations about Hollywood's treatments of the American Revolution—indeed, its treatment of many historical topics. We can posit three general rules.

First, for a film to be successful with a mass audience, it must contain scenes and characters with which the broadest possible group of people can identify—therefore *Drums* includes the roles played by Eddie Collins and Arthur Shields and accents weddings and births, experiences that every viewer is likely to have encountered at some time in life. The opening scene in *Drums,* the wedding at Lana's comfortable Albany home, does not appear in the novel. It was added by the scriptwriters in an obvious attempt to provide a colorful contrast to the Spartan life of the frontier and to allow the audience to relate immediately to Gil and Lana. This type of scene, of course, was John Ford's stock in trade and may have had special meaning for him, but its most basic function in a film such as this is in helping the audience relate immediately to characters from the past. The same end is accomplished in *The Patriot* with the poignant playing up of the widower father and his children. The relationship between Benjamin and his son Gabriel is central to *The Patriot's* drama. As Devlin explains, "It's an enormously emotional compelling story about a father and a son, which I think everyone can relate to, the idea of a father trying to keep his family together" (quoted in Fritz and Aberly 18). The scene of Gabriel and Anne's wedding at the beach is touching too. The film appealed to women as well as to men who might picture themselves fighting alongside Benjamin and his compatriots.

Second, characters who are meant to have broad appeal cannot be too intellectual or too radical; their personalities should be simple and their loyalties unconfused. One aspect of Gil's personality is forgotten in *Drums.* In the novel he, like Benjamin in *The Patriot,* has a troubling personal history—his previous experience in battle also showed a penchant for violence. The early chapters of Edmunds's book include reference to a bloody raid Gil and other colonists made against an Indian settlement, justifying their own savagery against the less-than-human "destructives." In the film, in contrast, there is no reference to specific earlier Indian conflicts, and Gil is shocked at the violence he encounters in his fight with the Indians. He remarks emotionally to his wife about the surprised look on one Indian's face as he fell on an upturned knife, and he expresses distress that some other colonists seem to be enjoying themselves in the fight. Driven though he is to acts of violence, he shows some sensitivity to the suffering and barbarity encountered on both sides. In *The Patriot,* several of Benjamin's violent outbursts appear, and viewers may be put off by his placement of a tomahawk squarely in the forehead of one of his foes. At another point he is drenched in the blood of one of his opponents, but perhaps the filmmakers resisted the temptation to show even more bloodletting.

Third, events and characters might have to be adjusted or their actions reordered to heighten the excitement and sharpen the climaxes. Therefore Gil rather than Adam Helmer makes the dramatic run, and a cavalry-to-the-rescue dramatic ending is grafted onto *Drums* to achieve the desired emotional crescendo. The clearest example of such creative adaptation in *The Patriot* is the shock value achieved by the burning of the church full of worshippers.

However indirectly these two important films on the American Revolution may have responded to the contemporary events of 1939 and 2000, impending wars in Europe and the Middle East helped set the tone for their interpretations of history. In addition, in their "adjustments" of plot and characterization (such as the cleansing of Henry Fonda's character in the film version of *Drums* and the sharpening of the violence in *The Patriot*'s church burning), both films reflect a twentieth-century worldview. The colonists in *Drums* are blameless victims of the Indians and Tories inflamed by the British, and the inhumanity of the church-burning enemy in *The Patriot* justifies any response. Taking a long view, both these films about the American Revolution answer the very challenging question of why we fought.

We can wish for more thoughtful and more accurate representations of our nation's founding struggle, ones more driven by scholarship than by perceived box office appeal. But as long as motion pictures remain a popular art form, historians who study them must remain cognizant of the pressures that inevitably come to bear in a film's production and must be sensitive to the concerns and perceptions of the audiences for whom the films were made. In the end, the analysis of popular historical dramas such as *Drums Along the Mohawk* and *The Patriot* can help us to understand the centuries-long confrontation between settlers and Native Americans, as well as the more specific struggle for American independence. Moreover, such study can inform us about how the nation's involvement in twentieth-century wars has helped shape modern portrayals of American history.

NOTES

Much of the material here on *Drums Along the Mohawk* was originally published in my article "A Reaffirmation of American Ideals: *Drums Along the Mohawk* (1939)," in O'Connor and Jackson (97–119).

1. Another Hollywood product of 1939 was *The Howards of Virginia*, which cast Cary Grant and Martha Scott as frontier settlers. They are at the center of revolutionary developments: Matthew Howard (Grant) is elected from his frontier district to sit in the House of Burgesses, where he votes for independence. As another interesting detail, Howard's brother-in-law, played by Sir Cedric Hardwick, was an unreconstructed Loyalist.

2. The memo was between two military consultants relied on by the studio to gain access to specialized information and to maintain good relations with the armed forces. Captain Lloyd Morris to Colonel Jason Joy, 27 June 1939, story editor's correspondence file, 20th Century-Fox Archives, Hollywood, Calif. Presumably, the author

was not thinking of the Indians' costumes when he suggested that the British might "weigh feathers."

3. Consider adaptations of other historical novels such as Margaret Mitchell's *Gone with the Wind* (1939) and Kenneth Roberts's *Northwest Passage* (1939).

4. Glancy argues that the event is a reference to the burning of a church in World War II. Although the scene was based on an actual wartime atrocity, he observes, it "was in the French village of Oradour-sur-Galne, and in 1944, that the German SS locked the villagers in their church and set it on fire." Others saw the burning of the church as a reference to the massacre of civilians at My Lai in Vietnam. Still others saw it as a reference to the siege of the Branch Davidian compound in Waco, Texas, in 1993 (Glancy 536, 538).

5. For example, one viewer noted that, although the film covers a seven-year span from 1776 to 1783, with one exception the children in the film do not age at all. *Movie Mistakes* <http://www.moviemistakes.com/film958>. See also http://www.moviemistakes. com/film958/corrections and http://www.saunalahti.fi/~frog1/goofs/patriot.htm.

WORKS CITED

Adams, James Truslow. *The Founding of New England*. Boston: Little, 1921.

Beard, Charles. *An Economic Interpretation of the United States Constitution*. New York: Macmillan, 1913.

Countryman, Edward. "John Ford's *Drums Along the Mohawk:* The Making of an American Myth." *Presenting the Past*. Ed. Susan Porter Benson, Steve Brier, and Roy Rosenzweig. Philadelphia: Temple UP, 1987. 87–102.

Drums Along the Mohawk. Press book. Library of the Performing Arts of the New York Public Library.

Edmunds, Walter. *Drums Along the Mohawk*. New York: Little, 1936.

Ferling, John. *Almost a Miracle: The American Victory in the War of Independence*. New York: Oxford UP, 2007.

Fritz, Suzanne, and Rachel Aberly. The Patriot: *The Official Companion*. London: Carlton, 2000.

Glancy, Mark. "The War for Independence in Feature Films: *The Patriot* (2000) and the 'Special Relationship' between Hollywood and Britain." *Historical Journal of Film, Radio and Television* 2 (2005): 523–45.

Hughes, Rupert. *George Washington: The Savior of the States, 1777–1781*. New York: Morrow, 1930.

Johnson, Julian. Memorandum to Darryl F. Zanuck. 31 July 1939. Story editor's correspondence file, 20th Century-Fox Archives, Hollywood, Calif.

Miller, Perry. *The New England Mind: The Seventeenth Century*. 1939. Cambridge, Mass.: Belknap, 1983.

Morison, Samuel Eliot. *Builders of the Bay Colony*. 1930. Whitefish, Mont.: Kessinger, 2004.

Morris, Captain Lloyd. Memorandum to Colonel Jason Joy. 27 June 1939. Story editor's correspondence file, 20th Century-Fox Archives, Hollywood, Calif.

O'Connor, John E., and Martin A. Jackson, eds. *American History/American Film: Interpreting the Hollywood Image.* New York: Frederick Ungar, 1979.

Shamaya, Angel. Online posting. 10 July 2000 <http://www.FreeRepublic.com/>.

Shipton, Clifford. "The New England Clergy in the Glacial Age." *Colonial Society of Massachusetts Publications* 32.1 (1933): 24–54.

Slide, Anthony, ed. and comp. *Robert Goldstein and* The Spirit of '76. Metuchen, N.J.: Scarecrow Press, 1993.

St. George, William Ross, Jr. Rev. of *The Patriot. Journal of American History* 87 (2000): 1146–48.

Zanuck, Darryl F. Comments on first-draft continuity script of 2 Dec. 1938. 30 Dec. 1938. Story file, 20th Century-Fox Archives, Hollywood, Calif.

———. Conference notes. 5 Apr. 1939. Story file, 20th Century-Fox Archives, Hollywood, Calif.

———. Conference notes on temporary script of 11 Mar. 1939. 5 Apr. 1939. Story file, 20th Century-Fox Archives, Hollywood, Calif.

———. Memorandum to Earl Carroll, Ray Griffith, Kenneth McGowan, Nunnally Johnson, Gene Markey, Lawrence Schwab, and Harold Wilson. 3 Mar. 1937. Story editor's correspondence file, 20th Century-Fox Archives, Hollywood, Calif.

REPRINTING THE LEGEND

The Alamo on Film

Back when schoolchildren actually knew something about history, the stirring and heroic saga of the siege and fall of the Alamo was as well known as Washington's crossing of the Delaware or Teddy Roosevelt's charge up San Juan Hill. To tell the story was to sing a hymn to gleaming, unassailable patriotism and, as Alamo commander William Barret Travis wrote in his most famous letter, "everything dear to the American character." Surely, the battle of the Alamo is a mythic event.

THE MYTHIC STORY

The story that those schoolchildren knew was roughly this: In February 1836 a small but determined band of Americans holed up in the Alamo, a crumbling old mission turned fort just outside San Antonio, Texas. Texas was at the time still a part of Mexico, and the cruel and despotic Mexican dictator General Antonio López de Santa Anna adjudged these Americans to be interlopers and revolutionaries. He and his army of thousands laid siege to the Alamo. What the defenders inside the walls of the Alamo lacked in numbers they made up for in ferocity, bravery, and sterling goodness. Young William Barret Travis, a firebrand lawyer and revolutionary, was in command. His cocommander, Jim Bowie, was too ill to take an active role in the defense of the fort, but his legendary knife and exciting exploits were such that his presence was as important as his actions.

But even Bowie's fame paled beside that of a recent arrival, Davy Crockett of Tennessee. Crockett's fellow fighters in the Alamo were inspired by his colorful history as a bear hunter and Indian fighter—not to mention congressman from 1826 to 1830 and from 1832 to 1834. He was possibly the greatest living

Frank Thompson Collection

The Alamo set from Errol Flynn's *San Antonio*.

frontiersman, and he had cast his lot with the outnumbered Texans in San Antonio.

Santa Anna's cannon pounded the walls of the Alamo for thirteen days. Despite Travis's repeated pleas for assistance, only one group of thirty-two reinforcements showed up. Finally, knowing all was lost, Travis gave a stirring speech to his men, telling them that they would surely die if they continued to defend the Alamo. He drew a line in the dirt with his saber and invited every man who volunteered to stay and fight to the death to cross over the line. Without hesitation, they all crossed over.

In the predawn hours of 6 March 1836, the Mexican army attacked. By sunrise the battle was over and every defender of the Alamo lay dead. But each Texan had taken scores of Mexicans with him into death. As Travis had promised in his letter of 24 February, Santa Anna's victory was "worse than a defeat."

A few weeks later, a vengeful Texas army under Sam Houston surprised Santa Anna at San Jacinto and defeated him in a battle that lasted a mere fifteen minutes. Santa Anna was captured and, in exchange for his life, gave the land we now call Texas to his victorious adversary. Now the territory was an independent republic, thanks to the martyrdom of the heroes of the Alamo.

THE BACKSTORY

Of course, as with all "true" stories, the actual event was far more chaotic and complicated than that pristine myth of patriotic sacrifice. Scholars and historians have spent decades uncovering new details, and every time they do, it seems that the legend of the Alamo is chipped away just a little more.

James Bowie was certainly an adventurer—but he was also a slave trader, land swindler, and sometime partner of the Louisiana pirate Jean Lafitte. And it appears that the famed Bowie knife was created by James's brother Rezin Bowie. William Barret Travis abandoned his pregnant wife to take up with a mistress and arrived in Texas under suspicion of murdering a man back in Alabama. And David Crockett, while admittedly a fine hunter, did not have much of a career as a fighter of Indians or anybody else. His most striking achievement in life had been serving three terms in Congress.

Nor was the Texas revolution quite the pure-hearted enterprise of which the storybooks sing. Settlers had been drawn to the Mexican territory of Texas by offers of no taxes and free land. But when Mexican dictator Santa Anna closed the borders, the settlers saw the action as downright un-American and started protesting and then fighting the new rulings.

In short, the battle of the Alamo was not a case of good guys being overwhelmed by bad guys but a conflict in which each side had uncompromising arguments that could be settled only by violence.

MY TWO VERSIONS OF THE ALAMO

For the movies, however, complexity has never been a comfortable attitude. Nearly every Alamo film over the past century has gone straight for the legend, erasing any ambiguity of motive. After all, if John Wayne is fighting for an ideal, who can doubt that he is firmly on the side of good and right?

John Wayne did not introduce me to the subject of the Alamo. In 1960, at the age of eight, I had lived through the backwash of the Crockett craze of 1955, even though I had been just a little too young to experience the real thing. Long before Wayne's *The Alamo* came along, I had spent countless hours defending the redoubtable fort in the backyard and re-creating the massacre with my precious 54mm plastic figures by the Louis Marx Toy Company. Thus I walked into the Wayne film somewhat familiar with the subject—but I walked out as a convert.

In the summer of 1963 my family took a road trip from South Carolina to San Antonio to let me see the Alamo in person. While we were there, I bad-

Frank Thompson Collection

The John Wayne version of the Alamo.

gered one of the Daughters of the Republic of Texas—the caretakers of the shrine since 1905—with questions. I couldn't quite reconcile the modern-day Alamo, which is essentially one building, with the massive mission compound that had served as the fort back in 1836. The caretaker suggested to my father that he take me down to Brackettville, a tiny town about 120 miles southwest of San Antonio, to see the set constructed for the Wayne film. My father thought that was a splendid idea, and we drove down the next day.

The Wayne set—or the Waynamo, as aficionados call it—was out in the middle of nowhere, in ruins from the blasts it took during production of the film four years earlier. It was magical—like a Marx play set come to life. From that day on, my imagination had room for two Alamos—the historical Alamo and the Alamo of popular culture. I kept them separate but equal. Others, as I was to learn over the years, did not bother to separate them at all.

In the late 1980s I began work on a book about the Alamo on film, which I titled, imaginatively, *Alamo Movies*. In it I charted the different ways Hollywood has approached the famous story. But I did not deal with how history has been mangled in these films. That struck me as pointless. No one had ever even tried to make an accurate depiction—although nearly every Alamo filmmaker made extravagant claims to authenticity. The artistic license started from the very beginning.

An Overview of the Movie Histories

In January 1910 the New York–based Star Film Company came to San Antonio, Texas, in search of sunny winter quarters to make moving pictures. The company, under the direction of Gaston Méliès, older brother of cinema pioneer Georges Méliès, came to San Antonio to populate its one-reel Westerns, comedies, and melodramas with "real cowboys" and "real Mexicans." The visitors stayed in the famous health resort Hot Wells Hotel and rented a house and barn on the banks of the San Antonio River. They called it the Star Film Ranch; it was the first moving picture studio in Texas. Given the location, it was probably inevitable that, in addition to the genre films they were producing, the Alamo would strike Méliès' troupe as a perfect subject—especially since no one had ever tried it before.

The *Film Index* reported that the company planned "a correct representation of the Alamo insurrection, famous in history, taken on the very ground where it took place. Many of the old houses which played an important part in the 'defense of the Alamo' are the scenes of the picture" (26 Feb. 1910, 3). The Alamo picture was among the first announced projects of the Star Film Company, but it took a year for the filmmakers to get around to it. When they did, director William Haddock stressed how hard they were working to fill the film with solid history. He told a *San Antonio Light* reporter in January 1911, "Already the scenario is being prepared and has necessitated delving into the old archives to obtain the correct historical setting and the infinite number of details to be known. Of course it would be impossible to give the siege in its entirety, but the incidents of most historic interest will be faithfully portrayed. The Alamo as it now stands does not resemble its appearance at the time of the famous battle, so we are building an exact reproduction of the structure as it then looked" (12–13). In 1911 the siege of the Alamo was still within living memory, closer in history than we are, for example, to Black Monday, which marked the stock market crash that precipitated the Great Depression. Many elderly citizens of San Antonio had witnessed the event. Indeed, at least one survivor of the battle—Enrique Esparza, who, as an eight-year-old boy, had watched his father die in the Alamo—still lived in the city, not far from where the film was produced.

Frank Thompson Collection

A scene from the first Alamo film, *The Immortal Alamo* (1911).

All the information from these witnesses and the records found in the "old archives" must have ensured that *The Immortal Alamo* would be as accurate and authentic a reproduction as was possible to make. But of course, it wasn't.

The "exact reproduction" turned out to be a painted canvas backdrop. Cadets from nearby Peacock Military Academy were pressed into service because their uniforms were vaguely similar to those worn by the Mexicans in 1836. And the plot was pure fictional melodrama about a pretty Anglo wife who survives the battle only to be nearly forcibly "married" to a lustful and deceitful Mexican (portrayed by Francis Ford, older brother of director-to-be John Ford). Luckily for her, her husband, Lieutenant Dickinson (a historical character who actually perished in the Alamo) has been sent out for reinforcements. He and Sam Houston's army arrive just in the nick of time, like the perennial cavalry, defeating the Mexican army and, more important, saving Mrs. Dickinson's honor.

The Immortal Alamo set the pattern for Alamo movies over the next nine decades. Claims of exhaustive research and rigorous attention to historical detail were regularly followed by cinematic depictions that were rarely anything other than pure fiction.

The press book for producer Anthony J. Xydias's *With Davy Crockett at the Fall of the Alamo* (1926) claims that the film bears "the stamp of authentic detail" and that the Alamo and San Antonio sets "are shown exactly as they were in those days," a lie made even odder by the fact that the city of San Antonio appears nowhere in the film, authentically or otherwise. And, needless to say, only tiny snippets of history were allowed to seep into the action-packed movie.

John Wayne loudly touted that the sets for his *The Alamo* (1960) were based precisely on the "original blueprints" in Spain and that screenwriter James Edward Grant had read scores of books on the Alamo. Of course, there are no "original blueprints." If they existed, perhaps art director Al Ybarra's sets would not have been so fanciful and inauthentic. And there is no evidence in Grant's dreadful, entirely fictional screenplay that he had read even a single book on the Alamo. Wayne did hire two of Texas's leading historians, Lon Tinkle and J. Frank Dobie, to act as historical consultants on the film, but both men left the set in disgust at the historical liberties being taken and asked Wayne to remove their names from the credits.

And the IMAX production *Alamo . . . The Price of Freedom* (1988), which even Alamo historians believed would be the most scrupulous film of all, was compromised by the reuse of Wayne's inaccurate set (which still stands near Brackettville, Texas), a cast of primarily amateur actors, and a simplistic screenplay written by one of the film's major financial backers. The creative forces behind the project crowed loudly about their careful adherence to fact, but even these history buffs were not immune to the lures of myth. The screenwriter, the late George McAlister, told me during production of *Alamo . . . The Price of Freedom* that whenever his research yielded more than one version of any given event, "we came down on the side of heroism every time."

So do nearly all Alamo films. Although the filmmakers want the public to believe they are witnessing precise reconstructions of events as they actually happened, the story of the Alamo has always been particularly problematic on this score. First, and perhaps most important, the myth of the Alamo is more persistent in the public's imagination than are the facts of the matter. Before the smoke of battle had cleared, the event was already inspiring poetry. Soon would follow songs, novels, plays, toys, games, souvenirs, comic books, and, of course, movies. And, in all these media, the battle of the Alamo is portrayed as an uncorrupted moment of heroism, the tale of an outnumbered band of patriots who stood bravely against an overwhelming, barbarous army led by a despot. That makes a shining legend, but it has little to do with the reality of the Alamo. Still, as the newspaper editor in John Ford's *The Man Who Shot Liberty Valance* (1962) says in one of the most quoted lines in movie history, "When the legend becomes fact, print the legend."

In 1955, when Fess Parker went down swinging his rifle at the onrush-

Frank Thompson Collection

Fess Parker as Davy Crockett.

ing Mexicans in the "Davy Crockett at the Alamo" episode of Walt Disney's *Disneyland* TV series, the image was fixed in the minds of millions of impressionable youngsters. The Crockett craze of that year was the big bang of the baby boom—more than three thousand items of Crockett merchandise were sold; Crockett-related clothing accounted for a whopping 10 percent of all children's clothes sold; and the theme song "The Ballad of Davy Crockett," recorded by a score of artists, sold millions of copies. There is almost nothing of real historical value in the program. The sets and costumes are all wrong, nearly all the characters are fictional, and there is no political context for the fight—just some vague lines about freedom. But none of that mattered to the kids who became Crockett fiends overnight. They followed the Liberty Valance principle: if this isn't what the battle of the Alamo was like, it's what it should have been like.

The release of John Wayne's epic five years later only compounded the problem. This huge Batjac/United Artists production was found wanting by many, but its homespun script, its outsized characters, and its colorful scenes of action were hugely attractive to those same kids who had lately been converted by the Crockett craze to the secular religion of Alamoism. The Wayne film contains not a word, character, costume, or event that corresponds to historical reality in any way. But in its heartfelt simplicity, it remains enormously entertaining and even moving. Its vast sets and location shooting even give it a powerful aura of reality. Unfortunately, many have confused this aura with genuine authenticity, of which the film contains not a whit.

I followed *Alamo Movies* with two more books on the subject: *The Alamo: A Cultural History* (2001) and *The Alamo* (2002). That seemed like enough for anybody, and I figured I had had my last word on the subject. But I was wrong.

MY CONTRIBUTION TO THE MOVIE MYTHS

In April 2002 producer Todd Hallowell asked me to attend a "summit meeting" with Ron Howard and several Alamo historians at the Omni Hotel in Austin. There had been rumblings for some time that a new Alamo film was in preproduction, and now I learned that the rumors were true.

Screenwriter Les Bohem had pitched the idea to Howard several years earlier and in 1998 had produced the first draft of a screenplay. But the project remained on the back burner until the terrorist attacks on the World Trade Center on 11 September 2001. Soon afterward, Disney head Michael Eisner put the dormant project on the fast track, apparently eager to get a good, patriotic, all-American story onto the screen. (It seems clear that Eisner's view of the Alamo came from other movies, not from history.) But Howard did not see the subject as a flag waver. Instead he wanted to tell the story of the Alamo with all the grimness and violence of *Saving Private Ryan* or *The Wild Bunch*. And overriding everything was his desire to take history seriously. Several other screenwriters contributed drafts, including one fascinating if rambling effort by independent filmmaker John Sayles, who was known for his original meditation on Texas history in *Lone Star*.

The summit meeting undoubtedly unnerved Howard far more than it enlightened him. He, his production designer Michael Corenblith, and his producer Todd Hallowell spent a very long day with the eight historians, discussing and debating every nuance of the Alamo narrative. Sometimes when Howard asked us a question, he would receive eight mutually exclusive answers. On some points, the authorities disagreed vehemently.

Howard left the project soon after and was replaced by John Lee Hancock. Happily, Hancock (a Texan) was even more determined to make the film as authentic as possible. He wrote a meticulously researched final draft of the script and kept two noted Alamo historians, Stephen Hardin and Alan Huffines, on the set with him nearly every day. Even so, he admitted that "each of us who attempts to tell the story of the Alamo, whether in words or images, is

An unused book cover for what would become *The Alamo: The Illustrated Story of the Epic Film*.

doomed to some degree of failure. Seemingly, every source one finds defends itself against a counter source; every bit of data carries an asterisk that puts its relevance or veracity in question." One day, in conversation with Corenblith, Hancock was reminded "that in any true story there exists both a factual and emotional truth. And that, to be faithful to the tale, you need a balance of both" (quoted in Thompson, *Alamo: Illustrated*).

During production, I learned that my Alamo book output was to rise from three books to a whopping five. I was assigned to write not only the "making of" volume, *The Alamo: The Illustrated Story of the Epic Film,* but also the novelization of the screenplay, *The Alamo.* I was given carte blanche to visit the set and was even asked to appear in a cameo role in the film as a Texas politician. All this, as you can well imagine, made me want to write a detailed postcard to the eight-year-old me.

The production of the Hancock version of *The Alamo* was one of the great events in my life. And part of the reason was that John Lee Hancock stayed true to his pledge of making *The Alamo* the most authentic and accurate film ever made on the subject. For the first time, all the events were based on what we know—or, at least, what we think we know—about the historical reality of the time and place. Also for the first time, the costumes evoked the top hat and tailcoat fashion of 1836 rather than the generic "frontier" style of other films on the subject; director Hancock took to calling the clothing style "dirty Dickens." Corenblith's sets, among the largest ever built at more than fifty acres, are very nearly perfect. The Alamo church—the only building standing today, the structure that we now call the Alamo—was reproduced in stunning detail based on its 1836 appearance. Indeed, each stone in the facade is the precise size and shape of the stones in the real thing. And the characters, Bowie (Jason Patric), Travis (Patrick Wilson), Crockett (Billy Bob Thornton), and Santa Anna (Emilio Echevarría), are thoughtful and multidimensional creations, built solidly on what we know about the real men. The film correctly depicts the climactic battle as a surprise attack under cover of night, meticulously re-created according to Santa Anna's original battle plans and the eyewitness accounts of survivors.

But even with all this, *The Alamo* presents a curious dichotomy: it is by far the most accurate and authentic Alamo movie ever made, yet, by its very nature, it can be neither accurate nor authentic; such a feat is simply beyond the capabilities of a single film—on any subject. Hence the hero worshippers may be offended by the distinctly human, and often fallible, portrayals of the Alamo heroes; the lovers of the myth can be dismayed that the motives of the Mexican army are presented with respect and understanding; and the hard-core Alamo buffs, each of whom clings to his specific set of beliefs as though they were handed to him by the angel Moroni, can endlessly nitpick each detail that differs from his own conception—and almost any detail of this particular moment in history can be nitpicked to death.

WHO WAS DAVY CROCKETT?

As an example of how impossible Hancock's task was, consider the character who was the most famous figure at the Alamo—David Crockett.

Who was he? What was he really like? It depends on who described him. To his political enemies, Crockett was an illiterate buffoon, a figure to ridicule. To his followers, he was a shining symbol of the frontier, clean, virtuous, and canny. To readers of the ubiquitous Crockett almanacs, he was a devilish and witty trickster, violent, racist, crude, and exuberant—"a ring-tailed roarer, half horse, half alligator and a little tetched with snapping turtle" (Clarke

Frank Thompson Collection

The real David Crockett.

164). To baby boomers in 1955 and ever after, he was the perfect hero—kind, principled, and brave.

But no movie has the luxury of exploring every aspect of a personality—especially one for which we have so relatively little to go on. John Lee Hancock had to do what any screenwriter must—create a character who is basically fiction but would seem real, based as closely as possible on the historical record. Billy Bob Thornton's portrayal of Crockett is the richest and most complex in any Alamo movie (sorry, Fess). It is a brilliant, nuanced performance that explores the duality of Crockett's life—"David" versus "Davy." There is plenty of evidence to support the idea that he did engage in such a struggle, that he felt limited, if not trapped, by the public's unrealistic perception of him.

One of the earliest scenes in the film depicts a true incident that speaks volumes about how the world viewed Crockett and how he viewed himself. In the scene, Congressman Crockett attends the performance of a play, *The Lion of the West* by James K. Paulding. The lead character, Nimrod Wildfire, was widely known to be a crude lampoon of Crockett, a buffoonish bull in a china shop who constantly enrages or embarrasses the high-society types on whom he imposes himself. The real Crockett was not pleased by the portrayal. When he showed up in the theater in Washington that night in 1833 (1835 in the film), the actor who played Nimrod, James Hackett, had every reason to be nervous; as far as he knew, Crockett really was a violent bumpkin like Nimrod. Before the play began, Hackett bowed to Crockett. As the audience applauded enthusiastically, Crockett stood and bowed back, a beautiful moment in which the real man acknowledged his own legend—however imperfect.

Thornton's Crockett understands the power of this legend. When he shows up in Texas, where he hopes to begin a prosperous new phase in his political career, he is dressed in buckskins and a coonskin hat—exactly as his constituents, or audience, expect to see him. Later, in the Alamo, when Bowie teases him about the hat, Crockett sheepishly admits, "I only started wearing that thing because of that play they did about me. People expect things." Throughout the film, this tug-of-war between the man and the myth continues. Trapped behind the walls of the Alamo, Crockett confides to Bowie, "If it was just me, simple old David from Tennessee, I might jump over that wall one night and take my chances. But that Davy Crockett feller—they're all watchin' him."

The struggle is resolved only at the point of his death. Of course, the manner of Crockett's death is among the most hotly and bitterly contested Alamo topics, even though there is virtually no real evidence to support any of the theories. But many historians take the word of one of Santa Anna's officers, Colonel José Enrique de la Peña, that Crockett was among the few Alamo defenders who survived the battle and were later executed. The film's purely speculative solution to this conundrum is slightly controversial but, dramatically, highly satisfying. As Crockett, on his knees before Santa Anna, faces death, he notices that one Mexican soldier is wearing his vest and another is sporting his coonskin cap. With a rueful laugh, Crockett realizes that he now has to choose for good—David or Davy. And he chooses Davy, the hero. He grins at his attackers and takes as his last words a line from the stage production of *The Lion of the West*—"I'm a screamer!"

Did this actually happen? Certainly not. Except for de la Peña's version, we have nothing reliable on which to base our guesses about Crockett's death. But this fictional moment seeks to illuminate a truth about Crockett, one that embraces the emotional truth of the moment while respecting the historical truth.

It is, in short, something that virtually no movie about the Alamo has ever attempted, preferring to look at Crockett and the others as men, not marble statues. The 2004 telling of *The Alamo* is not a documentary-style foray into unvarnished truth; it simply takes history seriously and tries its best to honor the reality of what those men and women in distant 1836 went through. I have watched, studied, and researched every Alamo film ever made, and I believe that this is probably the most we can ever ask of a movie with a historical subject. It is impossible to fully resurrect a time, a place, a people. But if those elements can be evoked with honesty, integrity, and sensitivity, the attempt can help ease us into a fuller appreciation and understanding of the subject. The result may be more emotional than historical, but when it comes right down to it, emotion is what the movies do best.

WORKS CITED

The Alamo. Dir. John Lee Hancock. Perf. Billy Bob Thornton, Patrick Wilson, Jason Patric. Touchstone Pictures, 2004.

The Alamo. Dir. John Wayne. Perf. John Wayne, Richard Widmark, Laurence Harvey. United Artists, 1960.

Alamo . . . The Price of Freedom. Dir. Kieth Merrill. Bonneville Entertainment, 1988.

Clarke, Matthew St. Clair. *Sketches and Eccentricities of Colonel David Crockett of West Tennessee.* New York: J. and J. Harper, 1833.

"Davy Crockett at the Alamo." *Disneyland.* Dir. Norman Foster. Perf. Fess Parker, Buddy Ebsen, Kenneth Tobey. ABC-TV, 23 Feb. 1955.

The Immortal Alamo. Dir. William Haddock. Perf. Francis Ford, Edith Storey, Gaston Méliès. Méliès Star Films, 1911.

"In San Antonio Plays Are Enacted Which Later Are Daily Viewed by Thousands of People in All Parts of the Country." *San Antonio Light.* January 1911.

Thompson, Frank. *The Alamo.* San Diego: Thunder Bay, 2002.

———. *The Alamo: A Cultural History.* Dallas: Taylor, 2001.

———. *The Alamo: The Illustrated Story of the Epic Film.* New York: Newmarket. 2004.

———. *Alamo Movies.* East Berlin, Pa.: Old Mill, 1991.

———. *The Alamo: A Novel.* New York: Hyperion, 2004.

With Davy Crockett at the Fall of the Alamo. Dir. Robert North Bradbury. Perf. Cullen Landis, Bob Bradbury. Sunset Pictures, 1926.

With Davy Crockett at the Fall of the Alamo. Press book. Frank Thompson Collection.

Assessing Television's Version of History

The Mexican-American War and the KERA Documentary Series

To better understand the Mexican-American War, we must place the conflict within the historical framework of the early and mid-nineteenth century, and especially in the context of how Americans viewed themselves and the world. The 1840s were years of rapid and dramatic territorial growth. This expansion, coupled with the ebullient popular attitudes, resulted in actions many Americans insisted were part of a "manifest destiny." The phrase was coined by John L. O'Sullivan in an editorial for the *Democratic Review* regarding the annexation of Texas in July 1845, and it quickly became the watchword for the mission of the republic and its citizens. Elected on a proexpansion platform in 1844, President Polk quickly moved to annex Texas and defiantly disregarded British claims to Oregon. Polk "incorrectly believed that the Mexican government was acting with Great Britain to thwart US territorial ambitions" (Haynes, "Manifest" par. 7), thereby fueling a distrust of Great Britain that lingered throughout the decade.

The gatherings and celebrations of American victories south of the border moved Walt Whitman to declare that there was no more "admirable impulse in the human soul than patriotism," which convinced him that the Mexican war was a great democratic mission; these military victories, he believed, would "elevate the *true* self respect of the American people" to a point equal to "such a great nation as ours really is" (82–85). This assertion of superiority and patriotism of the American ideal was but one element of manifest destiny; it also justified the extension of American democracy to the rest of the continent and placed a mantle of legitimacy over the entire expansionist effort. Of course, America's superiority assertion also contained the denigration of the enemy.

Though expansion and manifest destiny were inevitably linked, the expansionist agenda, never a clearly defined movement, did not enjoy what is now called bipartisan support. The fear and anxiety that Americans felt

KERA-TV

Manifest destiny was a dream of progress.

toward Great Britain—whose real and imagined designs involved blocking American territorial expansion at every turn and (what was feared by Southern landowners) actively engaging in a plot to abolish slavery throughout North America—changed the face of manifest destiny. Anglophobia converted support for gradual expansion to a more militant brand of American imperialism (Haynes, "Manifest" par. 1–2, 6–7).

In the years preceding the Mexican-American War, Great Britain was the dominant power opposed to the U.S. annexation of Texas. Her Majesty's government maintained extensive commercial and financial links with Mexico— Mexico owed a substantial debt to British stockholders, and the majority of foreign merchants living in Mexico were British. British policy essentially had two objectives: to secure Mexico's northern frontier against further encroachment by the United States and to reduce Britain's dependency on the American South by utilizing Texas's position as a great producer of cotton (Roeckell 182). Thus, according to historian Sam Haynes, there were much larger issues involved in the United States' expansion into Mexico (telephone interview).

Another aspect of the struggle between the United States and Great Britain was control of the western territories of Oregon and California. According to Haynes, "There was a fear that if the United States didn't acquire this territory now, Britain would acquire California; however, that does not diminish the Mexican role" (telephone interview). In fact, during the summer of 1845, Thomas O. Larkin, a U.S. merchant in California, warned the Polk administration that Britain, as well as France, had designs on the region. Mexican officials recognized California's vulnerability to American encroachment by land and sea and approached British minister Charles Bankhead for protection against potential U.S. expansion. But the British government was not prepared to contest America's move in California (Graebner 86–87). Once the annexation of Texas was accomplished, Great Britain abandoned further efforts to resist, rejecting opportunities to acquire California in 1845 and 1846.

Though the Mexican-American War has almost vanished from the American collective memory, it still remains very much alive south of the Rio Grande, where the war is called *la invasión norteamericana*, *la intervención norteamericana*, and *la guerra del 47*. Ironically, though the United States was victorious, the war is one that America strives to forget because it does not fit well with the preferred idea of American history; likewise, the war is one Mexico would like to forget, as it was lost in part because of internecine conflicts.

TELEVISED HISTORY

The television documentary has served a variety of functions since its inception in the early 1950s: it has been a focal point for national attention on complex issues, a record of human experience, and an instrument of social and artistic expression. Consequently, the genre is often a barometer of social and political dynamics. A nonfiction report devoted to a single thesis or subject overseen by a single producer, the TV documentary blends words, visuals, sound tracks, and individual aesthetic style to focus on singular moments or issues in history. But all too often, filmmakers are not content to merely depict the past; instead they turn out products designed to change attitudes and perspectives. When the work of these documentarians becomes popular, the films can serve to bridge the chasm between historians and the lay public (as evidenced by the success of Ken Burns's *The Civil War* [1990] and many programs on the History Channel), but they can also deepen the rift. The genre is judged not only by the standards of television but also by the standards of the academy. In achieving "resonance" (as Ken Burns terms a documentary's current social and moral relevance) with the modern mind as it places its subject in contemporary social and moral thought, the genre can fall victim to the dangers of historical manipulation and "presentism" (Melton par. 30).

Praised for its multiple-perspective approach and meticulous research, the KERA-Dallas/Fort Worth series *The U.S.-Mexican War (1846–1848)* (1998) embodies the tensions and compromises inherent in the production of any such historical documentary: the limitations imposed when presenting a historical event—and its subtleties—in a dramatic fashion; the presence of bias, even when attempts are made to avoid it; and the difficulties involved in creating an interesting and balanced product while remaining "true" to history, especially when focusing on a highly controversial period of conflict between two intricately connected nations. With its combination of contemporary visual materials, modern-day re-creations, and expert commentaries, *The U.S.-Mexican War* series is a case study for examining the creation of a compilation television documentary. Several key theoretical questions—and their very practical solutions—emerge: How can a narrator dramatically relate an event long ignored by some, yet significant and highly emotional for others? How can various contentious viewpoints be dealt with, both in preproduction and in the final product? Can such a project ultimately be fair and accurate, yet engaging enough for a general audience? The series applies current ideals, morals, and standards to historical figures and events, portraying the past through the prism of present-day standards. Even the series' title asserts a judgment, characterizing the United States as the aggressor.

Dallas-based columnist Ed Bark called *The U.S.-Mexican War (1846–1848)* a "triumph of the will" for KERA executive producer Sylvia Komatsu, who "wouldn't let the project die, despite innumerable rebuffs from potential major underwriters." The project began in 1991, when Komatsu saw an exhibition of daguerreotype images from the battlefields. After years of appealing, planning, and fund-raising, she won the aid of experts and historians steeped in the subject. She revealed to Bark that corporations were polite but "very frank" in declining to underwrite the project. "They told us, 'Fascinating subject, but it's simply too controversial for us to be associated with'" (C1). After finally receiving $672,000 in planning and production grants, including $527,000 from the National Endowment for the Humanities and generous support from Corpus Christie attorney J. A. "Tony" Canales, the series eventually attracted other funding from various foundations and councils. Komatsu, coproducer and screenwriter Rob Tranchin, director Ginny Martin, and the rest of the production team faced numerous challenges during production. Tranchin remembered that "it was a fight to get the show on the air. There was a certain lack of perspective, especially in the Northeast, and we were surprised by the

KERA-TV

Marines battle on the plain below Chapultepec Castle, September 1847.

feeling on the part of some that the war was of more regional interest than national significance" (telephone interview).

Essentially, the series presents a war fought in the name of manifest destiny. In 1846, the United States was looking well beyond the Rockies to expand all the way to the Pacific, but a vast wedge of Mexican territory inconveniently obtruded. The conflict with Mexico gradually escalated over the span of a decade: first came the Texas revolt of 1836, with the massacre at the Alamo followed quickly by a stunning victory for Sam Houston's forces in the Battle of San Jacinto; later came the more sustained conflict, involving the U.S. Army and Navy from 1846 to 1848 and the historic U.S. Marines' actions at the "Halls of Montezuma" (i.e., Chapultepec Castle, Mexico City).

The KERA series locates the conflict's origins in slavery, taxation, and an American settler rebellion against Mexico's central government. In the intervening nine years, President Polk annexed Texas all the way to the Rio Grande, deep inside territory claimed by Mexico. The unstable Mexico City regime was experiencing enough problems overseeing its own southern states, so many felt that it was impossible for Mexico to have much influence on its northern territory. Though Mexican officials knew their country was too weak to fight a war, their pride would not allow them to settle the issues diplomatically. When Polk declared war, it would be "the first time tens of thousands of [American] soldiers would be sent to fight on foreign soil," narrator Bruce Dubos intones (forgetting the incursions into Canada in 1776 and 1812). The series also asserts that, as the first war "fought in the media," the conflict fueled popular passions through heroic songs, plays, paintings, and lithographs, bringing the first reassurance since the War of 1812 that Americans could act heroically as a nation. By the 1840s, jingoistic cries arose from newspaper editors who wanted the country to exert its rightful interests and who whipped up war fever to bring about that end.

A darker consequence—internal division—threatened the movement toward war. The conflict was denounced as a cruel act of aggression by New Englanders as diverse as Henry David Thoreau, Frederick Douglass, and Daniel Webster, all of whom feared southern expansion. Conversely, it was celebrated as a necessary step in expansion and development by Polk and John C. Calhoun. As this division fueled the slavery debate, Massachusetts senator Webster opposed the antislavery position taken by his own Whig Party; he emphasized the party's need to remain flexible and abstained from voting on the declaration of war. Later, in response to the Wilmot Proviso, Webster stated that the United States should not wrest territory from the Republic of Mexico (Britt 477).

THE SERIES

On 13–14 September 1998 PBS affiliate KERA broadcast its four-hour documentary series *The U.S.-Mexican War (1846–1848)*. As an original broadcast, the series was shown in two-hour blocks over two nights. Produced in both English and Spanish, the series was KERA's first major PBS telecast since *LBJ* (1991). Interestingly, the series was not broadcast on KERA's Spanish-language partner network Canal Once (channel 11) or channel 13, the Mexico City educational station, until November of that year. The primary reason was that to air the Mexican version—which was a complete reproduction with Mexican actors and a complete reworking of the sound track—at that time was considered "too painful for their viewers" (Komatsu interview), since 13–14 September marked the 151st anniversary of the fall of Mexico City. Both sides paid heavily in blood. Of the 104,556 American men who served, 13,768 died—"the highest death rate of any war in our history," writes historian John S. D. Eisenhower (son of President Dwight D. Eisenhower) in *So Far from God: The U.S. War with Mexico* (quoted in Killian 2). Mexican casualties were considerably higher. But mention the U.S.-Mexican war, and most Americans react with a blank look. Mexicans, in contrast, remember more passionately. "It's a scar for them," Komatsu explained in an interview. Senior producer Paul Espinoza told journalist Diane Claitor that, when the war is mentioned in Mexico, "even a Mexican with a limited education will say, 'Oh, the war where the Gringos stole our territory,' while the Americans say, 'Which war?'" (par. 6).

The KERA series used a multiple-perspective approach to avoid historical inaccuracy.[1] The filmmakers provided commentary from both Mexican and American scholars. During preproduction, a panel of thirteen historians met in Dallas for a two-day seminar. Komatsu guided the discussions, soliciting advice and interpretive and factual information for the production.[2] Coproducers Paul Espinoza and Andrea Boardman, director Ginny Martin, and producer-scriptwriter Rob Tranchin often had to insert the working aspects of television production into a discussion that, at times, was "contentious" (according to at least one adviser) as the scholars lobbied, labored, and argued over points of particular concern (Haynes telephone interview). As David Weber remembered the process, "We read various drafts of the script and offered corrections or suggestions in our own areas of expertise. It seemed that those [corrections] were incorporated when possible."

The production team found itself in what amounted to a "scholarly war—with its own skirmishes, pre-emptive strikes, and sometimes full-fledged battles" (Claitor par. 13). Sam Haynes found the experience "frustrating and contentious and a rehash of old grievances." The older Mexican historians, he felt, often took "a position of victimhood," while the American historians examined the war in "broader, more objective terms." Ultimately, he thought that this "colored the editorial process"; "the battle lines were drawn and it was like we were fighting the war all over again." In his view, the Mexican historians on the panel exercised more editorial control over what was shown than the American historians, though he insisted that the traditionalist view was not shared by all attendant experts. Yet the traditionalist view does "make for more compelling television." In summing up the overall atmosphere of the meeting, Haynes said, "It may have started out as a turf war, but it didn't stay that way. Mexican historians were more passionate than the American historians" (telephone interview). The American advisers credited Komatso with moving the panel toward consensus on key points (Weber).

One of the most vocal members of the committee and the loudest critic of the series, Josefina Zoraida Vázquez argued that, in spite of the producers' earnest attempts at balance, a clear American bias surfaced. "I recognize the good intentions [of the production team] and it is difficult to overcome 150 years of trying to justify an unjust war," but she wished the Mexican advisers had been able to influence the makers of the series more. "In general," she said, it is unfortunate that the filmmakers "portray the standard U.S. view of the war . . . because most of the sophisticated university text books on U.S. history acknowledge U.S. provocation of the war" (quoted in Claitor par. 18–19). As Claitor explains, Vázquez is referring to "the presence of U.S. troops on the border, which led to border skirmishes that were used to justify the American invasion" (par. 19). Another Mexican adviser and critic of the series, Jesús Velasco-Márquez, further argues that, during the conflict, Mexico defended its territory not as "a result of arrogance, nor of irresponsibility, but rather the only [possible] response to the arguments and actions of the U.S. government. . . . The armed conflict between Mexico and the United States from 1846 to 1848 was the product of deliberate aggression and should therefore be referred to as 'The U.S. War Against Mexico'" (par. 15). As noted above, the title of the series certainly implies this viewpoint. According to Weber, "Each of us had our own particular interest and viewpoint, and not all of those could be accommodated. . . . Most of the scholars were very aware that the film could not be too didactic or it would lose its audience." Therefore, the advisers did not provide "easy" answers to the filmmakers, whose goal was not to cast blame for the war but to present a "neutral" narrative. "I remember a couple of occasions," Weber added ironically, "where the filmmakers seemed more concerned with historical accuracy than with filmic qualities, while the historians wondered how to make the narrative more crisp, increase the number of images, and make the film more visually interesting."[3]

Komatsu said that the production team "let the point of view come from historical characters and the historians themselves." Both Tranchin and Komatsu accept the criticism of the finished product: Said Tranchin, "It is natural, since different opinions were encouraged and those opinions were delivered in good faith and were reflective of difficult discussions." He pointed to the war itself as evidence of this natural reaction: "The subject for each audience is very different. Audiences come to the series with completely different emotional mind-sets" (telephone interview). Yet, Komatsu explained, "It wasn't simply a matter of U.S. advisers vs. Mexican advisers. Everyone involved felt that he or she had a 'particular take on the war,' not simply a matter of national bias. These divergent views were even present among the production team."

In the end, most of the historians agree that the other filmmakers "made a tremendous effort to include as many voices as possible. From Tejanos and women to Native Americans, there was a diversity of voices" (Haynes telephone interview). Weber concluded that "this was a fine collaboration, for each group was interested in advancing the fundamental goal of the other." Obviously, the participants prefer to cast a more positive light on these proceedings and to take a high ground over the disagreements. But it stands to reason that any product forged out of such contentiousness—and with such an earnest attempt to include as many voices as possible—might suffer from its own best intentions. In this atmosphere, political correctness would very likely arise to placate all sides, to soften and dilute any historical realities that might prove troublesome to any of the "voices."

Once the project was under way, points of contention multiplied exponentially. "Did Polk have a vision of how the war was going to take place when he sent [General Zachary] Taylor to the Rio Grande?" Tranchin asks. "In the main, our American scholars felt that he [Polk] didn't know—that he was reacting as much as acting. Our Mexican scholars felt Polk had a plan and was carrying out that plan. These are tricky shoals to navigate. When the narrator is involved, we make sure that the narrator doesn't plant a seed where we can't be sure" (quoted in Stabile 13). Despite the efforts of the production team to maintain an equilibrium, the series, as producer Andrea Boardman saw it, "was still television," meaning that the first priority remained presenting a story to an audience in an entertaining manner—which in so many telegenic studies of history leads to preferring drama over information and modern prejudice over truth about the past. From the producers' point of view, the need for a consistent narrative voice and clear, streamlined "story line" arose immediately. Tranchin recalled that "writing the script was excruciating because there were so many different points of view. The production was ongoing as the script was being constantly revised. It was a lot of work to get the visual track and narration to work together. Ginny [Martin] went through many revisions" (telephone interview).

A major challenge also lay in the actual storytelling, especially in describing the origins of the war. The producers felt it necessary to include basic information and history to set the stage. As Tranchin notes, "Most people imagine the war as the Alamo, which was a decade earlier." That meant the producers had to "get the viewers up to speed very quickly." The challenge to keep both the narrative development and the informative aspect provided yet another layer of tension: "We didn't want a spotty, superficial program, especially since a lot of TV history is bad history" (Tranchin quoted in Claitor par. 31, 36). To make this process as accessible as possible, the producers aimed to reflect the pulse of the past. They made an effort to incorporate a larger number of artifacts, portraits, and images of the period. "Paintings and lithographs are images," Tranchin said, "but they are also artifacts—they speak of a time and place in addition to the images they present. Daguerreotypes, photographs, and archival film footage are artifacts as well; they have a mechanical and optical

KERA-TV

A lithographic rendering of the Battle of Cerro Gordo, April 1847.

relationship to the world that most viewers accept as more authentic, though not necessarily more interesting" (e-mail). But one of the difficulties the team faced—surprisingly—concerned access to visual and written documents. For some, this inability to deal with primary materials might appear to be a major flaw. As Weber pointed out, "Visual materials for this period of time are scarce. With photography in its infancy, we had to depend on lithographs, paintings, historic places, and reconstructions. In the interest of historical accuracy, the producers did not employ photographs from later eras and present them anachronistically as of the era of the U.S.-Mexican War."

The producers sought to be authentic. "We were trying to balance the wealth of information from the U.S. side with a relative lack of information on the Mexican side," Tranchin said (telephone interview). English-language texts were available, but one challenging aspect, Komatsu said, was "our access to Spanish-language materials. Ultimately, our team of advisers would often be able to help us obtain translations of Mexican materials." Tranchin pointed out that the production team was "also fortunate to work with institutions that provided invaluable assistance. This testifies to a commitment to use historically accurate materials—a commitment that distinguishes most PBS productions" (telephone interview). Though such a statement rings of public relations posturing, the series does include these materials, which adds another layer of authenticity. The filmmakers combined these materials with scholar interviews, voice-over readings of period writers such as Walt Whitman, and scenes of battle reenactments. The producers rendered vignettes regarding events, individual battles, and interesting characters with historical accuracy.

One way the series attempted to reflect the pulse of the past was to include numerous landscape shots: "Landscapes are flexible because the viewer can accept them for what they are and imagine a past that took place 'there'" (Tranchin e-mail). Martin's challenge was to evaluate such perspectives and create a relationship between pictures and words. She was also in charge of the numerous historical re-creations; she "contacted several reenactor groups and set up a production schedule in Colorado, South Texas, and Mexico." Martin compiled and developed a wish list of historical moments to portray, sequences to set up, and shots to be taken at "a set of locations—like the California coastline, or a Santa Fe winter scene, or a South Texas plain" (Tranchin telephone interview). Tranchin explained, "Ginny would think . . . of shots that would convey a sequence—for example, introducing the battle of Palo Alto—and those locations would be approached with an eye towards recording the most important historical details. There was an enormous amount of footage, and only a fraction of it ended up in the final show." Re-creations are always perilous: "especially in documentaries," they "require a leap of faith. They function as moving illustrations and have to be produced well and used carefully because they can either enhance or distract" (Tranchin e-mail). The filmmakers found the reenactment groups to be as valuable as the advisory committee of scholars. "Our re-enactor groups were excellent to work with," Komatsu remembered. "They were very helpful and often served as advisers on historical detail." Of course, unless sketches or paintings are used instead, reenactors are necessary in a documentary depicting historical battles from periods before the advent of the motion picture camera to enable the audience to visually connect with the actions and the period. But this reliance on reenactors also proves problematic, because each reenactor has a personal view of the period and the conflict, and once again, the plethora of voices can overwhelm a visual history. Nevertheless, the production team was well aware of its responsibility to the public, and the final product demonstrates a responsible balance between reenactments and historical materials.

Though this approach is fairly standard for a historical compilation film, according to Tranchin, "there are so many different kinds of images and so many variables at work in each sequence. The images were chosen for their ability to carry the sense of the narration and dramatic readings, and sometimes

KERA-TV

Antonio López de Santa
Anna, president of Mexico.

because they enhanced the emotional quality of a certain passage." Various
images perform certain functions at key points in the narration. "Some [im-
ages] have a naturally introductory character—they set the scene. Others are
explanatory—they underline a point. Some enhance a particular mood or
emotion" (Tranchin e-mail). The series' visuals thus achieve Ken Burns's notion of resonance in placing the Mexican-American War squarely within the
present social and moral dialogue.

Along the way, the filmmakers created lively portraits of major personalities
of the war, such as generals Zachary Taylor and Winfield Scott and Ambassador Nicholas Trist, primarily through their own writings, contemporary news
accounts, and letters. The two most prominent and colorful characters to
emerge in the series are presidents Antonio López de Santa Anna and James
K. Polk—the former as a windbag of military bravado and foolhardy resolve
and the latter as a steely, intimidating agent of American expansion. Polk,
a dark-horse presidential candidate who won one of the closest elections in
American history, was unswervingly devoted to Jacksonian democracy and aggressively confrontational toward Mexico. As historian David Pletcher states in
the series, "When you face Santa Anna with Polk, you're facing one opportunist
with another. They both had that characteristic as part of their makeup. Polk
was using Santa Anna deliberately to gain negotiations with Mexico, but he

didn't count on Santa Anna rallying his people. Polk didn't realize this as a danger." An example of the series' portrayal of these two pivotal characters lies in Santa Anna's manipulation of Polk to enable the former to reenter Mexico from his exile in Cuba. Santa Anna persuaded Polk to let him slip through the naval blockade under the pretense of arranging negotiations between Mexico City and Washington. After Polk agreed and Santa Anna was safely back in Mexico City, he staged a coup, reinstalled himself as president, and declared war against the United States.

KEY FLAWS OF THE SERIES

Historians have been divided in their interpretations of the war since it ended in 1848. Some hold the United States culpable, while others blame Mexico; a survey of the historical literature indicates that the majority have taken a balanced view and consider neither country entirely blameless. Some, like John Eisenhower, see the annexation of Texas to the Union as the goal of the war (xix). Others believe that the fundamental conflict was a simple dispute: the United States demanded Mexico's land, and Mexico refused. The series returns to this particular point time and again. Vázquez argues in her commentary that "for North America, Texas was already a thing of the past. The only thing that interested them was to buy territory." Pletcher adds that "the one way to provoke the Mexicans into resistance was the one way Polk had chosen: to present a strong front and bluff the Mexican government into resisting—or into yielding—in other words, negotiating at cannon's point." The United States expected Mexico to willingly surrender half of its large territory, while Mexico expected, equally unrealistically, to fend off a U.S. military force.

Despite the resolve of the filmmakers to present an unbiased and factual look at the U.S.-Mexican war, the series demonstrates a tendency to downplay or omit significant elements that contributed to the conflict. One of the most obvious examples regards the role Great Britain played, if not in sparking the conflict then at least in exacerbating it. Not only does the series simplify the rather complicated role Britain played (only a fleeting reference is made in "The Terrible Word" and "The Other Shore" segments), but it omits that the British accused the United States of ignoring consequences to British trade and investments in Mexico and deliberately provoking an unjust war for the extension of slavery. (Mexico had abolished slavery in 1826; Britain abolished slavery and the slave trade in 1833.) Even more glaring, the series ignores the crucial role British diplomats played in facilitating communication between the United States and Mexico. In fact, thanks largely to British urging, Nicholas Trist remained in Mexico after being recalled by President Polk. In addition,

British agents assisted in the negotiations leading to the Treaty of Guadalupe Hidalgo (Roeckell 182). Ultimately, the series weaves all the various causes of the war into one simplistic and personalized thread: the U.S.-Mexican war was a result of President Polk's obsession with manifest destiny.

The series does note the war's military and journalistic significance. As mentioned above, except for incursions into Canada in 1776 and 1812, the Mexican-American War was the first occasion on which American troops were sent to fight on foreign soil. It was also the first war in which the United States raised and trained a large army, transported troops by railroad and by sea, and made a major amphibious landing. Significantly, it was the first war to be covered by mass circulation newspapers using dedicated correspondents. In the segment "Mr. Polk's War," the series shows the role the press played in affecting the public. It reveals that the war, for example, inspired Henry David Thoreau's famous treatise against war, "Civil Disobedience," and was the first major subject for mass-produced color lithographs and America's penny press.

Another area in which the series vacillates concerns President Polk's decision to go to war. According to the series' segment "Declaration of War," on Saturday, 9 May 1846, Polk met with his cabinet to "discuss" a declaration of war against Mexico—a document that had already been drafted. Later, at 6 P.M., Polk received Taylor's dispatch from two weeks earlier, detailing the commencement of hostilities. According to Weber, the production sidesteps that Polk had already decided to go to war but needed a plausible excuse to take to Congress:

> One of the points that I particularly wanted the film to make is that Polk had decided to declare war on Mexico even before he received the news of the skirmish on the Rio Grande. We know this from Polk's diary. At that point, many congressmen would have balked and war would have been a hard sell. Then came news of the episode on the Rio Grande that allowed him to make the specious claim that American blood had been shed on American soil and gave him a pretext for war that American congressmen found palatable. Although I'd suggested on more than one occasion that the script should include this small point, it didn't make it into the final cut.

This example illustrates the central problem with the series: the need for a narrative required the elimination of historical clutter. To appeal to the audience, the editorial desire for dramatic "story" took precedence over informational nuances. These particulars represented fascinating material that might provoke discussion, yet the producers' intention was to present a general overview for a general public that might be confused or bored by such historical sidelights.

This tendency to oversimplify extends to the treatment of the Saint Patrick's Battalion (Batallón de San Patricio). As depicted in the segment "The Naked Blade," the Mexican army, retreating to the Churubusco River, was pursued by U.S. troops, who came under heavy crossfire from the bridge and nearby convent. Here, the U.S. Army also clashed with two companies of Catholic immigrant deserters from the American army who had crossed over to the Mexican side. These deserters "stiffened the backbone of the Mexican resistance and brought about a more serious battle than Scott had any reason to expect," adds Eisenhower (quoted in Killian). The next mention the series makes of the deserter unit is in the segment "The Fate of Nations," where, as the battle at Chapultepec Castle rages on, thirty members of the Saint Patrick's Battalion watched from the gallows and, as the American flag was raised over the castle, were executed. According to Eisenhower, "if ever there were two points of view, this was one. To the Mexicans, the San Patricios were patriots. For the American military, there was little sympathy for deserters" (quoted in Killian). Yet the series offers no explanation for these soldiers' desertion. Though virtually none of the men left written records, as Robert Ryal Miller points out, other contemporary sources indicate possible factors (150). Brutal military discipline, hatred of and unsuitability for military life, harassment of and discrimination against foreign-born soldiers by native-born officers, religious sentiments and ideological beliefs, romantic entanglements, and, ultimately, material enticements by Mexican officers are all plausible reasons that the members of this battalion deserted (151). Yet the series offers little more than scant hints of the more complex issues within the Mexican army.

In contrast, MGM's feature film *One Man's Hero* (1999), which chronicles the life of Major John Riley and the Saint Patrick's Battalion, presents significant explanations for the Irish troops' desertion. According to the film, President Polk, with the backing of southern slave states, raised an army of the sons of Irish immigrants by promising them full citizenship for their families and forty acres of western land. After encountering pervasive nativism, the Irish troops deserted the army and fought for the Catholic Mexicans. Since the monumental volte-face, generations of Mexicans have regarded Riley as a folk hero. Director Lance Hool, who labored for three decades to bring the story to the screen, doubted whether American audiences would have the same sympathetic reaction: "After all, the Saint Patrick's were deserters. But they were also fighting for a cause they believed in [freedom from intolerance], a quality Americans still appreciate today" (quoted in Wherry 89). The film follows on the heels of Mark Day's 1996 documentary *The San Patricios*, which was shot on location in Ireland, Texas, and Mexico. Day's film includes interviews with American and Mexican historians, writers, and journalists and has been broadcast by RTÉ in Ireland, Televisa in Mexico, and more than a dozen PBS stations in the United States. In September 1997 the Saint Patrick's Battalion was honored in a commemoration ceremony in Mexico City involving Mexican president Ernesto Zedillo, Ireland's ambassador to Mexico, and other dignitaries. *One Man's Hero* did not benefit from this attention, however; controversy arose shortly after its release because of its seemingly anti-American flavor, and MGM stopped its U.S. distribution. To add insult to injury, the film was also critically assailed, often receiving a dismal rating of one star when it appeared on television listings.[4]

KEY STRENGTHS OF THE SERIES

Though effective in its military execution, the Mexican-American War was intensely ambiguous in the American national consciousness and remains controversial as a defining moment. *The U.S.-Mexican War* is successful in presenting these uncertainties for Mexico and offers some reflections on U.S. uncertainties as well. In the "Legacies" segment, Pletcher insightfully comments that America, "if not at fault, did not fully live up to its ideology of democracy. This was an aggressive war in which we attacked a neighbor. We do not like to look at the way in which we won it."

The series effectively discusses how this war ravaged Mexico. Though the Mexican cession of a half million square miles of new territory was the most important consequence of the war, the country also fell into political turmoil—France invaded in 1862 to collect a massive debt, and a series of brutal dictatorships further ravaged the country until 1910. Mexico remains economically underdeveloped. According to Israel Garza, "The only benefit is that we have found a spirit of Mexican identity."

The series is also strong in relating the differences in size between Mexico and the United States. In 1846 Mexico had a population of 7.5 million, compared with the United States' 20 million. The northern provinces in dispute were sparsely populated. California had only 7,000 residents, and except for Texas, what would become the American Southwest was desolate and isolated from central authority. Mexico received $15 million for lands lost to the United States, plus $10 million in other compensation. Before the war, Polk had offered $30 million to buy the territory outright. Miguel Soto adds in the "Legacies" segment, "The sooner we Mexicans confront how we have been in the presence of the United States, the better we will relate to North America. That we are victims of imperialism, yes, and many other ways as well. Certainly,

KERA-TV

A Mexican couple in the acquired territory.

our conditions helped the U.S. do what it did and to do what it does today. It is necessary to demystify our relationship with the U.S." Josefina Zoraida Vázquez adds, "To study that war will help those here to live together."

The Mexican-American War has long been eclipsed in the nation's popular memory by the American Civil War, which followed only a dozen years later, even though the war with Mexico ignited passions that would lead to the Civil War. For Mexico, the end of the war ushered in demoralization and turmoil, social restructuring, economic collapse, and the creation of "American" lands and Chicano culture.

REACTION TO THE SERIES

Verne Gray of *Newsday* commended the series for its "efficient, crisp script" and its stunning cinematography, remarking that it "looks fresh and feels energetic for the most part," but he criticized the extended commentary from Mexican and American historians. Gray opined that there was too much reenactment footage, "though it does, presumably, give a sense of what battle dress was like." He noted the density of detail in the series: "The producers seem to have found every illustration still extant of the war, including every early daguerreotype." Most critics held that the series' biggest accomplishment was the attempted conjoining of both national memories. As historian Eisenhower notes, "the biggest thing that Americans have to realize is that Mexicans have not forgotten this [war]" (quoted in Killian). Walter Goodman, in the *New York Times,* called the production "vigorous" and "fair-minded"; he appreciated that the main battles of the war were "effectively re-enacted in a rugged-looking terrain, and in the spirit of [Ken Burns's] *The Civil War,* soldiers' letters home provide personal touches." Goodman praised the producers for giving the Mexican defenders their due (1). In the *Columbia (S.C.) State,* Doug Nye found that the film "excellently blends daguerreotypes, lithographs, and paintings of the period with re-enactment footage shot at the actual battle sites" and commended the producers, who "strove hard to present a balanced and unbiased presentation of both sides of the story" (3). Ed Bark, in the *Dallas Morning News,* called the series "extraordinary save for its ordinary title" and characterized it as an "indelible, valuable retelling of this largely forgotten conflict" (C1). Tranchin noted that the series "had decent ratings, maybe not a home run like *The Civil War* was, but we had a uniformly good response" (telephone interview). In 1999, the series won an Emmy Award.

The most immediate impact of the series, according to the producers, was educational. The series "created more awareness about the war, and [it] is still being used in the classroom," Komatsu said; "it's helped to show how history and demographics change." The "balance of opinions" was key to the critical and commercial success of the series, and the panel of advisers reported "overwhelmingly positive responses" (Komatsu). The companion Web site to the series was identified by PBS as among its top visited. PBS was so pleased that PBS Educational Services funded a refurbishment of the site, including extensive video, sophisticated graphics, a brief episode summary, an interactive timeline map of events, and a large biographical section that covers the major figures involved on both sides of the conflict.[5]

The consensus among the production team was that Americans, especially Texans, would reject Mexican interpretations of the conflict. For many

Americans, who are accustomed to a stable government, there is a tendency to look at the disorganization and disunity in Mexico as a sign of ineptitude. To counter that stereotype, Tranchin said, one goal of the series was to portray Mexican society at the time as it emerged from imperial domination. "It had only been a nation for twenty years and was still operating with medieval institutions and a government it had inherited from the Spanish" (telephone interview). This colonial structure hampered the Mexican reaction to the U.S. invasion and severely handicapped efforts at national defense. But despite the mostly positive reviews from critics, the series' presentation of Mexico's view of the conflict as a war of Yankee aggression was repugnant to some viewers. Komatsu, for example, remembered that when KERA aired a short promotional spot before the series debuted, the station immediately received angry calls from Dallas viewers, who often began with phrases like, "My ancestors fought the Mexicans at San Jacinto" and "How dare you" (quoted in Claitor par. 49). Tranchin hoped that, when the series aired, Americans in all parts of the country would see how much more complex the issues were and still are. "The Mexicans didn't come to the U.S., the U.S. came to them," he said. After attending a San Antonio preview with a largely Mexican American audience, Tranchin said that he was struck by the "intensely emotional reaction" to the "Legacies" section. "Here the series makes it clear for the first time that the war between U.S. and Mexico was the birth event for the Mexican American [i.e., Chicano] people," he explained (quoted in Claitor par. 57). The war was assuredly pivotal for both nations in a variety of ways, and for many it is still an emotional firestorm 150 years later.

No matter how sincere the production team's effort was to achieve a balanced approach to presenting the war with Mexico, the divisive nature of the subject undermined the final product. The series suffers from trying to be all things to all sides: at times, it vocalizes the "victimhood" of the Mexican viewpoint while castigating the arrogant American motivations; at other times, it steadfastly presents the American viewpoint of expansionism and defense while demonstrating the Mexican arrogance and, ultimately, incompetence in provoking a war with its dynamic neighbor. The series shows the difficulty of maintaining balance in the face of fervent multiple perspectives. In the end, the series attains no single perspective but leaves it to the viewer to form a rationale for the nature and causes of the war—which is not necessarily a negative result. Ultimately, the series falls victim to its own ambitions: by concentrating on streamlining a clear, telegenic narrative, it loses significant historical subtleties, and by striving so diligently for multiple perspectives, it often succumbs to political correctness. These are critically missed opportunities to add layers of complexity and understanding for the viewer. The filmmakers fall back to the traditional question that has been asked from the first major project in the compilation tradition, *Victory at Sea* (1952–1953): what would be most interesting and engaging—and visually dramatic—to an audience?

History is not always well served by the methods of production that result from such a focus. *The U.S.-Mexican War (1846–1848)* is significant as the most comprehensive television treatment of this war. The impact of the series will continue to be felt, and the "almost forgotten war" will remain in the consciousness of two very different—yet very connected—nations. The U.S.-Mexican war gave shape not only to the borders but also to the populations and political identities of the two countries, an impact that has extended into the twenty-first century. KERA's *The U.S.-Mexican War* does not merely offer historical details but, more significantly, presents perspectives on an ambiguous and pivotal moment in U.S.-Mexican relations—a historical moment that may have more relevance as the twenty-first century progresses.

NOTES

1. From the outset, Komatsu and her production team resolved to present multiple perspectives to produce a balanced and compelling story. According to screenwriter-producer Rob Tranchin, "The bi-national nature of the project was our biggest challenge—it always, in a way, had two heads. We were trying to account for both the U.S. and Mexican perspectives without having each cancel out the other point of view" (quoted in Stabile 12). The extensive collaboration of experts from the United States and Mexico did, indeed, attract a wide range of views. KERA also provided a number of teaching materials, including a companion book (Christensen and Christensen), a curriculum kit designed for middle and secondary schools, and a thorough Web site (http://www.pbs.org/kera/usmexicanwar/educators) amplifying the issues broached by the documentary. A significant element of the KERA documentary is its emphasis on the Mexican point of view; some Mexican scholars view the conflict as not merely a war fought over territory but a spiritual violation by expansionist America—a violation of language, labor, and culture. Other Mexican sources view the war as a simple matter of self-defense that Mexican authorities were unable to meet—in addition to fighting the Americans, many Mexican factions were fighting one another. Still others come very close to echoing nineteenth-century Mexican nationalist José María Lafragua's demand that the United States return unjustly acquired territory to the nation from which it was wrested.

2. The advisory panel included R. David Edmunds, American history, University of Texas at Dallas; Mario T. Garcia, Chicano and American race and ethnicity, University of Santa Barbara; Deena Gonzalez, history of Chicano/a studies, Pomona College; Richard Griswold del Castillo, history, San Diego State University; the late David Pletcher, history, Indiana University; Miguel Soto, history, Universidad Nacional Autónoma de México; Ron Tyler, history, University of Texas at Austin; Josefina Zoraida Vázquez, his-

tory, El Colegio de México; Sam W. Haynes, history, University of Texas at Arlington; Robert W. Johannsen, history, University of Illinois at Urbana-Champaign; Robert Ryal Miller, history, California State University, Hayward; Jesús Velasco-Márquez, international studies, Instituto Tecnológico Autónomo; and David Weber, history, Southern Methodist University.

3. The historical commentary was provided by numerous scholars, including Antonia Castañeda, Israel Cavazos Garza, Richard Deertrack, William DePalo Jr., R. David Edmunds, John S. D. Eisenhower, Luis Garfias, Miguel González Quiroga, Sam W. Haynes, Robert W. Johannsen, Tony Mares, Genaro Padilla, David Pletcher, Carlos Recio Dávila, Miguel Soto, Josefina Zoraida Vázquez, Jesús Velasco-Márquez, and David W. Weber.

4. After *The U.S.-Mexican War* aired in September 1998, interest in the Mexican-American War grew as other films appeared on the small screen and in theaters, though not entirely without controversy. In 1998 the History Channel aired a four-part documentary titled *Mexico* that offers a different perspective on the war. The film's second episode, "From Independence to the Alamo," examines the initial conflict between Mexico and the United States. The third episode, "Battle for North America," treats the U.S.-Mexican war as a result of Polk's obsession with manifest destiny and Mexico's refusal to accept the annexation of Texas by another country.

In the fall of 2006 the History Channel presented a new two-hour documentary called *The Mexican-American War.* The documentary was shot in high-definition and was also broadcast on History en Español, the channel's Spanish-language sister network. Three of the KERA production's advisers, Sam Haynes, Jesús Velasco-Márquez, and Josefina Zaraida Vázquez, also served as advisers and interviewees on this documentary (Filmmakers 1–3).

5. The impressive Web site, http://www.pbs.org/kera/usmexicanwar/, is arguably the best Internet site dealing with the war. If one combines the Web site, the series, and the companion book written by Carol and Thomas Christensen, both accomplished translators and publishers, one has a full and detailed discussion of the broad strokes of the war and a good presentation of the subtleties of the conflict. Where the series often comes up short, the Web site and the book fill in numerous details. Although the Web site never contradicts the series, it does capture more of the nuances of the conflicts and broaches a wider spectrum of interpretations.

WORKS CITED

Bark, Ed. "War & Remembrance: First-Rate Production, Storytelling Bring U.S.-Mexican War to Life." *Dallas Morning News* 13 Sept. 1998: C1.

Boardman, Andrea. Telephone interview. 6 Sept. 2006.

Britt, Cassandra. "Daniel Webster." Frazer 477.

Christensen, Carol, and Thomas Christensen. *The U.S.-Mexican War: Companion to the Public Television Series.* San Francisco: Bay, 1998.

Claitor, Diana. "Producers Must Tell Mexican War from Two Viewpoints, Far Apart." *Current* 24 Aug. 1998. <http://www.current.org/hi/hi815m.html>.

Eisenhower, John S. D. *So Far from God: The U.S. War with Mexico, 1846–1848.* Norman: U of Oklahoma P, 1989.

"Filmmakers Reenact Epic Battles of the Mexican-American War with Panasonic's AG-HVX200 Hand-Held And AJ-HDC27 Varicam HD Camcorders: Two-Hour History Channel Documentary Will Air Fall 2006." *Panasonic Ideas for Life.*

Frazer, Donald S., ed. *The United States and Mexico at War: Nineteenth-Century Expansionism and Conflict.* New York: Macmillan, 1998.

Goodman, Walter. "Rattling Montezuma's Halls." *New York Times* 11 Sept. 1998, weekend ed.

Graebner, Norman A. "Causes of the War: U.S. Perspective." Frazer 86–87.

Gray, Verne. "A Mess with Texas: PBS Revisits War with Mexico." *Newsday* 9 Sept. 2006.

Haynes, Sam W. "Manifest Destiny." *The U.S.-Mexican War (1846–1848).* 14 Mar. 2006. PBS. <http://www.pbs.org/kera/usmexicanwar/prelude/md_manifest_destiny.html>.

———. Telephone interview. 30 Aug. 2006.

Killian, Michael. "'Mexican War' or 'U.S. Invasion'? PBS Series Looks at Both Sides." *Chicago Tribune* 11 Sept. 1998: 1.

Komatsu, Sylvia. Telephone interview. 29 June 2006.

Melton, Matthew. "Ken Burns' *Civil War:* Epic Narrative and Public Moral Argument." *Sync: The Regent Journal of Film and Video* 1.2 (Spring 1994). <http://www.regent.edu/acad/schcom/rojc/melton.html>.

The Mexican-American War. Dir. Jim Lindsey. History Channel, 2006.

Mexico. Dir. Michael Rodgers. History Channel, 1998.

Miller, Robert Ryal. *Shamrock and Sword: The Saint Patrick's Battalion in the U.S.-Mexican War.* Norman: U of Oklahoma P, 1989.

Nye, Doug. "PBS Special Is a Vivid Lesson of an Almost Forgotten War." *State* 13 Sept. 1998.

One Man's Hero. Dir. Lance Hool. MGM, 1998.

Roeckell, Leila M. "Great Britain." Frazer 182–83.

The San Patricios. Dir. Mark Day. Day Productions, 1996.

Stabile, Tom. "Crossroads of Conflict: Exploring the Legacy of the U.S.-Mexican War." *Humanities* 19.5 (1998): 12–16.

Tranchin, Rob. E-mail to the author. 15 Sept. 2006.

———. Telephone interview. 29 June 2006.

———. "U.S. MX War Notes Are Coming." E-mail to the author. 15 Sept. 2006.

The U.S.-Mexican War (1846–1848). Dir. Ginny Martin. KERA-Dallas/Fort Worth, 1998.

Velasco-Márquez, Jesús. "The Mexican Viewpoint on the War with the United States." *La Prensa San Diego* 11 Sept. 1998 <http://www.laprensa-sandiego.org/archieve/september11/view.htm>.

Weber, David. "RE: The U.S.-Mexican War Series." E-mail to the author. 2 Sept. 2006.

Wherry, Rob. "Tale of the Turncoats." *George*   Sept. 1998: 88–89.

Whitman, Walt. *The Gathering of Forces.* Ed. Cleveland Rodgers and John Black. New York: Putnam, 1920.

KEN BURNS'S REBIRTH OF A NATION

The Civil War as Made-for-Television History

It has been around eighteen years since *The Civil War* premiered over five consecutive evenings (23–27 September 1990), amassing a level of attention unsurpassed in public television history. Ken Burns's eleven-hour version of the war acted as a flash point for a new generation, attracting a spectrum of opinion that ranged from rapturous enthusiasm to milder interest in most segments of the viewing public, from outrage over Yankee propaganda in a few scattered areas of the South to both praise and criticism from the academy (Lord, "Did Anyone" 18; *Civil War Illustrated* July–Aug. 1991; *Confederate Veteran* Jan.–Feb. 1991, Mar.–Apr. 1991, July–Aug. 1991; Toplin). Burns employed twenty-four consultants on this project, including many prominent historians, but understandably, not all these scholars and filmmaking specialists agreed with everything in the final series.[1] With so many experts, and with a subject the size and scope of the Civil War as the historical terrain, a certain amount of controversy was unavoidable.[2]

One historian even concluded his analysis of *The Civil War* by calling the series "a flawed masterpiece" (Koeniger 233), evoking the customary judgment of D. W. Griffith's *The Birth of a Nation* (1915) that has been repeated in dozens of general film histories over the past seventy years.[3] This analogy goes only so far, however; it makes more sense on the grounds of shared cinematic brilliance than on the basis of any similarities in outlook or sensibility. Indeed, one of Burns's stated intentions was to amend the "pernicious myths about the Civil War from *Birth of a Nation* to *Gone with the Wind*," especially in regard to racial stereotyping and the many other bigoted distortions in plot and imagery (quoted in Milius 1, 43).

Still, *The Birth of a Nation* and *The Civil War* were similarly indicative of mainstream contemporary public opinion. For example, Russell Merritt has argued convincingly that the racist aspects of *The Birth of a Nation* were anything but the ravings of some "isolated crackpot"; rather, they were representative of white America at the time. According to Merritt, Griffith "attracted his audience . . . because the drama itself was one . . . Americans wanted to see" (167, 175). As a result, *The Birth of a Nation* was embraced by an estimated 10 percent of the U.S. population in its original release, making it the preeminent box office success in silent film history (166).

The popular reaction to *The Civil War* was likewise record setting. Public television achieved its highest ratings ever when 38.9 million Americans tuned in to at least one episode of the five-night telecast, averaging 12 million viewers at any given moment (Statistical Research Inc. 2.1–2.8). The audience research findings also indicated that half the viewership would not have been watching television at all if it had not been for this program ("CBS, PBS" 28; "Learning Lessons" 52–53; Gold 36; Carter C17; Gerard 46; Bickelhaupt, "'Civil War' Weighs" 61, 64). This fact was reflected in the range of published responses to *The Civil War*, which included pieces by political pundits who rarely, if ever, attend to the opening of a major motion picture or television series. George Will, for example, wrote, "Our *Iliad* has found its Homer. . . . If better use has ever been made of television, I have not seen it" (A23). David S. Broder and Haynes Johnson weighed in with similar high praise.

Film and television critics from across the country were equally effusive. *Newsweek* reported that *The Civil War* was "a documentary masterpiece" (Waters 68); *Time* called it "eloquen[t] . . . a pensive epic" (Zoglin 73); and *U.S. News and World Report* named it "the best Civil War film ever made" (Lord, "Unvarnished" 74). David Thomson in *Film Comment* declared that *The Civil War* "is the great American movie of the year—and one of the true epics ever made" (12). Tom Shales of the *Washington Post* remarked, "This is not just good television, nor even just great television. This is heroic television" (G5). And Monica Collins of the *Boston Herald* informed her readers that "to watch 'The Civil War' in its entirety is a rare and wonderful privilege." She then urged, "Keep in mind that the investment in the program is an investment in yourself, in your knowledge of your country and its history" (43).

Between 1990 and 1992, accolades for Ken Burns and the series took on institutional proportions, as it garnered more than forty major awards from the entertainment industry and the academic community combined. Burns was named producer of the year by the Producers Guild of America; the series won two Emmys for outstanding informational series and outstanding writing achievement, best foreign television award from the British Academy of Film and Television Arts, a Peabody Award, a duPont-Columbia Award, a Golden

Globe, a D. W. Griffith Award, two Grammys for best traditional folk album and best spoken word album, best special and best program from the Television Critics Association, and a People's Choice Award for best television miniseries. Gettysburg College also awarded *The Civil War* its first $50,000 Lincoln Prize as the "finest scholarly work in English on Abraham Lincoln or the American Civil War soldier" in competition with forty-one books ("Ken Burns Wins" 14). Burns was awarded eight honorary doctorates from various American colleges and universities in 1991 alone.[4] In retrospect, Burns said, "I don't really know how to put my finger on it. A generation ago as we celebrated, or tried to celebrate, the centennial, we seemed focused on the battles or the generals, and the kind of stuff of war, but here we seemed to respond to the human drama, and maybe it just resonated in a particular way with how we are. I feel a tremendous sympathy for this country and somewhere along the line that sympathy must line up with where we are now and whatever the subject is" (personal interview). *The Civil War* became a phenomenon of popular culture. The series was mentioned on episodes of *Twin Peaks, Thirtysomething*, and *Saturday Night Live* during the 1990–1991 television season. It was spoofed on National Public Radio and in a *New Yorker* cartoon. Burns appeared on the *Tonight Show* shortly after Johnny Carson took the unusual step of recommending the series to his audience on the Monday following the Sunday debut of the first episode. Burns was selected by the editors of *People* magazine as one of 1990's twenty-five "most intriguing people," along with the usual odd assortment of international figures, including George H. W. Bush, Julia Roberts, M. C. Hammer, Saddam Hussein, Bart Simpson, Sinead O'Connor, and Nelson Mandela.

The series also developed into a marketing sensation, as the companion book published by Knopf, *The Civil War: An Illustrated History,* became a runaway best seller. According to *Publishers Weekly*, "The celebrated PBS television series *The Civil War* certainly helped its eponymous companion volume sell enough books for the #2 slot. Knopf reported sales of 560,931 in 1990, and the book is still enjoying a brisk rate of sales in 1991" (Mayles 20). This hardcover title spent eleven straight weeks on the top-ten list during 1990 and then extended its streak for fifteen additional weeks in 1991 ("Longest-Running" 34). "Considering the $50 ticket price," *Publishers Weekly* related, "the book is easily the year's bestselling nonfiction grosser in dollars" (Mayles 20). The accompanying Warner sound track and the nine-episode videotape version from Time-Life were similarly successful. Burns noted that "the Civil War videotapes are the best-selling nonfiction documentary series on history ever made" ("Movie Maker" 1050). *Billboard* reported that the videotape set reached the 1 million plateau in aggregate sales as early as October 1993 (Fitzpatrick 9).

Several interlocking factors evidently contributed to the extraordinary level of interest surrounding *The Civil War,* including the overall technical and dramatic quality of the miniseries itself, its accompanying promotional campaign, the momentum of scheduling Sunday through Thursday, the synergic merchandising of all its ancillary products, and a TV industry strike earlier in the year that disrupted the fall season and caused the network competition to briefly delay its season premieres. Most significant, though, a new generation of historians had already begun addressing the war from the so-called bottom-up perspective, underscoring the role of African Americans, women, immigrants, workers, farmers, and common soldiers in the conflict. This fresh emphasis on social and cultural history had revitalized the Civil War as a subject, adding a more inclusive and human dimension to the traditional preoccupations with great men, transcendent ideals, and battle strategies and statistics. The time was propitious for creating another rebirth of the nation on film that included the accessibility of the bottom-up approach. In Burns's own words, "I realized the power that the war still exerted over us" (personal interview).

The Civil War has, indeed, fascinated Americans for more than 140 years. In his Pulitzer Prize–winning *Battle Cry of Freedom,* James M. McPherson estimates that the literature "on the war years alone . . . totals more than 50,000 books and pamphlets" (865). Reader interest had been increasing in the five years preceding the debut of *The Civil War;* 520 of the 1,450 titles that were still in print in September 1990 had been published since 1986. After the premiere of the series, however, fascination with the war became "higher . . . than it has ever been" (McDowell D10).

Shelby Foote was the first modern writer to liken the Civil War to the *Iliad,* in the third volume of his trilogy *The Civil War: A Narrative* (*Red River* 1064). His intent was to emphasize how "we draw on it for our notion of ourselves, and our artists draw on it for the depiction of us in the same way that Homer and the later dramatists—Aeschylus, Sophocles, Euripides—drew on the Trojan war for their plays" ("Conversation" 8). Much of the success of Ken Burns's *The Civil War* is linked to the extent that his version made this nineteenth-century conflict immediate and comprehensible to audiences in the 1990s. The great questions of race and continuing discrimination, of the changing roles of women and men in society, of big government versus local control, and of the individual struggle for meaning and conviction in modern life all remain. The Civil War captivates because its purposes endure; Americans are as engaged as ever in the war's dramatic conflicts. As Burns summarized,

There is so much about *The Civil War* that reverberates today . . . a developing women's movement, Wall Street speculators, the imperial presidency, new mili-

General Motors/Owen Comora Associates

Shelby Foote (seated left), the author and principal on-screen commentator for *The Civil War,* with producer-director Ken Burns.

tary technology, the civil rights question and the contribution of black soldiers. . . . There are also approximations and that sort of thing. You have to cut stuff out. I would have loved more on the congressional sort of intrigues during the Civil War. I would have loved to do more on women and more on emancipation and more on Robert E. Lee and more on the western battles, but limitations of photographs or just time or rhythm or pacing, or whatever it is, conspired against those things. And they were there, but they were taken out to serve the demands of the ultimate master, which is narrative. (personal interview)

THE FILMMAKER AS POPULAR HISTORIAN

Narrative is a particular mode of knowledge and means of relaying history. It is a historical style that is dramatic and commonly literary, although *The Civil War* does indicate that it can be adapted to electronic media as well. Burns strongly recognizes that "television has become more and more the way we are connected to the making of history" ("In Search" 1). In selecting the Homeric model, he chose certain narrative parameters that are epic and heroic in scope. The epic form tends to celebrate a people's national tradition in sweeping terms, and a recurring assertion throughout Burns's filmic history is that the Civil War gave birth to a newly redefined American nation. The final episode, "The Better Angels of Our Nature," for example, begins with three commentaries on nationhood that rhetorically set the stage from which the series will be brought to its rousing conclusion:

> Strange is it not that battles, martyrs, blood, even assassination should so condense a nationality. —Walt Whitman (spoken by Garrison Keillor)

> [The Civil War] is the event in American history in that it is the moment that made the United States as a nation. —Barbara Fields

> Before the war it was said the United States *are*, grammatically it was spoken that way and thought of as a collection of independent states, and after the war it was always the United States *is* as we say today without being self-conscious at all—and that sums up what the war accomplished: it made us an is. —Shelby Foote

These remarks are immediately followed by the bittersweet and tragic lament that serves as the series' anthem, "Ashokan Farewell," thus reinforcing the overall heroic dimensions of the narrative. Heroism, honor, and nobility are related Homeric impulses that permeate this series, shaping our reactions to the great men of the war, such as Abraham Lincoln, Frederick Douglass, and Robert E. Lee, along with the many foot soldiers whose bravery often exceeded the ability of their officers to lead them, resulting in the appalling carnage recounted in episode after episode.

History on TV tends to stress the twin dictates of narrative and biography, which ideally express television's inveterate tendency toward personalizing all social, cultural, and, for our purposes, historical matters within the highly controlled and viewer-involving confines of a well-constructed plot structure. The scholarly literature on television has established intimacy and immediacy (among other aesthetics) as inherent properties of the medium (see Newcomb, *Television* and *TV*; Fiske and Hartley; R. Adler; Allen; and Bianculli). In the case of intimacy, for instance, the confines of a relatively small TV screen, typically watched within the privacy of the home environment, long ago resulted in an evident preference for intimate shot types (i.e., close-ups and medium shots). Thus most fictional and nonfictional historical portrayals are fashioned in the style of the personal drama or melodrama, played out by a manageable number of protagonists and antagonists. When the effort is successful, audiences closely

This famous photograph of three Confederate soldiers captured at the Battle of Gettysburg is used several times during *The Civil War*. Shelby Foote discusses it for nearly a minute at the start of episode five, "The Universe of Battle," suggesting that it reveals the "attitude . . . determination . . . and individuality" of its subjects. He concludes, "There is something about that picture that draws me strongly as an image of the war."

identify with the historical actors and stories being presented and respond in intimate ways in the privacy of their own homes.

    The Civil War's most celebrated set piece, the poignant and eloquent voice-over of Major Sullivan Ballou's parting letter to his wife before he was killed in the First Battle of Bull Run (again accompanied by the haunting strains of "Ashokan Farewell"), illustrates the skillful way in which Burns infuses the epic sweep of the series with a string of highly personal and well-placed dramatic interludes. This scene, which lasts approximately three and one-half minutes, concludes episode one, "1861—the Cause," thus lending the preceding ninety-five minutes an air of melancholy, romance, and higher purpose. Poetic license is used throughout the segment, as Ballou's declaration of love is heard over

This photograph is used in *The Civil War,* in the accompanying book, and on the series' video jacket to portray a band of young Confederate soldiers. Taken before the Confederacy was even created, however, this photo actually shows the Richmond militiamen of the First Virginia Regiment, who were guarding John Brown in Charles Town, West Virginia, in November 1859, following his capture at Harpers Ferry. Such poetic license is a regularly acknowledged feature of TV histories.

images that have nothing factually to do with Sullivan Ballou but evoke the emotional texture of his parting sentiments: photographs of the interior of a tent where such a letter might have been written, a sequence of pictures portraying six other Civil War couples, and three static filmed shots of the Manassas battlefield as it looks today in a pinkish twilight.

After narrator David McCullough briefly begins the scene with the words, "A week before Manassas, Major Sullivan Ballou of the Second Rhode Island wrote home to his wife in Smithfield," actor Paul Roebling's serenely heartfelt and understated reading fades up quietly underneath the photographs:

> My very dear Sarah. . . . I feel impelled to write a few lines that may fall under your eyes when I shall be no more. . . . I have no misgivings about, or lack of confidence in the cause in which I am engaged, and my courage does not halt or falter. . . . Sarah my love for you is deathless. . . . The memories of the blissful moments I have spent with you come creeping over me . . . but O Sarah, if the dead can come back to this earth and flit unseen around those they loved, I shall always be near you . . . always, always, and if there be a soft breeze upon your cheek, it shall be my breath, as the cool air fans your throbbing temple, it shall be my spirit passing by. Sarah do not mourn me dead; think I am gone and wait for thee, for we shall meet again.

The effectiveness of this section, titled "Honorable Manhood," was immediately apparent, as Burns recalled a year later: "Within minutes of the first night's broadcast, the phone began ringing off the hook with calls from across the country, eager to find out about Sullivan Ballou, anxious to learn the name of Jay Ungar's superb theme music ('Ashokan Farewell'), desperate to share their families' experience in the war or just kind enough to say thanks. The calls would not stop all week—and they continue still" ("Mystic Chords").

Burns's plot structures are characteristically composed of four kinds of scenes. To start with, he employs narrative descriptions, which primarily move the story along. These sections follow a simple chronology and are designed above all to provide the audience with the basic historical facts: what is happening and who is involved. *The Civil War* was planned as a five-part, five-hour series, according to the National Endowment for the Humanities grant application written in late 1985 and early 1986 by Ken and Ric Burns, with each section "covering roughly one year of the conflict, 1861 through 1865. While the three central episodes will treat most of the major battles and campaigns, we will take advantage of the militarily less eventful years, 1861 and 1865, to explore the origins and consequences of the conflict. The war was, of course, a great epic, and episode by episode we will chart the large ebb and flow of the war: the mobilization of men and material, of industry and new technology, the deeds of generals and diplomats, the statistics of death, disease, and cost" (9). By the premiere telecast, *The Civil War* had more than doubled in length to eleven hours. Burns "eventually subdivided '62, '63, '64, and '65 into the first and second halves of the years, creating a total of nine episodes" (Burns, "Movie Maker" 1035). As Daniel Boorstin explains, the "most popular" method of organizing historical stories is in one-year, ten-year, and "hundred-year pack-ages. Historians like to bundle years in ways that make sense, provide continuity and link past to present" (37). Burns, first and foremost, then, creates descrip-tive scenes that provide the factual details needed to support and validate the larger historical outlines of the overall nine-episode structure.

Second, he designs what he calls emotional chapters, such as the afore-mentioned Sullivan Ballou set piece, that have the "ability to float between episodes" (Burns, "Movie Maker" 1037). This category of scene is bound less by chronological demands than by its capacity to affect mood and engage an audience emotionally at strategic moments within the plot. *The Civil War* is pep-pered, for instance, with the entertaining and informative anecdotes of writer, popular historian, and master raconteur Shelby Foote. His seemingly intimate asides about the human-interest aspects of the conflict add a needed personal dimension to the drier evidential framework of the broader historical narrative. Burns suggested, "Just go back to the section on the Gettysburg Address and watch Shelby's head twitch as he talks about Lincoln stepping down from the stand and, Shelby says, he came back and he turned to his friend Ward and he said, Ward, that speech won't scour. And he tilted his head as if, [had] the camera pulled back, you'd see next to Shelby, Abraham Lincoln, and on the other side of Lincoln, Ward Lamon. And to me, any man who puts you there, that's a great gift" (personal interview).

The third type of scene that Burns designs are those he calls "telegrams [or] short bursts that also have a certain potential to move but are more or less tied to a specific moment or a specific time" ("Movie Maker" 1037). Tele-grams are a mixture of both narrative description, because they are bound to whatever event is transpiring in the story line at the time, and emotional chapters, since these concise segments strongly contribute to viewer involve-ment. Prime examples of this sort of scene include the many private reactions to a wide array of historical developments throughout the series by Southern diarist Mary Chesnut (as spoken by Julie Harris) and Northern lawyer and civic leader George Templeton Strong (as spoken by George Plimpton). The most remembered telegrams, undoubtedly, are the ones built around single archival photographs featuring ground-level views of ordinary Union and Confederate soldiers before and after virtually every bloody engagement. These evocative images, once again, render the personal dimension of the conflict much more accessible to a modern audience of millions. As Burns disclosed,

> We wanted you to believe you were there. . . . There is not one shot, not one photograph of a battle ever taken during the Civil War. There is not one mo-ment in which a photographer exposed a frame during a battle, and yet you will

swear that you saw battle photography. . . . You live inside those photographs, experiencing a world as if it was real inside those photographs. . . . Once you've taken the poetry of words and added to it a poetry of imagery and a poetry of music and a poetry of sound, I think you begin to approximate the notion that the real war could actually get someplace, that you could bring it back alive. (personal interview)

Burns, fourth and finally, constructs editing clusters as his way of critically analyzing the various sides of a theme, question, or controversy that is central to a better overall understanding of his subject, such as "slavery and emancipation" in *The Civil War*, which he calls "the inner core of our story" ("Movie Maker" 1040). This type of scene involves editing together images of historical relevance with a montage of commentators who typically present both corroborating and conflicting opinions, creating a collage of multiple viewpoints. The "Was It Not Real?" segment of the final episode, for example, contains three commentaries presenting both confirming and dissenting points of view about the lasting meaning of the Civil War. Barbara Fields, who previously had suggested that Lincoln was actually a moderate on the issue of race in comparison to his contemporaries, begins by observing that "the slaves won the war and they lost the war because they won their freedom, that is the removal of slavery, but they did not win freedom as they understood freedom." Next, James Symington provides a different slant on the issue by declaring that "the significance of Lincoln's life and victory is that we will never again enshrine [slavery] into law." Yet he agrees with Fields that we should "see what we can do to erase . . . the deeper rift between people based on race . . . from the hearts and minds of people." Stephen Oates ends this section by shifting the focus to the survival and triumph of "popular government," ending with the assertion that the Civil War is "a testament to the liberation of the human spirit for all time." Oates's conclusion has little to do with the specific substance of the previous statements by Fields and Symington, but coming where it does, his testimony cannot help but soften the references to racial injustice that preceded it.

More important, this specific editing cluster establishes the liberal pluralist consensus: different speakers might clash on certain issues (such as what degree of freedom was won in the Civil War and by whom), but disagreements take place within a broader framework of agreement on underlying principle. In this case, the larger principle is Oates's evocation of popular government, which is understood to guarantee the democracy and human rights needed to eventually eradicate racial inequality and disharmony. A historical narrative does not merely record and dramatize what happens; it also at times interprets events and shapes the presentation of the subject at hand.

Furthermore, this particular example illustrates that the historical documentary is able to sustain a certain degree of analysis (although not nearly as deep and comprehensive an analysis as written discourse and public discussion and debate can provide). The expert testimonies and first-person reports that Burns employs provide shifting angles of vision that sometimes agree and at other times contrast with each other. These multiple voices, however, form a cultural consensus because of both the filmmaker's liberal pluralist orientation and, in Burns's words, "the power of film to digest and synthesize" (quoted in Weisberger 99). In the end, then, Ken Burns, the popular historian, is much more a committed storyteller than a reasoned and detached analyst. As he explains, "It is the texture of emotion that is important to me. And this is what television can do that all the texts cannot do" (quoted in Powers 218).

Burns's position as a historical documentarian, moreover, straddles two well-established and generally distinct professions. He is a highly accomplished television producer-director and, as he often characterizes himself, "an amateur historian" with a wide-ranging interest in American history but no particular scholarly training or specialization. His work habits, nevertheless, do have a great deal in common with many standard academic practices. Preparing a historical documentary includes the disciplined rigors of thoroughly researching his subject, writing grant proposals, collaborating and debating with an assortment of scholarly advisers, composing multiple drafts of the off-screen narration, and gathering and selecting the background readings and the expert commentaries. (The final 372-page script for *The Civil War* was its fifteenth version.)[5]

The academic community began paying far closer critical attention to Burns and his made-for-television histories after the remarkable public response to this miniseries. One historian, for example, chided Burns for utilizing the Sullivan Ballou letter without "report[ing] in *The Civil War* . . . that the letter was never sent; it was discovered among Ballou's possessions" (Sullivan 42). Other scholars pointed out that a number of versions of the letter exist (Donohoe 54–55; Bickelhaupt, "Civil War Elegy" 1, 5). Burns responded that "poetic license is that razor's edge between fraud and art that we ride all the time. You have to shorten, you have to take shortcuts, you have to abbreviate, you have to sort of make do with, you have to sometimes go with something that's less critically truthful imagery-wise because it does an ultimately better job of telling the larger truth, but who is deciding and under what system becomes the operative question" (personal interview).

Here Burns raises two fundamental differences between his own approach to producing history on television and the academic standards shared by most professional historians. First, he is far more concerned with the art of storytelling than with a fundamentalist sense of detailed accuracy, although he is always careful to marshal the facts of history as his stated goal of capturing the emotional truth of his subject allows (Burns, "Historical Truth" 752). As he explains, "The historical documentary filmmaker's vocation is not precisely the same as the historian's, although it shares many of the aims and much of the spirit of the latter. . . . The historical documentary is often more immediate and more emotional than history proper because of its continual joy in making the past present through visual and verbal documents" ("Mystic Chords"). Second, Burns is not as self-reflexive about historiography as are professional historians. He is aware that there are "systems" to history, but he has been criticized for stressing plot over historical analysis: "I am primarily a filmmaker. That's my job. I'm an amateur historian at best, but more than anything if you wanted to find a hybridization of those two professions, then I find myself an emotional archaeologist. That is to say, there is something in the process of filmmaking that I do in the excavation of these events in the past that provoke a kind of emotion and a sympathy that remind us, for example, of why we agree against all odds as a people to cohere" (personal interview).

At first blush, Burns's statement might appear to confirm the assessment offered in a 1992 *American Quarterly* essay, which suggests that "'The Civil War' stands as a new nationalist synthesis that in aims and vision can be most instructively compared to James Ford Rhodes's histories of the Civil War (written at the end of the nineteenth and in the early twentieth centuries)" (Censer 245). A 1991 appraisal in *American Historical Review* similarly takes the filmmaker to task: "Burns used modern historical techniques, at the level of detail and anecdote, to create an accessible, human-scale account of the Civil War. But, when it comes to historical interpretation, to the process by which details coalesce to make events meaningful, *The Civil War* is vintage nineteenth century." The severity of these judgments is encapsulated by the same author in a final dismissal: *The Civil War* "is the visual version of the approach taken by generations of Civil War buffs, for whom reenacting battles is a beloved hobby" (DuBois 1140–41).

Historical documentaries should certainly be subject to evaluation and criticism, especially if they are to be viewed by audiences of tens of millions and subsequently used as teaching tools in our nation's schools. *The Civil War*, for example, was licensed after its premiere telecast to more than sixty colleges and universities for future classroom use (Jones and Kelley D4). Burns reports that he has "received over 6,000 letters and cards from secondary school teachers alone, grateful for the series, pleased with how well it works" ("Mystic Chords"). Clearly, then, *The Civil War* should be assessed, and the authors of the *American Quarterly* and *American Historical Review* articles raise relevant questions of interpretation and detail. It is a welcome development that historians are increasingly attending to the validity of films and television programs.

These reviews, however, also demonstrate the academy's long-standing tendency to underestimate yet another motion picture or television series, which in turn shortchanges *The Civil War* as popular history. One of the primary goals of scholarship is to create new knowledge. No more thorough indictment exists, according to this frame of reference, than to reject a text for its obsolete conception and design, in this case, banishing it to the nineteenth century. *The Civil War,* however, deserves a more measured examination than dismissal as the stuff of "Civil War buffs."

In his widely acclaimed book *That Noble Dream* (1988), Peter Novick skillfully examines the controversies that have fundamentally affected the history discipline over the last generation. Current debates continue in the literature and at conferences over the relative merits of narrative versus analytic history, synthetic versus fragmentary history, and consensus versus multicultural history. Lawrence W. Levine suggests that all these historiographical exchanges make "sense only when it is seen as what, at its root, it really is—a debate about the extent to which we should widen our historical net to include the powerless as well as the powerful, the followers as well as the leaders, the margins as well as the center, popular and folk culture as well as high culture" (8).

The Civil War is a product of this intellectual climate. In this respect, it is not enough to focus on specific details from *The Civil War,* such as the Sullivan Ballou letter, without also considering Burns's ideological bearings and the scope of his historical net. This more comprehensive outlook reveals fragments of a nationalist approach to historiography, as the aforementioned reviewers suggest. *The Civil War* evinces elements of the romantic, progressive, social history, and consensus schools as well. As Burns explained, "In narrative history you have this opportunity, I believe, to contain the multitude of perspectives. You can have the stylistic, and certainly my films have a particular and very well-known style. You can involve yourself with politics, but that's not all there is. And that's what I'm trying to do, is to embrace something that has a variety of viewpoints" (personal interview).

The Civil War is essentially a pastiche of assumptions derived from a number of schools of historical interpretation. As just mentioned, the series is nationalistic in its apparent pride in nation building, but it lacks the nineteenth-century arrogance that envisioned America as the fulfillment of human destiny. *The Civil War* is romantic in its narrative, chronological, and quasi-biographical structure, but it lacks the unqualified, larger-than-life depictions of the unvarnished "great men" approach. *The Civil War* is progressive in its persistent intimation that the war was ultimately a struggle to end slavery and ensure social justice, although this perspective, too, is tempered by some passages, such as Barbara Fields's assertion in the final episode that the Civil War "is still to be fought, and regrettably, it can still be lost." *The Civil War* is also informed by social history, with its attention to African Americans, women, laborers, and farmers, and especially with its firsthand accounts in each of the nine episodes by two common soldiers (Elisha Hunt Rhodes, a Yankee from Rhode Island, and Sam Watkins, a Confederate from Tennessee), but the series is nowhere near as representative of the bottom-up view as is pure social history. In Burns's own words, "I try to engage, on literally dozens of levels, ordinary human beings from across the country—male and female, black and white, young and old, rich and poor, inarticulate and articulate" (quoted in *"Civil War"* 58).

What Burns is annunciating is his liberal pluralist perspective, where differences of ethnicity, race, class, and gender are kept in a comparatively stable and negotiated consensus within the body politic. Burns's brand of made-for-television history is marked more by agreement than is the multicultural or diversity model that grounds the social history perspective. The preservation of the Union and an emphasis on its ideals and its achievements are fundamental to consensus thinking; they are also some of Burns's primary themes throughout *The Civil War:*

> It is interesting that we Americans who are not united by religion, or patriarchy, or even common language, or even a geography that's relatively similar, we have agreed because we hold a few pieces of paper and a few sacred words together, we have agreed to cohere, and for more than 200 years it's worked and that special alchemy is something I'm interested in. It doesn't work in a Pollyanna-ish way. . . . We corrupt as much as we construct, but nevertheless, I think that in the aggregate the American experience is a wonderful beacon . . . and I think the overwhelming response to *The Civil War* is a testament to that. (Burns, personal interview)

Rather than being ideologically stuck in the nineteenth century, Burns and the audience for *The Civil War* were instead fully modern in their outlook. The tenets of liberal pluralism were prevalent throughout American culture during the 1990s and continue to be today. Popular metaphors such as the quilt, the rainbow, and, to a lesser degree, the old-fashioned melting pot are still used by public figures across the political spectrum to evoke a projection of America that is basically fixed on agreement and unity, despite whatever social differences may exist. By realizing this perspective on film, Burns has, moreover, usurped one of the foremost goals of social history, which is to make history meaningful and relevant to the general public. *The Civil War* brilliantly fulfills this objective as few books, motion pictures, television series, or even teachers, for that matter, have ever done.

BRIDGING THE DIVIDE BETWEEN POPULAR AND PROFESSIONAL HISTORY

The mutual skepticism that sometimes surfaces between popular and professional historians is understandable but unfortunate. Each usually works with different media (although some scholars do produce historical TV programs, videos, and films); each tends to evaluate differently the role of storytelling versus the role of analysis in relaying history; and each tailors a version of the past that is designed for disparate—though overlapping—audiences. These distinctions are real enough. Still, the artist and the scholar, the amateur and the expert can complement each other more than is sometimes evident. Both make their own unique contributions to America's collective memory—that is, the full sweep of historical consciousness, understanding, and expression that a culture has to offer.

Interdisciplinary work in memory studies now boasts adherents in American studies, anthropology, communication, cultural studies, English, history, psychology, and sociology.[6] The contemporary preoccupation with memory dates back to Freud, although recent scholarship focuses more on the collective nature of remembering than on the individual act of recalling the past, which is the traditional realm of psychological inquiry into this topic. Researchers today make distinctions between the academic historical record and the rest of collective memory. Professional historians, in particular, "have traditionally been concerned above all else with the accuracy of a memory, with how correctly it describes what actually occurred at some point in the past" (Thelen 1119). However, "less traditional historians have allowed for a more complex relationship, arguing that history and collective memory can be complementary, identical, oppositional, or antithetical at different times" (Zelizer, "Reading" 216). According to this way of thinking, more popular uses of memory have less to do with accuracy per se than with using the past as a kind of communal, mythic response to current events, issues, and challenges. The proponents of memory studies, therefore, are more concerned with how and why a remembered version is being constructed at a particular time, such as *The Civil War* in 1990, than with whether a specific rendition of the past is historically correct and reliable above all else. As Burns further clarifies his approach, "History . . . is an inclusion of myth as well as fact because myth tells you much more than fact about a people" ("Historical Truth" 749).

Rather than thinking of popular and professional history as diametrically opposed traditions (i.e., one unsophisticated and false, the other more reliable and true), it is more helpful to consider them as two ends of the same continuum. In his 1984 book *Culture as History*, the late Warren Susman first championed this more sympathetic appreciation of the popular historical tradition. Susman noted that myth and history are intimately linked. One supplies the drama; the other, the understanding. The popular heritage holds the potential to connect people passionately to their pasts; the scholarly camp maps out the processes for comprehending what happened with richness and depth. Susman's fundamental premise was that popular history and professional history need not always clash (7–26).

From this more inclusive perspective, popular history and professional history are seen less as discrete traditions and more as overlapping parts of the same whole, despite the many tensions that persist. For instance, popular histories can nowadays be recognized for their analytical insights, while professional histories can be valued for their expressive possibilities. Popular history, too, is built squarely on the foundations of academic scholarship; it provides professional historians, such as Fields and Oates in the case of *The Civil War*, with a platform from which to introduce their scholarly ideas and insights to a vastly wider audience. Together, popular history and professional history enrich the historical enterprise of a culture, and the strengths of one can serve to check the excesses of the other (Susman 7–26).

Any understanding of *The Civil War*, accordingly, needs to be based on the fundamental assumption that television's representation of the past is an altogether new and different kind of history. Unlike written discourse, the language of TV is highly stylized, elliptical (rather than linear) in structure, and associational or metaphoric in its portrayals of historical themes, figures, and events. *The Civil War* as popular history is above all an artistic attempt to link audiences immediately and intensely with the life stories of the people who were caught up in the conflict. A content analysis of "444 substantive letters from the more than 1,100 letters Burns had received as of March 1991" found that "more than one out of every four letters (27 percent) praised Burns for offering them a sense of direct, emotional connection with the past" (Glassberg 3). As with any mediated rendering of history, the main strength of *The Civil War* is experiential: it provides viewers with the dramatic illusion that they are somehow personally involved in the action, even as they are learning factual details about this vast subject through the course of the narrative. Popular history is always vicarious and participatory, rather than comparatively detached and analytical like most examples of written professional history.

Made-for-television histories are thus never conceived according to the standards of professional history. They are not intended chiefly to debate issues, challenge conventional wisdom, or create new knowledge or perspectives. *The Civil War,* more specifically, is designed for the far less contentious and communally oriented environment of prime-time television with its audiences in the tens of millions. In this way, producing, telecasting, and viewing this miniseries became a large-scale cultural ritual in and of itself.

This process, in turn, completed three important functions: First, *The Civil War* served as an intermediary site bridging the findings of professional historians with the interests of the general public. "There are levels of inquiry," according to Burns, "and we have to celebrate those that bring us to the door of the next level. And I think *Roots* brings in a huge audience. Maybe *The Civil War* has a little bit more select audience . . . but all of it is enriching the academy as well as the populace" ("Historical Truth" 757). Second, the series facilitated an ongoing negotiation with America's usable past by portraying those parts of the collective memory that were of most interest to the television producers as well as to the nearly 40 million viewers who decided to tune in: issues such as the residual effects of slavery and the continuance of racial conflict and discrimination in the United States, the influence of a strong federal presence in both state and local governments across the country, and the search for meaning and personal responsibility in national life. In this regard, Burns explains, "history is really not about the past; it's about the present. We define ourselves now by the subjects we choose from the past and the way each succeeding generation interprets those subjects. They are more a mirror of how we are now than they are a literal guide to what went before" ("Movie Maker" 1033). And, third, *The Civil War* loosely affirmed mainstream standards, values, and beliefs; in the filmmaker's own words, "there is more *unum* than *pluribus* in my work" ("Historical Truth" 747).

Burns, overall, articulates a version of the country's past that conveys his own perspective as a popular historian, intermingling many widely held assumptions about the character of America and its liberal pluralist aspirations. Like other documentarians of his generation, he too addresses matters of race, gender, class, and regional division, but unlike many of his contemporaries, he presents an image of the United States eventually pulling together despite its many chronic differences rather than coming apart at the seams. Exploring the past is Burns's way of reassembling an imagined future from a fragmented present. *The Civil War,* in particular, reaffirmed for the members of its principal audience—which, according to the ratings, skewed white, male, thirty-five to forty-nine, and upscale (Statistical Research Inc.)—the relevance of their past in an era of unprecedented multicultural redefinition. This aesthetic reintegration of the past into the present is one of the major purposes of popular history. For Ken Burns, it is a process of reevaluating the country's historical legacy and reconfirming it from a wholly new generational outlook.

In the end, Burns contends, "the Civil War compelled me to do this film," enabling him to establish "a dialogue with the past." As Fields reminds us in the final episode of the series, "The Civil War is in the present as well as in the past." In this sense, at least, all history is contemporary. We can never escape our own time or set of ideological predispositions, and within this context, no one has ever done a better job of "bringing [the Civil War] back alive" to more Americans through the power and reach of television than Ken Burns.

Notes

1. The consultants listed in the credits are Shelby Foote, Barbara J. Fields, C. Vann Woodward, Don Fehrenbacher, Stephen Sears, William McFeely, James McPherson, Bernard Weisberger, Mike Musick, Richard Snow, Eric Foner, Stephen B. Oates, Robert Johannsen, Tom Lewis, William E. Leuchtenburg, Daniel Aaron, Charles Fuller, Charley McDowell, Ira Berlin, Gene Smith, Robert Penn Warren, Jerome Liebling, Dayton Duncan, and Amy Stechler Burns.

2. Some of the more prominent critiques of *The Civil War* focus on its errors in detail, its abridgement of the origins of the war and Reconstruction, and its condensation of other complex issues, such as policy making and the formation of public opinion. For additional disagreements in interpretation, see J. Adler, Censer, DeCredico, DuBois, Koeniger, Marc and Thompson 307, May, Purcell, and Summers.

3. Echoing many film scholars before him, Louis Giannetti writes, "*Birth* is a diseased masterpiece, steeped in racial bigotry" (67). This critical ambivalence about *The Birth of a Nation* in general film histories dates back to Ramsaye, Hampton, and Jacobs.

4. Burns received the following honorary degrees in 1991: LHD, Bowdoin College; LittD, Amherst College; LHD, University of New Hampshire; DFA, Franklin Pierce College; LittD, Notre Dame College (Manchester, N.H.); LittD, College of St. Joseph (Rutland, Vt.); LHD, Springfield College (Ill.); and LHD, Pace University.

5. The final draft of the script, dated 17 July 1989, is in the Ken Burns Collection, Folklore Archives, Wilson Library, U of North Carolina, Chapel Hill. The materials on *The Civil War* include all drafts of the script, all the filmed interviews with various scholars and experts (including outtakes), other footage, notes on decision making, test narrations, some financial records, and correspondence.

6. See Fussell; Kammen; Le Goff; Lewis; Lipsitz; Schudson; and Zelizer, *Covering* and *Remembering*.

Works Cited

Adler, Jerry. "Revisiting the Civil War." *Newsweek* 8 Oct. 1990: 62.

Adler, Robert P., ed. *Understanding Television: Essays on Television as a Social and Cultural Force.* New York: Praeger, 1981.

Allen, Robert C., ed. *Channels of Discourse: Television and Contemporary Criticism.* Chapel Hill: U of North Carolina P, 1987.

Bianculli, David. *Teleliteracy: Taking Television Seriously.* New York: Continuum, 1992.

Bickelhaupt, Susan. "Civil War Elegy Captivates TV Viewers." *Boston Globe* 29 Sept. 1990: 1+.

————. "'Civil War' Weighs in with Heavy Hitters." *Boston Globe* 25 Sept. 1990: 61+.

Boorstin, Daniel J. "The Luxury of Retrospect." *The 80s.* Spec. issue of *Life* Fall 1989: 37.

Broder, David S. "PBS Series Provides a Timely Reminder of War's Horrors." *Springfield (Mass.) Sunday Republican* 30 Sept. 1990: B2.

Burns, Ken. "Historical Truth." Interview with Thomas Cripps. *American Historical Review* 100 (1995): 741–64.

————. "In Search of the Painful, Essential Images of War." *New York Times* 27 Jan. 1991: sec. 2, 1.

————. "The Movie Maker as Historian: Conversations with Ken Burns." Interviews with David Thelen. *The Practice of American History.* Spec. issue of *Journal of American History* 81.3 (1994): 1031–50.

————. "Mystic Chords of Memory." Speech. U of Vermont. 12 Sept. 1991.

————. Personal interview. 18 Feb. 1993.

Burns, Ken, and Ric Burns. "*The Civil War:* A Television Series." Grant application submitted to National Endowment for the Humanities 14 Mar. 1986. Ken Burns Collection, Folklore Archive, Wilson Library, U of North Carolina, Chapel Hill.

Carter, Bill. "'Civil War' Sets an Audience Record for PBS." *New York Times* 25 Sept. 1990: C17.

"CBS, PBS Factors in Surprising Prime Time Start." *Broadcasting* 1 Oct. 1990: 28.

Censer, Jane Turner. "Videobites: Ken Burns's 'The Civil War' in the Classroom." *American Quarterly* 44.2 (1992): 244–54.

"*The Civil War:* Ken Burns Charts a Nation's Birth." *American Film* Sept. 1990: 58.

Collins, Monica. "A Victory for 'Civil War.'" *Boston Herald* 21 Sept. 1990: 43.

DeCredico, Mary A. "Image and Reality: Ken Burns and the Urban Confederacy." *Journal of Urban History* 23 (1997): 387–405.

Donohoe, Cathryn. "Echoes of a Union Major's Farewell." *Insight* 5 Nov. 1990: 54–55.

DuBois, Ellen Carol. "The Civil War." *American Historical Review* 96 (1991): 1140–42.

Fiske, John, and John Hartley. *Reading Television.* New York: Methuen, 1978.

Fitzpatrick, Eileen. "Burns Sues Pacific Arts for Back Royalties on Videos." *Billboard* 22 Oct. 1994: 9.

Foote, Shelby. "A Conversation with Civil War Historian Shelby Foote." Interview with Lynne V. Cheney. *Humanities* 11.2 (1990): 8.

————. *Red River to Appomattox.* Vol. 3 of *The Civil War: A Narrative.* New York: Random, 1974.

Fussell, Paul. *The Great War and Modern Memory.* New York: Oxford UP, 1989.

Gerard, Jeremy. "'Civil War' Seems to Have Set a Record." *New York Times* 29 Sept. 1990: 46.

Giannetti, Louis. *Masters of the American Cinema.* Englewood Cliffs, N.J.: Prentice-Hall, 1981.

Glassberg, David. "'Dear Ken Burns': Letters to a Filmmaker." *Mosaic: The Newsletter of the Center on History-Making in America* 1 (Fall 1991): 3, 8.

Gold, Richard. "'Civil War' Boost to Docu Battle." *Variety* 1 Oct. 1990: 36.

Hampton, Benjamin. *A History of the Movies.* New York: Covici, Friede, 1931.

Jacobs, Lewis. *The Rise of the American Film.* New York: Harcourt, 1939.

Johnson, Haynes. "An Eloquent History Lesson." *Washington Post* 28 Sept. 1990: A2.

Jones, Dylan, and Dennis Kelly. "Schools Use Series to Bring History to Life." *USA Today* 1 Oct. 1990: D4.

Kammen, Michael. *Mystic Chords of Memory: The Transformation of Tradition in American Culture.* New York: Vintage, 1993.

"Ken Burns Wins First Lincoln Prize." *American History Illustrated* 26.3 (1991): 14.

Koeniger, A. Cash. "Ken Burns's 'The Civil War': Triumph or Travesty?" *Journal of Military History* 55.3 (1991): 225–33.

"Learning Lessons from 'The Civil War.'" *Broadcasting* 8 Oct. 1990: 52–53.

Le Goff, Jacques. *History and Memory.* New York: Columbia UP, 1996.

Levine, Lawrence W. *The Unpredictable Past: Explorations in American Cultural History.* New York: Oxford UP, 1993.

Lewis, Bernard. *History: Remembered, Recovered, Invented.* Princeton, N.J.: Princeton UP, 1975.

Lipsitz, George. *Time Passages: Collective Memory and American Popular Culture.* Minneapolis: U of Minnesota P, 1990.

"Longest-Running Hardcover Bestsellers for 1991." *Publishers Weekly* 1 Jan. 1992: 34.

Lord, Lewis. "'The Civil War': Did Anyone Dislike It?" *U.S. News and World Report* 8 Oct. 1990: 18.

———. "The Civil War, Unvarnished." *U.S. News and World Report* 24 Sept. 1990: 74–75.

Marc, David, and Robert J. Thompson. *Prime Time, Prime Movers: From* I Love Lucy *to* L.A. Law—*America's Greatest TV Shows and the People Who Created Them.* Boston: Little, 1992.

May, Robert E. "The Limitations of Classroom Media: Ken Burns' Civil War Series as a Test Case." *Journal of American Culture* 19.3 (1996): 39–49.

Mayles, Daisy. "1990 Facts & Figures: Fiction Sales Outpace Nonfiction." *Publishers Weekly* 8 Mar. 1991: 20.

McDowell, Edwin. "Bookstores Heed Call on Civil War." *New York Times* 1 Oct. 1990: D10.

McPherson, James M. *Battle Cry of Freedom.* New York: Oxford, 1988.

Merritt, Russell. "Dixon, Griffith, and the Southern Legend: A Cultural Analysis of *Birth of a Nation.*" *Cinema Journal* 12.1 (Autumn 1972): 26–45.

Milius, John. "Reliving the War between Brothers." *New York Times* 16 Sept. 1990: sec. 2, 1+.

Newcomb, Horace, ed. *Television: The Critical View.* 7th ed. New York: Oxford UP, 2006.

———. *TV: The Most Popular Art.* New York: Anchor, 1974.

Novick, Peter. *That Noble Dream: The "Objectivity Question" and the American Historical Profession.* Cambridge: Cambridge UP, 1988.

Powers, Ron. "Glory, Glory." *GQ* Sept. 1990: 216–18.

Purcell, Hugh. "America's Civil Wars." *History Today* May 1991: 7–9.

Ramsaye, Terry. *A Million and One Nights.* New York: Simon, 1926.

Schudson, Michael. *Watergate in American Memory: How We Remember, Forget, and Reconstruct the Past*. New York: Basic, 1992.

Shales, Tom. "The Civil War Drama—TV Preview: The Heroic Retelling of a Nation's Agony." *Washington Post* 23 Sept. 1990: G5.

Statistical Research Inc. "1990 Public Television National Image Survey." Unpublished report commissioned by the PBS Station Independence Program. 28 Sept. 1990. Ken Burns Collection, Folklore Archive, Wilson Library, U of North Carolina, Chapel Hill.

Sullivan, Robert. "The Burns Method: History or Myth-Making?" *Life* Sept. 1994: 42.

Summers, Mark Wahlgren. "The Civil War." *Journal of American History* 77 (1991): 1106–7.

Susman, Warren. *Culture as History: The Transformation of American Society in the Twentieth Century*. New York: Pantheon, 1984.

Thelen, David. "Memory and American History." *Journal of American History* 75 (1989): 1117–29.

Thomson, David. "History Composed with Film." *Film Comment* 26.5 (1990): 12–16.

Toplin, Robert B., ed. *Ken Burns's* The Civil War*: Historians Respond*. New York: Oxford UP, 1996.

"The 25 Most Intriguing People of 1990: Ken Burns." *People* 31 Dec. 1990: 46–47.

Ward, Geoffrey C., Ric Burns, Ken Burns. *The Civil War: An Illustrated History* (New York: Knopf, 1990).

Waters, Harry F. "An American Mosaic." *Newsweek* 17 Sept. 1990: 68.

Weisberger, Bernard A. "The Great Arrogance of the Present Is to Forget the Intelligence of the Past." *American Heritage* 41.6 (1990): 97–102.

Will, George F. "A Masterpiece on the Civil War." *Washington Post* 20 Sept. 1990: A23.

Zelizer, Barbie. *Covering the Body: The Kennedy Assassination, the Media, and the Shaping of Collective Memory*. Chicago: U of Chicago P, 1992.

———. "Reading the Past against the Grain: The Shape of Memory Studies." *Critical Studies in Mass Communication* 12.2 (1995): 214–39.

———. *Remembering to Forget: Holocaust Memory through the Camera's Eye*. Chicago: U of Chicago P, 1998.

Zoglin, Richard. "The Terrible Remedy." *Time* 24 Sept. 1990: 73.

"It's What People Say We're Fighting For"

Representing the Lost Cause in *Cold Mountain*

In the introduction to *Cold Mountain: A Screenplay,* author Charles Frazier describes a strange moment that occurred during the making of the film. As they were filming a Christmas celebration, director Anthony Minghella suddenly stopped the cameras and asked Frazier, "This scene is in the book, isn't it?" Remarkably, Frazier responded, "I'm not sure. I'd have to check" (xii). This unusual confusion over authorial paternity leads Frazier to speculate on the proper relationship between a book and its film version. On the one hand, he recognizes that "books are books and movies are movies. They should not be identical, nor can they be" (xii–xiii). Nevertheless, he insists that "the original work—if it is worth taking on in the first place—is owed something. Not perfect fidelity. Not excessive respect. But it is owed a degree of commitment not to violate its essence, its heart. Otherwise, go make up your own story" (xv).

The initial impression that Minghella's *Cold Mountain* (2003) creates is one of unusual fidelity to Frazier's novel. The costumes, the sets, and the music all capture the essence of the novel's time period. But a close analysis of the novel and the film reveals many differences. Scenes that are central to the novel's meaning did not make it to the screen, and other scenes, such as the Christmas party, are not in the literary version. As Frazier recognizes, many of the differences can be attributed to a film's need for compression: "a sort of agreed-upon shorthand of narrative and character development" (xiii). Other changes are harder to explain: for example, in the film, the corrupt minister, Veasey (Philip Seymour Hoffman), suffers ostentatiously from constipation, and Teague (Ray Winstone), the ruthless leader of the Home Guard, inexplicably joins in the singing of "I Wish My Baby Was Born" shortly before the shooting of Pangle (Ethan Suplee) and Stobrod (Brendan Gleeson). But the most consistent and intriguing differences between the novel and the film are in their representation of the ideology of the Lost Cause.

The expression the "Lost Cause" comes from the title of an 1866 history of the Confederacy by Edward A. Pollard.[1] The meaning of the phrase has shifted over time, but Thomas L. Connelly and Barbara L. Bellows suggest that, in its general sense, it refers to "the core of that enduring memory of southern defeat" (4). In the 1870s, the Southern Historical Society, led by its president, Jubal Early, formulated a discourse to help justify secession and account for the military defeat of the South. Through the society's journal, the *Southern Historical Society Papers,* members constructed a consistent interpretation of the war that promoted three main ideas. First, they insisted that the South fought for states' rights, not slavery. Second, they represented Robert E. Lee as a military genius and a perfect embodiment of the Southern gentleman. Finally, they claimed that, despite the heroism of the individual Confederate soldier, the North's overwhelming resources and numbers eventually forced the South to succumb. In the 1880s, this Lost Cause vision grew from the stubborn resistance of a few Virginia diehards into a widespread celebration of Southern culture and virtue. Indeed, as the two sections began to move toward reconciliation in the late nineteenth century, Northerners increasingly adopted elements of the Southern interpretation of the war, especially the deification of Lee and the celebration of the Southern soldier. Much of the nationalization of Lost Cause ideology can be attributed to two immensely popular epic films: D. W. Griffith's 1915 *The Birth of a Nation,* an adaptation of Thomas Dixon's *The Clansman* (1905), and David Selznick's 1939 version of Margaret Mitchell's *Gone with the Wind* (1936). While not as popular as these earlier works, *Cold Mountain* in its novel and film versions perpetuates the mythology of the Lost Cause.[2]

FRAZIER AND THE LOST CAUSE

An important figure associated with the historiography of the Lost Cause is Thomas L. Connelly, who was a professor of history at the University of South Carolina when Frazier was working on his PhD. In *The Marble Man: Robert E. Lee and His Image in American Society* (1977), Connelly traces the development of the Lee myth from the 1870s, when the Southern Historical Society represented him as the embodiment of the Southern chivalric ideal, to the Civil War centennial, by which time Lee had been transformed into a national hero and a representative of middle-class values (161). By the 1970s, historians such as Connelly had begun to complicate the Lee myth, and this revisionist history seems to have influenced Frazier's novel, especially the characterization of the protagonist, W. P. Inman. At the Battle of Fredericksburg (1862),

Photofest

Union troops under withering fire in *Cold Mountain*.

Inman's regiment is placed behind a stone wall on Marye's Heights, near Lee and Longstreet. Frazier writes that "the two generals spent the afternoon up on the hill coining fine phrases like a pair of wags" (12). However, unlike subsequent historians, Inman is not impressed:

> Old Lee . . . said it's a good thing war is so terrible or else we'd get to liking it too much. As with everything Marse Robert said, the men repeated that flight of wit over and over, passing it along from man to man, as if God amighty Himself had spoken. When the report reached Inman's end of the wall he just shook his head. Even back then, early in the war, his opinion differed considerably from Lee's, for it appeared to him that we like fighting plenty, and the more terrible it is the better. And he suspected that Lee liked it most of all and would, if given his preference, general them right through the gates of death itself. (12)

Proponents of the Lee myth attributed his military defeats to failures by his subordinates, especially Longstreet's alleged lethargy at Gettysburg in 1863. But when Inman compares Lee and Longstreet, he thinks "he'd any day rather have Longstreet backing him in a fight. Dull as Longstreet looked, he had a mind that constantly sought ground configured so a man could hunker down and do a world of killing from a position of relative safety" (10). Inman realizes that his thoughts about Lee are unspeakable, "as were his feelings that he did not enlist to take on a Marse, even one as solemn and noble-looking as Lee was that day on Maryes Heights" (12).

This passage raises the question of why Inman enlisted. As a deserter, he is in an ambiguous position between the two sides, and he frequently muses on his reasons for fighting. As he struggles through the foul flatlands near Raleigh, North Carolina, he wonders, "How did he ever think this to be his country and worth fighting for?" (85). When he passes through a region with large mansions, he bitterly realizes "he had been fighting battles for such men as lived in them, and it made him sick" (261). The most sustained discussion of the causes of the war occurs while Inman recuperates with the goat woman. She asks him, "What I want to know is, was it worth it, all that fighting for the big man's nigger?" (275). When Inman protests, she insists that slavery is the real cause of the war: "Nigger-owning makes the rich man proud and ugly and it makes the poor man mean. It's a curse laid on the land. We've lit a fire and now it's burning us down. God is going to liberate niggers, and fighting to prevent it is against God" (275). Inman then speculates aloud on the reasons that he and his fellow Southerners fought: "I reckon many of us fought to drive off invaders. One man I knew had been north to the big cities, and he said it was every feature of such places that we were fighting to prevent. All I know is anyone thinking the Federals are willing to die to set loose slaves has got an overly merciful view of mankind" (275). Finally, Inman realizes that he was motivated partially by the call of adventure: "The powerful draw of new faces, new places, new lives. And new laws where-under you might kill all you wanted and not be jailed, but rather be decorated. Men talked of war as if they committed it to preserve what they had and what they believed. But Inman now guessed it was boredom with the repetition of the daily rounds that had made them take up weapons" (276). When Sara tells him that her husband was killed at Gettysburg, he completes the process of effacing any meaningful cause for the war: "Every man that died in that war on either side might just as soon have put a pistol against the soft of his palate and blown out the back of his head for all the meaning it had" (305). Accordingly, at the end, when Inman must decide whether to return to the fighting or surrender to the Yankees, the decision is purely pragmatic. He decides to "put himself in the hands of the Federals, the very bastards who had spent four years shooting at him. They would make him sign his name to their oath of allegiance, but then he could wait out the fighting and come home" (436).

When the war is represented as being without larger purpose, the focus shifts from the legitimacy of the cause to the courage of individual soldiers. David Blight has pointed out that, in the late nineteenth century, the emancipationist implications of the war were neglected as both Northerners and Southerners enabled sectional reconciliation by developing amnesia over the causes of the war. Instead, they celebrated the heroism of the American soldier, whether Union or Confederate: "By the 1880s, Americans needed a social and moral equivalent of war. They would achieve this, of a kind, in the realm of sentiment—in a resurgent cult of manliness and soldierly virtues recycled in thousands of veterans' papers, speeches, and reminiscences. But such a moral equivalent of war came increasingly to exalt the soldier and his sacrifice, disembodied from the causes and consequences of war" (95). Ambivalent about the cause of the war to the point of desertion, Inman is nevertheless clearly not a coward. He reflects with some surprise on his ability to fight: "Before the war he had never been much of a one for strife. But once enlisted, fighting had come easy to him. He had decided it was like any other thing, a gift" (123). As he struggles to return home, he dispatches every enemy, regardless of the odds. As is the case in nearly all Civil War literature, both northern and southern readers can admire Inman's martial prowess.

In Lost Cause ideology, the courage of the Southern soldiers is linked closely with an insistence on the superior numbers of the North. Frazier describes the Battle of Fredericksburg from Inman's perspective as resembling "a dream, one where your foes are ranked against you countless and mighty" (11), and Inman becomes frustrated at the persistence of the seemingly limitless enemy: "The Federals kept on marching by the thousands at the wall all through the day, climbing the hill to be shot down. . . . The Federals kept on coming long past the point where all the pleasure of whipping them vanished. Inman just got to hating them for their clodpated determination to die" (11). When he is with the goat woman, Inman regrets his initial enthusiasm for the war: "The shame he felt now to think of his zeal in sixty-one to go off and fight the downtrodden mill workers of the Federal army, men so ignorant it took many lessons to convince them to load their cartridges ball foremost. These were the foes, so numberless that not even their own government put much value to them. They just ran them at you for years on end, and there seemed no shortage. You could kill them down until you grew heartsick and they would still keep ranking up to march southward" (276). But Frazier seems to undermine the Lost Cause emphasis on the Northern superiority of numbers. When Ada and Ruby visit Mrs. McKennet, she tells "a long and maudlin story she had read about a recent battle, its obvious fictitiousness apparently lost on her. It was fought—as they all were lately—against dreadful odds" (181). Like the Southern women who would maintain the altar of the Lost Cause throughout the postwar period, Mrs. McKennet "found the fighting glorious and tragic and heroic. Noble beyond all her powers of expression" (180). Ada dismisses the romantic story as "the most preposterous thing I have ever heard" (181).

To some extent, Frazier's ambivalent representation of the Lost Cause can be attributed to his protagonist: by focusing on a soldier from the mountains of North Carolina rather than a Tidewater cavalier, Frazier puts his fiction outside the mainstream of Lost Cause ideology. Nina Silber points out that in the 1880s Northerners looking to heal the wounds of the war turned with hope to the Southern mountaineer. Praised for his primitive virility and national loyalty, the mountaineer was especially valued for his racial purity: "Indeed, what began as an explanation of the mountaineers' isolation from the sectional politics of slavery and the slaveholder became a tribute to their detachment from the black people. . . . Suddenly, the southern mountaineers had become a people defined by their distance from African Americans, a point of considerable significance in a period when northern culture had begun to cast the black population aside as foreign and to embrace Anglo-Saxonism as pure Americanism" (146–47). Although Frazier does not completely avoid the racial implications of the war, they are not as central to his novel as might be expected for a work published in 1997. Mountaineer and deserter, Inman evades the complications that would have been inherent in a sympathetic protagonist fighting for the preservation of slavery.

MINGHELLA'S FILM VERSION OF COLD MOUNTAIN

In an interview, Minghella explained that when he read *Cold Mountain,* it appeared "to be a story about the American Civil War, and I don't necessarily have an interest in war stories. But then I realized that war was not the issue. It's more about a man's return from war, the after effects of war, and the effects of war on the world away from the battlefield" (quoted in Walsh par. 21). Given his lack of interest in war stories and his cultural distance from the American Civil War, it is not surprising that Minghella ignores much of Frazier's critique of the Lost Cause. Although some important elements of this ideology remain, they are transformed by Minghella's own cinematic vision.

Frazier's challenge to the idolization of Robert E. Lee is eliminated from Minghella's film. The screenplay does include a shortened reference to Lee's famous quote at Fredericksburg: before he is sent on his mission at Globe Tavern, an officer tells Inman (Jude Law), "It's what our general said, son: Good

Photofest

Inman (Jude Law) deserts the battlefield and returns to his roots.

thing war is so terrible, else a man might end up liking it too much" (22), but there is no irony to undercut the quote, and these lines were dropped from the film. Likewise, there is less emphasis on the overwhelming numbers of the North and the heroism of the individual Confederate soldier. In the film, Inman tells the goat woman (Eileen Atkins), "I could be at killing for days, my feet against the feet of my enemy, and I always killed him and he never killed me," but the cinematic version shows fewer of his battles during the war and on the way home to Cold Mountain. The Battle of the Crater in Petersburg is not as lopsided as the endless slaughter at Fredericksburg; Minghella deletes Inman's battle with the three men at the Cape Fear River; and Inman is assisted by Sara (Natalie Portman) in his fight with the three Yankees.

Minghella's *Cold Mountain* reflects the Lost Cause interpretation most pointedly on the origins of the war. In contrast to Lost Cause ideology, the film identifies slavery as the fundamental cause, but Minghella carefully distances the main characters from this issue. In the published screenplay, the hospital has been moved from Raleigh to a former mansion in Charleston, the location of Fort Sumter, where the war began. As Inman convalesces, he is surrounded by slaves in the fields, and the stage directions note, "He brings the wet bandage to his neck, considers the ocean, his fellow ragtag of wounded, the slaves, the great fields, the mansion. The whole meaning of this war around him" (43). Although this episode does not appear in the film, a similar scene makes the point even more clearly. The Charleston hospital is surrounded by cotton fields that are being worked by slaves, and as the doctor shows a group of women the horrors of the hospital, he comments, "Look out the window, ladies, and see what these poor fools are dying for. How many would still lose a leg for the rich man's slave?"

The film suggests that, before the war, the average Southerner was deluded about what was leading the South into war. Esco Swanger (James Gammon), who is described in the screenplay as having "no truck with a war he judges to be based on a conflict between one type of wealth and another," gets into a debate with young men enthusiastic about the prospect of going into battle:

ESCO: What do you fools think you're fighting for?

ROURKE: The South.

ESCO: Last time I checked, south was a direction.

In the screenplay, he continues, "You cut the wood, you carry the water for good old King Cotton. Now you want to fight for him. Somebody has to explain it to me" (9–10). As they are hammering nails into the church roof, one man says, "I call this nail Northern Aggression." In the screenplay, the next line is, "I call this nail a free nigger" (5–6), but in the film, it is changed to "Yankee skulls," and another man dismisses their enthusiasm: "Fightin' for a rich man's slave, that's what." Minghella represents the economic interests of the wealthy planters as the real cause of the war, a cause that is hidden from most of the men who will fight.

Inman's motives for enlisting are problematic. In the screenplay, he explains to Ada Monroe (Nicole Kidman), "I don't care much for a man from Washington telling me how to live" (20), echoing the Southern antigovernment individualism that W. J. Cash discusses in his classic study *The Mind of the South*. In the film, this scene is replaced by a conversation that occurs during Inman's walk with Ada's father, Reverend Monroe (Donald Sutherland). When Monroe comments on the beauty of the distant mountains, Inman replies, "It's what people say we're fighting for—to keep it that way." Thus in the film, he enlists to protect the South he loves, whereas in the novel, he comes to a more complex realization that it was boredom that seduced him into military service. In any case, both screenplay and film take pains to demonstrate that he does not enlist to defend slavery; indeed many of Minghella's changes to the novel distance Inman from the racism of the region. In a scene deleted from the final cut, Inman is "appalled" when Butcher (Trey Howell) kills a wounded black Union soldier after the Battle of the Crater (15–16).[3] In Frazier's novel,

Inman meets Veasey as he is about to murder his white mistress; Minghella makes her black, which gives Inman the opportunity to express his outrage: "So you reckoned to kill her because she's a slave." Similarly, when Inman attempts to buy eggs from the escaping slaves, he insists, "I've got no quarrel with you." Thus Minghella challenges the Lost Cause denial that slavery was the cause of the war, but his critique is compromised by Hollywood's need to make sure that a protagonist is free of racism—even more than Inman's status as a Confederate deserter would suggest.

Ada's racial attitudes in the film are equally modern. Minghella gives Reverend Monroe slaves; indeed, in the screenplay, he points out that they are the only slaves within twenty miles of Cold Mountain (28). When Ada arrives at Cold Mountain, a voice-over describes her happiness at escaping from Charleston, "a world of slaves, and corsets, and cotton." During a party, she demonstrates her compassion by serving root beer to the lowly inhabitants of the slave quarters (20). In the screenplay, the Home Guard drives Monroe's slaves away by burning their homes (35), but in the film Ada frees them herself. Commenting on the sorry state of Ada's farm, Sally Swanger points out, "Poor soul. She let those slaves go free and she's got nobody and nothing." Indeed, the only racists in the South seem to be the members of the despicable Home Guard. In a scene cut from the released version, Teague echoes the message of *The Birth of a Nation* when he promises to "guard against the Negro. They want what the white man got. Give them the chance, they'll carry rape and murder to your firesides" (28).

THE RESIDUAL LOST CAUSE

Modern interest in arguments about the causes of the war, the relative merits of its commanders, and the reasons that the North won is largely limited to Civil War historians. Yet key aspects of Lost Cause ideology have become embedded in popular culture. Connelly and Bellows define the modern Lost Cause as "an awareness of defeat, alienation from the national experience, and a sense of separatism from American ideals. It is not the totality of southern folk culture, but remains a strong central element" (137). They argue that America has alternated between two images of the South. One option, especially during the desegregation struggles of the 1950s, has been to see the South as a benighted contrast to mainstream America (138). The other option, evident in such films as *Walking Tall* (1973), *Smokey and the Bandit* (1977), and *Every Which Way but Loose* (1978), has been to see southern resistance to northern culture as a desirable alternative to the social turmoil of post-1960s America; in these films, "the stress was upon the protagonist, who, while fighting evil, exhibited human weaknesses slightly outside of the confining aspects of the law. To a nation emerging from civil turmoil and disillusionment with its political leaders, the southern image was a welcome change" (144). In other words, Inman might be seen as a Southern Dirty Harry who has exchanged his .44 Magnum for a LeMat pistol. Seeing Inman as an antiestablishment vigilante who uses violence for good ends creates a context for *Cold Mountain*'s selective embrace of Lost Cause mythology: like those Clint Eastwood antiheroes, Inman faces overwhelming numbers with courage, is ambivalent about the cause for which he fights, and has contempt for his superiors.

Another aspect of the Lost Cause that has persisted in American culture can be sensed in country music. Connelly and Bellows argue that "the core of this music is continual striving amid perpetual disappointment—that is the heart of the Lost Cause" (146). Music plays an important role in the novel, and much of the film's popularity may be attributed to Gabriel Yared's bluegrass score. Indeed, not one but three popular albums have been generated by the film: the original sound track (2003), *Return to Cold Mountain* (2004), and *Backroads to Cold Mountain* (2004). Songs such as "Wayfaring Stranger" and "I'm Going Home" evoke the heroic endurance of the Southern people.

This perseverance in the face of defeat is common to the endings of both novel and film. To provide narrative closure, Frazier adds an epilogue that balances the random, violent death of Inman with images of his child and Ada thriving on Black Cove Farm. Frazier sets the epilogue in 1874, midway between the 1872 reelection of Ulysses S. Grant (the last election in which the "bloody shirt" of the war was useful to the Republicans) and the 1876 election of Rutherford B. Hayes, which precipitated the end of Reconstruction by way of the Compromise of 1877. This period was the beginning of the celebration of the Lost Cause that would lead to a restoration of Southern confidence and ultimately to sectional reconciliation. The film does not make the time frame clear but instead concludes with Ada's mournful voice-over: "What we have lost will never be returned to us. The land will not heal. Too much blood. The heart will not heal. All we can do is make peace with the past and try to learn from it." Clearly, the lesson from the past is to avoid war, but the film's final image draws on Lost Cause affirmations of Southern perseverance, reinforced by images of music, family, and religion.

In his introduction to *Cold Mountain: The Journey from Book to Film,* director Anthony Minghella uses adoption as a metaphor for the process of converting a novel into a film: "Sitting with Charles Frazier on the porch where most of his novel was written, the mountains in front of us shrouded in mist, I was conscious of a strange moment, as if I were adopting someone's child. I was starting the long and painful journey to turn Charles Frazier's *Cold Mountain* into something of my own" (12). In his introduction to the screenplay, Frazier uses a slightly different version of the family metaphor. While recognizing the inevitability of difference, he insists, "If novel and film adaptation can never be twins, it seems to me that they ought to share significant amounts of DNA beyond just a correspondence of character names and the barest elements of plot, always the least interesting parts of a movie or a novel for me" (xiv). Adopted child or sibling, the film version is a creation of both parents and reflects the ideologies of both author and adapter. Of course, Frazier's novel is itself a retelling of Homer's *Odyssey*. Frazier explained that while writing *Cold Mountain*, "I realized that there are two kinds of books about a war: there's an *Iliad*, about fighting the war, and about the battles and generals, and there's an *Odyssey*, about a warrior who has decided that home and peace are the things he wants" (interview, par. 12). The choice of the *Odyssey* as a pattern does distinguish *Cold Mountain* from those Civil War novels that glorify war—for example, Michael Shaara's *The Killer Angels* (1974). And even more than the novel, Minghella's *Cold Mountain* focuses on Inman's disenchantment with the war and the manipulation of the common soldier. Inman tells the goat woman, "I'm like the boy who goes for wood in winter and comes back in the spring with a whistle. Like every fool sent off to fight with a flag and a lie." War was certainly a context for Minghella's involvement with *Cold Mountain:* he wrote the screenplay in the spring of 2001 and began filming in July 2002, during the buildup for the Iraq War.

Nevertheless, one wonders whether either the novel or the film is truly an effective antiwar protest or merely another opportunity to experience vicariously the thrill of battle, sheltered under reassuring platitudes about the evils of war. An entire chapter of *Cold Mountain: The Journey from Book to Film* is devoted to the filming of the battle sequence, and producer Bill Horberg describes the crew's painstaking quest for realism: "We wanted to avoid the sense of reenactment that turns up in most films of the Civil or Revolutionary War. We wanted a quality of first-time authenticity and nonvarnished life that didn't feel like it came out of the Smithsonian Museum" (quoted in Sunshine 77). The "thousands of extras and tons of explosives" (77) certainly did produce an exciting and memorable experience, but it seems less certain that filmgoers were any more repulsed by, or informed about, the horrors of war than they would have been at a Civil War reenactment.

In 1960, C. Vann Woodward, in *The Burden of Southern History,* warned that America might fall victim to its belief in its own innocence and the inevitability of success. Writing during the cold war, just prior to the buildup of Vietnam, Woodward described the paradox of America's situation in the world: "Having more power than ever before, America ironically enjoys less security than in the days of her weakness. Convinced of her virtue, she finds that even her allies accuse her of domestic vices invented by her enemies. The liberated prove ungrateful for their liberation, the reconstructed for their reconstruction, and the late colonial peoples vent their resentment upon our nation—the most innocent, we believe, of the imperial powers" (172–73). As southerner and Yale professor, Woodward called for the southern historian, infused with the Lost Cause understanding of limitations and defeat, to rescue America from its blindness. He warned of the potential consequences if the implications of the Civil War were not learned: "There is the danger that America may be tempted to exert all the terrible power she possesses to compel history to conform to her own illusions. The extreme, but by no means the only expression, would be the so-called preventive war" (173). Forty years later, both Frazier's novel and Minghella's film use the tragedy of Southern experience to represent the dangers of naïve idealism and the horrors of war. But recent events suggest that it remains unclear whether we have avoided Woodward's Cassandra-like prophecy that America might not learn the lessons of the Lost Cause.

NOTES

1. There has been much recent scholarship on the Lost Cause. Gaines M. Foster, in *Ghosts of the Confederacy: Defeat, the Lost Cause, and the Emergence of the New South, 1865–1913* (1987), sees the late-nineteenth-century popularity of the concept as a response to social tensions in the New South. Charles Reagan Wilson, in *Baptized in Blood: The Religion of the Lost Cause, 1865–1920* (1980), argues that the Lost Cause was a civil religion that linked Christianity and regional history. David W. Blight, in *Race and Reunion: The Civil War in American Memory* (2001), discusses the role that white supremacy played in Lost Cause ideology. Thomas L. Connelly and Barbara L. Bellows, in *God and General Longstreet: The Lost Cause and the Southern Mind* (1982), distinguish between the literary productions of diehard ex-Confederate political and military leaders that occurred before World War I and the timeless Confederate ideal that has evolved into a national Lost Cause.

2. Gross sales for *The Birth of a Nation* are difficult to determine with any accuracy, but according to the *Internet Movie Database*, it grossed $3 million, which adjusts to approximately $50 million today. *Gone with the Wind* remains the highest-grossing film of all time, with gross box office receipts at $198 million in the United States alone. *Cold Mountain* has grossed $95 million ("Business Data").

3. Although the Union attack at the crater was performed largely by African American troops, Minghella's soldiers are white, because he used the Romanian army as actors. There is, however, a brief scene showing the Native American swimmer (Jay Tavare) grappling with an African American soldier—perhaps to emphasize the irony of two oppressed groups fighting a white man's war.

WORKS CITED

Blight, David W. *Race and Reunion: The Civil War in American Memory.* Cambridge, Mass.: Harvard UP, 2001.

"Business Data for *The Birth of a Nation.*" *Internet Movie Database* <http://www.imdb.com/title/tt0004972/business>.

"Business Data for *Cold Mountain.*" *Internet Movie Database* <http://www.imdb.com/title/tt0159365/business>.

"Business Data for *Gone with the Wind.*" *Internet Movie Database* <http://www.imdb.com/title/tt0031381/business>.

Cash, W. J. *The Mind of the South.* New York: Knopf, 1941.

Cold Mountain. Dir. Anthony Minghella. Miramax, 2003.

Connelly, Thomas L. *The Marble Man: Robert E. Lee and His Image in American Society.* New York: Knopf, 1977.

Connelly, Thomas L., and Barbara L. Bellows. *God and General Longstreet: The Lost Cause and the Southern Mind.* Baton Rouge: Louisiana State UP, 1982.

Foster, Gaines M. *Ghosts of the Confederacy: Defeat, the Lost Cause, and the Emergence of the New South, 1865–1913.* New York: Oxford UP, 1987.

Frazier, Charles. *Cold Mountain.* New York: Vintage, 1997.

———. Interview with Random House <http://www.randomhouse.com/catalog/display.pperl?isbn=9780739308912&view=auqa>.

———. Introduction. Minghella, *Cold Mountain* xi–xv.

Minghella, Anthony. *Cold Mountain: A Screenplay.* New York: Miramax Books, 2003.

———. Introduction. Sunshine 11–17.

Silber, Nina. *The Romance of Reunion: Northerners and the South, 1865–1900.* Chapel Hill: U of North Carolina P, 1993.

Sunshine, Linda, ed. Cold Mountain*: The Journey from Book to Film.* New York: Newmarket, 2003.

Walsh, David. "Not Quite a Serious Work." Rev. of *Cold Mountain,* dir. Anthony Minghella. 7 Jan. 2004. World Socialist Web Site <http://www.wsws.org/articles/2004/jan2004/cold-j07.shtml>.

Wilson, Charles Reagan. *Baptized in Blood: The Religion of the Lost Cause, 1865–1920.* Athens: U of Georgia P, 1980.

Woodward, C. Vann. *The Burden of Southern History.* Baton Rouge: Louisiana State UP, 1960.

Part II

The Twentieth Century
Total War

THE GREAT WAR
VIEWED FROM THE 1920s

The Big Parade

The decade of the 1920s has long stood in the popular perspective as a unity, bounded by the ignoble brackets of war and economic crisis. The customary view of the period, kept alive by dozens of colorful book titles, is that it was a time of carefree hedonism and relentless materialism when American society unleashed the pent-up energies of the war years.

The traditional vision sees World War I not only as Woodrow Wilson's great crusade but also as the great watershed in modern American history. The war broadened the breakdown of the old moral code, particularly in relation to late Victorian concepts of femininity. It produced a universal social malaise that saw all gods dead, all heroes humbled, all causes exhausted. Americans responded to the Carthaginian peace of Versailles by withdrawing from world affairs and expressing a strong revulsion to war and militarism. The author of the League of Nations proposal died embittered and disowned by his own political party; Wilsonian idealism lay sacrificed on the altar of normalcy.

With the exception of the unfortunate Herbert Hoover and a few others, the decade was almost bereft of first-class political leaders at all levels. The economy, though it seemed to be booming right along, was disastrously uneven. By contrast, the nation's intellectual life flourished, particularly in areas of cultural criticism. The war produced a strong and antagonistic reaction from literature and the plastic arts. The postwar climate shaped by such "lost generation" authors as Ernest Hemingway, John Dos Passos, and e. e. cummings commonly is regarded as one of disillusionment.

The traditional interpretation is clear. A fatigued society, worn from patriotic exertion and with its almost hysterical idealism shattered, turned away from Progressive reform and ran the gamut of self-indulgence. Only with the convulsive shock of the stock market crash and the sickening slide into economic depression did Americans begin to pay for their excesses.

National Archives

President Woodrow Wilson promised to "make the world safe for democracy."

Yet this traditional view of the war-spawned 1920s is drawn largely from the evidence provided by cultural elites dissatisfied with their society. The war itself was at least as much an accelerator as it was a cause of the postwar mood of dissatisfaction and rebellion. Although many Americans doubtless took part in the war-induced climate of cynicism, historians have tended to overlook the continuities of the period. The flaming passions of the Jazz Age probably held more smoke than fire, for family and church life continued as the hubs of social activity for millions. The Progressive reform impulse still flickered; Robert La Follette was able to mount a strong third-party movement on its base in 1924, and watchdogs such as George Norris kept progressivism alive in Congress. Some old Progressives were still around to praise the New Deal, although many became as intensely displeased with the second Roosevelt as they had been enchanted with the first.

Overlooked in the minds of many Americans is the fact that the recent European war experience persisted as a legitimate theater for heroism and the display of national idealism. To be sure, this attitude was at a high pitch

U.S. Signal Corps

In 1919 General John J. Pershing helped create the Military Order of the World Wars, a distinguished veteran officers association that is still active on military issues.

between 1917 and 1919, when government, organs of public opinion, motion pictures, and popular literature allowed almost no dissent from total and un-compromising support of the war effort. But even in the years following the war, the general public was probably as supportive of this alternative vision as of the more pessimistic view that is much better known historically. With the nation in a conservative mood, the sacrifices of wartime met with approbation as well as disapproval. Veterans' organizations hawked their brand of patri-otism. The Veterans of Foreign Wars, founded in 1899, gained new life and new blood from World War I, while veterans of the American Expeditionary Force (AEF) developed the American Legion and the Military Order of the World Wars in 1919. These organizations had fond memories of the Great War and were assiduous in the cultivation of "Americanism" and militant patriotism in textbooks and among teachers.

Although it is fair to say that most of the elitist literature and art was intensely critical of the war and of America's role in it, newspapers, popular magazines, cheap books, and motion pictures did not advance beyond the common sentimentality of daring heroism and noble sacrifice. This view was particularly true of the motion picture industry, a young and growing busi-ness giant that advanced to the forefront of popular culture during the 1920s.

Americans became habitual moviegoers during these years, when the silent film reached its artistic and financial peak. What had once been an inexpensive source of amusement for lower-class urban workers blossomed into a major recreation for persons of every social and geographic background.

Historical evidence gleaned from commercial films is useful because of their appeal to a mass audience. Common themes in films often reflect the fears, desires, ideas, attitudes, and beliefs of the mass audience. Producers depend on this relationship, for profit is maximized in the dead center of audience desires. Such evidence is indirect, but it must be noted that traditional forms of evidence are also indirect in this regard. Historians using novels, memoirs, and other literary works often make assumptions about the impact when they have no audience on which to depend. The difference between using film and literature as historical evidence is one of degree, not of quality. If anything, film evidence may be more useful because of its wider audience. The American literary public for a Hemingway novel numbered in the thousands; the movie public for a Chaplin film was in the millions.[1]

The motion picture industry generally did well during the war years. Moviemakers dutifully cranked out hundreds of one- and two-reel features with war plots, most of which brought an average return of a few thousand dollars. Many of these films were of the trite heroic genre, although some moved far enough into the fantastic to be remembered today as examples of the extremism of war. *The Kaiser, the Beast of Berlin* (1918) might be regarded as the quintessence of the latter type. But with the armistice, the hate pictures quickly became ludicrous. War pictures were falling off as profit makers by November 1918. Caught with titles such as *Red, White and Blue Blood* and *Break the News to Mother,* industry flacks hastened to assure distributors that these were not war stories. Movie pioneer Fred J. Balshofer remembered that on the day of the armistice, he completed final cutting on a "six-reel all-out anti-Kaiser picture." The market was dead, and he lost $80,000 (Balshofer and Miller 139).

The immediate postwar climate continued to treat the war film as a pariah. Very few pictures with a world war background were made between 1919 and 1925. Almost all sank at the box office. The one major exception, Metro's *Four Horsemen of the Apocalypse* (1921), succeeded largely on the strength of its exciting new leading man—Rudolph Valentino. In general, the industry rode the crest of the broadening wave of materialism, sexual freedom, and sensation.

VIDOR, MAYER, THALBERG, AND STALLINGS

Riding this crest with everyone else was a young director named King Vidor. Vidor was born in Galveston in 1894, the descendant of a Hungarian grandfather who had immigrated to Texas at the close of the Civil War. In 1918, already a veteran maker of amateur newsreels, Vidor moved to Hollywood, the new golden land where the motion picture industry had firmly seated itself during the second decade of the century.

In 1918 and 1919 Vidor did a series of feature films for the Brentwood Corporation, a group of doctors and dentists seeking profits in foreign fields. Then, after a short stint with First National, he formed Vidor Village, his own independent production company. As was common in those days, he inserted his "Creed and Pledge" in *Variety* in 1920. It was couched in the purplish prose and hyperidealism of a young man, and an inevitable recession from its extremes soon occurred. But throughout his life Vidor remained committed to film as an art and as a noble device of human expression: "I believe in the picture that will help humanity to free itself from the shackles of fear and suffering that have so long bound it with iron chains" (quoted in Baxter 10).

In 1922 Vidor Village folded, and the young entrepreneur moved to the Metro Pictures lot. He then worked on "artistically respectable" productions for Louis B. Mayer, and in 1924 he moved with Mayer to the newly formed Metro-Goldwyn-Mayer Studios, where he was a staff director. By the age of thirty, Vidor had put a world of moviemaking experience behind him, a background not uncommon in an industry whose organizational and bureaucratic patterns were still congealing. Mayer regarded him as a reliable director of marketable films, and Vidor was entrusted with directing some of MGM's best talent, such as John Gilbert in *His Hour* (1924) and *Wife of the Centaur* (1925).

Irving Thalberg, Mayer's chief of production, was even younger than Vidor, having been born in 1899 in modest middle-class comfort in Brooklyn. His father was a lace importer, but the young Thalberg broke away from the world of trade and by 1919 was on the West Coast working for Carl Laemmle at Universal Studios. For four years he learned about motion pictures from the front office. In February 1923 he amicably left Laemmle to join Mayer. The division of labor worked out by the two men—which carried MGM to leadership of the industry in less than a decade—was for Thalberg to concern himself with the production end and Mayer to serve as administrator and link to the home office in New York. Thus, Thalberg was the man the restless Vidor approached late in 1924 with an idea for a film that would tackle an important question. As a child of the Progressive Era, Vidor was concerned with three major topics: war, wheat, and steel. Thalberg asked whether he had a particular subject in mind, and Vidor replied vaguely that the story would be about an average young American, neither patriot nor pacifist, caught up in war. Nothing was on paper yet, and the two men agreed to search for a good story centered on World War I (Vidor, *Tree* 111–12). Both knew of the chilly box office reception of war stories, yet each felt that a fresh and innovative treatment would find an audience. Thalberg, who had production control, was the key to script approval.

Weeks later, Thalberg returned from a trip to New York accompanied by a writer named Laurence Stallings and a story, tentatively titled "The Big Parade," typed on five pages of onionskin. Unlike Thalberg or Vidor, Stallings (who was the same age as Vidor) was an AEF veteran. As a captain in the U.S. Marines, he had lost his right leg at Belleau Wood in June 1918. When Thalberg met him, the young veteran and Maxwell Anderson had one of the hottest plays of the 1924 season, *What Price Glory?* running on Broadway.

The former marine had recently completed a semiautobiographical novel, *Plumes,* about the painful rehabilitation of a wounded war veteran. Overwritten and consciously tendentious, *Plumes* presented a weaker version of the postwar climate of disillusion that had been more artfully limned by such writers as Hemingway, Dos Passos, and cummings. For Stallings, the sound of the trumpets persisted among the carnage. Despite a shattered leg, his hero, Richard Plume, remained a patriot, albeit a troubled one.

Until his death in 1968, Stallings retained the love-hate relationship for the war that is so evident in *What Price Glory?* and in much of his later work. The memory of his doughboy comrades was constantly with him. "Why write of them at this hour?" he asked rhetorically in 1963. "Why open the door of a room sealed off in my mind for so many years?" In fact, the door was never sealed; the stump of his right leg was a daily reminder: "I have my Idaho willow foot to remind me now" (Stallings, *Doughboys* 1). As it did for many aging veterans, romanticism battled horror for memory's hand and won. Stallings claimed in his final testament concerning the earth-shaking adventures of his young manhood that he had written about the doughboy "conscious of being unable to summon him back in entirety, and heartsick of enduring the melancholy of trying to recover long-buried remembrances of the past" (6–7).

In 1924 Stallings's memory of the war was fresh and unencumbered by time. The theatrical realism of his brawling, cursing marines in *What Price Glory?* brought him to Thalberg's attention. Those first five pages were loosely based on *Plumes,* but what evolved bore little resemblance to the original. Whereas *Plumes* was concerned with a veteran's postwar struggles, the onionskin treatment dealt mostly with the war itself. Both Thalberg and Vidor believed that they had found their story. Vidor and writer Harry Behn traveled back to New York with Stallings, stayed a week, and returned with the completed script of *The Big Parade.* The title was a product of Stallings's romantic image of the transatlantic chain of doughboys fighting in defense of liberty (Vidor, *Tree* 113–14; Stallings, *Doughboys* 7). As the film would make clear, the vision included another less exhilarating "parade"—of the ambulances returning from the front with America's wounded.

Producing *The Big Parade*

Casting the film presented little problem, since MGM had a growing roster of contract actors from which to choose. Robert Sherwood, one of Stallings's friends at the celebrated Algonquin Round Table, would later claim that Stallings had been allowed to select the director and the leads. However, this was Stallings's maiden voyage in the hazardous seas of film creation, and though Vidor and Thalberg were young, they were not inexperienced in the industry. It is therefore most unlikely that Stallings had the final say in the casting process (Baxter 26).

The male lead, an average American boy, was cast against type. Thalberg, with Vidor's concurrence, selected John Gilbert, although Vidor had supposedly experienced some difficulties with the actor on the set of *Wife of the Centaur.* Thalberg convinced Vidor that Gilbert, shorn of his mustache, would fit the role of Jim Apperson nicely. The actor had developed a sophisticated, romantic acting style that began to attract public notice after Thalberg offered him a five-year contract with MGM (Crowther 103–4). The female lead, a French peasant girl, went to an unknown with the improbable name Renée Adorée. The roles of Apperson's two doughboy buddies were filled by raw-boned Karl Dane, who had just stepped up from a job as studio carpenter, and Tom O'Brien, a stocky "Irish" actor (Vidor, *Tree* 115).

The story line, a collaboration of Stallings, Vidor, Behn, and perhaps Thalberg, was modified slightly by Vidor a number of times during shooting, a common practice in the silent film era. What emerged was a tale hackneyed by today's standards but fresh and engaging to the motion picture audience of 1925.

As the film opens, the three principal characters are seen in their civilian occupations: Slim (Dane) at work as a steelworker on a skyscraper; Mike "Bull" O'Hara (O'Brien), as a bartender; and James Apperson (Gilbert) as a rich wastrel—a departure from Vidor's notion of an average young American. Apperson is persuaded to enlist by an exciting parade of recruits, leaping from his luxury car to join the marching men and their brass band.

A time-transition montage sequence follows the conversion of the raw recruits into doughboys, tracing the developing friendship of the central trio. The unit is sent to France, where the men are billeted in a small village and they begin to mingle with the local population. Apperson meets a pretty girl, Melisande (Adorée), in the first series of light romantic scenes. Rash youth

Photofest

Melisande (Renée Adorée) bids au revoir to James Apperson (John Gilbert) as he marches off to the battlefront.

that he is, Apperson attempts to kiss her but is met with a slap in the face. The budding romance is postponed by the movement of Apperson's unit to the front, a melee of scurrying soldiers, careening trucks, and hurried good-byes. The sequence includes one of the most famous separation scenes in cinema, in which Melisande has to be pried from her lover by a sergeant. Distraught, she clings to Apperson's leg, then to a chain dangling from the rear of his truck transport, and finally collapses in the dust of the road. Apperson throws her his dog tags, watch, and an extra boot as a remembrance. The fade-out is on the peasant girl clutching the precious boot (a symbol of Apperson's forthcoming injury) and gazing toward the front.

The battle sequences follow, most prominently a tense march through woods—resembling Belleau Wood, where Stallings was wounded—heavy with impending death. When Slim ventures into no-man's-land and is killed, an enraged Apperson engages in hand-to-hand combat. He holds a bayonet to a German soldier's throat but cannot follow through. Instead, he lights a cigarette for the German, who then dies of other wounds. Apperson takes the cigarette and calmly smokes it himself. (There is a matching shell crater scene with a German corpse in *All Quiet on the Western Front* [1930].)

A parade of trucks returning from the front disgorges Apperson, minus a leg. The village has been evacuated, and Melisande is nowhere to be found. Apperson is repatriated to America, where his family is shocked by his appearance and his deferred brother is courting Apperson's left-behind fiancée. Nothing remains but a postwar return to France; he and Melisande are reunited in an open field as the film ends.

Location shooting was rare under the studio system, and the adventures of Apperson and his buddies were mostly re-created on back lots. Many of the sets had an authentic air, a tribute to the talents of an artist named Warren Newcombe. Many of the bombed upper stories of French farmhouses and the roof of a cathedral used as a field hospital were expertly painted by Newcombe to match the action taking place in the lower half of the frame.

The technical skill behind the picture is not readily apparent today because the film is usually seen without the original orchestration. The most admired aesthetic aspect was the welding of visual imagery to music. As a young man, Vidor had shot footage of army maneuvers in Texas; some of these compositions helped him order the crowd shots of *The Big Parade*. In preparation for filming, the director screened almost a hundred reels of Signal Corps war footage. In the process, he was struck by the rhythmic cadence of the soldiers' images in combat—"the whole pattern spelled death." For the sequence of the doughboys advancing through the woods, filmed in Los Angeles's Griffith Park, Vidor used a metronome for pacing and had a bass drum keep the beat for the actors as they strode toward enemy positions in Belleau Wood. In theaters, the orchestra stopped playing during this sequence, and only a muffled bass drum kept cadence with the warily advancing soldiers on the screen, a highly evocative suspense mechanism (Vidor, *Tree* 156–57).

Vidor and his assistants also created distinctive orchestral rhythms for the love scenes and the hurly-burly of the movement to the front. Most of the war footage was shot for the film, adhering rigidly to Vidor's visual conceptions gleaned from the Signal Corps material. The director sent an assistant down to Fort Sam Houston to get shots of trucks, planes, and men all moving in a straight line (the "big parade" to the front). Although army personnel were cooperative, they convinced the assistant that the actual conditions on the western front had not allowed such geometry. Vidor was aware of this fact, but the convolutions in the resulting footage did not match his vision, so everything was reshot. Thus, realism and aesthetic considerations were interwoven, although some of the scenes of trucks moving at night look like model work. The director sometimes kept his camera running through three hundred to four hundred feet of film without a cut. This experiment was quite an innovation. Longer scenes would later evolve with the use of synchronized sound and what Vidor called "panning and perambulating cameras" (Vidor, *Tree* 120–21).

The picture had been intended as a standard production, budgeted at $205,000, but when Thalberg saw the rushes during filming, he decided to promote it as a major feature. An exhibitor named J. J. McCarthy, whose release of *Ben-Hur* would shortly give MGM another box office hit, viewed the finished print and offered to promote it if more battle scenes and romance were added. Under pressure, Vidor added the weak Apperson family sequences toward the end and created the subplot with Apperson's American fiancée. Since Vidor was already involved with his next project, *La Boheme,* director George Hill filmed additional night battle scenes at a cost of $40,000. This tinkering did not enhance the film, but it gave rise to the legend that Thalberg overhauled *The Big Parade* to make it a major release. Vidor later claimed that only about seventy feet of additional combat footage got into the final print (Baxter 21–24). Certainly the film is strongest in its re-creation of combat and in the romantic bits Vidor dreamed up for Apperson and Melisande. The next-to-closing sequences are conventional domestic soap opera.

With the studio firmly behind the picture, its New York release was heavily promoted. Vidor arrived in the city with a print of 12,800 feet. This running time was a bit too long for the distributor, who claimed that commuters in the audience would be put off their schedules by such a long film. The director was requested to pare 800 feet from his creation. Vidor was naturally averse to letting an editor hack away at the footage, so he took the print back to the coast with him. Each night, after a day spent working on *La Boheme,* Vidor snipped three frames from the beginning and end of each scene. Upon the completion of this labor, he was still 165 feet over the desired length, so he pruned one additional frame on each side of every splice. At that point, the total eliminated came to exactly 800 feet. This process of excision would have been impossible with a sound film (Vidor, *Tree* 123–24).

The orchestral scores were written in New York City after the distributors received the truncated version. A full orchestra was in the pit at the Astor Theater, but Vidor's idea of the single bass drum accentuating the foreboding walk into the forest was not used until the film opened at Grauman's Egyptian Theater in Hollywood (Vidor, *King Vidor* 142).

The Big Parade (1925) was a moneymaker from the beginning. At the Astor alone, the picture took in $1.5 million during a ninety-six-week run. By 1930 it had grossed more than $15 million nationwide. In 1931 it was rereleased with a musical sound track to capitalize on new audio technology. The final gross was in the neighborhood of $20 million. Vidor personally reaped little of this bonanza. Originally he had owned a 20 percent interest in the film, but his own lawyer convinced him that a fixed directorial fee was safer than a box office percentage. Later in life he sourly remarked, "I thus spared myself from becoming a millionaire instead of a struggling young director trying to do something interesting and better with a camera" (Vidor, *Tree* 125).

CRITICS AND AUDIENCES RESPOND

Critics nationwide generally applauded the picture, which played well in urban and rural areas alike. Both Stallings and Vidor burned with the desire to show war realistically, and this realism was the most common point of admiration among the critics. Gilbert Seldes, for example, thought the war scenes were magnificent. Stallings's friend Robert Sherwood was amazed that the war scenes actually resembled war (Seldes, review 169), while another admirer expostulated that "in every sense of the word, *it is the war!*" (Finch 25). Military organizations also favored the film's vision; that Vidor had used AEF veterans as technical advisers had been widely publicized.

The favorable critical reception reflected several themes infusing *The Big Parade* that were also congenial to Americans. The war was perceived not only as democracy's war, in a righteous sense, but also as an intrinsic leveler of class differences. The spoiled rich boss, Apperson, quickly fuses interests with the steelworker and the bartender; in avenging Slim, he is mourning a friend. His romance with a peasant girl furthers the democratization process, and his rejection of his former way of life affirms his commitment to a simpler, unostentatious existence.

The combat sequences did not part substantially from heroic, adventurous patterns. Several critics mistakenly praised the film as antiwar because of the shell-hole incident in which Apperson balks at killing. But Apperson, Bull, and Slim do their share. A publicity still for the picture had the primitive steelworker simultaneously bayoneting one German and decking another with his free hand. Virtually all the war films of the era preached the litany of commitment, duty, heroism, sacrifice, and *The Big Parade* made no innovations in this regard. The heroics are individualized by dramatic convention. Apperson's war is an intensely personal one: "I came to fight—not to wait and rot in a lousy hole while they murder my pal." His sacrifice (which is double—a friendship and his own body) is rewarded in the fade-out.

In this context, *The Big Parade* offers a most admiring view of the American soldier and his war efforts. The doughboy is a committed civilian who, when aroused, becomes a dominant warrior, only to yearn for the blessings of peace. Here Vidor's humanitarianism, which infuses the film, is unable to overshadow the ambiguities of Stallings's relationship to the war. Stallings and most of his comrades could never admit the possibility that the whole thing had been unnecessary, meaningless, and disastrous. This reconsideration would have made the loss of life and limb unbearable as well as tragic. So the war became a legitimate theater for the heroics of the democratic fighting man, the GI as New World Cincinnatus.

The general critical tone indicated appreciation of an epic entertainment grounded in human emotion. No one wanted to applaud the war itself, but *The Big Parade* did not indict the war aims or practices of the United States nor those of any of the Allies. This statement by an industry reviewer unintentionally keyed the significant qualities of the picture: "It is the first production that I have ever seen that has caught *the spirit of national pride* that makes the United States Army the greatest fighting organization on earth—that subtle yearning to acquit themselves honorably in doing *that which the situation demands,* that brings heroes out of the slums and the mansions of wealth alike" (Finch 59; emphasis added).

The themes of nationalism, honor, duty, and egalitarian heroism are all common to the war-adventure genre. Plots threaded with them cannot make a coherent antiwar or pacifist statement, since the focus of such themes is individualistic rather than situational. When another member of the Algonquin Round Table, Alexander Woollcott, viewed *The Big Parade,* he observed among his fellow moviegoers pity for the dying doughboys and satisfaction in the scenes of German deaths (40). The individualism of the film is sketched in the positive attributes of friendship and democratic solidarity. Transferred to the emotional level of the viewer, these become the admirable qualities of loyalty, devotion, and dedication to service. Here, patriotic impulse overcomes the horrors of war, not vice versa.

The mass audience that saw the film was probably unaware of the ambiguities actually underlying the plot. *The Big Parade*'s patina of realism was deemed to be significant comment in itself. Also, many in the audience doubtless shared these ambiguities without any intellectual tensions whatsoever. Thus, war could be applauded and excoriated at the same time. Thalberg in particular was convinced that his production marked a significant departure from earlier war films:

> The only difference between it and the other war pictures was the different viewpoint taken in the picture. We took a boy whose idea in entering the war was not patriotic. He was swept along by the war spirit around him and entered it but didn't like it. He met a French girl who was intriguing to him, but he wasn't really serious about her. The only time he was interested in fighting was when a

Jim Apperson in an archetypal World War I situation: alone in a shell crater. (Note the extra boot.)

Photofest

friend, who was close to him, was killed. It was human appeal rather than patriotic appeal, and when he reached the German trenches and came face to face with the opportunity to kill, he couldn't do it. In other words, a new thought regarding the war was in the minds of most people, and that was the basis of its appeal. (quoted in Thomas 129)

The producer offered a virtually complete list of mistaken reasons for the film's popularity. The basic appeal of *The Big Parade* was adventure and romance. None of its ingredients were new; they were only packaged differently. The theme of war as a democratic leveler stretched back in movie time at least to Thomas Ince's *Civilization* (1916). Rich boys democratized by war had been prominent in such earlier films as Edison's *The Unbeliever* (1918) and McManus's *The Lost Battalion* (1919). Apperson reaches romantic fulfillment with ingenuous Melisande at the war's end in spite of his being "not really serious about her." Finally, it is difficult to reconcile the audience partisanship observed by Woollcott and applauded by many reviewers with a "human" rather than a patriotic appeal.

The Big Parade is flawed as an antiwar statement by the very individualism Thalberg regarded as its primary virtue. Years later Budd Schulberg would succinctly call the film "second-rate perfection" for exactly this reason (Schulberg

117). In Seldes's terms, Vidor gave American audiences the spectacle of the war but "little else" (Seldes, "Two Parades" 111–12). As long as individuals stood apart from the mass and were made special through the devices of romance or action, the cinema could never come to grips with the true nature of twentieth-century warfare. The protagonists of *The Big Parade* did not lay down their arms and refuse to fight, nor were they left numbed by the potential nihilism of their situation. They dwelled in a rational, if horrible, condition and responded to it in necessary and rational ways. *The Big Parade* was thus a prisoner of dramatic convention, and, judging from its reception, so was its audience.

Although English and French viewers naturally tended to resent the film on chauvinistic grounds, its real difficulty lay in a fundamental misapprehension of the war itself. If international combat is conventionally seen as a process with winners and losers, the screen in the 1920s transmuted these into heroes and villains. *The Big Parade* marched in an intellectual arena heavily populated with the ghosts of nineteenth-century romanticism and the American cult of the individual. Here it tapped one of the deepest veins in the national character, and therein lay its success—not in any new conception of the war, for it had none. "No film dare show what [war] resembled," wrote critic Iris Barry. As she saw it, *The Big Parade* "wreathes machine-guns in roses" (946–47).

Vidor himself later admitted that his love for documentary realism had been dominated by conventional screen action and romance. He saw the picture as late as 1974 and stated: "I don't like it much. . . . Today I don't encourage people to see the film. At the time, I really believed it was an anti-war movie." Thus, even the director conceded that the basic appeal of the film was not the "parade" of young men marching toward the maelstrom of death but the romantic bits developed for Apperson and Melisande (Baxter 21).

What remains is nevertheless an exceptional piece of screen storytelling. By the standards of its day, *The Big Parade*'s battle scenes were realistic. A few critics derided the forest sequence as militarily inaccurate, but Vidor claimed to have received a letter from the War Department praising precisely those portrayals (Mitchell 180). The basic merit of the film lay in Vidor's ability to maintain the action without interrupting overmuch with titles; in this sense, the picture is a choice example of mimetic art.

MGM's box office success inevitably inaugurated a war-adventure film cycle throughout the industry. The cycle lasted for five years—at least through the release of Howard Hughes's *Hell's Angels* (1930). *What Price Glory?* and its brawling marines appeared in 1926, and William Wellman's aviation epic *Wings* appeared the next year; both spawned dozens of imitators. Vidor's original plot contributions became stale through reiteration, until Seldes finally threw up his hands in surrender when he wrote in the 3 July 1929 *New Republic:* "In all American films since *The Big Parade,* if a regiment is marching away, or a thousand trucks roll by, the hero or heroine staggers through the lines, fighting off the men in the trucks, trying to make his or her way to the beloved and departing one" (179). Not until 1930, when Universal gambled with a screen adaptation of *All Quiet on the Western Front,* did the American public see an American film that was truly antiwar in intent and execution. Even then, films depicting war as a worthy arena for heroic adventure and romance were not extinguished. The genre survived to fuel the buildup to a new and greater war.

After *The Big Parade*

Stallings stayed with motion pictures, working as an editor of Fox Movietone newsreels and turning out journeyman film scripts, several for Vidor. Stallings's documentary film *The First World War* (1934) was his harshest statement on the experience, but his bittersweet written history *The Doughboys* retained the essential ambiguities developed in *Plumes, The Big Parade,* and *What Price Glory?* Thalberg continued his record of high-quality film production until his untimely death from lobar pneumonia in 1936. John Gilbert's career faded in the late 1920s. His deterioration and early death, which also occurred in 1936, compose a case history that is often cited as a classic example of the decline and fall of a star. Vidor went on to become, by any standards, one of the finest directors in Hollywood history. He tackled a wide variety of projects, from socialist symbolism (*Our Daily Bread* [1934]) to Western epic (*Duel in the Sun* [1946]), before finally closing the books with the routine biblical tale *Solomon and Sheba* (1959). His original concerns—humanistic, idealistic, fraught with optimism—remained remarkably consistent throughout a career that spanned five decades.

Vidor, Stallings, and Thalberg, all of them thirty or younger at the time, bear the essential creative responsibility for *The Big Parade.* The realistic vision of the war is Stallings's; the aesthetic vision belongs to Vidor. Put another way, the story was an intensely personal one by Stallings, but the storyteller was Vidor. Their product is symbolic of an American view of the great crusade as seen from the 1920s, a vision that contrasts markedly with the traditional consensus to be found in elite histories and fictions.

Historian Otis L. Graham Jr., in a succinct study of continuity and discontinuity in the Progressive reform impulse, recently restated the traditional view. World War I was "the stimulus to private indulgence and social irresponsibility" (91). To Graham and many others, the war caused the spirit of reaction so evident in many of the social conflicts of the decade (109). This spirit suffused the

The popular consensus: World War I was an epic—albeit tragic—adventure.

debates over fundamentalism, rekindled nativist sentiment, and heightened the tension between urban and rural sectors of America. Reaction, like almost all American social trends, had no distinctive class basis. Thus, films like *The Big Parade* cannot be analyzed as mouthpieces of social thought from either the Left or the Right.

Instead, *The Big Parade* is an indicator of a broad, classless climate of opinion, circa 1925, concerning the nature of the Great War. *Consensus* is too strong a word, implying a reasoned decision based on choice. Evidence from films such as this resolves a seeming paradox concerning the historical analysis of the 1920s, which may be stated as follows: how can a decade usually classed as reactionary or conservative also be seen as one of intense antiwar sentiment? To be sure, conservatism and militarism do not always fit snugly, but the instinct for tradition and order implicit in the former camp usually finds a welcome home in the latter. There is sketchy evidence—for example, the empty pacifist idealism of the Kellogg-Briand Pact (1928)—to indicate that hostility toward war can encompass reformers and conservatives alike. But such evidence is sparse and does not drive a lasting wedge between conservatism and militarism as patterns of thought and behavior.

The paradox vanishes when the elitist basis of traditional 1920s historiography is recognized. Our evidence of the antiwar and antimilitarist condition of the period is drawn largely from professional cultural critics: novelists, journalists, artists, and others whose business it is to criticize. This is hard evidence and convincing in its sphere; the mistake lies not in accepting it but in allowing this material to dominate the historiography of the decade.

The Big Parade, touching a far wider audience than anything produced by cultural elites in the 1920s, departs from the common view. Its alternative vision, of course, does not stand alone—but neither should that of the antiwar elites. The foggy differentiation between art and entertainment, or high culture and popular culture, should not obscure the fact that in relying on film evidence to test the nature of American thought about the war, we are using precisely the same method as historians who rely on written materials. Only the nature of the evidence is different.[2]

The popularity of the war-adventure films of the 1920s strongly indicates that a considerable number of Americans retained an ambiguous relationship to the war experience. For many, the image of war persisted as one of a legitimate theater for heroism and nationalistic endeavor. America had confronted Europe with ancient European wrongs; having righted them on the battlefield, the young giant of the West rejected involvement in the corrupt diplomacy of a decadent continent. Thus, the feelings of frustration and disillusion strengthened the climate of isolation, which was indeed strong throughout the interwar period.

But isolationism is not antimilitarism. Intellectual elites might inveigh against the sword, but the qualities of patriotism, service, and social hierarchy implicit in a uniform remained positively symbolic of the essence of national idealism for many Americans. In this sense, the war was perceived as an unwelcome task that had to be undertaken. The passionate excesses of the war years had dampened even before President Wilson's debilitating stroke, but the conviction that the war was necessary survived in many quarters. The tragedy was thus not only one of lives destroyed and bodies shattered but also one of a task completed with an imperfect ending. Here there was no nation to forge, no sundered Union to reunite, no defeated Mexicans or Spaniards waiting to drop vast acreages into the lap of Uncle Sam.

In the final analysis, it was a war fought for ideals of the highest order. Human imperfection can suffer this strain for only so long, and the resulting disillusionment is compounded by the strength of the original moral fervor. The motion picture theater, however, is a house of dreams: there, ideals not

only achieve perfection but endure in screen time forever. The steadily un-
winding spools of celluloid may simultaneously reduce a world war to romance
and enshrine it as a fit pantheon for heroes. American filmmakers were only
beginning to learn the language of tortured ambiguity, and their audiences
remained largely unreceptive to this language when it spoke of war.

So Vidor and the others failed, in a sense, to make their antiwar statement.
Like all of us, they were culture bound, working in a medium that relied on
broad cultural acceptance for its livelihood. *The Big Parade* inspired no marches
to the recruiting station, but neither did the film indict the war itself. An era
rich in contradictions blandly ignored one of the most profound contradictions of all—the reconciliation of militancy and pacifism under the symbolic
blanket of democratic idealism.

NOTES

Isenberg's original essay on *The Big Parade* appeared in O'Connor and Jackson in 1979
and is republished here as a particularly fine example of historical film analysis.

1. This is not to argue that historical impact is measured in numbers alone. I
analyze the reasons for the mistrust of film evidence by the history profession in "A
Relationship of Constrained Anxiety."

2. We leave in abeyance the question of causation, which is exceedingly difficult
to resolve in the context of intellectual history. This difficulty is true regardless of the
nature of the evidence. I examine the contours of this question in "Toward an Historical Methodology."

WORKS CITED

Anderson, Maxwell, and Laurence Stallings. *Three American Plays*. New York: Harcourt,
1926.

Balshofer, Fred J., and Arthur C. Miller. *One Reel a Week*. Berkeley: U of California P,
1967.

Barry, Iris. Rev. of *The Big Parade. Spectator* 5 June 1926.

Baxter, John. *King Vidor*. New York: Monarch, 1976.

Crowther, Bosley. *The Lion's Share: The Story of an Entertainment Empire*. New York: Dut-
ton, 1957.

Finch, Robert M. Rev. of *The Big Parade. Motion Picture Director* Nov. 1925.

Graham, Otis L., Jr. *The Great Campaigns: Reform and War in America, 1900–1928*. Englewood Cliffs, N.J.: Prentice-Hall, 1971.

Isenberg, Michael T. "A Relationship of Constrained Anxiety: Historians and Film."
History Teacher 6.4 (1973): 553–68.

———. "Toward an Historical Methodology for Film Scholarship." *Rocky Mountain Social
Science Journal* 12.1 (1975): 45–57.

Mitchell, G. J. "King Vidor." *Films in Review* 15.3 (1964).

O'Connor, John E., and Martin A. Jackson, eds. *American History/American Film: Interpreting the Hollywood Image*. New York: Frederick Ungar, 1979.

Schulberg, Budd. "Movies in America: After Fifty Years." *Atlantic Monthly* 180.5 (Nov. 1947): 115–22.

Seldes, Gilbert. Rev. of *The Big Parade*. *Dial* Feb. 1926.

———. "The Two Parades." *New Republic* 16 Dec. 1925.

———. *New Republic* 3 July 1929: 179–80.

Stallings, Laurence. *The Doughboys: The Story of the AEF, 1917–1918*. New York: Harper, 1963.

———. *Plumes*. New York: Harcourt, 1924.

Thomas, Bob. *Thalberg: Life and Legend*. Garden City, N.Y.: Doubleday, 1969.

Vidor, King. *King Vidor on Film Making*. New York: McKay, 1972.

———. *A Tree Is a Tree*. New York: Harcourt, 1953.

Woollcott, Alexander. "'*The Big Parade*' of British Anger." *Literary Digest* 12 June 1926.

7 / James Latham

TECHNOLOGY AND "REEL PATRIOTISM" IN AMERICAN FILM ADVERTISING OF THE WORLD WAR I ERA

Advertising and publicity are forms of commercial speech that motivate moviegoing and shape the understanding of films. In fact, at times, advertisements are even more memorable, more evocative, and more widely seen than the films they promote. Although historians have studied the production and exhibition of war-related films, they have paid less attention to how these films were marketed. Advertising did more than simply tout movies; it conveyed cultural meanings of patriotism and national identity, as well as reasons why the country was at war and why the public should participate. This case study of seven advertisements reveals the ideological power of what Christian Metz describes as cinema's "third machine: after the one that manufactures the films, and the one that consumes them, the one that *vaunts* them, that valorizes the product" (14). Most of these advertisements promoted films exhibited in the latter years of World War I, when the United States and its film industry were fully engaged; other ads emphasized war-related issues that were of special concern to exhibitors, such as taxes on theater admissions.[1]

World War I–era advertisements for war films created rich rhetorical forms with words and images that could evoke the primal fear of victimization or the optimism of the modern technological age. Technologies were depicted in ads to encourage exhibitors to book movies and the public to see them. World War I marked the introduction or modernization of the submarine, machine gun, tank, airplane, artillery, radio, and chemical weapons, technologies that transcended conventional limitations of space and time to deliver destruction to distant military and civilian populations on an unprecedented scale. Film promotion both familiarized audiences with these technologies and used them rhetorically to signify the relative power of combatants and the righteousness of the Allied cause. When, for instance, ads depicted Americans with one of these new weapons, "we" were portrayed as effective and morally justified; in contrast, when a German wielded a machine gun, he was inept or evil. In addition to new technologies, film promotion depicted conventional and even primitive weapons, including knives and clubs, sometimes staging allegorical scenes with figures such as Uncle Sam and Kaiser Wilhelm II. These melodramatic images condensed the war into a conflict between two familiar combatants and alluded to the great historical significance, or the putative ancient animosities, of the democracy of the doughboy and the tyranny of the evil "Hun." Film promotion even depicted nonmilitary technologies being used as weapons, such as mechanical presses that squeezed the Kaiser to death. Thus, images of technology often went beyond the literal content of the films they promoted, as is typical with advertising—a practice prone to hyperbole and other means of playing on the emotions of consumers.[2]

Like the films they promoted, advertisements functioned to rally support for the war effort and to exploit the conventional movie attraction of technology as spectacle in such forms as action, novelty, and raw power. War film promotion also valorized the medium of cinema, itself a modern form of communication and a powerful technological weapon that served "our" interests. Ads touted the capacity of film to provide news and spectacular images from the war with greater verisimilitude than any other medium. They praised cinema's ability to serve the war effort, explaining how film could portray the leaders, heroes, villains, and victims of the war in ways that furthered national interests. Movies were likened to weapons such as the machine gun, with the information and persuasive content of film images being as powerful as bullets in combating the enemy. Alternatively, ads promoted cinema as a respite from the struggle, providing escapist entertainment that rejuvenated war-weary spirits. As providers of this potent new medium, local exhibitors were encouraged to see themselves not simply as merchants but as providers of a service for both their local communities and the country.

"Reel Patriotism" and the Early War Effort

American film advertising from World War I depicted technologies in ways that benefited the U.S. government's war effort while serving the film industry's own business interests. Advertising promoted movies and also the technological, economic, and moral superiority of the United States as part of what Leslie Midkiff DeBauche terms the film industry's wartime "reel patriotism." The industry's direct cooperation with the government functioned to promote the war to often indifferent Americans, improve cinema's public image and profitability, and help the industry achieve what would become its long-standing dominance of the global film market. Indeed, this period was pivotal for the U.S. film industry, which was just beginning to migrate toward Los Angeles while vertically integrating and rapidly expanding its distribution in both domestic and international markets—an expansion caused partly by the war's overseas socioeconomic and political disruption as well as America's prolonged neutrality.

Although the June 1914 assassination of Archduke Franz Ferdinand precipitated the war in Europe, the United States remained officially neutral until April 1917, for reasons that included widespread public sentiments of isolationism and pacifism. When the United States finally entered the war, among the government's immediate mobilization efforts was the formation of the Committee on Public Information (CPI), which conducted a massive advertising and public relations campaign to promote the war.[3] The CPI was unprecedented in its scale, sophistication, and interplay with the private sector, providing a model for conducting warfare through the modern mass media. The CPI's Division of Films enlisted the emerging Hollywood industry on many levels of production, distribution, and exhibition. Seeking cultural legitimacy and an outlet for its own patriotism, as well as the economic benefits of working with the government, the film industry responded by producing movies that derided Germany, praised the Allies, and urged public participation in the war effort. Film companies encouraged local exhibitors to show these movies and to promote the war to the public in various other ways, such as providing forums for the thousands of volunteer "four-minute men," who gave patriotic speeches about the war in movie theaters during reel changes.[4] Studios and exhibitors also produced advertising that stimulated the demand for films with a wartime fervor.

During the period of U.S. neutrality, Germany was not especially vilified in American film promotion.[5] Films about the war typically were not promoted in a manner that criticized Germany, and even some pro-German films were imported and distributed in the United States.[6] Among the more common types of films about the war during these early years were newsreels showing footage from Europe, including what were purported to be the front lines. A trade journal ad for one such series, *The Fighting Germans*, was typical in this regard. The ad contains no call to arms or moralistic fervor but instead depicts more neutral imagery of battles and anonymous soldiers. It refers to the spectacle of "marvelous," "bloody," and "giant" scenes of warfare and to the authenticity of the images of "actual" battles filmed by A. K. Dawson, described as "the most daring camera correspondent in the European war." The film is described as "showing the horrors of a desperately fought battle from

Moving Picture World 28.8 (20 May 1916): 1278–79.

the very beginning to the very end." Overall, the ad emphasizes the realism of actual footage and the spectacle of warfare rather than the melodramatic clash of good and evil that would dominate film promotions in 1917–1918. The emphasis on realism is a long-standing appeal of documentary footage and may have been especially compelling for films of the World War I period. The technological limitations of movie cameras made it difficult to perform location shooting even under the best of circumstances, much less in combat situations. Outdoor events were often reenacted in safe locations—whether controlled studio environments or neutral territories such as Scotland—and presented to viewers as authentic, with varying degrees of verisimilitude. Thus, while promoting a particular newsreel series, this ad also implies the developing power of cinematic technology to capture moving images from anywhere in the world for geographically dispersed audiences to see up close in the safety and convenience of their local movie theaters. The four separate images in the ad support this sense of ubiquity.

Although this advertisement may valorize cinematic images of actuality, it also encourages exhibitors to contact local newspapers for possible cross-promotions. This encouragement may reflect hierarchical assumptions about the credibility of the more established print news organizations in contrast to the new entertainment-dominated medium of film. More likely, however, it is an attempt to encourage exhibitors to work with local newspapers instead of viewing them as rivals. Probably this message is promoting a tie-in campaign, with serialized newspaper stories appearing in conjunction with regular installments of the newsreel and perhaps containing images from the film, thus capitalizing on the synergistic potential of print and moving image media.

PROMOTING WAR FILMS AND TECHNOLOGIES

German warfare technologies that appeared in American film promotion included zeppelins, U-boats, airplanes, artillery, guns, and explosives. In film promotion before and after the war, these technologies did not signify an immediate danger to the United States and even had benign connotations as novelties or symbols of modernity. But during 1917–1918 German weapons technologies were criticized as symbols of military power (malevolent forces to be reckoned with) or mocked as comically inept (nuisances that were easily overcome), such as the reference to an ineffectual "rubber periscope" in a promotion for the Charlie Chaplin film *Shoulder Arms* (1918).

Among the technologies most often depicted, zeppelins were usually associated with malevolent qualities and the entertainment value of spectacle. For example, a trade journal ad for *The Zeppelin's Last Raid* (1917) shows a dirigible being attacked by several biplanes and exploding while a city below is in flames, apparently from the bombs dropped by the zeppelin.[7] In addition to touting the involvement of producer Thomas Ince, a marketable name in 1917,[8] the ad emphasizes the entertainment value of dogfight imagery, explosions, and flames, in part by quoting several reviews of the film attesting to its ability to "thrill, entertain and impress all who see it." Although this image is ostensibly apolitical in its emphasis on spectacle as entertainment, in fact, it has an anti-German slant. The dirigible symbolizes ominous German power, although its destruction also suggests technological weakness; at the very least, it suggests that this particular lumbering airship is no match for the more mobile Allied planes. Thus, the message is that "they" may have modern weaponry, but "ours" is better. The strongest anti-German reference, though, may be the image of a city in flames; at least two church steeples are visible, and the one in the lower right is toppling. The violence of this image might have been compelling enough if it had depicted a battlefield, but showing "a raid upon a defenseless village" that might be located anywhere—perhaps even within the United States—likely enhanced the emotional and hence commercial impact of the ad.

In wartime film promotion, technology is often depicted serving the Al-

Exhibitor's Trade Review 2.25 (24 Nov. 1917): 1961.

lied cause, whether it shows American military might, the moral legitimacy of unleashing this power on the enemy, or the unified support among Americans for doing so. For example, an ad for *The Greatest Power* (1917), also known as *Her Greatest Power,* shows Ethel Barrymore (instead of a male soldier) dutifully grasping an artillery round at waist level and tilting it upward as she loads it into

James Latham Collection

Exhibitors Herald and Motography
7.15 (5 Oct. 1918): 9.

the breech of a cannon (*Exhibitors Trade Review* 9 June 1917: 23). Promotion
for *The Submarine Spy,* a film about the workings of a U.S. submarine, shows
Uncle Sam as a colossus holding the submarine in a phallic position (*Moving
Picture World* 12 Dec. 1914: 1460–61).

Although warfare typically involves a battle of the most advanced technologies, the weapons of war depicted in film promotion of this era were not
always modern. An ad for the early Raoul Walsh film *The Prussian Cur* (1918)
forgoes modern technology for hand-to-hand combat. Here the Kaiser is shown
lurking in an alley or a cave in the lower right, cringing in fear or perhaps
preparing to lunge with his long sword. He stands atop many victims whose
facial features and hair seem to code them mostly as women. (These figures
may simultaneously symbolize a captive Europe, allude to the abundant claims
of German atrocities circulating in the Allied media during the war, and
provide a counterpoint to the other, more visible female figure in the ad, the
Statue of Liberty.[9]) Whether protecting Liberty or empowered by her, Uncle
Sam dominates the scene,[10] standing tall and erect with his sleeve rolled up
and wielding a club in what is probably a reference to Theodore Roosevelt's

Moving Picture World 39.13 (29 Mar. 1919): 1753.

famous 1903 proclamation that, in its foreign policy, the United States should "speak softly and carry a big stick." Altogether, the blunt message here is that the Kaiser is an enemy to American values, institutions, and people; he must and will be beaten into submission.[11] The Kaiser may have some technological superiority (the relatively modern sword versus the primitive club), but this potential advantage is trumped by American democratic values and Uncle Sam's willingness to defend them. Thus, advertisers could have it both ways: in some images the enemy might be depicted as technologically inferior, whereas in others he might enjoy a degree of technical superiority but is ultimately defeated by other factors specific to "our" side.

Whereas some wartime film ads depicted premodern weaponry, others referenced technologies that were not weapons at all but symbolized the powers associated with them. One example promotes *Mutt and Jeff* cartoons by depicting the Kaiser cranking sausages out of a meat grinder into a container marked "Bill Hohenzollern and Son, Sausage Makers." This image, which appeared in the months following the war, depicts the Kaiser's son offering up Jeff, "der nice big fat von," to which the Kaiser responds in equally accented English, "Dot's nice! Chuck 'em in." Overhead, Mutt points a pistol at the Kaiser, ready to save Jeff from the meat grinder. The rhetorical techniques employed here include manipulating people's names, in one case by elevating filmmaker Bud Fisher to the status of "captain," and in another case by diminishing Kaiser Wilhelm to the status of "Bill." More significant, although the image does not depict battle scenes or German atrocities, it alludes to them, with the callous Kaiser and his son about to toss a sympathetic living victim into a meat grinder. Intended or not, this seems to satirize the relations among the German leadership, military, and public, especially late in the war, when nearly any adult male was deemed fit for active service. Thus, Jeff may symbolize a draft dodger being captured (his disguise has not saved him) and forced into the service of the German military.[12] Subordinated to the state, he is turned into a faceless cog in a deadly war machine. He also may represent an Allied prisoner of war or even Europe itself, similarly threatened with destruction at the hands of the Kaiser's war machine. Mutt's pointing a pistol toward the Kaiser could symbolize the United States' liberating Europe from evil, similar to Uncle Sam in the ad for *The Prussian Cur.*

This image satirizes Germany's role in the war as an absurd act of mass murder and conjures notions of a nation consuming itself and its neighbors and of people helplessly serving the twisted whims of their leadership. Further connotations include German desperation because of food shortages, the enemy as barbaric and cannibalistic, and the stereotyping of Germans as merchants (particularly butchers) and heavy consumers of processed meat. (Although this image likely had resonance for its period, it is even more chilling when viewed in relation to the later Holocaust, the epitome of modern Teutonic efficiency and mechanized mass murder.[13]) Finally, in the context of film promotion, this image may evoke the physical analogue between the meat grinder and the movie camera or projector, or even the industry in general. In a sense, cameras, projectors, and the industry crank out reels of film like sausages. If one observes this parallel, then it is possible to view Jeff here as a movie actor being turned into a character for the consumption of audiences "everywhere"; the Kaiser could be a director or producer figure conducting this commodification, with his lackey son being something like a casting director.

PROMOTING THE WAR EFFORT TO EXHIBITORS

The film industry promoted the war effort for its own patriotic reasons but also because producers, distributors, and exhibitors had strong incentives to create goodwill with the national government, local businesses, and the film-going public.[14] This compliance enabled the industry in general, and theaters in particular, to become more integrated with the fabric of American life by providing entertainment, information, and places for communities to gather, which in turn facilitated economic growth and stability for the film industry. Yet within the industry there was resistance to the war effort, particularly among exhibitors, who were generally more susceptible to local tastes and cultures than the regionally and nationally oriented distributors and producers. De-Bauche notes in *Reel Patriotism* that throughout America's involvement in the war, there was an ongoing debate within the industry about what films should be made. Some believed that escapist entertainment best served the public, while others advocated films that were more directly engaged in contemporary issues. Regarding the latter films, there was concern that overtly propagandistic films might be unpopular with audiences, and therefore harmful to business, because of their inflammatory content as well as the pacifist or even privately pro-German sentiments of some American filmgoers.[15] Exhibitors also resisted compulsory Monday theater closings for energy rationing, as well as war taxes that increased movie ticket prices.

The CPI and film studios responded to these concerns on several levels, as illustrated in the remaining images in this chapter. The studios carefully scheduled the production of war films so that they never constituted a dominant market share and overwhelmed audiences. The films were varied in genre and rhetorical tone to make them appealing to diverse audiences. Local exhibitors were targeted with promotions arguing that they could contribute to the war effort while making profits. For example, war taxes could be justified to filmgoers as a way for them to support the struggle while being informed and entertained at the movies.

Among the advertisements that targeted the concerns of exhibitors is one for Francis Ford's *Berlin via America* (1918). This image shows Ford dressed as an aviator along with an exhibitor; together they push the Kaiser through a meat grinder, with money pouring out the bottom and filling a "box office." The roles from the *Mutt and Jeff* ad are now reversed; this time, the heroic figures are using the meat grinder to serve "our" pro-social purposes, and the Kaiser is suffering as he is pressed through the machine and turned into dollars and cents. The costuming of the heroes facilitates a reading of them on

Moving Picture World 36.11 (15 June 1918): 1531.

James Latham Collection

different levels, suggesting a soldier (the film's star) representing the military and a civilian (the exhibitor) representing the general public. The moral value of a technology depends on who is using it, how, at what costs, and for what ends. The end in this case is defeating Germany while making money. The image asserts that war films and the broader war effort need not alienate audiences or channel revenues to the government or the studios. Instead, they allow studios and exhibitors to work together to make money because of the putative drawing power of the Kaiser and the war, especially when "big and timely stories [are] ably presented by artists of the highest order, and with Mr. Ford in the stellar role."[16]

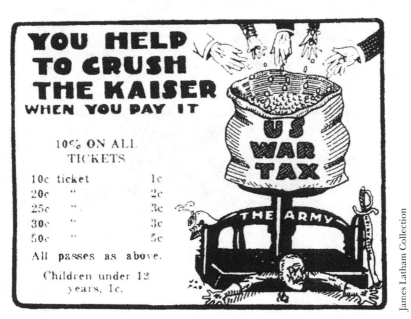

Moving Picture World 35.2 (12 Jan. 1918): 232.

Another advertisement speaks to the same issue and depicts a similar scene, but with interesting differences. This image, promoting the war tax on movie theater admissions, depicts the Kaiser being crushed in a press—"the army"—that is activated by the tax. The implication is that the money collected goes directly to the army to crush the Kaiser rather than to governmental bureaucrats. Here again, technology symbolically kills the Kaiser, though not for the purpose of making money. In fact, exhibitors may be losing money because of the war; this loss is downplayed, though, in several ways. One involves the depiction of the tax payment in the form of loose change, suggesting a minimal expense; recall that the previous image showed dollar bills as well as coins coming out of the meat grinder. In addition, the hands dropping the money into the bag represent not exhibitors but film audiences (one of the anonymous hands is a woman's, and another appears to be that of a child), thus minimizing the sense that the exhibitor is losing profits; instead, filmgoers are absorbing the cost of the tax. Also, the presence of multiple hands implies that costs are being distributed among a mass audience and that movies are popular even with a higher admission price. Finally, whatever burdens the tax may place on exhibitors or audiences, it is for a good cause and places far greater burdens on the enemy than on "us."

Whereas some of the previous ads depicted meat grinders that could be

analogues of movie cameras and projectors, a final one, for Paramount and Artcraft Pictures, more overtly associates cinema with a different technology—namely, the machine gun. This image depicts a battlefield scene of a dough-boy firing a modern water-cooled machine gun; behind him, soldiers charge up from a trench toward an unseen enemy. A parallel scene of the home front depicts a projectionist cranking a movie projector for a theater full of middle-class filmgoers. This imagery draws parallels between the machine gun and film projector (and camera) in terms of their general construction and functioning. The rotating motion rapidly and continuously feeds a strip of individual frames (or bullets) through an apparatus and sends them through space to their "targets"—namely, movie screens or enemy soldiers.[17] Perhaps more significant in this wartime context, though, is the value of these devices as weapons in the war effort, with images being potentially as powerful as bullets in defeating the enemy. As the copy asserts, "It is just as important to project the right sort of pictures as to fire the right sort of cartridges."

Probably alluding to the rectangular movie screen as a device that restricts our perception, the ad encourages exhibitors to keep Americans "in the right frame of mind" by showing the "right" kind of films—that is, those distributed by Paramount and Artcraft. This apparent certitude is undermined, however, when the copy simultaneously disparages "trashy entertainment" films and advocates films that evoke emotional responses of "laughter" and "tears." These contradictions may reflect the diverse range of films offered by Paramount and Artcraft, as well as the broader ambivalence within the industry about what kinds of films best served the war effort.[18] Curiously, the image does not show the film that is being projected in the movie theater, possibly to allow for this ambivalence. Perhaps the film is the scene shown on the left, and the audience is watching a movie about Allied soldiers rushing into harm's way. Or perhaps it is an escapist entertainment film that ignores the war altogether, with the audience literally looking away from scenes of battle. In either case, the message instructs exhibitors that they can both serve the community and make money during the national struggle. Exhibitors are likened to domestic soldiers, providing films that can inform or entertain, rally the public or provide a brief respite from everyday concerns; in so doing, exhibitors simultaneously help the war effort, serve the public, and generate revenues. This imagery is also consistent with an ongoing discourse in the trade press that depicted projectionists in heroic terms as people who served their customers (and theater managers) via their professionalism, technological prowess, and even bravery in risking their lives in the projection booths, where the highly flammable nitrate film stock could be deadly.

The depiction of technology in film promotion was only one of many elements in the larger campaign to persuade Americans to participate in both filmgoing and the war effort. But this depiction served multiple—and sometimes contradictory—purposes. Technology worked to attract filmgoers to see advanced weaponry in action or to persuade reluctant exhibitors that audiences indeed wanted to see such things. Technologies were praised when serving "our" interests but condemned or belittled when used by the other side. They were flaunted as modern marvels or crude instruments of power. Advertising promoted the medium of cinema as a new and powerful tool in shaping the hearts and minds of mass audiences as well as distracting and entertaining them.

All these meanings and more were combined in ads that were seemingly simple yet participated in complex dialogues about the intersections of war, culture, technology, and power in the modern world—a world increasingly shaped by both the illusions and the harsh realities portrayed in the media.

As Hollywood developed from an industry struggling for a foothold in the media landscape into a global multimedia empire, the messages in its films and promotion expanded in quantity and quality. The film industry has participated in new wars and reenacted previous ones, often perpetuating myths and sometimes revising them or creating new ones. Today, Hollywood and its audiences are more enamored than ever of new technologies, including those of warfare. The combatants and battlefields may have changed, and the ways of waging war through moving images may have proliferated, but the underlying fascination with technology continues to attract, inform, and entertain mass audiences across the divides of nation, language, and culture. The images discussed in this chapter come from a particular moment in early film history and reflect circumstances unique to that time. But they also speak to broader and deeper concerns about the human condition, including conflict resolution through violence. If, as suggested in *2001: A Space Odyssey* (1968), the invention of tools was the pivotal moment in the transition from ape to human—and if the first tool was not the wheel or fire but the club—then these ads may serve as examples of how far and yet how little humanity has progressed through the millennia.

NOTES

A previous version of this essay appears in *West Virginia University Philological Papers* 51 (2006): 61–76. I wish to thank Leslie Midkiff DeBauche, Kathryn Fuller-Seeley, and Mary Beth Haralovich for their thoughtful readings of this essay.

1. Although some of the advertisements examined in this chapter resemble posters, all are from the trade press, whose readership was relatively small but also highly influential in terms of local theater programming and promotion. As I have written elsewhere, ads in the trade press encouraged exhibitors to acquire films and related products, including ads for films ("Promoting Otherness in Films"). In its form and content, promotion in the trade press often resembled more general promotion, but it also addressed issues that were of specific importance to the film industry (including how to best attract and satisfy audiences)—issues that were downplayed or absent in more public venues such as posters and fan magazines. As a case study, my work here examines only one part of the promotional apparatus of the film industry, but it is an important part.

2. Jane Gaines discusses how the movie poster and its antecedent form, the circus poster, often used hyperbole to go beyond the literal attributes of the products they promoted. With the poster's garish colors and exaggerated scenes and verbal descrip-

tions, the "pleasure afforded by hyperbolic representation is actually in this going beyond the literal" (35). Gaines associates this pleasure with the Barnumesque notion of "humbug": the enjoyment of being tricked while knowing that one is not really being tricked, or being seduced by deceptions while not fully believing them.

3. For more on American wartime media propaganda, see Pratkanis, Rollins and O'Connor, Lasswell, Isenberg, and Vaughn.

4. Their name derives from both the Revolutionary War militiamen and the time limit on their speeches, which were monitored by the CPI to avoid "jeopardizing the hospitality of the theater owner" (Ross 245).

5. A search for promotional materials that overtly referenced "Germanness" in the fan and trade press from 1910 to 1925 yielded a total of 284 items, mainly advertisements, publicity articles, photos, and editorial cartoons. Quantitatively, this search showed that references to Germanness were relatively and consistently marginal before and after the war and in the years before America's involvement; the period covering America's involvement in the war saw a major increase in references to Germanness, amounting to about half of all the collected references. Similarly, in qualitative terms, Germanness was depicted mainly as benign or positive before and after the war; there was some ambivalence from 1914 to early 1917, and Germanness was couched in highly negative terms from April 1917 to the end of the war and a few months thereafter. One reason for the lingering of propaganda film promotion after the war may have been that some films simply were not ready for release until that time. For a study of race and dehumanization in these materials, see my article "The Kaiser as the Beast of Berlin."

6. A trade paper ad for a news film told exhibitors that they could "be neutral and still show your patrons the idol of the German army. The master mind on which the hopes of the German Empire rest—the man, who every day, bears the greatest weight of responsibility ever placed upon the shoulders of a human being—Field Marshall von Hindenberg" (*Moving Picture World* 13 Mar. 1915: 1698). This film supposedly contained "the first motion pictures of this colossus of the military world, taken at Army Headquarters in East Prussia." Another ad described official war pictures as having just arrived from Germany "by special permission of the Kaiser" and featuring "the latest German war news taken on the battle fronts," providing "Germany's side of the war"—what patrons wanted and otherwise could not get. The film was made by the Eiko Film Company, described as "the largest moving picture company in Germany" (*Moving Picture World* 15 May 1915: 1157).

7. The composition of this ad could suggest that the bottom image is for the other advertised Thomas Ince film, the Bessie Barriscale vehicle *Those Who Pay*, but the content, style, and position of this lower image in relation to the upper one make it more likely to be for *The Zeppelin's Last Raid*.

8. The reference to Thomas Ince may be surprising to those familiar with his earlier and more famous antiwar film *Civilization* (1916). In fact, the story line of *The Zeppelin's Last Raid* parallels that of *Civilization*. Ince's earlier film depicts a war-loving Teutonic count changing his mind because of a peace activist and then purposely sinking his own ship and drowning himself as a sacrifice to peace. Likewise, the later film depicts a zeppelin commander persuaded by both his activist fiancée and German atrocities to become an opponent of the war. While on a climactic bombing mission, "the zeppelin commander refuses to attack a British sea town and begs his crew to follow his

lead and join his crusade for peace. They ignore his pleas and continue preparations for the raid, but rather than kill civilians, the commander blows up the zeppelin in midair, destroying his crew and himself" (American Film Institute). Whereas the earlier Ince film was strongly antiwar, the later film apparently was more ambivalent, with its combination of anti-German rhetoric and antiwar sentiments affirming the German commander who makes the ultimate sacrifice to promote peace. The ambivalence of the film may reflect that of Ince or his perceived audience; put another way, the film may have been designed to maximize its audience by including elements that would appeal to both detractors and supporters of the war effort.

9. The work of Dutch graphic artist Louis Raemaekers contains several related themes, including images of Uncle Sam confronting German military leaders or the Kaiser himself. One image by Raemaekers depicts the Kaiser and probably his son standing atop a pile of dead soldiers while surveying the battlefield landscape; an accompanying poem by Eden Phillpotts, titled "A Higher Pile," likens this scene to Golgotha, "all shattered, torn, and sped, a mountain for these royal feet to tread" (Raemaekers, *Kultur in Cartoons* 18–19). See also *Raemaekers' Cartoons* and the three-volume *Raemaekers' Cartoon History of the War.*

Pamela Grace suggested to me that this image of a modern tyrant standing atop his people may refer to ancient images of tyrants and pharaohs standing atop their slaves and other subjects, or to religious images of bodies writhing in agony or in hell. Image makers always have a vast cultural intertext from which to draw, consciously or not; for a historical study of visual depictions of war that suggests this vastness, see Perlmutter.

10. From his beginnings, possibly in the War of 1812, Uncle Sam represented values such as loyalty, common sense, and hard work. In peacetime his politics were rather fluid, and he could appear in advertising as a congenial and apolitical authority figure comparable to a product spokesman. But in wartime he embodied a strident patriotism, translating complex national issues into categories of right versus wrong, or good versus evil, and acting symbolically on behalf of America (see Leeming and Page 42–43). His presence here as a single figure—not flanked by comparable Allied figures—may suggest American independence or a self-image as the one country that has the power and values to make a difference in the war. The Statue of Liberty references France, though indirectly and as something both inspiring Uncle Sam and being protected by him.

11. Although this cartoonish scene does not appear in the film, it does reflect the film's harsh anti-German animus. Indeed, *The Prussian Cur* was eventually removed from distribution because of its *Birth of a Nation*–style scenes in which American patriots dressed as Ku Klux Klansmen heroically lynch a group of pro-German "traitors." Apparently, what could be done to African Americans in films of the time was not acceptable to the mass audience when done to Aryans.

12. The diminutive Jeff resembles a child wearing pajamas, possibly alluding to Allied wartime propaganda depicting Germans as evil baby killers. Jeff's mask appears to be that of an animal, perhaps a dog. If so, this may add a layer of criticism leveled at violation of the Western taboo against eating dogs. Mary Beth Haralovich mentioned to me that this depiction may allude to an early Edison film, *Dog Factory* (1904), in which stray animals are turned into sausages. Indeed, the staging of this single-shot film

strongly resembles the ad discussed here, and in the background, among the labels for different kinds of sausages, is one prominently marked "mut."

13. Julian Putkowski mentioned to me that this ad may allude to contemporaneous British rhetoric about the German "corpse factory," where enemy corpses were allegedly turned into soap and other products (foreshadowing later Nazi practices).

14. Negative motivations included the possibility of the industry's being shut down as "nonessential" during the war or being subjected to strong governmental censorship (DeBauche, "United States'" 138).

15. By 1900, more than a quarter of the U.S. population was of direct German descent (Gatzke 31). German Americans varied in their loyalty to the German government, but many probably had deeper ethnic and familial ties to the homeland that complicated their attitudes toward the war, especially in immigrant communities such as Milwaukee and St. Louis.

16. Francis Ford's younger brother John would direct some of the major feature films and documentaries about World War II, including *They Were Expendable* (1945) and *The Battle of Midway* (1942).

17. Flexible film stock and an intermittent mechanism were prerequisites for cinema. The machine gun may have provided a model for the latter development; the sewing machine certainly did (Thompson and Bordwell 15). *Shooting* was used as a synonym for *filming* by the 1910s.

18. In a conference paper, Kathryn Fuller-Seeley presented a study of Paramount's ten-year public relations campaign that began in 1917 to promote not the studio's films or stars but the psychic and social values of filmgoing itself, in a manner consistent with the promotion of other consumer goods at the time. This Paramount and Artcraft Pictures ad apparently was part of that larger campaign.

WORKS CITED

American Film Institute. *Catalog of Motion Pictures Produced in the United States.* <http://www.afi.com/members/catalog/>.

DeBauche, Leslie Midkiff. *Reel Patriotism: The Movies and World War I.* Madison: U of Wisconsin P, 1997.

——. "The United States' Film Industry and World War One." *The First World War and Popular Cinema: 1914 to the Present.* Ed. Michael Paris. New Brunswick, N.J.: Rutgers UP, 2000. 138–61.

Fuller-Seeley, Kathryn. "Panacea for the Ills of Modern Life: The Movie-Going Consumption Ideal in Paramount's National Magazine Advertising, 1917–1927." Society for Cinema and Media Studies Conference, Denver, Colo., 24 May 2002.

Gaines, Jane. "From Elephants to Lux Soap: The Programming and 'Flow' of Early Motion Picture Exploitation." *Velvet Light Trap* 25 (1990): 29–43.

Gatzke, Hans W. *Germany and the United States: A "Special Relationship?"* Cambridge, Mass.: Harvard UP, 1980.

Isenberg, Michael T. *War on Film: The American Cinema and World War I, 1914–1941.* Rutherford, N.J.: Fairleigh Dickenson UP, 1981.

Lasswell, Harold D. *Propaganda Technique in World War I.* 1927. Cambridge, Mass.: MIT Press, 1971.

Latham, James. "The Kaiser as the Beast of Berlin: Race and the Animalizing of Germanness in Early Hollywood's Advertising Imagery." *West Virginia University Philological
   Papers* 50 (2003): 16–30.

———. "Promoting Otherness in Films: Blackness and the Primitive in Early Hollywood
   Advertising Imagery." *Velvet Light Trap* 50 (Fall 2002): 4–14.

Leeming, David, and Jake Page. *Myths, Legends, and Folktales of America*. New York:
   Oxford UP, 1999.

Metz, Christian. *The Imaginary Signifier: Psychoanalysis and the Cinema*. Trans. Celia Brit-
   ton, Annwyl Williams, Ben Brewster, and Alfred Guzzetti. Bloomington: Indiana
   UP, 1975.

Perlmutter, David D. *Visions of War: Picturing Warfare from the Stone Age to the Cyber Age*.
   New York: St. Martin's Griffin, 1999.

Pratkanis, Anthony R. *Age of Propaganda: The Everyday Use and Abuse of Persuasion*. New
   York: Freeman, 1999.

Raemaekers, Louis. *Kultur in Cartoons*. New York: Century, 1917.

———. *Raemaekers' Cartoon History of the War*. New York: Century, 1918–1919.

———. *Raemaekers' Cartoons, with Accompanying Notes by Well-Known English Writers*. Garden City, N.Y.: Doubleday, Page, 1916.

Rollins, Peter C., and John E. O'Connor, eds. *Hollywood's World War I: Motion Picture
   Images*. Bowling Green, Ohio: Bowling Green State U Popular P, 1997.

Ross, Stewart Halsey. *Propaganda for War: How the United States Was Conditioned to Fight
   the Great War of 1914–1918*. Jefferson, N.C.: McFarland, 1996.

Thompson, Kristin, and David Bordwell. *Film History: An Introduction*. 2nd ed. New
   York: McGraw-Hill, 2003.

Vaughn, Stephen. *Holding Fast the Inner Lines: Democracy, Nationalism, and the Committee
   on Public Information*. Chapel Hill: U of North Carolina P, 1980.

CULTURE WARS AND THE LOCAL SCREEN

The Reception of *Westfront 1918* and *All Quiet on the Western Front* in One German City

Six nights in December 1930 were all it took to make Lewis Milestone's *All Quiet on the Western Front* (1930) the most controversial film in Germany between the world wars. For six nights it played in Berlin, with protests inside and outside the theater and across the country, until Germany's Censorship Board reversed its earlier approval of the movie and banned it. For several weeks the conflict about the movie—Should it be shown or not? What does it mean for Germany?—grabbed front-page headlines, a singular feat that indicated the film's significance for national politics. Like the thirty films about the Great War produced in Weimar Germany between 1925 and 1933, Milestone's American film offered Germans a variety of ways to come to terms with a cataclysmic defeat (Kester 291–301). Since very few Germans actually saw *All Quiet* in 1930, it served chiefly as a political lightning rod in Weimar Germany. Its function as a symbol of the era's conflicts and vitriol has marked its place in the history of interwar German cinema and politics.

By contrast, less controversial films such as G. W. Pabst's *Westfront 1918* (1930) clearly illustrate the very real and significant function of the Great War in interwar German politics; it opened a dialogue among critics and viewers about the war through the era's most important mass medium. To use Carl Schorske's idea about a previous epoch, German politics in 1930 was performed in a "'sharper key,' a mode of political behavior at once more abrasive, more creative, and more satisfying to the life of feeling than the deliberative style of . . . liberals" (119). In that year of vituperative elections and street fighting, *Westfront* offered Germans across the political spectrum a rare opportunity to find common ground, whereas *All Quiet* served only to polarize.

This chapter analyzes reactions to *Westfront 1918* and *All Quiet on the Western Front* in the midsize German university town of Göttingen to investigate the process by which cinema both reflected and shaped perceptions about the Great

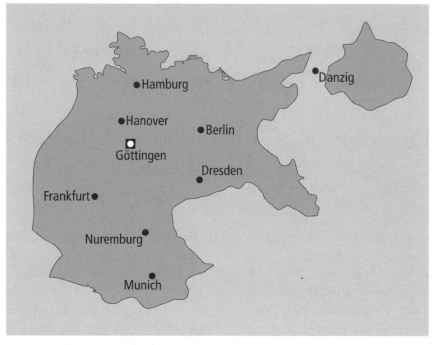

Map of Germany after World War I.

War and its role in German politics. The history of these two films in Göttingen demonstrates that local perspectives and experiences helped determine how national cultural products took root in everyday life. Eventually the experience of integrating external ideas and images into local cultural life taught Germans how to make Nazism a part of their daily lives too. Indeed, discussions surrounding these two films in Göttingen helped normalize ideas about culture and national identity that directly benefited Hitler's movement.

No matter where motion pictures originated, Germans experienced them in their own towns and neighborhoods. More than is often recognized, local cultural purveyors, institutions, and discourses molded the development of mass culture in interwar Germany. Celia Applegate and Alon Confino have shown that the most important negotiation of political and cultural change in modern Germany took place at the local level.[1] Like other cultural activities in Germany, local moviegoing in the interwar period aided the process of Nazification as much as national and international political events did. Discussions about movies such as *Westfront* and *All Quiet* articulated a homegrown set of notions with which Nazi ideas could resonate.

City Museum, Göttingen

The University of Göttingen's Auditorium, circa 1930.

GÖTTINGEN AS MISE-EN-SCÈNE

To quote Clifford Geertz, anthropologists and cultural historians "don't study villages . . . they study *in* villages. . . . The locus of study is not the object of study" (22). My analysis draws its significance from the fact that the location is both unique and representative. A city of about forty-five thousand between the world wars, Göttingen was large enough and diverse enough to experience a wide range of cultural activities, yet small enough to reveal the finer workings of local cultural practices. Located south of Hanover, Göttingen was a historically important trading and administrative city for the Kingdom of Hanover and then Prussia. Today it stands almost exactly at the center of Germany, along major north-south and east-west transportation routes. The George August University, which opened in 1737, has defined the city as a provincial intellectual center. The university has, for instance, produced more Nobel Prize winners than any other except Cambridge. Many of the scientists who worked on America's Manhattan Project trained there, and the city has hosted a number of important Americans, including historian George Bancroft, poet Henry Wadsworth Longfellow, President William Howard Taft, and, briefly,

Benjamin Franklin. The city's peaceful surrender to American forces in April 1945 helped engender good relations between Göttingen and the United States after the Second World War.

In the 1920s Göttingen was a conservative city: the many pensioners, military personnel, students, professors, and bureaucrats there exercised more influence than the working class, which was smaller than that of more industrialized German cities (Saldern 14–56). Cultural purveyors such as newspaper critics and cinema owners, in particular, reflected this social and political conservatism, since they often came from and worked closely with the local elite who held leadership positions in both the city administration and cultural organizations. Top city officials, who passed and enforced laws controlling cultural activities, remained much the same in terms of both personnel and perspective from before World War I through the end of the Third Reich.

Göttingen's conservative politics shaped cultural activities themselves and the ways in which they were discussed in the media. City leaders, for instance, viewed the expansion of leisure activities, especially mass culture, with some apprehension. As the mass culture medium par excellence in the 1920s, cinema was a particularly visible target for elite attempts to mold popular culture. Germany's reactionary Motion Picture Law of May 1920 and its taxation rules in particular enabled local governments to encourage the showing of some films rather than others in their towns. City leaders and newspaper critics generally favored historical dramas, documentaries, and films based on classical literature over the more popular musicals, melodramas, comedies, and mysteries that dominated the silver screen during these years. They could use their own prerogatives to set the tax levels for films, which in turn influenced the prices of individual tickets. Allowing an "educational" film to show tax free, for instance, meant that the cinema owner could lower ticket prices to attract patrons. In Berlin a group of movie industry leaders and government officials actually decided which films were deemed "culturally valuable" per the 1920 Motion Picture Law; local authorities then had the power to use those definitions to grant tax breaks. Such policies alone might not determine the success or failure of a particular film, but they could shape the size of the audience and bring in revenue for the city from the more popular films.

Cultural critics in Göttingen newspapers and periodicals, moreover, directly influenced how moviegoers thought about cinema by creating a common syntax for cinematic discussions that blended local, national, and international ideas and images. Commentators promoted cinema as a benefit to the local economy and civic prestige, offering tangible reasons for integrating mass culture into established local institutions and Göttingen culture. The cultural purveyors who regulated and promoted cinema in Göttingen pressed a traditional (essentially nineteenth-century) concept of culture, one that reinforced conservative politics in general. In particular, the Göttingen Magistracy, the highest elected body in the city, wrote local regulations for cinema and oversaw their application by the police. Its stable membership and general approval of nationalism (in both cinema and government) helped legitimize the city council's move toward the right that began in the late 1920s and culminated in a significant victory for nationalist parties in the May 1929 local elections.

As the economy worsened after the American stock market crash that October, Göttingers were increasingly attracted to the solutions offered by Hitler's party. The Nazis preached an antipolitics that rejected the efficacy of Weimar democracy and thus drew strength from both political maneuvering and cultural activities. Newspaper critics, who had also been slow to embrace cinema's value, often connected these two different public activities. Since they generally preferred to act as boosters rather than critics, the more powerful conservative newspapers extolled celebratory rather than critical cinema. The papers exercised considerable influence on local perspectives about cinema, often using reviews of a national premiere to set the terms of discussion about a specific film even before it arrived in Göttingen. Together, civic leaders and cultural purveyors thus endorsed motion pictures with more "traditional" subjects and positive visions of German history. Films based on the works of Goethe or Shakespeare, for instance, received tax discounts as "culturally valuable" films and positive reviews from critics, as did historical epics about Frederick the Great. By supporting such films over popular comedies or melodramas or any kind of critical treatment of the past, these influential Göttingers promoted a conservative vision of culture and ultimately helped politicize cinema in a way that fostered emerging Nazi notions about culture.

WAR FILMS AND THE WEIMAR REPUBLIC

Fictionalized cinematic depictions of the Great War illustrated the spectrum of thought on cinema's role in German society and politics. The First World War had served as midwife to both the Weimar Republic and the contemporary German film industry and therefore became integral to the post-1918 cultural scene. Memories and mythologies of the war defined and energized Weimar politics and ideology. Conservatives blamed Germany's subsequent problems at home and abroad on defeat and the Versailles Peace Treaty and challenged any attempt to portray the war in terms other than glory, heroism, and sacrifice on the part of German soldiers. For Social Democrats, in contrast, the war served as the tragic impetus for a new Germany; they saw it as a terrible event that the new republic must never repeat. The German Communist Party had actually formed as a result of a 1917 split over support for the war between the Independent Social Democratic Party and the Social Democratic Party. A number of left-wing artists used these political sentiments to portray a society broken by the war and unwilling to cope with its aftermath. George Grosz and Otto Dix, chief among German visual artists, rendered the war's effect: the glaring inequities it failed to change and the search for hollow sensation it engendered. Conservatives lamented what one columnist in Göttingen called the "pleasure craving" and "cocainism of the entertainment industry" that had been spawned by war and hardship (*Tageblatt* 2 Aug. 1925).[2] War films made this politically charged issue a part of mass entertainment.

By 1930 the Great War had already been the topic of seventeen German motion pictures. Some were hard-hitting and controversial, such as the antiwar *Nameless Heroes* (1925) and films about war guilt such as *The Double Murder of Sarajevo* (1920) and *The European Arsonist* (1926). Many others were documentaries or sentimental features, including *The Heart of a German Mother* (1926) and *German Women—German True* (1928). American war films such as *Havoc* (1925), *The Big Parade* (1925), *What Price Glory?* (1926), and *Wings* (1927) had also played in Germany, as had French films such as *Verdun* (1929). Popular knowledge about the vicious anti-German propaganda movies made in the United States during World War I raised concerns about Hollywood's fairness in portraying the conflict (especially if Germans chose to forget their own nation's vitriolic cinematic campaign during the war). No matter who made them, filmed versions of war offered potentially greater controversy and commercial windfall than did other cultural representations of the conflict (Saunders 29–31). The year 1930 represented a high-water mark for movies about the war—six productions premiered that year—and for violent political clashes across the country, including in Göttingen. The films *Westfront 1918* and *All Quiet on the Western Front* highlighted major fault lines in German politics in 1930 and the ways arbiters of culture articulated their differences.

WESTFRONT 1918

G. W. Pabst's *Westfront 1918* did not treat war romantically and seemed to advocate postwar rapprochement between France and Germany. Its realism prompted responses ranging from patriotic enthusiasm to strong antiwar sentiment, as had the 1927 UFA nationalist documentary *The World War* (Saunders 44–45; Korte 206).[3] Indeed, the various English translations of Pabst's German title—including *Comrades of 1918, The Western Front 1918, Four Infantry Men, Drums of Doom,* and *Shame of a Nation*—underscore the film's various valences. *Westfront 1918* was based on Ernst Johannsen's 1929 novel *Four from the Infantry*.

Max Fertig Collection

Westfront 1918: comradeship in the trenches.

It was Pabst's first effort with sound and the first German sound film about the war. The realistic representation of the horrors of trench warfare owed much of its power to the expressive cinematography of Fritz Arno Wagner, who also worked on the early silent classic *Nosferatu* (1922) and rich German sound films such as *M* (1931), *The Testament of Dr. Mabuse* (1932), and *Amphitryon* (1935).

Unlike *All Quiet on the Western Front,* which follows the hero's personal narrative and loss of innocence, *Westfront 1918* episodically portrays the daily experience of war. It is built on the connected stories of four seasoned soldiers—an aristocratic lieutenant, a wry Bavarian, a young student, and a middle-class family man named Karl—in the same company during the final year of the war. The love interests of two characters in particular illustrate the broader impact of war. The student falls in love with a French girl and volunteers for a dangerous assignment so that he can visit her. But his reward is a gruesome death at the hands of a French African, a scene that illustrates the implicit racism informing many Germans' thoughts about the war and their enemies. When middle-class and long-suffering Karl goes home on leave, he finds that his wife is having an affair with a butcher's assistant because she is lonely and hungry. Karl is bitter and wants to return to the front, preferring

Westfront 1918: ubiquitous death scene.

the comradeship of the trenches to the complexities of home. Likewise, the marked difference between the lieutenant's zeal and the Bavarian's mordancy encapsulates the breadth of attitudes about war. Ultimately, though, attitudes do not matter: for these four soldiers, death is the common outcome.

The film ends with a French soldier taking Karl's dead hand and saying, "My comrade . . . not my enemy!" But Pabst is telling a cautionary tale: he closes the film with "The End?!" Reviewers in and out of Germany remarked on the film's realism and its antiwar perspective (Kester 127–36). The *New York Times*'s Berlin correspondent, for instance, called it "the most vivid argument yet contrived against war" (Trask 4). The film's popularity—it was one of the ten top-grossing films of the season in Germany and had the second-longest-running premiere—indicates that Pabst's realism might have shocked but did not necessarily outrage.

In Göttingen *Westfront 1918* played in the Capitol Theater, the largest and most luxurious movie house in town. Ernst Heidelberg, the city's leading figure associated with cinema throughout the interwar period, built the theater in October 1929. He used this substantial landmark to secure more of the big films coming to Göttingen than the other five theaters in town. Heidelberg

Capitol Theater interior.

Capitol Theater exterior.

and other theater owners often made local premieres into important events that helped glamorize and localize the experience of moviegoing. By emulating gala national premieres in Berlin, theater owners and newspaper reviewers connected local activities and mass culture. At the grand opening of the Capitol, for example, one newspaper reporter concluded that this modern "big-city movie theater" would take up Göttingen's "great cultural obligation" and fulfill "a cultural mission in our city" (*Tageblatt* 3 Oct. 1929). Since cinema and other forms of mass culture introduced new cultural products to Göttingen, this "cultural mission" meant that local institutions and individuals integrated external ideas into local life. The rituals of moviegoing—national premieres and discussions in local papers, then local premieres, reviews, and discussions—gave Göttingers a process by which they could make the images and ideas of cinema parts of their daily lives. As an important film about an important subject playing in an important movie theater, *Westfront* therefore acquired special significance.

When *Westfront* opened in Göttingen on 1 July 1930, its premiere coincided with several events that underscored the continued local impact of the Great War. Just the day before, Allied forces had completed their evacuation of the area around the Rhine River that marked Germany's traditional western border, ending a humiliating legacy of the Versailles Peace Treaty. Marches and celebrations were organized by various groups in Göttingen and continued for several days thereafter. A collection of veterans' associations hosted a "German evening" on 1 July in honor of the event. That same day former prisoners of war in Göttingen marched to protest unemployment among veterans. And just a month and a half earlier, on 17 May, the American Young Plan, organized by the U.S. government and banks to refinance Germany's $9 billion wartime reparations payments, had gone into effect. Although this new payment plan attempted to address realistically Germany's ability to honor its massive debt, the October 1929 stock market crash that sent the world into depression seemed to nullify its potential benefit. Nationalists in particular chafed at this most recent American intervention in Germany's finances as the economic crisis intensified. In short, the loss of the war seemed doubly painful because the ramifications of the reparations payments hit vulnerable veterans especially hard. This mix of celebration, commemoration, and attention to the worsening depression meant that a movie about the Great War would be treated as a highly significant statement about something that directly impacted Göttingers' lives. And given that parliamentary elections were just two months away, it promised to reflect—and perhaps shape—political perceptions.

Reviewers from the three main local newspapers, each of which represented a different political perspective, enthusiastically endorsed *Westfront 1918* for very different reasons. The ultraconservative *Tageblatt* (2 July 1930) gravely commended director Pabst's depiction of valor and sacrifice, calling it "the cinematic gravestone of the unknown German soldier." The Social Democratic *Volksblatt* (2 July 1930) praised *Westfront* as an "accusation against the war and National Socialist supporters of war." Waxing literary, the cautiously liberal *Zeitung* (3 July 1930) maintained that the film reveals the "countenance of war" and condemns the "great senselessness" of 1914 to 1918. Both the *Tageblatt* and the *Volksblatt* mentioned one specific scene in which officers call the soldiers heroes. The conservative *Tageblatt* expressed approval, whereas the *Volksblatt* reminded readers that the sardonic Bavarian grumbles that if they really were heroes they would be home already. Likewise, the *Tageblatt* questioned the validity of a scene in which an officer tries unsuccessfully to rally the men to cheer, and the Social Democratic paper observed that the scene exemplifies one class's forcing another to continue a pointless war.

The conservative *Tageblatt* review came from Heinz Koch, the newspaper's local editor and chief cultural critic. Koch's steady stream of writing on all things cultural and local throughout the interwar period in the city's most widely read newspaper made him the premier cultural critic in Göttingen. Like many conservatives, Koch arrived late at the conclusion that cinema could serve a positive purpose, but he eventually became an ardent supporter and took his reviews of films as seriously as those of opera, music, theater, and art. Beyond noting the film's political implications, his review situated *Westfront* within the broader contexts of the many books and films about the war and the development of sound films, lauding its technical and topical efficacy. Koch was a well-known conservative who helped make the *Tageblatt* a nationalist and right-leaning newspaper (his incendiary work even prompted authorities to shut the paper down temporarily in 1922). But in *Westfront* he saw not antiwar or anti-German sentiments but a powerful, empathetic portrayal of the war and of soldiers' experiences. Anyone, he wrote, "who lived through those horrifying, hopeless final months of retreating battle in the west must admit: it was just like that!" Apparently politically neutral in this review, Koch concluded that the French saying "C'est la guerre!" would also make a suitable title for this film (*Tageblatt* 2 July 1930).

Westfront 1918's statement about the horrors of war was neutral enough to prompt discussion of the qualities of the film and to cause critics from across the political spectrum to praise it. As was the case for other cultural activities in Göttingen, though, this film's ability to unite conflicting political opinions bolstered conservatives (like Koch), who had consistently lamented Weimar's fragmented political scene. The common condemnation of the suffering portrayed in *Westfront* in all three newspapers lent some support to the conservative desire to honor fallen soldiers rather than address difficult issues such as the validity of the war, the experience of guilt, and the justice of the ensuing peace. Such sentiments, clearly visible in reviews of *Westfront*, underscored the growth of nationalist political parties—especially the Nazis—beginning in 1929 and gave nationalists a set of powerful images with which their ideas could resonate.

ALL QUIET ON THE WESTERN FRONT

In contrast to Pabst's film, *All Quiet on the Western Front* had the effect of pouring gasoline on an already fiery debate. Although the publication of Erich Maria Remarque's book in January 1929 had prompted attacks and protests, detractors lacked a specific time and place to stage their demonstrations; these elements were conveniently provided by the film's premiere. Controversy had already helped the novel become the world's best-selling book. Everywhere the discussions and anger surrounding *All Quiet* reflected both postwar disillusionment and malaise and disagreement about the Great War itself (Eksteins 60). In Göttingen and across Germany, the brouhaha surrounding the film illuminated the mutually reinforcing relationship between mass politics and mass culture.

After German studios declined to make the film, Universal Studios in Hollywood undertook the project, with Lewis Milestone directing. Like the book, the film follows a group of idealistic German high school students and their natural leader, Paul Bäumer, during four years of war. It portrays their growing up and camaraderie through scenes of battle, celebration, bitter trips back home, and death. Its American release in May 1930 generated both sharp criticism and strong support, and it won the Academy Award for best picture. In Paris, London, and Brussels, *All Quiet* garnered enormous attention and generally good reviews. Anticipating opposition in Germany, Universal made some judicious edits before the German-language dubbed version premiered in Berlin on 4 December 1930 (Eksteins 61–62).

Much had happened in Germany in the months since Remarque's book had been published and even since *Westfront 1918* had debuted. Democracy and liberalism had taken some heavy blows. A grand national coalition of various opposing parties fell apart in March 1930. In July President Paul von Hindenburg and Chancellor Heinrich Brüning (Catholic Center Party) invoked article 48 of the Weimar constitution, using its emergency powers to dissolve the existing Reichstag (parliament), call for new elections, and temporarily rule by presidential decree. (This move, aimed at squelching the Social Democratic opposition, provided precedent for Hitler's use of the same constitutional provision in 1933.) In the September 1930 elections the Nazi Party earned the second-largest majority in parliament, and voters increased their support for the Communists as well. Thus, although the agencies governing film policy and policing had not changed between the releases of *Westfront* and *All Quiet,* the tenor of government had shifted in Berlin and in Göttingen (Jelavich 157–90). In addition, just before *All Quiet* premiered, leftist artist Georg Grosz had been cleared of slandering the Catholic Church, invoking a storm of protests and outraged rhetoric from conservatives, who deplored his nightmarish postwar visions in which Germans embraced sex, violence, and brutality.

The 4 December 1930 opening night in Berlin proceeded without incident, and *All Quiet* garnered generally good reviews in most national papers. Protests began the second evening, most notably when Joseph Goebbels (then National Socialist German Workers' Party propaganda director and head of the party in Berlin) and a group of Nazis halted that night's showing by shouting "Jewish film," tossing stink bombs, and releasing mice in the aisles. Nazi agitators then used the film as an excuse to march, fight, and generally cause chaos at various points across Berlin for the next couple of days. Even though *All Quiet* had been approved by the national Censorship Board in November, elected representatives continued to debate fiercely in the Reichstag whether the film should be played. Together with the raucous protests in Berlin, direct appeals from politicians in Saxony, Brunswick, Thuringia, Württemberg, and Bavaria eventually convinced the Appellate Censorship Board to reconsider the approval of the film. Testimony from regional and federal government officials, some of whom had, in the meantime, reversed their opinions about *All Quiet,* gave the appellate board ammunition for labeling it anti-German and dangerous, and it decided to ban the film on 10 December 1930. Board members claimed that it represented a threat to public order and "German reputation" at home and abroad (Jelavich 157–77).

Göttingen newspapers reported these protests and debates in great detail. Even more than in their *Westfront* reviews, the papers used the film's debut and the ensuing scandal as vehicles to push their ideological lines about the war, the uneasy peace, and the republic that followed. The right-wing *Tageblatt* came out strongly against Milestone's film, which it called "a new anti-German hate film," and it celebrated the film's prohibition—"at last"—on the front page as "Goebbels's Victory!" (*Tageblatt* 8, 12 Dec. 1930). On 10 December the local section reprinted a speech by Hans Frick, an important regional Nazi Party minister,

Tageblatt 12 Dec. 1930.

in which he used the attack on *All Quiet* to promote the National Socialist fight against "cultural Bolshevism," specifically the threats represented by "Jews," "modernism," and "materialism."[4] Certainly, in many conservative minds, the fact that Americans had produced *All Quiet* (whereas Germans had made *Westfront*) made it more reprehensible. But the animosity toward Milestone's film says more about grave changes occurring in Germany during 1930 than it does about the films' national origins.

The left-leaning *Volksblatt* (11 Dec. 1930) called Goebbels's "hate speech" about the film a "witch hunt for Jews," a provocation for riots, and a call to replace the Weimar Republic with a "Third Reich." The Social Democratic paper also singled out the conservative press as a mouthpiece for Nazi ideas.

Volksblatt 12 Dec. 1930.

The *Volksblatt*'s front page on 12 December called the ban a "suppression of the truth" and featured a cartoon showing Prussian soldiers marching behind a triumphant (former) Kaiser Wilhelm II and crushing everyone in their way. The caption read: "This is how films must look to tell the truth in Germany." The following day the *Volksblatt* ran another cartoon, this one of an aggressive and "happy" Mars, dressed as a Roman warrior and surrounded by skulls, thanking the "brave" Nazis for securing the *All Quiet* ban. The *Tageblatt* also featured a front-page cartoon on 12 December, showing a packed Berlin movie house at the premiere of *All Quiet,* half of which was filled by local police officers. The next panel portrayed all the patrons fleeing, except for a few Communists. The caption exclaimed, "For four years Germany held the world at bay! Must

Volksblatt cartoon.

a self-respecting nation [*Volk*] now just collapse?" The moderate *Zeitung* (9, 12 Dec. 1930) carefully explained the reasons for the initial approval and the subsequent reversal, presenting both sides of the debate.

The controversy continued to dominate the Göttingen papers for days after the ban, and its echoes reverberated for months. A 12 December ban of a documentary about the Stahlhelm, a right-wing paramilitary group, for instance, demonstrated that the response to *All Quiet* had made film censors more cautious. Coverage in the *Zeitung* (13 Dec. 1930) about that prohibition ran as part of a front-page analysis of perspectives on war movies in and out of Germany. On its front page that day the *Tageblatt* derisively called the Stahlhelm film ban "revenge for Remarque" and attacked the fear instilled in censors as "a new disgrace for Remarque-types!" The *Tageblatt* reported extensively through the end of the year on the "echo of the film ban," detailing various reactions across Germany and beyond and describing the law and order that the ban had restored to the nation (*Tageblatt* 16, 19, 27–28 Dec. 1930). The *Volksblatt* also continued to cover the ban's ramifications. A 19 December article reported that leaders of the Austrian government had responded positively to *All Quiet* at a private screening in Vienna, maintaining that it was a pacifist but not anti-German film. Soon, however, Austrian censors banned the production because of embarrassing protests and the potential strain in Austro-German

Tageblatt cartoon.

relations (Simmons 56). As late as 31 March 1931, the *Volksblatt* reported that the Social Democratic faction of the Reichstag had formally protested the "illegal" ban of *All Quiet.*

The context of a recently empowered Nazi Party shaped perspectives about *All Quiet on the Western Front* at the local and national levels. Peter Jelavich argues that the ability of National Socialists to pressure the German government into banning *All Quiet* in many ways marked the demise of a "Weimar culture" that had previously promoted critical engagement, liberalism, and experimentation (Jelavich 176; see also Gay xii–xiv). He attributes the "death" of Weimar culture around 1930 to the fear and passivity that the *All Quiet* ban engendered among potentially critical artists. Although this narrow slice of cultural activity did not often affect the lives of many Germans, the particular cause célèbre of *All Quiet* defined the events of 1930 as a major turning point in Germany when mass culture became both the medium and the message for more aggressive politics and a less critical culture.

CINEMA'S ROLE IN POLITICAL TRENDS

Different responses in Göttingen to *Westfront* and *All Quiet* highlight local trends in political behavior and cinema's role as a vehicle for connecting political ideology with daily life, both of which explain the growing popularity of Hitler's party. The traditional elite and university students had supported Hitler since the early 1920s; beginning in 1929 the deepening world depression pushed the "floating" middle-class vote toward nationalist parties that had consistently challenged the Weimar Republic. Local elections in May 1929 gave a Nazi-led right-wing coalition an absolute majority on Göttingen's city council and placed key party members in the elite Magistracy. The September 1930 Reichstag elections prompted violent demonstrations in Göttingen against the national government and bloody street fighting between Nazis and leftists. More than one out of three Göttingen voters (37.8 percent) supported the National Socialists that year, more than double the party's 18.3 percent showing throughout Germany (Marshall 272–327). This growing political power emboldened those in Berlin and elsewhere in Germany who went to such trouble to stop the showing of a film. Against a backdrop of conflict and violence, therefore, conservative support for the banning of *All Quiet* made sense to many in Göttingen who voted for a "nationalist" solution to Germany's social and economic woes. Discussions in newspapers about the film's provocative and divisive nature jibed with campaign rhetoric from right-wing groups about the need to move beyond an unstable democratic "system" that kept Germany weak and fractured.

For very different reasons, both *Westfront 1918* and *All Quiet on the Western Front* bolstered conservative claims that ideological differences in the parliamentary system continued to divide Germans and that only "apolitical" solutions could unite them. Pabst's film illustrated that "safer" treatments of the war could garner a broad audience, whereas Milestone's epic underscored the danger of critical filmmaking. The controversy surrounding *All Quiet*, together with growing right-wing majorities in national, regional, and local governments, moved the national Film Censorship Board in a conservative direction. Thereafter, critical and controversial movies such as Pabst's *Three-Penny Opera* (1931) and the worker melodrama *Whither Germany?* (1932) lost some of their bite, as filmmakers censored themselves to assuage the Censorship Board. Yet they still faced difficulties passing the censors' scrutiny (Willet 207–8). In contrast, nationalist historical dramas such as the more neutral and sympathetic *Westfront 1918* fared well in the early 1930s because of their established tradition in German film, their less overtly political messages, and their broad popularity among both elites and average Germans (Korte 250; Murray 234).

The many Weimar-era motion pictures about Frederick the Great, the Napoleonic wars, and other moments of perceived national greatness, for instance, expressed nationalist sentiments in the context of a less controversial past. Such historical dramas formed an important thematic bridge between the Weimar and Nazi regimes, since Goebbels in particular liked to promote ideology through a two-pronged approach that celebrated the Third Reich in newsreels and entertained citizens through feature films that avoided controversial topics. Helmut Korte similarly points not to Hitler's assumption of power in 1933 but to late 1931 and early 1932 as the start of a steady growth in the production of nationalist epic films such as *Yorck, Blush of Dawn, Refugees,* and *Marshall Forward* (122–26). And even after 1933, Hilmar Hoffmann argues, the Third Reich chiefly used documentaries and newsreels to communicate its ideology rather than heavy-handed and largely unpopular "Nazi" feature films such as *SA Man Brandt, Hitler Youth Quex,* and *Hans Westmar* (115–97).

The two World War I films discussed here likewise reinforced the tendency of civic leaders and newspaper critics in Göttingen to describe and control cinema in a way that promoted conservative social and political values. Although *Westfront 1918* was not beloved by Hitler's National Socialists and was banned after they came to power in 1933, it did not elicit the ire of conservatives like Koch who, though not Nazis themselves, fostered many of the same ideas in their writing. This chapter has mentioned several possible explanations for the success of *Westfront* in contrast to the failure of *All Quiet:* xenophobia, episodic versus narrative structure, and especially the power over cultural decisions that electoral victories gave to Hitler's party. *Westfront* allowed members of the Göttingen Magistracy and leading cultural critics to promote film as an edifying medium and a potential source of tax revenue, whereas *All Quiet* generated only conflict that local leaders viewed as neither informative nor lucrative. The confluence of material interests and established conservative ideas meant that the debates surrounding these motion pictures in 1930 helped ensure that conservative films and reactions to them would have the most currency in Göttingen after 1930. This situation, in turn, helped normalize Hitler's aggressive nationalism in the two years before the National Socialist Party actually gained power in Germany.

More generally, the different experiences of these two films illustrate that culture and leisure pursuits mattered in interwar Germany. Indeed, these two films about the Great War helped make cinema an essential part of political life and mass culture a part of the syntax of interwar German politics. Cultural representations of politics raised the stakes of political difference because they were so pervasive and potentially powerful.[5] By 1930 Göttingers and other Germans had grown all too accustomed to political fighting in the Reichstag, in their local governments, and on the street. Still, not everyone cared about politics—but almost everyone went to the movies. Nazis, Communists, Social Democrats, middle-class liberals, elitists, and mass culture advocates all recognized that the film *All Quiet on the Western Front* had, to borrow a phrase, rewritten Remarque's book "with lightning" (Rosenstone 191). To be sure, this conflict crystallized political responses in Göttingen to cinematic depictions of the war and, by extension, other controversial subjects. Perhaps more important, these films wedded discussions of cinema with local political discourse. More than reflecting ideological conflict, therefore, cinema functioned increasingly as a popular platform for talking about politics. This synthesis of mass culture and mass politics would arguably become the Nazis' most powerful tool for promoting their vision for a new Germany.

NOTES

1. Notable local studies that bear out this general argument include Allen, Koshar, Heilbronner, Jenkins, and Bergerson.

2. In subsequent references to Göttingen's newspapers—the *Göttinger Tageblatt, Göttinger Zeitung,* and *Göttinger Volksblatt,* the city's name has been omitted. Since Göttingen newspapers of this era rarely numbered more than fifteen pages each day, I have likewise omitted page numbers. Reviews, when signed at all, were often merely attributed to initials that do not conclusively demonstrate the author's identity.

3. The German Reich founded UFA (Universum Film-Aktien Gesellschaft) in 1917 as a hybrid public-private enterprise that united several of Germany's largest film companies. Originally designed to produce nationalist entertainment and propaganda during World War I, the company was privatized in 1921 and made many pathbreaking films during the Weimar era, including *The Cabinet of Dr. Caligari* (1919), *Metropolis* (1927), and *The Blue Angel* (1930). National and local reviews of *The World War* in Göttingen newspapers endorsed this documentary, but chiefly for reasons stemming from political ideology.

4. Later, as the Third Reich's Minister of the Interior, Frick would draft laws that sent opponents to concentration camps, as well as the infamous 1935 Nuremburg race laws. He was one of the few Third Reich officials executed as a war criminal after World War II.

5. In a sense, the comparative impact of book versus film bears out the penetrating and psychological power that Walter Benjamin ascribes to motion pictures. Anton Kaes charts this relationship in more detail.

WORKS CITED

Allen, William. *The Nazi Seizure of Power: The Experience of a Single German Town, 1922–1945.* Rev. ed. New York: Franklin Watts, 1984.

Applegate, Celia. *A Nation of Provincials: The German Idea of* Heimat. Berkeley: U of California P, 1990.

Benjamin, Walter. "The Work of Art in the Age of Mechanical Reproduction." *Illuminations.* Ed. Hannah Arendt. Trans. Harry Zohn. New York: Schocken, 1968. 217–52.

Bergerson, Andrew Stuart. *Ordinary Germans in Extraordinary Times: The Nazi Revolution in Hildesheim.* Bloomington: U of Indiana P, 2004.

Confino, Alon. *The Nation as Local Metaphor: Württemberg, Imperial Germany, and National Memory, 1871–1918.* Chapel Hill: U of North Carolina P, 1997.

Eksteins, Modris. "War, Memory, and Politics: The Fate of the Film *All Quiet on the Western Front*." *Central European History* 12.1 (1980): 60–82.

Gay, Peter. *Weimar Culture: The Outsider as Insider.* New York: Harper, 1968.

Geertz, Clifford. *The Interpretation of Cultures.* New York: Basic, 1973.

Heilbronner, Oded. *Catholicism, Political Culture, and the Countryside: A Social History of the Nazi Party in South Germany.* Ann Arbor: U of Michigan P, 1998.

Hoffmann, Hilmar. *The Triumph of Propaganda: Film and National Socialism, 1933–1945.* Trans. John A. Broadwin and V. R. Berghahn. Providence, R.I.: Berghahn, 1996.

Jelavich, Peter. *Berlin Alexanderplatz: Radio, Film, and the Death of Weimar Culture.* Berkeley: U of California P, 2006.

Jenkins, Jennifer. *Provincial Modernity: Local Culture and Liberal Politics in Fin-de-Siècle Hamburg.* Ithaca, N.Y.: Cornell UP, 2003.

Kaes, Anton, ed. *Texte zum Verhältnis von Literatur und Film 1909–1929.* Munich: Taschenbuch, 1978.

Kester, Bernadette. *Film Front Weimar: Representations of the First World War in German Films of the Weimar Period (1919–1933).* Trans. Hans Veenkamp. Amsterdam: Amsterdam UP, 2003.

Korte, Helmut. *Der Spielfilm und das Ende der Weimarer Republik: Ein rezeptionshistorischer Versuch.* Göttingen: Vandenhoeck and Ruprecht, 1998.

Koshar, Rudy. *Social Life, Local Politics, and Nazism: Marburg, 1880–1935.* Chapel Hill: U of North Carolina P, 1986.

Marshall, Barbara. "The Political Development of German University Towns in the Weimar Republic: Göttingen and Münster, 1918–1933." Diss. U of London, 1972.

Murray, Bruce. *Film and the German Left in the Weimar Republic: From* Caligari *to* Kuhle Wampe. Austin: U of Texas P, 1990.

Rosenstone, Robert A. "Like Writing History with Lightning: Historical Film/Historical Truth." *Contention* 2.3 (1993): 191–204.

Saldern, Adelheid von. "Göttingen im Kaiserreich." *Von der preußischen Mittelstadt zur südniedersächsischen Großstadt 1866–1989.* Vol. 3 of *Göttingen: Geschichte einer Universitätsstadt.* Ed. Rudolf von Thadden and Günter J. Trittel. Göttingen: Vandenhoeck and Ruprecht, 1999. 5–62.

Saunders, Thomas. "Politics, the Cinema, and Early Revisitations of War in Weimar Germany." *Canadian Journal of History* 23.1 (1988): 25–48.

Schorske, Carl E. *Fin-de-Siècle Vienna: Politics and Culture.* New York: Vintage, 1980.

Simmons, Jerold. "Film and International Politics: The Banning of *All Quiet on the Western Front* in Germany and Austria, 1931." *Historian* 52.1 (1989): 40–60.

Trask, C. Hooper. "News of Berlin Screen." *New York Times* 22 June 1930: 4.

Willet, John. *Art and Politics in the Weimar Period: The New Sobriety, 1917–1933.* New York: Pantheon, 1978.

THE PEACE, ISOLATIONIST, AND ANTI-INTERVENTIONIST MOVEMENTS AND INTERWAR HOLLYWOOD

In studying U.S. foreign policy in the period between the two world wars, scholars have recently produced some important work on interventionism and the film industry, but the relationship of antiwar groups to motion pictures has been largely ignored. Such neglect is clearly unwarranted, since surveys indicated that throughout the 1930s, the overwhelming majority of Americans opposed U.S. intervention in another war. As late as July 1941, the final Gallup poll on the question revealed that 79 percent still advocated U.S. neutrality (Gallup 290). This chapter is intended to provide a fuller and more balanced account.

My exploration of the relationship between leading antiwar groups and the film industry has produced some new insights into the foreign policy debate in the interwar era and contributes to a broader understanding of the place of movies in American public life. It indicates how some interest groups sought to filter and interpret motion pictures to their membership and demonstrates how, for most of the 1930s, pacifists and isolationists sought to use films in a positive manner and to build a working relationship with the motion picture industry. It was only in 1941, with the advent of a new, more extreme anti-interventionist movement, that a vituperative campaign was launched against the Hollywood studios.

Unfortunately, all those who were opposed to U.S. military intervention overseas are often linked together as isolationists, but they are more accurately analyzed as three separate entities, at least in the interwar period: pacifists, isolationists, and anti-interventionists. The peace movement was composed of a variety of pacifist and peace advocacy groups; internationalist rather than isolationist, they opposed military force and collective security and advocated nonviolent methods to address the causes or consequences of war. In contrast, the isolationist movement was neither pacifist nor internationalist. Its member groups opposed U.S. political as well as military intervention overseas, but they supported military defense of the Western Hemisphere. The anti-interventionist movement, composed of an ad hoc coalition of groups ranging from the political Left to the Right, emerged in 1940 to prevent U.S. military intervention in World War II.

The archival records of groups from these three different antiwar movements can disclose much more than merely how they sought to increase their membership and political influence—the standard use of such records.[1] In this case, they reveal how such groups tried to shape members' attitudes and actions toward motion pictures, the film industry, and U.S. foreign policy. Here, I focus on one group from each of the three movements: the pacifist Women's International League for Peace and Freedom (WILPF); the peace-oriented, isolationist-influenced National Council for the Prevention of War (NCPW); and the anti-interventionist America First Committee (AFC). Both the WILPF and the NCPW existed throughout the interwar period. The AFC was a temporary coalition organization that existed only from 1940 to 1941.

The U.S. Section of the WILPF, founded in 1919 by Jane Addams and other women interested in working for peace and women's rights, was one of the most important pacifist pressure groups. It consisted of more than 13,000 women, most of them from the middle or upper class, in branches across the country. Mildred Scott Olmstead headed the influential Pennsylvania branch, and in 1934 she became chief administrator of the entire U.S. Section of the WILPF (Alonso; Bacon; Foster; Pois). The most influential umbrella organization that included an isolationist coalition was the NCPW, headed by its founder Frederick J. Libby. A large, assertive lobbying coalition made up of a wide spectrum of groups from the American Federation of Teachers to the Grange and the Veterans of Foreign Wars, the NCPW mailed out nearly 2 million pieces of literature each year to a large audience ranging from farmers and blue-collar workers to educators and editors (Kuusisto; Libby, To End). The anti-interventionist AFC was headed by Robert Wood, chairman of Sears Roebuck and Company, and counted a membership of some 850,000 persons, the majority in the isolationist Middle West (Cole, America First; Doenecke, In Danger; Moser, "Gigantic Engines").

During American intervention in World War I, pacifists had been appalled by Hollywood's "hate the Hun" silent films.[2] With the renewed peace and isolationist sentiment of the late 1920s, some antiwar leaders expressed an interest in using the new talking pictures to engage the mass audience in the task of building a better and more peaceful world. Olmstead, already emerging as

Swarthmore College Peace Collection

Frederick Libby (left) of the National Council for the Prevention of War sends college students off to work for peace in their local communities after a summer institute at Duke University in 1934.

a key figure in the U.S. Section of the WILPF, became a leading advocate of using cinema for peace. She was impressed by a December 1928 radio talk in which Harry M. Warner of Warner Bros. had called the moving picture "The New Ambassador of Good Will." He suggested that sound films could "reach directly the heart and mind of the individual," and he predicted that they could "contribute to abolishing war by engendering mutual understanding and empathy among the masses of every race and nation" (Weiss). By the following spring Olmstead was writing to colleagues that real "peace movies" were desperately needed, but she recognized that they were too expensive to be produced by peace organizations (Olmstead, letter to Fry).

In 1930 the film industry began to produce a series of antiwar films that appealed to an audience that was now disillusioned with World War I. The worldwide financial success of the book *All Quiet on the Western Front* by Erich Maria Remarque, a German veteran, led to an outpouring of similar "disillusionist" books and films about the senseless tragedy and horror of modern warfare. Universal Pictures turned Remarque's book into a powerful antiwar movie, released in the spring of 1930. Combining new sound technology with some fast-paced action editing, the film shocked audiences with its battlefield slaughter and its poignant conclusion. *All Quiet on the Western Front* played to packed houses around the world in 1930 and 1931 and was rereleased in 1934 during the "merchants of death" hearings by Congress. An augmented version was released in the United States in September 1939, a shortened version was distributed worldwide in 1950 during the Korean War, and a color remake was produced in 1979 in the wake of the Vietnam War (Chambers, "*All Quiet*"; Chambers and Schneider).

The awards and profits garnered by *All Quiet on the Western Front* demonstrated that such antiwar pictures, exciting as well as disillusioning, could produce major profits. Consequently, movie theaters between 1930 and 1934 were filled with disillusionist antiwar films both American and foreign, including *Westfront 1918* (Germany, 1930), distributed in America under such titles as *Four from the Infantry* and *Drums of Doom; Journey's End* (England, 1930); *Dawn Patrol* (Warner Bros., 1930); and *A Farewell to Arms* (Paramount, 1932). Most popular with the peace and isolationist organizations were *All Quiet on the Western Front* and *Broken Lullaby* (Paramount, 1931). The latter, later retitled *The Man I Killed*, emphasized sorrow rather than action and centered on the guilt of a French poilu who killed a German soldier and later tried to make amends to the dead man's family and sweetheart. The wave of disillusionist films ebbed by 1933–1934 with less well-known pictures such as *The Eagle and the Hawk* (1933), *Ace of Aces* (1933), and *Crimson Romance* (1934), many of which combined thrilling aerial combat with a condemnation of wartime slaughter and a plea for peace. So powerful was the disillusionist theme that it permeated many nonwar films as well, with references to the Depression's unemployed veteran (the "forgotten man").

ANTIWAR ORGANIZATIONS MOBILIZE

After the premiere of *All Quiet on the Western Front* in the spring of 1930, Mildred Scott Olmstead began to create a list of films to recommend to WILPF members, and in 1931 she queried other peace-oriented organizations about their use of motion pictures. Their replies showed that they too saw movies as an important influence. The Federal Council of Churches, a liberal Protestant umbrella organization, reported that it had frequently protested against films with the "military spirit" (Gulick). Suffragist-pacifist Carrie Chapman Catt's National Conference on the Cause and Cure of War, a moderately conservative coalition of women's organizations, had no film-related program, but Catt noted in a letter that "the moving picture is a tremendous education—a few times for good and a great many times for bad." Most prominently, Libby's NCPW had already recognized film's potential for peace, compiling a list of short educational films that could be rented by local antiwar groups ("Educational Films"; "Motion Picture").

But as the antiwar organizations recognized, such limited efforts were inadequate. As a result, a gathering in 1930 hosted by the NCPW commissioned a study by Raymond T. Rich, head of the World Peace Foundation. After consulting producers of newsreels and educational and feature films, Rich recommended that the peace organizations shift away from complaining about the films they did not like and begin active programs to promote and develop films that contributed to world peace. Rich suggested, for example, that peace organizations should have actively publicized *All Quiet on the Western Front* and urged their members to patronize its exhibitors. They had to demonstrate that peace and antiwar films could be profitable. "The answer rests with box office receipts or other income," Rich asserted, "for no business is more strictly business than is the motion picture business."

"The field of visual education, as regards peace work, is practically untouched," a WILPF executive concluded after the organization's own survey. The reason was a lack of funds. "Until the peace organizations can supply the moving picture corporations with free reels depicting peace events, as the War Department now supplies them with free pictures depicting military manoeuvres," a WILPF executive wrote, "we cannot do a great deal" (Jones, letter to Schaffner). As a start, the WILPF established a Motion Picture Committee and began sending warnings to its members about newsreels or feature films that were particularly "militaristic." It urged members to voice their disapproval of such films to local exhibitors as well as to Hollywood studios, but it also urged members to buy tickets for movies on the WILPF's list of films "showing the cost, horrors, and futility of modern warfare" and those that portrayed what these pacifists called the "new patriotism," which was "international rather than national" (Jones, form letter; Springer).

The women's peace organization took the campaign further in February 1933 when Olmstead committed the WILPF to encouraging the production of motion pictures promoting international understanding and peace. In a letter to film distributors, she indicated that the WILPF would help them and local theater managers promote any film of an "antimilitaristic nature or any picture which would create a better understanding between nations." The WILPF had already endorsed pictures that showed the common humanity between former enemies, among them G. W. Pabst's German film *Kameradschaft* (1931), Ernst Lubitsch's *The Man I Killed* (Paramount, 1932), and Frank Lloyd's *Cavalcade* (20th Century-Fox, 1933) (Olmstead, letter to Goldman).[3]

The WILPF's designation of *Cavalcade* as an "antiwar" movie illustrates the complexity of categorizing films. *Cavalcade,* 20th Century-Fox's Oscar-winning adaptation of a Noel Coward play, emphasizes disillusionment with the war and

Advertisement for *Must War Be?* This 1932 peace film was shown in schools and churches.

its results, particularly the end of the old way of life among the two English generations it portrays. However, with a less preconceived antiwar view, the film could more accurately be seen as a fond if nostalgic portrayal of British society, and a picture that was more internationalist than pacifist.

The peace movement also made some films of its own. In 1932 the Peace Films Foundation, headed by Walter Niebuhr (related to theologian and social activist Reinhold Niebuhr), produced a five-reel educational sound film, *Must War Be?* According to Walter Niebuhr, the film, which focuses on the League of Nations, dramatically depicts the struggle "between the forces trying to organize permanent peace and those tending to perpetuate the war system." It was shown to religious, educational, peace, and foreign policy groups throughout the Northeast. Olmstead praised the project. "It is through such popular forms," she wrote to Niebuhr, "that we have to work to reach the millions of people who would not dream of attending a peace lecture. Yet these are the people who are the first to suffer in a war, and for many years after, and it is their votes which affect the most vital issues of war and peace. It is the mobilization psychology and the instinctive emotional reactions of the unthinking which must be changed if wars are to be averted."

To bypass the film industry's controlled distribution system, some peace advocates employed imaginative methods to bring antiwar and pro-peace films directly to the masses. The Peace Films Caravan was such an example. It was established by Francis Skillman Onderdonk, a religious pacifist of New York Dutch ancestry who taught architecture at the University of Michigan. Onderdonk created a "peacemobile," an automobile that he used to bring a traveling antiwar show to churches, clubs, fraternal organizations, schools, and colleges in half a dozen states in the early 1930s ("Biographical Sketch").

In addition to lecturing and exhibiting devastating photographs from the war, this peace showman mounted a 16mm projector on top of his car, set up a ten-foot portable screen, and showed peace films at night in parks, town squares, campuses, and fairgrounds. *All Quiet on the Western Front* was initially his most popular film, even though Universal would only sell him the silent version.[4] (Ironically, Onderdonk's road show provided extended life for this silent version long after most American theaters had converted to sound or had closed their doors.) Several peace groups endorsed the Peace Films Caravan, which made nearly one hundred presentations to some seventeen thousand persons between 1930 and 1935 (Onderdonk, form letter to Dear Friend). Three peacemobiles brought antiwar films to an even larger audience in 1936 and 1937.

Although it excited the opponents of war, the flood of antiwar books and films between 1929 and 1934 dismayed others. The leadership of the American Legion, for example, denounced such works as distorted, "sentimental pacifism" and protested that they undermined patriotism and national defense ("Keeping Step" 28; "Real" 18). Some conservative civilian organizations sought to have them banned on the grounds that they were Communist propaganda. *All Quiet on the Western Front* was denounced by one conservative patriot as Communist subversion that "undermines belief in the Army and in authority" and "will go far to raise a race of yellow streaks, slackers and disloyalists" (Pease; "Pease Porridge"). Despite calls from legionnaires to ban movies such as *All Quiet on the Western Front*, the American Legion's headquarters ignored such films ("Sound Film").

Even during the peak of the disillusionist antiwar films, Hollywood continued to churn out other pictures emphasizing the romance, excitement, and adventure of war and the military. Some dealt with World War I in sagas of love and glory with popular stars and upbeat endings, among them *Hell's Angels* (Caddo, 1930), *Today We Live* (MGM, 1933), and *Road to Glory* (20th Century-Fox, 1936). In addition, a slew of newsreel stories and feature films (dramas or even musicals) was made with the cooperation of the armed services. Although the peace organizations decried this cozy, self-serving relationship, recent

Mildred Scott Olmstead of the Women's
International League for Peace and
Freedom, circa 1932.

research indicates that there were often conflicting agendas, and the navy, at
least, was not always cooperative with Hollywood (Suid, *Guts* and *Sailing*).

NEW THREATS TO WORLD PEACE

With the emergence of new threats to world peace in the early and mid-1930s,
pacifists and isolationists were alerted to the possibility that the United States
might face another foreign war. Mussolini's fascist regime invaded Ethiopia
in 1935, leading to a public outcry. The League of Nations proved ineffectual
without the United States, but the Senate rejected even U.S. participation in
the World Court. Consequently, a number of peace organizations, such as the
WILPF, and peace-oriented isolationist bodies, such as the NCPW, joined in
launching a nationwide Emergency Peace Campaign in 1936.

As part of the planning for the Emergency Peace Campaign the previous
year, Frederick Libby of the NCPW had created a Motion Picture Department
and hired Albert "Benny" Benham, an old Hollywood hand, to run it. Benham
had worked at several Hollywood studios—United Artists, RKO-Pathé, and
Paramount—in various capacities from script clerk to film editor, assistant
director, and production manager. He had also served as vice president of an
independent film production company. Libby explained the goal of the NCPW's

Motion Picture Department in a form letter: "to lessen the great amount of militaristic propaganda in newsreels and features, and to increase the use of peace films." Within a year, Benham had organized a national network of some two thousand persons connected with various organizations, newspapers, and magazines who would receive a biweekly newsletter, the NCPW's *Bulletin on Current Films*. By labeling particular movies as pro- or antiwar, Benham sought to generate pacifist and isolationist pressures on exhibitors and studios ("Militarism" 118; Bromley; "Film Makers").

One of the first feature films praised by the NCPW's Motion Picture Department was *The President Vanishes* (Paramount, 1935), produced by Walter Wanger. It portrays a cabal of American capitalists trying to whip up a mob spirit against the wishes of a pacifistic president in order to plunge the country into a European war and maximize their profits. However, the president pretends to be kidnapped and foils the conspirators' plan. Castigated by conservatives, *The President Vanishes* was hailed by radicals and many liberals. The NCPW championed it as "a splendid peace document" that showed "how wars are made and who profits from them" (*Bulletin on Current Films* 22 June 1935: 2).[5] As with *Cavalcade* and many other films, *The President Vanishes* was open to different interpretations. Libby's organization brought its own peace-oriented perspective to it, but Wanger was hardly a pacifist or even an isolationist. His ideological purpose was to address what he saw as the threat of fascism in the United States, and Wanger's biographer indicates that the pacifist message had been added to the opening and closing purely as "bookends" to the film (Bernstein 97–102).

The threat to world order by the Italian invasion of Ethiopia, the beginning of German rearmament, and the increasing militarization of Japan coincided with a burst of Hollywood films that treated war as a just and exciting adventure. Many of these movies were Kiplingesque melodramas, such as the highly popular *Lives of a Bengal Lancer* (Paramount, 1935), that glamorized the wars of the British Empire against threats to "civilization" in the nineteenth century.[6] Pacifist and isolationist organizations vigorously protested them. Assailing *The Last Outpost* (Paramount, 1935), which depicts "civilizing" British soldiers holding off onrushing hordes of "savage" Africans, the NCPW opined: "There is a strange similarity between the episodes in this film and Mussolini's apparent conception of his campaign in Abyssinia [Ethiopia]" (*Bulletin on Current Films* 20 Nov. 1935: 2). *The Charge of the Light Brigade* (Warner Bros., 1936) was a romantic swashbuckler, with Errol Flynn as a British cavalry officer leading successful charges against rebellious Afghans and expansionist Russians. The jingoistic, imperialistic nature of such films was obvious to the mainstream press as well as to antiwar organizations and came under considerable attack.

Frank Onderdonk (left) and associates with one of his three "peacemobiles" in 1936.

Not only did the NCPW protest them, but some of its chapters urged that the war-glorifying *Charge of the Light Brigade* be publicly boycotted (*Bulletin on Current Films* 4 Dec. 1936: 2).

Opposing such films, the Emergency Peace Campaign expanded its own rating system, made more use of peace-oriented educational films, and increased its support for Frank Onderdonk's Peace Films Caravan, which he billed as "not 'another' peace organization—rather [a] specialization in the visual techniques for peace" (Onderdonk, form letter to Dear Secretary; Peace Films Caravan brochure).[7] Now with three peacemobiles, the Caravan was able to reach fourteen thousand people with presentations at fifty-six different high schools, colleges, churches, YMCAs, and union halls during the 1936–1937 academic year ("Peace Councils").

With the outbreak of the Spanish Civil War in 1936, a number of radical left-wing organizations joined with more moderate antiwar groups such as the WILPF and the NCPW to form the New Film Alliance to combat Hollywood's production of films that were seen as hostile to peace and social justice. The organizational meeting in November 1936 included representatives of the YWCA, Federal Council of Churches, American Jewish Congress, New York branch of the WILPF, NCPW, National Student Federation, Teachers' Union, National Negro Congress, and Communist-led American League Against War and Fascism (ALAWF).[8] The Communists sought to control the organization and proposed to boycott not just offensive films but every film made by the studios that produced offensive films. This radical proposal worried Benham of the NCPW, who confided privately, "I do not think that such a move could be successful; and I think that if a movement, dominated by Communists, is set up to clean out films, Hollywood will retaliate by starting a campaign to glorify preparedness, etc., and to discredit the whole peace movement" (Benham, letter to Dale, 16 Nov. 1936).[9]

The mass boycott idea was dropped, and although Benham was apprehensive about Communist influence and the goals of the New Film Alliance, which were much broader than the prevention of war, the NCPW, WILPF, and Emergency Peace Campaign worked with the new organization, at least on issues of war and peace.[10] In what they viewed as one of their major achievements, the NCPW and the New Film Alliance pressured 20th Century-Fox into canceling plans for *The Siege of the Alcazar,* a proposed celebration of a bloody victory by General Francisco Franco in the Spanish Civil War.[11]

In its attempt to keep the horrors of modern war in front of the public, the NCPW convinced owners of large, second-run movie theaters to show the full sound version of *All Quiet on the Western Front* during the Armistice Day holiday each year from 1935 to 1937. The showings filled the theaters, and local activists sometimes linked them to larger peace meetings (Benham, announcement card; *Ohio State U Bureau of Educational Research Newsletter* April 1937: 3; *Bulletin on Current Films* 17 Nov. 1936: 2–3).

"The number of theatrical features like ALL QUIET is pitifully small," Benham complained (letter to Dale, 25 Nov. 1936). Several newspaper columnists, educators, and businesspeople joined the NCPW in advocating the production of more peace films and publicizing movies that they considered antiwar. Edgar Dale, director of the Bureau of Educational Research at Ohio State University, had published the results of a study emphasizing the influence of motion pictures, particularly on young people (*Content*). In the 1930s he was also an activist in the Columbus, Ohio, chapter of the NCPW. Public opinion studies, he wrote to Benham, showed that there was strong public interest in the production of peace films, antiwar movies, and pictures dealing with relations among nations, races, and social groups (Dale, letter to Benham, 18 Dec. 1936).

"Motion picture producers have no mandate from the people for their overemphasis of war and *violence* on the screen," Dale fumed. "On the contrary, the success of *All Quiet on the Western Front, Cavalcade,* and other peace movies shows that the reverse is true" (Dale, letter to Benham, [Feb.? 1937]). Although many viewers undoubtedly appreciated the antiwar messages in the two films Dale cited, he ignored the fact that many other viewers had probably seen *All Quiet* as an exciting action movie, and others had enjoyed *Cavalcade* because of Noel Coward's caustically witty dialogue and the film's lavish Hollywood sets.

When Congress adopted a comprehensive neutrality act in May 1937, designed to keep the United States out of foreign wars, the ad hoc Emergency Peace Campaign was ended because isolationists concluded that it had been a success. Traditional peace and isolationist organizations continued their own work, and during 1937 they expressed some optimism because antiwar films were being producing by two major studios—*The Road Back* (Universal, 1937) and *They Gave Him a Gun* (MGM, 1937). They were, however, disappointed in the final versions. Universal had miscast John King as the leading character in Erich Maria Remarque's sequel, and MGM had watered down the powerful condemnation of war in William Joyce Cowan's novel. Neither film fared well at the box office.

In response to pacifists' and isolationists' protests against newsreels glorifying war and the military, managers at the newsreel companies in New York and Chicago countered that they were simply reporting current events, although they agreed to seek a reasonable balance. In Hollywood, studio executives replied that their feature films were designed as entertainment, not propaganda.[12] Even studios that made antiwar films denied that they did so for propaganda purposes. They stressed the antiwar message to peace organizations and urged them to generate ticket sales among their members (Cochrane).

Isolationists and peace advocates had considerable success in obtaining Hollywood celebrity endorsements. They hailed Gary Cooper's refusal to join the "Hollywood Hussars," a quasi-military unit formed by pugnacious, British-born actor Victor McLaglen, who starred in many jingoistic films. Even more helpful was Francis Lederer, a frequent male lead, who refused to star in a film glorifying war in 1935 and instead delivered more than eighty speeches on world peace to an estimated 100,000 people (*Bulletin on Current Films* 9 July 1935: 1–2, 22 July 1935: 2). The NBC radio network carried a nationwide broadcast of the NCPW's program "Women Want Peace" on 9 October 1935;

Swarthmore College Peace Collection

Movie stars Jean Muir (left) and Anita Louise buy "peace bonds" from Frederick Libby to help finance the NCPW's peace campaign in 1936.

it was presided over by first lady Eleanor Roosevelt. To help finance the Emergency Peace Campaign in 1936–1937, actresses Jean Muir and Anita Louise led off the purchase of "peace bonds." Silent-era film star Lillian Gish began a public commitment against war that lasted until 1941, when she abandoned her opposition, claiming that she had been blacklisted for supporting the anti-interventionist AFC (Affron).

Clark Gable made a strong radio plea in October 1937 for the United States to keep out of war. The next month he starred in a radio play version of *All Quiet on the Western Front* (*Bulletin on Current Films* 18 Oct. 1937: 2). In October 1938 Swedish-born actress Greta Garbo, unmarried and retired, issued a statement that she would have no babies to be used as "cannon fodder." Advocating a tactic used successfully by labor unions, Mary Pickford, also retired from stardom but still a successful businesswoman, called for women to refuse to work and to stage a universal "sit-down strike" in the event of war (*Bulletin on Current Films* 14 Oct. 1938: 3).

International tensions escalated in 1937 when Japan launched a war to conquer China. Many Americans condemned the savage aggression. Although Americans had long seen the United States as a special friend of China, they also viewed that country as continually plagued by floods, famines, bandits, warlords, and civil wars, a perspective shaped in part by Hollywood films from

Shanghai Express (Paramount, 1932) to *The Good Earth* (MGM, 1937). In 1937 the horrors perpetrated by Japanese forces in the bloody siege of Shanghai and the "Rape of Nanking" were graphically displayed in newsreels in the United States (Fielding, *American Newsreel* 260). The NCPW believed that such images confirmed the terrible human costs of war and reinforced Americans' disinclination to become involved in a land war in Asia. Antiwar activists were more concerned with the United States being drawn into a war in Europe.

SLOW RESPONSE TO THE NAZI MENACE

Rearmed and expansionist, Nazi Germany escalated its aggression dramatically in 1938 with the annexation of Austria and increased persecution of the Jews. On 9–10 November 1938—known as *Kristallnacht,* "the night of the broken glass"—German dictator Adolf Hitler let loose his thugs in a brutal campaign against the Jews of Germany. Hollywood studios had avoided any direct attack on the Nazi regime since Hitler took power in 1933, partly to avoid losing the lucrative German market, but in 1938 Hitler cut off their access to movie theaters in Germany (Vasey 155–56). American audiences were divided over the proper U.S. response to Nazi brutality. The newsreel companies could hardly avoid dealing with the repressive aspects of Hitler's regime, and that year some began to focus on its evils, most prominently Henry Luce's *March of Time* documentary *Inside Nazi Germany* (1938). The film showed an armed and regimented Germany preparing for aggression, but viewers differed over the nature of its message.[13]

With the public still divided over how the United States should respond to totalitarian expansion and repression, Hollywood remained reluctant to address the issue directly. In 1937–1938 the trade press debated what the film industry should do. From an antiwar perspective, Welford Beaton's gadfly *Hollywood Spectator* asserted that the studios had both a moral obligation and an economic incentive to make films that reflected the widespread American sentiment for peace and isolationism (*Bulletin on Current Films* 15 Nov. 1937: 1; 15 Mar. 1938: 2). Others suggested taking a stand against Nazism. Martin Quigley's conservative and influential *Motion Picture Herald* countered repeatedly that propaganda had no place as a motive for motion pictures and that their sole purpose was to entertain (*Bulletin on Current Films* 10 May 1938: 2–3). This was the position of most studio heads.

Although Hollywood remained aloof from the issues posed by Nazism, the film companies continued to churn out flag-waving, military service films—adventures, comedies, and musicals—much to the chagrin of the peace and isolationist movements (Dale, letter to Benham, 6 June 1936). But as

President Franklin D. Roosevelt initiated a rearmament program in 1938, the armed forces adopted more stringent policies toward cooperating with film companies, demanding the right to control the way the military was portrayed. This new censorship policy angered the film industry as well as the antiwar movement.[14] Antiwar activists were particularly incensed when the Army Air Corps pressured Paramount into eliminating all pacifist preachments in William Wellman's saga of aviation, *Men with Wings* (1938), including dropping the original ending in which the heroine strongly denounces war (*Bulletin on Current Films* 2 June 1938: 1–2).

By 1938 it was becoming clear that the bloody Spanish Civil War (1936–1939) was being lost by outgunned Loyalists defending the left-wing Republican government in Madrid against Franco's right-wing forces supported by Nazi Germany and fascist Italy. Although the Loyalists were aided by Communists and left-wing groups from the Soviet Union and elsewhere, the Western democracies had declared neutrality; the resulting blockade of arms and other supplies hurt the Loyalists more than Franco's fascist-supplied forces. *Blockade* (United Artists, 1938), Walter Wanger's controversial Spanish Civil War drama, was touted by some as Hollywood's first serious look at the challenge posed by the expansion of fascism. Henry Fonda played a peace-loving young Spanish farmer who takes up arms to defend his land and the elected government against better-armed and brutal "militarists" who ruthlessly bomb towns and cities. The film ends with a plea by Fonda's character for an end to the blockade, because the war in Spain is, he says, a new kind of war, a war against civilians: "Stop the murder of innocent people! The world can stop it! Where's the conscience of the world?"[15]

In retrospect, the released version of *Blockade* is a rather mediocre melodrama. But at the time, even though the words *fascists, Franco, Communists,* and *Loyalists* were never mentioned (at the insistence of the Production Code Administration), the film intensified an ongoing and divisive debate over the Spanish Civil War. The New Film Alliance as well as many Communists and many left-leaning liberal internationalists applauded the film. But many Roman Catholics and conservatives attacked it because they supported Franco's nationalists against the anticlerical, anticapitalist actions of Madrid. The Knights of Columbus, Legion of Decency, and Catholic Youth Organization denounced the film as "Marxist propaganda" and picketed exhibitors.

Many saw in *Blockade* what they wanted to see. Although contending that it might have been stronger in some places, the NCPW effused that, "just as it is, 'Blockade' is head and shoulders above any anti-war movie that has been made since 'All Quiet on the Western Front.' It strikes so loud a note not only in its cry against war but in its plea that the screen fulfills a mission deeper than mere entertainment" (*Bulletin on Current Films* 20 June 1938: 1–2). This was certainly not what writer John Howard Lawson and producer Walter Wanger had intended. Lawson and Wanger were not antiwar but antifascist; they wanted to help the Loyalists win the war (Bernstein 129–38).

CHANGING AMERICAN ATTITUDES

The brutality of the Nazi regime in Germany and the threat of expanding fascism in Europe led a growing number of Americans, though still a minority, to urge the United States to take an active role abroad where moral issues as well as national interests were involved. In January 1939 President Roosevelt raised the possibility of boycotting what he called "aggressor governments." Hitler occupied the remainder of Czechoslovakia in March 1939 and increased his demands on Poland.

Film industry spokesman Will Hays announced a change in Hollywood's policy in January 1939, conceding that pure entertainment might not be enough with the world in such crisis. The film industry, he said, had a responsibility to inform, not just entertain, the public. Beginning in 1939 Warner Bros. decided to make an army and a navy picture and half a dozen others with patriotic significance in the next two years, and other studios joined this "Americanism" campaign. Exhibitors started to play the national anthem at the top of each show. Some antiwar groups hoped that the campaign would emphasize democracy and the threat war posed to it, rather than the kind of flag-waving patriotism that, they feared, could easily become war fever (*Bulletin on Current Films* 20 Feb. 1939: 2).

As the studios produced a larger number of patriotic films, new antiwar films became increasingly rare. The most important antiwar film, French director Jean Renoir's *La Grande Illusion* (1937), was released in a subtitled version mainly in art houses on the East and West coasts in 1938 (*Bulletin on Current Films* 14 Oct. 1938: 4; 10 Jan. 1939: 3). In addition, the NCPW designated *Idiot's Delight* (MGM, 1939) an antiwar picture. An adaptation of Robert Sherwood's stage play set in a hotel on the Swiss border at the outbreak of World War II (*Bulletin on Current Films* 14 Mar. 1939: 2), *Idiot's Delight* can more accurately be characterized not as antiwar but as an early challenge to Hitlerism by Hollywood.

The NCPW vigorously protested the growing tendency of American newsreels and feature films to create a war spirit by stirring up fear. In a letter to Will Hays, Albert Benham referred to half a dozen films, especially *Confessions of a Nazi Spy* (Warner Bros., 1939), that overemphasized the extent of Nazi espionage in the United States (*Bulletin on Current Films* 10 Jan. 1939: 2–3). A lesser-known film was *Espionage Agent* (Warner Bros., 1939), a domestic thriller in which an American peace group is depicted as a Nazi front organization. Although Warner Bros. took the lead, it was some time before other studios began to make such stridently anti-Nazi films. Yet, even as the NCPW issued its warning against increasingly interventionist productions, it announced in October 1939 the closure of its Motion Picture Department, which was apparently no longer considered a viable voice (*Bulletin on Current Films* 26 Oct. 1939: 1).

EMERGENCE OF THE AMERICA FIRST COMMITTEE

The start of World War II in September 1939, and especially the German conquest of France and the bombing of Britain in the summer of 1940, began a shift in American opinion and launched a major debate over U.S. policy. The story of the isolationist-interventionist debate of 1939–1941 is an oft-told tale (see Langer and Gleason, *Challenge* and *Undeclared;* Divine; Cole, *America* and *Roosevelt;* Doenecke, *Storm*). New interventionist groups such as the Committee to Defend America by Aiding the Allies and Fight for Freedom were formed to mobilize sentiment in favor of assisting Britain and eventual U.S. intervention. Among antiwar groups, the internationalist peace movement saw membership plunge; isolationist support eroded more slowly but steadily.

Seeking to halt the decline, a diverse body of isolationists joined a new, ad hoc anti-interventionist coalition, the America First Committee, established in September 1940. Dominated by conservative, Republican elites, the new organization also drew on a wide range of support, including, for different reasons, some liberals and even a number of radicals on the Left. Largely isolationist and anti-Roosevelt, its leadership feared both the foreign and the domestic impact of U.S. entry into the war (Cole, *America;* Doenecke, *In Danger*). The AFC was headed by Robert Wood, chairman of Sears Roebuck, and it drew its greatest popular support from the Midwest. Although President Roosevelt and the interventionist organizations were the main targets of the AFC, it also focused on companies producing newsreels and feature films that seemed to be preparing Americans for war. In July 1941 the AFC created a list of such films, among them *The Great Dictator* (Chaplin, United Artists, 1940), *Foreign Correspondent* (Wanger, United Artists, 1940), *The Mortal Storm* (MGM, 1940), and *That Hamilton Woman* (Korda, United Artists, 1941); later that summer it called for boycotts of theaters showing such films.

Despite the flood of interventionist films after 1939, some of the most popular antiwar films continued to be shown. *All Quiet on the Western Front* was rereleased in September 1939, augmented with a new preamble that was anti-

Antiwar, anti-Hollywood postcard, circa 1939–1941.

Nazi but also promised that "there shall be *no* blackout of peace in America!"[16] It played at theaters throughout the winter of 1939–1940 (*Motion Picture Herald* 28 Oct. 1939: 70; 2 Dec. 1939: 73). Indeed, *All Quiet on the Western Front* stayed in circulation as late as April 1942, when protests led to its withdrawal (Glassman; Director).

To counter the horrible image of ground warfare portrayed so vividly in *All Quiet on the Western Front,* Warner Bros. produced two films that provided a more positive view of World War I. Although scholars differ on whether *The Fighting 69th* (1940) and *Sergeant York* (1941) were preparedness productions, my own reading is that they were messages of support for a military buildup and ultimately for U.S. entry into the war against Germany.[17] They certainly were celebrated by interventionists and decried by anti-interventionists at the time.

Desperate to counter the increasing support among the mass media and the entertainment industry for the United States' movement toward war, the most extreme isolationists in Congress and the AFC decided to launch an attack on the major Hollywood studios, accusing them of unduly influencing Americans through pro-Allied propaganda. The resulting 1941 investigation by a Senate subcommittee has been described by a number of historians. The records of the three antiwar organizations examined here indicate that the AFC, supported by the NCPW but not the WILPF, was responsible for that assault.[18]

BATTLE ON CAPITOL HILL

The AFC planned, initiated, and supported the attack on Hollywood. In August 1941 the head of its New York chapter, John T. Flynn, a former columnist for the liberal *New Republic* who had turned against Roosevelt's domestic and foreign policies, urged isolationist Senator Burton K. Wheeler (D-Mont.) and the AFC's executive committee to expose "collaboration between the film magnates and the government to whip up [war] propaganda" (Flynn, letter to Wheeler; Flynn, letters to Wood).[19] With AFC encouragement, Wheeler appointed an investigating subcommittee cochaired by isolationists D. Worth Clark (D-Idaho) and Gerald P. Nye (R-N.D.).[20]

Recent scholarship has shown that a number of the major film studios were consciously producing movies designed to emphasize the Nazi menace and encourage support for those nations fighting against it; in addition, the studios and newsreel companies were privately being encouraged to do so—actively by the British government, and cautiously by the Roosevelt administration (see Birdwell; Brewer; Cull; Mahl; Steele). But motion pictures were only one of the many foreign and domestic forces affecting the shift in American public opinion. Even more quickly than members of Congress, the American people recognized the magnitude of the Nazi threat and supported those nations fighting against it, although they continued to hope that American troops would not need to be sent overseas.[21]

The Senate hearings of September 1941 failed to demonstrate any connection between the film industry and the government. They failed partly because of the ineptitude of the isolationist majority on the subcommittee and partly because of the skill of the studio heads and their spokesman, former GOP presidential nominee Wendell L. Willkie.[22] But the primary cause of their failure—indeed, their collapse—was the charge of anti-Semitism. The hearings and the AFC itself were attacked and largely discredited by Willkie and the press, which charged, not without some basis, that they were engaged in a scheme to focus on foreign-born Jews in the motion picture industry as unduly influencing public opinion.[23]

Willkie's charges gained credibility with the public when aviator Charles Lindbergh, at an AFC rally in Iowa on 11 September 1941, declared that the United States was being pushed toward war by the Roosevelt administration, the British, and the Jews. Lindbergh depicted Jewish Americans as a powerful

Gerald Nye (second from left) and Bennett Champ Clark (right) were among the sponsors of the Senate investigation of Hollywood propaganda in 1941. In this earlier photograph, they and fellow isolationist senators Arthur Vandenburg (left) and Homer Bone (second from right) celebrate the passage of neutrality legislation.

alien group that was acting against the interests of the United States (Berg 425–28).[24] Although Lindbergh's anti-Semitic remarks reflected the privately held views of some of the more reactionary anti-interventionists, they were condemned by many pacifists, isolationists, anti-interventionists, and, of course, interventionists.[25] They threw the entire antiwar movement into disarray ("Senate Isolationists" 21, 25; "Hollywood in Washington" 13; Straight 363; Moffitt 1).

Less than two months later, the Japanese attack on Pearl Harbor ended the debate over intervention and brought the United States into World War II. The Senate subcommittee disbanded without issuing a report. Motion pictures would play an important role in the war, helping to forge national consent for wartime policies and build a public culture with a unity and reach never achieved before or afterward.

Without resuming the partisan debate of the 1930s, it should now be possible, with most of the relevant archives open, to explore more fully and fruitfully the relationships among the antiwar and interventionist movements, motion pictures, public opinion, and U.S. foreign policy in the interwar era. The standard narrative emphasizes the shortsightedness and negativity of pacifists and isolationists, who are generally linked with anti-interventionists. It also stresses the timidity of Hollywood, which only belatedly began to alert Americans to the dangers posed by Nazi Germany.

The present study, like some other recent scholarship,[26] indicates that the story is more complex. The antiwar movement, for example, did not simply bemoan what were considered war-mongering films. And despite the 1941 diatribes of some anti-interventionist extremists such as Lindbergh and Nye, the antiwar movement did not, for the most part, employ anti-Semitic tactics against Hollywood. Instead, throughout much of the 1930s, the peace and isolationist movements, unlike the anti-interventionist America First Committee of 1940–1941, sought to use motion pictures in a positive manner. They employed antiwar movies and educational films in imaginative ways, such as peacemobile caravans and annual Armistice Day showings, to reinforce their messages. Rather than trying to foster animosity toward the film industry, the Women's International League for Peace and Freedom and, for most of the period, the National Committee for the Prevention of War, unlike the America First Committee, tried to work with studios, distributors, and exhibitors, encouraging profitable nonchauvinistic motion pictures to educate the public in the interest of peace.

A related question, of course, is whether Hollywood could make films that explored larger issues or clarified policy choices in an educated, sophisticated manner. Most of the antiwar films of the early 1930s merely encouraged excitement and revulsion against the horrors of warfare. Few of them explored in any depth the causes of wars or the moral issues raised by aggression. When Hollywood eventually became committed to the anti-Nazi cause in 1939–1941, the studios again produced rather simplistic, one-sided propaganda, this time in support of war. Admittedly, the chances for more complex explorations either way were slim, not merely because of external forces, such as propaganda connections with the British, but more importantly because of a system that encouraged the use of generic plot structures. Hollywood was geared toward producing entertaining, moneymaking movies for a wide audience, not providing sophisticated education for the public.

It was widely believed at the time that motion pictures influenced public attitudes, but it was not clear how. The present study shows some of the ways pressure groups sought to filter films and interpret their meaning to their members. Research on spectatorship has emphasized the degree to which viewers bring their own preconceptions to the theater. These preconceptions are sometimes shaped by ideological organizations. That helps explain why, as shown in this study, radically different messages can be, and often are, derived from the same film.

In the interwar period, leaders of the peace, isolationist, and anti-interventionist movements tried to actively influence the way motion pictures affected the public's attitudes about war and peace. They did so in various ways. The traditional view of the antiwar movement and the film industry between the two world wars has ignored the significant diversity among the groups and their attitudes and policies with regard to war and the movies. The dominant perspective has focused on vigorous anti-Hollywoodism, culminating in the abominable anti-Semitic accusations that accompanied the Senate hearings of September 1941. But as my study has shown, exclusive focus on that deplorable episode distorts the larger and longer relationship between the antiwar movement—especially the peace and peace-oriented movements—and motion pictures. Wider research and broader perspectives have revealed more positive attitudes about movies and the film industry and active attempts to use the new technology of "talking pictures" to steer public opinion toward a culture of world peace.

NOTES

1. The organizations' attitudes and actions with regard to motion pictures are ignored in their institutional histories, which focus on other, admittedly main, aspects of their agendas. For a discussion of the recent literature on interventionism and the film industry, see Chambers, "Movies."

2. See, for example, the recent collection of essays in Schneider and Wagener.

3. Some motion picture executives and theater owners responded to the WILPF's campaigns by seeking the women's endorsement for films with pacifist or antiwar themes. Despite several entreaties, the WIPLF declined to endorse any films between March 1933 and October 1934. However, at the end of 1934 it gave enthusiastic support to two new antiwar films: *The First World War,* a documentary based on Laurence Stallings's book of the same title, and *The Man Who Reclaimed His Head,* a feature film starring Claude Rains as a pacifist writer who struggles against manipulation by capitalist munitions makers trying to use him for their own selfish purposes.

4. Onderdonk's program usually began with a thirty-minute sound film, *The Next War,* about the evolution of increasingly lethal weaponry. He also showed three short silent films—*The Zeppelin Raid on London, The League of Nations,* and *New York's 1934 Peace Parade*—followed by the silent version of *All Quiet on the Western Front* (Onderdonk, form letter to Dear Sir).

5. Two years earlier, Wanger had produced a somewhat similar political allegory and fantasy, *Gabriel Over the White House* (MGM/Cosmopolitan, 1933), involving conspiratorial forces seeking to block a U.S. president from achieving peace and justice.

6. The *Motion Picture Herald,* a trade journal for exhibitors, expressed the connection

as follows: "The thunder of hob-nailed marching feet of Mussolini's Italian infantrymen . . . echoes with the roar of bombing planes from Abyssinia across 3,000 miles of ocean and then 3,000 miles of land, and Hollywood is listening" ("Hollywood Starts" 18).

7. When Universal Pictures rejected his request for the sound version of *All Quiet on the Western Front,* Onderdonk continued to show the silent version, but in 1936 he began to emphasize the "talkies" he had, including *The Man I Killed.* In 1937 his other feature sound films included *Dealers in Death,* four reels on munitions makers and the international arms trade, and *Drums of Doom (Four Infantrymen from the Western Front in 1918),* an English-dubbed, seven-reel version of G. W. Pabst's *Westfront 1918.*

8. American Communists joined with reformist groups in establishing the New Film Alliance as part of the Communist Party's Popular Front policy of cooperating to oppose fascism during this period.

9. Benham did not allow the New Film Alliance to control the NCPW's *Bulletin on Current Films;* consequently, the New Film Alliance published its own weekly cinema bulletin, *Film Survey.*

10. The WILPF also worried about Communists in its own and other peace organizations—ideologically, because the Communists did not oppose all wars, and politically, because Communist members made the organization vulnerable. Yet the WILPF worked with organizations that were Communist influenced or even dominated, such as the American League Against War and Fascism, because of their larger membership. This was true until 1937, when the WILPF broke with the ALAWF to work with the isolationist Keep America Out of War Congress, which relied on pacifist, labor, and socialist support rather than the Communist Party.

11. Joseph M. Schenck, president of United Artists, credited the NCPW and the New Film Alliance with Fox's cancellation of *The Siege of the Alcazar.* Fox had received nearly four thousand letters of protest (Benham, letter to Dale, 28 Nov. 1936).

12. An executive of the *March of Time* series assured an isolationist Ohio manufacturer that the preparedness emphasis in a newsreel about the Spanish Civil War would be matched by a new release on the Sino-Japanese War that included a strong protest against U.S. involvement by House leader Bennett Champ Clark (de Rochemont).

13. Some active anti-Fascists such as Dorothy Thompson applauded *Inside Nazi Germany* as an appropriate attack on the German regime, but others denounced it. The Warner brothers banned it from their four hundred theaters because they said it appeared to be "pro-Nazi," given its use of German propaganda footage, even though the narration condemned Nazism (*Bulletin on Current Films* 5 Feb. 1938: 1–3).

14. In an editorial reprinted in the *Bulletin on Current Films,* the editors of the New York–based trade journal *Box Office* declared that the military's new policy suggested "a very definite warning that the move is launched to smack a military censorship on peacetime enterprise." The motion picture industry, *Box Office* warned, "should seriously watch its step to the end that it is not unwittingly caught in the meshes of rabid jingoism" ("New Brand" 1–2).

15. *Blockade* was the first film to take a stand on the Spanish Civil War, but it was not the first to use it as a setting. *The Last Train from Madrid,* made by Paramount a year earlier (1937), was a thin melodrama set amidst the flight of civilians from the war zone.

16. Director Lewis Milestone later wrote that he had been appalled by the 1939 version, which he saw as Universal's response to isolationist sentiment.

17. Daniel J. Leab ("Viewing the War") asserts that *The Fighting 69th* and *Sergeant York* were not primarily designed to stimulate sentiment for war, as suggested by Basinger (98) and Sklar (99, 105). Leab develops this argument further in *"The Fighting 69th*: An Ambiguous Portrait of Isolationism/Interventionism." My own view of these two films is that, although they did not praise war and even included some gestures to the still strong isolationist sentiment in the United States, they reversed the pessimistic emotional position of antiwar films that had portrayed the war's senselessness and its breaking of the human spirit. Instead, the films of 1940 and 1941 emphasized the need for a patriotic willingness to do one's duty for the nation and a view of combat that highlighted bravery, courage, camaraderie, and even redemptive glory. Granted, Warner Bros.' primary aim was to earn a profit, and it made a handsome one, particularly on *Sergeant York*. But preparing the country to fight the Nazis was another important motive behind both films. The latest study of Warner Bros. agrees that *Sergeant York* became an interventionist vehicle for the studio and for Alvin York himself (Birdwell 131–53).

18. In fact, both the NCPW and the WILPF cooperated with the AFC beginning in the winter of 1940–1941, and they received some financial support from it (Doenecke, *In Danger* 59n). But only the NCPW supported the assault on Hollywood and its leaders. See Libby, letter to Stuart [AFC's founder], and Detzer [WILPF's lobbyist].

19. See also the confidential memorandum to members of the executive committee of the AFC. For Flynn's plan, see Flynn, letter to Stuart. Earlier, Flynn had been research director for Senator Gerald Nye's 1934 hearings on profits of the munitions industry during World War I, and he continued to be concerned with oligopoly, profiteering, and interventionism. The Scripps-Howard chain continued to publish his column after the *New Republic* dropped it in November 1940. See Doenecke, *In Danger* 16; Stenehjem; Moser, *Right Turn*. AFC chairman Robert Wood later disingenuously wrote to an executive of Columbia Pictures that the Senate investigation was in no way sponsored by the AFC.

20. Wheeler, chair of the Senate Interstate Commerce Committee, introduced Senate Resolution No. 152, 77th Cong., 1st sess., on 1 Aug. 1941, to authorize the investigation. The full Senate was never given the chance to vote on the resolution. Instead, Wheeler simply appointed an investigating subcommittee. In an otherwise well-researched account, Steele, in *Propaganda in an Open Society* (65), misidentifies the cosponsor of the resolution as D. Worth Clark. Clark, an Idaho Democrat, was made cochair of the subcommittee, but Wheeler's cosponsor of the resolution was actually Senator Bennett Champ Clark (D-Mo.).

21. In a Gallup poll at the end of June 1941, 79 percent of respondents said that they would vote to stay out of the European war. Although that question was not used again by Gallup, when Americans were asked in October and November 1941 which was more important—that the United States keep out of war or that Germany be defeated—only 32 percent said that it was more important to stay out of war, and 68 percent said that it was more important that Germany be defeated.

22. Nye and other isolationists on the subcommittee admitted that they had not seen the films they were condemning as propagandistic; their hostile questions were also offset by the lone interventionist on the committee, freshman senator Ernest McFarland (D-Ariz.). Industry leaders testifying included Barney Balaban of Paramount, Nicholas Schenck of Loew's, Darryl Zanuck of 20th Century-Fox, and Harry Warner

of Warner Bros. Warner, in the most quoted testimony, asserted that his company's films were not anti-American propaganda but were accurate and patriotic and that the American public should see the truth about Hitler and Nazism (U.S. Congress 57–60, 91–116, 213–66, 338–48, 337–92, 427–31).

23. Indeed, Robert S. Allen, coauthor with Drew Pearson of the widely syndicated column "The Washington Merry-Go-Round," reported confidentially to the interventionist group Fight for Freedom before the hearings began, "The whole movie affair is part of a deliberate anti-Semitic campaign" to reinvigorate the flagging anti-interventionist movement. "I heard on the Hill yesterday that this was deliberately cooked up for the double purpose of terrorizing the Jews, on one hand to keep them from active participation in the anti-isolationist fight and on the other to arouse public prejudice against the interventionist cause on the Jew angle. This is one of the most sinister and vicious schemes yet undertaken by the isolationists and I think that the FFF ought to hit very hard with the biggest speaker it can get to do the job. . . . The whole purpose of these so-called hearings will be to drag up Jews in the movie industry and parade them across the headlines."

The AFC's main attack was clearly against the motion picture industry for presenting, as Nye said in the hearings, "one-sided" propaganda. However, there were some anti-interventionists in the AFC and in Congress who were willing to play on anti-Semitism, most notoriously Charles Lindbergh and Gerald Nye. In a major radio address to an AFC rally in St. Louis on 1 August 1941, Nye declared that motion picture companies had "become the most gigantic engines of propaganda in existence to rouse the war fever in America and plunge this Nation to her destruction." He named the heads of the eight largest film studios as the responsible parties. Although Nye talked about the studios' economic connections to Britain and the number of British actors working in Hollywood, his recital of the names of seventeen men who were either Jewish or had Jewish-sounding names (Darryl Zanuck was Protestant), as well as his emphasis on their immigrant origins from central and eastern Europe, indicates a clear appeal to the strong current of anti-Semitism in the United States in the 1930s. Although the list of names is the same, some of the remarks in the printed version (Nye) differ from the broadcast version transcribed by a stenographer hired by Fight for Freedom ("Senator Gerald"). In describing his plan for the hearing, John T. Flynn thought it would help publicize the AFC's case about Hollywood propaganda; he did not know whether "the movie moguls" would agree to come to the hearing. "But in any case, it will obtain our objective in focusing attention on the movies and on them" (Flynn, letter to Stuart). At the hearing, Nye emphasized the oligopolistic nature of the film industry, dominated by the "big eight" firms, rather than emphasizing the names of their leaders. This and a debate over the issue of anti-Semitism can be seen in U.S. Congress 14–22, 26–29, 67–69. For an attempted defense of Senator Nye against charges of anti-Semitism, see Shapiro. Moser, in "'Gigantic Engines,'" seeks unsuccessfully (in my view) to shift the Senate subcommittee's main motivation from anti-interventionism and an anti-Semitic "witch hunt" to an ongoing effort by progressive insurgents against "the increasing corporatization of society" and in favor of greater regulation of the motion picture industry.

24. Two days after his radio address, Lindbergh returned to New York City and went to see *Sergeant York*. He noted in his diary that it was "good propaganda for war—

glorification of war, etc. However, I do not think a picture of this type is at all objectionable and dangerous." The next day he left for his home on Martha's Vineyard, still believing, despite the public outcry, that he had spoken "carefully and moderately" in Iowa (Lindbergh 538–39).

·   25. Anti-interventionists were divided on the issue, but many of them, particularly in conservative circles, had been privately condemning Jewish interventionists for some time. Anti-interventionist Joseph P. Kennedy, U.S. ambassador to Great Britain, had warned studio executives in November 1940 that they, and particularly the Jews among them, would be in jeopardy because of their propagandistic war films (Fairbanks). For Kennedy's anti-interventionism, see Kennedy 221–508. For condemnation of Lindbergh's anti-Semitic remarks within the antiwar, isolationist, and anti-interventionist movements, see Cole, *Charles A. Lindbergh* 171–85, and Doenecke, *In Danger* 37–40. In the second week of October 1941, the Gallup poll asked, "What persons or groups do you think are most active in trying to get us into war?" Listed in decreasing order of frequency were the Roosevelt administration and the Democratic Party; big business and profiteers; British organizations and agents; American groups with pro-British sympathies; and Jews. The most frequently mentioned individuals or groups "trying to keep us out of war" were Charles Lindbergh, Burton Wheeler, and Gerald Nye; America First Committee; Roosevelt administration; Nazi agents and fifth columnists; and church groups (Gallup 302–3).

26. See, for example, Felicia Herman's "Hollywood, Nazism, and the Jews, 1933–1941," which reveals how Hollywood films indirectly attacked Nazism before 1938. Herman acknowledges that the studios avoided explicitly anti-Nazi films for most of the 1930s, but she contends that one of the many reasons was the fear by Jewish organizations that films that overtly condemned Nazism or directly defended Jewry would intensify the growing anti-Semitism. The 1941 Senate hearings raised the charge that Jews controlled Hollywood and were interventionists and propagandists. But instead of seizing on that accusation, the American press and much of the public repudiated it. See also Gabler 338–47. Todd Bennett places Will Hays, the head of the Motion Picture Producers and Distributors Association, rather than the studio heads, at the center of Hollywood's shift to anti-Nazi films beginning in 1939. Bennett contends that Hays asked for the Roosevelt administration's help in reopening the British market, since London had frozen the American studios' assets there to help the British balance of payments. In return for the administration's success in getting the British government to unfreeze those assets a year at a time, Hays relaxed his previous ban on interventionist films, such as those directly attacking Nazism. Thus, London made an economic sacrifice to gain a political objective: increasing interventionist propaganda in the United States.

Works Cited

Affron, Charles. *Lillian Gish: Her Legend, Her Life.* New York: Scribner's, 2001.
All Quiet on the Western Front. Continuity and dialogue script. 8 Sept. 1939. New York State Motion Picture Division Records.
Allen, Robert S. Letter to Merle Miller. 9 Aug. 1941. Fight for Freedom Inc. Records.
Alonso, Harriet Hyman. *Peace as a Women's Issue: A History of the U.S. Movement for World Peace and Women's Rights.* Syracuse, N.Y.: Syracuse UP, 1993.

America First Committee Records. Hoover Institution, Stanford, Calif.

Bacon, Margaret Hope. *One Woman's Passion for Peace: The Life of Mildred Scott Olmstead.* Syracuse, N.Y.: Syracuse UP, 1993.

Basinger, Jeanine. *The World War II Combat Film: Anatomy of a Genre.* New York: Columbia UP, 1986.

Benham, Albert. Announcement card. 4 Nov. [1935]. NCPW Records.

———. Letters to Edgar Dale. 16, 25, 28 Nov. 1936. NCPW Records.

Bennett, Todd. "The Celluloid War: State and Studio in Anglo-American Propaganda Film-making, 1939–1941." *International History Review* 24.1 (2002): 64–102.

Berg, A. Scott. *Lindbergh.* New York: Putnam, 1998.

Bernstein, Matthew. *Walter Wanger: Hollywood Independent.* Berkeley: U of California P, 1994.

"Biographical Sketch." Onderdonk Papers.

Birdwell, Michael E. *Celluloid Soldiers: The Warner Bros. Campaign against Nazism.* New York: New York UP, 1999.

Brewer, Susan A. *To Win the Peace: British Propaganda in World War II.* Ithaca, N.Y.: Cornell UP, 1997.

Bromley, Dorothy Dunbar. "Hollywood Isn't Deaf to Voice of People." *New York World-Telegram* [March 1937?]. Box 116. NCPW Records.

Catt, Carrie Chapman. Letter to Mary Hobson Jones. 21 Aug. 1931. WILPF Records.

Chambers, John Whiteclay II. "*All Quiet on the Western Front* (U.S. 1930): The Antiwar Film and the Image of Modern War." *World War II, Film, and History.* Ed. John Whiteclay Chambers II and David Culbert. New York: Oxford UP, 1996. 13–30.

———. "The Movies and the Antiwar Debate in America, 1930–1941." *Film & History* 36.1 (2006): 44–57.

Chambers, John Whiteclay II, and Thomas F. Schneider. "*Im Westen nichts Neues* und das Bild des 'modernen Krieges.'" *Text + Kritik* 149 (2001): 8–18.

Cochrane, R. H. Letter to Trevor Lloyd. 14 July 1937. NCPW Records.

Cole, Wayne S. *America First: The Battle against Intervention, 1940–1941.* Madison: U of Wisconsin P, 1953.

———. *Charles A. Lindbergh and the Battle against Intervention in World War II.* New York: Harcourt, 1974.

———. *Roosevelt and the Isolationists.* Lincoln: U of Nebraska P, 1983.

Confidential memorandum to members of the executive committee of the AFC. 16 Sept. 1941. Flynn Papers.

Cull, Nicholas J. *Selling War: The British Propaganda Campaign against American "Neutrality" in World War II.* New York: Oxford UP, 1995.

Dale, Edgar. *The Content of Motion Pictures.* New York: Macmillan, 1935.

———. Letter to Albert Benham. 6 June 1936. NCPW Records.

———. Letter to Albert Benham. 18 Dec. 1936. NCPW Records.

———. Letter to Albert Benham. [Feb.? 1937]. NCPW Records.

de Rochemont, Louis. Letter to Gardner Lattimer. 16 Sept. 1937. NCPW Records.

Detzer, Dorothy. Letter to Emily Greene Balch. 22 Sept. 1941. WILPF Records.

Director of the New York State Motion Picture Division. Letter to Samuel M. Glassman. 17 Apr. 1942. *All Quiet on the Western Front* (1939) file. New York State Motion Picture Division Records.

Divine, Robert A. *The Illusion of Neutrality.* Chicago: U of Chicago P, 1962.

Doenecke, Justus D., ed. *In Danger Undaunted: The Anti-interventionist Movement of 1940–1941 as Revealed in the Papers of the America First Committee.* Stanford, Calif.: Hoover Institution P, 1990.

———. *Storm on the Horizon: The Challenge to American Intervention, 1939–1941.* Lanham, Md.: Rowman, 2000.

"Educational Films for Peace and International Conflict." Ts. 1931. WILPF Records.

Fairbanks, Douglas, Jr. Letter to President Roosevelt. 19 Nov. 1940. (Returned to Roosevelt in memorandum from Sumner Welles. 26 Nov. 1940.) President's secretary's file, diplomatic correspondence: Great Britain; Kennedy, Joseph P., 1939–1940, box 37. Franklin D. Roosevelt Papers. Franklin D. Roosevelt Lib., Hyde Park, N.Y.

Fielding, Raymond. *The American Newsreel, 1911–1967.* Norman: U of Oklahoma P, 1972.

———. *The March of Time, 1935–1951.* New York: Oxford UP, 1978.

Fight for Freedom Inc. Records. Seeley G. Mudd Manuscript Lib., Princeton U, Princeton, N.J.

"Film Makers Besought to Push for Peace in Pictures of War." *Christian Science Monitor* 1 Aug. 1936. Box 116. NCPW Records.

Flynn, John T. Letter to R. Douglas Stuart Jr. 4 Aug. 1941. America First Committee Records.

———. Letter to Burton K. Wheeler. 6 Aug. 1941. Flynn Papers.

———. Letters to Robert E. Wood. 8, 12 Aug. 1941. Flynn Papers.

———. Papers. U of Oregon, Eugene.

Foster, Carrie A. *The Women and the Warriors: The U.S. Section of the Women's International League for Peace and Freedom, 1915–1945.* Syracuse, N.Y.: Syracuse UP, 1995.

Gabler, Neal. *An Empire of Their Own: How the Jews Invented Hollywood.* New York: Crown, 1988.

Gallup, George H. *The Gallup Poll: Public Opinion, 1935–1948.* New York: Random, 1972.

Glassman, Samuel M. Letter to the governor of New York. 1 Apr. 1942. *All Quiet on the Western Front* (1939) file. New York State Motion Picture Division Records.

Gulick, Sidney L. Letter to Mary Hobson Jones. 10 June 1931. WILPF Records.

Herman, Felicia. "Hollywood, Nazism, and the Jews, 1933–1941." *American Jewish History* 89.1 (2001): 61–89.

"Hollywood in Washington." *Time* 22 Sept. 1941: 13.

"Hollywood Starts War Cycle." *Motion Picture Herald* 19 Oct. 1935: 18.

Jones, Mary Hobson. Form letter. 30 July 1931. WILPF Records.

———. Letter to Gerta H. Schaffner. 9 July 1931. WILPF Records.

"Keeping Step." *American Legion Magazine* Apr. 1930: 28.

Kennedy, Joseph P. *Hostage to Fortune: The Letters of Joseph P. Kennedy.* Ed. Amanda Smith. New York: Viking, 2001.

Kuusisto, Allan A. "The Influence of the National Council for the Prevention of War on United States Foreign Policy, 1935–1939." Diss. U of Nebraska, 1955.

Langer, William L., and S. Everett Gleason. *The Challenge to Isolation, 1937–1940.* New York: Harper, 1952.

———. *The Undeclared War, 1940–1941.* New York: Harper, 1953.

Leab, Daniel J. "*The Fighting 69th:* An Ambiguous Portrait of Isolationism/Interventionism." *Hollywood's World War I: Motion Picture Images.* Ed. Peter C. Rollins and John E. O'Connor. Bowling Green, Ohio: Bowling Green State UP, 1997. 101–20.

———. "Viewing the War with the Brothers Warner." *Film and the First World War.* Ed. Karel Dibbets and Bert Hogenkamp. Amsterdam: Amsterdam UP, 1995. 223–33.

Libby, Frederick. Form letter to Dear Friends. 12 June 1935. NCPW Records.

———. Letter to R. Douglas Stuart Jr. 22 Sept. 1941. America First Committee Records.

———. *To End War: The Story of the National Council for the Prevention of War.* Nyack, N.Y.: Fellowship, 1969.

Lindbergh, Charles A. *The Wartime Journals of Charles A. Lindbergh.* New York: Harcourt, 1970.

Mahl, Thomas E. *Desperate Deception: British Covert Operations in the United States, 1939–44.* Washington, D.C.: Brassey's, 1998.

McMillan, James E., Jr. "McFarland and the Movies: The 1941 Senate Motion Pictures Hearings." *Journal of Arizona History* 29 (1988): 227–302.

Milestone, Lewis. Letter to James Sheehan. 6 Apr. 1964. Folder 1. Lewis Milestone Papers, Margaret Herrick Lib., Academy of Motion Picture Arts and Sciences, Los Angeles, Calif.

"Militarism in the Films." *Peace* Oct. 1936: 118.

Moffitt, Jack. "Senators' Case Bogs to Zero." *Hollywood Reporter* 26 Sept. 1941: 1.

Moser, John E. "'Gigantic Engines of Propaganda': The 1941 Senate Investigation of Hollywood." *Historian* 63.4 (2001): 731–52.

———. *Right Turn: John T. Flynn and the Transformation of American Liberalism.* New York: New York UP, 2005.

"Motion Picture Films." Ts. 1932. WILPF Records.

National Council for the Prevention of War Records. Swarthmore College Peace Collection, Swarthmore, Pa.

"A New Brand of Censorship." *Bulletin on Current Films* 23 Nov. 1938: 1–2.

New York State Motion Picture Division Records. New York State Archives, Albany.

Nye, Gerald P. "War Propaganda—Our Madness Increases as Our Emergency Shrinks." *Vital Speeches of the Day* 15 Sept. 1941: 720–23.

Olmstead, Mildred Scott. Letter to Lucretia Fry. 19 Apr. 1929. WILPF Records.

———. Letter to William Goldman (Stanley-Warner Co.). 23 Feb. 1933. WILPF Records.

———. Letter to Walter Niebuhr. 24 Mar. 1933. WILPF Records.

Onderdonk, Francis S. Form letter to Dear Friend. 31 Jan. 1935. Onderdonk Papers.

———. Form letter to Dear Secretary. 4 Sept. 1937. Onderdonk Papers.

———. Form letter to Dear Sir. 28 Aug. 1934. Onderdonk Papers.

———. Papers. Swarthmore College Peace Collection, Swarthmore, Pa.

"Peace Councils." Ts. [1937]. Onderdonk Papers.

Peace Films Caravan brochure. Onderdonk Papers.

Pease, Frank. Telegram to the president (copy to chief of Military Intelligence Bureau, War Department). 27 Apr. 1930. File 10604-211. U.S. Army Military Intelligence Division Records.

"Pease Porridge Not So Hot." Clipping. 18 June 1930. File 10604-211. U.S. Army Military Intelligence Division Records.

Pois, Anne Marie. "The Politics and Process of Organizing for Peace: The Women's International League for Peace and Freedom, 1919–1939." Diss. U of Colorado, 1988.

"Real versus Unreal." *American Legion Magazine* June 1930: 18.

Rich, Raymond T. "The Problem of Moving Pictures in the Promotion of Peace." Ts. Peace and AV Material, 1926–1982. Swarthmore College Peace Collection, Swarthmore, Pa.

Schneider, Thomas F., and Hans Wagener, eds. *"Huns" vs. "Corned Beef": Representations of the Other in American and German Literature and Film on World War I.* Osnabrück, Ger.: V&R unipress/Universitätsverlag Osnabrück, 2007.

"Senate Isolationists Run Afoul of Willkie in Movie 'Warmonger' Hearings." *Life* 22 Sept. 1941: 21+.

"Senator Gerald T. [*sic*] Nye over Columbia Broadcasting System." 1 Aug. 1941. Ts. Fight for Freedom Inc. Records.

Shapiro, Edward. "The Approach of War: Congressional Isolationism and Anti-Semitism." *American Jewish History* 74 (1984): 45–65.

Sklar, Robert. *City Boys: Cagney, Bogart, Garfield.* Princeton, N.J.: Princeton UP, 1992.

"Sound Film of Convention." *American Legion Monthly* (Sept. 1931): 80.

Springer, Mrs. Eugene. Letter to WILPF's Radio and Motion Picture Committee. 4 Mar. 1932. WILPF Records.

Steele, Richard W. *Propaganda in an Open Society: The Roosevelt Administration and the Media, 1938–1941.* Westport, Conn.: Greenwood, 1985.

Stenehjem, Michele Flynn. *An American First: John T. Flynn and the America First Committee.* New Rochelle, N.Y.: Arlington, 1976.

Straight, Michael. "The Anti-Semitic Conspiracy." *New Republic* 22 Sept. 1941: 363.

Suid, Lawrence H. *Guts & Glory: The Making of the American Military Image on Film.* Rev. ed. Lexington: UP of Kentucky, 2002.

———. *Sailing the Silver Screen: Hollywood and the U.S. Navy.* Annapolis, Md.: Naval Institute P, 1996.

U.S. Army. Military Intelligence Division Records, 1917–1941. Record group 165, box 3618. National Archives II, College Park, Md.

U.S. Congress. Senate. Committee on Interstate Commerce. *Propaganda in Motion Pictures: Hearings on Senate Resolution 152 . . . September 9 to 26, 1941.* 77th Cong., 1st sess. Washington, D.C.: GPO, 1942.

Vasey, Ruth. *The World According to Hollywood, 1918–1939.* Madison: U of Wisconsin P, 1997.

Weiss, Anna. Letter to Mildred Scott Olmstead (ts. of Warner radio talk enclosed). 7 Jan. 1929. WILPF Records.

Women's International League for Peace and Freedom Records. Swarthmore College Peace Collection, Swarthmore, Pa.

Wood, Robert. Letter to Stanton Griffis. 31 Oct. 1941. America First Committee Records.

THE B MOVIE GOES TO WAR IN *HITLER, BEAST OF BERLIN*

During the 1930s, the neighborhood movie house was a place of refuge for many. The pressures and strains of the world vanished amidst the laughter, thrills, and chills of the golden era of the B movie. In the world outside, people were weighed down by the burdens of the era—memories of family, friends, and neighbors who had died in World War I; the effects of the Great Depression; and the strife of the Spanish Civil War. But once they were behind those movie house doors, the tensions of everyday life melted away, as the Bs brought low-budget action, suspense, comedy, and melodrama into the lives of the moviegoing public. With a shriek, a pratfall, or a fiendish glare, B movies served up extra helpings of escapism; however, by the end of the decade, the boundaries between the world of the cinema and the world outside began to erode. The question of whether to become involved, once again, in Europe's recurring struggles was beginning to creep into popular thought, and as the conflicts in Europe and Asia escalated, the film industry once again engaged with the more serious affairs of the world.

Hollywood's "Poverty Row," known for its quick, low-budget B productions pandering to the desire for over-the-top entertainment, produced a small film, *Hitler, Beast of Berlin* (1939), that played a striking role in the national tug-of-war over military preparedness. While other films of the interwar era whispered words of fear or caution in the ears of American moviegoers, *Beast of Berlin* screamed—it mocked, shocked, and menaced in defiance of the Third Reich. Dismissed by critics as an artistic flop but a masterful work of propaganda (Crowther; Morrison; Thirer), *Beast of Berlin* combined images of life inside the Third Reich and slap-in-the-face, exploitation-style public relations to create one of the first blatantly interventionist films of the prewar years, and also one of the first to openly cast the Nazi regime in a villainous

Cynthia J. Miller Collection

The press kit for *Hitler,
Beast of Berlin* urges theater owners to promote
the film "boldly, and
without reservation."

light. The film brought vivid, tangible oppression onto the screen and into
the lives of theatergoers.

Produced by Ben Judell, *Hitler, Beast of Berlin* was one of the inaugural
efforts of the small, independent Producers Distributing Corporation (PDC;
renamed Producers Releasing Corporation in 1943), infamous for its low
production standards and sensationalism. When the joint German and Soviet
invasion of Poland in September 1939 produced widespread concern in Hollywood, Judell's low-budget studio was one of the first to act, and it did so in
sensationalist form, setting aside other projects to rush into the production of
Hitler, Beast of Berlin, based on the novel and screenplay *Goose Step* by Broadway
producer-director Shepard Traube. In line with the studio's lowbrow dedication
to "high entertainment and exploitation values" (Fernett 99), Judell changed

the title to the more dynamic *Hitler, Beast of Berlin,* hoping to capitalize on the notoriety of the 1918 film *The Kaiser: Beast of Berlin,* which, during the previous worldwide struggle, had incited American audiences to anti-German riots in several cities. Subsequently the PDC project became *Beasts of Berlin,* but as public sentiment mounted in favor of the Allied cause, the *Hitler* title was reinstated and shouted at audiences from marquees and lobby posters. At the time of its official release (15 October 1939), *Beast of Berlin* was a "hot" item, regardless of its B status. Cited as prowar, inflammatory, and offensive to Germany, it was quickly shut down by the Production Code Administration and censorship boards in several states. After a month of editing, it reopened to reviewer praise as the first fiction feature to depict the terrors of life inside the Third Reich.

HOLLYWOOD AND INTERVENTION

Before 1936, the idea of meddling in world affairs was a complex and unpopular one, and it would continue to be so until it became clear that American involvement was unavoidable. At home, pressures and tensions ran high. The German-American Bund, with about twenty-five thousand dues-paying members, carried out a high-profile, often volatile campaign for neutrality, while influential figures such as pro-German aviator Charles Lindbergh and Senator Gerald Nye (R-Ohio) would soon create and support the nation's most powerful isolationist group, the America First Committee. By 1937 the political lines were drawn. On one side, President Franklin D. Roosevelt warned in his "quarantine" speech (15 October 1937): "If those things [war] come to pass in other parts of the world, let no one imagine that America will escape" (Akers 81). On the other side, Senator Nye spoke for the isolationists: "There can be no objection to any hand our government may take which strives to bring world peace to the world so long as that hand does not take 130,000,000 people into another world death march. I very much fear that we are once again being caused to feel that the call is upon America to police a world that chooses to follow insane leaders. . . . Once again we are baited to thrill to a call to save the world" (Akers 81–82).

With the formal outbreak of war in Europe in September 1939, the debate in the art, literature, and film communities took a more tangible form. Roosevelt still publicly pledged neutrality, but the Hollywood community was becoming a hotbed of debate between isolationists and interventionists (Birdwell; Ross; Alpers). While Popular Front groups such as the Hollywood Anti-Nazi League used demonstrations, weekly radio shows, and their own newspapers to establish a public voice against neutrality, much of the Hollywood Left believed that the Soviet Union was aligned with the world's democracies against fascism and resisted U.S. action toward the Stalin regime. But in 1939, when Hitler signed a nonaggression pact with Stalin and invaded Poland, the Anti-Fascist Refugee Committee (with such prominent members as writers Dashiell Hammett and Lillian Hellman) rapidly transformed into the Hollywood League for Democratic Action.

Economic factors complicated Hollywood's position as well. As Allen Rostron points out, the advance of fascism and the outbreak of war in Europe offered enticing subject matter for films: "Wars have obvious dramatic potential, and the studios knew a story 'ripped from the headlines' could draw audiences" (85). At the same time, studios had tangible reasons for their caution. Overseas box office receipts were a substantial part of their profits, while at home, most of America's heartland was fervently isolationist. Films stepping too far into controversial territory risked hostile reactions, including censorship (Rostron 85).

And censorship was active in the late 1930s. The presumed power of the movies made their content a hot issue. Scores of cities and many states had set up censorship boards early in the century, and in the late interwar era, they were becoming more active. Fearing federal censorship or a breakup of the film industry, the Motion Picture Producers and Distributors of America preached for Hollywood to purvey only "pure entertainment"—wholesome films that avoided social and political issues. The Motion Picture Production Code, which imposed stringent restrictions on the portrayal of a wide range of subjects both political and moral, had largely been ignored since its inception in 1930 but was reinvigorated in 1934, causing a sharp cutback in the treatment of social and political issues by the major studios (Bernstein). The war was an irresistible subject for Hollywood, but it also threatened the doctrine of "pure entertainment." As the nation geared for battle, the movies became a prime instrument for public persuasion—so much so that Joseph Breen, head of the Production Code Administration, accused Hollywood (in particular, the Hollywood Anti-Nazi League) of attempting to "capture the screen of the United States for Communistic propaganda purposes" (Koppes and Black 22).

In 1939 Warner Bros. broke through the barrier on political topics and premiered the controversial *Confessions of a Nazi Spy,* which revealed, in melodramatic fashion, that Germany sought to conquer the world. The picture's release netted a host of problems for the studio: an injunction from the German-American Bund; official protest from the German ambassador, Hans Heinrich Dieckhoff; and threats on the lives of Jack Warner and the film's star, Edward G. Robinson (Shane 40; Birdwell 76). PDC's low-budget but even more riveting *Hitler, Beast of Berlin* (shot in less than a week) was scheduled to open soon after, but it ran into opposition from the Production Code Administration as well as from local censorship boards. Michigan, Pennsylvania, and New York wanted *Hitler* deleted from the title (Fernett 103). The war still had not hit close enough to home, and the film's detractors found it offensive to Germans and German Americans alike. Chicago and Providence turned the film down completely, as an organized opposition gathered steam. After a title change to *Beasts of Berlin* and a wide range of edits, including the deletion of several remarks about Roosevelt, the film opened in New York in late November. Shortly after its premiere, a reviewer for *Box Office* cited the film as being "a timely picture, filmed with the realization of what was happening in Germany" (Fernett 103). The stage was then set for the appearance of a rapid succession of prointervention films, including Charlie Chaplin's *The Great Dictator* (United Artists, 1940), *I Married a Nazi* (20th Century-Fox, 1940), and *A Yank in the R.A.F.* (20th Century-Fox, 1941). In 1939, however, only six titles dealt directly with Germany and the European situation, and of those, all but *Hitler, Beast of Berlin* were tales of espionage (*Television Spy, Espionage Agent, The Lone Wolf Spy Hunt, They Made Her a Spy,* and *Confessions of a Nazi Spy*).

The Rhetoric of Intervention

Propaganda is a vague concept. As Koppes and Black note, "Propaganda is a bit like pornography—hard to define, but most people think they will know it when they see it" (49). And in *Hitler, Beast of Berlin,* critics, censors, and audiences alike knew what they were seeing. In classic B movie fashion, viewers are dragged headlong into a Manichaean battle of good and evil, absolute right versus absolute wrong, where characters, dialogue, and ideological positions all work in concert to drive home the point that intervention in Europe is the only logical and moral course of action for the United States.

The film focuses on a small group in Germany's underground, actively resisting the growing Nazi power until the male members are apprehended and sent to a concentration camp. Roland Drew plays Hans Memling, the group's dedicated leader and a former pilot in the German military. Because of his combat background, Hans is not merely some easy-to-write-off idealist; his resistance to the Third Reich is rooted in moral and political principles rather than pacifism or fear.

Alan Ladd (as Karl) and Steffi Duna (as Hans' wife, Elsa) play the doubters—sympathetic, yet raising all the arguments, questions, and what-ifs that a typical isolationist might entertain about the necessity of intervention, the costs of the fight for democracy, and the ethical dilemma of sacrificing individual happiness and comfort for the vague concept of a greater good. With a lack

Cynthia J. Miller Collection

Elsa (Steffi Duna) and Anna (Greta Granstedt) print handbills in support of the resistance fighters.

of pretense and subtlety typical of B movies, the film blatantly foregrounds doubts about the wisdom of resistance in order to allay them. Elsa asks, "Will democracy happen in our lifetime? Are we fighting for something we'll never see the results of?" Karl presents the well-intentioned counter to intervention, taking an academic and historical perspective that there has never been a tyrant in history who has ruled permanently—that eventually, this Nazi regime too shall pass. Hans admonishes him that "people have to want democracy" and that Germans must experience true self-government to know what it is really like, and they must be willing to rise up in its defense. He responds to Karl's fear of the futility of a small resistance effort by reminding him (optimistically), "We have friends everywhere."

Finally, Anna (Greta Granstedt) is the modern American-type woman who has a sense of duty to her country and political convictions that override any feminine stereotype. Anna is paired with doubting Karl, in parallel to Hans and the fearful Elsa. Strong, independent, and dedicated, Anna places her ideal of the greater good before personal happiness. When Karl asks her to marry him, she says no—she needs to continue to work for the cause. "If we marry, the state will demand children of us. That's what a woman is for in the New Germany." Anna chooses "the fight" over marriage and children, as her means of resisting Nazi ideology.

Supporting characters run the gamut from good to evil. There is the sympathetic storm trooper who is punished for rejecting the brutality of the concentration camps yet still clings to the notion that "all will be corrected in time. Hitler will see that justice be done to all people." In contrast are the corrupt, high-ranking Gestapo officers, driven by ego and embodying the "insanity" and lack of reason that would later be used to characterize the Third Reich. This strategy of depicting good versus evil in the German characters—the humane yet faithful storm trooper, members of the resistance, and the dissatisfied but compliant townspeople versus the corrupt lawyers and dogmatic military officers—was also an effective means of assuring that *Hitler, Beast of Berlin* did not fall into the Production Code's "hate film" category. Such films were subject to additional sanctions and editing because the "national feelings" section of the code required that "the history, institutions, prominent people and citizenry of other nations, shall be represented fairly" (Koppes and Black 29). And "fairness," in the case of motion pictures, meant that no group—be it national, ethnic, political, or occupational—could be portrayed as innately, overarchingly evil. According to the code, immorality could be attributed to particular leaders of the Nazi regime but not to the German people as a whole.

The code-satisfying concept of "fairness" is established early in the film; it opens with newsreel footage of an ominous sea of storm troopers, parading by torchlight with Nazi flags flying, blended into fictional scenes of average townspeople complying with the Nazi salute but with resentful looks, subtle head shaking, and downcast eyes. Their demeanor forecasts the unrest of the story line, which begins in a secret room where members of the underground resistance are printing flyers to be disguised as official leaflets. The text reads: "To all Peace-Loving Germans: The National Socialist Party is leading the German people to destruction and war. Hitler and his murderers have suppressed the true state of world opinion concerning what is happening within Germany. The entire world is horrified by the brutalities that have been visited upon our once civilized nation. This constant betrayal of the people can lead to but one end—complete annihilation of the German nation." The rhetoric here is designed to convey an alignment between the audience and "real" Germans. It alludes to the horrors of the Nazi regime while reinforcing the notion that "civilized" Germans, who undoubtedly share the moral convictions of middle-class American filmgoers, are unaware of foreign support for their plight.

As the film continues, so does its appeal to democracy and similarity on various social and ideological levels. Bracketed vignettes provide dialogue from characters who represent sectors significant to U.S. audiences, as they note how Hitler's war machine has undermined the nation's resources and economy. A woman in a grocery store complains bitterly that, under the Third Reich, food prices have gone up while quality has gone down; rail workers grumble about the destruction of independent unions. A church sermon adds the issue of religious freedom to the mix, when a priest reminds his parishioners that "dissenters are suffering and dying to keep the love of God in the hearts of your children and your children's children." Even nature is invoked to support intervention, when—during a picnic—Elsa contemplates the tree she's lying under and comments, "This is the Germany we love. This tree has been here since before Hitler and Goebbels and it will be here long after they're gone. . . . Perhaps if they thought of that, they'd take it down."

The counter to these positive images is, of course, demonizing images of the hostile, aggressive, overtly anti-American Gestapo and storm troopers. Stark lighting, melodramatic dialogue, and harsh camera angles invoke the power of the B film to create menacing Nazi figures eager to display their military power. One trooper asks another, "Do you think there's going to be another world war?" His companion responds, "Let it come—today, we have the greatest army in the world. Today the German people are united. The English will never fight us."

When the subject of world war is introduced again, the camp's commanding officer tells his subordinates that he welcomes the prospect of battle. When his newspaper is delivered, he reads aloud, "Roosevelt appeals to Hitler for peaceful solution" and then tosses the paper to the floor with scorn. It is clear that the avoidance of confrontation, through either diplomacy or isolation, is seen as a sign of weakness by the Third Reich's true believers. Although several of these anti-Roosevelt scenes were allowed to remain in the final cut, one in which the colonel refers to Roosevelt as a "meddling fool" was excised by censors (Rostron).

In another scene, a direct confrontation takes place between Hans and the concentration camp's commanding officer. After several days of numbing detention, an exhausted Hans is summoned for an "interview." The colonel, who served with Hans in the army, attempts to turn his loyalties: "At Versailles, the rest of the world robbed Germany, the Fatherland, from everything we hold dear—our possessions and our honor. Now, with Hitler's leadership and direction, Germany holds its head high." Hans resists and ultimately counters: "If I find myself in a mad house and I'm still sane, I cannot believe I must submit myself to the rule of a lunatic!" In response to this cri de coeur, he is dragged away to be "reeducated."

IMAGE POLITICS

Continuing the trend begun in the films of World War I and used heavily during the Spanish Civil War, *Hitler, Beast of Berlin* used "factual" footage to blur the line between fiction and reality. Utilized primarily at the film's beginning and end, this footage frames the scripted drama in ways that were familiar to American audiences, who were regular consumers of the newsreel series *March of Time*. *Beast of Berlin* opens with newsreel scenes of storm troopers parading through small towns, dominating the otherwise peaceful landscape. These clips are intermingled with dramatizations of women, children, and elderly towns-people with wary demeanors offering reluctant salutes—delivering an image of the Third Reich as a grim force choking the flow of everyday German life and reinforcing earlier vignettes of oppression. At the film's end, Hans, Elsa, and their new baby escape to Switzerland, but Hans is determined to return to Germany. As Elsa begs him to stay, Hans attempts to explain to her why he must leave her, their child, and their newfound safety. A montage of newsreel images of warfare and death supports his admonishment that they can never truly be free as long as Germany is a dictatorship. The scene closes with Elsa winning him over by reminding him, "Here, you are free to tell the rest of the world what is happening in Germany, and that what is going on does not speak the hearts of the German people."

Although the controversial *Confessions of a Nazi Spy,* released earlier that fall, was the first anti-Nazi film produced by a major studio and constituted the film industry's wake-up call to American audiences about the Nazi threat, *Beast of Berlin* was the first to actually dramatize horrific Nazi excesses. Its concentration camp scenes were considered inflammatory to the Hitler regime at a time when diplomatic solutions were still being entertained, and many were lost to censorship edits (Rostron). Still, the remaining scenes effectively convey the hopelessness and brutality of the early camps. Arriving prisoners are told that they are under "protective arrest" and will be considered enemies of the state until proved otherwise. At intake, they are fingerprinted, weighed, and measured—objectified as the sum total of so much flesh. Once processed, they are beaten, humiliated, exercised in the yard, or worked on road crews until they drop from exhaustion and malnourishment.

As the resistance members acclimate to the camp, an already established prisoner is pointed out to them as being "not right"—insane. He shuffles through the barracks like a robot, disoriented and unaware of his surroundings. The ensuing dialogue reveals that his arrest was at the hands of his own son, who had joined the Hitler regime: "When he found out his son joined the Nazis, he tried to shoot him" rather than see his offspring betray basic German values and ideals. The old man is broken—handed over by the son he tried to save. When the two later meet in the barracks, the father pleads, "Wilhelm! Take off that uniform! Please!" The soldier reacts with scorn, grab-bing his father by the shirt and hurling him onto the floor and then out into

Cynthia J. Miller Collection

Hans (Roland Drew) is weighed and measured as he becomes a concentration camp commodity.

the yard with the other prisoners—a vivid symbol of families torn apart by brutal dogmatism.

Another polarizing scene, illustrating the Nazi threat to the fabric of society, shows a guard tearing the rosary beads from around the neck of a priest and crushing them. A close-up shows the guard's boot heel smashing the beads to bits, callously shattering the priest's hope and faith underfoot and demonstrating that Catholicism—or any other competing ideology—is powerless against the Nazi regime.

The harshness of the Third Reich is also made tangible through depictions of the prisoners' quarters. The barracks are concrete and barren, consisting only of bunks with a water trough for cleaning and drinking in the middle of the room. The specter of the ominous "Room 14," where "instruction," "convincing," and interrogation occur, hangs over the prisoners. As the disappearance of several prisoners illustrates, it is a place from which there is often no return. When one of the resistance supporters fails to reappear in the barracks, Hans demands to know what happened to him. The guard smiles broadly and says, "He fell down the stairs and broke his neck"; he then becomes menacing as he warns, "And if you don't mind your business, the same could happen to you!" Later, when Hans defies the commanding officer, he is taken off-camera to Room 14 and beaten senseless while his fellow captives listen to his screams.

Cynthia J. Miller Collection

Hans requires convincing that Hitler will lead Germany to glory.

When he is subsequently returned to view, barely able to stand, he is forced into a torture box—an upright coffin with only a barred opening across the face—and left alone murmuring Elsa's name.

EXPLOITATION GOES TO WAR

Mysterious deaths, implements of torture, shrieks of pain—this sort of gut-wrenching B movie sensationalism was not unfamiliar to Ben Judell, who came to PDC with a track record in exploitation films. Prior to filming *Beast of Berlin*, his credits included a trio of 1938 celluloid scandals: *Rebellious Daughters*, *Delinquent Parents*, and *Slander House*, followed in 1939 by the pulp shockers *Torture Ship*, *Buried Alive*, and *Invisible Killer*, all produced either during or immediately after *Hitler, Beast of Berlin* (Dixon). Suspense, terror, and melodrama drove the thin plots of these low-budget pictures, electrified by fiendish killers and mad scientists. Judell's flair for exploitation led *Hitler, Beast of Berlin* to make its strongest mark on the politics of prewar films. The film's promotional strategy was an odd mixture of the approach taken for earlier films such as *Three Comrades* (1938) and *Blockade* (1938), which expressly disavowed any propagandistic intent yet utilized a sensational publicity approach generally reserved for mainstream exploitation films. The main title image of *Hitler,*

Beast of Berlin announces that it reflects no bias, prejudice, or hatred of any individual, group, or nation; a critic for the *New York Sun* reported that this disclaimer prompted a roar of laughter (Creelman). The movie explicitly depicts brutal atrocities suffered by the resistance heroes, as well as verbal abuse and scorn toward not only the resistance but also Jews, Catholics, and, of course, fainthearted Americans.

Similarly, the press kit for *Beast of Berlin* contains a remarkable combination of material urging the aggressive exploitation of anti-Nazi sentiment while vehemently denying that the film takes any position either for or against Nazism. The posters and advertisements for the film contain ominous images of Gestapo officers standing over bloody and beaten prisoners: "A wail of anguish from a nation in chains," screams the copy. The ads describe the film as "written with the hearts' blood of innocent people" and made "as a monster ravishes a continent"; yet every review and publicity story prepared by the studio takes pains to disclaim that the film reflects any partisan intent. For instance: "*Hitler, Beast of Berlin* is not propaganda. It is not a preachment for or against Nazism. It is not a screen editorial. It does not violate good taste nor is it in any manner offensive." In a prime example of this hypocritical juxtaposition of damnation and denial, one sentence in the promotional materials describes the film as "shorn of all propaganda and without prejudice," while at the same time previewing the story line as the saga of a fearless young German risking all to bring down the Nazi regime so that his unborn children "shall not feel the iron heel of despotism."

In the portion of the press kit meant for exhibitors' eyes only, PDC encourages theaters to adopt this same strategy of ambiguity. The studio requests that each exhibitor place a poster in a prominent lobby position bearing the text, "NO WAR, NO HATE, NO PROPAGANDA. Just eloquent and dramatic ENTERTAINMENT." The press kit then recommends that "all exploitation should be BOLD and FLAMBOYANT!" Exhibitors were advised to hang giant blow-up photos of Hitler in their lobbies and on their marquees, and they were told that maps of Europe and provocative newspaper headlines about war would make an eye-catching lobby display under this caption: "A Madman Redrawing the Map of Europe with a Sword Dipped in the Blood of Innocent Children! Will America Be Next?" The press kit also suggests that each theater hire a "stockily built young man with Teutonic features, dress him in a Storm Trooper uniform with a swastika armband," and have him stationed to open car doors and to attract attention in front of the theater. Finally, the kit recommends building a concentration camp "torture box" to drive home "the brutality of Hitler's Gestapo." The film "pulled no punches" in addressing a topic that no other American studio had as yet dared to touch (Boehnel).

Cynthia J. Miller Collection

A neighborhood theater follows the studio's promotion advice and flamboyantly beckons moviegoers.

OPPORTUNISM AND OPPORTUNITY

Controversial in a way that was good for the box office, *Hitler, Beast of Berlin* was profitable for PDC. It took B movie melodrama and a stark moral battlefield to the controversy over intervention, creating a familiar framework for grappling with the nation's involvement. Judell's exploitation-style strategies and blood-and-guts sensationalism offered, or perhaps confronted, audiences with new opportunities to consider Hitler and Nazi expansionism. While the film's dialogue acknowledges isolationist arguments, it counters the heartland's objections with even more compelling American values. "Good" Germans were not the cultural "others" of American film audiences; they were reflections of them. Viewed in that light, Germans not only deserved America's help; their plight constituted a moral obligation to intervene.

These moral and intellectual appeals were supported by visual and tactile affronts delivered by the film and its promotion in ways that were largely unfamiliar to film-going audiences outside the exploitation genre. Judell brought the horrors of concentration camps onto the screens and into the lobbies of movie houses, forcing Americans not only to look at but also to feel and interact

Cynthia J. Miller Collection

Handbills dare audiences to view the film exposé that no one wants them to see.

with the realities he constructed, blurring the boundaries between drama and fact. Newspaper ads and handbills asked, "What don't they want you to see?" and advertised rewards for the return of "stolen" copies of the film. Cardboard stand-ups of Hitler looked on as moviegoers were encouraged to touch and open and even climb inside the torture boxes built for theater lobbies—to better imagine the atrocities depicted in the film and identify with the fictional protagonists. The closer that identification became, the more difficult it would be to maintain a neutral stance.

As it was mobilizing political sentiments, *Hitler, Beast of Berlin* also made another contribution—to the movement to loosen the moralistic fetters on the motion picture industry. The stringent restrictions of the Production Code Administration (along with general pressure from the Catholic Church's Legion of Decency) had begun to "cut the film industry off from the realities of American experience" (Schlesinger 77), and a combination of government censorship and self-regulation threatened to suffocate creativity and social relevance in American films. Only Warner Bros. studio, with its production of *Black Legion* (1937) and *Confessions of a Nazi Spy* (1939), has received any significant recognition for making socially conscious films about Nazism prior to 1939 (Birdwell; Schwartzman). Despite the pressure against making "interventionist" films (which would remain in force until the bombing of Pearl

Harbor in 1941), fifty anti-Nazi films were released between 1939 and December 7, 1941 (De Grazia and Newman 60), and *Beast of Berlin* was one of the earliest. Judell's bent for exploitation-style sensationalism broke new ground, and the film's scandalous, rousing promotion made up for what was lost on the screen to censorship. In 1942, after the United States had officially joined the war, *Hitler, Beast of Berlin* was rereleased with even better box office returns and far less scandalous marketing, since war was now part of everyday American life. And instead of Hitler, another name now dominated *Beast of Berlin*'s marquees—Alan Ladd, Hollywood's newest star to rise from the B list—and memories of the film's role in shaping American prewar sentiment faded in its glow.

WORKS CITED

Akers, Stanley. *The Role of Rhetoric in American Cinema in the U.S. Interventionist Movement, 1936–1945.* Ann Arbor, Mich.: University Microfilms International, 1990.

Alpers, Benjamin. "History and Controversy in 1930s Hollywood: The Case of Borzage's Weimar Trilogy." Paper presented at the Film and History Conference, Cape Town, South Africa, 2002.

Bernstein, Matthew. *Controlling Hollywood: Censorship and Regulation in the Studio Era.* New Brunswick, N.J.: Rutgers UP, 1999.

Birdwell, Michael. *Celluloid Soldiers: Warner Bros.' Campaign against Nazism.* New York: New York UP, 1999.

Boehnel, William. "'Beasts of Berlin' Opens at Globe." *New York World-Telegram* 20 Nov. 1939: 39.

Creelman, Eileen. "Rev. of 'Beasts of Berlin.'" *New York Sun* 20 Nov. 1939: 42.

Crowther, Bosley. "Rev. of 'Beasts of Berlin.'" *New York Times* 20 Nov. 1939: 15.

De Grazia, Edward, and Roger Newman. *Banned Films: Movies, Censors and the First Amendment.* New York: Bowker, 1982.

Dixon, Wheeler. *Producers Releasing Corporation: A Comprehensive Filmography and History.* Jefferson, N.C.: McFarland, 1986.

Fernett, Gene. *Hollywood's Poverty Row.* Satellite Beach, Fla.: Coral Reef Publications, 1973.

Hitler, Beast of Berlin. Press kit. Hollywood: Producers Distributing Corporation, 1939. Author's collection.

Koppes, Clayton, and Gregory Black. *Hollywood Goes to War.* New York: Free Press, 1987.

Morrison, Hobe. "Rev. of 'Beasts of Berlin.'" *Variety* 22 Nov. 1939: 16.

Ross, Steven J. "Confessions of a Nazi Spy: Warner Bros., Anti-Fascism, and the Politicization of Hollywood." *Warner's War: Politics, Pop Culture, and Propaganda in War Time Hollywood.* Ed. Martin Kaplin and Johanna Blakley. Los Angeles: Norman Lear Center, 2004. 48–59.

Rostron, Allen. "'No War, No Hate, No Propaganda': Promoting Films about European War and Fascism during the Period of American Isolationism." *Journal of Popular Film and Television* 30.3 (2002): 85–96.

Schlesinger, Arthur, Jr. "When the Movies Really Counted." *Show* Apr. 1963: 77.

Schwartzman, Roy. "Hollywood's Early Cinematic Responses to Nazism." *Review of Communication* 2.4 (2002): 373–77.

Shane, Russell. *An Analysis of Motion Pictures about War Released by the American Film Industry, 1930–1970.* New York: Arno, 1976.

Thirer, Irene. "'Beasts of Berlin' Anti-Nazi Film on View at the Globe." *New York Post* 20 Nov. 1939.

WHY WE FIGHT AND PROJECTIONS OF AMERICA

Frank Capra, Robert Riskin, and the Making of World War II Propaganda

In an overview of America's then-recent documentary tradition, Robert and Nancy Katz observed in 1948 that the welter of outstanding World War II documentaries had only a limited impact on the genre in the United States due to their restricted viewing at home. They reserved special praise, however, for the *Why We Fight* series directed by Frank Capra and for a series of films commissioned and organized by Robert Riskin for the Overseas Branch of the Office of War Information (OWI)—a series referred to here as *Projections of America*.[1] According to the Katzes, "Frank Capra's series set a successful pattern for the hard-hitting newsreel type of political education film, explaining the causes of the war, the issues at stake, and helping the GI to know and appreciate his allies." They also assert that "the Overseas Branch of the OWI, under the leadership of Robert Riskin and his group of documentary writers and producers, executed a number of films that are still outstanding in their field" (426–27).

The Katzes' appreciation of these two series, and of the talents of Capra and Riskin in particular, was part of an argument for a distinctive gap between the kind of work emerging from the United States before and after the war compared with the quality and sophistication of documentaries in other national film cultures. But the real significance of the Katzes' assessment is that their article was virtually the last time Capra's and Riskin's films were mentioned in the same breath. Nearly a decade after the Katzes' study, Douglas Gallez asserted that the Korean War had failed to produce anything like the quality of documentary filmmaking that had emanated out of World War II. The reason, thought Gallez, was that Korea was a limited war and therefore did not pose an all-encompassing global threat to humankind; nor was it able to galvanize the righteousness of the cause overlaid by the ruthlessness of the enemy be-

Museum of Modern Art/Film Stills Archive

Robert Riskin and Frank Capra—two visions of
America.

ing opposed. Hence, Korea could not provide anything as melodramatic as,
for example, Capra's series: "Much of the content of *Why We Fight* hits us with
great impact even today," opined Gallez (133). In contrasting this collection
with the work of John Ford and John Huston, he concluded that themes of
humanism, the incalculable cost of war, and the need to be restrained and
respectful of defeated peoples were motives endemic and necessary for the
pattern of future wartime documentaries. By this argument, *The Battle of Midway, Memphis Belle,* and the seven *Why We Fight* films had already defined the
documentary motifs of World War II film.

Riskin's series was absent from Gallez's account, and the pattern became a
familiar one. In the sixty years since the end of the war, *Why We Fight* has risen
to become an exemplary stalwart of not just the World War II documentary
tradition but of all propaganda filmmaking. In contrast, with the notable exception of his film about conductor Arturo Toscanini (1943) and *Autobiography of*

a Jeep (1944), Riskin's *Projections of America* was seen by only a select few of the general public. The first question to ask is why this was so. Are we to assume that Capra's series was simply better than Riskin's? Were there issues over the permission and distribution of the material in each series? Was Capra's name a bigger and better draw than Riskin's, leading companies to believe that there was a market for *Why We Fight* beyond the war that could not be reached by *Projections of America*? There is evidence to answer all these questions.

At least some of the reasons for Capra's ubiquitous popularity and Riskin's relative anonymity had to do with the types of films the two made and commissioned, as well as the concerns they had about aesthetic and ideological conceptions. But the reception they each enjoyed also had to do with their respective outlooks on film. Riskin's early wartime experiences in London, his interest in New Deal projects and the artists working for the various administrations, as well as his humanist, egalitarian instincts toward repressed or disadvantaged people made him believe that film could improve and uplift society. He asserted quite vigorously at the close of the war that the German people could be rehabilitated in part by a diet of good feature films allied to documentaries extolling the virtues of American life ("Riskin"). And he was never afraid to assert the view that film and politics had always been closely related. He commented: "Hollywood has been in the political field ever since they made the first motion picture. Every picture that has to do or concerns itself with the interests of the people whether it's social, or whether it's an economic, or whether it's a religious subject is definitely in the field of public opinion" ("ABC's Town Meeting").

Capra sought impact too, but his attention was drawn to the simple but challenging idea of rebuttal: a rebuttal of all things totalitarian. He found his answer by cloning the master-race histrionics and affirming a religious devotion to freedom through one overarching principle. "I needed one basic idea, an idea that would spread like prairie fire, an idea from which *all* ideas flowed. I thought of the Bible. There was one sentence in it that always gave me goose pimples: 'Ye shall know the truth, and the truth shall make you free'" (330). Riskin saw his films as an extension of American liberty and freedom conveyed to a changing world in calm and measured tones. Capra, in contrast, beat a drum for the Allies against the obdurate fanaticism of the enemy. In their two approaches lay different but equally enduring aims: Riskin's vision was to contribute to the rich and voluble American documentary tradition, while Capra's was to make propaganda accessible and pertinent to the masses in a time of crisis and conflict. Both achieved spectacular results, but the real legacy and approbation have been somewhat misplaced.

Main title of *Why We Fight,* Episode Seven.

WAR AND MEMORY

What is the relationship between politics and propaganda? Indeed, what is the nature of the relationship between warfare and the modern aesthetic experience, between art and perception? How has a cinematic representation of war contributed to popular consciousness about the horrors and sacrifices of conflict? These are some of the questions posed by David H. Culbert and John Whiteclay Chambers in *World War II Film and History.* They suggest that the public memory of war in the twentieth century was conceived not out of a real or remembered past but from a manufactured one in which documentaries and fictions shaped popular recollection. Every film explores the relationship between art and society, they explain, between the culture where they were produced and the culture where the films are seen. They argue: "The unifying theme is that the visual representation of past wars is itself a cultural construction. To an increasing degree, memory of wars won and lost, like other public memories, is a social construct" (10).

The themes outlined by Culbert and Chambers are useful starting points in trying to understand both the concept and the ideology behind *Why We Fight* and *Projections of America*. Capra and Riskin understood the power of cinematic construction, and both had collaborated on fables that had repositioned American attitudes toward society and democracy during the Great Depression (1929–1941). Ensconced within a worldwide conflict, they were now charged with the task of shaping public consciousness about war, but each took his own path toward the building of memory, tradition, and ideology.

Bernard Dick in *The Star-Spangled Screen* provides an important clue to Capra's outlook. Dick recounts the day he saw *Prelude to War* (1943), the first of the *Why We Fight* films, in a Saturday double bill at his local movie theater. Its aim was to provide factual information of events leading up to the war. The implication, says Dick, was that such information had not been imparted before, at least in this context. Rather like an academic lecture, here was a summary of events set in the context of post–World War I history. "Capra applied methods of film to the lecture hall, by lumping Italian Fascism, German Nazism, and Japanese imperialism into one collective enemy. The Audience becomes the class called to attention by teacher Walter Huston who begs the question, 'Why are we fighting?'" (4).

In Dick's assessment, what was most interesting about the film was the way a variety of techniques that had characterized Capra's fictional films—montage, superimposition, and newsreel footage—were all brought forth in the documentary context. History took on a well-defined narrative that encompassed a strong Christian ethos and was, he states, plainly interpretative. Suddenly, his understanding of what had been the limits of World War II up to that point differed from the claims being made in the film. "A date bears only a synecdochal relationship to an event, but is not the event. Chronology also was only sequence, not configuration," Dick suggests. He remembers being transfixed by the idea that 18 September 1931 was the real start of World War II, according to Capra's film. This was the day that Japanese troops invaded Manchuria and thus, according to *Prelude to War*, was the real initiation of the world's descent into global strife (Dick 6–7).

Dick's personal account offers the prospect of a unified spirit among people who were naïve about documentary propaganda, insinuating a naïveté to the point that the central tenet of the genre was not fully grasped: that it was produced on behalf of, and with the intention of promoting, the state. This basic philosophy was intrinsic to *Why We Fight* and, in truth, equally so to *Projections of America*. But herein also lies a distinction between the wartime oeuvre of the two filmmakers. Robert Riskin never felt that his films needed, and his writers and directors did not engage in, anything that explicitly affirmed the principles of the state or the bankrupt corruptibility of ideas on the other side. Riskin's history lesson, such as it was, only reaffirmed the status of the United States as a nation of immigrants unified by a vitality and belief in the country they had created. *Projections* films such as *Cowboy* (1943) and *People to People* (1944) were, by World War II standards, strangely restrained about victory and defeat, about the awakening from a "long night" (Dick 7). The series strove to be, instead, a quiet affirmation of life in America, of accomplishment, and, indeed, of social attainment and cultural appreciation. The films had a religious dimension that was broadly Christian in tone, rather like *Why We Fight*. Films such as *The Town* (1944) and *Swedes in America* (1943) observed a secular devotion to faith, hope, and charity but also took pains to spotlight communities, ethnic enclaves, and social and even class empathies, all working toward the cause of reaffirming democracy and freedom, but not proclaiming it from the rooftops. In the latter film, narrator Ingrid Bergman walks graciously around the American Swedish Historical Museum in Philadelphia, talking in measured tones of her immigrant people's great contribution to the history of America.

The aim of these basic comparisons, practical as well as ideological, is not to provide a strict reevaluation of *Why We Fight* or to promote applause for *Projections of America* over and above its more famous contemporary. In a way, the interest here is in thinking through the approaches taken by each series and to ask why two filmmakers so in tune with each other's cinematic sensibilities would produce such very different cinematic portraits. In addition, the analysis asserts that *Projections* deserved, and continues to deserve, a more honored place than it now occupies in America's documentary heritage.

There are practical factors to consider when explaining the differences between the two collections. It should be noted that one major dissimilarity involved the management of the series. Riskin had far less hands-on involvement with *Projections*. He was the overseer, the orchestrator of the project rather than the director or, conceptually, the dominant author. Capra was far more of a controlling force; when it comes to *Why We Fight,* it seems apt to describe him as director, producer, and—often—editor of the final cut. But it should also be remembered that Capra's 834th Signal Corps, rather like the Overseas Bureau of the OWI, was a team that included many other prominent filmmakers and producers. The 834th did in fact engage in a number of other projects made with Capra's approval but not directly overseen by him; *Know Your Enemy: Germany* (1945) and *The Negro Soldier* (1944) are good examples.[2] Nevertheless, Capra did not exactly recruit these people himself. In contrast, the personnel that Riskin engaged reflected his personal philosophy about filmmaking as

University of Southern California

Robert Riskin, spokesman for American values.

well as his attitudes toward the world conflict. Staff members of the Overseas Branch were stylish, attentive filmmakers—people with wit, imagination, and social and cultural concerns. With the likes of Alexander Hammid, Willard Van Dyke, and Philip Dunne, Riskin's filmmaking horizons appeared broader and more diverse than Capra's. It should also be conceded that Capra worked from within the military—rather than a civilian agency—and so had additional restrictions placed on him. *Why We Fight* received a clear mandate from General George C. Marshall that Capra was, to a certain extent, obliged to follow. Therefore, to suggest that these films were the singular visions of Capra or Riskin is not accurate. Still, even allowing for such constraints on their work routines, there are important comments to be made about the films, their ideological outlook, and their legacies.

PROPAGANDA VERSUS DOCUMENTARY

Technically, conceptually, and structurally, *Why We Fight* is very different from *Projections of America*. As Charles Maland indicates, apart from some footage shot by Robert Flaherty for *War Comes to America* and some specially composed Disney animation, the Capra films are compilations derived from enemy battle footage or prewar documentaries such as Leni Riefenstahl's notorious *Triumph of the Will* (1935) (123). The example of Riefenstahl does much to demonstrate the attitudes of both Capra and Riskin when it came to the subject matter. Capra was startled by the power of her films, but to the point of having an almost revelatory exposure to documentary as propaganda. "Satan couldn't have devised a more blood-chilling super-spectacle," he shares in his autobiography, barely able to believe that a film documenting the ascendancy of the Nazi Party could have such a profound impact (328). So dumbstruck was he by the force of Riefenstahl's imagery that Capra felt compelled to resist it by using it. Thomas Doherty describes the director as "compulsively scaveng[ing] *Triumph of the Will*. Riefenstahl's Nazis are not denied their power, only their affirming mythos," he asserts, as though Capra could do no more than invert the mastery of the image in order to master it for his own means (74). But master it he did, and such were the timing and touch of Capra's expropriation of footage from *Triumph of the Will* that he created caricature and buffoonery where they appeared impossible to exist. In the end, "Riefenstahl's dynamic forces became Capra's deluded automatons" (Doherty 407).

Riskin, meanwhile, staked his claim on a keen awareness of and admiration for documentary that had been instilled in him since arriving in Hollywood in the early 1930s. His choice of people at the Overseas Bureau was more or less a conscious wish list of filmmakers whose work he had applauded over the previous decade. As a consequence, although *Projections* did include some archival footage (*Autobiography of a Jeep* is a good example of a compilation film taken from other sources), the series was filled with new, original film shot largely on location. Josef von Sternberg's short *The Town*, Helen Grayson's film *The Cummington Story* (1945), and the pictorials of New York and Chicago (both 1943) all featured fresh footage shot at the source. The result of these opposing techniques was clear to see: Capra's triumph in *Why We Fight* was to undermine Nazi iconography by using it against the enemy; Riskin's achievement in *Projections* was to extend the scope and tradition of the American documentary by going back to the roots of the genre and its love affair with ordinary life.

In terms of the composition of both series, narration was clearly very important to *Why We Fight,* as was music. Commentaries by Walter Huston, Lloyd

U.S. Signal Corps

Another "big parade," this time with motor vehicles, from *Autobiography of a Jeep*.

Nolan, and John Litel, as well as the musical scores of Dmitri Tiomkin, Alfred Newman, and Meredith Willson, added dramatic effect and depth to the images, an indelible legacy in this field of filmmaking (Nichols 49). *Projections* also used music and narration, but both functions became embedded elements in the narrative of Riskin's series, not just overlaid accompaniments for effect. Riskin's narration was not so much directed—as teacher or instructor—as it was incorporated into the cinematic fabric. The narration was not just authoritative but attributable to the story, not just an implicit frame of reference but rather an explicit inducement to share in the values and ideals on offer. In *Swedes in America*, for example, Ingrid Bergman is both the messenger and the message; her personal pilgrimage to sites of Swedish cultural and historic interest is a counterpoint to the collective example of wider immigrant pride and heritage. In *Toscanini*, Riskin conceives of the maestro's very presence in America, reaffirmed in the narration and through pieces such as Verdi's *La forza del destino* and the conductor's own *Hymn of the Nations*—notably featuring work by Beethoven, an important gesture in itself—as a call to arms for the world to understand that artistic freedom in the United States goes hand in hand with other basic human and civil rights. "When the night of fascism darkened most of Europe," Burgess Meredith informs in the commentary, "Toscanini brought his music and his democratic faith to the new world."

WAR AIMS AND SMALL-TOWN VALUES

Only in the seventh and final *Why We Fight* episode, *War Comes to America* (1945), do the influence and images that Capra and Riskin employ come together in anything like a complementary way. The film was shot partly in California, but more importantly in its evocation of the fundamentals of American life, it spliced together footage that displayed the talents of New Deal filmmakers Pare Lorentz and Willard Van Dyke. But if the crossover in style and pastoral domesticity of America seemed familiar with this propaganda effort, it was because these filmmakers were the very people who were actually working on the *Projections* series for Riskin. Capra's seventh *Why We Fight* episode (produced by him but directed by Anatole Litvak) goes on to extol Americans as hardworking but fun loving, committed to their communities and disciples of sport, leisure, and the outdoor life in an Edenic paean to the richness and vibrancy of American society. The tone was as close in aestheticism and meaning as Capra's films ever came to Riskin's.

The social vision of *War Comes to America* is therefore inherent, translated through symbols and values, just as it was in many of the *Projections* films. But social causation was much more of a question for Riskin. Assimilation in particular, the melting pot ideal, ethnic and racial integration, urban and rural distinctions, and the value of governmental intervention and direction as a means of social and cultural advancement are not so much implied as heavily weighted investigations in many of Riskin's films. Hans Borchers emphasizes the way many of these ideals came to fruition within the small-town locale: "Unquestionably, the myth of the small town was seen by the OWI as an important chapter; *Steel Town* and *The Cummington Story* exploit this myth in more or less subtle ways" (174). Although the latter film offers an agenda couched within a rural idyll, Borchers underlines the mythology at work in Willard Van Dyke's account of Youngstown, Ohio. In *Steel Town* (1945), the title place is not really a "small town" in the agrarian mold but a bustling industrial center. Nevertheless, immigrant integration is represented through the factory workers from different backgrounds; religious observance and tolerance are displayed in scenes of Christmas celebrations, and cultural attainment is presented via the town's orchestra. As Borchers indicates, *Steel Town* involves no literal personification of the small town, but "the values conveyed by the film are central to the myth" (171).

U.S. Signal Corps

America's children: citizenship as a journey in *War Comes to America*.

Both films preach communal tolerance and individual identity, but *The Cummington Story* goes further in examining the root-and-branch democratic ideals extending into such communities. The film's rendition of a New England town meeting not only offers foreign audiences a glimpse of participatory politics, but it also casts a spotlight on a tradition of public involvement in the democratic process stretching back to the beginnings of Anglo-American settlement. Indeed, the political content of the whole *Projections of America* series speaks to a much more forceful and personal agenda at work in Riskin's mind than was necessitated by *Why We Fight*, but aided also by Capra's conservative instincts. Each series was catering to a different audience, of course—Capra's principally a military one, Riskin's initially a foreign civilian populace—but in taking on subjects like the Tennessee Valley Authority, immigration in midwestern America, and the construction of the United Nations organization, *Projections* laid down a marker for liberal change and social responsibility that directly flowed out of the New Deal and into the postwar world. Indeed, Riskin could be seen as documenting a social and cultural optimism that would, in Henry Luce's telling phrase, define an American century.

Riskin's films clearly adhered to John Grierson's idea of documentary as the "creative treatment of actuality" (Hardy 13). For him, documentary narrative meant creating scenes and scenarios that followed a linear progression of ideas and discovery. One empathized with the people in *Projections* films because their story was symbolically cast as a meta-narrative for the story of the nation. Once this premise had been accepted, propaganda no longer needed to be assertive and demanding of the audience, only identifiable and receptive. Riskin's "eaves-dropping method" of filming, as he called it, was a marvelous evocation of this approach (Crowther 3). It was concerned with national character, with communal hopes, beliefs, and values testified to by the people themselves in a lucid and sober style. As critic Bosley Crowther wrote at the time: "Significant in all this product is the simple and unpretentious way in which the character of America and Americans is displayed" (3). Indeed, one may suggest that Riskin never actually entered the debate that was subsequently characterized by Michel Foucault as the public battle for the memory of World War II ("Interview with Foucault"). With a few notable exceptions, Riskin's films consciously disengage from situating the most profound iconographic images within the textual space, preferring instead to covertly ground their narratives in a dialogic counterreading of fascism and imperialism. In other words, the battle is not simply America repelling a totalitarian menace with democracy and freedom—which is certainly asserted in a number of the films—rather, it is striving all the time to come to terms with the ideals it has set for itself, such as assimilation, libertarianism, and individualism. Linked to these beliefs is a broadly Christian message of love thy neighbor, be true unto thyself, and stand by fundamental principles. In *The Town, The Story of the TVA, Swedes in America,* and the pictorials of New York and Chicago, Riskin places the city, the small town, and the people in these narratives in a familiar American context: they are all in the process of becoming. America, asserts Riskin in these films, has not *arrived* at some political, social, or even religious Shangri-La—a nod to his and Capra's account of the mythic city in *Lost Horizon* (1937)—and that is the most potent argument against Nazism. Instead, the nation is forever striving to achieve the next state of being for its citizens: America is an unending journey, states *Projections,* and that is the temperate but insistent message of all the films in the series. The promises of Hitler, Stalin, and Hirohito, therefore, remain fabrications, ideological constructs that hold a haven of state benevolence over the loyal citizenry but whose rhetoric always engenders the need for action, the striving for conquest. In other words, in their own brilliant ways, Capra and Riskin depict two different visions of the Axis's passion for lebensraum. In Capra's version, their ideology is conceived of as ridiculous and nebulous, constructed through the lens of Riefenstahl's carefully positioned camera and helped by her masterful editing. Riskin's idea is to contrast lebensraum with American exceptionalism and visualize the United States as a gleaming city on a hill.

TWO LASTING LEGACIES

These two philosophies—Capra's explicit rejection of tyranny and Riskin's more subtle affirmation of the American way of life—both of which were wound into the fabric of the films they were overseeing, say something about the kind of filmmakers Capra and Riskin were and had become. In 1941 they made one of their most profound, striking, and ambitious social statements under the auspices of their own production company. The film was *Meet John Doe,* a fable considering the possibilities of fascist takeover in America. More important, it was the last film they ever made together, and *Why We Fight* and *Projections of America* are small demonstrations of why the two men's working relationship ended the year World War II began for America. A rather harsh comparative reading of their careers from this point on would suggest that Riskin was the one who strove for meaning and depth in his work as he became concerned about postwar American society and began to reflect on its darker, ambiguous underpinnings; he wrote dialogue for *The Strange Love of Martha Ivers* (1946), was writer and producer for *Magic Town* (1947), and served as writer on *Mr. 880* (1950). Capra, in contrast, not only stopped striving but actually set about putting his social vision into reverse by reclaiming a nostalgic bygone era for America as well as for his own career with *It's a Wonderful Life* (1946) and re-makes in the form of *Riding High* (1949, previously *Broadway Bill* [1934]) and *A Pocketful of Miracles* (1961, previously *Lady for a Day* [1933]). Yet this assessment may be a little too harsh. Capra did make an intriguing postwar film about developments in American politics, *State of the Union* (1948), which was argu-ably a more pointed and revelatory exposé of political culture than the more celebrated *Mr. Smith Goes to Washington* (1939). And Riskin, in contrast to the rich pickings noted above, harked back to light and airy screwball comedy in the decidedly underwhelming *Half Angel* (1950).

Nevertheless, beyond fictional screenplays, Riskin's immediate postwar concerns were more politically and socially ambitious. His work for the OWI had given him an even greater predisposition toward progress and activism in the film industry once hostilities ceased. At the close of the war he directed his attention toward government and Hollywood in a bid to establish a documen-tary film unit that would continue his work at the OWI. He was disillusioned and dismayed once the investigations of the House Un-American Activities

Committee beckoned in 1947, and he felt that the industry was losing creativity and failing to fashion stories about people and events in the corporate, financially constrained postwar atmosphere. Riskin championed independent producers in the classic mold, such as David O. Selznick, who could maintain the levels of dynamism and originality that had so defined prewar output. "The independents have been around a long time," he said. "They [are the ones] who built up this industry" (Scott 215).

It was true that Capra had similar concerns, but *Why We Fight* seemed to bring out in him an omniscient fear about where too much propaganda might lead. He did not seek to embrace the power of his wartime filmmaking so much as to reject it out of hand. Capra's reflective mood at the end of the war was certainly engendered by the force of the propaganda he had witnessed, which seemed to oppose the American way of life so totally. But he also took on a renewed faith in religious principles, a faith that was reflected in the neo-orthodox movement emerging in America after the war. Some of this secular devotion had surfaced earlier in *Mr. Smith Goes to Washington* and *Meet John Doe*, whose heroes poignantly espouse biblical scripture. It also took a personally tragic form, derived from the loss of Capra's young son John in 1938. As a result, the director could not raise any great enthusiasm for the host of realistic, social inquiry films that emerged in the months after the war. He commented openly that he did not care for these social-reflections-on-the-war-type pictures and their impact on society, pointedly dismissing his friend William Wyler's immediate postwar success *The Best Years of Our Lives* (1946) as too grave and bleak. When asked what his first postwar film would be about, Capra said that he knew what it would not be; it would not be a film about the war (Capra 374–75).

Capra had, in fact, immersed himself so totally in fascist iconography that it almost infected his vision. He spent the next few years trying to drain it from his system but never really succeeded. *Why We Fight* was a masterpiece of sorts and the culmination of years of storytelling, political imagery, and cinematic technique honed into one striking articulation of the dangers of master-race ideology. But somewhere along the line, Capra realized that there was nothing else he could say on the subject.[3] Riskin, it could be argued, was inspired and galvanized into action by his wartime filmmaking and was only just getting started on another phase of his career when creative and financial disputes—and then illness—intervened. Without these roadblocks, there is evidence that his writing and producing would have taken many different and creative turns. Indeed, his work in World War II almost confirmed a state of mind that he sometimes intimated during the conflict—that he had worked with Capra for the last time, and their paths had begun to diverge.

A year after the end of the war, Philip Dunne, who had been Riskin's chief of production at the Overseas Bureau, wrote a piece urging Hollywood to demonstrate more appreciation for documentary filmmakers, the work they were doing, and the contributions they had made during the war. Dunne praised what he called the factual film of World War II and went on to cite *Why We Fight*, claiming that "the Capra films are classics of their kind" (167). But for Dunne, the factual film was not made in the same vein or with the same predispositions as the documentary. For him, documentary conveyed ideas and philosophy; it could be factual as well as fantasy, inventive and even quirky. Moreover, he saw it as having traditions and a lineage that recent factual films, made for the emotional mood of the times, might be unable to sustain. "The true documentary," wrote Dunne, "is usually limited in pictorial scope, though the idea it espouses may be as large as democracy itself. It strives for uniformity in quality and mood and, like the entertainment film, achieves it by shooting original material to express its central idea" (168).

In other words, for Dunne, the documentaries of World War II were part and parcel of an era that constituted another chapter in the American tradition of the genre. And he had no doubt that the tradition had been ably served. "I learned about documentaries the hard way," he said, "in the process of directing the production activities of Robert Riskin's [Overseas Bureau]. My associates and teachers were all veterans of the American documentary movement, such as Willard van Dyke, Irving Lerner, Sidney Meyers and Roger Barlow. I should guess that most of these names are unknown to a majority of Hollywood picturemakers. They will continue to be unknown as long as some in Hollywood persist in looking on documentary as a poor relation of 'The Industry'" (166). Dunne's argument was not so much a putdown of Capra's type of propaganda—and the use of the "Hollywood" director by some agencies—as it was an endorsement of Riskin's vision at OWI. *Projections* nurtured ideas and built an unprecedented team. The films followed no comprehensive pattern, but, as Dunne asserted, they encompassed a master theme that was the hardest one of all: to "make friends for America" (167). In the end, the Manichaean clarity of Capra's vision won out when it comes to remembering World War II, but the complexity of Riskin's vision deserves recognition and renewed appreciation.

NOTES

1. *Projections of America* was a common moniker for the series during the war but has since fallen out of usage—along with any recognition of the collection as a group. The films themselves are not even clustered under any unifying heading within the National

Archives or in any other special collections. The rehabilitation of the title in this chapter is therefore an important signal of Riskin's contribution and the significance of the films overall. For recognition of the collective heading, see Pryor and Callender.

2. See, for example, Charles Maland (121–22), who notes that William Wyler, John Huston, George Stevens, Stuart Heisler, and Robert Flaherty came to work for the 834th Signal Service Photograph Detachment.

3. McBride (497, 504–6) tells two interesting stories in this regard. One involves a 1982 interview with Bill Moyers, at which Capra turned up with pictures of the death camps from his personal files to justify that his propaganda role had been necessary, even though he was uncomfortable talking about it after the war. The second account comes from those close to Capra, principally Chet Sticht and Joe Walker, who noticed a major change in him after the war, when he became less happy-go-lucky, less carefree and enthusiastic. Capra turned to his faith and to a kind of neo-orthodoxy that was prevalent at the time and expressed in literary terms through the likes of Flannery O'Connor. For Capra, the close of the conflict put the events of the past few years into stark relief. It was as though his efforts to create the *Why We Fight* series had revealed to him how vicious and unrelenting man's inhumanity to man could be, how harsh and unrelenting the world had turned out to be.

WORKS CITED

"ABC's Town Meeting of the Air." Ts. of radio broadcast, 6 Sept. 1945. Riskin Papers. U of Southern California.

Borchers, Hans. "Myths Used for Propaganda: The Small Town in Office of War Information Films, 1944–45." *American Popular Culture at Home and Abroad*. Ed. Lewis H. Carlson and Kevin B. Vichcales. Kalamazoo, Mich.: New Issues Press, 1996. 161–76.

Callender, Harold. "Suspicious Senate Eye upon OWI Role Abroad." *New York Times* 25 Apr. 1943: E6.

Capra, Frank. *The Name above the Title*. New York: Macmillan, 1971.

Crowther, Bosley. "Speaking Up for America: The OWI Overseas Film Bureau Pictures US to the Peoples in Other Lands." *New York Times* 21 May 1944: X3.

Culbert, David H., and John Whiteclay Chambers. *World War II Film and History*. New York: Oxford UP, 1996.

Dick, Bernard. *The Star-Spangled Screen*. Lexington: UP of Kentucky, 1996.

Doherty, Thomas. *Projections of War: Hollywood, American Culture, and World War II*. New York: Columbia UP, 1993.

Dunne, Philip. "The Documentary and Hollywood." *Hollywood Quarterly* 1.2 (1946): 166–72.

Gallez, Douglas W. "Patterns in Wartime Documentaries." *Quarterly of Film Radio and Television* 10.2 (1955): 125–35.

Hardy, Forsyth, ed. *Grierson on Documentary*. New York: Praeger, 1971.

"Interview with Michel Foucault." *Cahiers du Cinéma* 13 (July–Aug. 1974): 251–52.

Katz, Robert, and Nancy Katz. "Documentary in Transition, Part 1: The United States." *Hollywood Quarterly* 3.4 (1948): 426–35.

Maland, Charles. *Frank Capra*. New York: Twayne, 1995.

McBride, Joseph. *Frank Capra: The Catastrophe of Success*. London: Routledge, 1992.

Nichols, Bill. *Introduction to Documentary*. Bloomington: Indiana UP, 2001.

Pryor, Thomas M. "Dispelling a Harmful Illusion." *New York Times* 7 Mar. 1943: X3.

"Riskin Emphasizes Documentaries' Value." *Exhibitor* 30 May 1945: 17. Riskin Papers, U of Southern California.

Scott, Ian. *In Capra's Shadow: The Life and Career of Screenwriter Robert Riskin*. Lexington: UP of Kentucky, 2006.

On Telling the Truth About War

World War II and Hollywood's Moral Fiction, 1945–1956

The Homecoming

There is a scene in *The Best Years of Our Lives,* the Academy Award–winning film of 1946, in which an army veteran of the Pacific war presents his teenage son with a souvenir—a samurai sword. The boy hesitates a moment and says flatly, "Thanks very much, Dad." The father then holds up a Japanese flag and tells his son that he took it off "a dead Jap soldier." He points out the various good-luck wishes inscribed on the flag. The son, looking at the object, instructs the father, "The Japanese attach a lot of importance to their family relationship." With no little irony the father replies, "Yah, entirely different from us." Suddenly, the boy becomes interested in the conversation, remembering that his father had been stationed in Hiroshima at the war's end. "Did you happen to notice the effects of radioactivity on the people who survived the blast?" he asks. "No," the combat veteran says, "I've seen nothing." The son takes the opportunity to tell his father that his high school physics teacher has been lecturing on the dangers of nuclear war. "I should have stayed home," the father states, "and found out what was really going on." Later, as the boy is about to leave, his mother reminds him not to forget the war trophies. He picks up the sword and the flag and, with a pointed lack of emotion, says, "Gee, thanks an awful lot for—these things." The scene predicts the problems the veteran will face in his return to normal life. Who can really understand his experience, since the home front he fought to save is out of joint with his perceptions?

The homecoming reflects Hollywood at its best; it demonstrates what the film industry was capable of producing—a truthful, moral statement about human behavior and the human condition. The film's ultimate happy ending and celebration of the American Dream, however, have led skeptics, unwilling to accept its deeper moral meaning, to judge the movie to be a well-crafted

U.S. Signal Corps

Those wounded in combat receive immediate care.

lie—a movie that did not have the courage of its convictions or the integrity to recognize the story's potential for tragedy. Other critics have seen the film as realistic and a projection of moral truth. Which is it?

There are essentially two opposing positions from which to view Hollywood's World War II and its consequences. The first school demands that war films represent the "real thing" in graphic detail—gaping wounds, traumatic amputations, disfigurement, and mental disorders. Those who take this view demand a grim documentary image of the experience of combat, even in fictional stories, and they hold that the film industry was at heart incapable of such truth. Their reasoning is that market interests and fear of government censure controlled the studios; as a result, producers, directors, and screenwriters were incapable of creating anything of lasting value. World War II, contrary to Hollywood history, was the story of tragedy, lies, and stupidity.

The second school contends that despite the economic, social, and political limitations and the compromises with reality, Hollywood was capable of picturing the truth about war and the American people. This school holds that myth is about truth—truth reflected in moral fiction. True art, as novelist and literary critic John Gardner asserts in his controversial essay *On Moral Fiction* (1978), must be life affirming. Moral works seek meaning and provide hope even in hopeless situations. "In the past few decades," he writes (in 1978), "we have shaken off, here in America, the childish naïveté and prudishness we see in . . . movies of the thirties and forties, in which killers say 'Jeez' and reporters say 'Gosh,' but in our pursuit of greater truth we have fallen to the persuasion that the cruelest, ugliest thing we can say is likely to be truest" (126). But "when a novel or poem, a film or play, achieves some noble end," he insists, "the critic should not hesitate to mention the fact and comment . . . on how the effect is achieved" (145). Thus, the question should be asked: was wartime and early postwar Hollywood capable of producing moral fiction?

TRAGEDY, LIES, AND STUPIDITY

Paul Fussell, in his *Wartime: Understanding and Behavior in the Second World War* (1989), has nothing good to say about the war on celluloid. In his reflection on how Hollywood sold the war to the American people, Fussell presents an uncompromising indictment of Hollywood as a base propaganda shill in the service of government and industry seeking to cover up the ugly nature of war in the interest of national morale or corporate profits. Influenced by his own bitter personal experience of combat (Fussell was a second lieutenant with the 410th Infantry Regiment, 103rd Infantry Division, in World War II and was wounded in eastern France in the spring of 1945), he castigates all attempts to find this war (even if it was a necessary or just war) and its aftermath as anything but the history of petty tyrannies, deadly blunders, gruesome death, mutilation, sinful deception, and tragedy. Certainly, there was heroism, he acknowledges, and a general adherence to duty, but cowardice, desertion, lying, and atrocity were also characteristic of the so-called Good War. In truth, Hollywood's Good War was no more realistic than MGM's *The Wizard of Oz* (1939) or Disney's *Pinocchio* (1940). According to Fussell, Hollywood consciously created a "fairy-tale world of un-complex heroism and romantic love, sustained by toupees, fake bosoms, and happy endings," in contradiction to what was really happening (*Wartime* 189). Fussell only admits that by 1945, "a Hollywood film could go so far as to suggest that wounded men scream and cry and the men losing limbs experience severe shock." The true story of the war (292,000 killed in battle, 671,000 wounded) subverted the false promise of a "silver lining" for veterans: "At home salvation waits, for their women will comfort them. In all these films, no matter how temporarily damaged the personnel, good triumphs, which means that the success story, Hollywood's dominant narrative model, was easily accommodated to the demands of wartime moral meaning" (*Wartime* 191).

Fussell finds no truth at all in "high-minded" prose and poetry, magazine advertisements, official and unofficial propaganda, or Hollywood war films. Truth lies only in the hard and bitter realities of war and the serviceman's vile language—the "fresh idiom" of the common soldier and his "little folk-poems" of profane verse (*Wartime* 257). This language of "verbal subversion and contempt" communicated the "conviction that optimistic publicity and euphemism had rendered their experience so falsely that it would never be readily communicable" (*Wartime* 268). His uncompromising disgust and loathing for his own experience has led film historian and Vietnam combat veteran Peter Rollins to conclude, "Fussell's bitterness reads like a plea from someone with PTSD (Post Traumatic Stress Disorder)" (106). Indeed, Fussell admits that he never got over his experience of combat: "The Second World War . . . has pursued me all my life and has helped determine my attitudes and my behavior. The point is, wars are not easily forgotten. They tend to linger socially and psychologically" ("Initial Shock"). Further, he asserts that only those who have actually been in combat, especially as infantry soldiers, can understand what really happens on a battlefield: "Some acquaintance with actual warfare ought to be a legal requirement for anyone writing about or giving his views about it" (Interview). In his view, only frontline soldiers have any right to comment on the hardships of war, which excludes Hollywood filmmakers and almost everyone else. If wartime combat films were, in Fussell's view, dishonest in their depiction of the experience of combat, Madison Avenue was utterly disgraceful in turning the tragedies of war and a soldier's longing for a normal life into an opportunity for a *Saturday Evening Post* advertisement.

MORALITY AND MATERIALISM

Advertisements, as well as Hollywood movies, reflected and exploited the desires of the returning American serviceman, whose simple hopes and aspirations included a wife, a home, and a good job: "Out here," says a tank commander in a Nash-Kelvinator Corporation magazine ad of January 1944: "I dream of peace—and coming home to showers and clean sheets and Christmas trees and apple pies and my job . . . and the girl I love." . . . "I'll turn to the job I want to do, when I'm done with this job that must be done . . . and not before" (quoted in Nelson 134). Consider too, the potential home of one "Pvt. Perkins" in this ad by the same company: "Tomorrow's Victory Home will have *better living built in!* A new age of electrical living is going to bring untold comforts and convenience.

U.S. Signal Corps

Fatigue: a reality of combat.

There will be a place for everything and everything in its place . . . the kind of home we want" (quoted in Nelson 121, emphasis in original). Private Perkins and the tank commander will, the company hopes, return to new Nash-Kelvinator automobiles, refrigerators, and ranges and "a new age of electrical living" in "tomorrow's Victory Home," all "compact, efficient, complete" (Nelson 121). "So acceptable were those (commercial) sentiments," Fussell writes, "that the same message could have been conveyed without variation by radio, popular song, or film, to be greeted by universal applause" (*Wartime* 194–95).

Madison Avenue was not necessarily without a conscience or motivated entirely by the desire to sell products or maintain brand loyalty. Nor were the American people uncritical of corporations' exploitation of the war to promote their products. The story is more nuanced than critics will allow. An appeal run by the Magazine Publishers of America in February 1943, for example, advocated participation in the Civilian Service Corps, a home-front organization committed to community solidarity. The illustration accompanying the message shows a dead marine on a beach. He is facedown in the sand with two holes in his helmet. One arm is draped over a machine gun. His right arm stretches out with his hand frozen into a claw. The script reads:

> What did *you* do today . . . for freedom?
> Today, at the front, he died . . . Today what did *you* do?
> Next time you see a list of the dead and wounded, ask yourself:
> "What have *I* done today for freedom?
> What can I do tomorrow that will *save* lives of men like this and help them win the war?" (Nelson 133)

True, readers did not see the dead marine's destroyed face, but the message was truthful as well as moral when it spoke to the wartime necessity of maintaining a commitment to victory and sacrifice. At the same time, of course, newspaper and magazine ads were overwhelmingly positive as well as self-serving, assuring Americans of both victory and prosperity.

American films echoed the consumerism proclaimed in advertisements. Audiences applauded because the aspirations of the Nash-Kelvinator ad's tank commander were their own values. They were hopeful and, yes, materialistic; they were innocently optimistic in many ways, but guarded in their expectations.

Hollywood and Madison Avenue, of course, did not create the American Dream, but they portrayed its possibilities. Movie audiences at home and men at war hoped for a normal life and the material comforts that went along with it. It was returning veterans, men who had lived through the Great Depression and survived the war, who populated the mass-produced houses of the postwar suburb Daly City, California, the archetypal middle-class environment. These were the kinds of people with middle-class aspirations (veterans, perhaps, like the character Tom Rath in *The Man in the Gray Flannel Suit*) satirized in 1962 by Malvina Reynolds, a socialist songwriter, in "Little Boxes":

> And they all play golf on the golf course
> and drink their martinis dry
> And they all have pretty children
> And the children go to school. . . .
> And the boys go into business
> And marry and raise a family
> In boxes made of ticky tacky
> And they all look just the same (quoted in Smith and Schimmel)

In this same spirit, historian Michael C. C. Adams declares that it is time to recognize the "moral smugness" and "posture of moral innocence" that characterized the Allied cause by 1945 (137). A disciple of what might be called the "Fussell school," he demands that Americans stop seeing World War II as a patriotic adventure sponsored by Coca-Cola with a score by Glenn Miller. In a chapter entitled "Mythmaking and the War," he argues that Hollywood, more than any other agency, metamorphosed this brutal experience into "the best war ever." The popular image of World War II reflects a collective need to find a useful past—a good war story that ignores the tragedy, lies, and stupidity at the heart of the real historical events. The movie industry, with the encouragement of the government in Washington, explained the meaning of the war to the American people, who "preferred the film version" over the real thing (11). It was not the Good War or "the best war ever," Adams reminds us. And it was certainly not "the best years of their lives" for the thousands of disfigured or traumatized combat veterans or, reflecting today's emphasis on the litany of class, race, and gender, for the Japanese Americans, African Americans, homosexuals, and women who faced discrimination during the conflict. Fussell and Adams react to attempts by politicians, journalists, historians, advertisers, novelists, poets, and Hollywood filmmakers to glorify the gruesome, vile business of war or transcribe the cacophony of the battlefield into a romantic symphony. They staunchly seek only to recover the "memory" of what really happened.

Critics miss the appeal of the popular arts when they take this unvarnished "realism" approach. They also fail to realize or refuse to recognize that there is more than one way to tell a story and more than one truth to tell. Their general dismissal of Hollywood's war ignores the role that motion pictures play in an optimistic, consumer society. Americans were aware of the artificiality of movies; filmgoers were not entirely innocent of the realities of war, but they were often enthralled by the stories and images of war on film.

Hollywood as a narrative center for America tapped into a deep human need for myth regarding the experience of 1941 to 1945. Despite its commercialism and easy patriotism, Hollywood provided the American people with a usable myth—"that imaginative ordering of experience which helps the group or person giving it assent to enjoy or endure life and to accept death" (*Oxford English Dictionary*). *Guadalcanal Diary* (1943), for example, does not picture a wounded marine the way Richard Tregaskis describes it in his book of the same name:

His face and shoulders lay in the center of a sheet of gore. Face wounds rained blood on the ground. A deep excavation through layers of tissue had been made in one shoulder. The other shoulder, too, was ripped by shrapnel. I could see now how he made the terrible noise. He was crying, sobbing, into a pool of blood. The blood distorted the sound of his wailings, as water would have done, into a bubbling sound. The sound still came in cycles, raising to peaks of loudness. One of the wounded man's hands moved in mechanical circles on the ground, keeping time with his cries. (159–60)

That the movie does not show the bloody details or describe the horrible sounds uttered by the man demonstrates that, in important respects, the film is not "real" in the sense urged by Fussell and Adams, but that does not mean that the film is not "true." Nor does it mean that Hollywood was dishonest, unmindful of moral obligations, or unrealistic about the nature of war. That Hollywood often failed to achieve its moral potential or that it failed to picture events through the lens of historical, social, or political realism, as Fussell and Adams demand, should not lead to a general condemnation.

Fussell insists on the experience of the combat infantryman as the only true experience of war. His contempt for Hollywood is an extension of his contempt for those who "fought" the Good War safe behind the front lines as staff officers, supply clerks, administrative assistants, USO entertainers, cooks, typists, artillerymen, and the like. He is certainly right in this regard: out of the millions who served, only a few actually saw real or sustained combat. Few men merited the coveted Combat Infantryman Badge (CIB) that the army awarded only to the real fighters—to those who actually faced the enemy in battle and endured the greatest danger and hardship. Despite this reality, others, civilians as well as veterans, have stories to tell about sacrifice and about the homecoming. These alternative stories (alternative histories?), though not as gruesome as Fussell and Adams would want, are no less true and honorable. They are not necessarily dishonest or infected with moral smugness, even if they are told without a sense of guilt or remorse about the experience of war. "Yet perhaps if we have learned through our difficult passage out of the Vietnam era," Philip D. Biedler writes, "that there is actually more than one kind of national experience of war, so perhaps we may now see that there is also more than one way to make a film that confronts the problems of return, especially to an America once flushed with victory and not without reason deeming itself the geopolitical hope of a new order of history"(6).

Consider, too, the limitations that politics imposed on filmmakers. Hortense Powdermaker notes that the moral vision of producers, directors, and writers was often based on the matrix provided by the motion picture industry's Production Code rather than on a firm foundation of moral values. According to the self-regulatory code created in 1933, a moral film was one that represented good taste over hard reality. In relation to war films, this meant no words that repeated the vile lexicon of the combat soldier (the names of God and Jesus, for example, could not be used in vain, and SOB could not be used at all, even though real soldiers went much further with their creative profanity). The code was less strict regarding violence, but combat wounds or death in battle could not be shown in explicit detail. With a wisdom that suffuses her study of Hollywood, Powdermaker observes that "a system of morals which includes truthfulness, understanding and a concept of freedom cannot be achieved by men whose ideas of morality are limited by a set of taboos imposed out of fear" (79). For its part, the Office of War Information (OWI) wanted reality in film, but without excessive brutality: "The mortal realities of war must be impressed vividly on every citizen. This does not mean dwelling at length on pain, anguish, and bloodshed. Nor does it mean sugar-coating the truth" (quoted in Roeder 21). Moviemakers did not have to be fearless to produce movies that reflected a basic honesty; rather, they needed a moral compass and enough integrity to see possibilities beyond their own immediate concerns for profit and the limitations of the Production Code or OWI guidelines. With such restrictions, how could filmmakers tell the truth?

MORAL FICTION

By 1945, the film industry assumed that the market for the genre had dried up, but it also produced three of its best war films at that time: *The Story of G.I. Joe* (released 13 July 1945), *A Walk in the Sun* (released 25 December 1945), and *Battleground* (1949). All are moral fictions in line with the aesthetic wisdom of Gardner and Powdermaker—a school of interpretation that accepts the idea that Hollywood can transcend its limitations and create moral and truthful films. Films like these, to apply Powdermaker's standard, "are not necessarily great pictures, but they are all exceptional to the general run of movies because in each case someone, with power enough to leave his stamp on the film, really cared for and respected mankind—someone who was truly moral" (79). The courage to make moral films such as these emerged as World War II entered its final phase. By 1944, Americans understood that the Axis powers would be defeated; nevertheless, the hard fighting continued, and the last steps to the end were deadly and measured. Those who lived through the "duration" were impatient with the progress of the war by this time, but they were also much more aware of the true meaning of events and much less inclined to accept larger-than-life melodramas as the image of that experience. World War II was the "last war that involved the passions of a people, and even that is a generalization we have learned did not hold true for many Americans," film critic Judith Crist conceded. "In our present cinematic sophistication (and perhaps it involves our psychological and social growth as well) most films of World War II will tell us relatively little about the long-ago conflict." Yet, Crist argues, "they can tell us, largely through indirection, a great deal about the American people of the time—and therein is recorded history" (7).

Skeptics also miss or refuse to accept the fact that some of those who made war films spoke from experience. Director William Wellman (*Wings* [1927], *Battleground,* and *The Story of G.I. Joe*) served in World War I in the Lafayette Escadrille, was shot down in 1918, and received the Croix de Guerre for valor. Richard Pirosh, who wrote the screenplay for *Battleground,* was a combat veteran of the Battle of the Bulge and later toured the battlefield to jog his memories. Additionally, he based the plot on his diary and his observations of the men he served with in 1944 (McAdams 114). For his achievement, he won the Oscar for best screenplay in 1949.

THE STORY OF G.I. JOE

The Story of G.I. Joe takes place in September 1943 during the march on Rome. It depicts urban warfare and the controversial bombing of the Monte Casino, the founding house of the Benedictine monks. Like *A Walk in the Sun,* the action is largely understated. The film tells the story of Company C of the 18th Infantry and is based on the reporting of Ernie Pyle (played by Burgess Meredith), the news writer who became famous for chronicling the tale of the common soldier. One sequence, based on the real death of Captain Henry Waskow of Belton, Texas (Langman and Borg 556), comments on the death of an infantry officer, Captain Bill Walker (Robert Mitchum). Critics praised Mitchum's "underplayed demonstration of exhaustion, disillusionment, and deep care for his men" (Dolan 56). His acting was a true and moral statement about combat and leadership As the scene is played out, soldiers come by to honor their deceased leader. One holds the dead man's hand; another tenderly touches his face. Fussell nevertheless judges that Pyle's reporting, like that of all other journalists, was "fueled [by] . . . misconceptions" and characterized by "gentle vagueness" about how men really die in battle. Movies, even good ones, lack a commitment to hard truth. Fussell demands more, unsatisfied unless the story of the death of GI Joe is told his way: "Where was his wound? How large was it? Was it a little hole, or was it a great red missing place? Was it perhaps in the crotch . . . ? Were his entrails extruded . . . ? How much blood was there? Was the captain's uniform bloody? Did the faithful soldier wash off his hands?" (*Wartime* 287–88). Such are the "probing" questions of a realist. Reviewers, nevertheless, have been nearly universal in their praise for the film's careful depiction of the experience of combat. *G.I. Joe* "avoids inflated rhetoric, grandstand heroics, and stereotyping that characterized most other World War II films" (Auster and Quart 7). For his part, James Agee, novelist, screenwriter, and film critic, thought it true enough and moral. The dead were not shown as they would have been in a real killing zone, but "with a slight shift of time and scene, men whose faces have become familiar (during the course of the film) simply aren't around any more. The fact is not commented on or in any way pointed; their absence merely created its gradual vacuum and realization in the pit of the stomach" (172). Agee understood that—at critical moments in the arts—understatement can be more persuasive and powerful than the blare of trumpets or the sight of blood and guts. He called it a "war poem." The scene may not be bloody, but "the sudden close-up . . . of a soldier's loaded back, coldly intricate with the life-and-death implements of his trade, as he marches away from his dead captain, is as complete, moving, satisfying, and enduring as the finest lines of poetry." Agee thought it as good as anything by Walt Whitman, the poetic memorialist of the American Civil War (173–74).

A WALK IN THE SUN

Based on the 1944 novella by Harry Brown, *A Walk in the Sun* is a "gritty tone poem" (Rotha 466) that spoke honestly to the audience about the nature of war. In September 1943, a Texas platoon lands on the shore at Salerno, Italy; the American GIs advance six miles inland and capture a German-held farmhouse. The platoon exists in a self-contained world, isolated from the rest of the landing force. The greater war is remote and over the horizon. The story is simple—no love interests, no complex relationships, and certainly no Hollywood heroics. The movie focuses narrowly on the intimate world of the combat infantryman. It is less a combat film and more a commentary on the infantryman's fears, anxieties, humor, inner thoughts, and dedication to getting the job done. The men talk to themselves and to one another about the futility of war, their loved ones, and the return home:

> PRIVATE FRIEDMAN (George Tyne): You ever think you'll live long enough to make corporal?
>
> PRIVATE RIVERA (Richard Conte): Baby, I just want to live long enough to make civilian.

The nervous breakdown of Sergeant Porter (Herbert Rudley) illustrates the psychological pressures of combat. Sergeant Tyne (Dana Andrews), who moves up to take Porter's place in command, is the model of a noncommissioned officer capable of leadership. Violence in the movie is understated. For example, during the approach to the beachhead, Lieutenant Rand (Robert Lowell) is hit in the face by a shell fragment as he looks out over the side of the landing craft through field glasses. Moviegoers do not see the wound, as they would in post-Vietnam films, but the scene is powerful nonetheless—half his face is blown away. Later, a Nazi fighter plane strafes the unit. One soldier is intent on going back to see what is happening on the beachhead, and his curiosity results in his death. The platoon stages an ambush and destroys a German armored car. The film ends with the successful attack on the farm building.

By the time *A Walk in the Sun* appeared in 1945, American audiences had a "widespread sense of the reality of combat." War "was a subject about which people (not just combat veterans) knew something about and felt deeply" (Rotha 466). The film communicated a "genuine feeling for its melting-pot infantry unit's fear and anxiety about fighting and dying" (Auster and Quart 7). This was no sugarcoated view of war.

Fussell admits that the book was "honorable," but for him, neither this book nor any other novel or film would ever convey the "real war" to those who had not experienced it, and there was no way of "persuading readers that the horrors have not been melodramatized" (290). Adams, too, concedes that this film is one of the "dissonant voices" of wartime Hollywood (14). Indeed, *A Walk in the Sun* provided "a high note of quality and maturity," observes film historian Clyde Jeavons, "to conclude Hollywood's contribution to the war effort" (140). Important to this discussion is that, for Fussell and Adams, this film and a few others were surprising aberrations in a four-year wartime history of cinematic whitewashing.

BATTLEGROUND

Battleground is also narrowly focused on the intimate experience of combat. It is the story of a company of the 101st Airborne at the Siege of Bastogne during the German winter offensive of 1944 (the Battle of the Bulge, 20–26 December). If *A Walk in the Sun* is about inner thoughts and dialogue and *The Story of G.I. Joe* is about comradeship, *Battleground* is about the imagery of battle, without the compulsion to describe the physical trauma in gruesome detail.

The movie depicts the experience of combat as a series of discrete encounters with both the enemy and other soldiers. The film does not build up the usual momentum of plot device "A" leading to plot device "B" and so on to the end. Each episode seems nearly self-contained, with an occasional overlapping reference to something that came before. The role of Denise (Denise Darcel) is

MGM

Battleground dramatizes the anxieties and exhaustion of combat infantrymen. Sgt. Kinnie (James Whitmore) is at far right.

illustrative of the film's approach. Early in the film, the men take shelter in her home. There is some flirtatious banter, especially from Pfc. Holly (Van Johnson), but nothing comes of it. Then the men move up to the front lines—such as they are—and Denise disappears from the film. No one speaks of her or refers to the time spent with her. Much later, during a lull in the action, Pfc. Holly races back to her house, obviously in pursuit of some kind of intimacy, only to find that a new guy, Jim Layton (Marshall Thompson), is already there enjoying a bottle of cognac.

Battleground does not indulge in pulp heroics. Only at the very end, as the weary troops march away from the battlefield, does the sound track provide the kind of swelling chords so common to war films. The one big combat scene is an accidental ambush of some German soldiers. The survivors are rounded up and taken away as prisoners, and nothing more is said. The American casualties, such as Johnny Rodriquez (Ricardo Montalban) and Abner Spudler (Jerome Courtland), are mourned briefly, but the emphasis is always on surviving and avoiding foolish risks. The film stresses character, and each man is given a distinctive touch, but in a very low-key fashion. Donald Jervess (John Hodiak), a journalist before the war, reads *Stars and Stripes* and compares what he reads to

MGM

Donald Jervess (right), played by John Hodiak, tries to stay warm in the foxhole he shares with another paratrooper in this scene from *Battleground.*

what he is experiencing. Kipp Kippton (Douglas Fowley) is more concerned about his false teeth. His comments are mostly gripes about army life. Ernest "Pop" Stazak (George Murphy), scheduled to rotate home as the battle begins, finds himself trapped at Bastogne along with everyone else. The men endure a variety of hardships, including winter in the Argonne forest, but in the end, they can march away from their battlefield proudly counting cadence.

It is unlikely that any real soldiers sang as they marched away from battle, but the film is making a comment about the men's relief at surviving and the pride in their achievement. It may be the one false note in the movie. Although the scene is certainly unhistorical, it is not dishonest. In any event, there is no suggestion that some great homecoming awaits them, but they have not been so traumatized, the film implies, that they will not be able to function as civilians and citizens.

The commitment to telling the truth about the war in *The Story of G.I. Joe, A Walk in the Sun,* and *Battleground* carried over to three films about the war's consequences: *Pride of the Marines* (1945), *The Best Years of Our Lives* (1946), and *The Man in the Gray Flannel Suit* (1956).

PRIDE OF THE MARINES

Pride of the Marines (based on a biography by Roger P. Butterfield titled *Al Schmid, Marine*) was released in August 1945. It tells the true story of a marine blinded by a Japanese grenade. The film opens with Al Schmid (John Garfield) living in a boardinghouse, where he falls in love with Loretta (Ann Todd). They hear a radio announcement of the Pearl Harbor attack, and Al joins the Marine Corps. The film's short battle scene (lasting about ten minutes) in which Schmid is wounded is so realistic that one commentator thought it could serve as a training film on the proper use of the .30-caliber machine gun. In reality, as well as in the film, Schmid is a machine gun loader with the 1st Marine Division at Guadalcanal (August 1942), where the men are holding out against incessant enemy attacks. After the gunner (Johnny Rivers—a Native American) is killed and a corporal (played by Dane Clark) is wounded, Schmid takes over firing the gun until he is severely injured in both eyes by hot metal fragments. Nevertheless, he continues to fire his pistol even though he can no longer see. (Schmid and his comrades may have killed as many as two hundred Japanese infantrymen during the night of continual attacks.)

The film implies that Schmid will regain at least partial vision (which was not the case in real life), and in one scene "men debate postwar prospects in an immaculate San Diego veteran's hospital," where they can be optimistic. Though wounded, their "military experience culminated in upward mobility—a societal expression of personal fulfillment," and "they expect their prewar fantasies to be realized" (Koppes and Black 308).

The film argues that it will take teamwork, optimism, and a patient woman—the standard ingredients of a happy ending—to reintegrate Al into society. Curiously—and awkwardly for the Fussell and Adams school of war stories—that is what actually happened to Schmid. Not surprisingly, real life was more complex than the movie depicted. After initial indications that he might regain some sight in his right eye, that prognosis proved wrong. Schmid adjusted to his blindness by relying on his wife and even kept up an elaborate masquerade that convinced many, long after the war was over, that he was not blind at all. Decorated for his bravery, he tried to play the role of national hero: "Like many other twentieth century soldiers, much of what Al knew about how he should behave as a soldier and a patriot, and then a hero, came from both oral traditions that the soldiers, beginning in basic training, hand down to one another, and war movies he had seen" (Gerber, "In Search" 6–7). The Marine Corps, always astute about public relations, encouraged hometown folks to watch *Pride of the Marines* as a recruiting event and then sponsored it at various Guadalcanal Day banquets across America (Caute 495). The message was simple: "We can make it work in peace as we did in war" (Dick 229). The movie is "sincere and realistic (notably in its handling of the climactic battle scene in which Schmid receives his wounds) and spoke with a liberal voice" about anti-Semitism, social class, and hopes for a better life (Jeavons 159). Warner Bros. was apparently worried at first about moviegoers' reception of its grim subject, because at least one lobby card showed Garfield, Todd, and Clark dancing down the street arm in arm as if in a musical, though another showed that the hero was blind.

John Garfield lived with the real-life hero of the film for a while in preparation for the role. In a periodic series in the *Saturday Evening Post* titled "The Role I Liked Best," Garfield said that the movie "told the story of the boy's struggle to adjust himself and work out a romance to a happy conclusion after returning from the war. . . . I found him the kind of kid we like to think of as the wholesome American type—brave, determined, resourceful, fun loving, but not without some of the faults that are American, too." Schmid thought that Butterfield's biography was more accurate than the film, but both told the true story of a common man thrown into uncommon circumstances—an American "Everyman" (Gerber, "In Search" 1). Thus, "the thing Al believes most strongly," Butterfield writes, "is that he is no different from any other young American in uniform. He expects no special credit or sympathy for what he did, and he feels no bitterness over his personal tough luck" (13).

Initially disgusted, angered, and fearful about his fate, Al Schmid survived the war and his brief moment of fame to lead a productive and, by all appearances, a relatively happy if unremarkable life until his death from cancer some forty years later.

THE BEST YEARS OF OUR LIVES

Of all the films released in the postwar era, certainly *The Best Years of Our Lives* is still the most famous and probably the most influential. The interlocking stories of three veterans who meet when they hitch a ride home to "Boone City"(obviously in the American heartland) concentrates on Al Stephenson (Fredric March), a banker who served as an army sergeant with the 25th "Tropical Lightening" Division in the Pacific; Fred Derry (Dana Andrews), a soda jerk who rose to captain as a bombardier in the Eighth Air Force in the war over Germany; and Homer Parrish (Harold Russell), who served in the navy and lost both hands in a fire. Stephenson has a wife and two children and his banking career to restart; Derry, after being an officer, does not wish to return to his menial prewar role; and Parrish is apprehensive over how he will cope with his traumatic disability.

Despite the surface tranquility of Stephenson's life, he must cope with a drinking problem. Derry must deal with his reckless and unfaithful wife, Marie (Virginia Mayo), and the unexpected developments when he falls in love with Stephenson's daughter, Peggy (Teresa Wright). Parrish must face the fear that he will be burdening his fiancée with his handicap, and he initially rejects any thought of marriage. The film slowly unravels these fears and concerns and leads to a reconciliation and a modest sense of hope that a better future awaits all three veterans, despite the trauma of their wartime experiences and the obstacles before them.

Stephenson, back at the bank, risks his career by advocating for "character loans" to veterans, even when they have little or no collateral. To counter the argument that the bank would be gambling with shareholder money by making such loans, Stephenson argues, successfully, that the risk is worth it because "we'll be gambling with the future of America." The film, in this regard, is an ode to the virtues of small-town capitalism, but Stephenson knows that the purpose of the bank is to make profits and that unsecured loans, even to salt-of-the-earth veterans, are a risky investment. In addition, his patient wife, Milly (Myrna Loy), convinces him to give up the drinking habit that he, and many others, brought home from the service. It is truly an uneasy peace.

Derry meets and falls in love with Stephenson's daughter, and the feeling is mutual. Derry is still married, however, although he is coming to realize that his marriage is an empty charade, so he acquiesces when Stephenson asks him to stop seeing Peggy. Derry finally breaks with his wife when he sees her with another man; then he loses his job and decides to leave town. As he waits for a flight, he visits an aircraft "graveyard" and sits in one of the abandoned B-17 Flying Fortresses, reliving his days as a captain flying raids over Germany. (In fact, director William Wyler used an actual site in Ontario, California, where the junked aircraft were stored.) By chance, a work crew salvaging metal from the discarded bombers comes along, and Derry lands a job converting swords into plowshares—the building of suburbia.

Parrish, after nearly losing the girl he loves because of his anxieties, comes to accept that his disability has not affected her feelings for him, and he decides that they should marry after all. At the wedding the three men meet again, and Derry, now free of his philandering floozy of a wife, can honestly court Stephenson's daughter. It is a happy ending for all three veterans—a model for the nation.

The government never "encouraged Hollywood to concoct happy endings or painless outcomes" (Roeder 90), but a movie like *The Best Years of Our Lives* could help "man understand himself and his complicated world, and thereby reducing his confusion and fear . . . could also be considered a moral matter" (Powdermaker 79). Agee argues that to judge a film by a standard that always insists on surface realism misses an opportunity to see its underlying meaning and purpose. Though he is clear about the problems in *The Best Years of Our Lives*—"the movie has plenty of faults, and the worst of them are painfully exasperating" (221)—he concludes that "it is easy, and true, to say that it suggests the limitations which will be inevitable in any Hollywood film, no matter how skilful and sincere. But it is also a great pleasure, and equally true, to say that it shows what can be done in the factory by people of adequate talent when they get . . . the chance" (226). The happy ending in *The Best Years of Our Lives* is a celebration of the American culture and a hopeful message about survival and recovery.

In an essay published in 1947 in *Partisan Review* entitled "The Anatomy of Falsehood," Robert Warshow contradicts Agee, stating that *The Best Years of Our Lives* is simply unrealistic about the realities of postwar American life. "The falsehood has many aspects," he observes, "but its chief and most general aspect is the denial of real politics, if politics means the existence of real incompatibilities of interest and real social problems not susceptible to individual solution" (128). Manny Farber, known for his acerbic film reviews, is harsher, condemning the film as "a horse-drawn truckload of liberal schmaltz," one of those "solemn goiters" that pretends to high "ART" (15). *Time* film critic Richard Schickel, writing about his memories of movies during the war, shares Farber's view, calling it "the last great wartime lie, a fantasia of good feelings . . . eerily out of touch with human reality" (270). Audie Murphy, the boy-hero of World War II turned movie actor, is especially scornful, calling the "part with the kid with no hands" not serious drama but "a kind of circus act" (quoted in Graham 146). (This response may have had less to do with the quality of the film than with Murphy's postwar struggle with combat flashbacks.)

As the film *accurately* suggests, the vast majority of veterans adjusted amazingly well to civilian life. These young men, and their wives, "threw themselves into civilian life with unanticipated success," historian William O'Neill notes. "The men went to school in astonishing numbers" and "the women supported them and bred prodigiously. Together they created a domestic environment of exceptional health and vigor and a unique if controversial social ethic" (6–7).

One postwar study of the World War II veteran came to this conclusion: "It is true that some men were physically ruined by the war and others bear scars which will never disappear. Others broke under the strain." Nevertheless, "there seems little reason for doubting the reabsorption of the vast majority of American soldiers into the normal patterns of American life" (Stouffer et al. 643). These were middle-class men who, in the words of Adams, were "dull, anti-intellectual, and obsessed with buying right and looking right" (152). Film scholar and biographer David Thomson notes, "No one should forget that *Best Years* spoke for 1946 with a directness that helps reveal film's eloquence as *a kind of history*"

(257, emphasis added). The vast majority of veterans felt no shame in the lives they were creating, nor did they exhibit "personal bitterness" about the recent experiences they had been forced to endure (Kennett 232). America at the end of World War II was not only victorious; it was the richest and most powerful country in the world. More than that, it was the richest and most powerful country in the history of the world. Americans may have been smug and materialistic, but they were also rightly proud of the achievements of the American military and American industry. The GI Bill, veterans' reward for service, offered opportunities only dreamed of by the majority of men before the war.

Harold Russell, for his part, had a difficult time conveying Homer's anger and humiliation because of his own rapid recovery, natural optimism, and patriotism, despite his initial anger and outrage (Gerber, "Heroes and Misfits" 567). Here was a unique backstory in Hollywood history. Russell really was a disabled veteran—a former paratrooper who had lost both hands when a demolition exercise went horribly wrong (one of sixty-four veterans who suffered such wounds in World War II). Russell, against the odds, recovered emotionally. Years later, he reflected on his survival and that of America as well: "I could give you a long lecture on what went wrong. However, the important thing is that the postwar years were a great period for our country, and you had a tremendous feeling just being alive, periods of adjustment are always difficult, but they are interesting. We had problems, sure, but they didn't dominate us; we face the same things now, and we despair" (quoted in O'Connor and Jackson 162).

The Best Years of Our Lives reflects a truly "realistic" national experience—a happy, middle-class ending. Al makes his peace with the Cornbelt Loan and Trust Company; Fred, now divorced from his narcissistic and unfaithful war bride, finds happiness in the arms of a devoted woman and fulfillment in a job building new housing developments. Homer, secured by his disability pension and the love of his girlfriend, is able to adjust to his condition. The protagonists of the film find—as millions of real veterans found—a certain peace and material success, even though they still have anxieties about the future. Powdermaker observes that Americans believe in the American Dream but are never quite "sure of the happy ending" (307). As Butch (Hoagy Carmichael), the owner of the bar where the veterans gather from time to time, says to Homer: "Give 'em time, kid; they'll catch on. You know your folks'll get used to you, and you'll get used to them. Then everything'll settle down nicely. Unless we have another war. Then none of us have to worry because we'll be blown to bits the first day. So cheer up, huh?"

The Best Years of Our Lives is an "American masterpiece" because it "came as near perfection as popular art contrives to be. . . . It showed Americans as they are, presented their problems as they themselves see them, and provided only such solutions—partial, temporary, personal—as they themselves would accept" (Jeavons 159).

THE MAN IN THE GRAY FLANNEL SUIT

The films discussed so far in this chapter all appeared within the first four years after the end of the war. Moving into the next decade—the 1950s—the depiction of veterans continues to reveal an obsession with the memories of their experiences, both combat and noncombat; anxieties about the future; and, importantly, the belief that reconciliation, along with peace and material success, can be found.

Sloan Wilson's best-selling novel *The Man in the Gray Flannel Suit* appeared in 1955; the film version, directed by Nunnally Johnson, opened in New York in April 1956 and was a popular success. Gregory Peck hoped the film would be another *Best Years of Our Lives*. The central figure, Tom Rath (Peck as a former paratrooper), survives both the European and Pacific wars, but at great personal cost. At one point Tom tells his wife, Betsy (Jennifer Jones), that he killed seventeen men, one of them a teenage German soldier he first attempted to strangle and then stabbed to death. More traumatically, Tom lives with the memory that he accidentally killed his best friend, Hank Mahoney, with a hand grenade while attacking a Japanese pillbox. The film provides flashbacks to both incidents, including Tom's unwillingness to accept his friend's death and his demand that the corpse receive medical attention. It is, however, a third set of memories that both provokes a crisis in Tom's life and finally leads to reconciliation with his war experiences. While stationed in Rome between the end of the European war and his transfer to the Pacific theater, Tom has an intense love affair with a young Italian woman. He then leaves for the Pacific and never hears from her again, and by 1955, he has only his memories of their relationship to balance his memories of combat.

In a plot twist, Tom accepts a new job with the United Broadcasting Corporation television network as an assistant to Ralph Hopkins (Fredric March), the dominating founder and president of the company. There, Tom discovers that an elevator operator in the UBC building is a former comrade and, even more surprisingly, is married to the cousin of the woman in Rome. He is told that he has fathered a child and is asked to make some small contribution to support mother and son. Tom, depicted as a "good man," feels compelled to reveal to his wife the story of his affair and the existence of the child. Naturally, his wife is devastated, but she soon comes around to both understanding and accepting the situation, especially after Tom reveals the extent of his combat

Museum of Modern Art/Film Stills Archive

Tom Rath's (Gregory Peck) wartime affair with a young Italian woman (Marisa Pavan) will complicate his adjustment to peacetime in *The Man in the Gray Flannel Suit*.

experiences, including his certainty that, after surviving the war in Europe, he would surely be killed in the Pacific.

As the film concludes, Tom and his wife arrange for a $100-a-month dependence allowance for the woman and child. The film ends with their driving off to suburbia—if not into the sunset, at least into the sunshine of a happier and more honest relationship. Tom prospers materially as well. Hopkins takes a liking to him, even though Tom tells his boss that he cannot and will not become a work-obsessed figure like Hopkins. Family comes first, he tells Hopkins, who accepts Tom's decision, especially in the light of his own dysfunctional private life. The film makes it clear that Tom has a hard time adjusting to civilian life, both emotionally and morally. He is addicted to martinis and cannot forget the war. But in the end, Tom gets over it. His generation stands in contrast to contemporary America and its "Culture of Trauma"—a preoccupation with post-traumatic stress disorder (Shepard 385–99) and the image of Vietnam veterans' combat experience (Shewring 65). Tom survives his experience and his nightmares. He is able, in the end, to find a mature happiness, just as most American veterans did. Like most other veterans, he welcomes the material comforts of Middle America and comes to terms with the agony of combat memories (Gladwell).

MacKinlay Kantor, in *Glory for Me,* the verse novel that was the initial basis for *The Best Years of Our Lives,* speaks for all these celluloid heroes about the American Dream—for Homer Parrish, Al Stephenson, Fred Derry, and, by extension, Al Schmid and Tom Rath—in a passage that describes the neighborhoods in which these veterans find happy endings—in their dreams:

> The street was lilac in its lengthened ease—
> Some maple trees, some elms, a vacant lot,
> And houses set above their sloping lawns . . .
> And boys rode bicycles in circles
> With auto traffic thin.
> An old man walked; he turned to talk
> With someone sitting on a porch.
> It was the sober, verdant kind of street
> Where God is middle-class. (29)

Hollywood's moral fiction was, in the words of John Gardner, "a game played against chaos and death"(6). The producers, screenwriters, directors, and actors created a certain kind of history—part myth and part reality, yet essentially true to the American experience of war.

Works Cited

Adams, Michael C. C. *The Best War Ever: America and World War II.* Baltimore: Johns Hopkins UP, 1994.

Agee, James. *Agee on Film: Reviews and Comments by James Agee.* Vol. 1. New York: Wideview/Perigee, 1983.

Auster, Albert, and Leonard Quart. *How the War Was Remembered: Hollywood and Vietnam.* Westport, Conn.: Praeger, 1988.

Battleground. Dir. William Wellman. Perf. Van Johnson, John Hodiak, Ricardo Montalban, George Murphy, Marshall Thompson. MGM, 1949.

The Best Years of Our Lives. Dir. William Wyler. Perf. Fredric March, Myrna Loy, Teresa Wright, Dana Andrews, Virginia Mayo, Cathy O'Donnell, Harold Russell, Gladys George, Steve Cochran, Hoagy Carmichael. RKO, 1946.

Biedler, Philip D. "Remembering the Best Years of Our Lives." *Virginia Quarterly Review* 72.4 (1996). <http://www.vqonline.org.printmedia.php/prmMediaID/742/>.

Brown, Harry. *A Walk in the Sun.* 1944. Philadelphia: Blakiston, 1945.

Butterfield, Roger P. *Al Schmid, Marine.* New York: Norton, 1944.

Caute, David. *The Great Fear: The Anti-Communist Purge under Truman and Eisenhower.* New York: Simon & Schuster, 1978.

Crist, Judith. "Introduction." *The Films of World War II: A Pictorial Treasury of Hollywood's*

War Years. Ed. Joe Morella, Edward Z. Epstein, and John Graggs. Secaucus N.J.: Citadel, 1973.

Dick, Bernard. *The Star-Spangled Screen: The American World War II Film.* Lexington: UP of Kentucky, 1985.

Dolan, Edward F. *Hollywood Goes to War.* New York: Smith, 1985.

Farber, Manny. *Negative Space: Manny Farber on the Movies.* New York: Praeger, 1971.

Fussell, Paul. "The Initial Shock: A Conversation with Paul Fussell." Host: Sheldon Hackney. Nov./Dec. 1996 (National Endowment for the Humanities). <http://www.neh.gov/news/humanities/1996–11fussell.html>.

———. Interview with Alex Beam. The Connection.org. 23 Dec. 2003. <http://www.theconnection.org/shows/2003/12/20031223_b_main.asp>.

———. *Wartime: Understanding and Behavior in the Second World War.* New York: Oxford UP, 1989.

Gardner, John. *On Moral Fiction.* New York: Basic Books, 1978.

Garfield, John. "The Role I Liked Best." *Saturday Evening Post* 12 Jan. 1946: 94.

Gerber, David A. "Heroes and Misfits: The Troubled Social Reintegration of Disabled Veterans in *The Best Years of Our Lives.*" *American Quarterly* 46.4 (1944): 545–74.

———. "In Search of Al Schmid: War Hero, Blinded Veteran, Everyman." *Journal of American Studies* 29 (1995): 1–32.

Gladwell, Malcolm. "Getting over It: The Man in the Gray Flannel Suit Put the War behind Him. What Changed?" *New Yorker* 8 Nov. 2004: 75–79.

Graham, Don. *No Name on the Bullet: A Biography of Audie Murphy.* New York: Viking, 1989.

Jeavons, Clyde. *A Pictorial History of War Films.* Secaucus, N.J.: Citadel, 1974.

Kantor, MacKinlay. *Glory for Me.* New York: Coward-McCann, 1945.

Kennett, Lee. *G.I: The American Soldier in World War II.* New York: Scribner's, 1987.

Koppes, Clayton R., and Gregory D. Black. *Hollywood Goes to War: How Politics, Profits and Propaganda Shaped World War II Movies.* New York: Free Press, 1987.

Langman, Larry, and Ed Borg. *Encyclopedia of American War Films.* New York: Garland, 1989.

The Man in the Gray Flannel Suit. Dir. Nunnally Johnson. Perf. Gregory Peck, Jennifer Jones, Fredric March, Marisa Pavan, Lee J. Cobb. Fox, 1956.

McAdams, Frank. *The American War Film: History and Hollywood.* Westport, Conn.: Praeger, 2002.

Nelson, Derek. *The Ads that Won the War.* Osceola, Wis.: Motorbooks International, 1992.

O'Connor, John E., and Martin A. Jackson, eds. *American History/American Film: Interpreting the Hollywood Image.* New York: Frederick Ungar, 1979.

O'Neill, William. *American High: The Years of Confidence, 1945–1960.* New York: Free Press, 1986.

Powdermaker, Hortense. *Hollywood, the Dream Factory: An Anthropologist Looks at the Movies.* Boston: Little, Brown, 1950.

Pride of the Marines. Dir. Delmer Davis. Perf. John Garfield, Eleanor Parker, Dane Clark, John Ridgely, Rosemary DeCamp, Ann Doran, Ann Todd, Warren Douglas. Warner Bros., 1945.

Roeder, George H. *The Censored War: American Visual Experience during World War Two.* New Haven, Conn.: Yale UP, 1993.

Rollins, Peter. "America, World War II, and the Movies: An Annotated Booklist." *Film & History* 27.1–4 (1997): 96–107.

Rotha, Paul. *The Film till Now: A Survey of World Cinema.* London: Spring Books, 1967.

Schickel, Richard. *Good Morning, Mr. Zip, Zip, Zip: Movies, Memory, and World War II.* Chicago: Ivan R. Dee, 2003.

Shepard, Ben. *A War of Nerves: Soldiers and Psychiatrists in the Twentieth Century.* Cambridge, Mass.: Harvard UP, 2001.

Shewring, Anne L. "We Didn't Do that Did We? Representations of the Vietnam Experience." *Journal of American and Comparative Cultures* 23.4 (2000): 51–66.

Smith, Charles C., and Nancy Schimmel. "Malvina Reynolds: Song Lyrics and Poems." <http://www.wku.edu/~smithch/MALVINA/homep.htm>.

The Story of G.I. Joe. Dir. William A. Wellman. Perf. Burgess Meredith, Robert Mitchum, Freddie Steel, Wally Cassell, Jimmy Lloyd. United Artists, 1945.

Stouffer, Samuel A., Arthur A. Lumsdaine, Marion Harper Lumsdaine, Robin M. Williams Jr., M. Brewster Smith, Irving L. Janis, Shirley A. Star, and Leonard S. Cottrell Jr. *The American Soldier: Combat and Its Aftermath.* Vol. 2. New York: Wiley & Sons, 1949. Science Editions, 1962.

Thomson, David. *The Whole Equation: A History of Hollywood.* New York: Knopf, 2005.

Tregaskis, Richard. *Guadalcanal Diary.* New York: Random House, 1943.

A Walk in the Sun. Dir. Lewis Milestone. Perf. Dana Andrews, Richard Conte, Sterling Holloway, George Tyne, John Ireland, Herbert Rudley, Lloyd Bridges, Huntz Hall. Fox, 1945.

Warshow, Robert. *The Immediate Experience: Movies, Comics, Theater and Other Aspects of Popular Culture.* New York: Doubleday, 1964.

Wilson, Sloan. *The Man in the Gray Flannel Suit.* New York: Simon & Schuster, 1955.

James Jones, Columbia Pictures, and the Historical Confrontations of *From Here to Eternity*

James Jones spent his career writing about the average American soldier's experience immediately prior to and during the Second World War, from his "fictional" combat trilogy *From Here to Eternity* (1951), *The Thin Red Line* (1962), and *Whistle* (published posthumously in 1978) to his popular history *World War II* (1975). Nevertheless, historians and literary critics have tended to downplay his investment in the Second World War as a site of historical speculation and critique and have emphasized instead the more limited, historically ambivalent discourses of personal memory controlling the popular novelist's creative drives (Giles; MacShane). Because the content of *From Here to Eternity* originated from Jones's own experience in the peacetime army on Hawaii between 1939 and December 1941, his potential historical perspective on this period could be marginalized or ignored in favor of vaguer arguments about "social protest" or "personal vision." Jane Hendler's recent study of *From Here to Eternity* and its 1953 film adaptation by Columbia Pictures assesses Jones and the filmmakers' preoccupation with prewar army life as "the nostalgic recreation of a world in which males coexisted outside the confines of domesticity" (30). Rather than being a historical re-creation of prewar army life at the frontier of America's Pacific empire, Hendler views the novel and film as contemporary texts exposing "the postwar crisis in masculinity." According to Hendler and other film scholars, the historical contextualization of *From Here to Eternity* in 1941 Hawaii serves only to alleviate the conflicted gender dynamics facing American men in 1951 and 1953; the past functions as pure nostalgia, as masculine myth, where contemporary cultural contradictions can be reconciled temporarily (Bell-Metereau 92).

Both these views in American literature and film studies neglect *From Here to Eternity*'s critical historical attitude toward the 1941 peacetime army as well as Jones's class-based indictment of traditional historiography on prewar America and the military. Although not discounting the novel's and film's status as icons of the 1950s controversy over the representation of sex, violence, and language (Bell-Metereau 102–3), this chapter asks new questions about *From Here to Eternity*'s production history, its place within Hollywood's World War II genre, and its unconventional attitudes toward national history.

Jones's historical sensibilities, though neglected by critics, had a powerful impact on the development of the film adaptation between 1951 and 1953. The novel, Jones's original screenplay, and Daniel Taradash's adapted script were written deliberately as prewar narratives of the lives of marginal Americans—Robert E. Lee Prewitt, a southern cracker enlistee; First Sergeant Milton Warden, the perfect soldier with no identity outside the army; Angelo Maggio, an Italian American enlistee from Brooklyn; Lorene, a Hotel Street prostitute; and Karen Holmes, an army wife. Although Columbia's filmmakers showed some deference to the Production Code by editing the novel's explicit sexual content and language, film historian Lawrence Suid's series of interviews with director Fred Zinnemann, screenwriter Taradash, and others from the Department of Defense's Motion Picture Production Office reveals the controversy over filming such a representation of the U.S. military (Suid, *Guts* 117–29). While Suid relates Columbia's partial accommodation of the military's demands, other film critics such as Peter Biskind claim—without any tangible evidence—that *From Here to Eternity* was essentially a "conservative" film (222), reinforcing the dominant 1950s corporate ideology. This chapter, which focuses on the extant production correspondence and script notes, reveals that the filmmakers' major concerns were to retain Jones's portrayal of a corrupt and brutal American military system and to engage the myth of the officer-hero, the U.S. Army, and Pearl Harbor through multiple personal narratives of American misfits. This chapter also reexamines Jones's preliminary script for Columbia and the extent to which he and others shaped the film's historical content, for the film is more than a controversial adaptation of a controversial best seller, and more than a reflection of contemporary gender conflicts. *From Here to Eternity* represents a major revision of the World War II genre and a partial reversion to the conventions of the popular prewar historical cycle. Its antiheroicism and historical structures combine to undermine both the visual and the textual establishment histories of the war.

JAMES JONES AND REVISIONIST HISTORY

Jones would express his distaste for traditional historical writing in his 1975 account of the Second World War, heading an entire chapter with the question, "Is History Written by the Upper Classes for the Upper Classes?" (*World War II* 70). For Jones, traditional histories of World War II were inescapably constructed from the mind-set of officers, who shared the same privileges and social background as historians. Historical writing was therefore "always filtered through the ideals system [that the historian] and other members of his class, the commanders, shared and adhered to." Soldiers like Jones could therefore read histories of campaigns in which they had fought and realize that "the history doesn't at all tally with the campaign [they] remembered." There were two competing historical discourses of World War II, but establishment histories tended to dominate public perceptions of the war. Jones's work, both popular history (*World War II*) and historical fiction (*From Here to Eternity, The Thin Red Line, Whistle*), not only was an antidote to the grand studies of foreign policy and military biography proliferating since the mid-1940s but also attempted to reconcile the discrepancies among soldiers' memories, military history, and popular consciousness.[1]

There was never any doubt about Jones's historical loyalties. *World War II* is a soldier's perspective, a history from below that mixes rarely seen graphic art with memories of his combat experience at Guadalcanal, where he was wounded and later decorated. But *World War II* is not just a memoir; it was designed and marketed as a popular history by Grosset & Dunlap. As Jones writes, "The whole history of my generation's World War II has been written, not wrongly so much, but in a way that gave precedence to the viewpoints of strategists, tacticians and theorists, but gave little more than lip service to the viewpoint of the hairy, swiftly aging, fighting lower class soldier" (71).

Jones had been practicing his unique revisionist history since 1951 and *From Here to Eternity*. His on-the-job research began in 1939, when he joined the U.S. Army Air Corps. In the space of a few weeks, however, he was transferred to the more proletarian infantry. On Sunday, 7 December 1941, he was at Schofield Barracks in Hawaii, eating breakfast, when the Japanese attacked Pearl Harbor. After being wounded at Guadalcanal in 1942, he was shipped back to the States. Struggling with depression and injuries, he went AWOL, was thrown into more than one army prison, and was finally discharged in mid-1944 (MacShane 60–70). In 1948 Norman Mailer's *The Naked and the Dead* made the American war experience in the Pacific even less idyllic than it seemed in World War II combat films and on the pages of *Time* and *Life* magazines, but Jones's novel was unique. It was the first sustained portrayal of the pre–World War II army on Hawaii, and it was not flattering. Graft, corruption, sadism, adultery, prostitution, and homosexuality were all part of not only the prewar army but also prewar America. By writing about men and women like Milton Warden, Robert E. Lee Prewitt, Angelo Maggio, Lorene, and Karen Holmes,

Jones attacked traditional historical accounts on two fronts. These were the stories of average people, unknown to traditional narratives of military culture and the war. But more significantly, these men and women lived their lives outside the myth of the old army and of continental America itself. Pushed beyond the borders of the United States into a new, peripheral twentieth-century American "frontier," these people projected an oppositional perspective on the "Stateside" nation's social and cultural norms.

When *From Here to Eternity* was at the proofs stage, Jones's editor at Scribner's, Burroughs Mitchell, sent it out to several prominent American novelists, including Norman Mailer and John Dos Passos. Mailer's response was generally positive; he would later meet Jones in New York, and the two would remain friendly. But Dos Passos, whose *U.S.A.* trilogy (*The 42nd Parallel* [1930], *1919* [1932], and *The Big Money* [1936]) was then one of the most ambitious and well-known works of twentieth-century American historical fiction, had a more specific comment: "It is an impressive book. People will buy it for the smut but there's more to it than that. Prewitt and Angelo and Sergeant Warden and the rest of them reach something of the greatness of figures of tragedy because their hopeless dilemma expresses so glaringly the basic tragic dilemma of our time. There's considerable valuable folklore in the book, and as history . . . well it's the only account of the events leading up to Pearl Harbor I've seen that doesn't have some damn selfserving axe to grind" (quoted in Mitchell, 3 Jan. 1951). Dos Passos recognized that Jones's work both resonated with contemporary America and offered a powerful synthesis of American myth and history. Its most obvious historical ties were to the attack on Pearl Harbor, an event that triggered national involvement in the global war and became the basis for a modern American myth. Dos Passos was well aware of the way the disaster at Pearl Harbor had been used as a propaganda tool, as a means of justifying the internment of Japanese Americans and focusing on Japanese treachery rather than on the incompetence of the military establishment.[2]

From the moment that news of the attack reached Washington, Pearl Harbor was censored, managed, and packaged as a national myth. Within the first few months of the war, the public was inundated by press coverage, but the information was limited, restricted mostly to set text and official quotations from President Franklin D. Roosevelt and the Joint Chiefs of Staff. The *New York Times*' spread on 7 December included no photographs at all. In fact, the naval department, evidently frightened by the potential public reaction, did not release photos of the damage until they appeared in the February 1942 issue of *Life*, and not until December 1942 was *Life* allowed to publish an extensive spread ("Pictures"; "Pearl Harbor"). Instead, the government identified Pearl Harbor with simplified slogans and later a carefully vetted series of images emphasizing Japanese treachery and selfless American heroism, whether through FDR's rhetoric to Congress ("Always will we remember the character of the onslaught against us") or director John Ford's government-approved filmed reconstruction *December 7th* (1943) (Rosenberg 20–21). During wartime, the government exerted substantial control over the production of history, whether setting the rhetorical tone for its popular remembrance or commissioning a canned version for movie theaters. It had not always been that way.

THE FEAR OF FILM AND HISTORY

During the 1930s and early 1940s, Hollywood specialized in high-profile historical films and war epics (*The Last of the Mohicans* [1936], *The Buccaneer* [1938], *Gone with the Wind* [1939], *The Fighting 69th* [1940], *Sergeant York* [1941]), attracting audiences and cultural power that mainstream historians could only dream of. But after Pearl Harbor, the studios gave up major American historical productions for contemporary war films such as *Across the Pacific* (1942), *So Proudly We Hail* (1943), and *Objective, Burma!* (1945)—films that relied increasingly on a sense of immediacy, a borrowed documentary aesthetic, and realistic violence (Smyth). The relationship between the studios and the federal government was necessarily close during World War II. The Office of War Information (OWI), established in June 1942, was essentially a centralized propaganda agency that liaised with the studios (Schatz 268–80; Koppes and Black; see also chapter 11 in this collection). In exchange for supporting the armed forces and the government in an unequivocal way, Hollywood received massive foreign distribution rights. John Ford and Gregg Toland's *December 7th* was a product of this new era of Hollywood filmmaking and was the first attempt to narrate the attack and its effect on the nation. This government-approved history, though claiming to be the definitive view of Pearl Harbor, with voice-over narration and document inserts, had almost no actual footage from 7 December. Although they shot "on location," the attack footage was nothing but simulated reenactment, process photography, rear projection, and miniatures (Basinger 128; Skinner). Nevertheless, the film was marketed and received as a true documentary, supplemented by text inserts in the opening sequences in which Secretary of War Henry Stimson and Secretary of the Navy Frank Knox asserted that the film was "factual." Like many great American war myths, the government ripped the event from the tangle of classified political and military details and used the press and culture industries to revision it as a set of often spurious printed documents and reconstructed images.

When Harry Cohn, head of Columbia Pictures, paid James Jones $82,000 for the film rights for *From Here to Eternity* in 1951 (*New York Times* 6 Mar. 1951),

December 7th and the constructed documentary footage.

his decision signaled a return to the old-style war films made in the 1930s, when the studios routinely paid high prices for the rights to best-selling memoirs (*Sergeant York*), historical novels (*Gone with the Wind*), and other presold material (*The Roaring Twenties* [1939]). Unlike the modern war features produced during the time of U.S. combat involvement, which were frequently based on cheap original scripts churned out by studio writers, *From Here to Eternity* was intended as a major prestige production. It was based on a historical novel published ten years after Pearl Harbor, and the accuracy of its historical content would prove to be the major source of contention in terms of censorship and army cooperation. To make *From Here to Eternity*, Cohn had to enter into censorship negotiations unlike any faced before by the Hollywood studios. Even though the OWI had effectively been disbanded after the war, filmmakers still had to handle the armed forces carefully. If the film in any way remained faithful to the novel, it promised to revise the heroic war genre, correcting the fallacies of *December 7th*. It would also break with the carefully monitored propaganda of Hollywood's wartime genre (*Wing and a Prayer* [1944]; *Objective, Burma!*; *Back to Bataan* [1945]). But in order to film with any degree of authenticity, the studio needed the army's cooperation to shoot at Schofield Barracks in Hawaii (Suid, "Zinnemann" 50; Bell, letter to Towne).

Jones's book was a bit too historically "authentic" for the army. He literally created the problem with his author's note: "This book is a work of fiction. The characters are imaginary and any resemblance to actual persons is accidental. However, certain of the stockade scenes did happen. They did not happen at Schofield Barracks post stockade but at a post within the U.S. at which the author served and they are true scenes of which the author had first-hand knowledge and personal experience." Jones trod a fine line as a historical novelist—the major officers who had served at Schofield were still alive and could sue successfully for libel. Asserting its fictional basis in a disclaimer was a standard safety mechanism, but Jones mischievously problematized this convention by mentioning his personal story. He and his editor had to word the note with care. At one point, they even submitted it to Scribner's lawyer Horace Manges for comment. Manges responded that the note was "extremely dangerous to the book, from the point of view of libel" (10 Nov. 1950). Filmmakers concurred. As director Fred Zinnemann recalled, "The book, fiercely critical of the pre-war U.S. Army, had created a sensation . . . filming a book so openly scathing about the peacetime army . . . was regarded by many as foolhardy if not downright subversive" (*Autobiography* 117, 119). In a letter to Harry Cohn, Ray Bell, the studio's Washington representative, estimated that there would be four major sources of trouble if the studio tried to release the film: military, censorship, religion, and politics. But the first two really worried him.

> From the Pentagon point of view the Army personnel are most unfavorably shown. Corruption, incompetence, goldbricking, and preoccupation with sex and gambling seem to be the army's sole concern. I do know that there exists in Washington a feeling against this book because, according to an officer who volunteered this information, "the book portrays a rotten and corrupt army, it propagandizes against officers and the traditions of the service, and it could be a demoralizing influence at a time when this country's trying to build a big army, draft eighteen year olds and win the confidence of parents and Congress."

Bell knew that the U.S. military's involvement in Korea in 1951 made *From Here to Eternity* an especially irritating and even dangerous project. Embroiled in an increasingly unpopular, limited war, the army must have taken one look at Cohn's plans and wished for reinstatement of the OWI. Studio employees were fazed at first by the government's attitude; a week after Bell's report, another studio employee submitted that "this story must be Pro-Army." He also attacked the antiofficer slant of the book and said that "99% of the dialog in this book cannot be transferred to the screen. . . . We intend to show all of our officers as intelligent officers of whom the army would be proud" (Report). A military adviser, Colonel E. P. Hogan, had similar criticisms and concluded, "The flag should be waved more." At first, Cohn paid attention to the army perspective, but the postwar relationship between Hollywood and Washington was becoming strained. Bruised by the House Un-American Activities Committee hearings and crippled by the 1948 *Paramount* antitrust decision, Hollywood had been shouldering burdens from an increasingly antagonistic Washington. Cohn, tired of knuckling under government pressures, was tempted to produce a faithful, high-profile production of Jones's work.

But for the first year of preproduction, Cohn and Columbia tried to negotiate the novel's historical controversy by bringing in a series of advisers and commentators. Columbia officials were very nervous about acquiring Pearl Harbor footage (*From Here*, conference notes; Towne memo, 2 Apr. 1953). For this film, historical authenticity mattered so much that no one even considered restaging Pearl Harbor. Ironically, though, the army did not hold the copyright to the combat footage of Pearl Harbor. Fox Movietone cameraman Al Brick had been up early that morning, getting some authentic Pearl Harbor material for the feature *To the Shores of Tripoli* (1942), when the Japanese began their attack (Doherty 231–32). The government declassified the combat footage in December 1942, so *From Here to Eternity*'s filmmakers had the best of both worlds and combined Brick's actual combat footage with extensive sequences from Toland's reenactments for *December 7th*. However, the army threatened to prevent crews from shooting at Schofield Barracks in Hawaii if the script were not tailored to its specifications. As Colonel (later General) Frank Dorn wrote, "Army cooperation in production of this film is extremely doubtful" (letter to Columbia Pictures).

Dorn, the U.S Army's deputy chief of information, was particularly concerned with the screen representation of Private Angelo Maggio, the working-class Italian American who voices some of Jones's toughest critiques of the military. Dorn advised Columbia to portray Maggio as "a parasite on society" because he failed to fit in with the army. Colonel Clair Towne of the motion picture section of the Defense Department's Office of Public Information was equally against Maggio, but he also disliked the cynical Warden and the individualistic Prewitt. Towne thought that he had a solution, though: "By making it clear that while Warden, Prewitt and others might dislike their officers, this dislike stems from the realization that they, as individuals, do not have the stuff to become officers . . . the officers might be placed in a better light" (undated comments). In effect, the army was working overtime to label any of its ethnic or critical components as aberrant and to rewrite Jones's working-class social history, where traditionally marginalized, "voiceless" men could not speak. As Jones memorably writes in his novel, "The clerks, the kings, the thinkers: they talked and with their talking ran the world. The truckdrivers, the pyramid builders, the straight-duty men; the ones who could not talk, they built the world out of their very tonguelessness—so the talkers could talk about how to run it, and the ones who built it. And when they had destroyed it with their talking the truckdriver and straight duty man would build it up again, simply because they were hunting for a way to speak" (130).

Even before Cohn bought the film rights, Jones and Mitchell had low expectations of Hollywood. In one exchange, the editor commented, "God knows what Hollywood would do with your book," and Jones replied, "I don't give a damn what they do to the movie" (Mitchell, 26 Apr. 1950; Jones, letter to Mitchell). Columbia evidently cared, for in an unusually brave move, Cohn hired Jones to write the script in early 1951. Jones did not push for an accurate adaptation. His preliminary script, dated 16 May 1951, indicates the extent to which he saw *From Here to Eternity* as a traditional historical film along the lines of *Young Mr. Lincoln* (1939) and *Citizen Kane* (1941). The narrative opens with a flashback to Harlan, Kentucky, in 1932. Sergeant Warden narrates the film in a voice-over, which had been a standard component of the biopic genre since the 1930s. Jones also employed other tricks of historical filmmaking, including montages and document inserts. The montage covering Prewitt's youth and early army experiences was an extraordinarily lengthy fifteen pages, ending with Prewitt's arrival at Schofield (Jones, preliminary treatment 3–18). But Jones's use of these old historical signifiers had an innovative edge: Prewitt was not a famous, successful man like Abraham Lincoln or Charles Foster Kane; he was an unknown, Depression-era "forgotten man." It was no accident that Jones named him Robert E. Lee Prewitt. He may have been just as proud and devoted to the army as his namesake, but Prewitt was not a privileged West Point graduate from Virginia. He was a twentieth-century rebel who had grown up in a depressed southern mining community. He had seen his father and uncle killed by the police during labor riots, and he had watched his mother die of tuberculosis. Prewitt left home to ride the rails as a kid and was raped by an older man. He joined the army in 1936 because he had nowhere else to go. Prewitt was not just a literary exception; during the Depression, many young men joined the army to avoid unemployment and starvation (Jones, *From Here* 367; MacShane 38).[3]

Surprisingly, even Jones's script shows evidence of the self-censorship that was endemic in much of classical Hollywood. Perhaps as a means of placating the censors, he turns the adulterous Karen Holmes into "the Captain's younger sister." Also, the corrupt Captain Dana Holmes of the novel is transformed into a good guy who pressures Warden to "lay off" his hazing of Prewitt. In this early version, Prewitt is killed by a Japanese Zero pilot rather than by American soldiers from another unit, thereby absolving the army of any blame for his death. Even Prewitt's term in the stockade is construed as a misunderstanding after another soldier lies about his confrontation with Prewitt. Major Thompson, the head of the stockade, eventually busts Fatso Judson for killing Maggio, so the army looks better on all fronts. Jones did not document his feelings about the script, and it is difficult to assess how much of it was his own idea and how much was dictated by Sylvan Simon, the producer then in charge of day-to-day preproduction. Nevertheless, it is significant that Jones was willing to adopt old-fashioned historical elements and censorship in these early stages.

Jones did not remain a screenwriter for long, and the job was eventually given to Daniel Taradash. Cohn hoped to bring Jones back on the project, but he declined, stressing his frustration with Simon's pressure to make Captain Holmes a more sympathetic character. In a 29 June letter to Jones, Cohn tried to change his mind, citing his own anger at the need to pacify the army:

> Have we not changed certain characters in order to pacify the Army and thus lost the quality and theme which you tried to put forth in your novel? I feel that the implications in the novel of officer laxity and improper use of authority were so astonishing that it opened the eyes of all who read it. If in making the movie we eliminate this entirely, then we have bastardized the book and cleaned it up to present it for screen purposes without integrity or purpose. It is my candid opinion that we do not have to lose this idea.

Jones still refused to participate.

After getting the army's temporary approval based on the novelist's expurgated script, Cohn kept any further rewrites quiet for a year (Brown).[4] The secrecy worked in Cohn's favor for a while. As Suid has pointed out, even Taradash's carefully revised script of February 1952 took a year to receive the army's grudging approval (*Guts* 120; Towne memo, 11 Feb. 1953; Towne letter, 30 Mar. 1953). Ironically, though, most of the military's requests for changes involved issues more suited to the Production Code: changing the New Congress Club from a bordello to a nightclub, editing language, eliminating the suggestion of Karen's other affairs, making Holmes "a more positive character who exerts an influence for good on Prewitt" (Hogan), removing Warden's drunk scene, and cutting Maggio's descriptions of his beatings in the stockade. Most of these requests were carefully ignored (Towne letter, 21 Jan. 1953; Adler). Taradash's main concession was to have the U.S. Army brass dismiss the incompetent Holmes rather than promote him.

Taradash kept the harsh edge of Jones's original, which pleasantly surprised Hollywood critics in August 1953, when the film was finally released (see reviews in *Cue, Hollywood Reporter;* Weiler). Even the culture of Hotel Street prostitution, which Taradash semidisguised as a "private club," was easily translatable: "There has, for example, been no attempt to make angels of the playful girls in the New Congress Club," wrote one critic after the premiere (review in *Variety*). Film publicity in the press book emphasized Lorene's commodified sexuality ("Sure I'm nice to you. We're nice to all the boys"), and in a *New York Post* interview with Archer Winsten, actress Donna Reed mused on her role, "How would I have made all that money in two years, enough to buy a house back home, join the country club, become respectable. I couldn't make that much just being a dance hostess. No, I suppose it wouldn't make much sense unless you were a prostitute." But *From Here to Eternity* was not just remarkable for its frank discussion of female sexuality in the 1950s; it was a startling, critical picture of the much-honored American army that helped win the war. The book's and film's representation of the army's long-standing exploitation of women added a new historical dimension to the popular understanding of the recent national past.

TARADASH AND ZINNEMANN'S HISTORICAL ICONOGRAPHY

From Here to Eternity was a turning point in the World War II film genre for another reason. Although films made about the Pacific campaigns began to "document" World War II events with more historical text toward the end of the 1940s (*Battleground* [1949], *Sands of Iwo Jima* [1949]), it was not until 1953 and *From Here to Eternity* that Hollywood really looked at World War II as a finite historical era. Perhaps it was partially because America was involved in another war in the Pacific, this time in Korea.

But *From Here to Eternity* certainly did not supply a "Good War" alternative to the increasingly unpopular stalemate in Korea. Instead, the film makes military apathy and incompetence a feature of World War II's historical context. The revised final script begins with an intertitle, "June 1941," and Taradash introduces key scenes with a soldier reading a newspaper with headlines such as "JAPS ADVANCE IN CHINA" and "LOU GEHRIG DIES" (Taradash 1, 17, 60). When outlining the 7 December attack, Taradash's script notes, "Stock shots bombing Hickam Field, Wheeler Field and Pearl Harbor from 'December Seventh' and other available material" (148, 152). During the 1940s, newsreels and fictional films about the war used reconstructions and limited government and military combat footage (often not from Pearl Harbor). Even during the 1930s, Hollywood had borrowed footage from the military to make films about World

From Here to Eternity's historical intertitle.

War I (*The World Moves On* [1934], *The Roaring Twenties* [1939]). The World War II footage in war films of the 1940s was contemporaneous and largely interchangeable with the cinematography of the "fictional" Hollywood footage. But in *From Here to Eternity* there is a definite visual contrast in the quality of the documentary and "fictional" cinematography. The 1953 shots of the fictional historical content are in clear, sharp black and white. The documentary footage is grainy, dark, and blurred, with abrupt editing cuts. Even the character of the sound is different—the engines, guns, and bombs in the documentary footage are almost deafening compared to the scenes of Sergeant Warden attempting to manage the chaos in Schofield after the attack. The footage acts like a historical artifact—something from the vaults of history. This is what the American Stateside public saw in 1942 and at intervals in newsreels thereafter, but in 1953 it had aged visibly and did not fit with the pristine cinematography and modulated sound of the rest of the narrative. The filmmakers' refusal to conceal this obvious contrast in cinematography and sound foregrounds a sense of historical discontinuity.

Is this simply a case of seamless Hollywood fiction juxtaposed with rough documentary accuracy, a historical touch added to bolster a romantic fabrica-

There is an obvious visual contrast between the fictional and documentary footage. Here, Zinnemann's history of 7 December captures First Sergeant Milton Warden (Burt Lancaster).

The "official view": Al Brick's documentary footage shows its age in 1953.

tion of Hawaii in 1941? Hardly. These contrasting forms of cinematography and sound represent equally contrasting historical views of Pearl Harbor. What Zinnemann shows Americans in 1953 also happened in 1941 Hawaii—the disparate, private, painful stories of Prewitt, Lorene, Maggio, and Karen. Taradash's script streamlined the 850-page narrative and connected four of the protagonists to devastating personal stories: Karen's miscarriage and hysterectomy, Lorene's decision to become a prostitute, Prewitt's accidental crippling of his best friend during a boxing match, and Maggio's death scene, in which he tells Prewitt of repeated beatings in the stockade. These kinds of people never made the headlines; they were not interviewed after Pearl Harbor. Their stories, related in the film as lengthy personal narratives, were lost to traditional history, which emphasized Japan's treachery and the horror of the attack. In contrast, the filmmakers retain and expand the marginal narratives, making them central to their film.

From Here to Eternity reuses much of the iconography of the old historical film—the opening intertitle identifying the historical locale and period, the use of dates (such as one glimpse of a calendar reading "7 December" on the wall beside Warden), the documentary footage and location shots, the contrasting personal narratives. But ironically, it lacks one of the hallmarks of the genre: a credited military adviser or endorsement. Although the army allowed Zinnemann to photograph army personnel around Schofield, it "did not authorize Columbia Pictures to include in the picture the fact that Army cooperation had been given" (Parks). Zinnemann, however, may have realized that obtaining and displaying army approval in the credits would have invalidated the accuracy of Jones's perspective. Instead, the film constructs a historical world that does not rely on the spurious endorsement of the establishment. Zinnemann's vision was not confined to the events of Pearl Harbor and World War II. He heavily underlined passages in his copy of Jones's novel where the Depression is credited with causing Prewitt to enlist (Zinnemann, marginalia 7, 676, 854–55). As he commented after reading Taradash's script, he did not want to lose the feeling of history in the novel: "If at all possible, reference should be made to Prew's childhood—the fact that he was from Harlan County, Kentucky, that he grew up in the Depression—bummed all over the country and finally got into the Army because, 'he wasn't ready to starve yet'" (Zinnemann, notes 6). Zinnemann also underlined an unusual passage in which Jones, via Prewitt, speculates on the untold histories "written" in the scars on a soldier's body. "Each one had its own story and memory, like a chapter in a book. And when a man died they buried them all with him and then nobody could ever read his histories and his stories and his memories that had been written down on the book of his body" (marginalia 669). Prewitt is a work of living history: "Robert E. Lee Prewitt, a history of the U.S. in one volume, from the year 1919 to the year 1941, uncompleted, compiled, and edited by We the People." But Jones recognized the tenuousness of the historical trace left by the ordinary soldier, and Zinnemann, though intrigued, never pushed Taradash to incorporate it in the script.

Taradash did retain some aspects of Jones's comments on the frontier myth and its relevance to the 1930s army. In the novel, Prewitt's and Warden's different attitudes toward the army are based on the conflict between the traditional, nineteenth-century frontier discourse and a more skeptical view of America's international, twentieth-century frontiers. Prewitt had been drawn to the army by stories told by his uncle John, who had briefly served during the Spanish-American War (1898). Later, Jones explicitly links Prewitt's desire to join the army to the old nineteenth-century frontier myth and a desire to be an active participant in history. According to Jones, farming—associated with 1920s agricultural depressions, southern tenant poverty, stasis, and anonymity—is the antithesis of American romanticism. Although Prewitt is convinced that the agrarian ideal kills the American spirit, the army "impressed him with a sense of seeing history made," since it carries on the "noble" frontier tradition (17). So he moves out of the South and heads west—as did millions of Americans during the Depression.

The frontier no longer exists: Prewitt wins no new territory, but he does follow in the footsteps of many pioneers by forming a relationship in Hawaii with a "native" Asian woman, whom he later discards.[5] Like the pioneers and their historians from George Bancroft to Frederick Jackson Turner and Theodore Roosevelt, Prewitt forgets this mixed-race union in order to pursue individual achievement. But even though he doggedly hangs on to the idea of the past, others remind him that it is only a myth. A friend warns him (Warden in the film), "Maybe back in the old days, a man could do what he wanted to do, in peace. But he had the woods then. . . . And if they followed him there for this or that, he could just move on. There was always more woods up ahead. But a man can't do that now" (Jones, *From Here* 11).[6] To a certain extent, Jones attributes the prevailing public romanticism of the army to the dominance of an officer culture: "It is hard to be Romantic about the cavalry when you have to curry your own horse, and it is hard to be adventurous about the uniform when you have to polish your own boots. And this explains why officers, who are above such menial tasks, are capable of such exciting memoirs of war" (79). These memoirs and their heroic, establishment-derived discourse would later become the foundation for historical interpretations of U.S. conquest and "development."

Jones undercuts these myths of progress and development with Warden's and Maggio's perspectives on officers. Both believe that there is no essential difference between nineteenth- and twentieth-century army life. Class clashes are not defined by historical change, and there is no such thing as nostalgia or historical progress; the army has always been a grim place for the common soldier. When Maggio complains to Prewitt about the corruption and nepotism in their infantry company, he growls, "This is the Army, they can give it back to Custer" (40). Warden, too, uses the Custer analogy to describe Captain Holmes. "Boots and Saddles," he sneers at his egomaniacal chief's back, a pointed reference to officers whose greatest feats of military incompetence (such as Little Big Horn, in 1876) are written into memoir and history as tragic-heroic events (Slotkin). For Jones, Pearl Harbor was America's next Little Big Horn.

Not without irony, Taradash and Zinnemann decide that Lorene should have the last word in *From Here to Eternity*—not the heroic Warden or any high-ranking army officer. *From Here to Eternity* is a series of untold narratives excised by establishment history, related by people who have literally been pushed to the very edges of America. But even these personal histories begin to be corrupted by the effects of Pearl Harbor. The events of 7 December unleash a rabid historical consciousness. Within minutes of the bombings, Hawaiian civilians are calling the event "history" (Jones, *From Here* 763). On their way home, Lorene and Georgette meet a professor who is already planning a book about the attack. As soon as the new draftees begin arriving, Washington pressure groups begin to close down the Hotel Street brothels, wiping the peacetime army experience from the islands. But Lorene's final personal narrative is the most sustained example of reconstructing the past in the aftermath of the attack. Lorene, who has fallen in love with Prewitt, remakes herself into a prosperous businesswoman. Once she has enough money, she tells Prewitt, she will refashion her identity in the States and become an upper-middle-class housewife. Soon after Prewitt is killed, she begins to "fix" her official story in the same way that Warden managed the infantry company's records. On board a ship that will take them back to the States, Lorene tells Karen Holmes that her "fiancé" was killed during the Japanese bombing of Hickam Field. According to her, Prewitt was a bomber pilot and was awarded the Silver Star. Although Lorene retains Prewitt's southern heritage, she transforms the poor white cracker and common soldier into a fine gentleman and a pilot. The war has just started, and already the civilian population is joining the army in rewriting its history, in constructing a heroic image. Although Karen recognizes that Lorene's story is false, she does not challenge the myth.

More than ten years separated the attack on Pearl Harbor from the publication and film production of *From Here to Eternity*. Were Jones's novel and Hollywood's adaptation of it merely reflections of the cultural mythmaking that began in December 1941, or was the historical perspective more defined? In her recent study of Pearl Harbor in American memory, Emily Rosenberg contests the discursive divide between serious history and popular memory (of which historical fictions are a part), writing that "memory and history are blurred forms of representation whose structure and politics need to be analyzed not as oppositional but as interactive forms" (5). Although the recent interest in memory studies has elevated the method's importance as an interpreter of history, the effort has been to see collective, public memory as a constructed and managed form of historical interpretation, much like traditional historiography (Rosenberg 4–6; Halbwachs). And there persists a sense that memory, regardless of its oppositional stance on historical issues, does not have the clout of official history. Jones had a lifelong distrust of traditional history and official views because of their tendency to obliterate other perspectives on the past. Historical fiction, rather than the more traditional memoir or military history, enabled him and Columbia Pictures to place marginalized perspectives on Pearl Harbor back into the popular understanding of American history.

Recent scholarly studies of homosexuals in the World War II military (Allan Bérubé's *Coming Out Under Fire*) and the racial and sexual tensions in wartime Hawaii (Beth Bailey and David Farber's *The First Strange Place*) do not raise new questions about the wartime military. Decades before a revamped cultural studies began to alter the perspective of American historical research, James Jones and Columbia Pictures wrote their own controversial versions of Pearl Harbor and the American military. But Jones, Taradash, and Zinnemann were not just unconventional historians whose iconoclasm spurred developments in American social and cultural history of the 1990s. In his novel and, to a certain extent, in his original screenplay, Jones was equally concerned with the authenticity of history, the politics of memory, and the fragility of historical experience. Harry Cohn, Daniel Taradash, and Fred Zinnemann also pursued these ideas as contrasting forms of narrative and cinematography. In foregrounding the myth, in drawing attention to the discrepancy between popular views of American militarism, heroism, and World War II and the more complex social histories of Depression-era America, Jones and Columbia's filmmakers did what other historical novelists and filmmakers before them had done only rarely—confronted the process by which Americans reconstruct a mythic past.

NOTES

1. See, for example, U.S. Army; Halsey; Kimmel; Hoehling; Waller; Brownlow; Baker; and Editors.

2. Among the many accounts and analyses of Pearl Harbor are Clark; Lee; Flynn; and Sweeny. For more contemporary accounts, see Lord; Melosi; Collier; Prange, *At Dawn* and *Pearl Harbor;* and Stinnett.

3. During the 1920s the army was scaled back to around 150,000 men; by 1939, it had only 174,000 men, most of whom never saw action until 1941.

4. Rebecca Bell-Metereau mistakenly states that *From Here to Eternity* never received army approval (104).

5. Prewitt's relationship with this native woman was not included in any of the early scripts.

6. Jones's idiomatic syntax is retained throughout.

WORKS CITED

Adler, Buddy. Opinion of the requested changes on the part of the Department of Defense to Col. Dorn. Jan. 1953. Department of Defense Files.

Bailey, Beth, and David Farber. *The First Strange Place: Race and Sex in World War II Hawaii.* Baltimore: Johns Hopkins UP, 1992.

Baker, Leonard. *Roosevelt and Pearl Harbor.* New York: Macmillan, 1970.

Basinger, Jeanine. *The World War II Combat Film: An Anatomy of a Genre.* New York: Columbia UP, 1986.

Bell, Raymond. Letter to Harry Cohn. 13 Mar. 1951. Folder 342. James Jones Collection, Yale U.

———. Letter to Lt. Col. Clair Towne. 19 Jan. 1953. Department of Defense Files.

Bell-Metereau, Rebecca. "1953: Movies and Our Secret Lives." *American Cinema of the 1950s: Themes and Variations.* Ed. Murray Pomerance. New Brunswick, N.J.: Rutgers UP, 2005. 89–110.

Bérubé, Allan. *Coming Out Under Fire: The History of Gay Men and Women in World War II.* New York: Free Press, 1990.

Biskind, Peter. *Seeing Is Believing: How Hollywood Taught Us to Stop Worrying and Love the Fifties.* New York: Pantheon Books, 1983.

Brown, Ned. Letter to Jones. 22 May 1952. Folder 526, James Jones Collection, Yale U.

Brownlow, Donald Grey. *Accused: The Ordeal of Rear Admiral Husband E. Kimmel.* New York: Vantage Press, 1968.

Clark, Blake. *Remember Pearl Harbor!* New York: Modern Age Books, 1942.

Cohn, Harry. Letter to Jones. 29 June 1951. Folder 490, James Jones Papers, Yale U and U of Texas, Austin.

Collier, Richard. *Road to Pearl Harbor—1941.* New York: Atheneum, 1981.

Department of Defense Files. Record group 33, entry 141, box 705. National Archives, College Park, Md.

Doherty, Thomas J. *Projections of War: Hollywood, American Culture, and World War II.* New York: Columbia UP, 1999.

Dorn, Frank, Col. Letter to Columbia Pictures. 31 Mar. 1951. Folder 342, James Jones Collection, Yale U. Also Comments and References. Undated. Department of Defense Files.

Dos Passos, John. *U.S.A.* New York: Modern Library, 1937.

Editors of the *Army Times*. *Pearl Harbor and Hawaii: A Military History*. New York: Walker, 1971.

Flynn, J. Thomas. *The Truth about Pearl Harbor*. New York: Flynn, 1944.

From Here to Eternity. Conference notes. 13 Mar. 1951. Folder 345, James Jones Papers, Yale U.

Giles, James R. *James Jones*. Boston: Twayne, 1981.

Halbwachs, Maurice. *On Collective Memory*. Chicago: U of Chicago P, 1992.

Halsey, William Frederick. *Admiral Halsey's Story*. New York: Whittlesey House, 1947.

Hendler, Jane. *Best-Sellers and Their Film Adaptations in Postwar America*. New York: Peter Lang, 2001.

Hoehling, A. A. *The Week before Pearl Harbor*. New York: Norton, 1963.

Hogan, E. P., Lt. Col. Notes on *From Here to Eternity*. 22 Mar. 1951. Folder 342, James Jones Papers, Yale U. Also Department of Defense Files.

Jones, James. *From Here to Eternity*. New York: Scribner's, 1951.

———. *From Here to Eternity*. Preliminary treatment. 16 May 1951. Folders 340–41, James Jones Papers, Yale U.

———. Letter to Burroughs Mitchell. Dec. 1950. Folder 537, James Jones Papers, Yale U and U of Texas.

———. *World War II*. New York: Grosset & Dunlap, 1975.

Kimmel, Husband E. *Admiral Kimmel's Story*. Chicago: Regnery, 1955.

Koppes, Clayton, and Gregory Black. *Hollywood Goes to War*. London: Taurus, 1988.

Lee, Amy Freeman. *Remember Pearl Harbor*. New York: Fine Editions Press, 1943.

Lord, Walter. *Day of Infamy*. New York: Holt, 1957.

MacShane, Frank. *Into Eternity: The Life of James Jones, American Writer*. Boston: Houghton Mifflin, 1985.

Manges, Horace. Letter to Burroughs Mitchell. 10 Nov. 1950. Folder 536, James Jones Collection, Yale U.

Melosi, Martin V. *Shadow of Pearl Harbor: Political Controversy over the Surprise Attack, 1941–1946*. College Station: Texas A&M UP, 1977.

Mitchell, Burroughs. Letter to Jones. 26 Apr. 1950. Box 36, folder 538, James Jones Papers, Yale U.

———. Letter to Jones. 3 Jan. 1951. Box 36, folder 529, James Jones Papers, Yale U.

Parks, Lewis S., Rear Adm. Letter to Ray Bell. May 1954. Department of Defense Files.

"Pearl Harbor Damage Revealed." *Life* Dec. 1942: 31–37.

"Pictures of the Nation's Worst Naval Disaster Show Pearl Harbor Hell." *Life* Feb. 1942: 30–35.

Prange, Gordon William. *At Dawn We Slept*. New York: McGraw-Hill, 1981.

———. *Pearl Harbor: The Verdict of History*. New York: McGraw-Hill, 1986.

Report on *From Here to Eternity*. 20 Mar. 1951. James Jones Papers, Yale U.

Rev. of *From Here to Eternity*. *Cue* 8 Aug. 1953: 16.

Rev. of *From Here to Eternity*. *Hollywood Reporter* 9 July 1953.

Rev. of *From Here to Eternity*. *Variety* 29 July 1953.

Rosenberg, Emily. *A Date Which Will Live: Pearl Harbor in American Memory*. Durham, N.C.: Duke UP, 2003.

Schatz, Thomas. *Boom and Bust: American Cinema in the 1940s*. Berkeley: U of California P, 1997.

Skinner, James M. "*December 7:* Filmic Myth Masquerading as Historical Fact." *Journal of Military History* 55.4 (1991): 507–16.

Slotkin, Richard. *The Fatal Environment.* Norman: U of Oklahoma P, 1985.

Smyth, J. E. *Reconstructing American Historical Cinema from* Cimarron *to* Citizen Kane. Lexington: University Press of Kentucky, 2006.

Stinnett, Robert B. *Day of Deceit: The Truth about FDR and Pearl Harbor.* New York: Free Press, 2000.

Suid, Lawrence H. *Guts and Glory: Great American War Movies.* Reading, Mass.: Addison-Wesley, 1978.

———. "Zinnemann on Working with the Military and *From Here to Eternity*" [1974]. *Fred Zinnemann Interviews.* Ed. Gabriel Miller. Jackson: UP of Mississippi, 2005. 47–54.

Sweeny, Charles. *Pearl Harbor.* Salt Lake City: Arrow Press, 1946.

Taradash, Daniel. *From Here to Eternity.* Revised final script. 24 Feb. 1953. Folder 334, Fred Zinnemann Collection.

Towne, Clair, Lt. Col. Letter to Ray Bell. 21 Jan. 1953. Department of Defense Files.

———. Letter to Ray Bell. 30 Mar. 1953. Department of Defense Files.

———. Memo for Chief of Information, Department of Army. 11 Feb. 1953. Department of Defense Files.

———. Memo for Chief of Information, Department of the Army. 2 Apr. 1953. Department of Defense Files.

———. Undated comments. Folder 342, James Jones Papers, Yale U.

U.S. Army, Pearl Harbor Board. *Report on Pearl Harbor.* Washington, D.C., 1945.

Waller, George Macgregor. *Pearl Harbor: Roosevelt and the Coming of the War.* Boston: Heath, 1965.

Weiler, A. H. "Rich Dividend." Rev. of *From Here to Eternity. New York Times* 9 Aug. 1953.

Winsten, Archer. "Reviewing Stand." *New York Post* [Aug. 1953]. Unmarked press clipping. Academy of Motion Picture Arts and Sciences.

Zinnemann, Fred. *Autobiography.* London: Bloomsbury, 1992.

———. Collection. Academy of Motion Picture Arts and Sciences, Los Angeles, Calif.

———. Marginalia on director's copy, *From Here to Eternity.* Folder 333, Fred Zinnemann Collection.

———. Notes on *From Here to Eternity* script. 30 Sept. 1952. Folder 360, Fred Zinnemann Collection.

HOLLYWOOD'S D-DAY FROM THE PERSPECTIVE OF THE 1960s AND 1990s

The Longest Day and *Saving Private Ryan*

Cinematic history from Hollywood is intriguing not only for its perspectives on the past but also for what it says about the times in which the films were being produced. Often the creators of motion pictures address concerns of the present when they fashion stories about the past. This characteristic is certainly evident in the case of movies depicting events associated with World War II. For instance, *Bataan* (1943) shows U.S. forces fighting bravely in the face of an overwhelming enemy. The movie's tragic conclusion, in which all the Americans die, symbolizes the difficult position of American soldiers in the Pacific during the early war (Basinger 45–46). In another example of present conditions weighing heavily on a cinematic treatment of the past, the creators of *Patton* (1970) planned to tell the story of a heroic general as they moved their project toward production in the 1960s. By the time they were ready to begin major photography, however, controversies over the Vietnam conflict made the intended gung-ho portrait of General Patton problematic. Consequently, the filmmakers shaped their story and advertising in ways that suggested a complex and sometimes critical portrait of their subject's militarism (Toplin, *History* 163–64).

It is useful, then, to consider the message and appeal of two films that are among the most influential American movies about the Second World War: *The Longest Day* (1962) and *Saving Private Ryan* (1998). Both deal with the invasion of France's beaches on 6 June 1944; each became a blockbuster, drawing large audiences in the United States and abroad; each proved to be a surprising success, because in both 1962 and 1998 the traditional war film seemed to have run its course; and each film was the project of a leading Hollywood mogul who had racked up a long list of movie successes. Darryl Zanuck was the major force behind *The Longest Day* (he produced the movie and directed

Photofest

The Longest Day features a large cast of notables: Steve Forrest (as Captain Harding), John Wayne (as Lieutenant Colonel Benjamin Vandervoort), Tom Tryon (as Lieutenant Wilson), and Stuart Whitman (as Lieutenant Sheen).

more than half its scenes), while *Saving Private Ryan* owed its success largely to Steven Spielberg.

Why did these movies resonate with audiences in 1962 and 1998? In what ways did Zanuck's and Spielberg's films address different or similar concerns of the American people in 1962 and 1998? How did critics' reactions differ, and in what ways do these distinctions throw some light on changing attitudes toward war? Above all, did these films contribute to the public's appreciation of history, even though each communicated very different impressions of warfare and history?

THE LONGEST DAY

Darryl Zanuck took a substantial risk when he made *The Longest Day*. After years of splendid successes (including many Academy Awards) as a producer and as head of production at 20th Century-Fox, he seemed to be losing his magic in the early 1960s. Zanuck's work on *Cleopatra* turned out to be a fiasco (the long-delayed picture eventually appeared in theaters in 1963). That expensive historical epic left Fox stretched financially. Yet, while *Cleopatra* was in production, Zanuck proposed to make the most expensive black-and-white war epic in Hollywood history. His $10 million gamble succeeded magnificently. *The Longest Day* grossed $17 million in the United States and reaped millions more abroad, and it is still shown on network TV at least once annually.

Zanuck's movie carries a symbolic message about the Cold War: it shows that American, British, and French troops could cooperate to defeat a common enemy. In 1944 the Allies had successfully challenged Nazi Germany; in the 1960s, the movie seemed to suggest, those same allies could successfully confront the Communists (Ambrose, "Longest Day"). Zanuck made this message more workable by depicting the German leadership with a modicum of empathy. German military commanders in *The Longest Day* seem confused, fumbling, and sometimes comic. They are not enthusiastic about Nazi policies, and in one telling moment, a general complains about Hitler's foolish leadership, blaming the Führer for the failure of the German counteroffensive (Custen 362). Zanuck's rather friendly portrait of America's erstwhile enemy was appropriate for the times; Germany, of course, was a democratic ally of the United States in 1962 and represented an important pillar in the West's strategy of collective security in Europe.

Americans soon needed to practice Zanuck's preachment about collective security. In October 1962, just a few weeks after *The Longest Day* appeared in American theaters, the Cuban Missile Crisis flared. During that confrontation, President John F. Kennedy relied on support from European and Latin American allies. As in the assault on Normandy's beaches in 1944, the successes of October 1962 depended on multilateral cooperation.

Zanuck employed two techniques to make his three-hour war film appealing to the audiences: he engaged numerous Hollywood stars, and he tried to make the war scenes look authentic. *The Longest Day*'s all-star cast included forty-two notable actors appearing in various roles, often in cameos. Among them were John Wayne, Henry Fonda, Robert Mitchum, Peter Lawford, and Richard Burton. This technique helped audiences follow the movements of the many characters in the story, since they could recognize the famous faces. The only woman to have a significant role was Zanuck's mistress at the time, Irina Zemick, who played a French resistance fighter. She had met Zanuck at a cocktail party. "This creepy old man started asking me out on dates," she reported. "He was so ugly and obnoxious, but he offered me a part in the movie, so I thought, 'What the hell. I've nothing to lose'" (quoted in Silverman 85). That role won Zemick international attention.

To make his war story look realistic, Zanuck incorporated a veritable army and navy in the production, obtaining many ships, planes, tanks, and trucks from the NATO allies. The French loaned him two thousand soldiers, even though France was involved in a long and difficult war at the time against guerrillas in Algeria (Suid 172). One amused observer claimed that Zanuck was in control of the ninth biggest military force in the world when he staged the invasion of Normandy for the silver screen (*Time* 19 Oct. 1962: 91). The Pentagon came through with men and equipment too, but its participation became controversial because *The Longest Day* shows Allied troops shooting Germans who are attempting to surrender. Overall, the availability of thousands of men and considerable military hardware allowed Zanuck to give his film a documentary look. As one reviewer noted, the movie was "a tour de force of audio-visual verisimilitude—surely if this is not precisely how it was, it's as close to the genuine article as any imitation is likely to come" (Gill 188).

Zanuck spent a lot of money to obtain authentic-looking airplanes, ships, and tanks for his film, but with regard to another aspect of authenticity, many critics blasted him for failing to deliver. They noted that *The Longest Day* depicts combat death as rather painless. The sensibilities of critics and audiences in 1962 called for a more realistic portrayal of the idea that war is hell and that soldiers suffer terribly. Many reviewers expressed disappointment in the movie's presentation of slaughter on the beaches. Hundreds of extras fall into the sand, they observed, but each victim appears to be unscathed. The troops "die handsomely and intact, with their box-office appeal unimpaired," reported Jay Jacobs in *The Reporter:* "One gets the impression that each death is instant, sanitary, and the result of a mercifully accurate shot to the heart. Nobody has the bad taste to be shot in the face or the belly" (18 Nov. 1962: 50–51). *Time*'s critic complained that "Zanuck shamelessly sugars his bullets—men die by the thousands, but not one living wound, not one believable drop of blood is seen on the screen" (19 Oct 1962: 91). Similarly, *Newsweek*'s reviewer observed, "Nobody bleeds, or groans, or cries out"; the critic noted that although the director seemed determined to show audiences that 6 June 1944 was a big day, he also needed to indicate that it was a terrible day (15 Oct. 1962: 105).

Even before *The Longest Day* appeared in theaters, various Hollywood filmmakers had been more honest in depicting the impact of war on soldiers, although much more realistic depictions would be possible once the Production Code Administration was no longer an obstacle. More grisly images of combat became available to audiences through Oliver Stone's *Platoon* (1986) and Stanley Kubrick's *Full Metal Jacket* (1987).

Darryl Zanuck provides an expansive view of the battlefield in *The Longest Day*.

SAVING PRIVATE RYAN

No movie portrays the violence of wartime combat more memorably than Steven Spielberg's 1998 classic *Saving Private Ryan*. David Denby of *New York* magazine succinctly identified the significance of Spielberg's film: "In this one scene [near the beginning], as in another battle at the end, Spielberg knocks into oblivion every World War II movie ever made, and not even *Platoon* or *Full Metal Jacket* has brought us so close to the experience of men facing live fire at close range" (17 July 1998: 44).

More than any other aspect of the movie, critics and audiences focused on the emotional impact of watching the first half hour of *Ryan*. They sensed the soldiers' fear in the midst of danger, chaos, and confusion on the beaches. Through abundant use of the shaky handheld camera, numerous loud and distinct noises, occasional silences, and shocking imagery, Spielberg gives his movie the appearance of a documentary shot by combat cameramen. These opening sequences lack the heroics that might be expected from such figures as John Wayne or Robert Mitchum in earlier war movies. Men traveling on the Higgins boats vomit from seasickness and fright; many are cut to ribbons

Photofest

Saving Private Ryan stars: Tom Hanks (as Captain Miller), Matt Damon (as Private James Ryan), and Edward Burns (as Private Richard Reiben).

as they charge the beaches. Others fall quickly in horrible deaths that involve mangled torsos and spilled intestines. Some cry in fear.

Spielberg relied heavily on Stephen Ambrose's book *D-Day* for the details in the movie's first twenty-seven minutes. Those memorable scenes of chaos, confusion, and bloodshed are described at length in Ambrose's volume. Even the lead character in the movie is based, to some degree, on a figure described by Ambrose. Tom Hanks's role as the likable Captain Miller resembles the character of Tom Howie, a mild-mannered teacher of English literature before the war. Howie led his men brilliantly in the actions immediately following D-day. He died in combat, and *Life* magazine described "The Major of St. Lo" as a hero (Ambrose, *Citizen Soldiers* 74–76.)

Is *Saving Private Ryan* an antiwar film or a celebration of courage in combat? It is both. Spielberg's complex message communicates the sensibilities of Hollywood and the American people at a time quite different from the 1960s, when Zanuck created *The Longest Day*. In fact, *Saving Private Ryan* communicates attitudes about warfare that are different from today's outlooks as well.

For many Americans in 1998, combat in foreign wars seemed largely a thing of the past. Americans had enjoyed relative peace for several years. When the nation's soldiers became bogged down in Somalia's troubles in the early 1990s, Americans were horrified. They reacted strongly to the disturbing news that eighteen U.S. troops had been killed in urban fighting—with some of the bodies dragged through the streets. Sensitivities over combat losses in that African nation weighed heavily on President Bill Clinton as he contemplated action in later international crises during his two terms in office (1993–2001). Clinton demonstrated a reluctance to commit U.S. soldiers to combat. When intervention seemed necessary in the Balkans, Clinton operated primarily through air campaigns. Military actions by the United States and NATO in 1998 brought down Serbia's Slobodan Milosevic without American combat fatalities. *Saving Private Ryan*'s reminder of the horrors of warfare nicely served an American and global population that held strong hopes for cost-free international strides toward peace in the post–Cold War world.

Yet *Ryan* is also a commentary on history, and in that regard, it provides an inspiring message about the nobility of sacrifice for a greater cause. It portrays World War II in the way many Americans recalled it in the 1990s—as the "Good War," a worthy struggle against the evils of tyranny, oppression, and militarism. Spielberg opens his film by showing the U.S. flag flapping in the breeze, and he leaves audiences with the memorable question of whether the aged Private Ryan has led a life worthy of the tremendous sacrifices made to rescue him. Spielberg reminds audiences that sometimes wars are, indeed, necessary, and for good causes (Doherty).

The director delivers a useful commentary for the time. For years, many Americans had been sharply critical of military engagement because of their disillusionment over the Vietnam conflict. Spielberg shows audiences that some battles are worth fighting, and the men who risk their lives in worthy causes deserve to be honored. Film reviewer Karen Jaehne identified the public's sense of distance from the war experience at the time, as well as the public's need to recognize war's potential to serve noble purposes. "Ultimately," she states, "we watch this film as a generation of Americans who have never risked their lives to defend the free world or gone hungry because there was scarcely enough food for the entire family. In short, to those of us who have never made a personal sacrifice for the greater good, Steven Spielberg brings us the ersatz opportunity of the experience we missed because of the Pax Americana" (39).

Although the combat scenes are largely a product of Spielberg's genius (and that of cinematographer Janusz Kaminski, who worked with Spielberg previously on *Schindler's List, Amistad,* and *The Lost World: Jurassic Park*), the structure of the story emerges largely from the imagination of writer Robert Rodat, who cleverly mined numerous elements of old World War II combat

Photofest

Soldiers prepare to rush the beach in Steven Spielberg's *Saving Private Ryan.*

movies to make an interesting tale. Most young movie patrons of 1998 were unfamiliar with these techniques, but some of the older audience members may have recognized them. Perhaps Rodat honed his skills by reading Jeanine Basinger's magnificent primer on the genre, *The World War II Combat Film.* For instance, *Saving Private Ryan* features a small U.S. military unit made up of diverse ethnic types. There is a smart aleck from Brooklyn, a Jew, a religiously inclined southern sharpshooter (who resembles Sergeant York), and other stereotypes that fit right into Basinger's formula for the World War II combat film. Some of the soldiers in *Saving Private Ryan* doubt their mission, and there is tension between the captain and his troops. Combat waxes and wanes, and during quiet periods the soldiers talk about their girls back at home and jest with one another. When a soldier violates military discipline, an enemy sniper shoots and kills him. The message: follow orders in combat situations (Basinger 37–82). In these and many other ways, *Saving Private Ryan* references the combat genre. It borrows many of its principal characteristics, but, as in all successful war pictures, it also tweaks and revises traditions of the narrative to meet the needs of the age and to respond to the constantly changing expectations of movie audiences.

CINEMA HISTORY: FACT, FICTION, AND "FACTION"

Which film offers a better depiction of history? Does *The Longest Day* or *Saving Private Ryan* present a better and more informative portrayal of the past? At first glance, *The Longest Day* appears to win the contest for historical verisimilitude. After all, Darryl Zanuck's production, based on Cornelius Ryan's book of the same name, portrays the experiences of real-life people; the book relies on interviews with numerous participants in the 1944 invasion. Lawrence H. Suid, author of an important study of war films, praises *The Longest Day* considerably but takes Steven Spielberg to task for relying mainly on fiction rather than fact. He notes that Spielberg "appropriated virtually every scene in *Saving Private Ryan* from other films" and complains that "nothing on the screen actually happened, despite the violence, blood, and gore" (627). He also claims that many of the events depicted in the movie could not have happened. Spielberg's film, Suid concludes, "strains and even far exceeds the limits of dramatic license" (630).

Nevertheless, we can recognize and appreciate the achievements of these two fine movies by noting the distinctive conditions of their production. *The Longest Day* appeared when Hollywood was still making the traditional big-budget, big-cast epics. That movie's didactic style, brimming over with details about strategies for the invasion of Europe, was suitable to filmmaking in the early 1960s. Zanuck's technique was not easy to imitate, as the makers of *Tora! Tora! Tora!* (1970) and *Midway* (1976) discovered. The expectations of audiences changed, and cinema changed as well, partly because of the expansion of television. A vision of the future appeared in the mid-1970s when network television introduced *The Missiles of October* and *Eleanor and Franklin,* character-driven stories that became identified as "docudramas." Soon cable television would expand the offerings, as numerous biographical films and documentaries about historical events appeared on PBS, the History Channel, HBO, and other venues. By the 1990s, Americans expected to receive semieducational entertainment on the small screens in their homes; they ventured out to movie theaters for a different kind of experience.

Experience is the right word to employ when considering modern cinematic histories (Turan). In recent years, such movies' primary contribution to historical appreciation relates to the audience's emotional connection to another time, place, and situation. Steven Spielberg's motion picture accomplishes that goal splendidly by giving viewers the *feeling* of combat and sacrifice on the beaches of Normandy and in the cities of France (Rosenstone 19–24). The movie's success in touching emotions was abundantly evident as patrons left the theaters—many of them in complete silence. To speak would have been tantamount to dishonoring the men who had lost their lives on the altar of freedom.

Saving Private Ryan is a much more modern combat film than *The Longest Day*. It contrasts notably with the old-fashioned war films of the 1940s, 1950s, and early 1960s. *Ryan* accentuates the experience of combat but offers few historical markers about the purpose and strategy of the war planners. There are no speeches about Hitler's tyranny or comments about the events that led America to join the fight in Europe. It communicates messages about the past, but in distinctive ways.

Saving Private Ryan, like most of today's cinematic history, is what I call *faction,* and we cannot hold faction to the traditional standards of authenticity. In faction, the history we are familiar with through our textbooks is in the background, but the stories of people in the foreground—the narratives featuring lead characters—are pure fiction. Faction is the format in *Titanic* (1997), *The Patriot* (2000), *U-571* (2000), and many other modern historical films. The litmus test for judging faction's value in advancing historical appreciation cannot relate solely to its treatment of historical details. This genre demands, by its very nature, a great deal of creative and artistic license (Toplin, *Reel History* 94–97). Faction cannot be truthful in its many small details. Our judgments of it must be based on a film's potential for delivering larger truths in sophisticated ways. By that measure, *Saving Private Ryan* succeeds as an important cinematic commentary on the past.

Both *The Longest Day* and *Saving Private Ryan* engage audiences impressively, but in very different ways. *Saving Private Ryan* is more emotion driven. *Ryan* offers representations of World War II to moviegoers who, for the most part, have little or no personal connection to the war. By contrast, *The Longest Day* is essentially information driven. It provides historical interpretations of epic proportions for Americans who participated in the war themselves or whose parents were intimately connected to it. The cinematic approaches of the two films are quite distinctive, yet the movies' impact on audiences is similar. As visually stunning depictions of historical situations, both films arouse the public's interest in reading and learning about the past.

WORKS CITED

Ambrose, Stephen. *Citizen Soldiers: The U.S. Army from the Normandy Beaches to the Bulge to the Surrender of Germany, June 7, 1944–May 7, 1945.* New York: Simon & Schuster, 1997.

———. *D-Day, June 6, 1944*. New York: Simon & Schuster, 1994.

———. "The Longest Day." *Past Imperfect: History According to the Movies*. Ed. Mark C. Carnes. New York: Holt, 1995. 236–41.

Basinger, Jeanine. *The World War II Combat Film: Anatomy of a Genre*. 1986. Middletown, Conn.: Wesleyan UP, 2003.

Custen, George F. *Twentieth Century's Fox: Darryl F. Zanuck and the Culture of Hollywood*. New York: Basic Books, 1997.

Doherty, Thomas. "Cost of Good War." *Cineaste* 24.1 (1998): 68.

Gill, Brendon. *New Yorker* 13 Oct. 1963: 188.

Jaehne, Karen. Rev. of *Saving Private Ryan*. *Film Quarterly* 53.1 (1999): 39–41.

Rosenstone, Robert A. *Visions of the Past: The Challenge of Film to Our Idea of History*. Cambridge, Mass.: Harvard UP, 1995.

Silverman, Stephen M. *The Fox that Got Away: The Last Days of the Zanuck Dynasty at Twentieth Century-Fox*. Secaucus, N.J.: Lyle Stuart, 1988.

Suid, Lawrence H. *Guts & Glory: The Making of the American Military Image in Film*. Lexington: UP of Kentucky, 2002.

Toplin, Robert Brent. *History by Hollywood: The Use and Abuse of the American Past*. Urbana-Champaign: U of Illinois P, 1996.

———. *Reel History: In Defense of Hollywood*. Lawrence: UP of Kansas, 2002.

Turan, Kenneth. *Los Angeles Times* 24 July 1998. <http://www.calendarlive.com/movies/reviews/cl-movie980723–5,0,6595970.story>.

Part III

Cold War and Insurgency
The Paradox of Limited Wars

COLD WAR BERLIN IN THE MOVIES

From *The Big Lift* to *The Promise*

Although a sizable literature exists on the "Berlin film" (Byg), relatively few authors have explored filmmakers' use of Berlin as a political space during the twentieth century. They have devoted considerably more attention to issues such as modernity and postmodernity, gender, urban culture, and aesthetics.[1] After 1945, however, filmmakers represented Berlin not only as an important part of their mise-en-scène but also to comment on life in divided Germany and on the larger Cold War itself. These symbolic presentations evolved over time in several distinct patterns that closely coincided with changing developments in the city. In the late 1940s, as the Cold War was beginning to unfold, the cityscape communicated ambiguity and uncertainty about the future of Germany. During the next decade, however, both Western and German Democratic Republic (GDR) filmmakers began to portray the "other" Berlin as a source of danger, both in the political and in the cultural sense. The construction of the Berlin Wall on 13 August 1961 was a major turning point. Until 1989, East German filmmakers continued to portray the GDR as a safe haven, but the Wall itself became a taboo theme for them. In contrast, Western filmmakers, both German and non-German, frequently minimized the Wall's function as a divider in a return to the more ambiguous themes that characterized the immediate postwar years.

POSTWAR BERLIN MOVIES IN THE EARLY COLD WAR

In films made in Berlin right after the Second World War, the shattered cityscape represents the morally ambiguous human landscape and the still fluid and uncertain political situation of postwar Germany. These "rubble" films stress the need for a clean break with the past and a new start, although the future

National Archives

Berlin's Brandenburg Gate was behind the Wall.

remains uncertain. In *Berlin Express* (1948), a Hollywood production, the Nazi threat is still overt. An American, an Englishman, a Frenchwoman, and a Russian on a military train from Frankfurt to Berlin unite to thwart an attempt by Nazi underground agents to kill a prominent German resistance member. At the end of the film, the four Allied heroes and the resistance member go their separate ways under the shadow of the Brandenburg Gate; it is unclear whether they will cooperate in the future (Fujiwara 150–57; Christopher 68–69).

German rubble films set in Berlin did not ignore the Nazi past but were much more concerned with the problems of everyday life and themes such as the redemption and reconciliation of "normal" Germans (Shandley). By 1948 some of them were also cautiously addressing Cold War themes, a difficult task due to the need to secure Allied licensing for films. *'48 All Over Again* [*Und wieder '48*] (1948), a production of DEFA studios in the Soviet zone, tells the story of students involved in a film production on the 1848 revolutions. Songs from a cabaret scene make a plea for German unity (also the official Soviet position in the late 1940s and early 1950s) but also imply that the failure to establish a democratic, united Germany in 1848 eventually led to Nazism and the present-day division of the country (Shandley 141–48). Instead of going one hundred years into the past, *The Ballad of Berlin* [*Berliner Ballade*] (1948), a film licensed in the American zone, starts off one hundred years in the future in a prosperous, modern Berlin. In doing so, it validates the current struggles of the city's population and effectively encourages it to keep going despite the

Photofest

In *The Big Lift,* Danny MacCullough (Montgomery Clift) and Frederika Burkhardt (Cornell Borchers) find love among the ruins of Berlin.

onset of the Berlin Blockade in June 1948. In this popular parody of previous German rubble films, the hero, Otto Normalverbraucher (Otto "Average Consumer," played by Gert Fröbe), represents the average Berliner who is increasingly caught between East and West and is uncertain about the political future (Shandley 174–79). In the film, the city and its citizens "are transformed from perpetrators to victims of international disputes" (Shandley 179).

The Big Lift, a 1950 Hollywood production written and directed by George Seaton, tells the story of the 1948–1949 Berlin Airlift. It is one of the last rubble films and also the first true Cold War Berlin film. Shooting began even before the airlift ended with the full cooperation and encouragement of the U.S. Air Force, which also provided most of the actors (Seaton 119–33; Lipschutz 16–18, 25). Central to the plot are uncertainties about the reliability of the Germans as new partners in the Cold War. Danny McCullough (Montgomery Clift) and Hank Kowalski (Paul Douglas) play two American servicemen in the air force with very different views on the people they are aiding. Danny is sympathetic toward the Berliners and tries to learn their language, while his friend Kowalski, a Polish American and a former prisoner of war, has difficulty even being civil to them. He believes that were the situation reversed and the Americans in need of aid, the Germans would sooner kick them in the teeth.

Berlin's geography demonstrates similar doubts. The Soviet zone is portrayed as a potentially dangerous place; indeed, Soviet border guards arrest Berliners and seize their goods with impunity. But as Danny's German girlfriend Frederika (Cornell Borchers) points out, the zonal boundary is important only for the Allies—Berliners travel back and forth across it all the time. In some circumstances, moreover, the Soviet zone can be a haven. Günther (Fritz Nichlicsh), once a German camp guard, unsuccessfully tries to flee to the Soviet zone to escape his vengeful former charge, Kowalski. Danny stops Kowalski from beating Günther senseless just as American MPs arrive. However, Danny is temporarily out of uniform due to an accident, and because of this disciplinary infraction, he and Frederika must cross the border themselves to escape the MPs. There follows one of the most memorable scenes in the film in which the zonal boundary itself seems to be fluid. Soviet guards apprehend the two just as they are about to cross Potsdamer Platz back into the West, but this is exactly where the Soviet, U.K., and U.S. zones meet. American and British MPs physically prevent their arrest until the officers present can resolve whether the interzonal border runs fourteen meters from *this* curbstone or *that* curbstone. Forgotten in the jurisdictional debates, Danny and Frederika slip off unnoticed.

Further complicating Berlin's geography is the fact that spies are everywhere. While visiting Frederika's West Berlin apartment building, Danny meets Herr Stieber (O. E. Hasse), who cheerfully informs him that he is a Russian spy whose job is to record the number and type of Allied planes landing at Tempelhof Airfield. The Soviets doubt the accuracy of the official figures published daily in the newspapers and are especially pleased when Stieber neglects to record a few aircraft, which makes Western reports look exaggerated. He never pays for these omissions because the Soviet spy checking up on him is his own brother-in-law. Stieber estimates that there are fifteen thousand Soviet and ten thousand Western spies in Berlin and at least five hundred double agents. He himself is helpful, honorable (although not totally honest), and an admirer of the United States due to his past travels there. The film portrays the spy situation in an almost comical manner. But it also sends the message that Stieber and many other Berliners are willing to collaborate with either the Soviets or the Western powers in order to get along.

The Big Lift also uses two love affairs to demonstrate German unpredictability. While Frederika is working to clear rubble from the city streets, Danny confronts her about the lies she told concerning her family's resistance activities during the Third Reich. Frederika excuses her actions by pointing to the "sewer" that the Berliners live in and comparing the Berliners themselves to "rats." "Look around you—that's why we lie," she tells him. As Danny walks away, part of a building behind Frederika crumbles to the ground, as if to symbolize their relationship. Yet after seeing scenes of intense devastation and privation during a walk through the streets, Danny accepts the truth of her statement, and they are reconciled. Just before they are to be married, however, Danny learns from Stieber that Frederika is using him solely as a means to get to the United States, where she plans to rejoin her real husband, a former SS man, in St. Louis. Frederika is indeed a rat and a "bad" German, and Danny breaks off their relationship. She contrasts poorly with Gerda (Bruni Lobel), Kowalski's girlfriend, a "good" German who learns the true meaning of democracy.

Cold War Berlin between the Blockade and the Wall, 1949–1961

George Seaton was right when he said that *The Big Lift* "wasn't really anti-Russian" (131). It was more about the Germans and their uncertain future. Over the next decade most of the ambiguities in films about Berlin faded as the Cold War intensified. Despite assertions by both German governments that there was only one city, events clearly belied this claim. During the blockade, separate administrations sprang up and asserted control over public services in their respective halves of the city, which increasingly began to operate independently. Urban planners tried to turn their halves of Berlin into showcases for their respective systems (Ladd 178–89; Large 417–25). Personal contacts between East and West Berliners, as measured by indicators such as mail traffic and Eastern visitors attending West Berlin cultural events, also seemed to decline across the board between 1949 and 1961 (Merritt 170–73). Even if both halves of the city remained united by their relative poverty in the 1950s—due to its "island" status, West Berlin did not enjoy the full fruits of the "economic miracle" of the Federal Republic of Germany (FRG) and, like East Berlin, remained dependent on government subsidies—they were obviously drifting apart as municipalities.

The city also became an ideological battlefield. West Berlin "represented the door in the Iron Curtain. It became the meeting point for East and West. It was a showplace of Western Civilization that countered the influence of Communist indoctrination and provided an outlet for psychological pressures" (Engert 151). West German and Western Allied authorities realized that their part of Berlin served as an open provocation to the communist East and did what they could to emphasize its function as an "outpost of freedom," including making discounted cultural and educational opportunities available to East

Germans (Large 416; Engert 451; Fehrenbach 234–53). As a 1953 short documentary produced by West Berlin authorities put it, their city was an "island of hope" [*Insel der Hoffnung*] for those who had fled the "people's prison of the GDR" (Heimann 90–91). Between 1949 and August 1961 an estimated 2.6 million East Germans—approximately one-sixth of the population—crossed the still-open municipal border and were received in refugee camps before being relocated in the FRG (McAdams 5). West Berliners themselves were intensely politicized during the 1950s, with approximately one-half regularly taking part in mass demonstrations, most of them directed against communist policies (Prowe 265). East German Socialist Unity Party (SED) chairman Walter Ulbricht was not totally off the mark when he claimed that West Berlin was being used as a "front-city" for Western aggression and "subversion" directed against his state (McAdams 29ff.).

The deep ideological cleft that sundered the city in the years between the blockade and the Wall was reflected in the Berlin films made by both Western and communist filmmakers. Each half of Berlin had now become a clear danger to the other side, and the political loyalties of the Berliners, though sometimes initially hidden from outsiders and even from the audience, were increasingly clear-cut. *Night People* (1954) stars Gregory Peck as CIA Colonel van Dyke, whose job it is to free a young GI who has been abducted in East Berlin. In exchange, the Soviets want a former German general involved in the 20 July 1944 plot against Hitler; they intend to turn him over to some former SS men who want revenge.[2] Van Dyke's moral dilemma is resolved when the general and his wife decide to commit suicide rather than face the prospect of certain death in the East, but now he has no one to exchange for the soldier. He and his colleagues then successfully substitute a "bad" German woman, their associate "Hoffy" (Anita Bjork), after discovering her true identity as a Soviet agent.

Escape to Berlin [*Flucht nach Berlin*], a 1960 American–Swiss–West German production, dramatizes East German farmers' resistance to collectivization. One of the farmers flees across the open border to West Berlin, where he is followed by one of the SED officials sent to his village who has had his own falling out with the party. Frank Arnold has described *Flucht nach Berlin,* as well as other Western films made after the construction of the Berlin Wall and having a similar escape motif, as a genuine cinematic "Go West!" movement. GDR films could counter it "with only the rhetorical movement forward into a better future" (Arnold 11).

These Western productions found their counterpart in the GDR's Berlin films of the 1950s, which had a common theme of portraying West Berlin as an unjust society and a source of social pathologies such as crime and delinquency (Feinstein 59–60). DEFA now stood under communist control, and its films from the early 1950s were painfully true to the party line (Allan 6–11; Schittly 39–69). Kurt Maetzig's 1952 film *Story of a Marriage* [*Roman einer jungen Ehe*] portrays a marriage between two actors, Agnes (Yvonne Merin) and Jochen (Hans-Peter Thielen), who live in West Berlin. Jochen succumbs to the temptation of furthering his career there and takes roles that Agnes believes are crude attacks against the East or celebrate militarism. Moreover, she sees cultural figures from the Nazi era rehabilitated in the FRG. Agnes eventually decides that her future lies in East Berlin, where she recites a poem in Stalin's honor to workers who are building the Stalinallee (this construction project is one of the film's leitmotifs). For his part, Jochen objects to his wife acting in what he believes are propaganda films for the GDR. But after he witnesses East German peace demonstrators being beaten by West German police, he sees the light, deciding to follow his wife and reconcile with her (Schenk 61).

Yet another DEFA film from 1952, *Fates of Women* [*Frauenschicksale*], is about three East Berlin women who have bad experiences with the same dashing but heartless West Berlin Casanova, Conny (Hanns Groth). They then succeed in building new lives in East Berlin (another woman, a member of the communist Free German Youth, turns Conny down during their first encounter). Besides contrasting the two halves of the city and implying that women's emancipation is possibly only in the East, director Slatan Dudow demonstrates that personal happiness can be realized only in the context of the creation of a socialist society.[3]

Director Gerhard Klein and screenwriter Wolfgang Kohlhaase made a trio of important films about Berlin between 1953 and 1958, a period in which GDR filmmakers enjoyed a relatively more open political atmosphere following the death of Stalin. Horst Claus writes that this work "established [both men] as creators of the so-called '*Berlin-Filme*'—films set in Berlin during the first two decades after World War II which focus on the personal experiences of working-class people under twenty-five in the divided city. Though rooted in fiction, these films are generally regarded as the most authentic portraits of a generation which was expected to realize the dream of a fair and equal German society in the East" (94). Even though both men were far more interested in neorealism than socialist realism, their Berlin films drew a clear contrast between the two halves of the city that fit within the official communist paradigm (Claus 96–110; Schenk 127–31).

Alarm at the Circus [*Alarm im Zirkus*] (1954) is a children's film about two working-class West Berlin boys, Max (Ernst-Georg Schwill) and Klaus (Hans Winter), who have very limited prospects for the future. The economic situation is so bleak that they cannot hope for a position or even proper job training.

Many young people they know are being "ruined" by American music and cheap comics. Max and Klaus dream of becoming champion boxers—if only they could afford the gloves. In the meantime, local West Berlin thugs are plotting to steal valuable horses from an East Berlin circus with the complicity of American soldiers. They hire the boys to help them without fully initiating them into their plans. The boys visit the circus themselves and meet the East German girl Helli. She informs them of her plans to attend university, which they cannot hope to do in the West, although they are from the same social class. Klaus later discovers that he and Max are actually involved in an attempt to steal the horses and tries to warn the authorities. When the West Berlin authorities do not respond, he gets Helli's father to call the East German police, who foil the crooks after a chase and a shoot-out. At the end of the film both boys are rewarded by the circus with the desired boxing gloves.

A Berlin Romance [Eine Berliner Romanze] (1956) tells the story of an East Berlin teenager working in a department store on Alexanderplatz who dreams of a modeling career in the West. Uschi (Annekathrin Buerger) is encouraged when a major Berlin paper runs a picture of her in an amateur fashion show. While strolling along the Kurfürstendamm she encounters Hans (Ulrich Thein), an unemployed West Berliner. Hans is smitten with Uschi, manages to win her, and finds several jobs to help pay her tuition at modeling school. But he is soon injured due to inadequate safety precautions at a demolition site. Realizing the foolishness of having run away to live in West Berlin and faced with her inability to pay her own tuition, Uschi returns home. After a talk with her mother, she asks Hans to come with her to East Berlin, where he finds a good job as a mechanic. The film presents West Berlin as glamorous and attractive but also as cold and materialistic, while human warmth, common sense, and full employment prevail in the East.

Finally, in Berlin—Schönhauser Corner [Berlin—Ecke Schönhauser] (1957) Klein and Kohlhaase attempt to present the problems of working-class youth who are enthralled with Western and especially American pop culture, the so-called Halbstarken ("teddy boys," or "hooligans").[4] The protagonists spend much of their time hanging out on a street corner under an elevated train provoking the passers-by with their rock-and-roll dancing and fresh comments. It is clear that their behavior originates in conditions such as problems at home, bad parenting, frustration with regimentation, and generational conflict. However, West Berlin also exercises an enormous attraction. Karl-Heinz (Harry Engel) becomes involved in an illegal money-changing operation and unsuccessfully tries to get two of his friends to join him. Fearing that they will be charged with murdering Karl-Heinz after a confrontation, the friends flee to West Berlin and have an extremely unpleasant experience in a refugee camp, where one

President John F. Kennedy visits Berlin in August 1961 and rides with Mayor Willy Brandt and President Konrad Adenauer. In his remarks JFK declares, "Ich bin ein Berliner."

of them dies. *Berlin—Schönhauser Corner* marks something of a shift in East German cinematic portrayals of a divided Berlin. Joshua Feinstein remarks that previous DEFA films had presented "the GDR as a place where dreams—or at least the aspirations of the working class—came true." In *Berlin—Schönhauser Corner* the characters abandon their fantasies about the West; however, now the alternative offered by the East is not a dream but "the realization that their own lives are already sufficient" (60). The film was a popular success in the GDR, and both East and West German critics praised its realism, although it drew fire from GDR cultural critics due to the "predominance of misfits" among the main characters (Feinstein 45–77).

FILMS OF THE SECOND BERLIN CRISIS

The Second Berlin Crisis (1958–1962), which culminated with the construction of the Berlin Wall on 13 August 1961, represented the height of the Cold War propaganda battle in Berlin. It also saw the premiere of two films, one Western and one Eastern, whose tenor directly reflected the ideological shouting match.

One, Two, Three, director Billy Wilder's 1961 political satire set in Berlin, did not appeal to most critics. Some still dislike its madcap pace, driven by James Cagney's abrasive and jingoistic performance as Coca-Cola executive

C. R. MacNamera, which they believe limited opportunities for both plot and character development (Dick 72–73; Chandler 240). Supposedly, the film also oversimplified the political situation and even threatened to complicate American-Soviet relations, which were at a boiling point already (Armstrong 5; Dick 70). Many contemporary critics simply found it crass and shallow. The final blow came when the Wall went up just before filming finished on location in Berlin. This compelled Wilder both to construct a papier-mâché version of the Brandenburg Gate and other exteriors in Munich (where the interior scenes were being shot) and to attach a short prelude spoken by MacNamera (Cagney) referring to the events of 13 August 1961 (Sikov 453–65). Nonetheless, audiences found *One, Two, Three*'s subject matter already outdated when it appeared in theaters. Wilder's lighthearted treatment of the Cold War also seemed, in his own words, "a great miscalculation [at a time when] people were being shot trying to climb the Wall" (Chandler 237–38; Wilder, "Billy Wilder" 107; American Film Institute 125). The film bombed at the box office (Sikov 465). However, more than thirty years later, *One, Two, Three* was rediscovered in unified Germany, where it is still shown in theaters and on television (Chandler 242; Crowe 165). On one level, it is a successful throwback to the screwball comedies of the 1930s;[5] on another, it seems far ahead of its time in its treatment of American culture—in this case, Coca-Cola—as a powerful weapon in the Cold War.[6]

MacNamera's boss from the Atlanta headquarters, Wendell P. Hazeltine (Howard St. John), asks him to take care of his hot-blooded seventeen-year-old daughter Scarlet (Pamela Tiffin) on the Berlin segment of her European tour. Scarlet is known for her multiple wedding engagements. Although her arrival will cause major difficulties for MacNamera's family, including the cancellation of their vacation plans, he can hardly refuse. He has ambitions to become leader of Coca-Cola's European operations in London, and he is on the verge of a major coup that he thinks will secure the job for him: a deal with three commissars from the Soviet Trade Commission to sell Coke for the first time behind the Iron Curtain. Scarlet's two-week visit turns into two months due to an illness and her secret romance with an East German communist, Otto Piffl (Horst Buchholz). The MacNameras are alarmed when she does not come home one evening, but the next morning she turns up in MacNamera's office and announces that she is married and that she and Otto are planning to leave that day for Moscow, where Otto will begin his studies as a rocket scientist.

After each defends the merits of his respective system (MacNamera: "To hell with Khrushchev!" Otto: "To hell with . . . Frank Sinatra!"), MacNamera rigs a booby trap to get rid of the problematic Otto. This involves giving him a "Yankee Doodle" cuckoo clock wrapped in the *Wall Street Journal* as a gift and secretly putting a "Russki go home" balloon on the exhaust of his motorcycle. On cue, Otto is arrested as soon as he crosses the Brandenburg Gate on his way home to pack. Unfortunately for MacNamera, it turns out that Scarlet is pregnant and that her parents are arriving the next day. He races to East Berlin and spends the entire night at a seedy hotel pretending to peddle his sexy German secretary, Ingeborg (Lilo Pulver), to the three Soviet commissars in exchange for their help in freeing Otto. They successfully intervene with the GDR police but get a big surprise when MacNamera puts his hopelessly obsequious personal assistant Schlemmer (Hanns Lothar) in Ingeborg's dress before making the exchange. Just before his release, Otto confesses to being an American spy after being tortured by the repeated playing of the song "Itsy-Bitsy, Teeny-Weeny, Yellow Polka-Dot Bikini." He can no longer return to the East, and the remainder of the film depicts Otto's implausible instant conversion into a German count and Coke bottling plant manager in an effort to make him acceptable to Scarlet's parents.

One, Two, Three does a good job of evoking the political tensions of the time. One of the first scenes in the film portrays mass demonstrations in East Berlin featuring posters of Khrushchev and signs with slogans such as "What's Going on in Little Rock?" Balloons, as well as other flying and floating devices, were indeed used to carry political slogans across the zonal boundaries as displayed in the film. Wilder also parodies a West German society that only twenty years earlier had firmly supported National Socialism in the form of the heel-clicking West Germans on MacNamera's staff and several scenes with references to the Third Reich. Unlike the Berliners in *The Big Lift*, these Germans are clearly on the side of the West, although MacNamera has good reason to question whether they are being completely honest about their past activities. Moreover, the Second Berlin Crisis is always lurking in the background. Again and again the political situation in the city is referred to as dangerous or explosive.

The basic East-West divide is also present. West Berlin is clearly the more desirable place to live. MacNamera explains early in the film that one of his major problems is East Berliners who bring Coke home and then forget to return the bottles. To make this point, Wilder wildly exaggerates the poverty of East Berlin, even though by 1961 the GDR government had already devoted considerable resources to renovating the downtown government districts around Unter den Linden, which are supposedly featured in several scenes (Sikov 458). There are a few brief mentions of the actual refugee crisis, and one of the Soviet trade commissars, Peripetchikoff (Leon Askin), decides to defect so that he can go into business in the West (and be with Ingeborg). In the process, he preemptively betrays the other two commissars, who have similar plans, to the communist authorities. Disgusted at Peripetchikoff's actions and at the tactics used to secure his own confession, Otto decides to renounce communism as well as capitalism. In the funniest exchange in the film, he cries out, "Is *everybody* in this whole world corrupt?" to which Peripetchikoff matter-of-factly replies, "I don't know everybody." Wilder is saying, as he did in his 1948 Berlin film *A Foreign Affair,* that people are people, regardless of the political and social system, and they have the same basic desires and, perhaps, the same capacity for shenanigans. Yet he clearly thinks that it is much better to be corrupt in the prosperous West than in the poor and politically repressive East. If Otto and Scarlet's baby grows up to be a socialist, at least he or she will be a rich one.

Look at This City [*Schaut auf diese Stadt*], an East German documentary, premiered exactly one year to the day after construction began on the Berlin Wall.[7] Its director, Karl Gass, remarked that he and his colleagues wanted to "create a national document" that made the historic importance of 13 August clear ("Gass' Experimentierküche" 45). Film historian Hans-Jörg Rother's appraisal of the film is far more accurate: "Never before and never again in the history of the DEFA documentary film would a work turn so hard-heartedly and maliciously against its own public." It was arguably the most polemical and "hateful" documentary by Gass, a filmmaker known for his ideological fervor (95–96).

Look at This City, which is based primarily on GDR newsreel footage, presents a history of Germany and Berlin since 1945 from a communist perspective. Beyond the film's undisputable technical qualities, it is interesting for two reasons. First, it faithfully repeats the SED's official rationale for building the Wall as an "anti-Fascist protective bulwark" designed to preserve the achievements of socialism in the GDR.[8] The screenplay was even written by Karl-Eduard von Schnitzler, who, as chief commentator of the GDR's *Deutschlandsender* [Germany Service], was "the public voice of the East German cause" (Hanwehr 92–94); he would remain in that role in radio and television until the fall of the Berlin Wall on 9 November 1989. Second, preparations for the film began even before construction of the Wall. As Gass states, events transformed a film initially intended merely to highlight West Berlin's "abnormal [*anomal*]" situation into a "national document" ("Gründlicher analysieren" 46; Rother 95). Therefore, *Look at This City* provides the clearest and indeed most wildly exaggerated version of the "West Berlin as a danger" motif evident in pre-Wall GDR feature and documentary films.

This theme, by the way, was not a new one in Gass's work. His 1960 documentary *Freedom . . . Freedom . . . über alles* [*Freiheit . . . Freiheit . . . über alles*], which deals with contradictions between political rhetoric and actual conditions in the West, begins with theme music and broadcasts from the Voice of America and the Radio in the American Sector (RIAS) in West Berlin. At suitably ironic points it also features the chimes of West Berlin's Freedom Bell [*Freiheitsglocke*] located in the Schöneberg Rathaus (Kleinert). An exact model of the Liberty Bell in Philadelphia cast to commemorate the Berlin Airlift, it rang every Sunday just before the noon broadcast of RIAS Berlin, which always started with a spoken "Liberty Oath." These sounds, as well as the images of radio towers, would have been very familiar to East German and especially East Berlin audiences (Baumgärtel; Kundler).

Look at This City argues that even though the people of West Berlin have the same desire to work, live, and love as their compatriots in the East, they allow their city to be used by imperialists who want to overthrow the GDR. West Berlin Lord Mayor Ernst Reuter's appeal to the people of England, France, and America during the 1948 Berlin Blockade to "look at this city" as an outpost of freedom becomes the film's ironic leitmotif. West Berlin's streets are filled with Western troops and jazz and rock and roll music, "strange sights and sounds for a German city." Its street names commemorate "warmongers" such as General Lucius D. Clay and revolts in the GDR (the *Straße des 17. Juni* honored the major uprising in 1953). West Berlin is home to the RIAS and other organizations that continually stir up trouble and even sabotage in East Germany. The imperialists abuse the transit routes across the GDR by sending their troops to West Berlin and allowing East German refugees out of it, the latter mainly by air. West Berlin also hosts conferences of expellees, German veterans, and, in July 1961, the Evangelical Church (the tenth annual *Evangelischer Kirchentag*). All these groups are anticommunist and, in the case of the first two, also revanchist. To underline this theme of Western subversion, Reuter's appeal to "look at this city" is repeatedly paired with the statement by his successor as Lord Mayor, Willy Brandt, that he is proud that West Berlin is a troublemaker [*Störenfried*] for the GDR. If Wilder makes the East German population appear militant, Gass does the same with the West Berliners.

One can also "look at this city" to see high rates of criminality, suicide, and unemployment (based on actual statistics from the FRG), along with other forms of social depravity. Gass contrasts the state of affairs in West Germany with repetitious footage of workmen, apartment houses, schools, and a mother with child to emphasize the positive accomplishments of the East German social state. To make West Berlin harmless, the obvious solution is to construct the "anti-Fascist defensive bulwark" along the dividing line long established by the Western powers. Although portrayed as a heroic act, footage of the construction of the Wall is literally tacked on to the end of *Look at This City* and in no way changes the film's basic arguments about the Berlin situation.

Look at This City also skillfully employs music to underline the differences between the two parts of Berlin. Classical music provides the sound track

**YOU ARE LEAVING
THE AMERICAN SECTOR
ВЫ ВЫЕЗЖАЕТЕ ИЗ
АМЕРИКАНСКОГО СЕКТОРА
VOUS SORTEZ
DU SECTEUR AMÉRICAIN
SIE VERLASSEN DEN AMERIKANISCHEN SEKTOR**

National Archives

A Berlin sign reflects the city's divided consciousness.

when the GDR or the USSR is featured. The "fate theme" from Beethoven's Fifth Symphony is used to demonstrate East German and Soviet heroism and resolve, such as when East German militia secures the Brandenburg Gate on 13 August 1961. Shostakovich's Symphony no. 7 (the Leningrad Symphony) plays during scenes of the Soviet conquest of Berlin. Finally, music by Johann Sebastian Bach (who, like SED chairman Walter Ulbricht, was from Saxony) figures prominently whenever the GDR's accomplishments are being featured. According to Wolfram von Hanwehr, Bach represents a perfected harmonic order; therefore, the use of his music "represents the order of the East German state contrasting the 'decline and fall' of the order of the capitalist world" (337). In contrast, Gass uses rock and jazz to accompany images of West Berlin. "Yakety Yak" ("Take out the papers and the trash") and "Take the A-Train" play when GIs appear. British troops march to the World War II hit "Hanging out the Washing on the Siegfried Line" (an ironic reference to the poor U.K. performance in the first years of the war), and NATO troops to "Lili Marlene," a Nazi favorite. The popular West German song "Tomorrow [*Morgen*]" ("Tomorrow, tomorrow, life will finally be beautiful again") and the Hitler Youth song "Today Germany Is Ours, Tomorrow the Whole World [*Heute gehört uns Deutschland, Morgen die ganze Welt*]" are used in tandem to represent German revanchism (Hanwehr 300–58).

THE GREAT DISAPPEARING BERLIN WALL

One, Two, Three and *Look at This City* represent an era in Berlin's history in which the two halves of the city were drifting apart and communication between them represented a shouting match rather than a dialogue. The construction of the Wall, of course, completed the city's division. In his book *The Ghosts of Berlin,* Brian Ladd argues that the Wall "was antithetical to the mobility and circulation characteristic of a modern city." Pollution, radio and TV signals, and the sound of rock concerts still passed across it, and it was possible for Westerners to travel underneath it through the city's historical central district (*Berlin-Mitte*) on two subway lines that linked the northeastern and southeastern parts of West Berlin. Otherwise, the Wall now blocked streets and tram lines, and even gas and water mains had been cut. East German guards would kill at least seventy-eight people trying to cross it illegally (Ladd 18–19, 24). The inner-German détente of the 1970s and 1980s did relatively little to revive personal contacts in the divided Berlin, even after East Germans received increasing opportunities to visit relatives in the West starting in 1984 (Merritt 174–81; McAdams 166–67). The city also clearly began to drift apart economically. In the words of *Der Spiegel* magazine in 1966, West Berlin and its 2.2 million residents had become "the glittering thing" (Ladd 469). Even though East Berlin enjoyed the highest standard of living in the communist bloc, the GDR's economy as a whole went into a long and irreversible decline during the 1970s. Its inhabitants realized that West Berliners had it much better (Ladd 463–515; Maier 59–107; Fulbrook 37–38).

By the mid-1980s some observers were also pointing to a much more serious source of division that was psychological in origin. Political scientist Richard L. Merritt wrote in 1985 that "as each year passes, the underlying basis of political community in Berlin as a whole erodes a bit more. . . . In place of community, estrangement was growing" (183). East and West Berliners had lived parallel but separate lives for too long. Three years earlier, Peter Schneider had similarly noted in his influential novel *The Wall Jumper: A Berlin Story* [*Der Mauerspringer. Eine Berliner Geschichte*] that "it will take us longer to tear down the Wall in our heads than any wrecking company will need for the Wall we can see" (119).

Cold War Berlin films made after 1961 display a similar radical break between East and West. After the early 1960s the Berlin Wall—and indeed the East-West conflict as a whole—began to disappear from the East German cinema. There were several reasons why GDR filmmakers began to avoid addressing the problems of the divided city. Everyday life in East Berlin was no longer dominated by the open border and its temptations, so GDR directors started to focus instead on the social world of Berlin's residents and the difficulties they faced (Richter; Claus 110–14). Documentary filmmakers, too, turned their view inward, often in the hope of creating an attractive image for the GDR's welfare state (Rother 108).

If some East German filmmakers initially believed that construction of the Wall would give them more artistic freedom, which seemed desirable to attract more visitors to movie theaters, they soon found that they were sorely mistaken (Schittly 101–24; Allan 11ff.). Mid-1960s films that tried to depict the division of Germany in a nuanced way, such as Konrad Wolf's 1964 film *Divided Heaven* [*Der Geteilte Himmel*] (based on Christa Wolf's 1963 novel), enjoyed a controversial reception. East German critics disliked the heroine Rita (Renate Blume), who, despite her commitment to socialism, was a "weak" and "passive" character, torn between the GDR and her lover who had fled to West Berlin. They accused both the book and the film of making the division of Germany look like a greater misfortune than West German "imperialism" (Richter 175; Schittly 125–27). Starting with its Central Committee's Eleventh Plenum in 1965, the SED increasingly demanded that works of the GDR's artistic community conform to its ideological line. In response, the party banned twelve films from theaters in 1965 and 1966. After construction of the Wall, the SED de-emphasized national unification in order to dwell on the construction of socialism in East Germany, and by the early 1970s it had normalized relations with the West, including the FRG. Therefore, any film that addressed the East-West divide risked official disfavor.

Last but not least, it was difficult for East German filmmakers to portray the Berlin Wall in a positive light in any way that was plausible and believable. It hardly represented a "victory" for socialism and in fact had been constructed against the wishes of the majority of the East German population. DEFA produced only four feature films in the 1960s in which the Wall played a central role. Two of them, . . . *And Your Love Too* [. . . *und Deine Liebe auch*] (1962) and *The Hook to the Chin* [*Der Kinnhaken*] (1962), deal with East Berliners who try to get to their West Berlin jobs on 13 August 1961.[9] A third, *Sunday Drivers* [*Sontagsfahrer*] (1963), is a *comedy* about several Leipzig families whose attempt to flee to West Berlin by car on 13 August is frustrated by the construction of the Wall. Since not all the passengers wish to leave the GDR, the disloyal ones can be portrayed as unsympathetic caricatures. Although . . . *And Your Love Too* has some cinematographically important sequences that use documentary techniques to re-create the bustle of Berlin's streets, none of these films was popular or a critical success. The final film, *Stories of that Night* [*Geschichten jener Nacht*] (1967), attempts to justify the Wall in four vignettes, but it can also be understood primarily as a declaration of party loyalty by its directors, two of whom, Frank Vogel and Gerhard Klein, had their films banned after the Eleventh SED Plenum (Richter 164–71).

After *Stories of that Night*, both the division of Germany and the Wall itself became virtually taboo subjects in GDR cinema. Only in 1990 would an East German director, Jürgen Böttcher, focus on this theme with his documentary *The Wall* [*Die Mauer*], which, notably, depicts its fall (Richter 171; Allan 11). It was much safer and more effective to concentrate on unfavorable developments in West Germany's capitalist society such as high rents, on laws that unfairly favored business, or even on the few cases of West Germans who decided to settle in the GDR. These themes were made more credible to audiences by the fact that the West German media also discussed them openly, as most East Germans would know from their consumption of Western television and radio (Heimann 99–100). Yet even such comparisons found limited appeal because of another trend, which found East German directors concentrating on the portrayal of everyday life rather than the progress made in "constructing socialism."[10]

For Western filmmakers, Cold War Berlin with its Wall had an obvious appeal as a setting for escape films featuring tunnels (*Escape from East Berlin* [1962]), buses (in Alfred Hitchcock's *Torn Curtain* [1966], Paul Newman and Julie Andrews flee from Leipzig to East Berlin by bus on their way to Sweden), and trains (*Durchbruch Lok 234* [1963]) (Arnold 11). In some cases they were based on true stories, such as the American made-for-TV film *Berlin Tunnel 21* (1981) and the German miniseries *The Tunnel* [*Der Tunnel*] (2001), about the business of tunneling under the Wall that flourished for a brief time in the early 1960s. An escape to West Berlin is even the central plot element in a rather forgettable comedy called *The Wicked Dreams of Paula Schultz* (1968), starring Elke Sommer as an East German athlete who wants to defect. The good Westerners and bad East Germans are played by the lead actors from the TV series *Hogan's Heroes*.[11]

However, most filmmakers in the FRG joined their East German colleagues in avoiding portrayals of the inter-German border. In a book that first appeared in 1985, West German film critic Hans Günther Pflaum noted:

> If foreigners totally unfamiliar with the German situation were to view those films set in West Berlin, they would hardly become aware of an essential aspect of this city: the wall that effectively seals off the western part of the city from East Berlin and the German Democratic Republic. No other taboo has been so consistently observed by German filmmakers in recent years than the taboo of the border

Photofest

Alec Leamas (Richard Burton) and Nan Perry (Claire Bloom) are caught on the Wall between East and West.

between the two Germanys. The causes of this restraint are most likely to be found in the feature films produced during the cold war era, especially American productions. No director of the new German cinema wanted to be associated with any of those films, and most of them systematically avoided the problem of the border, which, as recently as 1982, was the subject of an American film with a decidedly propagandistic tone, *Mit dem Wind nach Westen* [*Night Crossing*], a Walt Disney production. (97)

This observation seems even more remarkable when we consider that West Berlin was an important center for the FRG's movie industry and, for that reason alone, an obvious setting for films (Pflaum 91).

Yet it is not true that the Wall disappeared from Western films. American and British directors never shied away from it, and Pflaum acknowledges that a few younger West German filmmakers such as Helke Sander and Reinhard

Hauff featured it in their films. In the late 1980s they would be joined by a number of others. What had changed, however, was that the most significant Western films on Cold War Berlin had lost their propaganda function and instead returned to the ambiguities of the late 1940s in their portrayals of the divided city. Especially by using the genre of the spy film, some filmmakers blurred the distinction between East and West politically and tended to make both sides appear amoral or even immoral in their behavior. Meanwhile, West German filmmakers began to de-emphasize the physical barriers between East and West Berlin. In these films the Wall is no longer a particular obstacle to movement, and the city itself is portrayed as an organic whole. Finally, due to Peter Schneider's direct influence, filmmakers began to emphasize that the true walls dividing Germans were internal instead of external, psychological instead of physical.

THE BERLIN WALL AND THE WESTERN ESPIONAGE FILM

Starting in the mid-1960s several important Berlin films appeared with the theme of international espionage. By then directors could draw on a considerable number of popular spy novels set in that city, either in whole or in part, as the basis for screenplays (Mews; Kamm). Of course, this was also the era of the James Bond films starring Sean Connery, which inspired many imitators on both the silver screen and the television screen (G. Miller 80). In 1965 John Le Carré's novel *The Spy Who Came in from the Cold* was filmed, followed a year later by Len Deighton's *Funeral in Berlin*. Gritty realism and a sense of history pervade these films. Although not devoid of charm and sophistication, Le Carré's Alec Leamas (Richard Burton) and Deighton's "Harry Palmer" (the nameless Cockney spy in his early novels played in several films by Michael Caine) are expendable foot soldiers instead of glamorous superspies.[12] Leamas and Palmer are assigned to the often cold and dreary Berlin, not to the sunny locales frequented by 007. They do not battle megalomaniacal supervillains armed with high-tech gadgets but instead have to deal with plausibly conceived representatives of the Soviet bloc's security agencies using primarily their own wits. *The Spy Who Came in from the Cold* and *Funeral in Berlin* also represent a return to the ambiguities found in the Cold War Berlin films of the late 1940s. Leamas and Palmer are not sure who is friend and who is foe or, more importantly, whose side in the Cold War holds the moral high ground.

Throughout *The Spy Who Came in from the Cold* the East and West are portrayed as moral equivalents. Control (Cyril Cusak) informs Leamas, "I'd say since the war, our methods, our techniques that is, and those of the communists have become very much the same . . . yes. I mean, occasionally we have to do wicked things, very wicked things indeed. But you can't be less wicked than your enemy just because your government's policy is benevolent, can you?" Leamas tells his lover Nan Perry (Claire Bloom) much the same thing, even saying, "communism, capitalism. It's the innocents who get slaughtered." Nan is portrayed as naïve, not so much because she is a British communist but because she is a true believer in a cause. During the film's climactic dialogue she asks Leamas, "How can you turn the whole world upside-down? What rules are you playing?" To which he replies, "There is only one rule—expediency." The character Nan is also of interest because she participates in the Campaign for Nuclear Disarmament, which reminds us of the nuclear anxieties prevalent in the late 1950s and early 1960s and suggests another area in which parallels can be drawn between the superpowers.

In the film East and West are also linked by anti-Semitism. In his mission to eliminate the head of East German intelligence operations, Hans-Dieter Mundt (Peter van Eyck), Leamas plays a defector. He confirms the suspicions of Mundt's deputy, Fiedler (Oskar Werner), that his boss is a double agent working for the British. Fiedler is an honest man who is in some respects like Nan: he thinks that spies should at least work for a cause they believe in if they must commit evil acts. His colleagues also know that he is a Jew and dislike him for that reason. As it turns out, Mundt is actually London's man in East Germany, and Leamas unknowingly has been sent as part of a scheme to save him from Fiedler's investigations. Helping to seal Fiedler's fate is doubly bitter for Leamas. Many British agents that he controlled in Berlin had been eliminated by the "bastard" Mundt, and he has grown to respect Fiedler. Yet he believes that something else is rotten about the situation, too. "London made us kill him," he tells Nan, "kill the Jew." Four years after the verdict against Adolf Eichmann in Jerusalem, the film raises the ultimate damning analogy, comparing Cold War espionage to the Holocaust.

"Berlin," or, more precisely, a massive reconstruction of the Berlin Wall (the film was shot in England and Ireland), appears as a setting only twice in *The Spy Who Came in from the Cold*, but it also frames the entire movie. In the opening scene, accompanied by Sol Kaplan's haunting theme music, the camera pans back very slowly from barbed wire on the Eastern side toward Checkpoint Charlie, giving the viewer an impression of the immense obstacles separating East and West. It is the middle of the night, and Leamas is waiting nervously for Karl Riemek, an East German spy in his charge. He must watch helplessly as the East German border guards shoot Riemek down just as it seems that he will cross to West Berlin without incident. In the closing scene, once again at night, but this time on the Eastern side, Leamas and Nan are on the verge of climbing over the Wall when they are betrayed and killed. Thus these scenes at the Wall underscore the film's portrayal of international espionage as characterized by death, betrayal, and drabness. In being drab, Berlin is no different from London or any other locale in the movie, another parallel. Director Martin Ritt intentionally filmed in black and white to create the dreary world in which Leamas and other intelligence agents live and in which there are no clear standards of right and wrong (G. Miller 81, 85; T. Miller 113).

Funeral in Berlin is the second Harry Palmer film. Due to his criminal past, Palmer's bosses in British intelligence are sure of his loyalty: he must either do as they say or serve time in prison for theft. In a comparable situation are two other agents, J. B. Hallam (Hugh Burden) and Johnnie Vulkan (Paul Hubschmid), who are plotting to secure $2 million stolen from Jews during World War II and locked away in a secret Swiss bank account. Hallam, who provides Palmer with aliases, eventually loses his job because he is considered a "security risk"; the film subtly implies that he is a homosexual. Vulkan is Palmer's contact in West Berlin, as well as a former guard at Bergen-Belsen and the son of the Nazi who deposited the stolen money. His real name is Paul Louis Broum. Broum is supposed to be dead, and British intelligence keeps his identity papers on file to ensure Vulkan's loyalty. If Hallam can get Vulkan these papers by issuing them as an alias to the unsuspecting Palmer, both men will have access to the bank account.[13]

Before these plot details fully unfold, Palmer has been to Berlin twice, the second time as "Broum," to arrange the defection of Soviet Colonel Stok (Oskar Homolka), head of the KGB's Berlin section.[14] The colonel insists that he is not a traitor and is still a good communist, but unfortunately, his record in preventing people from fleeing to West Berlin has been poor lately. He recommends that West German underworld figure Otto Kreuzman (Günter Meissner), the most successful people smuggler in the city, be hired to get him across the Wall. Palmer has many reasons to suspect that Stok is lying but finally authorizes the flight attempt. Kreuzman's team poses as undertakers to get the colonel through the checkpoint at the Bornholmer Straße bridge in a hearse. When Kreuzman's corpse is found in the coffin, it is obvious that the "funeral in Berlin" has gone awry. Being right about the colonel is of little consolation to Palmer, who has not only blown his mission but also lost Broum's papers. His boss Ross (Guy Doleman) then tells him to eliminate Vulkan, who can no longer be blackmailed and may sell himself to the highest bidder in the Cold War, but Palmer now has to worry about the Israeli secret service too.

Funeral in Berlin has a less somber tone than *The Spy Who Came in from the Cold,* if no less somber an ending. Palmer cracks jokes throughout. Moreover, the film was shot in color and on location and portrays downtown West Berlin as the "glittering thing," complete with transvestite cabarets. The Wall features prominently, but the majority of the outside scenes were filmed around the Zoologischer Garten and Kurfürstendamm in the West, including atop the newly built, twenty-two-story Europa-Center, with its revolving Mercedes-Benz symbol. While in the bar at the Berlin Hilton, another major symbol of postwar reconstruction,[15] Vulkan agrees with Palmer's comment that the division of the city has not hurt business and adds that many people "make a great living out of the Wall." Yet the films are similar in portraying spying as a dirty business. A West Berlin police official tells Palmer how much he hates Western agents because they operate in league with every criminal in the city. Although he pretends that he works only for money, Palmer is troubled by his situation. He agrees with Stok that Kreuzman is a "fascist," but he does not like sending him to his death. Nor does he want to kill Vulkan in cold blood, in part because he recognizes that their cases are similar. Ross underlines this point. When Palmer asks, "Do you mean Her Majesty's Government employs ex-Nazis, sir?" he replies, "And thieves, Palmer." By the end of the film Palmer has demonstrated that he does indeed have some principles, but we are left wondering whether British intelligence is any better than the KGB.

A West German variation on the themes in *Funeral in Berlin* appeared in 1976, when Roland Klick directed a film based on Johannes Mario Simmel's novel *Dear Fatherland* [*Lieb Vaterland magst ruhig sein*] (1965). Tunnels are a central plot element. A small-time East German crook is told by the authorities that he will be pardoned if he helps kidnap the West Berliner responsible for smuggling people out. In West Berlin he becomes a double agent in the hope of starting a new life there with his lover. He is to expose the East Germans trying to crack the smuggling ring but finds that he cannot trust his new Western bosses either, who see him as expendable.

Spy stories were not the only way filmmakers could demonstrate that both sides in the Cold War sat in the same boat when it came to their principles. Kenneth Loach's 1987 film *Singing the Blues in Red* is about an East German writer and singer, Klaus Drittemann, who is kicked out of the country by the authorities. When he arrives in West Berlin, those who hope to make a propaganda coup out of his expulsion are shocked to find that Drittemann is just as critical of Western capitalism as he is of communism (appropriately, his surname means "third man") (Canby).

THE WALL IGNORERS AND THE WALL JUMPERS

By the mid-1980s many West German filmmakers had begun minimizing or even ignoring the Wall's significance as a physical divide. Peter Timm's *Meier*

(1985) is about a young East German who inherits a considerable sum of money, 30,000 deutsche marks, from his father, who had settled in the West. After making a world tour, the young man uses the rest of the funds to buy a counterfeit West German identity card and thereby secure the right to travel whenever he wants, the dream of all GDR citizens. When officials from the East German State Security [*Stasi*] catch him and ask whether he is West or East German, Meier automatically replies, "all German [*gesamtdeutsch*]." Although he decides to remain in the East, it is clear that he is not quite at home in either the FRG or the GDR (Nadar 252).

Once to the Ku'damm and Back [*Einmal Ku'damm und Zurück*] (1985) is an adventure-romance based on a true story from 1974. Thomas Stauffer (Christian Kohlund), a cook at the Swiss embassy in East Berlin, is well known to the border guards since he travels back and forth between the two halves of the city every day. He meets the East German woman Ulla Haferkorn (Ursela Monn), who is a secretary at a government ministry. Ulla gets the urge to visit the fancy shops on the Kurfürstendamm, and one day she hops in his trunk and goes. One trip leads to others, until the authorities discover and stop them. Ulla goes back to East Berlin, no sentences are leveled, and the love affair simply dies. The real-life couple, Peter and Christa Gross (née Feurich), disliked the film, and with good reason. It does not portray how an informal *Stasi* collaborator at the Swiss embassy betrayed them just as Christa attempted to permanently flee to the West (as opposed to merely making another shopping trip, as portrayed in the film). It also ignores the almost five years each spent in jail and their later marriage. According to the *Süddeutsche Zeitung, Once to the Ku'damm* was practically an informational film for the *Stasi*, which imprisoned more than seventy-two thousand East Germans for "fleeing the Republic [*Republikflucht*]" during the Wall years (Schade; "Einmal Ku'damm"). In comparison to reality, the film is a fleeting fairy tale.

Other West German films suggest that in spite of the Wall, Berlin is united through a common past and a common humanity. In the documentary *Location: Berlin* [*Drehort Berlin*] (1987), director Helga Reidemeister interviews people from both halves of the city in an attempt to capture the rhythms of life there. She strives to demolish the prejudices, clichés, and sheer ignorance about the "other side" that developed in Germany as a result of the Cold War (Hickethier). Although the Wall and the city's politicized history are present throughout the film, the audience is repeatedly left guessing whether the people are from East or West. A decade earlier, Sander's *Redupers, or the All-Around Reduced Personality* [*Die allseitig reduzierte Persönlichkeit*] (1977) also highlighted the similarities between the two halves of the city through the pictures taken by members of a women's photography collective. The main character, Edda (played by Sander), mentions that contrary to popular wisdom, it is actually the West Berliners who are trapped behind the Wall, not the East Berliners (Knight 83, 87).

Wim Wenders's *Wings of Desire* [*Der Himmel über Berlin*] (1987) also plays fast and loose with geography, since its main characters are angels who can move about the city freely. Although most of the scenes are shot in West Berlin, the location is never entirely certain except when there are outward signs such as automobiles, advertising, clothing, and the occasional landmark. The Wall is present, but politics plays a limited role. The sole important exception comes when Damiel (Bruno Ganz) chooses to transform himself into a human being—with all the senses, feelings, and emotions he lacks as an angel—at the Wall. It is unlikely that Wenders chose this site randomly, and the scene might be interpreted as a protest against the dehumanizing role of Cold War politics in Berlin. But Wenders has said that his angel characters like to walk at the Wall simply because it is quiet there. Otherwise, it has been around for such a short time compared to them that they are not impressed by it (Fusco 16).

Besides humanity, history is another factor that *could* unite Berliners in *Wings of Desire*. In one scene, the angel Cassiel (Otto Sander) pictures the destroyed Berlin of 1945 in his mind while driving through the streets in the 1980s. In another, the elderly Homer (Curt Bois), accompanied by Cassiel, returns to the site of the Potsdamer Platz, once Europe's busiest traffic center but now a ghostly, divided wasteland due to the Wall. He knows where he is but cannot understand why he no longer sees his favorite cigar shop, café, and other familiar sights. One gets the impression that few Berliners in the film besides Homer and the angels are conscious of the city common's history anymore. In fact, it was the intention of screenplay writer Peter Handke for Homer to lose his human audience in order to suggest a general loss of innocence (one line in the film states, "if a nation loses its storytellers, it loses its childhood") (Johnston).

On one level, these West German films from the 1970s and 1980s that allow movement between the two halves of Berlin or that stress the similarities shared by both parts of the city offer a critique of the Cold War. They suggest in various ways that the postwar division of Berlin and Germany, though understandable, probably permanent, and even justifiable, violates an underlying unity of the human beings who live there, their way of life, and their history. By largely ignoring Berlin's political divisions, they can focus on more universal human issues. Wenders, for example, uses Berlin as a metaphor not only for his own country but also for the entire world and the human condition in general (Fusco 16; Caltvedt 122; Paneth 2). However, on another level, these films and their characters frequently convey uneasiness, incompleteness, and indeed division—Meier's inability to be happy in either the East or the West, Edda's dual roles as worker and mother, Damiel's desire for true human feelings. In the "New German Cinema" of the 1970s and 1980s, the real divisions in Germany were those in the national community, especially those that led to the catastrophe of the Third Reich. Neither of the postwar German states was ideal, but to a great extent, both they and their defects were simply legacies of a fractured national life from before 1945 (Elsaesser 239–78). Wenders said, "It is only in Berlin that I could recognize what it means to be German . . . for history is both physically and emotionally present. . . . No other city is to such an extent a symbol, a place of survival" (Paneth 2). Perhaps these films are also trying to tell us that Germans during the Wall years were united by their divisions.[16]

Finally, in two films whose screenplays Peter Schneider helped write, the thesis of his novel *The Wall Jumper* is followed. The films emphasize that the true walls dividing Berliners and, by implication, Germans are internal or ideological. The protagonists can travel easily enough across the Wall, at least on occasion, but being able to do so does not bring them happiness. The first film is *The Man on the Wall* [*Der Mann auf der Mauer*] (1982), which features one of the characters from *The Wall Jumper*, Kabe (Marius Mueller-Westernhagen). Kabe lives in East Berlin and is obsessed with jumping over the Wall. After repeated attempts lead to his being thrown into a mental institution and then jail, he is finally allowed to settle in the West, but he then finds that he is unhappy because he is separated from his wife. So Kabe begins jumping again, but in the wrong direction for most people.

Schneider also cowrote the screenplay for Margarethe von Trotta's *The Promise* [*Das Versprechen*] (1994), which is really a "microhistory" of divided Germany from 1961 to 1989. Two East Berlin lovers, Sophie (played by Meret Becker and Corinna Harfouch to reflect the passage of time) and Konrad (Anian Zollner and August Zirner), are separated when she successfully flees with a group of friends through the sewer tunnels under the Wall. The police arrive just as Konrad is about to go through the manhole cover. He can only shout to Sophie that he will follow later. He never does and instead becomes a successful astrophysicist in the GDR. *The Promise* shows how their lives drift apart, including in material terms, despite the fact that they meet on several occasions. During an extended stay in Prague in 1968, Sophie becomes pregnant with their son Alexander (Christian Herrschmann and Jörg Meister). Forced to leave Czechoslovakia due to the Soviet invasion, they find that for various reasons they are unwilling or unable to continue to live together. By the 1980s Sophie is living in West Berlin with her French boyfriend, while in East Berlin Konrad has married and has another child. He is able to visit Sophie briefly while at a scientific conference in West Berlin, but direct contact between them is now superseded by preteen Alexander's visits to his father. Unfortunately, his first meeting with Konrad's family at their apartment goes poorly. Young Alex has culture shock and painfully, albeit unintentionally, reminds the family that they do not enjoy the life of privilege that he does. Eventually, the *Stasi* will prevent him from visiting East Berlin altogether. Yet his parents will meet again. The film closes with Sophie and Konrad simply staring at each other on the Bornheimer Bridge in Berlin on 9 November 1989, as people all around them celebrate the fall of the Wall. Although they are physically together once more, it is obvious that the emotional distance that separates them has become immense.

Trotta uses a number of strategies to create a very convincing illusion of historical realism throughout *The Promise*, which was filmed on location in Berlin and Prague. Several scenes feature re-creations of the Berlin Wall and its guard posts, and the crowd scenes on the Bornheimer Bridge closely resemble news broadcasts of the opening of the border in 1989. Other parts of the film incorporate actual newsreel or television footage. These include the opening scenes of the creation of the Wall in August 1961, the depiction of the Warsaw Pact invasion of Czechoslovakia, and an East German broadcast of a GDR May Day parade in the 1980s that Sophie watches in her apartment in the West. *The Promise* "draws the Wall and the division of Germany as a larger-than-life tableau of the fantasies and aspirations of the 1960s generation" (Byg). Its last scene in particular suggests the ambivalence of the German "New Left" about how reunification took place. Some critics have disparaged *The Promise*'s conclusion because it contrasts so starkly with the joy that most Germans felt. Others found it too sentimental and believed that its portrayal of the GDR was unrealistically negative (Wydra 201–6; Hehr 50). Nonetheless, due to its sweeping vision and its sense of history, it remains the definitive film on the division of Germany.

THE PERSISTENCE OF THE WALL

Since 1989 there has been little reason to doubt the actual existence of the cleft between East and West Germans addressed in *The Promise*. It includes a stubbornly persistent gap in income, employment, and living conditions, but also important psychological divisions. Residents of the old West Germany resent what they see as a drain of their resources on behalf of Easterners, while the latter believe that they are negatively stereotyped and forced to assimilate into a new state on terms that were not of their making (Naughton 12–22). The invisible barriers have proved more difficult to overcome than the visible ones, just as Schneider predicted.

The Promise appeared at a time when German filmmakers had discovered a new interest in themes relating to national unification. Starting around 1990, a wave of documentaries appeared that the German film industry collectively labeled the "Wall film." Although not all of them dealt directly with the fall of the Berlin Wall, they explored issues relating to life under communism and the events leading to reunification (Naughton 98–101). In feature films, notes Leonie Naughton, the division of Germany is still perceptible. Most West German productions about unification, which have ranged from docudramas to comedies, focus on what happened after the Wall fell. They also tend to present an idealized view of East Germany as "part rural idyll and part preindustrial paradise" (Naughton 239), in an often condescending attempt to positively address existing tensions. In contrast, in East German productions the events of 1989 often represent the climax of the film rather than the departure point, and the personal costs of unification also figure prominently (in these respects, *The Promise* is an atypical Western unification film). Despite these differences, Naughton remarks, "unification films from both the east and west present a generally consistent portrait of German-German relations. Mostly, these films suggest that those relations do not exist. No alarm is displayed about this situation, which is accepted as perfectly normal. . . . What these films ultimately effect is a segregation of East and West Germans" (242–43).

Several recent films on Cold War Berlin heavily reflect the current *Ostalgie* (a combination of the words *East* and *nostalgia*) phenomenon among former East Germans who want their everyday lives under communism validated, even if they do not wish to return to the past politically (Theil). Accordingly, the popular 1999 comedy *Sonnenallee* depicts life in the shadow of the Wall in East Berlin during the 1970s as rather bucolic and safe. Wolfgang Becker's *Goodbye, Lenin!* (2003), which also has its farcical elements, is a serious statement about the problems many former GDR citizens experienced in adjusting after the Wall came down.

Robert Brent Toplin has noted that "cinematic history speaks to the present" (41). This survey of films about Cold War Berlin confirms his point. Cold War Berlin continues to fascinate filmmakers and moviegoers who themselves remain divided about life in Germany since reunification.

NOTES

1. Exceptions include Schulte-Sasse and Heimann.
2. This plot device probably did not bother 1950s audiences, who were used to equating "Red" and "Brown" totalitarianism (Gleason).
3. Despite this ideologically correct message, GDR cultural authorities criticized

the film. They could not understand why a figure like Conny was the "hero" of a socialist production. Dudow, of course, intended the women to be the heroines (Schenk 74–76; Schittly 60).

4. On the *Halbstarken* in East and West Germany, see Poigner.

5. Wilder based the film's plot on *Egy, ketto, három* [*One, Two, Three*], a 1930 one-act play by Ferenc Molnár featuring a fast-talking banker and his socialist would-be son-in-law, but he changed the setting from Sweden to Berlin. The plot also echoes that of a 1939 comedy whose screenplay Wilder helped write, *Ninotchka,* about a Soviet agent, played by Greta Garbo, who succumbs to the temptations of capitalism while on a mission in Paris to retrieve three wayward commissars (Dick 28–29, 70–72). Wilder also had *Duck Soup* (1933) in mind and wondered how the Marx Brothers would have approached the Cold War as a subject (Chandler 237).

6. A point made by Crowe (165). Wilder, however, had other motivations for picking Coke as a central plot device: "I happen to think Coca-Cola is funny. A lot of people didn't. Maybe that's why the picture bombed out. I still think it's funny. And when I drink it, it seems even funnier" (Sikov 465).

7. Icestorm International recently released the original film with English subtitles as *Look at This City.* The dubbed English-language version from the 1960s was called *Berlin Wall,* but this title was neither an exact translation nor particularly accurate in terms of summarizing the film's content (Hanwehr 1–2).

8. East German authorities officially prohibited use of the word *wall* [*Mauer*] to describe it (Ladd 18; Large 454; Wyden 358; Ward).

9. This was not an uncommon occurrence. In August 1961 fifty-three thousand East Berliners still worked in West Berlin, and twelve thousand West Berliners had jobs in the East (Engert 151).

10. This is a major theme in Feinstein.

11. This film is so bad that it has achieved cult status. Quentin Tarantino references it in *Kill Bill, Volume II* (2004).

12. Burton was nominated for an Academy Award for his portrayal, but director Martin Ritt had to get him to tone down his romantic leading man persona in order to play the Leamas role convincingly (G. Miller 80).

13. Since Hallam is a proper British bureaucrat, stealing the papers is not an option. A signature (in this case, Palmer's) is required before they can leave his office.

14. In the novel, a Soviet scientist, not Stok, is supposed to defect.

15. Like the Europa-Center, the Berlin Hilton was built to see over and to be seen from both sides of the Wall, thereby suggesting to the East Germans what they did not have (Wharton 71–88).

16. Of course, the Wall could also be used as a metaphor for other types of divisions that had nothing to do with Germany in the Cold War. In Andrzej Zulawski's *Possession* (1981), Isabelle Adjani plays a Berlin housewife who suffers from schizophrenia and goes on a murder spree. She and most of the other characters have not only split personalities but also look-alikes with different character traits from the "originals." Ewa Mazierska and Laura Rascaroli note that in Sander's *Redupers,* "the Wall stands for sexual difference, as argued by some feminist critics, or for the divisions of the female self." In Park Kwang-Su's *Berlin Report* (1991), the city represents the divided Korean peninsula (Mazierska and Rascaroli 118–19).

WORKS CITED

Allan, Seán. "DEFA: An Historical Overview." Allan and Sandford 1–21.

Allan, Seán, and John Sandford, eds. *DEFA: East German Cinema, 1946–1992*. New York: Berghahn Books, 1999.

American Film Institute. "Dialogue on Film: Billy Wilder and I. A. L. Diamond" (1976). Wilder, *Interviews* 110–31.

Armstrong, Richard. *Billy Wilder, American Film Realist*. Jefferson, N.C.: McFarland, 2000.

Arnold, Frank. "Der Kalte Krieg im Kino." *EPD Film* 8.6 (1991): 10–13.

Baumgärtel, Martin. "Die Freiheitsglocke." *Deutschlandradio Kultur*. 17 June 2007. <www .dradio.de/dkultur/sendungen/freiheitsglocke/beitrag/>.

Byg, Barton. "The Berlin Film." DEFA Film Library at the U of Massachusetts, Amherst. 17 June 2007. <www.umass.edu/defa/filmtour/essay.shtml>.

Caltvedt, Les. "Berlin Poetry: Archaic Cultural Patterns in Wender's *Wings of Desire*." *Literature Film Quarterly* 20.2 (1992): 121–26.

Canby, Vincent. "From Germany, 'Singing the Blues in Red.'" Rev. of *Singing the Blues in Red*, dir. Kenneth Loach. *New York Times*, 29 Jan. 1988: C8.

Chandler, Charlotte. *Nobody's Perfect. Billy Wilder: A Personal Biography*. New York: Simon & Schuster, 2002.

Christopher, Nicholas. *Somewhere in the Night: Film Noir and the American City*. New York: Owl Books, 1998.

Claus, Horst. "Rebels with a Cause: The Development of the '*Berlin-Filme*' by Gerhard Klein and Wolfgang Kohlhaase." Allan and Sandford 93–116.

Crowe, Cameron. *Conversations with Wilder*. New York: Knopf, 2000.

Dick, Bernard F. *Billy Wilder*. Updated ed. New York: Da Capo Press, 1996.

"Einmal Ku'damm und ab nach Bautzen." *Frankfurter Allgemeine Zeitung* 18 July 2001: BS 3.

Elsaesser, Thomas. *New German Cinema: A History*. New Brunswick, N.J.: Rutgers UP, 1989.

Engert, Jürgen. "Berlin between East and West: Lessons for a Confused World." Merritt and Merritt 149–65.

Fehrenbach, Heide. *Cinema in Democratizing Germany: Reconstructing National Identity after Hitler*. Chapel Hill: U of North Carolina P, 1995.

Feinstein, Joshua. *The Triumph of the Ordinary: Depictions of Daily Life in the East German Cinema, 1949–1989*. Chapel Hill: U of North Carolina P, 2002.

Fujiwara, Chris. *Jacques Tourneur: The Cinema of Nightfall*. Baltimore: Johns Hopkins UP, 2001.

Fulbrook, Mary. *Anatomy of a Dictatorship: Inside the GDR, 1949–1989*. Oxford: Oxford UP, 1995.

Fusco, Coco. "Angels, History and Poetic Fantasy: An Interview with Wim Wenders." *Cineaste* 16.4 (1988): 14–17.

Gass, Karl. "Gass' Experimentierküche. Interview mit Karl Gass." Interview in *Der Morgen* 14 Aug. 1962. Gass, *Ich glaube* 45–46.

———. "Gründlicher analysieren." Interview in *Neue Berliner Illustrierte* 4 Aug. 1962. Gass, *Ich glaube* 46–48.

————. *Ich glaube an den Dokumentarfilm, wenn. . . . Auswahldokumentation.* Ed. Hermann Herlinghaus and Brigitte Gerull. Aus Theorie und Praxis des Films 2.87. Berlin: VEB DEFA Studio für Dokumentarfilme und Betriebschule des VEB DEFA Studio für Spielfilme, 1987.

Gleason, Abbott. *Totalitarianism: The Inner History of the Cold War.* Oxford: Oxford UP, 1996.

Hanwehr, Wolfram von. "A Critical Analysis of the Structure of the East German Film *Berlin Wall.*" Diss. U. of Southern California, 1970.

Hehr, Renate. *Margarethe von Trotta: Filmmaking as Liberation.* Stuttgart: Edition Axel Menges, 2000.

Heimann, Thomas. "Deutsche Brüder und Schwester im Kalten Krieg der Medien. Beobachtungen zum deutsch-deutschen Dokumentärfilm nach 1945." *Der geteilte Himmel. Arbeit, Alltag und Geschichte im ost-und westdeutschen Film.* Ed. Peter Zimmermann and Gebhard Moldenhauer. Close Up 13. Konstanz: UVK Medien, 2000. 77–102.

Hickethier, Knut. *Drehort Berlin.* Goethe Institute, N.Y., 2005. <www3.inter-nationes .de/in/?MIval=fzfass_e.html&in_nr=1508&css=http://www.goethe.de/ins/us/ ney/pro/filmkat/css2x.css&sk=0&bu=0>.

Johnston, Sheila. "Wim Wender's New Romanticism." *World Press Review* 35.8 (1988): 59.

Kamm, Jürgen. "The Berlin Wall and Cold-War Espionage: Visions of a Divided Germany in the Novels of Len Deighton." Schürer, Keune, and Jenkins 61–73.

Kleinert, Marianne. Rev. of *Freedom . . . Freedom . . . über alles. Karl Gass.* Ed. Manfred Lichtenstein, Evelyn Hampicke, and Kleinert. Filmdokumentaristen der DDR. Berlin: Staatliches Filmarchiv der DDR, 1989. 86.

Knight, Julia. *New German Cinema: Voices of a Generation.* Short Cuts. London: Wallflower, 2004.

Kundler, Herbert. "RIAS Berlin and the Americans." RIAS Berlin Kommission. 17 June 2007. <www.riasberlinkommission.de>.

Ladd, Brian. *The Ghosts of Berlin: Confronting German History in the Urban Landscape.* Chicago: U of Chicago P, 1997.

Large, David Clay. *Berlin.* New York: Basic Books, 2000.

Lipschutz, Ronnie D. *Cold War Fantasies: Film, Fiction, and Foreign Policy.* Lanham, Md.: Rowman & Littlefield, 2001.

Maier, Charles A. *Dissolution: The Crisis of Communism and the End of East Germany.* Princeton, N.J.: Princeton UP, 1997.

Mazierska, Ewa, and Laura Rascaroli. *From Moscow to Madrid: Postmodern Cities, European Cinema.* London: Tauris, 2003.

McAdams, A. James. *Germany Divided: From the Wall to Reunification.* Princeton, N.J.: Princeton UP, 1993.

Merritt, Richard L. "Interpersonal Transactions across the Wall." Merritt and Merritt 166–83.

Merritt, Richard L., and Anna J. Merritt, eds. *Living with the Wall: West Berlin, 1961–1985.* Durham, N.C.: Duke UP, 1985.

Mews, Siegfried. "The Spies Are Coming in from the Cold War: The Berlin Wall in the Espionage Novel." Schürer, Keune, and Jenkins 50–60.

Miller, Gabriel. *The Films of Martin Ritt: Fanfare for the Common Man.* Jackson: U of Mississippi P, 2000.

Miller, Toby. *Spyscreen: Espionage on Film and TV from the 1930s to the 1960s.* Oxford: Oxford UP, 2003.

Nadar, Thomas R. "The German-German Relationship in Popular Culture: Recent Literary, Musical and Cinematic Views." Schürer, Keune, and Jenkins 250–55.

Naughton, Leonie. *That Was the Wild East: Film Culture, Unification, and the "New" Germany. Social History, Popular Culture, and Politics in Germany.* Ann Arbor: U of Michigan P, 2002.

Paneth, Ira. "Wim and His Wings." *Film Quarterly* 42.1 (1988): 2–8.

Pflaum, Hans Günther. *Germany on Film: Theme and Content in the Cinema of the Federal Republic of Germany.* 1985. Ed. Robert Picht. Trans. Richard C. Hecht and Roland Richter. Detroit: Wayne State UP, 1990.

Poigner, Uta G. *Jazz, Rock, and Rebels: Cold War Politics and American Culture in a Divided Germany.* Berkeley: U of California P, 2000.

Prowe, Diethelm. "Brennpunkt des Kalten Krieges: Berlin in den deutsch-amerikanischen Beziehungen." *Die USA und Deutschland im Zeitalter des Kalten Krieges 1945–1990. Ein Handbuch.* Ed. Detlef Junker with the assistance of Philipp Gassert, Wilfried Mausbach, and David B. Morris. Stuttgart: DVA, 2001. 1:260–70.

Richter, Erika. "Zwischen Mauerbau und Kahlschlag 1961 bis 1965." Schenk, *Das zweite Leben* 158–211.

Rother, Hans-Jörg. "Auftrag: Propaganda, 1960 bis 1970." *Schwarzweiß und Farbe. DEFA Dokumentarfilme 1946–1992.* Ed. Günther Jordan and Ralf Schenk. Berlin: Jovis, 1996. 93–127.

Schade, Eberhard. "Einmal Ku'damm und zurück." *Süddeutsche Zeitung* 8 Sept. 2000: 11.

Schenk, Ralf, ed. *Das zweite Leben der Filmstadt Babelsberg. DEFA-Spielfilme 1946–1992.* Berlin: Henschel Verlag, 1994.

———. "Mitten im Kalten Krieg, 1950 bis 1960." Schenk, *Das zweite Leben* 51–157.

Schittly, Dagmar. *Zwischen Regie und Regime. Die Filmpolitik der SED im Spiegel der DEFA-Produktionen.* Berlin: Links Verlag, 2002.

Schneider, Peter. *The Wall Jumper: A Berlin Story.* 1982. Trans. Leigh Hafrey. Chicago: U of Chicago P, 1983.

Schulte-Sasse, Linda. "Retrieving the City as *Heimat:* Berlin in Nazi Cinema." *Berlin: Culture and Metropolis.* Ed. Charles W. Haxthausen and Heidrun Suhr. Minneapolis: U of Minnesota P, 1990. 166–86.

Schürer, Ernst, Manfred Keune, and Philip Jenkins, eds. *The Berlin Wall: Representations and Perspectives.* Studies in Modern German Literature 79. New York: Peter Lang, 1996.

Seaton, George. *George Seaton: Working as a Writer-Director.* Interview with David Cherichetti. The American Film Institute/Louis B. Mayer Oral History Collection, Part 1, 18/The New York Times Oral History Program. Glenn Rock, N.J.: Microfilming Corporation of America, 1977.

Shandley, Robert R. *Rubble Films: German Cinema in the Shadow of the Third Reich.* Philadelphia: Temple UP, 2001.

Sikov, Ed. *On Sunset Boulevard: The Life and Times of Billy Wilder.* New York: Hyperion, 1998.

Theil, Stefan. "Red Again." *New Republic* 229.15–16 (13 and 20 Oct. 2003): 16–20.

Toplin, Robert Brent. *Reel History: In Defense of Hollywood.* Lawrence: UP of Kansas, 2002.

Ward, James J. "Remember When It Was the 'Antifascist Defense Wall'? The Uses of History in the Battle for Public Memory and Public Space." Schürer, Keune, and Jenkins 11–24.

Wharton, Annabel Jane. *Building the Cold War: Hilton International Hotels and Modern Architecture.* Chicago: U of Chicago P, 2001.

Wilder, Billy. "Billy Wilder." Interview with Gene D. Phillips. 1976. Wilder, *Interviews* 99–109.

———. *Interviews.* Ed. Robert Horton. Conversations with Filmmakers. Jackson: U of Mississippi P, 2001.

Wyden, Peter. *The Wall: The Inside Story of Divided Berlin.* New York: Simon & Schuster, 1989.

Wydra, Thilo. *Margarethe von Trotta—Filmen, zu überleben.* Berlin: Henschel Verlag, 2000.

Invaders of the Cold War

Generic Disruptions and Shifting Gender Roles in *The Day the Earth Stood Still*

In *The Fifties*, David Halberstam writes, "In retrospect the pace of the fifties seemed slower, almost languid. Social ferment, however, was beginning just beneath this placid surface" (ix). He further notes, "Few Americans doubted the essential goodness of their society. After all it was reflected back at them not only in contemporary books and magazines, but even more powerfully and with even greater influence in the new family sitcoms on television" (x). TV programs such as *The Donna Reed Show* and *Leave It to Beaver* belied any sense of turmoil or tension, yet while these programs showed, in black-and-white simplicity, American families leading idyllic lives in the suburbs, the nation was in the grip of rapid social, political, and economic changes. Besides the beginning of the Cold War, a wide range of other issues was contributing to the anxiety of the era, including postwar affluence, the development of atomic power for defense and its promise of unlimited energy, the Korean War, and the beginning of the civil rights and women's movements. The apparent advances, benefits, and changes in the 1950s were met with excitement, but also with a great deal of anxiety.

Hollywood was also affected by these changes. From the mid-1940s through most of the 1950s, a new conservatism took root in Hollywood. Still shaken from the House Committee on Un-American Activities' trial of the "Hollywood Ten" and the communist blacklists that put more than three hundred directors, technicians, writers, and actors out of work, Hollywood vowed, in the words of Eric Johnston, head of the Motion Picture Producers Association, "We'll have no more films that show the seamy side of American life" (quoted in L. May 145). Though many Hollywood figures such as Arthur Miller, Paul Robeson, Lester Cole, Dalton Trumbo, and the rest of the Hollywood Ten stood firmly against this trend, others were naming names, confessing their past communist affiliations, asking for forgiveness, or adding their voices to the vanguard of conservatism that culminated with Ronald Reagan's election as president of the Screen Actors Guild in the early 1950s. As Paul Carter notes, "Hollywood had always been chicken-hearted about social and political controversy. . . . The Cold War reinforced these intrinsic tendencies" (209). Hollywood's goal, if not to support Cold War ideologies openly, was to stay on the *right* side of the controversy.

Cultural artifacts of the 1950s, including film, provide a less than complete picture of the time. Wheeler Winston Dixon notes that "mainstream films tell us what we *wish* to remember about the 1950s, as seen through the lens of the dominant cinema, but not what is necessarily an accurate record of the times as we lived them" (8). He states that another difficulty with understanding the 1950s has to do with the films that scholars and critics have chosen to discuss: "One of the essential problems with any canon, filmic or otherwise, is that it limits one's scope of inquiry" (9). By focusing on A films, the cultural importance of B, C, and D films, including the subject of this study—science fiction—is often lost or forgotten, leading to the misconception that there was one unified voice emerging from 1950s Hollywood, a voice concerned with playing it safe.

Even with pressure to produce films that supported dominant ideologies, some films—either by design or by accident—resisted or were critical of hegemonic narratives and ideologies. Marginalized films—what Dixon refers to as "phantom" films or "purely entertainment" genres—such as horror and science fiction, were often allowed special license. This is not to say that all popular genre films were critical of the politics of the time; many science fiction films, for example, supported and promoted dominant values. In *This Island Earth* (1955), much of the opening sequence features a Lockheed jet, and the ensuing dialogue ensures that everyone is aware that it is a Lockheed product. The film also stresses the importance of continued technological research and development, made possible by government contracts with private industry. It was common practice for the military to lend or rent equipment to filmmakers as long as the subject matter of the film did not conflict with the military's agenda (Turner 80). As Lawrence Suid notes, "The military has seen these films as a superb public relations medium" (8). And since the equipment enhanced the documentary style of many science fiction films, studios "regularly sought assistance from the armed forces in the form of technical advice, men, and hardware" (Suid 8). The arrangement not only gave an "authentic" look to the films but also provided free advertising for the military.

Other science fiction films, however, particularly invasion films, were critical of the social and political status quo, often challenging narrowly defined gender roles and Americans' fear of the "Other." These films, such as the one examined here—Robert Wise's 1951 classic *The Day the Earth Stood Still*—provide important alternatives to dominant cinema's "record of the times," presenting a more "accurate record" of the tensions and anxieties that plagued the postwar era (Dixon 8). By disrupting narrative conventions of the genre—specifically, the representation of gender roles, the hero, and the alien Other—Wise's film addresses and interrogates not only 1950s masculinity and conformity but also Cold War ideologies.

Gender in the 1950s

That gender was a central issue in 1950s media is not at all surprising. As Elaine Tyler May notes, "Fears of sexual chaos tend to surface during times of crisis and rapid social change," and this was true of the turbulent 1950s (93). A variety of cultural artifacts were educating Americans about the proper roles for women. This kind of information filled the pages of popular women's magazines such as *Redbook, McCall's, Housekeeping Monthly,* and *Ladies' Home Journal,* as well as Federal Civil Defense Administration pamphlets and popular guidebooks by doctors and other "experts." For example, in *The Modern Woman: The Lost Sex* (1947), Ferdinand Lundberg and Dr. Marynia Farnham blame feminism and career women for an assortment of social problems. They warn that "the more educated the woman is, the greater the chance there is of sexual disorder, more or less severe. The greater the disordered sexuality in a given group of women, the fewer children do they have. Satisfactory sexuality, therefore, is linked for a woman with wanting and having children" (270–71). In their opinion, women who decide not to have children or who choose to stay single are deviant. More important, they claim that women's mental health depends on their focusing on the roles of wife and mother.

Being a good woman in 1940s America was not always an easy task, as Philip Wylie announced in his book *Generation of Vipers* (1942). Wylie discusses two types of women: the Cinderella, who wants only to marry a "good-looking man with dough" who will reward her "for nothing more than being female," and the mom (46, 47). "Mom" is the central target of Wylie's chapter "The Common Women." In his "sermon," he charges that overindulgent, over-bearing, or obsessively nurturing moms are to blame for the sad state of the American male(xxii). The power of "momism" and its effects are far-reaching, Wylie warns: "Good-looking men and boys are rounded up and beaten or sucked into pliability, a new slave population continually goes to work at making more munitions for momism, and mom herself sticks up her head, or maybe a periscope of the woman next door, to find some new region that needs taking over. This technique pervades all she does" (193–94). According to Wylie, momism was creating a generation of dependent, foolish, and weak men who were easy marks for all sorts of corrupting forces, including the allure of communist ideology and unfettered sexuality.

Besides Lundberg and Farnham, Wylie, and Dr. Benjamin Spock, popular genre writers such as Mickey Spillane were warning that female desire and sexuality, if not properly contained, could distract men, destroy families, and make the nation ripe for communist infiltration. Female sexuality, in fact, was quickly linked to the destructive power of the atom. Not long after the atomic bomb was dropped on Hiroshima, the concept exploded in the American popular imagination. Businesses were having "Atomic Sales," and bars were mixing "Atomic Cocktails" while people danced to the "Atom Polka" (Boyer 10–11). General Mills "offered an 'Atomic Bomb Ring' for fifteen cents and a Kix cereal box top" (Boyer 11). As Benjamin Shapiro notes, the "link of atomic power with female sexuality has been widely noted as a broad phenomenon in American popular culture. The bomb dropped on Bikini Island, for example, was itself nicknamed for *femme fatale* 'Gilda' and adorned with a picture of Rita Hayworth," who played the title role in the 1946 noir film (109).

Science fiction films such as *The Leech Woman* (1959), *The Attack of the 50 Foot Woman* (1958), and *The Wasp Woman* (1960) exploited the link that already existed between technology and the feminine, featuring females made powerful and monstrous by science. These characters are the science fiction equivalents of the vamp or female vampire figures that have "sucked men dry physically, financially, or morally for centuries on stage, in literature," and more recently in film (George 1). Janet Staiger observes that the vamp appears as a staple in early U.S. films such as D. W. Griffith's *The Mothering Heart* (1913) and Frank Powell's *A Fool There Was* (1915). The tales of the science fiction vamps, like the stories of their predatory sisters before them, provide cautionary tales as they feed on an assortment of male figures from innocent and unsuspecting men to criminal and deviant ones.

A different strategy needed to be developed to deal with the new global politics and the changing gender roles evident in postwar America. That strategy was "containment" on all fronts, foreign and domestic. George Kennan first offered the political policy of containment in a 1947 *Foreign Affairs* article about the Soviets. "Containment," as Eric F. Goldman states, "better than any other term, was the expression of the emerging Truman policies in foreign and domestic affairs" (80). The policy of containment, like the power of the atomic bomb, quickly became a significant tenet of the popular imagination.

The nuclear family: a post–World War II ideal.

Socially, containment signaled a concentrated effort by the media, government, and business to force women out of the workforce and back into the home. For instance, a 1955 issue of *Housekeeping Monthly* noted, "A good wife always knows her place" ("Good Wife's"). She is to stay at home and make sure the children are good citizens. Her goal is to "try to make sure [her] home is a place of peace, order and tranquility where [her] husband can renew himself in body and spirit" ("Good Wife's"). In the domestic sphere, containment was accomplished through marriage and the establishment of a "nuclear" family residing in the suburbs, with a husband as the breadwinner and a woman as his hausfrau.

THE MYSTIQUE MODELS

Many female characters in 1950s science fiction invasion films, those most often remembered by fans and scholars alike, fit this prescribed model. These characters exemplify what Betty Friedan would describe in 1963 as the "feminine mystique." They are constructions of hegemonic forces speaking for the status quo and dominant ideologies. These are the 1950s women who were featured in countless movie trailers and lobby poster displays: high-heeled, well-dressed damsels who scream when threatened and who represent traditional American notions of hearth, home, and family. They include Ellen Fields (Barbara Rush) in *It Came from Outer Space* (1953) and Cathy Barrett (Lola Albright) in *The Monolith Monsters* (1957). The social and political forces that produced what I call the "mystique model" were so powerful that some female science fiction characters became case studies in or step-by-step manuals on how to behave.

One fine example is Sylvia Van Buren (Ann Robinson) in the big-budget adaptation of H. G. Wells's *The War of the Worlds* (1952). Although Sylvia starts out as an educated and intelligent woman, she quickly transforms into a mystique model. When a strange object crashes outside a small Southern California town, the townspeople, including Sylvia and some vacationing scientists, all go to investigate the crash site. From the beginning, it is clear that Sylvia is rather "star struck" with the scientist hero of the film, Dr. Clayton Forester (Gene Barry), even though she has never met him. When she does, she fails to recognize him in his casual fishing clothes and a few days' growth of beard. She tells the vacationing stranger what she knows or presumes about the "meteor" and predicts that all their questions will be answered when Dr. Forester, who is the "top man in astro- and nuclear physics," arrives.

As she goes on about Forester, a medium close-up shows her smiling, admiring face. He comments that she seems to know an awful lot about this "Forester fellow," and she tells him that she wrote her master's thesis on modern scientists; it would seem that he was her favorite. At this point in the narrative Sylvia speaks for the many U.S. women who went to college after World War II. The GI Bill increased the number of veterans in college, and there was also an increase in the number of women entering college (E. T. May 78). While many of these women got married and dropped out to help support their husbands, Sylvia completed her degree. In addition, after graduation Sylvia was able to find a job in her area of study—something most women of the decade found difficult, if not impossible. When the film begins she is an instructor of library science at the University of Southern California.

Later, when the meteor turns out to be a spacecraft and the aliens demonstrate their hostile intentions, the film shifts its focus away from Sylvia's education and knowledge. Indeed, as the alien threat increases, Sylvia's objectivity and IQ seem to rapidly decrease, and when troops arrive to take charge of the situation, Sylvia's role becomes completely domestic. The next sequence shows her wearing a Red Cross volunteer armband and serving coffee and doughnuts to the men mobilizing a defense. Her new role as a symbol of all that needs protecting (hearth, home, white womanhood) is emphasized when General Mann (Les Tremayne) arrives. When she is introduced to him all she says is, "Hello, General, would you care for some coffee?" She then hands him a cup and moves on with her tray. This scene marks the beginning of her transformation from active participant—a bright young woman who knows about meteors and modern scientists—into inactive damsel, a perfect mystique model.

Sylvia's position as someone who needs caring for and protecting—and as a commodity of exchange—is highlighted later in this same sequence. She lives with her Uncle Matthew (Lewis Martin), who is the town pastor. As the military prepares to attack and eliminate the aliens, Uncle Matthew decides that someone should first try communicating with them.

> MATTHEW: I think we should try to make them understand we mean them no harm. They are living creatures out there.
>
> SYLVIA: But they're not human. Dr. Forester says they are some kind of advanced civilization.
>
> MATTHEW: If they are more advanced than us they should be nearer the creator for that reason. No real attempt has been made to communicate with them, you know.
>
> SYLVIA: Let's go back inside, Uncle Matthew.
>
> MATTHEW: I've done all I can in there. You go back. Sylvia, I like that Dr. Forester. He's a good man.

After this dialogue, Sylvia returns to the bunker, and Uncle Matthew attempts to communicate with the invaders. With his Bible held out in front of him and reciting the twenty-third psalm, "though I walk through the valley of the shadow of death," he approaches the spacecraft, blocking its advance. In response, the ship incinerates him as the others watch from the bunker. This scene, linked with the first scene between Sylvia and Forester, lays the groundwork for her affections and attention to pass, with Uncle Matthew's blessing, from her father-daughter relationship with him to the compulsory and "proper" heterosexual love relationship with the "good man" Forester.

Sylvia's transformation, the mystique models in many other science fiction films, and the cautionary tales of the science fiction vamps make Helen Benson (Patricia Neal) in *The Day the Earth Stood Still* a unique and curious aberration as she offers an alternative to these representations. Though she is not the lone hero in the film, she plays a central and active role in the narrative and, by doing so, rejects the Cold War values exemplified by the mystique model and the fears of female sexuality and power evident in the science fiction vamp films.

THE DAY THE EARTH STOOD STILL

The Day the Earth Stood Still begins when a very human looking alien, Klaatu (Michael Rennie), comes to earth with a message of welcome and a warning for humankind now that it has discovered atomic power and can venture into space. He is the spokesman from a group of planets where the inhabitants have given their power "in matters of aggression" over to powerful robots so that they can "pursue more profitable ventures. At the first sign of violence [the robots] act automatically against the aggressor." Unfortunately, Klaatu is wounded by a nervous soldier before he can deliver his message; when he is later told that the current political landscape makes a meeting of all the world's leaders impossible, he decides to find out what humans are really like and whether they are worth the trouble of saving. He takes a room in a Washington, D.C., boardinghouse under the name Carpenter and is introduced to Helen, her son Bobby (Billy Gray), and her boyfriend Tom (Hugh Marlowe).

From the beginning, Helen appears to be a different kind of woman. Charles Ramírez Berg observes that, in most science fiction films, a character from "the less powerful group is often typed along a spectrum of possibilities from harmless and childlike to dangerous" (6). However, these stereotypical possibilities are never consistently applied to Helen. She is presented as an intelligent and capable person. A working war widow supporting herself and raising her son, she is thoughtful, understanding of the alien's point of view, and she is usually placed in a powerful position within the mise-en-scène. For example, early in the film, when the boarders are all having breakfast and listening to a radio broadcast regarding the invader's recent escape from Walter Reed Hospital, Helen sympathizes with the alien's position and takes an active role in the discussion:

> HELEN: This space man, or whatever he is, we automatically assume he's a menace. Maybe he isn't at all.
>
> MR. BARLEY: Then what's he hiding for? Why doesn't he come out into the open?

20th Century-Fox

By declining Tom's (Hugh Marlowe) marriage proposal, Helen (Patricia Neal) rejects both the gender standards of the decade and the masculinity represented by Tom.

MR. KRULL: Yea, like that Heatter fella says, "What's he up to?"

HELEN: Maybe he's afraid. [. . .] After all, he was shot the minute he landed here. I was just wondering what I would do?

CARPENTER/KLAATU: Well, perhaps before deciding on a course of action, you'd want to know about the people here.

Helen is seated at the head of the table and is the focus of much of the scene. A medium shot shows her filling her coffee cup and that of another boarder, but this "domestic" act does not hinder her participation in the conversation, as it did with Sylvia in *The War of the Worlds*. Instead, this domestic scene places the woman, Helen, and her thoughts at the center instead of on the periphery.

In addition, the fact that Bobby, Helen's son, is a bright, friendly child and not on the verge of delinquency because of a lack of paternal love, as is the case in many 1950s family melodramas, further validates Helen's position within the film. She is a different kind of woman, one who can work, have her own opinions, and still raise a healthy, well-adjusted son.

Helen does not break the narrative trajectory of the mystique model completely, since she is dating an insurance salesman named Tom, who, early in the film, asks her to marry him. When Tom is introduced to the narrative, generic expectations dictate that he will be the protagonist who protects Helen and Bobby from the invader so that, when the crisis has passed, they can become a typical postwar family. Instead of fulfilling this convention—common in other invasion films such as *It Came from Outer Space* (1953), *The Beast from 20,000 Fathoms* (1953), and *20 Million Miles to Earth* (1957)—this film takes another direction. Later, when Klaatu tells Helen who he is and why he has come to earth, she decides to help him evade the authorities long enough to deliver his message to the scientists that Professor Barnhardt (Sam Jaffe) has managed to assemble. Meanwhile, Tom has decided to go to the military with his information about Klaatu. Helen tries to change Tom's mind but fails. Earlier, Helen has told Tom that she needs time to think about his marriage proposal, but during the following exchange, she makes up her mind:

> HELEN: That's what I'm trying to tell you, we mustn't do anything about it. Believe me Tom, I know what I'm talking about.
>
> TOM: He's a menace to the whole world. It's our duty to turn him in.
>
> HELEN: But he's not a menace. He told me why he came here.
>
> TOM: He told . . . he told you, oh don't be silly, honey, just because you like the guy. You realize, of course, what this would mean to us. I could write my own ticket. I'd be the biggest man in the country. [. . .]
>
> HELEN: [. . .] Tom you mustn't. You don't know what you're doing. It isn't just you and Mr. Carpenter, the rest of the world's involved.
>
> TOM: I don't care about the rest of the world. You'll feel different when you see my picture in the papers.
>
> HELEN: I feel different right now.
>
> TOM: You wait and see. You're gonna marry a big hero.
>
> HELEN: I'm not going to marry anybody. [She exits.]

While 1950s cultural politics and media representations were telling women that their role was to find a good husband, stay at home, and raise the requisite number of children, Helen rejects the prevailing standard. Her rebuff of Tom's proposal disrupts both dominant ideologies and the "drawing together of the heterosexual couple," which "occurs with such consistency [in science fiction films] that we may consider it an integral part of the generic formula" (Shapiro 108).

20th Century-Fox

Klaatu's (Michael Rennie) gentler masculinity presents a different
role model for young Bobby (Billy Gray).

In addition, when Helen rejects Tom, she rejects a masculinity forged and
supported by Cold War values that "demanded ideological vigilance, crew-
cuts, and a talent for rigid self-control," in favor of the gentler masculinity of
Klaatu/Carpenter (as well as Barnhardt and Bobby) that would not be widely
acknowledged in the United States until the 1960s and 1970s (Ehrenreich
104). Since the film resists the temptation to have Helen and Klaatu develop
into a couple, she becomes more autonomous and functions as a hero in the
film. Through Helen's role as hero and the contrasting masculinities presented
by Tom and Klaatu, *The Day the Earth Stood Still* draws into question dominant
ideologies about gender and containment in ways that other 1950s science
fiction films rarely did.

However, Tom serves as more than just a foil to Klaatu; he also foregrounds the fact that alongside the preoccupation with getting women back into the home and containing female sexuality, there was also a crisis in masculinity. Returning veterans found more than a grateful nation when they returned; they also found a changing political and social landscape. Although some veterans were able to return to the jobs they had left behind, displacing their replacement workers, others were not so fortunate. The influx of servicemen and their new families added to the existing housing shortage, forcing many young couples to live with their parents or in makeshift arrangements—even trailers and campers. Halberstam notes that in Chicago the housing crisis was so severe that "250 used trolley cars were sold for use as homes," and other newlywed veterans were living in army Quonset huts (134). These factors and the added stress of readjusting to civilian life left many veterans feeling ill equipped to fulfill their roles as breadwinners and providers. Moreover, the definition of masculinity, of what it meant to be an American male, was undergoing major revisions.

Early in U.S. history John Locke and Adam Smith made popular the notion "that there is a natural and harmonious relationship between the desires of individuals and the demands of social necessity, that individuals who act out of self-interest will automatically move the society as a whole in the direction of natural perfection" (Samuels 210). This notion of "natural harmony" was predicated on the belief that nothing in the system—including class, gender, religion, or race—could prevent people from achieving their goals. Thus, any failure on the part of the individual was a result of personal shortcomings, not social or political impediments. The individual, then, was the proper driving force in the development of the society. This archetypal image of the rugged individualist was a staple of U.S. social policy and narrative tradition at least as far back as the novels of James Fenimore Cooper and the tales that grew out of the exploits of historical figures such as Daniel Boone and Davy Crockett, but it came under fire in the 1950s. There was a new, strong desire for conformity—a conformity that would lead to a united and stable nation able to repel the threat of communist infiltration as well as withstand domestic problems such as the rising divorce rate and juvenile delinquency. Conformity and maintaining the status quo were the new standards of the decade, and they were being examined, promoted, and critiqued in a wide range of cultural texts, including David Riesman's best seller *The Lonely Crowd* (1950), William Whyte's *The Organization Man* (1956), and Sloan Wilson's *The Man in the Gray Flannel Suit* (1955).

In *The Day the Earth Stood Still*, Tom is well aware of the new model of masculinity. He is concerned with respectability and upward mobility, and he knows that "compliance with the system" is the road to success (Samuels 207). He tells Helen that "turning in" Klaatu will allow him to "write my own ticket. I'd be the biggest man in the country." In a decade in which loyalty oaths and "turning in" friends, coworkers, or family members who might have communist leanings or were simply outside the norm in terms of individuality, sexual orientation, or race had become commonplace, Tom speaks for the new conformist masculinity of the time. Tom's actions attest not only to his understanding and acceptance of conformity but also to the xenophobia generated by Cold War rhetoric. Furthermore, Tom's dismissive treatment of Helen is indicative of the decade's attitude toward women. As William O'Neill observes, "Sexism flourished. Today nothing about the postwar era seems more peculiar than the universal indifference to women's rights. At the time gender stereotyping and discrimination, far from embarrassing anyone, were staples of humor" (39). They are also staples of Tom's behavior.

In addition to the scene quoted above, in which Tom dismisses the notion that the "spaceman" would entrust Helen, a woman, with the purpose of his mission, several others demonstrate Tom's sexism. For example, on the day he wants to propose, Helen has no one to watch Bobby. She suggests that they take Bobby with them, but Tom is less than keen about the idea. When Carpenter/Klaatu offers to stay with Bobby, Tom quickly and enthusiastically replies, "Say, that would be great!" Helen is not so sure, and she gives him a sideways look of caution; she is concerned about leaving her son with a virtual stranger. While her apprehension is lost on Tom, Klaatu understands her concern, assuring her that he and Bobby had "a fine time yesterday afternoon" and that he was hoping Bobby "might like to show [him] around the city." Helen is still not convinced and gives Tom another meaningful look that he clearly does not comprehend. Finally, they decide to leave the choice up to Bobby. Once Carpenter exits, Helen, still unsure, asks Tom, "You think it's all right?" and with vigor he replies, "Sure." In this scene Tom is more than ready to speak on Helen's behalf regarding arrangements for her son and is completely oblivious to her valid concerns.

As the film continues, Tom's actions become more hypocritical and his attitude more patronizing. Tom finds Helen talking to Mr. Carpenter when he arrives for their next date and becomes jealous, making a rude remark within earshot of Carpenter. When Helen comments on his behavior, Tom, who only days before had willingly left Bobby in Carpenter's care, tells her, "I guess I'm just tired of hearing about Mr. Carpenter. . . . I don't like the way he's attached himself to you and Bobby. After all, what do you know about him?" Helen is speechless. Her only reply is a look of unbelieving irritation before she coolly leaves the room to get her things. By the end of the film Tom is ready to turn Klaatu in to the authorities, saying that he "never did trust him."

Tom's behavior sets Klaatu's masculinity up as an attractive alternative. Besides running contrary to the generic conventions established for the white male love interest in science fiction films, Tom's character destabilizes audience identification with the male protagonist. Film scholar Laura Mulvey and others have noted that the assumed or "perfect" film spectator is the white male, and "as the spectator identifies with the main male protagonist he projects his look onto that of his like . . . so that the power of the male protagonist as he controls events coincides with the active power of the erotic look, both giving a satisfying sense of omnipotence" (34). As Tom's behavior becomes more and more suspect, the identification process is disrupted, and the spectator has to look toward other characters to identify with, others who are not "of his like" (including an alien, a woman, an aging scientist, or a young boy), thus calling into question not only Tom's attitude and behavior but also the spectator's own assumptions about masculinity in the atomic age.

To be fair to Tom and the military (the other representative of patriarchal authority in the film), in most cases they would be correct in thinking that Klaatu presents a threat and should be destroyed. Most alien invaders of the era are bug-eyed monsters with only one thing on their minds: the destruction of the planet and the extermination of the human race. Klaatu is quite different, a figure that Berg terms a "sympathetic alien." Spectators of science fiction films today have become familiar with this figure through characters in films such as *ET: The Extra-Terrestrial* (1982), *Close Encounters of the Third Kind* (1977), and *Star Man* (1984), but the "wise, understanding extraterrestrial was an oddity back in the 1950s when it appeared in the memorable form of Michael Rennie's Klaatu" (Berg 4). Klaatu is so conscious of the effects of his actions that, when he arranges to have the electricity neutralized all over the world at noon (as a demonstration of his power), he makes sure that "hospitals, planes in flight, those sorts of things" are not affected. Still, the military and Tom mark him for extermination. What, then, is Klaatu's crime? He is an elusive and powerful Other who cannot be contained and therefore cannot be tolerated or allowed within the rigid confines of 1950s masculinity and society. What Robin Wood observes about the treatment of the Other in Westerns is evident in Tom's and the military's response to Klaatu; it is "a classic and extreme case of the projection onto the Other of what is repressed within the Self, in order that it can be discredited, disowned, and if possible annihilated" (199).

This rather unusual science fiction invasion film disrupts narrative expectations and Cold War values on several levels. By placing the woman in an active role, breaking the narrative conventions of the genre, and questioning the notion of gender containment, the film challenges the status quo. It shows that the best prospect for survival and peace may lie not in military prowess and personal gain but in "oppositional values and meanings" of those that are typically labeled "Other." Raymond Williams notes that both alternative and oppositional values and meanings exist within a dominant culture. He writes that "there is a simple theoretical distinction between alternative and oppositional, that is to say between someone who simply finds a different way to live and wishes to be left alone with it, and someone who finds a different way to live and wants to change the society in its light" (Williams 11). The characters in this film clearly want to change society. By shifting the focus of the narrative and visual images away from Tom and the military and centering on the actions, reactions, and reasoning of Helen and Klaatu, the film suggests a "different way to live"—a way based less on aggression and more on tolerance and understanding.

The Day the Earth Stood Still can also be read as an antiwar film that is critical of U.S. expansionist tendencies and national myths and 1950s xenophobia. For example, while Helen, Bobby, and Barnhardt accept Klaatu, those with political and social power treat him like a monster come to earth to wreak havoc. Their reaction to Klaatu, like the reaction to real bug-eyed monsters in other films such as the giant queen ants in *Them!* (1954) and the "Gillman" in *The Creature from the Black Lagoon* (1954), demonstrates that the national response to the Other was still entrenched in Cold War rhetoric and negative stereotypes. Few science fiction films were able to negotiate the issue of difference, especially when difference could not be easily seen or "lack[ed] fixity," as in the case of the all too human Klaatu and "takeover" films such as *Invasion of the Body Snatchers* (1956) and *Invaders from Mars* (1953) (Ono and Sloop 44). It mattered little if the invader was a bug-eyed monster, took the form of a loved one, or was a soft-spoken humanoid; from the 1950s standpoint, all aliens were dangerous invaders that needed to be destroyed.

Moreover, by altering generic conventions, the film cast a critical gaze on conformist masculinity. Though the film fails to present complete alternative models or strategies to replace dominant ones, it does disrupt the conventions of a popular genre enough to raise questions about men's roles in the atomic age. Still, the concluding sequence confirms that the most significant generic variation is the representation of Helen. In most invasion films the woman watches from afar or is completely absent from the closing scenes as the male protagonist saves the day so "the status quo can be maintained" (Berg 7). In *The Day the Earth Stood Still* it is Tom, the model of 1950s masculinity, who is missing from the closing sequence. The military, though present, is ineffectual and barely visible in the distance behind a group of assembled scientists and

20th Century-Fox

Significantly, Helen and the alien Other, Klaatu—not Tom or the military—are the central figures in the film's closing sequence.

religious leaders, both male and female, of many races, nationalities, and ethnicities. In a series of medium close-ups, it is the faces of these people, rarely seen even in the crowd scenes of most 1950s invasion films, and Helen and Klaatu who are the central figures in the closing scene.

Helen Benson is presented in stark contrast to the dominant culture's "poster woman," the mystique model. Though she has her moment of weakness, including the obligatory blood-curdling scream, she still offers the 1950s woman alternative choices as she remains a good mother and a working woman and functions as the film's protagonist as well, while still maintaining her femininity and her keen fashion sense. Her characterization suggests that a woman can think for herself, choose to stay single (or widowed, as in Helen's case), and be an active participant outside the home without her child paying for it—disproving the denunciations about "mom" made by Lundberg and Farnham, Wylie, and other pundits of the day. Unfortunately, 1950s science fiction films contain far more mystique models who "serve the interests of the ruling class" and are rewarded with the promise of marriage for maintaining traditional gender roles than women like Helen (Wright 41).

Many film theorists claim that genre films are solely tools of the dominant culture, so it is not surprising that mystique models outnumber any other type of woman in science fiction films. The dominant culture, as Christine Gledhill notes, repeatedly tries to "turn artistic practice to it own ends," but is not always successful. As she explains: "Due to a complex of contradictions in the socio-economic and cultural conditions of the mass media and aesthetic production, the hegemony of the dominant ideology is always in question. Despite the claim that all mainstream production is tainted with realist reaction, genre has been seized on by radical cultural analysts as the ground on which 'progressive' appropriations may be made of bourgeois and patriarchal products" (10). *The Day the Earth Stood Still* opens a space for emergent ideologies and "progressive appropriations" of "patriarchal products" such as the narrowly defined or "traditional" gender roles imposed on women and men, the move from individualist to conformist as the model for masculinity, and the fear of the Other that permeated the era. Moreover, the film offers a different world-view, one in which the earth is saved not through dominant cultural dogma but through the progressive vision of those who are traditionally marked as Other and thus less valued in the culture, such as "other people, women . . . [and] children" (Berg 4). Therefore, the film stands as another "phantom" production that offers an oppositional voice and a more complete understanding of what Goldman identifies as the "crucial decade."

WORKS CITED

Berg, Charles Ramírez. "Immigrants, Aliens and Extraterrestrials: Science Fiction's Alien 'Other' as (Among Other Things) New Hispanic Imagery." *CineAction!* 18 (1989): 3–17.

Boyer, Paul. *By the Bomb's Early Light: American Thought and Culture at the Dawn of the Atomic Age.* Chapel Hill: U of North Carolina P, 1994.

Carter, Paul A. *Another Part of the Fifties.* New York: Columbia UP, 1983.

The Day the Earth Stood Still. Dir. Robert Wise. 1951. Videocassette. 20th Century-Fox Film Corp., 1979.

Dixon, Wheeler Winston. *Lost in the Fifties: Recovering Phantom Hollywood.* Carbondale: Southern Illinois UP, 2005.

Ehrenreich, Barbara. *The Hearts of Men: American Dreams and the Flight from Commitment.* Garden City, N.Y.: Anchor Press/Doubleday, 1983.

George, Susan. "Pushing Containment: The Tale of the 1950s Science Fiction Vamp." *Reconstruction: Studies in Contemporary Culture* 5.4 (Fall 2005). <http://reconstruction.eserver.org/054/george.shtml>.

Gledhill, Christine. "Klute 1: A Contemporary Film Noir and Feminist Criticism." *Women in Film Noir*. Ed. E. Ann Kaplan. 1978. London: British Film Institute, 1994. 6–21.

Goldman, Eric F. *The Crucial Decade—And After: America, 1945–1960*. 1956. New York: Vintage Books, 1960.

"The Good Wife's Guide." *Housekeeping Monthly* 13 May 1955.

Halberstam, David. *The Fifties*. New York: Villard Books, 1993.

Lundberg, Ferdinand, and Marynia F. Farnham, MD. *The Modern Woman: The Lost Sex*. New York: Harper & Brothers, 1947.

May, Elaine Tyler. *Homeward Bound: American Families in the Cold War Era*. New York: Basic Books, 1988.

May, Lary. "Movie Star Politics: The Screen Actor's Guild, Cultural Conversion, and the Hollywood Red Scare." *Recasting America: Culture and Politics in the Age of the Cold War*. Ed. Lary May. Chicago: U of Chicago P, 1989. 125–53.

Mulvey, Laura. "Visual Pleasure and Narrative Cinema." *Screen* 16:3 (1975). Rpt. in *Issues in Feminist Film Criticism*. Ed. Patricia Erens. Bloomington: Indiana UP, 1990. 28–40.

O'Neill, William L. *American High: The Years of Confidence, 1945–1960*. New York: Free Press, 1986.

Ono, Kent A., and John M. Sloop. "Shifting Borders: Rhetoric, Immigration, and California's 'Proposition 187.'" Personal copy of unpublished manuscript. 2001.

Samuels, Stuart. "The Age of Conspiracy and Conformity: *Invasion of the Body Snatchers*." *American History/American Film: Interpreting the Hollywood Image*. Ed. John E. O'Connor and Martin A. Jackson. 1979. New York: Ungar, 1988. 203–17.

Shapiro, Benjamin. "Universal Truths: Cultural Myths and Generic Adaptation in 1950s Science Fiction Films." *Journal of Popular Film and Television* 18.3 (1990): 103–11.

Staiger, Janet. *Bad Women: Regulating Sexuality in Early American Cinema*. Minneapolis: U of Minnesota P, 1995.

Suid, Lawrence H. *Guts & Glory: The Making of the American Military Image in Film*. Lexington: UP of Kentucky, 2002.

This Island Earth. Dir. Joseph Newman. 1955. Videocassette. Universal Pictures Company, 1983.

Turner, George. "Howard Hawks' *The Thing*." *Cinefantastique* 12 (1982): 78–85.

The War of the Worlds. Dir. Byron Haskin. Prod. George Pal. 1952. Videocassette. Paramount Pictures, 1980.

Williams, Raymond. "Base and Superstructure in Marxist Cultural Theory." *New Left Review* 82 (1973): 3–16.

Wood, Robin. "An Introduction to American Horror Films." *Movies and Methods*. Ed Bill Nichol. Berkeley: U of California P, 1985. 2:195–220.

Wright, Judith Hess. "Genre Films and the Status Quo." *Jump Cut* 1 (1974): 16–18. Rpt. in *Film Genre Reader II*. Ed. Barry Keith Grant. Austin: U of Texas P, 1995. 41–49.

Wylie, Philip. *Generation of Vipers*. New York: Rinehart, 1942.

USING POPULAR CULTURE TO STUDY THE VIETNAM WAR

Perils and Possibilities

The Vietnam War is not over for the United States. It is still being fought in our popular culture, and the struggle provides rich opportunities for researchers and teachers of contemporary literature, mass media, and culture. The secret for exploiting this opportunity has less to do with identifying the kinds of materials to use in the classroom than with defining the right approach to them, for while there are possibilities, there are also perils. Existing Vietnam texts are short on hard, irreducible facts and long on bias; as a result, historians should look upon popular culture as a subjective prism of intense feeling rather than as Clio's reliable mirror.

Disagreements about interpreting Vietnam can lead to heated debates that echo the confrontations of the 1960s. For example, James Webb (later to become a U.S. senator from Virginia) stepped on a rhetorical land mine at a 1985 conference on "The Vietnam Experience in American Literature" when he defiantly questioned the willingness of assembled academics to consider perspectives other than those that portrayed America as exploiter, manipulator, and villain. As a highly decorated marine combat veteran who believed that our cause in Vietnam was not only just but also vindicated by the post-1975 experience of the "killing fields" and the boat people, Webb deplored the uniformity of perspective along academe's postwar paper trail. Although Webb's position is overstated—he is well known for his combativeness—it deserves consideration, especially his complaint about what he calls the influence of an "academic-intellectual complex": "In media and publishing circles, supporting government policy of almost any sort becomes akin to selling out. Such a writer is quite often viewed by his peers and by critics to be either stupid or a pawn. Awards are lavished on those who discover new ways to question or attack government policy. Sometimes it takes more courage to confront the

National Archives

A marine and his flag, 1968.

hostility of one's peers than it does to attack that amorphous dragon called government policy" (Lomperis 18–19).

Many present at the conference complained that Webb's remarks were not helpful, although a few of the assembled authors who were veterans confirmed Webb's charges by recounting their own struggles with publishers who rejected manuscripts that "did not exhibit enough guilt" (Lomperis 22). Scholars who have taken an empathetic stand toward government policies or who have defended public figures such as General William C. Westmoreland against attacks by programs such as *The Uncounted Enemy: A Vietnam Deception* (1982) have been picketed at conferences and blacklisted from speaking engagements. (During a job interview, one veteran I know was refused employment and called "war criminal" for serving in the armed forces during the Vietnam conflict.) Thus, although Webb's statement oversimplifies, it points to a real question: in publishing, on television, and in the classroom, have Americans been exposed to a full spectrum of perspectives on our tragic experience in Vietnam?

I think not. The purpose of this chapter is to briefly illumine the problems of using existing histories, fictions, films, and television programs to study Vietnam. I do not wish to argue that these materials should not be used—indeed, I feel that the opposite is the case, that they provide excellent teaching

U.S. Army

Is Iraq Vietnam? What are the lessons to be applied?

instruments. What I do offer is that while there are wonderful possibilities in using existing texts in the classroom, there are also perils. The opportunity exists to show that the study of Vietnam—like virtually every other war era—is rich with differing perspectives and redolent with many "truths." The danger lies in relying on any one document for the total picture. The first half of this chapter surveys the various documents and indicates potential pitfalls in using them; the second half tries to account for the biased consensus of approach to Vietnam. Along the way, I speculate about the possible impact of two Gulf wars on our evolving, retrospective images of Vietnam.

GENRES USED TO INTERPRET VIETNAM

Novels and Autobiographical Fiction

Vietnam fictions are so charged with feeling because veteran authors strive to dramatize the trauma inflicted on them and their friends. Shortly after graduating from the Marine Corps' Basic School for officers at Quantico, Virginia, Philip Caputo found himself in Vietnam as an infantry platoon commander; *A Rumor of War* (1977) is his elaborate novelistic effort to depict himself as a youthful victim of war. W. D. Ehrhart's *Vietnam-Perkasie: A Combat Marine Memoir* (1983) similarly traces the frontline devolution of a young boy fresh from the backwoods town of Perkasie, Pennsylvania. James Webb's *Fields of Fire* (1978) traces the combat experience of officers and men in a tightly knit marine infantry platoon; in an unusual coda for this literary genre, the narrative follows one of the protagonists back to a university campus, where he rebukes the college peace movement for taking the easy way out. Personal narratives such as Michael Herr's *Dispatches* (1977) promote empathy for the pain and death Herr witnessed during his psychedelic tour as a "new journalist" for *Esquire*. Each of these writers faithfully recounts his personal story; each comments implicitly and explicitly on the "big picture." Webb and Herr create an intense identification with their subjects, whom we gradually see as the victims of an inept, but dangerous, killing machine: the hateful war itself. Caputo's work is more narrowly autobiographical; much of the novel tries to explain how the Marine Corps and America have brought young Philip to commit murder and perjury. These infantry fictions are colorful evocations of Vietnam; what makes them perilous as documents is that the authors ask that their personal tales be accepted as reliable microcosms. Most of these "corruption of innocence" books draw heavily on the American Adam motif, a topic discussed later in this chapter. The motif has deep roots in our Romantic culture, but it clearly skews interpretations toward a melodramatic mode of good versus evil rather than promoting a wiser, tragic sense of life. Historians have long understood that a participant in a historical event may lack the perspective needed to identify larger patterns of meaning. War viewed from a foxhole shows vivid pyrotechnics, but the view is often as narrow as it is intense.

Letters, Diaries, and Oral Histories

Likewise, anthologies of letters, diary entries, and collected oral histories from Vietnam have their perils. Although such collections are promoted as argument free, their editors inevitably shape the presentations. Stanley Beesley's *Vietnam: The Heartland Remembers* (1987) is a case in point. Beesley's own tour in Vietnam came during the later years of the war. He believes—with many others—that the Vietnam War had two phases for the ordinary fighting man: during the first phase (1965–1969), units were committed to the field after training together; in the second phase (1969–1973), replacements were inserted as individuals among complete strangers. As a result, according to this interpretation, the second phase was characterized by a breakdown of discipline and a precipitous decline in morale. According to Beesley, second-phase army units refused to go out on combat operations; furthermore, such insubordination did not lead to disciplinary action. *Vietnam: The Heartland Remembers* appears to be merely a collection of oral history statements from veterans across the state of Oklahoma, but the evocative anthology misleads the reader by painting the *entire* war with second-phase colors.

The New York State Vietnam Veterans Association collected a similar volume of letters entitled *Dear America: Letters Home from Vietnam* (1985). Interestingly, that book does *not* try to pour the experience into a preconstructed mold; instead, the anthology clusters letters around such topics as arrival in country, the experience of battle, what it means to be "short" on time, and other "generic" experiences (Edelman). In 1987 HBO came out with a special broadcast (very) loosely based on the anthology. This program could be used as a textbook in media manipulation. The visual rendering of *Dear America* places more than 70 percent of the anthology's letters out of chronological order to support the "two-phase" thesis. Filmmaker Bill Couturie, with the help of actors Charlie Sheen, Matt Dillon, and others, transforms an act of devotion into a diatribe. HBO's *Dear America* was circulated theatrically in 1989 so that it could be considered for an Academy Award. (It won an Emmy and a Sundance Film Festival Award.)

The lesson from these experiments is that oral histories and anthologies of personal documents are indeed perilous if approached as mere repositories of "fact." When the subject is Vietnam, many anthologists find it hard to avoid shaping the raw materials into their own messages about the evils of a purposeless war.

Television

Our students are visually oriented, if not visually literate: some brag that they have seen major Vietnam movies more than once; others own large off-air collections of Vietnam documentaries. Yet the visual route can be the most perilous of all, because teachers are often as ill prepared as their students to analyze the visual rhetoric that the media giants of both coasts, and places in between, have so effectively mastered.

There are a number of prominent documentaries that purport to probe issues related to Vietnam. As late as 1983, the Organization of American Historians' newsletter recommended *Hearts and Minds* (1974), directed by Peter Davis, as a perfect companion to *Vietnam: A Television History,* a series purveyed by WGBH-TV (Boston)—one of the major centers for educational television in this country. The reviewer's suggestion was right, but not in the positive way it was intended. In an early review, even *Time* magazine noticed that the historical interpretation of Davis's *Hearts and Minds* was simplistic, that its rhetoric was strident. By 1977 April Orcutt had laboriously dissected the propagandist techniques of Davis's *Hearts and Minds* in an excellent master's thesis. (See chapter 21 for a discussion of the influence of the Davis blockbuster on later war films.)

That much-touted, prize-winning WGBH-TV series has not lacked its informed critics. *Vietnam: A Television History* was first broadcast in the fall of 1983. Shortly after the third episode aired, Vietnamese refugees incensed by the programs staged demonstrations in Paris, London, Washington, D.C., New Orleans, Houston, and Los Angeles. The grievances against the series were consolidated by James Banerian in a book entitled *Losers Are Pirates* (1984), a volume that analyzes the flaws of the series, episode by episode. Accusations of bias are substantiated in prolix detail. Editor Banerian and his staff also took Stanley Karnow's best-selling companion volume to task. Of *Vietnam: A History*, they ask rhetorically, "Has history come to this?" (36). Historians joined the criticism. Writing for the *Newsletter of the Organization of American Historians* in 1984, R. C. Raack noted that the series "developed no sufficient methodology and seemed to be unaware of the nagging problems deriving from missing as well as mendacious documentation." As a result, Raack concludes, "They failed to confront the 'television war' and made up their own television war" (8). Despite such criticism, the WGBH series won numerous awards and was purchased for instructional purposes by countless school systems and universities.

In 1984 Accuracy in Media (AIM), a Washington-based public interest group, received a controversial $30,000 grant from the National Endowment for the Humanities (NEH) to produce a video critique of *Vietnam: A Television History*. (NEH had previously awarded WGBH more than $1 million to produce the series in a "noncontroversial" grant.) Two programs emerged from a Washington, D.C., conference called by AIM to examine the PBS series. *Television's Vietnam: The Real Story* (1985) spells out some of the points later made by Banerian in his book-length critique. Some of WGBH-TV's own consultants appear on the program to voice objections to the Boston station's historiography. As Banerian observes, WGBH saw Vietnam as "America's war. America's mistake. America's responsibility" (28). With Banerian, AIM's conference faulted WGBH not only for showing bias in favor of the communists but also for displaying an unremitting, almost racist view of our allies, not to mention the terrible portrayal of America's fighting men as drug addicts and war criminals. AIM's video critique was itself criticized (but its major arguments found accurate) by an *Inside Story Special* broadcast by PBS in the fall of 1985. *The Real Story* has received a number of awards from Vietnamese groups worldwide for setting the record straight (from their point of view). It was favorably reviewed by the

National Archives

The media record ignores the heroic performance of our South Vietnamese ally.

New York Times and *TV Guide*. A number of PBS stations carried the rebuttal as a fourteenth episode when they reran the WGBH series in 1985 and 1986.

A second program from AIM entitled *Television's Vietnam: The Impact of Media* (1986) focuses on the Tet Offensive of 1968, comparing news reports with contrasting versions of the same stories by diplomats and soldiers involved in the actions. Drawing heavily on Peter Braestrup's *Big Story* (1977), *Impact of Media* dramatizes the now widely accepted notion that the Tet Offensive was so misreported by our media that a North Vietnamese military defeat in Vietnam was transformed electronically into a psychological victory in the United States. To support its thesis, the program examines three microcosmic stories from the Tet Offensive of 1968: the Saigon embassy incident, the Battle of Khe Sanh, and the Colonel Loan photograph. In each case, the media image is contrasted with what actually happened. Although *Impact of Media* does not eschew point of view in its presentation, it states its bias up front rather than smuggling it into the work sub rosa. Because the AIM shows are so candid about their point of view, Dr. Martin Medhurst describes them as "bad" propaganda—as opposed to the WGBH shows, which he ironically praises as "good" propaganda (192). It would seem that there are many perils for students and teachers when they approach "good" propaganda programs in search of truth. (Both AIM programs were rereleased on DVD in 2007, with special features that include a thirty-minute video with the director, along with substantive articles and reviews readable with Adobe software. See "AIM store" at www.aim.org.)

The publication of Burton Benjamin's *Fair Play: CBS, General Westmoreland, and How a Television Documentary Went Wrong* (1988) revived interest in a CBS Special Report entitled *The Uncounted Enemy: A Vietnam Deception* (1982). That program promised to reveal "shocking decisions made at the highest level of military intelligence to suppress and alter critical information on the number and replacement of enemy troops in Vietnam." Once again, General Westmoreland was the villain of a CBS melodrama, and a long and inconclusive libel trial resulted. Subsequently, books such as Don Kowet's *A Matter of Honor* (1984) allege that producer George Crile and media star Mike Wallace cooked up their own brew of deception in *The Uncounted Enemy*. In addition, a CBS internal report by Burton Benjamin was published after it was "leaked" to the press by in-house sources who felt that the general was being treated unfairly. (This "source" was subsequently identified and fired by CBS.) Perils indeed seem to lie ahead for those who put their trust in this and other network exposés.

Hollywood Cinema

Hollywood's Vietnam has also been laden with tendentious metaphors and allegories. *Coming Home* (1978) is the story of a paraplegic veteran who makes a successful adjustment to civilian life and finds love. The film teaches that individuals should avoid military service because there is no moral basis for our involvement in far-off lands. In addition, viewers are asked to believe that antiwar activists have better sex than whose who serve. That same year, *The Deer Hunter* attempted a mythopoetic approach to Vietnam as it follows the tour of duty of steelworkers from Pennsylvania who are physically or emotionally crippled by a repulsive Asian war. In *Apocalypse Now* (1979) the American presence in Vietnam is depicted as an unmitigated "horror" that deserves the purging incineration it receives at the end of the film.

Within a twelve-month period in 1986–1987, five films saturated the Vietnam target. Viewers of Oliver Stone's *Platoon* are led to believe that American troops regularly shot civilians, that our field commanders used troops as "bait," and that our servicemen were so undisciplined that they spent nearly as much time "fragging" one another as they did pursuing an elusive enemy. *Platoon*'s Hollywood auteur comments broadly about American history when the most sympathetic father figure in the film, Sergeant Elias, explains, "We've [the United States] been kicking ass for so long, it's about time we had ours kicked."

U.S. Marine Corps

Which platoon was real—the disciplined or the undisciplined?

Stanley Kubrick's *Full Metal Jacket* looks back on the marines: the first half of the film shows how basic training perversely redirects the natural energies of young men from love to war; the second half of the film traces the degradation that occurs in combat to the point where the narrator, "Joker," reflects, "I am in a world of shit, but I am alive and I am not afraid." Such is the result— Hollywood's Kubrick, looking backward, asserts—of Marine Corps brainwashing and Vietnam service. In *Good Morning, Vietnam,* Robin Williams is given his best screen opportunity for nonstop hilarity. Between riffs, the film stresses that the United States is fulfilling a French imperialist design—although the notion itself goes unexplored. Looking within the American "Establishment," the film portrays those who plan American policy as hypocritical, manipulative, and—like the top brass in *Platoon*—willing to endanger the precious lives of young men. These messages are particularly memorable because Williams, himself, is genuinely funny. (The *real* Adrian Cronauer gladly lectures on the notable differences between his Vietnam experience and that portrayed by *Good Morning, Vietnam*—for which he provided the original screen treatment.)

Two films stand out from the 1986–1987 pack. *Hanoi Hilton* (1987) tells the story of American pilots held captive in the Hoa Lo Prison in Hanoi from 1964 to 1973. Director Lionel Chetwynd's film is unlike its contemporaries because it portrays American servicemen as dedicated professionals whose military training gives them inner strength and discipline. The North Vietnamese, in contrast, are shown as cruel and manipulative captors. Finally, the American peace movement is criticized for its naïveté. For taking such unorthodox positions, *Hanoi Hilton* was condemned by the Hollywood community and major critics. David Denby of *New York Magazine* challenged the research behind the film, decried its treatment of Jane Fonda, and concluded by describing the "tedious" production as suffering from "the grinding vindictiveness of an old Patrick Buchanan column" (91). Stanley Kauffman of the *New Republic* dismissed *Hanoi Hilton* as "filth" (26). In response to critical denunciations, Canon Films withdrew the offending film from circulation soon after its release, followed by a mini-revival of interest when veterans groups—including the POWS depicted—protested to local distributors.

A combat film entitled *Hamburger Hill* (1987) can be viewed as a cinematic rebuttal to Stone's *Platoon*. The film shows troops working together cohesively, respecting military discipline, and fighting courageously to complete their assigned mission, despite occasional friction within the unit. Like *Hanoi Hilton*, *Hamburger Hill* quickly disappeared from theaters. As Harry Summers of *U.S. News and World Report* observed in an early review, critics "will reject it as they rejected *Hanoi Hilton*, because it recalls shameful [wartime] events that they would rather not remember." Former Colonel Summers (who died in 1999) was right about the rejection, but his attempt to identify its motivation needs further thought.

UNDERSTANDING THE VARIOUS FRAMES OF INTERPRETATION

Ideological Elements

Objections by Those Who Served: Can They Be Ignored?

A cursory study of statistics from a 1980 Louis Harris poll shows some glaring contradictions between the depressing portrait of the American fighting man in Vietnam novels, documentaries, and feature films and the self-image of large numbers of veterans who were *not* part of the literary and movie communities. The executive summary of the Harris poll brings the following disturbing conclusions to light (28–33): 90 percent of those polled were happy to have served, 54 percent enjoyed their experience, and 79 percent denied that the United States had taken advantage of them.[1] Harris and later pollsters also found that Vietnam veterans were more likely to have gone to college and to have purchased a home than others of their age; they were also more likely to have a

U.S. Army

An American soldier's noon-hour recreation: not every moment was stressful.

better income than their peers. Syndicated editorialist Tom Tiede responded to these and other "surprising" statistics with the following observations:

> Ticking bombs? The people who were on duty in Vietnam are nothing of the kind. And they did not kill babies in the war. Rare exceptions to the contrary, the American troops were good, moralistic, and compassionate, and those are the principal characteristics for which they should be remembered.
>
> But they probably won't. The ugly image of the Americans in Vietnam may be permanent. It was a war in which slander became a national obsession, in which Jane Fonda is remembered while the heroes are forgotten, and in which we didn't have the determination to win or the good sense to abandon before losing. (1)

Tiede's statement underscores the frustration of veterans (and some veteran correspondents) when they see negative images of the American fighting man in popular culture.

The Wish to "Freeze" History

During the Vietnam conflict, opponents of the war depicted America's presence in Southeast Asia as the cause of regional suffering. Alas, when the United States withdrew in 1975, the predicted era of peace and tranquility did not come to pass; instead, Americans saw "killing fields" in Cambodia and "reeducation" camps in South Vietnam. Some 2 million Cambodians lost their lives during the murderous reign of Pol Pot. During the 1980s, Vietnamese American students on my campus reported that their fathers had died from malnutrition or from unattended health problems while in communist gulags; these wonderful kids strove for perfect academic records as a tribute to their lost fathers. And in 2007, news headlines showed that Vietnam still imprisons religious and political dissidents to encourage proper "reeducation."

The revelation of these cruelties should have cast a new light on the meaning of the American struggle in Vietnam. For many, it did. There has been a "Second Thoughts" movement led by Peter Collier and David Horowitz, two former editors of the New Left magazine *Ramparts*. They were shocked by the unwillingness of their colleagues on the American Left to criticize the postwar outrages in Vietnam: "No matter that our old allies the National Liberation Front were among the first to be crushed; no matter that South Vietnam was conquered by the North; no matter that the Khmer Rouge, which we had supported with great enthusiasm, had embarked on a policy of genocide. There were no enemies on the Left" (19). Collier and Horowitz claim that they were forced to reconsider their antiwar positions because of world developments after 1975, including the reluctance of the American Left to criticize communist excesses. These "lefties for Reagan" began to realize that "the Communists were every bit as bad as American supporters of the war said they would be" (26). For rethinking their historical commitments, former members of the New Left were ostracized by their erstwhile comrades. Jeffrey Herf, once a leader of the Students for a Democratic Society (SDS), reports that "to take such a political position was just more than a number of old friends on the left could stomach. At their initiative, old friendships ended or cooled" (quoted in Collier and Horowitz 30).

The roster of those who have changed their minds is formidable. In addition to Collier, Horowitz, and Herf, there is Lloyd Billingsley, a leader of the antiwar movement, and David Ifshin, Michael Dukakis's transition team leader who, in his student days, broadcast over Hanoi Radio. Michael Medved cohosted the PBS version of *Sneak Previews* and went on to be a syndicated, conservative talk-show host, but in the 1960s he was chairman of the Vietnam Moratorium in Connecticut. That student group succeeded in forcing the ROTC off the

Orion Pictures

The narrator of *Platoon* associates Staff Sergeant Barnes (Tom Berenger) with Herman Melville's demonic Captain Ahab.

Yale University campus—and it is still off in 2007. Stephen Schwartz, a leading Trotskyite during the 1960s, now works with a conservative think tank in San Francisco. The list of those who have had second thoughts is long (Collier and Horowitz 263–67).

However long the list, the majority of those who participated in the antiwar movement—including those who were eligible for the draft but found a way to avoid it—have a vested interest in "freezing" history circa 1968. By retaining the United States as the international villain, their opposition to the war during the 1960s continues to be vindicated. Unwillingness to serve their country in the war goes unquestioned. Even *Tonight Show* host Johnny Carson could observe that *Platoon* was a movie that reflected well on the draft dodger. What sensible person would want to serve in such a dispirited and conflicted army? And how could those who did serve emerge as anything but desperately wounded—psychically, if not physically? As one indignant reviewer of *Platoon* observed, "Needless to say, there are many people who think this movie is a tribute to those Americans who died in Vietnam. Needless to say, people who think so never knew anybody who went anywhere near Vietnam—Canada, yes, and Sweden, but not Vietnam" (Podhoretz). More research is needed to probe how and why Vietnam stories (and some popular histories) are designed to vindicate the judgments of those who opposed the war. Why are auteurs unwilling to reevaluate their positions in the light of subsequent developments? Do they truly believe that the "radical chic" of the 1960s caught the real nature of events?

Radical Chic in Hollywood: From Cuba to Vietnam to Nicaragua and on to Iraq

Traditionally, certain artistic people in Hollywood and the media in general have been attracted to utopian radicalism. In the 1930s and 1940s John Howard Lawson, Dalton Trumbo, Lillian Hellman, and others clung overlong to the dream of a "Soviet America." In the 1960s the Beverly Hills and New York radicals tuned their political antennae to Fidel Castro of Cuba and then switched channels to Vietnam's Ho Chi Minh. Chairman Ho was portrayed as a Jeffersonian democrat who reluctantly turned to communism when we rejected him, a preposterous view reiterated by George McGovern at an Air Force Academy Military History Symposium in 1990.

Many of these creative people still share the desire of the Left to cling to 1960s myths about Vietnam, despite the tragic repression in Cambodia and in Vietnam after 1975. For some, it would be spiritually disastrous to admit that support for the North Vietnamese army brought about the deaths of millions and the misery of thousands of "boat people," some 300,000 of whom died gruesomely at sea.

Central American was chic in the late 1980s. To many media celebrities, Daniel Ortega looked like a Jeffersonian democrat, while Mrs. Ortega became a special darling of the "cocktails for Nicaragua" crowd in Beverly Hills. TV star Edward Asner established a nonprofit organization that financed aid to rebels in El Salvador, some of whom have been identified as terrorists. The election of Violeta Chamorro to the presidency of Nicaragua came as a big surprise and disappointment to the American intelligentsia—if not to ordinary Nicaraguans who exultantly exercised their franchise. For many American observers, Central America was Vietnam redivivus. The alleged Vietnam analogy to events down south was invoked constantly in Congress; in this period, even Richard Nixon authored a book entitled *No More Vietnams* (1985).

But the Vietnam analogy is a two-edged sword: on the one hand, for neo-isolationists it means that the United States should never intervene because Vietnam proved that our meddling inevitably leads to tragedy; on the other hand, to Richard Nixon it meant that we should intervene decisively when doing so is in our national interest—a policy that later became known as the "Powell

Doctrine." Shortly after our hundred-day victory in Operation Desert Storm, President George H. W. Bush (1989–1993) visited the White House Press Room to announce that, as of 1 March 1991, "the Vietnam Syndrome is over."

Hollywood has not been passive in the Vietnam analogy debate: Oliver Stone's historical drama *Platoon* reached theaters the same month that his *Salvador* went into distribution. Other films such as *The Mission* (1986) and *Walker* (1988) further drove home the Vietnam message, although *Walker* so overstated the lesson as to draw critical guffaws. In the penultimate scene, as William Walker's pre–civil war Nicaraguan empire crumbles, an American helicopter lands near his palace. Out springs a U.S. State Department official who explains that he is authorized to remove all U.S. citizens. This tendentious anachronism, a heavy-handed parallel to the 1975 evacuation of the U.S. embassy in Saigon, has actually been praised by some reviewers. More sensible critics have described the scene as silly at best.

After the initial success of Operation Desert Storm in 1991 and in the wake of Operation Iraqi Freedom in 2003, the analogy lost its flavor. Public response to Hollywood criticism of the 2003 war was swift and took an entirely new direction. After her pronouncements about the war, Susan Sarandon was canceled as a speaker for a celebrity event in Florida. Not long thereafter, her *Bull Durham* costar and longtime partner Tim Robbins was informed by the Baseball Hall of Fame that the controversy over the war had made both of them undesirable speakers at an institution devoted to the national pastime. In March 2003, at a concert in England, Dixie Chicks singer Natalie Maines apologized to the audience for being from Texas, the home state of America's president. Within days, country western stations pulled Dixie Chicks records, and an angry constituency of country western fans made their displeasure known through protest calls and chain letters on the Internet. One wag even proposed to give a "Dixie Chicks Award" to Hollywood ideologue Janeane Garofalo, another celebrity activist. These reactions were 180 degrees from the Vietnam-era responses; an active public—assisted by the Internet, talk radio, and cable television news—refused to accept the posturing of the Hollywood elite. Indeed, it launched an aggressive counterattack, which was then condemned in the press as a new form of McCarthyism.

Some two years later, moribund Vietnam models and critiques regained viability as American troops encountered delayed resistance; for example, Michael Moore's major commercial success *Fahrenheit 9/11* borrowed heavily from the Vietnam epic by Peter Davis. On the political front, in May 2007 Congress haggled with President George W. Bush over the war budget. For some, it appeared to be an attempt to relive the glory days of the 1970s, when support for

South Vietnam had been undermined by the War Powers Resolution (1973) and subsequent congressional moves such as the Case-Church amendment. Led in the House of Representatives by Vietnam veteran John Murtha (D-Pa.), the 2007 ploy to encumber the supply of men and materiel was nearly successful. This mercurial change of national mood was reflected by a debate over the release of previews for Sylvester Stallone's new *Rambo IV*. Internet reactions varied from a fan who urged that "Chuck Norris needs to make another MIA film now" to a war-weary blogger who opined that "Stallone looks ridiculous. Please let Rambo rest in the 80s" (www.flynetonline.com).

Formal Factors

The Premise of a Lost War

James Banerian drew on a Vietnamese proverb to title his book *Losers Are Pirates*. In thinking about popular culture in relation to Vietnam, the proverb provides valuable insight. People naturally want to jump on the bandwagon. In relation to the WGBH-TV history of the war, Banerian saw two related trends: the Boston-based producers—none of whom had substantial training in history—wanted to produce empathy for the then current (i.e., 1980s) regime in Vietnam so that wartime enmities could be transcended; as a dramatic by-product, the "losers" in the war—the South Vietnamese and their American ally—had to occupy unsympathetic roles in the thirteen-chapter story.

The same perspective can easily be applied to other renderings of the Vietnam experience. Suppose you were involved in writing a novel or a screen-play or assembling an anthology; how would you conduct yourself if your basic premise was that we were the losers—and moral reprobates to boot? First, you would have to explain how the most technologically advanced and mobile armed force in world history was defeated by an agrarian, Third World nation. Second, your task with respect to individual motivation would be to explain how good American boys could be involved in such a dirty and disgusting foray. If possible, you would try to link these two themes.

Consider some eligible (and ineligible) themes. Prohibited would be the following: any intelligent defense of the concept of containment by sympathetic characters (only "lifers" would swallow such claptrap), good relations between American fighting men and local civilians (strictly for rebels against a callous establishment), concern for innocent human life or the destruction of civilian property (all Vietnam as a free-fire zone), racial harmony and teamwork on the front lines (rampant racism), mutual trust between officers and men (frequent fraggings), religious faith by fighting men (spiritual alienation only), intelligent conversation by officers or troops (f-words ad nauseam). At no time would commanders above the squad level be concerned about troop morale and safety. Whenever possible, include President Lyndon Johnson's picture in the same frame with the face of a high-ranking villain. Never show that leadership experience can help a young person grow in confidence so that he will make a contribution to society upon his return to the United States. Vietnam narratives are stories of losers who return to our country as pathetic remnants, "walking wounded." Years after they return, PBS can sponsor programs for them, such as the PBS special *For Vietnam Veterans and Others Who Should Care* (SONY Home Video). During such "happenings" we are urged to commiserate with the poor dupes. These are some of the spin-offs of the ubiquitous "lost war" premise, results demanded by the artistic form more than by the actual experience of veterans. (See note 1.)

The American Adam Motif

Concomitant with the "losers" premise is the American Adam motif. The novels by Caputo and Ehrhart, as well as the personal narrative by Herr and Beesley's collection of letters—but *not* Webb's *Fields of Fire*—draw on this familiar American literary motif. Dark romantics such as Nathaniel Hawthorne, Herman Melville, and Edgar Allan Poe ridiculed the motif's limitations when it became popular in the early nineteenth century, but the scheme is extremely useful in the Vietnam context, where the rhetorical strategy is to condemn the nation while forgiving the soldiers. (See Maland for a survey of this motif in American films.)

The American Adam leaves a placid, civilian environment to become immersed in a war that leaves him devastated. Ron Kovic's *Born on the Fourth of July* (1976) is a model text: films and television shape young Kovic's attitudes toward war; after high school, the Marine Corps adds its perverting influence. When combat experiences further erode his spirit, Kovic reaches a dead low: he kills a friend by accident and participates in the accidental shooting of Vietnamese children. His spinal wound comes as a blessing of sorts; through it, he learns to fight back against the official authorities—"Them." Caputo's *A Rumor of War* follows a similar outline in its effort to exculpate young Philip from his war crimes. At the climax of *Vietnam-Perkasie*, another tale of disillusionment, Ehrhart participates in the battle for Hue with demented fury:

> I fought back passionately, in blind rage and pain, without remorse, conscience or deliberation. I fought back . . . at the Pentagon Generals and the Congress of the United States, and the *New York Times;* at the draft card burners, and the Daughters of the American Revolution . . . at the teachers who taught me that America always had God on our side and always wore white hats and always won;

at the Memorial Day parades and the daily Pledge of Allegiance . . . at the movies of John Wayne and Audie Murphy, and the solemn statements of Dean Rusk and Robert MacNamara. (246–47)

In literary terms, the corrupted innocent is always pathetic, never heroic. From the opening scene of Stone's *Platoon* to the closing scene of Kubrick's *Full Metal Jacket,* the motif presents American boys who merit our pity—never our admiration. We feel compelled to honor their broken and faltering requests for forgiveness. Big-heartedly, they are welcomed home to whatever redemption a misdirected nation can offer.

The lost war premise and the American Adam motif work together. Even the *Rambo* fantasies tap them. John Rambo (Sylvester Stallone) is an alienated vet; when society pushes him too far, he erupts into violence. In *Rambo II* he asks an oft-quoted question: "Do we get to win this time?" Thus Rambo is an angry American Adam, flailing against "Them" as well as the evil enemy, rather than being an alternative heroic figure. Most critics have missed this important likeness between the maligned Rambo figure and his much-praised Adamic cousins in literature and film. As indicated earlier, John Rambo came back in 2007, again reflecting the ambivalence toward American soldiers and their mission in Iraq.

Search for a New Genre: The Vietnam Film

John Wayne's *Green Berets* (1968) was actually a World War II film that conformed to well-established genre conventions; it cannot really be counted as an attempt to break ground for a new Vietnam-based genre. In subsequent efforts such as *The Deer Hunter* and *Apocalypse Now,* filmmakers groped toward the right metaphors and the proper formula to cope with the complexities of a limited war that America could not win. Robert Baird argued that *Platoon* was such a box office success because it included good and evil characters in a way that allowed the protagonist (and the audience) to be exposed to the purported horrors of Vietnam without being fully corrupted. Chris Taylor (Charles Sheen) never suffers the full disillusionment of the American Adam. Audiences scratched their heads over *The Deer Hunter* and blew their minds over *Apocalypse Now,* but *Platoon* worked so well as a cathartic fiction that a now hip *Time* magazine (which had long since abandoned the cold warrior stance of its original publisher, Henry Luce) joined legions of reviewers in a cover story that (incorrectly) honored *Platoon* for portraying "Viet Nam, the way it really was." Baird's thesis seems more convincing: *Platoon* was so powerful as a metaphor for Vietnam because it seemed real as a war *film,* conforming to key elements of the genre while cleverly modifying factors to suit a new setting and special tensions. *Casualties of War* (1989) was an unsuccessful bid to repeat *Platoon*'s generic success. Not even Michael J. Fox could save Brian De Palma's jejune, sadopornographic attempt to decry America's "rape" of Vietnam; the story was revived, in an Iraq context, by De Palma's *Redacted,* a film that received kudos from professional reviewers but failed miserably at the box office, drawing no more than three thousand viewers nationwide.

Visual Language: Learning to "Read" Television and Film

For years, journals such as the *History Teacher* and *Film & History* have been exhorting historians to learn the language of film and television. Without such preparation, they are at a disadvantage—one that media producers cherish for the license it gives them—when they approach productions about Vietnam. Here are a few obvious examples of distortion.

In *Hearts and Minds,* General Westmoreland says something along the lines that "the oriental doesn't value human life the way we do." Filmmaker Peter Davis then cuts away to a graveyard in Vietnam, where the wife of a Vietnamese soldier grieves for her husband; she becomes so overwrought with anguish that she jumps into the grave! It is a heart-rending, "documentary" contradiction of the American general's apparently heartless observation. What really happened? General Westmoreland told Davis that in *Korea,* the Chinese routinely anticipated high casualties during attacks—casualty counts that would be inconceivable for American commanders who wanted to retain command. That experience, Westmoreland said, taught him that Asian commanders do not place the same value we do on individual human life. Davis extracted Westmoreland's observation and recontextualized it with the graveyard material to make the good general look callous, even racist. (Orcutt identifies other such editing legerdemain in *Hearts and Minds.*)

Westmoreland was bushwhacked again in the CBS documentary *The Uncounted Enemy,* where responses to very different questions were edited to appear as answers to the *same* question. This is a notorious trick of the trade, and it was expressly prohibited by CBS News guidelines at the time the show was broadcast, although that did not deter CBS's producers in their zeal to prove the malicious and untrue thesis of the program—that General Westmoreland hid intelligence information from President Lyndon B. Johnson and the American people.

Vietnam: A Television History employed Nguyen Vinh Long as its translator, yet Mr. Long had been exposed in public court as a paid employee of Hanoi. Banerian's *Losers Are Pirates* documents numerous critical translation errors in the series, all of which point to a consistent intent to hide communist rhetoric.

Film students know that narration can determine what audiences see on the screen.

Montage is a basic technique, but *Good Morning, Vietnam* has a particularly significant example as Louis Armstrong sings "What a Wonderful World." Ostensibly, this is a laid-back segment, but a close reading of the shot sequence, as well as the interaction between pictures and words ("film irony"), reveals a very serious message. Simply stated, the message is that Americans like Lieutenant Hauk (pronounced "Hawk") are inflicting pain on a placid and peaceful nation; communist aggression is the natural response of a wronged people to the violence perpetrated by us and our ally. As the aggressors, we have taken a lovely and wonderful world and transformed it into a bloody battlefield.

Producers will be forever grateful to historians and teachers who ignore the place of visual language. They know that their messages are more readily absorbed by the visually illiterate and that they will remain society's true teachers with "mass-pop" as content.

If popular culture novels, personal narratives, anthologies, and visual media dealing with Vietnam pose so many perils, why should we study them? The answer seems clear: our students, like us, are significantly influenced by the popular culture around them. We can let them make up their own minds about Vietnam, but we need to give them the tools to identify opinion and point of view as they consider the meaning of our longest war. We can make them sensitive to the contexts from which novels and films are produced; we can prepare them with some notion of the formal and artistic elements that make "the medium the message." As we do so, we will be giving them analytical skills that they can apply to other issues with high emotional stakes. In the 1990s and early 2000s, it seemed conceivable that the sea change in our national mood following Operation Desert Storm and Operation Iraqi Freedom could help Americans gain perspective and understanding of both the Vietnam experience and the various artistic renderings of it. The domestic and war-front turbulence of the postoffensive Iraq experience has delayed any expected exorcism of the "Vietnam Syndrome"; the perils of using popular culture to study Vietnam have been revived and intensified as our fellow citizens are asked to apply the putative "lessons of Vietnam" to the War on Terror.

NOTE

1. The executive summary of the 1980 Harris poll contains some interesting findings in response to questions put to veterans:

"Looking back, I am glad I served my country." Agree: 90 percent
"The United States took unfair advantage of me." Disagree: 79 percent
"The country owes me a great deal more in return for my military service than I've gotten." Disagree: 75 percent
"If I were asked to serve again, I would refuse." Disagree: 67 percent
"I enjoyed my time in the service." Agree: 54 percent

Students are shocked by these statistics for obvious reasons; almost everything they have seen in the media is contradicted by the figures. This Harris poll should be in most libraries and will definitely be in any library designated a "Federal Repository." As a commissioned work for the Veterans Administration, it is a government publication and contains both statistics and analysis.

WORKS CITED

Apocalypse Now. Dir. Francis Ford Coppola. Perf. Marlon Brando, Martin Sheen. United Artists, 1979.

Baird, Robert. "Perceptions of *Platoon*: Vietnam Myth or Vietnam Reality?" Master's thesis. Oklahoma State U, 1989.

Banerian, James, ed. *Losers Are Pirates: A Close Look at the PBS Series "Vietnam: A Television History."* Phoenix, Ariz.: Tieng Me Publications, 1984.

Beesley, Stanley, comp. *Vietnam: The Heartland Remembers.* Norman: U of Oklahoma P, 1987.

Benjamin, Burton. *The CBS Benjamin Report.* Intro. by Robert Goralski. Washington, D.C.: Media Institute, 1984.

————. *Fair Play: CBS, General Westmoreland, and How a Television Documentary Went Wrong.* New York: Harper & Row, 1988.

Braestrup, Peter. *Big Story: How the American Press and Television Reported and Interpreted the Crisis of Tet 1968 in Vietnam and Washington.* 2 vols. Boulder, Colo.: Westview Press, 1977.

Caputo, Philip. *A Rumor of War.* New York: Holt, Rinehart & Winston, 1977.

Casualties of War. Dir. Brian De Palma. Perf. Michael J. Fox, Sean Penn. Columbia Pictures, 1989.

Collier, Peter, and David Horowitz, eds. *Second Thoughts.* Lanham, Md.: Madison Books, 1989.

Coming Home. Dir. Hal Ashby. Perf. Jane Fonda, Jon Voight. United Artists, 1978.

Confronting Iraq: What America Should Know. Dir. Roger Aronoff. Autumn Documentary Productions, 2004.

Culbert, David. "Television's Vietnam and Historical Revisionism in the United States." *Historical Journal of Film, Radio, and Television* 8.4 (1988): 253–67.

The Deer Hunter. Dir. Michael Cimino. Perf. Robert De Niro, John Cazale, Christopher Walken, Meryl Streep. Universal Pictures, 1978.

Denby, David. "Movies: Flea-bagged." *New York Magazine* 13 Apr. 1987: 90–91.

Edelman, Bernard, ed. *Dear America: Letters Home from Vietnam.* New York: Norton, 1985.

Ehrhart, W. D. *Vietnam-Perkasie: A Combat Marine Memoir.* New York: Zebra Books, 1983.

Full Metal Jacket. Dir. Stanley Kubrick. Perf. Matthew Modine, Adam Baldwin. Warner Bros., 1987.

Good Morning, Vietnam. Dir. Barry Levinson. Perf. Robin Williams, Forest Whitaker. Touchstone Pictures, 1987.

The Green Berets. Dir. Ray Kellogg, John Wayne. Perf. John Wayne, David Janssen. Warner Bros., 1968.

Hamburger Hill. Dir. John Irvin. Perf. Anthony Barrile, Michael Boatman. RKO Pictures, 1987.

The Hanoi Hilton. Dir. Lionel Chetwynd. Perf. Michael Moriarty, John Edwin Shaw. Cannon Group, 1987.

Harris, Louis, and Associates, Inc. *Myths and Realities: A Study of Attitudes Toward Vietnam Era Veterans.* Washington, D.C.: Veterans Administration, 1980. Government document 792801.

Hearts and Minds. Dir. Peter Davis. Perf. Georges Bidault, Clark Clifford. Touchstone Pictures, 1974.

Herr, Michael. *Dispatches.* New York: Knopf, 1977.

Karnow, Stanley. *Vietnam: A History.* New York: Viking, 1983.

Kauffman, Stanley. "Hanoi and Elsewhere." *New Republic* 27 Apr. 1987: 26–27.

Kovic, Ron. *Born on the Fourth of July.* New York: Simon & Schuster, 1976.

Kowet, Don. *A Matter of Honor: General William C. Westmoreland vs. CBS.* New York: Macmillan, 1984.

Lomperis, Timothy. *"Reading the Wind": The Literature of the Vietnam War—An Interpretive Critique.* Durham, N.C.: Duke UP, 1987.

Maland, Charles. "The American Adam." *The Columbia Companion to American History on Film.* Ed. Peter C. Rollins. New York: Columbia UP, 2003.

Medhurst, Martin J. "Propaganda Techniques in Documentary Film: *Vietnam: A Television History* vs. *Television's Vietnam: The Real Story.*" *Television Studies: Textual Analysis.* Ed. Gary Bums and Robert J. Thompson. New York: Praeger, 1989. 183–205.

The Mission. Dir. Roland Joffe. Perf. Robert De Niro, Jeremy Irons. Enigma Productions, 1986.

Nixon, Richard. *No More Vietnams.* New York: Arbor House, 1985.

Orcutt, April Coleen. "An Eisensteinian Analysis of the Documentary Film *Hearts and Minds.*" Master's thesis. California State U, Fullerton, 1977.

Platoon. Dir. Oliver Stone. Perf. Tom Berenger, Willem Dafoe. Orion Pictures, 1986.

Podhoretz, Jonathan. "*Platoon:* Painful, Brutal, Much-Praised Movie on Vietnam Dishonors Veterans of America's Longest War." *Washington Times* 30 June 1986: IB, 6B.

Raack, R. C. "*Vietnam: A Television History:* Yet Another Vietnam Debacle? Caveat Spectator." *Newsletter of the Organization of American Historians* Feb. 1984: 8–10.

Rambo: First Blood. Dir. Ted Kotcheff. Perf. Sylvester Stallone, Richard Crenna. Orion Pictures, 1982.

Rambo: First Blood Part II. Dir. George P. Cosmatos. Perf. Sylvester Stallone, Richard Crenna. TriStar Pictures, 1985.

Rambo III. Dir. Peter MacDonald. Perf. Sylvester Stallone, Richard Crenna. Carolco Pictures, 1988.

Redacted. Dir. Brian De Palma. Perf. Sahar Alloul, Eric Anderson. The Film Farm, 2007.

Rollins, Peter C. "Historical Interpretation or Ambush Journalism? CBS vs. Westmoreland in *The Uncounted Enemy: A Vietnam Deception* (1982)." *War, Literature, and the Arts* 2 (1990): 23–61. Also *Journal of the Vietnam Veterans Institute* 1 (1990): 13–41.

———. "The Uncounted Expert: George Carver's Views on Intelligence 'Deception' Reported by CBS in *The Uncounted Enemy: A Vietnam Deception* (1982)." *Journal of American Culture* 31.1 (1997): 111–30.

———. "The Vietnam War: Perceptions Through Literature, Film and Television." *American Quarterly* 36.4 (1984): 419–32.

———, dir. *Television's Vietnam: The Impact of Media.* Washington, D.C.: Accuracy in Media, 1986.

———. *Television's Vietnam: The Real Story.* Washington, D.C.: Accuracy in Media, 1985.

Television's Vietnam: The Impact of Media. Dir. Peter C. Rollins. Sony Video, 1986. Re-released on DVD by Accuracy in Media, 2007.

Television's Vietnam: The Real Story. Dir. Peter C. Rollins. Sony Video, 1985. Rereleased in DVD by Accuracy in Media, 2007.

Tiede, Tom. "Writer Knows Vietnam First Hand." Nationally syndicated column published in *Stillwater (Okla.) News-Press* 10 Feb. 1987.

The Uncounted Enemy: A Vietnam Deception. Narr. Mike Wallace. CBS Special Report. 23 Jan. 1982.

Vietnam: A Television History. Ex. Prod. Margaret Drain, Richard Ellison. 13 episodes. PBS. 4 Oct. 1983.

Walker. Dir. Alex Cox. Perf. Ed Harris, Richard Masur. Universal, 1987.

Webb, James. *Fields of Fire.* Englewood Cliffs, N.J.: Prentice-Hall, 1978.

FRAGMENTS OF WAR

Oliver Stone's *Platoon*

The Hollywood image of war, and of Americans in battle, has been almost universally positive. Many Hollywood combat films begin with the training of a single unit and follow it into battle. American troops are depicted as heroic; the enemy fanatical. Our men are portrayed as reluctant soldiers more interested in the girl back home, their families, and baseball than they are in international politics. A number of early war films, and especially those about the war in Vietnam, fit that pattern.

After the United States entered World War II, and again during the war in Korea, there was a tremendous increase in the number of war films—most about combat—but there was no similar spurt of war film production from 1963 on, as more and more American troops served, and died, in Southeast Asia. Since that time, there have been few major theatrical films that deal with the American fighting man in Vietnam. This void was partly responsible for the tremendous reception of Oliver Stone's *Platoon* (1986). No earlier Vietnam feature film was so narrowly focused on the plight of the "grunt."

PLATOON'S PREDECESSORS

The lack of early films about the Vietnam War can best be explained by a brief review of three previous films that deal primarily with men fighting in Vietnam, each of which detours into propaganda, downright silliness, or dark personal confusion.

The Green Berets and The Boys in Company C

The first of these films to appear after the big buildup of American troops in Southeast Asia was John Wayne's *The Green Berets* (1968), which resembles

Orion Pictures

Platoon: the agony of Vietnam.

a Western rather than a film about the war Americans were watching on the TV news each night.

Between 1965 and 1975—from the landing of American combat troops to the final withdrawal of Americans from Saigon—*The Green Berets* was the only major American film about combat in Vietnam. In August 1965, just after President Lyndon B. Johnson promised to provide General William C. Westmoreland with the troops he needed to fight the war, Art Buchwald of the *Washington Post* observed: "Every war deserves a war movie and the Vietnamese War is no exception. . . . We have a part for John Wayne, as the tough paratrooper colonel." But as Buchwald also explained, under the guise of a fictitious studio head, there are other problems associated with making a film about the Vietnam War: "No one knows how to tell the South Vietnamese from the Viet Cong. They all look alike. . . . Our research indicates the Viet Cong are always smiling and looking friendly. . . . The Defense Department is against it. They say they don't want to show American soldiers attacking a South Vietnamese village because the Americans are in South Vietnam to protect the villages and not to attack them. We had a great scene when the paratroopers couldn't find any Viet Cong, so they burned every straw hut to the ground." And so Buchwald has his fictitious studio head conclude that the "Defense [Department] said if they have to fight a different kind of war we should be willing to make a different kind of war picture."

But almost as Buchwald had predicted, John Wayne wrote to President Johnson in late 1965 suggesting a movie based on Robin Moore's book *The Green Berets,* published earlier that year. Although the book relates stories of the Special Forces, screenwriter James Lee Barrett admitted that "the film makes wide departures from the book—but stops short of going on a propaganda foray" ("Studios Reject" 5). Most viewers would probably not agree. A subplot centering on a reporter is introduced into the film to make the political points Wayne wanted. At the beginning of the film the reporter (David Janssen) asks, "Why is the United States waging this ruthless war?" Sergeant Muldoon (Aldo Ray) makes the case in favor of the war and shows captured Communist Chinese weapons, explaining that the press seldom gives any of the arguments *for* the war. By the end of the film the reporter, who went to see for himself, is fighting side by side with the troops. But the reporter observes that if he had to write about his views of the war now, he would be out of a job. Michael Wayne, the film's producer and John Wayne's son, observed in the May 1968 issue of *Esquire:* "I'm not making a picture about Vietnam, I'm making a picture about good against bad. I happened to think that that's not true about Vietnam but even it isn't as clear as all that. That's what you have to do to make a picture. It's all right, because we're in the business of selling tickets."

In March 1968 a majority of Americans thought it had been a mistake to send troops to Vietnam, and 56 percent agreed with the statement that the best thing would be to "stop the bombing and the fighting and gradually withdraw from Vietnam." As more Americans had been killed, and there seemed to be no progress in spite of optimistic statements from officials, support for the war had declined steadily since Wayne's letter to Johnson in December 1965 (Mueller 52–65).

The world premiere of *The Green Berets* was 19 June 1968—after the Tet Offensive, Johnson's announcement that he would not seek the Democratic nomination again, and the beginning of peace talks in Paris. The critics were harsh, calling *The Green Berets* "cliché ridden," "dull," "stupid," "rotten and false in every detail," "foolish," "vile and insane," "absurd and blundering," and so on. But it sold tickets. British journalist John Pilger called it "so unwittingly silly that it was funny," which was surely true if one expected a truthful representation of the way war is fought or the issues involved. Yet Pilger also noted that when he saw the movie in the summer of 1968 at a theater in the American South, many in the audience cheered (353).

The film cost $6 million to make, according to Warner Bros. ($7.7 million, according to Michael Wayne); when distribution and other costs were added, it totaled more than $10 million. But by the end of 1968 *The Green Berets* had earned nearly $11 million and was one of the most successful Warner Bros. releases in the previous five years; *Bonnie and Clyde*, released a year earlier, had earned $26 million (Kessler; "Berets"). However, a decade later *Variety* listed the film's total rentals at only $9.75 million, compared with more than $22 million for *Bonnie and Clyde* by that time ("All-Time").

Not until five years after the last American combat troops and POWs came home did other films address the combat experience. One of these, *The Boys in Company C* (1978), based on a script by Rick Natkin, a nineteen-year-old student at Yale, was advertised as "Vietnam as it really was." But the film is a mediocre copy of *M*A*S*H* (1970), even down to a final soccer game substituted for football. One critic concluded: "The best thing to be said for this blithering, disjointed chronicle of a group of Marine recruits from boot camp to combat duty (of a sort) in Vietnam is that it scrapes the bottom. It will require truly subterranean ineptitude to sink lower. . . . [This film] gets the heralded cycle of Vietnam movies off to such a flying catastrophe that, everything that follows is bound to look relatively respectable" (Arnold, "Boys" B13). But attention was already being directed at Francis Ford Coppola's promised *Apocalypse Now* (1979), which industry analysts thought would be a "critical test of whether the wounds of war have healed enough for American audiences to pay money to relive the painful experience" ("Viet War Films" 7).

Coppola's Vietnam Epic

Francis Ford Coppola frequently boasted that he was "the only one making a picture about Vietnam" (McArthur 37). But because of numerous delays in filming, which generated nearly as much print as the final film, it was the last combat film produced in the 1977–1978 cycle. (Coppola had even asked the

Pentagon for support, but the Department of the Army was not interested.) Yet *Apocalypse Now* was really the first combat film since *The Green Berets* more than ten years earlier. Production began in March 1976, was stopped and then resumed in August of that year—taking 167 and then 230 shooting days. The budget was announced at nearly $31 million.

After much anticipation, the film was first publicly shown as a "work in progress" and, as such, received a great deal of publicity. *Variety* and *Newsweek* both said that it was "worth the wait," while other reviewers called it alternatively "brilliant and bizarre" and "extraordinarily powerful" ("Film Reviews" 21; Michener 100). It was also previewed in Los Angeles with a questionnaire from Coppola inviting viewers to "help me finish the film" by describing their favorite or disliked scenes and providing suggestions for the ending (Denby 101). Indeed, compared with the 70mm limited theater version, the 35mm print does include, under the credits, an additional ending as the jungle hideout of the mad Colonel Kurtz (Marlon Brando) is bombed to bits.

When *Apocalypse Now* was finally released in August 1979, correspondent Morley Safer, on the CBS *Sunday Morning* show, observed that the film reminded him of "Vietnam only in the sense that they tried to win it with money." Most critics were not kind. However, Vincent Canby argued that in many scenes it did live up to its title, "disclosing not only the various faces of war but also the contradictions between excitement and boredom, terror and pity, brutality and beauty. . . . When [the film] is thus evoking the look and feelings of the Vietnam War, dealing in sense impressions for which no explanations are adequate or necessary, [it] is a stunning work" ("The Screen").

Yet Coppola's film is really two movies—one about the many absurdities of the Vietnam War, the other based on Joseph Conrad's *Heart of Darkness,* James Frazer's *The Golden Bough,* and even T. S. Eliot's *The Waste Land* (Tessitore; Chiu). Many of the incidents on the trip up the river show the "real" Vietnam, with reasonable allowances for exaggeration and contraction. Patrols were startled by tigers and other animals in the jungle, and although there is no record of surfing in Vietnam, one navy commander did arrange for his men to water-ski behind patrol boats. And Americans did broadcast music and propaganda to the enemy over loudspeakers aboard helicopters. When, in the midst of carnage on the beach, Lieutenant Colonel Kilgore (Robert Duvall) says, "I love the smell of napalm in the morning . . . the smell of gasoline smells like—victory," it is only an echo of General George S. Patton Jr. describing his men as "bloody good killers." At one point on the trip upriver, Captain Willard (Martin Sheen) and his men stop a sampan. When a Vietnamese woman moves too quickly to protect something, all the Vietnamese in the boat are killed. The lone survivor

Orion Pictures

Chris Taylor (Charlie Sheen) on patrol.

is the small puppy she had tried to shield. This scene is frighteningly real to anyone who witnessed men on river patrol boats conduct just such searches.

Most of the rest of the film is a "profoundly anticlimactic intellectual muddle" and "a ruinously pretentious and costly allegorical epic." Coppola admitted as much himself, saying, "The movie is a mess—a mess of continuity, of style—and most important, the ending neither works on an audience or philosophical level" (Arnold, "Mangled" B12). But *Time* critic Frank Rich said more: "In its cold, haphazard way, *Apocalypse Now* does remind us that war is hell, but that is not the same thing as confronting the conflicts, agonies and moral chaos of this particular war. . . . The Vietnam War was a tragedy. *Apocalypse Now* is but this decade's most extraordinary Hollywood folly" (57). As a study of filmmaking, celebrity, or egotism, *Apocalypse Now* may be worthy of note, but for someone who wishes to understand Vietnam, it has very limited value (Coppola).

OLIVER STONE: VIETNAM VETERAN

In September 1967 Oliver Stone reported for duty in Vietnam as a member of the 2d Platoon, Bravo Company, 3d Battalion, 25th Infantry. During his tour he served in two other units and was wounded twice. In 1976, the year he arrived in Hollywood, Stone wrote a screenplay about his comrades and their war: "*Platoon* in many ways is a chapter in [Oliver Stone's] autobiography. The character of Chris Taylor has the psyche of Oliver Stone, and when the director is asked a question, he will sometimes refer the interviewer to his screenplay for the answer" (Norman 17). At age nineteen Stone quit Yale, taught in a Vietnamese school, served in the Merchant Marine, and worked on a novel in Mexico—all before his stint in the army and Vietnam. In 1969, after Vietnam and a scrape with the law over marijuana possession, Stone enrolled in the New York University film program, where he studied with Martin Scorsese. After moving to Hollywood in 1976 Stone served as coauthor on a number of scripts and eventually wrote the screenplays for *Conan the Barbarian* (1982) and *Midnight Express* (1978), winning an Academy Award for the latter. Even with that success, Stone struggled for years to get the script based on his Vietnam experiences produced. It was the dedication of the Vietnam Veterans Memorial in Washington, D.C., that marked a turning point. That event led to increased sales of books about the war, two TV documentary series, and a new willingness to talk about the war by those who knew and those who wanted to know. Yet it would take financing from Britain (two-thirds of the production costs) for the film to finally be made. *Platoon* was initially released in December 1986 for a very short run to qualify for the Oscars. It opened generally in January 1987, heralded by a very good publicity campaign, much press attention, and word of mouth. By mid-February it had become the top-grossing film and remained so for several weeks.

PLATOON AND THE VIETNAM WAR

Like Stone, Chris Taylor (Charlie Sheen) arrives in Vietnam in September 1967. As he disembarks a troop carrier plane, he passes body bags and seasoned soldiers so dirty and tired that they look dead. As a greenhorn, Chris has to learn on his own—the more experienced grunts rarely help and do not trust newcomers. On patrol, Staff Sergeant Barnes (Tom Berenger) argues with Lieutenant Wolfe (Mark Moses), who is portrayed as a wimp. While out on ambush, a GI falls asleep on guard duty; there is a firefight, and Taylor is wounded.

During one scene in the jungle—it is 1 January 1968—Sergeant Elias (Willem Dafoe) enters a tunnel to find an enemy hospital and emerges in a hooch. The unit then moves up the river toward a village, where they find a GI who had been missing from their outfit tied to a tree, tortured, and killed. As

Orion Pictures

Staff Sergeant Barnes (Tom Berenger) resorts to brutality.

they advance into the village they see a civilian running away, and he is shot. A GI trips over a cooking pot, and a pig is shot. Civilians come out of one of the holes, and an explosive charge is thrown in. Bunny (Kevin Dillon) uses his rifle butt to smash an old retarded man's skull. Prisoners are rounded up, and the enraged Sergeant Barnes shoots a woman amid the sound of children crying.

To this point, many moviegoers who had served in Vietnam were noting how realistically the frustrations were portrayed. It was clearly the milestone movie for the evocation of jungle combat. Yet everything in the film happens so fast, the images are so rich, the action so compacted, that even in several viewings it cannot all be absorbed. The fast pace of the film's action seems to trivialize what is happening. There may be a perception that the men's actions are not justified, and some in the audience may withdraw in disgust.

Back in the village, Sergeant Barnes interrogates an old woman and an older man. Growing impatient, he grabs a young girl and holds a pistol to her head. Sergeant Elias approaches and, seemingly in a single motion, asks what is going on and smashes Barnes in the face. They then engage in a fistfight. The lieutenant orders the village burned and blown up. Taylor then comes upon some of his team members forcibly raping a young girl. When he tries to stop them, he is called a homosexual and spat on.

Later the same day, after an artillery barrage that drives the enemy back,

Elias pursues the enemy. This pursuit results in the climactic battle of the film, which is based on a real battle that took place on New Year's Day 1968. But rather than pursue the enemy, Barnes stalks and then shoots Elias. The wounded Elias flees, running in the open in front of enemy soldiers. The action is observed from a helicopter hovering over the battlefield. Unfortunately, this scene looks as though it is staged, rather than a natural part of the film's action, and it tends to reduce the credibility of the rest of the film.

Later, after others learn that Barnes has shot Elias, he taunts and disdainfully urges his own men to kill him. Meanwhile, the firefight with the enemy continues throughout the next day and becomes even more ferocious: the captain faces annihilation of his company in an air strike on his position, Junior is bayoneted in the throat several times, and Bunny is killed when his foxhole is overrun. Barnes is wounded and tries to kill Taylor just as an air strike comes in. At dawn, Taylor finds Barnes still alive and shoots him. At the end of the battle, all the enemy dead are bulldozed into a bomb crater, and the wounded Americans are evacuated.

Occasionally Taylor narrates his story in voice-overs from letters to his grandmother. Without this continuity, the film might be hopelessly muddled. Much of the swirling confusion seems to be a deliberate attempt to capture the reality of a surreal experience. *Platoon* provides little or no information to help viewers understand why the men in the infantry unit are so abusive toward one another—especially the new members of the group. This is not the traditional "group-at-war" genre combat film. War here is depicted from the perspective of the individual, not from the group or from a national perspective. The film effectively reveals Taylor's confusion and disorientation from beginning to end. As Taylor is evacuated from his last battle, his narration concludes:

> I think now, looking back, we did not fight the enemy, we fought ourselves. And the enemy was in us.
>
> The war is over for me now, but it will always be there, for the rest of my days, as I'm sure Elias will be, fighting with Barnes for . . . "possession of my soul." There are times since then I've felt like a child born of those two fathers.
>
> But be that as it may, those of us who did make it have an obligation to build again, to teach to others what we know, and to try with what's left of our lives to find a goodness and a meaning to this life.

This same dichotomy is required for an understanding of the two parts of this one film. One part is an incredibly contracted but realistic visualization of what it was "really" like for some men in Vietnam. For those who were there, and even for those who watched at home, the images are incredibly vivid and evocative, sometimes appearing unreal or dreamlike. The other part is a question

Orion Pictures

Chris Taylor and the platoon leave a My Lai–like situation.

of finding purpose and meaning in the war experience, and the film presents confusing images of multiple enemies, both without and within.

MOVIES AND COMBAT

A GI pulls another dead soldier on top of himself in an attempt to hide; on night ambush a GI falls asleep as the enemy sneaks up; smoking drugs through the barrel of a shotgun; hooches set on fire with a lighter and a flamethrower; GIs wounding themselves to get out of battle; a GI cuts off the ear of a dead enemy; enemy bodies are stacked and buried. As Canby put it: "The movie is a succession of found moments. It's less like a work that's been written than one that has been discovered, though, as we all probably know, screenplays aren't delivered by storks" ("Film" 12).

Here for the first time in a theatrical film about Vietnam is the "small war" fought by the ordinary grunt. Literally the only settlement shown during the film is the village that is burned and many of its civilian inhabitants killed. There are no dramatic shots of choppers in flight. Except for one complaint about the bureaucrats in Washington who make them fight the war with one hand tied behind their backs, the only "politics" discussed is the preferential treatment given to other soldiers. After the village is burned and the civilians killed, Sergeant Elias can only say that he believed in the war in 1965, "but now it just bugs me." The platoon's war is being fought not for ideology but for survival. They are draftees, living in fear, counting the days they are "short."

These are finely drawn characterizations developed by the writer-director and the actors—especially with the aid of technical adviser Dale Dye, a retired Marine Corps captain who worked his way up through the ranks and has a few moments on-screen as the battalion commander. Dye put the actors and extras through "twelve unique days of hard, no-slack field training" (Sharbutt 32).

Anne Taylor Fleming, on PBS's *MacNeil-Lehrer News Hour,* noted that the My Lai–like destruction of the village and its people is the "shining moment of truth" in the film. But when the bad soldier kills the good soldier, and young Taylor must avenge the act, how are we to think about heroes or murderers? Thus, she argues, the film is no less sentimental about the Vietnam War than its predecessors: "[The film is] full of the old notion, [that] war is the ultimate male romance. War is the place where men go to learn about themselves and each other. That is the enduring myth Oliver Stone is not ready to let go of, nor judging from the huge success of this film, are many of the rest of us."

All artists manipulate history, and *Platoon,* as art, can be freely interpreted, but the main questions we ask here are these: What is the film's value in helping us understand some of what actually happened in 1967–1968? What did the war mean at the time to Oliver Stone and his fellow grunts? And how, if at all, had their thoughts changed by 1985, when the film was made? Finally, what does all this mean to viewers of the film in 1987 and beyond?

Those who have lived through combat like that in Vietnam understand how accurately parts of this film catch the fevered pitch of battle. *Platoon* can help others who were in Vietnam but only heard of such experiences or who saw only occasional glimpses of frenetic battles in news reports and documentaries to understand the frustrations and madness of men under such conditions. *Platoon* allows its audience to imagine what that kind of combat was like and perhaps, with that insight, to read other documents and sources in a more illuminating light.

But without the context provided by personal experience, will others (it is too easy to say younger people who did not experience that time) turn away? Many have seen *Platoon,* but as writer Charles Krauthammer has asked, how many can understand it? He states:

A filmmaker is not obliged to give context. It is perfectly legitimate to choose a narrow focus. But he should not then pretend to a cosmic message, such as the narrator's conclusion that in Vietnam the enemy was us.

War is hell, and *Platoon* does hell well. That is a considerable achievement. What *Platoon* does not do, despite its pretensions, is tell us anything more than that. (A19)

The men of the platoon are frightened draftees, counting the number of days they have left in Vietnam. They carry with them the character flaws that so typify ordinariness, existing unfettered by the conventions in force "back in the world." The believability of these characters is the film's strength, which magnifies its greatest weakness. Staff Sergeant Barnes is the manifestation of man's most ignoble instincts unchecked. The brooding and brutal Barnes seems to have wrenched his destiny from fate, whereas the others—the ordinary ones—seem propelled by a milieu that catches them up and overwhelms their inhibitions. Courage and restraint took on much different meanings in 'Nam.

Control—or its abandonment—permeates the film. Some of the characters seem predisposed to unconscionable behavior. Others are pushed to hysteria by horrific circumstances. For Bunny, the loud, not very bright, working-class kid who drinks beer and listens to country music, war is hell—except the good parts. He summarizes: "I like being here. You get to do what you want, nobody fucks with you. The only worry you got is dying. If that happens you won't know about it anyway." But the central figure in *Platoon* is Chris Taylor, the college dropout who seems to be characterized by both perceptiveness and indecisiveness. He is neither good nor bad. He is neither held up for admiration nor reviled for his conduct. His role is to "be there," to act as a surrogate for you and me.

In the end, *Platoon* is not a film in which the classic notion of "justice" is carried out when protagonist and antagonist have a final showdown. Instead, *Platoon* offers a nasty ending. In the ambiguity of war (or are we to believe it was only the Vietnam War?), Taylor's cool execution of Barnes is depicted as justice. Viewers may dismiss that act as inevitable, assuming that Sergeant Barnes would not hesitate to kill Taylor. Thus, the ending of the film plays out its greatest flaw. In the character of Barnes, Stone's film has succumbed to the temptation of a Coppola-like treatment of a universal madness personified in an individual. Neither Colonel Kurtz nor Sergeant Barnes have human frailties that are truly comprehensible; they are more akin to Herman Melville's Captain Ahab—who is referenced in the film—than to any actual Vietnam veteran. That flaw in the direction of literary allusion and symbolism is all the more regrettable because the totality of the war's madness, and what it does to the human beings who populate the platoon, is so finely drawn and credibly conveyed.

We are *not* asking that one film tell the whole story of the Vietnam War. No film, novel, or history book can do that. But more than any other feature film to date, *Platoon* demands that the viewer experience what is portrayed on

Orion Pictures

Sergeant Elias (Willem Dafoe) crucified by Vietnam.

the screen. Nor do we find fault with the film because it is not the final word on Vietnam. This is a Vietnam War story from the perspective of Oliver Stone, which carries more credence in its telling by virtue of his having served there. The writer-director makes no pretense of dealing with the gamut of events and places that was Vietnam; instead, he limits his account to that of a single platoon serving in War Zone C, in a place the Americans called the HoBo Woods, in 1967–1968. It is, Stone says, "one reality" (Phillips).

Yet on 26 January 1987, *Time*'s cover story went overboard by announcing, "Viet Nam as It Really Was," causing former marine and *Washington Post* writer Henry Allen to retort: "[It] is silly and decadent, this willful confusion of life and art. And it's dangerous. War is too wildly stupid, glorious, hideous, huge and human for us to think that art can tell us what it really is. War is a little like God—when we start thinking we understand it, we're heading for trouble" ("Why" 25). In the past two decades Oliver Stone has continued to make controversial films, and the American public has had many opportunities to watch wars on the big and little screens. Still, *Platoon,* as David Edelstein recently summarized, remains an important portrait of war "as moral hell." The many facets of Stone's powerful epic are still worthy of examination and interpretation.

As is so often the case, the interpretations say as much about the "readers" of the film as they do about the work of a great American filmmaker working in the tradition of the Hollywood war film.

WORKS CITED

Allen, Henry. "Why We Aren't in Vietnam." *Washington Post* 25 Jan. 1987: 25.

"All-Time Rental Champs." *Variety* 17 May 1978: 123.

Arnold, Gary. "'Boys in Company C': First Bomb in the Vietnam War Movie Cycle." *Washington Post* 9 Feb. 1978: B13.

———. "Mangled Revelations: 'Apocalypse' at Last." *Washington Post* 3 Oct. 1979: B12.

"'Berets' Brings in the Green." *Wisconsin State Journal* (*New York Times* News Service) 20 Jan. 1969.

Buchwald, Art. "War Is What?" *Washington Post* 12 Aug. 1965.

Canby, Vincent. "Film: The Vietnam War in Stone's 'Platoon.'" *New York Times* 19 Dec. 1986: 12.

———. "The Screen: 'Apocalypse Now.'" *New York Times* 15 Aug. 1979.

Chiu, Tony. "Francis Coppola's Cinematic 'Apocalypse' Is Finally at Hand." *New York Times* 12 Aug. 1979: 1.

Coppola, Eleanor. "Diary of a Director's Wife." *New York Times Magazine* 5 Aug. 1979: 31.

Denby, David. "'81/2' Now: Coppola's Apocalypse." *New York* 28 May 1979: 101.

Edelstein, David. Rev. of "World Trade Center." *CBS News Sunday Morning*. CBS-TV 13 Aug. 2006.

"Film Reviews." *Variety* 16 May 1979: 21.

Fleming, Anne Taylor. *MacNeil-Lehrer News Hour*. PBS 11 Feb. 1987.

Kessler, Felix. "Green Berets, Rapped as 'Vile, Insane' Film, Is 'Boffo' at Box Office." *Wall Street Journal* 3 July 1968.

Krauthammer, Charles. "'Platoon' Chic." *Washington Post* 20 Feb. 1987: A19.

McArthur, George. "Coppola Storms Philippines for Re-creation of Viet War." *Los Angeles Times Calendar* 6 June 1976: 37.

Michener, Charles. "Finally, *Apocalypse Now*." *Newsweek* 28 May 1979: 100.

Mueller, John E. *War, Presidents and Public Opinion*. New York: John Wiley & Sons, 1973.

Norman, Michael. "'Platoon' Grapples with Vietnam." *New York Times* 21 Dec. 1986: 17.

Phillips, Stone. "Platoon." *20/20*. ABC-TV 26 Mar. 1987.

Pilger, John. "Why the Deer Hunter Is a Lie." *New Statesman* 16 Mar. 1979: 353.

"Platoon." *Time* 26 Jan. 1967: 54–61.

Rich, Frank. "The Making of a Quagmire." *Time* 27 Aug. 1979: 57.

Sharbutt, Jay. "The Grunts' War, Take 1." *Los Angeles Times Calendar* 25 May 1986: 32.

"Studios Reject Viet Scripts." *Film Daily* 8 Jan. 1968.

Tessitore, John. "The Literary Roots of 'Apocalypse Now.'" *New York Times* 21 Oct. 1979: 2.

"Viet War Films Get Marching Orders." *Variety* 10 Aug. 1977: 7.

THE QUIET AMERICAN

Graham Greene's Vietnam Novel through the Lenses of Two Eras

Graham Greene's *The Quiet American,* published in 1955, has twice caught the interest of respected filmmakers. Joseph Mankiewicz directed his adaptation of the novel in 1958, and Phillip Noyce returned to the text nearly a half century later. These radically different presentations reflect the different historical contexts in which they were filmed and show how America's involvement in Vietnam from the early 1950s through the fall of Saigon in 1975 continues to be revisited and revisioned. The American director, Mankiewicz, transposed what he called a "cheap melodrama in which the American was the most idiotic kind of villain" into a dramatization of America's fledgling foreign policy in Indochina (quoted in Geist 269). By returning to *The Quiet American* with four decades of hindsight, Noyce, an Australian director, was able to treat his film with full awareness of America's pending escalation and ultimate defeat in Vietnam. Mankiewicz ennobles the political idealism of the quiet American, Pyle, while simultaneously emptying the protagonist, Fowler, of diplomatic wisdom. Noyce's departure from the novel also centers on the characterization of the American; this time, however, Pyle is more menacing. Mankiewicz privileges the murder investigation and Fowler's jealousy of Pyle as a motive, while Noyce favors the self-reflective intimacy of Greene's work. The 1958 screenplay, written by Mankiewicz, and the 2002 script, written by Christopher Hampton and Robert Schenkkan, both adhere closely to the novel. What separates the two films is the reimagining of the character of Pyle, the quiet American.

THE QUIET AMERICAN AS LITERATURE

Greene's controversial and popular novel provided attractive adaptation possibilities: it is part political thriller, part romance, and part detective story set in

Graham Greene
(1904–1991)—a literary
source for many filmmakers.

exotic French Indochina in 1952. Thomas Fowler, a washed-up reporter for the *London Times,* pits his fatalistic experience against the newly arrived American's youthful innocence in an effort to keep Phuong, his Vietnamese mistress—a contest that symbolizes Old and New World designs on Southeast Asia. The novel begins at the end of the story, with the investigation into the murder of Alden Pyle. Fowler, the lead suspect, tells Vigot, inspector for the French Sureté, how he became friends with the American. Pyle had come to the region to spread the ideals of a "third force," a third alternative to French or communist rule in Vietnam. Carrying books by fictional political scientist York Harding, Pyle embodies the democratic idealism that Louis Hartz describes in *The Liberal Tradition in America:* "the current struggle against Communism is in significant part an ideological competition for human loyalties; it has brought into the plainest view America's psychological pattern. One of the issues it involves is the issue of social 'message' to compete with the appeal of Communism in various parts of the world" (305). After befriending Fowler, Pyle meets and pursues the lovely Phuong. He unaccountably travels north through the war zone to Phat Diem, where Fowler has gone to report on an alleged massacre. Once there, the gentlemanly Pyle declares to Fowler his intention to tempt Phuong away from the elder man with the promise of marriage (an offer the married Fowler cannot make). The young suitor succeeds, and Fowler begins to struggle with the loss of his mistress and the increasingly suspicious behavior of this quiet American.

Pyle's chivalry is lambasted by the cynical expatriate. The young American's approach to women and politics is viewed as woefully naïve, and in the novel, Fowler underscores the danger of Pyle's innocence: "He was too innocent to live. He was young and ignorant and silly and he got involved. He had no more of a notion than any of you what the whole affair's about, and you gave him money and York Harding's books on the East and said, 'Go ahead. Win the East for Democracy'" (Greene, *Quiet* 31–32). The love triangle among Fowler, Pyle, and Phuong drives the plot of the novel as well as both screenplays. Fowler is threatened by the younger suitor and goes to extreme lengths—including deceit and murder—to keep Phuong. He is also moved to action against what he considers to be Pyle's lethal innocence. The shading between personal motives and political cover underscores the differences between the novel and the two films.

Greene's novel is highly autobiographical. He served as a correspondent in Saigon in the early 1950s, and most of the historical events were re-created from his dispatches and journal entries. Like Fowler, he smoked opium, frequented brothels, and intended to divorce his wife, Vivian, during his long affair with Catherine Walston (who was not Vietnamese). As the dedication to the novel suggests, Greene borrowed from his friend René Berval details about his apartment, the name of his girlfriend, and even his dog.

Fictional characters are often composites of real individuals melded by the author's imagination. Such is the case with *The Quiet American,* and even Greene would have trouble denying the similarities between author and protagonist. Fending off criticism, Greene offered a feeble disclaimer that he did not share Fowler's anti-Americanism because, unlike Fowler, he did not lose his girlfriend to an American. A few of the characters are more fact than fiction—Trinh Minh Thé, for example, is portrayed with historical accuracy. Thé led the Lien Minh platform, which supported an independent Vietnam and was both anti-Vietminh and anti-French, a veritable third force. To his biographer, Norman Sherry, Greene admitted that the bullying American correspondent Granger was based on Larry Allen, the Pulitzer Prize–winning World War II reporter who had, by 1951, "sadly lost his heroic qualities, had been drinking too much, and was rather obese and sloppy in manner, in his personal demeanor and in his work as well" (400). Likewise, Phuong and Miss Hei were based on the Mathieu sisters, whom Greene had met through his friend Berval.

The American (Audie Murphy) and Phuong (Giorgia Moll) in the 1958 version.

PHUONG RISES FROM THE ASHES:
THE FEMINIZING OF VIETNAM

The character of Phuong is central to the story. To Fowler, she is "the hiss of steam, the clink of a cup, she [is] a certain hour of the night and the promise of rest" (Greene, *Quiet* 12). She is a meal ticket for her sister, Miss Hei, who, having lost her Mandarin father to the communist Vietminh, aggressively calculates the dollar value of Pyle's marriageability. And to Pyle, she is a mission—a citizen, like the nation, in need of saving by the West. He sees himself rescuing her from a life in the House of the Five Hundred Girls: "You know, I think it was seeing all those girls in that house. They were so pretty. Why she might have been one of them. I wanted to protect her" (58). Pyle's desire to protect Phuong and her country echoes the paternalistic attitudes of many American policy makers in the early 1950s. Consider an excerpt from a speech by Senator John F. Kennedy (D-Mass.) in 1956:

Vietnam represents a test of American responsibility and determination in Asia.

If we are not the parents of little Vietnam, then surely we are the godparents. We presided at its birth, we gave assistance to its life, we have helped to shape its future. As French influence in the political, economic and military spheres has declined in Vietnam, American influence has steadily grown. This is our offspring—we cannot abandon it, we cannot ignore its needs. And if it falls victim to any of the perils that threaten its existence—communism, political anarchy, poverty and the rest—then the United States, with some justification, will be held responsible; and our prestige in Asia will sink to a new low. (quoted in Herz 17)

In many ways Phuong symbolizes Vietnam. She is beautifully exotic and much stronger than she appears. Fowler describes her this way: "She's no child. She's tougher than you'll ever be. Do you know the kind of polish that doesn't take scratches? That's Phuong. She can survive a dozen of us" (Greene, *Quiet* 133). Fowler notes that her name, Phuong, means "phoenix" but adds ruefully, "nothing nowadays is fabulous and nothing rises from its ashes" (11).

The feminization of Vietnam through Phuong is not unique to Greene. This form of reductive symbolism is common in films and literature about the conflict. Early films such as *Saigon* (1948), starring Alan Ladd and Veronica Lake, capitalize on Vietnam's exotic allure. Stanley Kubrick's *Full Metal Jacket* (1987) depicts the pitfalls of succumbing to the seductive beauty while underestimating the strength of the Vietnamese. His "in-country" half of the film begins in Saigon with a Vietnamese prostitute strutting to Nancy Sinatra's pop tune "These Boots Were Made for Walking"; it ends in Hue with a squad of marines being picked off by a female sniper. The eventual execution of the sniper—looking much like a gang rape—eerily mixes sex and violence in what one of the participants describes as "hard-core" and worthy of "the Congressional Medal of Ugly." Kubrick's female sniper subverts the image of a powerless Vietnam. Her plea to "kill me" is as much a challenge to the impotent soldiers with their guns in hand as it is a cry for mercy.

Vietnam has often identified itself through its resilient heroines; for example, the story of the Trung sisters continues to inspire generations of Vietnamese. In A.D. 40, Trung Trac and her sister Trung Nhi rallied thirty thousand troops to fight the occupying Chinese. They regained control of sixty-five citadels and ruled as queens for two years before their enemy amassed an overwhelming force and reoccupied the territory. Rather than surrender to their conquerors, the queens committed suicide by drowning in the Hat River. Theirs is an inspiring story of courage, resilience, and independence.

Female suffering and perseverance are also associated with *The Tale of Kieu,* the national poem of Vietnam. In the introduction to Nguyen Du's epic, translator Huynh Sanh Thong writes, "[*The Tale of Kieu*] has stood unchallenged since its publication and dissemination in the second decade of the nineteenth

Colonel Edward Lansdale (second from left) and President Ngo Dinh Diem (center) with colleagues, circa 1957.

century as the supreme masterwork of Vietnamese literature" (xx); "Kieu stands for Vietnam itself, a land well-endowed with natural and human resources, but too often doomed to see such riches gone to waste or destroyed" (xl). Graham Greene's tale of Phuong is much like *The Tale of Kieu:* both women are forced into a life of submission, but time and again they prove their resilience. Kieu's successes and failures are much more numerous and tragic than Phuong's, but in the end she serves as a model of hope and perseverance:

> Heaven appoints each human to a place.
> If doomed to roll in dust, we'll roll in dust;
> We'll sit on high when destined for high seats.
> Does Heaven ever favor anyone,
> Bestowing both rare talent and good luck?
> In talent take no overweening pride,
> For talent and disaster form a pair. (lines 3242–48)

Like the phoenix, Phuong rises from the ashes. Fowler frees her from a life as a taxi dancer, but when his efforts to obtain a divorce from his wife in England fail, she leaves him for a more secure life with his American rival. Upon Pyle's death she bounces back to Fowler. According to Cynthia Fuchs, "Phuong has will and determination, . . . she fully understands her situation, and . . . she doesn't much care what either of her would-be saviors wants of her. She is autonomous and resolute, long before they are willing or able to see it" (1). Thus, although Phuong is a metaphor for Vietnam, she is not a representation of subordination—a possession to be used or protected—but a symbol of survivability and independence.

EDWARD LANSDALE: A VERY QUIET AMERICAN IN VIETNAM

Controversy surrounding the character of Pyle contributed to the allure and longevity of *The Quiet American*. Speculation over who was the model for the quiet American narrowed to one man—Colonel Edward Lansdale. Sporting a background in advertising, he was sent to Vietnam from the Philippines immediately after the French loss at Dien Bien Phu in 1954 to "win the hearts and minds" of another country in turmoil. He had become a bit of a celebrity in the Philippines, where his propaganda operations helped subdue the Huk rebels; he was hoping to duplicate his success in Vietnam. Through his numerous State Department and Vietnamese contacts, he knew more than any American about a "third force." Sherry addresses the almost mythic connection between Graham Greene and Lansdale by stating, "It's rare to find a book on Vietnam which doesn't automatically accept that Greene used Lansdale as his source [for Pyle]" (416). Even Lansdale's biographer, Cecil Currey, perpetuates this tantalizing but inaccurate belief: "One of the book's two focal characters was Alden Pyle, patterned after Lansdale and other Americans Greene observed in Vietnam, and thus Greene became the first author to caricature Lansdale's real-life exploits" (196). Lansdale recounted to Currey that he had overheard Greene say that he had definitely not had Lansdale in mind when he created the character Alden Pyle: "I sure hope not. . . . On the other hand, Pyle was close to Trinh Minh Thé, the guerilla leader, and also had a dog who went with him everywhere—and I was the only American close to Trinh Minh Thé and my poodle Pierre went everywhere with me" (198).

Pyle's dog is prominent in the novel. The detail about Lansdale's dog accompanying him everywhere was something that could have made its way to Greene; it was certainly the type of authentic detail of espionage he cherished. When Lansdale arrived in 1954, he offered assistance to Captain Pham Xuan Giai, head of G-5, the psychological warfare division of the Vietnamese army. Lansdale taught the spy trade to his protégés at G-5, including Giai's cousin Pham Xuan An, who learned about using dogs for intelligence work. An said, "I trained my dog so that he could alert me when the police were searching people's houses, even a kilometer away. He was a good spy" (Bass 58).

Greene and Lansdale were like two alpha dogs fighting over the same backyard, and Saigon was not big enough for both of their larger-than-life personas. Lansdale recalled meeting Greene at the Continental Hotel and walking away, thinking, "I'm going to get written up someplace as a dirty dog" (Currey 198). He was convinced that he was being mocked by Greene, and none of Greene's denials stuck. The two Cold War celebrities fought over the Pyle connection until their deaths, but it was exactly through this association that their celebrity was reinforced. Jonathan Nashel, in his recent history *Edward Lansdale's Cold War,* writes: "Yet like so much about the nature of celebrity, Greene's denials concerning Pyle as Lansdale were drowned out by the far more intriguing tale of a British novelist and a CIA agent fighting their own personal Cold War. In ways neither could have appreciated at the time, Greene's novel created Lansdale's celebrity more than any single thing Lansdale actually did. One need only to consider that after 1955 it is rare to encounter a story about Lansdale that does not refer to him as the 'quiet American'" (150).

Despite popular belief, Pyle is not based on Lansdale. In his autobiography *Ways of Escape*, Greene writes of a trip in 1951 to visit Colonel Leroy, who was the French officer in charge of the Bentre province at the time. On the drive back to Saigon, Greene met the inspiration for *The Quiet American:*

> I shared a room that night with an American attached to an economic aid mission—the members were assumed by the French, probably correctly, to belong to the CIA. My companion bore no resemblance at all to Pyle, the quiet American of my story—he was a man of greater intelligence and of less innocence, but he lectured me all the long drive back to Saigon on the necessity of finding a "third force" in Vietnam. I had never before come so close to *the great American dream* which was to bedevil affairs in the East as it was to do in Algeria. (127)

Sherry identifies Leo Hochstetter, public affairs director for the economic aid mission in Saigon, as Greene's traveling companion. Other than sharing his political views, Hochstetter was nothing like the quiet Pyle; he was known to be talkative and gregarious (Sherry 419). Greene gave Hochstetter a photograph of their visit with Colonel Leroy, and on the back, Greene wrote everyone's name; behind Hochstetter he wrote "Q.A." (Quiet American) (417).

The meeting with Hochstetter preceded Lansdale's arrival in Vietnam. By the time Greene and Lansdale met, Green was almost finished with *The Quiet American*. Lansdale arrived in May 1954, and Greene had begun writing the novel as early as March 1952 and had a working draft finished long before completing it in June 1955 (Sherry 417). Greene hinted that Pyle's naïveté, particularly regarding women, was actually a caricature of how Greene viewed himself in his youth. Still, in much the same manner that Phuong was written as a metaphor for Vietnam, Pyle became a metaphor for American foreign policy.

Greene's "anti-American" novel touched off a firestorm of criticism when it was published in the United States in early 1956, but it grew in popularity with the rise of the antiwar movement a decade later. Both supporters and critics of America's involvement in Southeast Asia took the novel as fact. Nashel suggested that "this quality of 'real' fiction, verging on the *reportage* method, lies at the heart of the book's success in depicting the country, but it also leaves open the question of whether we should read it as a journalistic account of the period or primarily as a fictional meditation on American power. Greene essentially wanted to have it both ways: a piece of nonfiction masquerading as a novel" (151). Many of the scenes described in *The Quiet American*—Phat Diem, bombing runs along the Red River with the Gascogne Squadron, and the Place Garnier explosion—have their counterparts in newspaper stories bylined by Greene.

Martin Herz, a career diplomat, ambassador, and historian, addressed the influential role of the media (including, in this case, a work of fiction) in a series of lectures given just before his death in 1983. He suggested, "The thing to retain here is that the press had become a major factor in the drama unfolding in Vietnam; that it tended to have its own point of view, sometimes single-mindedly committed to a particular purpose; and that already under Kennedy our government often believed the vivid reporting of the media more than it believed its own representatives on the spot" (36). He added that once images such as Nick Ut's famous "napalm girl" photograph (1972) "entered people's consciousness one cannot rectify the impression—people are no longer interested in hearing that the Buddhist monks of Hue were totally unrepresentative or that the little girl was the victim of a military accident. Visual paradigms have been suggested, and once created in people's minds they persist" (46–47). Like the iconic photographs, *The Quiet American* took on the status of a paradigm for the conflict.

People will believe what they want to believe, and people wanted to believe *The Quiet American*. Nashel recorded Congressman William Lehman (D-Fla.) using fiction to describe reality when questioning CIA Director William Colby in a 1975 congressional hearing on the accuracy of the CIA's intelligence about the North Vietnamese and the Vietcong:

MR. LEHMAN: Just thinking back to some of the things I have read. I wonder how many of you gentlemen ever read any of Graham Greene's books? Have you read *The Quiet American?*

MR. COLBY: I have.

MR. LEHMAN: Graham Greene . . . seems to have a conceptual understanding of the impossibility of understanding the motivations and what you called the capabilities of the armed services of that particular kind of culture. . . . I am just concerned about how can we possibly prevent the kinds of miscalculations, the misconceptualizing or lack of understanding of what is going on—the basic limitations of someone like this fellow Pyle, and Graham Greene, who was dealing from one culture into another culture without knowing what the hell he was doing. (quoted in Nashel 162)

As Congressman Lehman's muddled inquiry evidences in substance and style, the real danger is not only that Greene's fiction verges on reportage but also that because of this style and the readership's overwhelming desire to make fiction fact, we have fiction serving as history.

THE MANKIEWICZ VERSION

Joseph Mankiewicz bought the movie rights to *The Quiet American* just a few months after it was published in the United States. Although the director-producer claimed he was not pressured by United Artists to put a pro-American spin on the story, Robert Lantz, executive vice president of Figaro Productions (the film's production company), claimed that the filmmaker boasted about the change: "I will tell the whole story anti-Communist and pro-American" (quoted in Geist 268). According to Mankiewicz's biographer, Kenneth Geist, the director later denied making this boast; however, interviews promoting the film displayed both Mankiewicz's seething anger toward Greene's anti-Americanism and his goal of reversing America's Cold War image. In the 25 January 1958 *Saturday Review,* Mankiewicz said he "often wanted to do a picture about one of those ice-blooded intellectuals whose intellectualism is really just a mask for completely irrational passion" (Knight 27). And while speaking with James O'Neill Jr. of the *Washington Daily News,* Mankiewicz made it clear that he saw Fowler, like Greene, as the real villain: "Here is a man whose lack of any real moral fiber made him far more dangerous than the stupid, idealistic American" (24).

While scouting for locations in Vietnam, Mankiewicz met Colonel Lansdale, and the two became allies. "Mankiewicz found in Lansdale the perfect source for the host of questions he had about Vietnam, its people, and the nature of the war. In turn, Lansdale found in Mankiewicz an American who could counter Greene in a way no one else had done" (Nashel 164). The partnership with Lansdale made clear the direction Mankiewicz intended for his film and provided Lansdale with a soapbox to promote America's involvement. Mankiewicz set out to shift the blame for the terrorist bombing of the Place Garnier in Saigon on 9 January 1952 from Colonel Thé (Pyle's third-force leader—Greene promoted him to general) to the communists. In a letter dated 17 March 1956, Lansdale identified Trinh Minh Thé as the mastermind behind the bombing and included details about how and where he had acquired the melenite (plastic explosive) and how the bombs had been detonated; amazingly, Lansdale continued to support the spin Mankiewicz wanted to place on the event: "in keeping with your treatment of this [incident] actually having been a Communist action, I'd suggest that you just go right ahead and let it be finally revealed that the Communists did it after all, even to faking the radio broadcast (which would have been easy to do)" (quoted in Nashel 165).

Government support for Mankiewicz's script extended above Lansdale's pay grade. Lantz met with Allen Dulles, director of the CIA. Dulles liked the idea of the film and how its message countered the novel's depiction of Americans abroad and offered Lantz U.S. government assistance (Nashel 166). On 28 October 1957 Lansdale wrote to Vietnamese president Ngo Dinh Diem:

> Just a little note to tell you that I have seen the motion picture, "The Quiet American," and that I feel it will help win more friends for you and Vietnam in many places in the world where it is shown. When I first mentioned this motion picture to you last year, I had read Mr. Mankiewicz' "treatment" of the story and had thought it an excellent change from Mr. Greene's novel of despair. Mr. Mankiewicz had done much more with the picture itself, and I now feel that you will be very pleased with the reactions of those who see it. (quoted in Pratt 307)

Diem should have been pleased; in the film Pyle refers to meeting an impressive Vietnamese while taking classes at Princeton. Pyle believes that this man (Diem, though he is not directly named) will be the third force and that Thé with his army will be one of his chief supporters. On the same day that Lansdale wrote to Diem he also wrote to his friend and supervisor General John W. O'Daniel: "Thanks to you, I attended the screening of 'The Quiet American' in Washington last Thursday. It was quite an experience to see and listen to a mature approach to such recent events in Vietnam, and one so understanding of the things free men believe in" (quoted in Pratt 308). Mankiewicz had endorsed the government's position on Vietnam and, judging by Lansdale's praise, created a film that forwarded the government's foreign policy agenda.

Audie Murphy: Cold War Symbol

Eight weeks of filming began on 28 January 1957, with Michael Redgrave as

Fowler and Audie Murphy as Pyle. Mankiewicz originally wanted Montgomery Clift to play the part of Pyle opposite Lawrence Olivier. Clift, who was recovering from an auto accident, canceled. Angered by the recasting of his costar, Olivier pulled out, and Michael Redgrave signed on for the role of the British reporter. Audie Murphy was a bold but logical choice for the role of Pyle, given Mankiewicz's revision of the novel. By 1958 Murphy, the most decorated soldier of World War II, had established himself as a motion picture action star. He had initially become a national celebrity with a *Life* magazine cover story on 16 July 1945, and his boyish good looks and battlefield credentials opened the doors to Hollywood. Murphy played himself in *To Hell and Back* (1955), but his brief rise to stardom was short-lived, and he soon found himself knocking on closed doors in Hollywood. *The Quiet American* would be his only dramatic departure from more formulaic Westerns and combat films. Still, the war hero was just the image Mankiewicz needed to sell his version of *The Quiet American*. In an interview with the *New York Times*, Mankiewicz bragged that Murphy was "the perfect symbol of what I want to say" (Pryor 35). The American hero-turned-actor in a supporting role received top billing over Michael Redgrave, his far more accomplished costar and the lead in the film. Audie Murphy, with his supportive fan base and remarkable military record, was ideal to represent an aggressive American presence.

Murphy was not a versatile actor; he largely played himself, which worked well for Mankiewicz's concept of the film. Possibly to increase the sincerity of the character or to make Murphy more convincing in the role, Pyle's home was switched from Boston to Murphy's native Texas. Mankiewicz did little to downplay the actor's heroic status. In an early scene in the film, when Pyle rescues Fowler from a burning watchtower, Fowler sarcastically remarks, "We're not a couple of movie Marines. You won't even get the girl in the end." Oblivious to the snide remark, Pyle responds, "This is the fireman's lift. I learned it in the Boy Scouts—my good deed for the day." Murphy fashioned Pyle into the consummate do-gooder without a hint of irony.

With the two principal actors cast, Mankiewicz needed to find an actress. *The Quiet American* was the first Hollywood feature filmed in Vietnam. Given the fact that he had invested a great deal both financially and emotionally (Mankiewicz was suffering from bouts of depression made worse by the location shooting) for an authentic setting, his choice of Italian actress Giorgia Moll came as a bit of a surprise—even though most of the interior shots were filmed at Figaro's soundstage in Rome. Mankiewicz had more convincing Asian actresses to choose from: France Nuyen tested for the role but was passed over. Nuyen became Joshua Logan's discovery in the stage version of *The World of*

Suzie Wong and his film version of *South Pacific* (Geist 273). Moll's character was an unconvincing Asian mistress, but Mankiewicz gave her Phuong more influence than she had in the novel. Her most empowering moment occurs in the final sequence, when she publicly rejects Fowler.

Greene was enraged by the American filmmaker's reworking of his novel and openly criticized the project. His harshest attack, appearing first in the *International Film Annual* (1958), left no question about his feelings: "The most extreme changes I have seen in any book of mine were in *The Quiet American;* one could almost believe that the film was made deliberately to attack the book and the author, but the book was based on a closer knowledge of the Indo-China war than the American director possessed, and I am vain enough to believe that the book will survive a few years longer than Mr. Mankiewicz' incoherent picture" (quoted in Geist 278). Greene's prediction that his novel's popularity would outlast Mankiewicz's film proved to be accurate.

THE NOYCE VERSION

Whereas Mankiewicz's film premiered just a little over a year after Greene's novel was published in the United States, the second film version had a fifteen-year production history. Sydney Pollack initially acquired the rights in 1988 and "promised a more faithful remake" of the novel ("*Quiet American* Remake" 10), but following the commercial and critical success of *Platoon* (1986), Vietnam combat films saturated the market for the remainder of the 1980s. Pollack held on to the rights for seven more years without getting so much as a script drafted.

Phillip Noyce stumbled onto the idea for a remake of *The Quiet American* by accident while vacationing in Vietnam in 1995. He had just toured the Ho Chi Minh Museum in Hanoi and left with what he thought was a volume of Chairman Ho's poetry (in translation). On the train ride from Hanoi to Ho Chi Minh City (formerly Saigon), Noyce discovered that he had bought a copy of Greene's novel by mistake. In an interview with Rob Blackwelder, Noyce recalled, "I thought at the time, it's weird how his [Greene's] portrait of the American political evangelist of the early '50s contained the same zeal that has guided American foreign policy through to the present—a zeal born out of the best intentions." And in a similar interview with Martin Grove for the *Hollywood Reporter,* Noyce recounted how Greene's novel particularly attracted him, "having lived in a country, Australia, that went through an almost identical journey (as America did with the war in Vietnam) and nationally believing in the necessity to take a stand against communism and believing in the domino theory, particularly as Australia was the final domino."

Thomas Fowler (Michael Caine) and Alden Pyle (Brendan Fraser) discuss their beloved Phuong (Do Thi Hai Yen) in the 2002 version.

Calling serendipitously from the Graham Greene suite in the Hotel Continental, Noyce tracked the film rights to Sydney Pollack at Paramount. Another six years transpired before the estimated $30 million could be raised to fund the picture. Completed in 2001, only to be shelved by Miramax for a year after the 9/11 attacks, the Noyce version finally premiered at the Toronto International Film Festival in September 2002. Four weeks later, Congress would authorize military force to disarm Iraq. America's foreign diplomacy would once again be examined through the lens of *The Quiet American,* this time through a historical perspective.

Although not as transparent as Mankiewicz about his desire to mold *The Quiet American,* Noyce's direction reflects his post-Vietnam, post-Watergate sensibility in the same way Mankiewicz's film was a product of the early Cold War. In particular, Noyce's film perpetuates a distrust of government, mostly in what is perceived as the government's abuse of power, as well as the popular myth that the press saved us from ourselves in Vietnam. Noyce vilifies American intervention by thrashing Pyle and valorizes the media through the rebirth of Fowler as a prescient reporter.

The Vietnam conflict has often been characterized as America's first televised war. Peter C. Rollins, summarizing the media's influence on the conduct of

Miramax Films

The lovely Phuong (Do Thi Hai Yen in the 2002 version) is a symbol for Vietnam in both films.

the war in *The Columbia Companion to American History on Film,* observes: "Night after night, American viewers saw their boys hurt or dying on the nation's television screens in a conflict insufficiently justified by their government. Especially during the Tet offensive of 1968, the stories from Vietnam stressed ineptitude and defeat, disaffecting the public permanently" (94). Most significantly, in the final newsreel montage, Noyce's valorization of the media presents as fact stories that many historians now contend were misleading interpretations of events. Despite an abundance of historical reassessments of the media's role during the Vietnam conflict, Noyce's film simply reinforces attitudes about the media that other historians and filmmakers explore more objectively.

Finding Phuong in the Era of the New Woman

Robert Schenkkan, writer of the first draft of Noyce's script, spoke with Richard Stayton about the difficulty of creating the female lead. Schenkkan said of Phuong:

> She's pretty much just treated as an object without a point of view. I don't think that Greene is particularly interested in her point of view, and that was one of the major character issues. We needed to understand Phuong as a human being, as

a woman living, admittedly, in a time period and culture that presented her with a very limited range of choices. But that she was an independent woman within that culture, that she had her own mind, her own point of view, that she made choices. And often she didn't have a wide range of choices, but she knew what was going on. She could see these two men's advantages and their disadvantages. (quoted in Stayton)

Noyce had difficulty finding an actress who could personify traditional Vietnamese womanhood to a globalized culture: "Every other girl we tested," said Noyce, "seemed polluted by the body language that you inherit from TV commercials, magazines, movies" (quoted in Corliss). Noyce finally cast newcomer Do Thi Hai Yen. Yen's performance offers the ethnic authenticity that Giorgia Moll's 1958 performance lacks, but as the credibility of Phuong's character increases, her influence in the film decreases.

Pyle for a New Generation

Brendan Fraser, who lacks Audie Murphy's status as a highly decorated war hero, is best known as an action and comedy star. The critical praise he earned as Clayton Boone in *Gods and Monsters* (1998) has been overshadowed by popcorn hits such as *The Mummy* (1999), *George of the Jungle* (1997), and *Dudley Do-Right* (1999). Casting an underestimated actor against the more experienced Michael Caine resembled Mankiewicz's strategy of putting Audie Murphy opposite Michael Redgrave. Just as audiences believed in Murphy's sincerity, they were equally willing to accept Fraser's do-gooder oafishness in the role of Pyle. Noyce voiced his enthusiasm for Fraser in an interview: "Fraser brings to his performance a sense of innocence and even a kind of goofiness that turns out to be a marvelous cover for a character who we learn soon enough is really an American spy. . . . All of the light-weight roles that he's been playing hopefully contribute to catching the audience off-guard" (Grove 6). Fraser also possesses an athletic physical presence that works remarkably well in the film. When Pyle first arrives in Saigon, his size and enthusiasm remind the viewer of a clumsy youth, but by the time of the terrorist bombing, Pyle intimidates like a seasoned soldier.

Pham Xuan An: History Reveals Itself

One of the most compelling aspects of Noyce's film is the last-minute compression of the communist characters (Dominguez, Mr. Heng, Mr. Moi, and Mr. Chou) into one individual. Noyce not only consolidates the characters but also expands the role and makes Hinh, Fowler's assistant and confidant, the one who actually assassinates Pyle. The change adds some credibility to a weakness

Miramax Films

Hinh (Tzi Ma) closely resembles Vietcong colonel Pham Xuan An, who "helped" American correspondents in Vietnam.

in Greene's plot. The novel never explains why Fowler needs to be involved in the assassination in the first place. Ostensibly his role is to get Pyle to a specified place at a specified time, but the tension comes from Fowler's moral struggle over whether or not to participate in the plot. By making the assassin Fowler's aide, Noyce puts the knife much closer to Fowler's own hand. Just as the audience is duped by Pyle's cover, it is also misled by the "loyal" Hinh.

What makes Hinh so believable is that Noyce bases the character on an actual double agent, Pham Xuan An. Noyce recalled the following meeting:

> We just combined the two [Dominguez and Mr. Heng] after I met a guy named General An. He wasn't a general until the day after Saigon fell, when he could come out of the closet and reveal that he had been a double agent, he had worked as a censor for the French at the Saigon post office, where foreign correspondents would come in and present their copy that they were asking to be telegraphed (to their newspapers) overseas. They warned him to be very careful of this Graham Greene character and read his communiqués very carefully. (Blackwelder)

An's own story is so remarkable that it makes Hinh's actions seem plausible.

In 1952 An began his work as a spy by practicing his English as a press censor at the central post office in Saigon. He was told to black out the dispatches written for British and French newspapers by Graham Greene, a "troublemaker" whom the French assumed was working for British intelligence (Bass 60). The French were convinced that Greene was an "honourable correspondent"—in the vocabulary of espionage, a "spy with cover"—according to a report sent to General de Lattre de Tassigny, commander of French forces in Indochina (Sherry 481). General de Lattre responded to the report: "All these English, they're too much! It isn't sufficient to have a consul who's in the Secret Service, they even send me their novelists as agents" (482). Beginning with his censoring of Greene's dispatches in 1952, Pham Xuan An would infiltrate *The Quiet American* in one way or another for the next fifty years.

An's communist case officer next instructed him to take a position in the Army of the Republic of Vietnam (ARVN). Through family connections, he found an assignment at G-5, the army's psychological warfare department. As noted earlier, An's cousin Captain Pham Xuan Giai was the commander of G-5 when Lansdale was sent by the CIA to run covert operations in Vietnam. "Finding a promising student in the young Pham Xuan An, Lansdale and his colleagues began teaching him the tradecraft that he would employ in his next twenty years as a Communist spy" (Bass 60). Next, the neophyte was sent to the United States to be trained as a journalist. In 1957, after much difficulty and several delays, the thirty-one-year-old communist spy, retired customs officer, and psywar specialist enrolled at Orange Coast College in California. Called "Confucius" by his classmates, An spent much of his time practicing his craft on the *Barnacle*, the school newspaper. Ironically, one of his articles was a review of Mankiewicz's *The Quiet American* (1958), in which he called the movie confusing and wrote that it should "not be shown in Vietnam" (Bass 61).

Returning to Vietnam, An was hired by the Office of Political, Cultural, and Social Research, a CIA-sponsored network of spies (Bass 62). He then went to the Vietnam News Agency, Reuters, and finally *Time* magazine, where he worked as a double agent until 1975 and the fall of Saigon. An wrote his dispatches, some as long as a hundred pages; photographed them; and hid the undeveloped film in baskets of fish. According to members of the Vietnamese Politburo, "the writing was so lively and detailed that General Giap and Ho Chi Minh were reported to have rubbed their hands with glee on getting these dispatches from Tran Van Trung—An's code name" (Bass 56). An served as *Time*'s sole correspondent in postwar Vietnam until it closed its Saigon bureau in 1976. Ordered to a reeducation camp in 1978 and then promoted to general in 1990, An was not allowed to retire until 2002, at the age of seventy-four.

Noyce met General An just before he started filming in 2001. In addition to making Hinh reflect An's real-life exploits, Noyce got a firsthand account of the 1952 terrorist bombing that is central to the plot of the story. An was running an errand that day and arrived at the Place Garnier by bicycle just as the bomb detonated. Noyce filmed the scene exactly from An's recollection. The bicycle figures in the film again as Hinh rides across the Dakow bridge after Pyle's assassination and looks back into the knowing stare of Fowler.

A STYLISTIC COMPARISON

The two films vary stylistically and emphasize different themes. Mankiewicz stresses the detective story and political intrigue of the novel, while Noyce devotes more interest to the character relationships and the introspective quality of Greene's text. Robert Krasker, director of photography, shot *The Quiet American* (1958) in a style reminiscent of his film noir classic *The Third Man* (1949). In contrast, Christopher Doyle, Noyce's cinematographer for *The Quiet American* (2002) and *Rabbit-Proof Fence* (2002), captured a richly textured mood warmed by the glow of an opium pipe and cooled by the damp rottenness of Phat Diem. He frequently shot in close-ups, hanging on the actor's eyes. The final newsreel montage zooms in on the wounded eye of an American soldier, carrying out the leitmotif of bearing witness that orders the film.

These two opposing approaches to Greene's novel suggest gross differences between the films. Their effects are vastly different, but ultimately, not until the end. Mankiewicz takes his shots at Greene's anti-Americanism, mostly by capitalizing on what Greene offers in the text. The most damning line of Fowler's is lifted verbatim from the novel: "Suddenly I couldn't bear his boyishness any more. I said, 'I don't care for her interests. You can have her interests. I only want her body. I want her in bed with me. I'd rather ruin her and sleep with her than, than . . . look after her damned interests'" (59). Noyce depicts Fowler's love for Phuong more favorably than Mankiewicz does and omits the misogynistic line. He also takes liberties in building a friendship between Pyle and Fowler and evokes a more disingenuous American than Greene intended.

THE LAST REEL

The novel and the two films diverge most clearly in what Pauline Kael, reviewing the earlier film, refers to as "the offending compromises of the last reel" (336). The terrorist bombing at the Place Garnier resolves both films with contrary actions by Pyle. The scene in the novel begins with Fowler sitting in the Pavillon (a café he would normally shun because of its crass American clientele) to avoid an awkward encounter with Phuong. While at the bar he finds himself for a moment "envying them [two American women] their sterilized world, so different from this world that I inhabited—which suddenly inexplicably broke in pieces" (160). After the explosion, Fowler runs to save Phuong, whom he believes is at a milk bar at the epicenter. He meets Pyle in the chaos, and both witness the carnage. Here is the precise moment of departure for Mankiewicz and Noyce. In the novel Greene writes:

> Pyle said, "It's awful." He looked at the wet on his shoes and said in a sick voice, "What's that?"
> "Blood," I said. "Haven't you ever seen it before?"
> He said, "I must get them cleaned before I see the Minister."
> I don't think he knew what he was saying. He was seeing a real war for the first time. . . . He looked white and beaten and ready to faint, and I thought, "What's the good? He'll always be innocent, you can't blame the innocent, they are always guiltless. All you can do is control them or eliminate them. Innocence is a kind of insanity." (162–63)

It is not surprising that Mankiewicz alters Pyle's action in this scene, but the extent of the change galled Greene and led many critics to call it a "travesty." As in the novel, Mankiewicz's scene begins in the Pavillon. Fowler rushes to find Phuong but is held back by Vigot and the Vietnamese police, who treat the desperate Fowler as a nuisance. In contrast to the helpless Fowler, Pyle, looking like George Washington crossing the Delaware, rides into the square on the running board of a vehicle marked "United States Operations Mission." Fowler manages to slip into the trunk of Pyle's car as it slowly passes through the crowd. Pyle, more astute than the flagging reporter, has arranged to have Phuong skip her afternoon break because he has "heard rumors that there might be a demonstration." When Fowler connects Pyle to General Thé and the bombing, Pyle incredulously reproves him: "What are you talking about? You must be out of your mind." Angered by Fowler's insinuation and inaction during the melee, Pyle condemns Fowler: "Why don't you just shut up and help somebody!" The blood on the shoes is gone: Pyle's innocence is not naïveté; it is guiltlessness.

This moment is also the point at which one would expect Noyce to hold to his promise to be faithful to the novel. Brendan Fraser is no Audie Murphy in this scene, but neither is he, as described in the novel, "impregnably armoured by his good intentions and his ignorance" (163). As Mankiewicz is faithful to the Cold War ideology of his day, Noyce is faithful to his era and overcompensates for a painful history by making Pyle sinister. Noyce flinches in the face of Greene's moral and political challenge: that America's foreign policy in Indochina is dangerously naïve—so dangerous as to necessitate murder. Assassinating a deceitful spy for his zealotry is more palatable than killing an indefatigable naïf. According to Greene, Pyle must be stopped because he "comes blundering in and people have to die for his mistakes" (174). The Pyle in Noyce's 2002 film does not blunder; he is neither ignorant nor innocent. Rather, he is driven by his myopic political idealism.

In the 2002 film, the revelation that Pyle is not what he appears to be occurs slowly as Fowler, back in his office, reflects on the massacre. Washing blood off his hands, Fowler says, "Did you see Pyle? He spoke Vietnamese like it was his native language." At the scene, Pyle barks orders at an American photographer to get shots of the wounded and bullies a Vietnamese police officer to stay out of the way. While doing so, he wipes blood off his pant leg with casual indifference. Pyle's actions at the bombing could not have been more different between the novel and the two films, nor could they be any more telling of each creator's general theme.

From the explosion until the respective endings, each work continues on its own trajectory. In the novel, Fowler meets with Pyle at his apartment and recalls the words of Captain Trouin and Mr. Heng that "one has to take sides. If one is to stay human" (174). Fowler becomes *engagé*. He takes a volume of poetry to the window, the prearranged signal to the communist assassins that Fowler will have Pyle on the bridge to Dakow at nine o'clock, and reads from Arthur Hugh Clough's *Dipsychus,* a nineteenth-century poetic dialogue between a tempting spirit and an idealistic youth:

> I drive through the streets and I care not a damn,
> The people they stare, and they ask who I am;
> And if I should chance to run over a cad,
> I can pay for the damage if ever so bad.
> So pleasant it is to have money, heigh ho!
> So pleasant it is to have money. (177)

Pyle responds disapprovingly, "That's a funny kind of poem," missing the gibe. Up to his last meeting with Fowler, Greene's Pyle projects an ignorance that cannot be controlled or cured, only eliminated (163).

Mankiewicz not only changes the delivery of the lines but also replaces Clough's poem altogether. Four lines from *Othello* reinforce Fowler's jealousy about losing Phuong:

> Though I perchance am vicious in my guess,
> As I confess it is my nature's plague
> To spy into abuses, and oft my jealousy
> Shapes faults that are not. (3.3.146–49)

Mankiewicz then delivers his most strident attack on Greene himself in a dialogue directed at Fowler. Pyle accuses the burnt-out Englishman of being "an adolescent boy who keeps on using dirty words all the time because he doesn't want anyone to think he doesn't know what it's all about. You're going to hate this; I think you're one of the most truly innocent men I'll ever know." Mankiewicz redirects the innocence that was once projected onto Pyle, betraying Fowler as the political naïf. In the 1958 film Pyle wrongfully dies because Fowler, driven by jealousy, is duped by the communists' manipulations.

In the 2002 version, Brendan Fraser's Pyle knowingly finishes the poem for Fowler, making him Fowler's intellectual equal as well as signifying his identification with Clough's indifferent driver. Pyle's youthful power and his pugilist's stance dominate the frame as he commands more than questions Fowler: "We can disagree and remain friends, can't we, Thomas?" The assumed naïveté is gone. Fowler confronts his friend's deceit: "It's you, isn't it? Joe Tunney, the staff at the Legation, General Thé, they all take their fucking orders from you, Pyle." Pyle ends the scene by lecturing on the amount of financial aid the United States has provided to France, the domino theory, and the claim that today's bombing will save lives in the long run.

Fowler's fortunes in the last scene provide the final departure. All three works—the novel and the two films—end with his stating, "I wished there existed someone to whom I could say that I was sorry" (Greene, *Quiet* 189). In the novel, the jaded reporter ostensibly gets everything he wants—a divorce, an extension from the *Times,* and the lovely Phuong—but he is existentially alone.

In 1958 Mankiewicz punishes the guilty for the murder of Pyle. Fowler delivers the sorry line to Vigot, the French investigator, as a confession. Mankiewicz continues the sentence by having Phuong publicly reject Fowler when he pleads for her return. Wilkins, a fellow correspondent at the club, predicts tomorrow's news story, suggesting that Fowler is washed up: "Let me put it to you as a reporter. The celebration of the Chinese New Year was briefly interrupted at the Cholon Restaurant by a shabbily dressed, middle-aged Caucasian who appeared suddenly on the dance floor, unshaven, unwashed, and unwanted and made a nuisance of himself by haranguing a young Vietnamese girl." The film ends with the defeated Fowler retreating into the crowd.

Noyce ends his adaptation with the hindsight of almost fifty years of history. Again, Fowler wishes he could apologize, but this time, Phuong is there to reply, "Not to me," while affectionately hugging him. Fowler continues busily at his typewriter, getting out the day's dispatch. An extreme close-up of the keys striking the paper dissolves into a montage of headlines detailing the escalation of America's involvement in Vietnam, each one bylined "Thomas Fowler." Thus, as circumstances worsen for the United States in Vietnam, Fowler actually benefits personally and professionally.

The headline montage begins with the French defeat at Dien Bien Phu and the Geneva accords ending the war with France, dividing Vietnam at the seventeenth parallel. A series of headlines follows, indicating the escalation of U.S. involvement: "August 24, 1965. Ground Operations Begin. 184,300 troops in Vietnam." The final image settles on a wounded soldier with a heavily bandaged eye. The date of the article is 23 December 1966, and the headline reads: "495,000 U.S. Forces Now in Vietnam. President Johnson Reinforces Commitment to Fight Communists." The actual troop strength at the end of 1966 was 383,500, 100,000 less than the 495,000 listed in the news article. More than just a quibble over numbers, Noyce puts the troop strength near the maximum of 540,000, which was not reached until 1968. An escalation of this magnitude did not occur until after the Tet Offensive in 1968 and was designed to reconstitute the army's strength worldwide and not, as Noyce's misleading article suggests, to send more troops to Vietnam.

The negotiations behind General Westmoreland's infamous troop request were explained as far back as 1977, when Herbert Schandler published *The Unmaking of a President: Lyndon Johnson and Vietnam*. Relying on the government study *United States–Vietnam Relations, 1945–1967*, better known as the Pentagon Papers, Schandler mentioned a 23 February 1968 meeting between General Wheeler and General Westmoreland in Saigon, where they discussed the current military situation and projected materiel and troop requirements: "The troop list developed in Vietnam by the two military leaders [Wheeler and Westmoreland] had been designed to serve many purposes. Under the best possible circumstances, it would provide some additional troops to the Vietnam commander, but most importantly, it would allow reconstitution of the strategic reserve" (115). Noyce's finale montage recycles the myth that the press somehow saved the United States from itself and fabricates a false visual paradigm to support it.

Much of the power of Greene's novel, when read in the new millennium, is due to its prophetic qualities. In the dedication, Greene insists, "This is a story and not a piece of history." Unfortunately, *The Quiet American* has become a chillingly accurate foreshadower of events. Mankiewicz's 1958 film remains an artifact of Cold War ideology, frozen in history. Likewise, Noyce's 2002 film is wedded to a post-Vietnam subjectivity and is no less a product of an era. And yet, the prescience of *The Quiet American* continues to strike new chords. When asked whether he intended his 2002 film to be a cautionary tale, Noyce replied, "I don't believe that one makes films to be cautionary tales, but they become them" (Blackwelder). Noyce's film may caution, but most of all, like Fowler, it wishes to say "sorry."

WORKS CITED

Bass, Thomas A. "The Spy Who Loved Us." *New Yorker* 23 May 2005: 56–67.

Blackwelder, Rob. "Noyce Delights in Double Duty." *SPLICEDwire* 7 Oct. 2002. <http://www.splicedonline.com/02features/pnoyce.htm>.

Corliss, Richard. "The Quiet Vietnamese." *Time Asia* 28 Oct. 2002. <http://www.time.com/time/asia/magazine/article.html>.

Currey, Cecil B. *Edward Lansdale: The Unquiet American.* Washington, D.C.: Brassey's, 1998.

Du, Nguyen. *The Tale of Kieu.* Trans. Huynh Sanh Thong. New Haven, Conn.: Yale UP, 1983.

Fuchs, Cynthia. "Willful Blindness." *PopMatters* 13 Feb. 2003. <http://www.popmatters.com/film/reviews/q/quiet-american.shtml>.

Full Metal Jacket. Dir. Stanley Kubrick. Perf. Matthew Modine, Adam Baldwin, Vincent D'Onofrio, Lee Ermey. Warner Bros., 1987.

Geist, Kenneth L. *Pictures Will Talk: The Life and Films of Joseph L. Mankiewicz.* New York: Charles Scribner's Sons, 1978.

Greene, Graham. *The Quiet American.* 1955. New York: Penguin Books, 2002.

———. *Ways of Escape.* New York: Simon & Schuster, 1980.

Grove, Martin. "Noyce's 'Quiet American' Something to Shout About." *Hollywood Reporter.com* 22 Nov. 2002. <http://www.hollywoodreporter.com/thr/article>.

Hartz, Louis. *The Liberal Tradition in America.* New York: Harcourt, Brace, 1955.

Herz, Martin F. *The Vietnam War in Retrospective.* Washington, D.C.: School of Foreign Service, 1984.

Kael, Pauline. *Kiss Kiss Bang Bang.* Boston: Little, Brown, 1968.

Knight, Arthur. "One Man's Movie." *Saturday Review* 25 Jan. 1958: 27.

Nashel, Jonathan. *Edward Lansdale's Cold War.* Amherst: U of Massachusetts P, 2005.

O'Neill, James, Jr. "A Director's View: Mankiewicz Backs Right to Alter Novels for Screen." *Washington Daily News* 8 Jan. 1958: 24.

Pratt, John Clark, ed. *The Quiet American: Text and Criticism.* New York: Penguin Books, 1996.

Pryor, Thomas M. "Producer Finds 'Quiet American.'" *New York Times* 14 Dec. 1956: 35.

The Quiet American. Dir. Joseph Mankiewicz. Perf. Audie Murphy, Michael Redgrave. United Artists, 1958.

The Quiet American. Dir. Phillip Noyce. Perf. Michael Caine, Brendan Fraser. Miramax, 2002.

"*The Quiet American* Remake." *Daily Variety* 1 Mar. 1991: 10.

Rollins, Peter C. "The Vietnam War." *The Columbia Companion to American History on Film.* Ed. Peter C. Rollins. New York: Columbia UP, 2003.

Schandler, Herbert Y. *The Unmaking of a President: Lyndon Johnson and Vietnam.* Princeton, N.J.: Princeton UP, 1977.

Sherry, Norman. *The Life of Graham Greene.* Vol. 2. New York: Penguin Books, 1995.

Stayton, Richard. "Greene's Men in Vietnam." *Written By* Feb. 2003. <http://www.wga.org/WrittenBy/0203/vietnam_chris.htm>.

Part IV

The Twenty-first Century
Terrorism and Asymmetrical Conflicts

OPERATION RESTORE HONOR IN
BLACK HAWK DOWN

On 3 October 1993 a group of U.S. Army Rangers and Delta Force operators, acting in support of a United Nations relief mission in Somalia, mounted a surprise raid into the urban center of Mogadishu. Task Force (TF) Ranger, as it was called, hoped to capture leaders of the Habr Gidr clan, which was leading the resistance to the UN presence in the country. The commando attack met fierce resistance from clan fighters; eighteen U.S. soldiers were killed, many more were wounded, and two Black Hawk helicopters were destroyed. Despite the adversity, TF Ranger seized several clan leaders and managed to extricate itself after a seventeen-hour battle. The mission exemplified remarkable heroism and discipline, yet to many within the military, it also represented a failure of command at high levels. For Jerry Bruckheimer, producer of the film *Black Hawk Down* (2001), it presented an opportunity to celebrate American heroism. He approached the Pentagon for equipment and personnel to heighten the feel of cinematic realism—without being quite so blunt about it. General John M. Keane, the army's vice chief of staff, remembers his first meeting with Bruckheimer: "He came into my office and said 'General, I'm going to make a movie that you and your Army will be proud of.' He did, so we thank him for it" (Kozaryn).

The book by Mark Bowden on which the film is based, along with the video game and the television documentaries on Operation Restore Hope in Somalia (1992–1993), have all cultivated among the public a sense that they have been historically informed through exposure to the dramatic narratives of the Battle of Mogadishu. The deluxe DVD edition of the Ridley Scott–directed film, which offers a running commentary by key veterans of the mission, is an unusually rich resource for the study of history presented in film, as are two major documentaries included in the three-disc set—PBS/Frontline's

Ambush in Mogadishu (1998) and the History Channel's *The True Story of Black Hawk Down* (2003). Although the film *Black Hawk Down* is a case of "mutual exploitation," Lawrence Suid's phrase for productions that employ Department of Defense (DOD) resources (Seelye A1), it has earned a reputation as a truthful telling that justified the Pentagon's faith in the production. The military's commitment was significant. Bruckheimer persuaded the Pentagon to lend one hundred troops and eight helicopters, all shipped to Morocco for location shooting, at a cost of only $2.2 million (USAPA 2). Two retired army officers, Lieutenant Colonel Tom Matthews and Colonel Lee Van Arsdale, veterans of the battle, served as technical advisers for location shooting. To develop the proper military stances and maneuvers, actors trained at Fort Benning, Georgia (Rangers), Fort Bragg, North Carolina (Delta Force), and Fort Campbell, Kentucky (helicopters). During this training, even the self-described "arty-farty" among the actors bonded with the soldiers and became outspoken advocates of their courage and patriotism.[1] The startling documentary-like scenes of expert aerial maneuvers, Rangers "fast roping" into rotor-washed streets, and furious firefights offer a visceral sense of skill, risk, and danger seldom experienced on film.

The result so pleased the George W. Bush administration that on 15 January 2001 top civilian and uniformed leaders attended the Washington premiere. In addition to General Keane, who at one time commanded the XVIII Airborne Corps, the audience included Army Chief of Staff General Eric Shinseki and General Peter Pace of the Marine Corps, vice chair of the Joint Chiefs of Staff. The civilian contingent included Vice President Richard Cheney, Defense Secretary Donald Rumsfeld, and Deputy Defense Secretary Paul Wolfowitz (Kozaryn). *Black Hawk Down* was praised by most mainstream critics and was well received by the public. When producers, actors, military professionals, civilian and political leaders, film critics, and the general public all agree on both the artistic merits and the accuracy of a popular film about a controversial episode, a historically minded person cannot resist asking a few questions: What kind of film could produce such a remarkable consensus? How could Bruckheimer and Scott transcend the Hollywood reluctance that kept big-budget, "mutual exploitation" Vietnam films—with the exception of John Wayne's *Green Berets* (1968)—away from the screen for a full decade? Was this American film culture's *The Charge of the Light Brigade,* praising the courage of soldiers in combat while rebuking the folly of their commanders?[2] This chapter examines such questions by exploring the background of the Somalian campaigns and the book that became the film. The focus then turns to the Bruckheimer-Scott collaboration that dramatized the book so effectively for popular audiences. The chapter concludes with some troublesome questions of historical truth that remain after the film and its numerous documentary and video game spin-offs have been played.

OPERATION RESTORE HOPE

The topic of *Black Hawk Down* is plucked from a complex, UN-requested engagement that began as a humanitarian mission in 1992, became a nation-building exercise in 1993, and finally evolved into U.S.-dominated warfare directed at capturing the leader of the Habr Gidr clan, Mohamed Farah Aideed.[3] Aideed had led the Somalian army under President Mohamed Siad Barre during a late 1970s war with Ethiopia, but he launched a successful rebellion against the president in 1989, pushing him into exile by 1991. The expulsion of Barre brought no stability, since Somalia had never had a functioning national government. In the absence of civil authority, warring clans and subclans fought with one another for dominance, while banditry flourished and relief agencies suffered from extortion.[4] The civil war was fought with leftover weapons from Somalia's past as a Soviet and then an American client state under the Carter administration. During the miseries of 1991–1992, television news, led by CNN, conveyed a picture of such desperate suffering and hunger that the U.S. Congress and President George H. W. Bush felt they could not ignore the situation, even though Bush had just lost the presidential election to Bill Clinton. The emotional appeal was this: having triumphed in the Cold War, how could the surviving superpower, so often animated by its humanitarian impulses, let the wretched of the earth die in the streets of their hopeless cities?

On 4 December 1992 President Bush sent twenty thousand marines to Somalia in a mission called Operation Restore Hope. The marines restored some stability, and under their protection, the United Nations and several non-governmental organizations (NGOs) set up an effective distribution system for humanitarian aid. Months later, in June 1993, U.S combat troops were drawn down to twelve hundred after a multinational peacekeeping force under UN command (UNOSOM) had been put in place.

Operation Restore Hope and its UN-commanded successors intermittently found Aideed and his clan antagonistic if not outright deadly. Aideed believed that the equitable distribution of aid and entreaties for reconciliation would permit rival clans a share of national power that they had not earned. Aideed also believed that the UN peacekeeping force was a personally motivated subterfuge by UN Secretary-General Boutros Boutros-Ghali to undermine and ultimately depose him. On 5 June 1993 twenty-four Pakistani soldiers were killed in ambushes and their bodies dragged through the streets. U.S. and UN leaders believed that Aideed had ordered the murders in response to aggressive searches of his clan's compounds by UN forces. Although Aideed's involvement could not be proved, the inference was reasonable. Anger and frustration among U.S. and UN forces were compounded by deadly attacks on U.S. servicemen. After four military policemen were killed on 8 August, U.S. commanders decided to assign top priority to the capture of Aideed. A special operations task force—TF Ranger (consisting of 440 men and code-named Operation Gothic Serpent)—was sent to Mogadishu on 24 August to take more aggressive action against armed disorder and resistance; it became, in effect, the counterinsurgency component to nation building (Karcher 27–29). TF Ranger's rules of engagement did not respect the limits of humanitarian peacekeeping: within the new campaign of raids to decapitate Habr Gidr's leadership, a significant escalation from the UN-U.S. side occurred on 12 July 1993 during the so-called Abdi house raid (Operation Michigan) in Mogadishu (Bowden, *Black Hawk* 72–74). Intelligence reports suggested that several leaders directing attacks on UN activities would be gathered at the house. According to U.S. military historians Robert F. Baumann and Lawrence A. Yates, U.S. air and ground forces attacked the building with antitank missiles and 20mm cannon fire. "Somalis who did not evacuate the building were 'fair game.'" Dozens of Somalis died or suffered injuries, "including Sheik Aden Mohammed, the movement's spiritual leader." There was collateral damage as well; the French embassy was struck by a missile and 20mm shells (Baumann et al. 118).[5]

Every kind of observer in Mogadishu as well as subsequent historians have called this tactical application of the Powell doctrine (overwhelming force) in an urban setting a grim turning point that elevated hatred for Americans and guaranteed the strategic failure of their nation-building mission. Four journalists were immediately murdered at the Abdi house site by angry mobs, their corpses displayed for television. Some of the journalists had been working for American publications (Hirsch and Oakley 121). Mark Bowden, who interviewed one surviving American-educated Somali who had been present at the Abdi house meeting, reported that clan leaders, fatigued by the chaos of Aideed's anarchism, had gathered on that day to discuss a moderation of their militancy and whether to accept peace proposals sent from Admiral Jonathan Howe, the U.S. special representative to the United Nations. After seeing ninety-year-old Sheik Aden and poet Moallim Soyan, as well as judges and lawyers, shredded by the missiles, the surviving Habr Gidr leaders felt threatened and naturally found support from other clans, who saw American bellicosity as intolerably destructive to the interests of all Somalis (Bowden,

Black Hawk 72–74). As John L. Hirsch and Robert B. Oakley, key U.S. diplomats present during 1992–1993, put it, "The change in atmosphere was evident; the effect of the raid irrevocable" (121).[6]

OPERATION IRENE

Thereafter, events spiraled toward 3 October 1993 and another exercise of overwhelming force. That mission, code-named Operation Irene, was a daylight Ranger–Delta Force urban assault aimed at neutralizing the leadership of the Habr Gidr clan. Aideed and other clan leaders were to be snatched from a site in south Mogadishu by Delta Force and conveyed to imprisonment by ground vehicles with a Ranger escort. The mission succeeded in snatching a pair of Habr Gidr leaders and a few other clan members at a cost of eighteen U.S. servicemen and perhaps as many as a thousand Somalis, but the mission as a whole failed. Aideed and other clan leaders remained at large, causing the Americans to convert Mogadishu into a battle zone. Operation Irene was retrospectively described as an attempt merely to arrest two Habr Gidr leaders, but most observers reject that description. Hirsch and Oakley, who worked intimately with the U.S. military principals, flatly say, "U.S. Rangers launched another attempt to find the elusive general [Aideed]" (127).

The title of Frontline's documentary, *Ambush in Mogadishu* (1998), may exaggerate the notion of a planned entrapment, but among a militia with plenty of Soviet-made rocket-propelled grenades (RPGs), it seems obvious that angry, drug-assisted (khat) shooters operating in full daylight would go for the tails of the low-altitude Black Hawks and the Little Bird choppers that provided battle command and control. Aideed and his lieutenants understood that if they shot down a helicopter or two, the resulting rescue missions through the narrow streets would be vulnerable. The thin-skinned Humvees would be easy targets for the thousands of lightly armed and hostile militia in the neighborhoods the vehicles would have to drive through. Having Aideed as a target for this mission helps explain the high level of risk accepted (Drew 312; Drysdale 210; Rosegrant 15; Loeb W06).[7] Two MH-60L Black Hawks were in fact shot down by RPGs, while three others were crippled and forced to land; recovery and escape efforts resulted in the eighteen soldiers killed, and one pilot, Michael Durant, was taken prisoner. The warriors exhibited high levels of courage, loyalty to one another, and ingenuity. At the same time, they were not prepared for the fierce, well-armed resistance. Drivers made wrong turns, circling back to be fired on in the neighborhoods they were trying to escape. Expecting a quick thirty-minute extraction, the Rangers and Delta men found themselves engaged in a battle lasting seventeen hours that produced seventy-six casualties in addition to the eighteen deaths.

THE POLITICAL FIRESTORM

An angry Congress and a very disappointed Bill Clinton quickly decided that the militarized nation-building mission was over. Talks resumed with Aideed, who even received a marine escort on one occasion for his own security. Those arrested on 3 October were released. By 25 March 1994, all U.S. troops had been withdrawn (U.S. GAO 1).

Called the Battle of the Black Sea, the Battle of Mogadishu, and the Day of the Rangers (the name of a Habr Gidr clan holiday), superlatives of U.S. and worldwide historical significance have been attributed to it.[8] It was the largest loss of life in a firefight since the Vietnam conflict and an unsurpassed humiliation as the world watched on CNN while American soldiers were mutilated and dragged through the streets. Many saw it as the death of the "superpower fantasy" of a U.S.-controlled new world order. Major Timothy Karcher of the U.S. Army sees Mogadishu in the light of the "victory disease," whose symptoms are "arrogance, complacency, and the habit of using established patterns to solve military problems" (v). Regarding the United States and the United Nations, some concluded that multilateral actions were irrelevant to U.S. national interests. As for military power's role in foreign policy, some despaired about the ineptness of Clinton, Secretary of State Warren Christopher, and National Security Adviser Anthony Lake. Widespread suspicions of timid incompetence were compounded by preoccupations with "force protection" that led to an exaggerated display (but not use) of force in Haiti (1994), ignoring of the Rwandan genocide (1994), and the stand-away war in Serbia over Kosovo (1999). Operation Allied Force in the airspace above Serbia was fought without a single American death but at the cost of target errors that claimed civilians in a dozen embarrassing incidents, include the bombing of the Chinese embassy in Belgrade, a misdirection that killed four staffers and sent twenty-six to the hospital (Lambeth 136–47). The late 1990s and eventually post-9/11 hindsight brought the severest interpretation of all: that the hasty accommodation of Aideed in Somalia and withdrawal in the face of his ragged militia advertised American weakness and lack of resolve.

The Battle of Mogadishu's aftermath was retrospectively seen by both hostile and friendly critics as nothing less than an invitation to al Qaeda. Osama bin Laden himself commented sarcastically on how quickly the Americans departed: "The American troops left after achieving nothing. They left after claiming that they were the largest power on earth. . . . The Americans ran away from those fighters who fought and killed them, while the latter were still there" (Arnett). Al Qaeda followed with attacks in Nairobi, Kenya, and Dar es Salaam, Tanzania; on the USS *Cole;* and ultimately with 9/11. Consistent with this portrait of humiliation, *Newsweek* reporters at the Battle of Fallujah in April 2004 encountered street vendors selling a $1 video calling for "brave men to slaughter the occupiers." The invocation to a showdown "was accompanied by grainy footage pirated from a copy of 'Black Hawk Down' with words from a singer telling that 'They [the Americans] were left on the ground. No one came to help them'" (Nordland 28).

The Battle of Mogadishu became the subject of dozens of anxious DOD examinations focused on training, weapons, tactics, foreign policy, and inter-agency coordination. It is obvious that *Black Hawk Down*'s topic was deeply political. Given the sense of failure clouding the mission as a whole and the perpetual search in American politics to identity *someone else* as the goat, the principals who had been responsible for authorizing, planning, and executing the mission had motives to be less than candid. Among them were figures still esteemed by the Pentagon who had to grant approval to the script and final cut. Major General William F. Garrison, who had commanded TF Ranger on that day, had been promoted to commander of the JFK Special Warfare Center at Fort Bragg (1995–1996) after Gothic Serpent (Bowden, *Black Hawk* 337). Thus the Pentagon's film liaison was an auteur with a stake in protecting the reputations of the commanders as well as building goodwill toward the military and an aura that would invite recruits to join. But how could such a film revisit a topic that was a source of dishonor for so many people? If the military itself was responsible for the heavy weight of failure placed on the events of those seventeen hours, how could its reputation be reclaimed? The DOD's own guidelines for assistance to filmmakers demand that a "production must be authentic in its portrayal of actual persons, military operations, and histori-cal events" (Department of Defense Instruction 3.1.1). But was this possible? What compromises with historical accuracy might be necessary for the movie to complete its mission successfully?

Black Hawk Down: The Literary Base

Mark Bowden's articles and book offer an eye-of-God narrative that incor-porates the views of soldiers, officers, diplomats, policy makers, observers, and noncombatants in Mogadishu. He made a wise choice in publishing his material first as a series of *Philadelphia Inquirer* articles, posting them on the

Internet, and inviting comments from anyone who could help him improve the accuracy of his treatment and lead him to new interviews. Veterans and military buffs were generous in responding (Bowden, "Narrative Journalism" 25). To achieve comprehensiveness, Bowden traveled to Somalia at some personal risk. His book carefully identifies its sources, both oral and written, sometimes noting discrepancies among the informants. Bowden shuns jingoism by sometimes complementing Americans' perceptions with those of Somalis. Although the battle scenes in the book are short melodramas, the whole story is conceived as a dramatic tragedy in which failures of planning, understanding, and communications spread harm in every direction. While Bowden presents the mission of 3 October as heroic, he believes that everyone ended up losing. In a concluding, cautionary comment he says, "The Battle of the Black Sea is another lesson in the limits of what force can accomplish" (*Black Hawk Down* 337).

In Bowden's larger ironic view, the bored young Rangers who quest for battle are naïve and arrogant about their prospects for success. His narrative voice frequently echoes their language of conquest and subordination, recording the fact that they see themselves in "Indian Country" fighting "Skinnies" and "Sammies," their terms of derision for Somalis. He seems condescending when he writes, "Most of the Rangers were practically kids. They had grown up in the most powerful nation on earth, and saw these techno-laden, state-of-the-art choppers as symbols of America's vast military might, all but invulnerable over a third world dump like Mog" (*Black Hawk Down* 88). But he is also the soldiers' affectionate champion, someone who sees their idealism and vulnerability and reports the remarkable things they do with little prospect of reward. He is quite sensitive to their deprivations, far from home and female companionship. To a lesser extent, Bowden is also moved to sympathy for the fate of the Somalis, who squandered their loyalty on leaders who offered nothing more than a life of continued anarchy and poverty or death in a city relentlessly perforated by shells long before outside powers ever arrived.

BLACK HAWK DOWN: THE DEMANDS OF CINEMA

Books are generally richer in sheer information than the films derived from them. Bowden's complex portrayals of politics, policy, and points of view hardly lent themselves to the combat film genre. The fuller, policy-laced story would be told on the screen by PBS and History Channel documentaries. Although Bowden contributed an initial screenplay, he had a subordinate role in shaping a predominantly visual and auditory battle film.[9] Director Ridley Scott's postrelease interviews emphasized his quest for factual truth, an attempt to "bring it as close to documentary accuracy and credibility as possible." Putting it in military terms, he said, "It was about the insertion and the exit and how it felt afterwards" ("Battlefield" 8:40–9:12).[10] Yet "documentary accuracy" does not hint at the most apparent techniques of transforming prose into the film's aesthetics of bloodstained fatigue: filmic condensation, mythic condensation, truthful fiction, and purposeful omission. The cinematic rhetoric occasionally veers subjectively toward slow-motion, balletic nightmare during scenes of extreme danger. The actors reported being so frightened by the explosive sounds on the set that their own real fear rather than acting technique drove their performances in the battle scenes. Jerry Bruckheimer wryly remarked, "Ridley doesn't interrupt weapons fire for dialogue" ("Battlefield" 17:49–18:45). Slawomir Idziak's daring camera technique records events using multiple viewpoints and relies on brilliant editing to create narrative drive. It was no surprise when the film received Oscars for best editing (Pietro Scalia) and best sound (Minkler, Munro, and Nettzak) and Oscar nominations for best cinematography (Slawomir Idziak) and best director (Ridley Scott). Such awards and nominations, also conferred by the American Film Institute, the Art Directors Guild, and other organizations, testify to the high production values achieved despite the recording of dangerous aerial maneuvers in a gritty shooting environment while using a crew and cast who spoke several languages.

Filmic Condensation

The film's story line simplifies TF Ranger's life in the hangar, and its projection into the city for a single battle creates an unusually tight thread. The frame of Operation Restore Hope in Somalia is foreshortened to Operation Irene on 2 and 3 October 1993, without any backward references to explanatory contexts rooted in prior hostilities; the "irrevocable turning point" of the Abdi house raid on 12 July is missing, as is a Black Hawk downing in Mogadishu on 25 September. With its hell in a small time period, the film becomes exhausting as Operation Irene offers terrifying moments that repeatedly flay the arrogance, idealism, and flesh of the Rangers.

An important example of this filmic condensation is the character of Todd Blackburn (Orlando Bloom), a cocky, chatty kid who arrives on base with the announcement that he is "excited in a good way" and "ready to kick some ass."[11] Then, as his Ranger "chalk" (a squad assigned to a helicopter) fast-ropes down to provide covering fire for the convoy of captured clan leaders, Blackburn misses and drops seventy feet to the street; his near fatality becomes Operation Irene's first liability. The resulting confusion hinders the squad's momentum,

Sergeant Matt Eversmann (Josh Hartnett) smiles indulgently as his men decide to leave behind water, flak jackets, and night-vision goggles. The real Sergeant Eversmann claims that, as chalk leader, he, not his men, chose the equipment for the mission.

making the point regarding Blackburn's youthful naïveté. Blackburn's fellow Rangers, faithful to their code of "Leave No Man Behind," will not abandon him even when withering militia fire falls on their positions. "Leave No Man Behind" is the movie's tagline, suggesting that the operational difficulties reflect this commitment to save lives and bodies. It is one of several displacement strategies that divert attention from the serious tactical miscalculations and command failures.

Another piece of condensation relates to the theme of neglected duties of command. As the men pack their gear for the 3 October mission, Grimes (Ewan McGregor) fills his canteen but is stopped by Nelson (Ewen Bremner), who says, "You're not going to need that, dude." Then, as Yurek (Thomas Guiry) gets his night observation gear ready, Twombley (Tom Hardy) says, "You're not going to need that either." Yurek drops the gear. As Casey Joyce (Chris Beetem) pulls the back panel out of his protective vest, he complains about "another 12 pounds" he does not need. "I'm not planning on getting shot in the back running away" (Nolan and Zaillian 26–27). Sergeant Eversmann watches all this and smiles serenely. Captain Mike Steele (Jason Isaacs) fails to make a premission inspection. The battle—and the film—ends with the dramatic scene of the "Mogadishu Mile." When the relief column makes a dash back to safety at the base, a dozen Rangers and Delta Force men are left behind by the rolling rescue column, forcing them to run to safety through intense fire.

Behind these three scenes that condense so much of the movie's version of Operation Irene is a story of blatant failure at all levels. Not since Vietnam has the army sent soldiers into battle before they have been integrated as a trained fighting team with their units, their officers and noncommissioned officers (NCOs), and their fellow troopers. Yet in the film, Blackburn, a rookie just assigned to the unit, is ordered to fast-rope seventy feet into a free-fire zone. The soldiers in Eversmann's chalk are seen deciding for themselves what gear to bring into battle and what to leave behind, while their sergeant passively watches. This casual take-whatever-you-want demeanor falls below the standard for a Boy Scout campout. It demonstrates a cavalier disregard at all levels of command for military regulations and basic principles of military organization and discipline. It is not the individual soldier's job to decide what equipment and supplies (including sufficient water) to bring on a mission. This responsibility of mission commanders extends all the way up the chain (Department of Army Headquarters Field Manual [FM] 7–8; FM 7–10, ch. 8 §III). The virtual abandonment of the squad of Delta Force men and Rangers is portrayed as the product of confusion and the fog of war, or perhaps the indifference of the Malaysian drivers for the armored column, but the survival of all twelve men is attributable only to luck or a miracle, not to the competence of command.

How do these details of neglect square with the film's DVD commentary by the soldiers themselves, including technical advisers Matthews and Van Arsdale? According to Matt Eversmann, Blackburn was not a callow recruit but a trained Ranger.[12] Eversmann says that his unit had trained as an organic rifle team and that even those who, like Blackburn, were sent to Mogadishu as replacements were fully trained and known to the other members of the team ("Task Force Ranger Veterans Commentary" [TFRVC] 11:45–12:30). (Was the film at this point attempting to evoke the Chris Taylor character in Oliver Stone's *Platoon* [1986], a young soldier who arrives fresh from basic training?) Eversmann also comments that it was *he,* not the individual soldiers under his command, who decided what to carry. Based on the unit's experience in six prior raids, he expected to return to base in less than an hour. He decided to leave extra water and night-vision gear behind to enable the men to carry more ammunition and, it can be inferred from his and Colonel McKnight's comments, to lighten the loads they would have to carry on the rope (TFRVC 30:00–31:00, 32:00–32:20).

Speaking to the issue of the ragged "Mogadishu Mile" run, Colonel Van

Arsdale says that the depiction is fictitious. He reports that, as the field commander, he followed the "time-honored combined arms technique," which requires that armor moving in urban territory be accompanied by infantry on foot (FM 71–2, App. A §4). He says that the plan was to carry the wounded out of the battle zone in the armored vehicles while the rest of the troops, including Van Arsdale himself, walked with the column. He reports that the column proceeded at a walking pace, with the foot soldiers between the armored vehicles. He adds that the column had air cover the whole way and that once outside the area controlled by Aideed's fighters, the foot soldiers mounted the vehicles and rode the rest of the way to the base (TFRVC 2:04:30–2:06:16).

But why, given the DOD's insistence on truth in historical fact and in the depiction of army procedure, and with veterans of the battle as technical advisers, does the film itself contradict its own tagline premise of "no man left behind" and falsely denigrate TF Ranger's leadership? None of these scenes is essential to the point the movie seeks to make about the valor of the soldiers on the ground. Blackburn could have served equally well—or perhaps even better—as an example of a cocky, experienced trooper rather than a rookie. The soldiers' ability to persevere in battle, even without their high-tech gear and enough water, might have been seen as even more heroic if the movie had accurately presented their ill-preparedness as the product of misjudgment on the part of their leaders. The scene of the abandoned soldiers running through smoke and fire to safety allows for high drama, great cinematography, and swelling music. But one can conceive of an equally dramatic climax showing the unit as it actually was: disciplined and cohesive to the end, truly leaving no man behind.

How, then, in a movie meant to make the U.S. Army proud, one that was subject to Pentagon approval, did these false implications of command failure make their way onto the screen? Colonel Tom Matthews, air commander of TF Ranger, says that he tried to ensure complete technical accuracy, but his recommendations were frequently rejected by the filmmakers as "not Hollywood entertainment." Dramatic entertainment values trumped the requirements of factual accuracy and plausible renditions of military procedure. Nevertheless, Matthews and other military commentators agree that the movie portrays the reality of urban combat (TFRVC 2:11:30–2:12:50). Perhaps the answer to these questions lies in the film's effect of shifting the responsibility for miscalculations in Operation Irene downward to the battlefield soldiers—and away from policy makers and military commanders.

There were certainly many instances of command failure during the Task Force Ranger mission. The army itself included a highly critical evaluation of

Revolution Studios/Jerry Bruckheimer Films

"Well this is my safety, sir," Hoot Gibson (Eric Bana) responds defiantly when Captain Mike Steele (Jason Isaacs) rebukes him for carrying a "hot" M16 in the chow line. Gibson personifies the lone warrior's scorn for army discipline.

the operation in its Field Manual 3–06 on urban operations (App. C). One particular instance highlights the movie's compromises with reality. In the movie, during his premission briefing, General Garrison (Sam Shepard) warns the assembled officers and NCOs that the mission will be a dangerous one. But according to the DVD commentaries, the NCOs were never given such a warning. When Eversmann comments that he based his decision not to carry night-vision gear or extra water on his experience with six previous missions, Matthews tells him that there was "significant concern" at higher levels that the extraordinary danger of the mission had not been passed down to Eversmann's level of command (TFRVC 32:30–33.30). So Eversmann apparently learned something in a film studio that would have had much greater survival value if he had been told a decade sooner.

Mythic Condensation

Most characters in the film are based on real soldiers who participated in the Battle of Mogadishu: despite fumbles, panics, and traumatic wounds, the fighting men are individually and collectively heroic, and their cohesiveness enables their survival. Within their collective bravery, two figures become the symbolic anchors that convey the film's ambivalent message about success in war. A mythic polarity is established between the real Staff Sergeant Matt Eversmann (Josh Hartnett) and the fictional, superheroic Sergeant First Class Hoot Gibson (Eric Bana), the "Delta boy" who is presented as realistic, apolitical, and superbly calm in facing every test of his military skill and courage. Hoot's character was invented for the film; he does not appear in Bowden's book.[13] A symbolic bonus of the film characters' names is that Eversmann suggests "Everyman," while Hoot Gibson points toward a cowboy film star of several decades' duration. The heroism of the group is thus distilled into these two characters, with Hoot's battle-earned wisdom emerging as dominant.

The Somalis themselves undergo a mythic diminishment that renders them as embodiments of tribal primitivism, warlordism, and cynicism about the death of their own people and as suicidal in battle. Rather than complaining about the Americans' indifference toward the value of their lives (as they do in Bowden's book), the film Somalis simply urge the United States to butt out, because war is their way of life. For example, when captured Chief Warrant Officer Michael Durant (Ron Eldard) explains that he cannot negotiate for his own release, Firimbi (Treva Etienne) replies, "Course not, you have the power to kill, but not negotiate. In Somalia, killing is negotiation. . . . There will always be killing, you see. This is how things are in our world" (Nolan and Zaillian 102).

Eversmann is portrayed as the trained but not battle-tested NCO who un-expectedly receives the call to lead his chalk. He articulates the humanitarian aspect of the U.S. commitment, conveyed in a piece of dialogue about whether he really likes the "Skinnies." Kurth (the only black in the movie's elite unit) has observed that "the Sergeant here is a bit of an idealist. He believes in the mission down to his very bones."

> EVERSMANN: Look, these people, they have no jobs. No food, no education, no future. I just figure that . . . we have two things we can do, we can either help, or we can sit back and watch a country destroy itself on CNN. Right?
>
> KURTH: I don't know about you guys, but I was trained to fight. Were you trained to fight Sergeant?
>
> EVERSMANN: Well, I think I was trained to *make a difference* Kurth. (Nolan and Zaillian 18)

Eversmann is presented as wanting to help the Somalis, not simply "kick some ass," as Kurth and Blackburn seem inclined to do.[14] But such optimism is in-sufficient, as shown when a Somali woman holding a baby aims her pistol at Kurth: "Don't damn do it," he yells before he shoots her.[15] During the raid, hordes of American-hating Somalis come out with their automatic rifles, RPGs, machine guns, and rockets mounted on pickup trucks (called "technicals"). How can you help people who are raging to kill you?

The philosophical solution comes from the laconic Hoot Gibson, a Delta Force operative who emerges early in the film as a traditional American superhero type. He takes spying assignments in the city; he wears no insignia or uniform and has the grizzled, wild look of a drifter in exotic lands. He shuns the Ranger spit and polish. During a helicopter ride, he becomes the hunter and brings back a wild boar for a welcome barbecue in the hangar. He breaks into the mess line, offending the callow Blackburn, who expects him to follow the rules. He carries his weapon in the mess hall with the safety off, defiantly telling Captain Ṣteele of the Rangers, "Well this is my safety, sir," as he lifts his index finger to eye level (Nolan and Zaillian 14). In a conversation with Eversmann about the mission in Somalia, we hear this dialogue[16]:

> HOOT: Know what I think? Don't really matter what I think. Once that first bullet goes past your head—politics and all that shit—just goes right out the window.
>
> EVERSMANN: I just wanna do it right today.
>
> HOOT: Just watch your corner . . . get all your men back here alive. (Nolan and Zaillian 31)

Hoot is shown saving the green tactician Eversmann in battle by advising him to stand away from a wall. And once Operation Irene is over, Hoot—like a much older brother—explains to Eversmann why he is going back into the city: "There are still men out there. When I go home and people ask me, 'Hey Hoot? Why do you do it man? Why? You some kind of war junkie?' I won't say a god damned word. Why? They won't understand why we do it. They won't understand, it's about the men next to you and that's it. That's all it is. Hey. Don't even think about it, all right? I'm better on my own" (Nolan and Zaillian 126).

Hoot resides in that mythic zone where warriors bond, love, and save one another, dying honorably together—evoking (if not borrowing from) scenes of *The Deer Hunter* (1978), where comrades transcend the national purpose of fighting in Vietnam by ignoring it. Hoot's character counters any interpretation of the film as mere American jingoism. Hoot takes its ideology beyond war's instrumentality into the region where war is transcendent. His character offers war as romance: to be at war with comrades is a fulfillment that lies beyond any rational justification or need. Hoot is as archaic as Homer's Achilles, who rages against the dishonoring of his comrade Patroclus's body, and as up-to-date as the night-vision goggles he remembers to take on Operation Irene.

Truthful Fiction

The film's opening scene on 2 October 1993 shows BH *Super Six Four,* an MH-60 Black Hawk, hovering over a food distribution site in Mogadishu. Men in technicals machine-gun the hungry who have come to be fed as Mo'Alim (Razaaq Adoti), wearing a do-rag and aviator sunglasses, megaphones to the crowd: "This food is the property of Mohamed Farah Aideed. Go back to your homes." Eversmann requests permission from his commander to engage and hears on the radio, "UN's jurisdiction, 6–4. Cannot intervene. Return to base. Over" (Nolan and Zaillian 4). This is cinematic mood and context setting. There is no mention of such an incident in the voluminous record of events in Mogadishu during TF Ranger's tour there. Colonel Van Arsdale reports that he never saw "a crew-served weapon" (i.e., a heavy machine gun, recoil-less rifle, or other heavy weapon) during his entire tour of duty in Somalia, including the days of 3–4 October (TFRVC 4:20–5:56, 1:50:46–1:50:57). He also says that the rules of engagement authorized TF Ranger to fire on such weapons without warning (TFRVC 4:42–4:48). As for jurisdiction, it is true that the United Nations and TF Ranger had separate chains of command. However, the UN mission was headed by Admiral Jonathan Howe of the United States, who, prompted by UN Secretary-General Boutros-Ghali, sought an aggressive military response to Aideed. Although the implication of this scene is that too little military power has been applied in support of the humanitarian effort, most interpretations suggest an excessive use of force along with collateral damage—as in the infamous Abdi house raid. Yet there is truth here. Aideed's militia harassed aid workers. And there was confusion about jurisdiction and command responsibility in Mogadishu.

Purposeful Omission

Other aberrations from history of the academic kind are major omissions that seem designed to please the Pentagon and make the film more acceptable to American audiences. General Garrison tells the troops leaving on Operation Irene that "the rules of engagement are that you do not fire unless fired upon." In the film, there is not a single scene in which a U.S. soldier fires at an unarmed civilian. But at several points in the book's narrative, Bowden reports that the rules of engagement broke down as soldiers fired into groups that contained both civilians and militia (76, 78, 187). Somali casualties ranged as high as one thousand to two thousand in Oakley's estimate, and hundreds of these would have been civilians, since high-caliber weapons were fired into residential structures. In the History Channel's *The True Story of Black Hawk Down*, several American soldiers show defensive sensitivity about the killing of civilians and say, "You can't look at this man and say he was a bad man."[17] They and Bowden both report that armed militia (including women and children) mixed in with bystanders as a tactic to restrain the fire of Americans.

Another kind of serious omission relates to the command responsibilities within Operation Irene. The film shows General Garrison making the decision to carry out the raid designed to snatch "tier one" clan leaders from a building in Mogadishu. In the film, he clearly has the command authority to make such a decision in the battle theater. But as noted later in this discussion, there were many other minds and hands involved. That they have successfully eluded official disclosure is another "story of modern war"—to borrow the subtitle from Bowden's book—that throws light on how military adventures of the Mogadishu sort get cooked up in high councils whose subalterns draw the curtains when things go wrong.

The Mythic Premise

"No Man Left Behind" is presented not merely as the movie's tagline theme but also as an immutable principle of the Rangers' code. The climactic moment of the film is the relief column's arrival at the "Alamo," the place chosen to make their stand. The wounded are loaded into armored vehicles, but all must wait for the body of pilot Cliff Wolcott (Jeremy Piven) to be recovered. Hours drag by and daylight comes, while the Rangers fight off furious attacks. A smoldering General Garrison radios Colonel McKnight (Tom Sizemore), commander of the relief column (in the movie), demanding an explanation for the delay. McKnight replies that they are trying to recover the pilot's body from the wreckage. A grim, determined Garrison tells McKnight, "Danny, no one gets left behind. Do what you have to do." It is a powerful scene meant to show both the force of the Rangers' code and the loneliness of command, but it is perhaps the movie's most extreme compromise with the truth. Van Arsdale, the actual commander of the relief column on 3 October, says in his commentary that he alone made the decision to delay the departure of the relief column until the pilot's body was recovered. "It was my call as the ranking man . . . and I determined that we were not going to leave him behind. We weren't taking any casualties. It wasn't a question of sacrificing live people for one dead guy. Had that been going on, I would have had to make a different decision." Although he pays "tribute to General Garrison and the guys in the C2 bird, that was my decision to make" (TFRVC 2:02:50–2:03:20).[18] Van Arsdale says earlier in his commentary that Garrison did not give instructions to his field commanders; "he only interjected by exception." The commanders on the scene made all the decisions and gave all the orders. The movie's Garrison shows "much more hands-on action" (TFRVC 9:36–10:00). Van Arsdale's explanation of his reason for waiting to recover Wolcott's body shows the thinking of a field commander who is careful with his men's lives, but these words could not be shaped into a ringing slogan that would bring the Pentagon's top brass to a premiere. It speaks well of General Garrison that he permitted his field commanders to exercise discretion, and to their credit, they exercised it prudently. But what they actually did was not the premise of the "no man left behind" tagline. Just as the blame for fatal choices in terms of combat gear is shifted downward to the young Rangers, the upward shift of credit for the retrieval of Wolcott's body gives the top command a more heroic aura. This dance of reassignment reflects a standard bureaucratic practice: push blame downward; pull credit upward.

RECEPTION OF THE FILM

Not since Richard Nixon repeatedly watched *Patton* (1970) at the White House has a Hollywood film become so historically intertwined with a sitting administration. In addition to its gala, Pentagon-blessed Washington premiere, *Black Hawk Down* had its own White House screening for George W. Bush. Bravo's documentary on presidential film-watching reported his comment that "his military would always get everything it needed" (Pedersen 2). Vice President Cheney cited *Black Hawk Down* on the campaign trail when he argued that insufficiently resolute military power in Mogadishu had led to later attacks on the United States: "If you saw the movie 'Black Hawk Down' it portrays the events where we lost nineteen soldiers in the battle in Mogadishu, and within weeks, we'd pulled all of our forces out of Somalia. So two lessons, one, they could strike us with impunity; and, two, if they did hit us hard enough, they could change U.S. policy" ("Vice President and Mrs. Cheney's Remarks").[19] In the context of the Iraq war launched in 2003, U.S. military leaders informed *Time* that Saddam Hussein was recommending *Black Hawk Down* as training for urban counterinsurgency against U.S. invaders (Ratnesar).

A film so firmly embedded in the policy struggles of its era guaranteed controversy. But perhaps because of the post-9/11 sense of urgency about the need for prolonged military sacrifice, it achieved success with critics and popular audiences. Like the award-granting film organizations, most reviewers for mainstream periodicals accepted it in the spirit Bowden expressed about the participants: "They returned to a country that didn't care or didn't remember. Their fight was neither triumph or defeat; it just didn't matter. . . . I wrote this book for them" (*Black Hawk* 346). Reflecting this memorial attitude, Roger Ebert lamented the "gung-ho capers" of films such as *Behind Enemy Lines* (2001) while praising *Black Hawk Down* because it helped "audiences understand and sympathize with the actual experiences of combat troops, instead of trivializing them into entertainments." However, the "gung-ho" *Behind Enemy Lines,* which was also made with Pentagon support and script review, shares *Black Hawk Down*'s tendency to shift blame down and credit up. The film's hero, navy flier Chris Burnett (Owen Wilson), is shot down over Bosnia and miraculously escapes a heavily armed force of Serb troops in hot pursuit as he seeks to rendezvous with rescuing helicopters. Scripted as a bored young whiner, Burnett is shot down after defiantly steering into a no-fly zone. But, inspired by brief pep talks given over his radio by the gruff but kindly Admiral Reigart (Gene Hackman), he perseveres and is rescued at last in a mission led—Captain Kirk style—by the grizzled old admiral himself. As in *Black Hawk Down,* the junior man in the field is saved from his folly by a senior officer's wisdom. This attribution of success to the brass is not an accurate or fair portrayal of the actual event that inspired *Behind Enemy Lines,* which is based on the experience of air force captain Scott O'Grady, who was shot down over Bosnia in 1995. He evaded Serb pursuers for six days, quietly hiding and eating "clean leaves" from a tree (O'Grady 114).

In *Behind Enemy Lines,* Burnett's violation of orders leads to his being shot down, just as the troopers in *Black Hawk Down* are made responsible for going into battle without the proper equipment. The real O'Grady followed orders, but like the troopers of Operation Irene, he failed to receive some vital information. NATO's threat warning network had detected a surface-to-air missile battery in O'Grady's vicinity, but the information was not relayed in time for him to take defensive action (O'Grady 196). As Deputy Secretary of Defense John White put it, "We failed O'Grady. We had the information that the pilot needed and we didn't get it to his cockpit" ("O'Grady, Con't"). The Pentagon also belatedly recognized its inadequate preparation for O'Grady's mission, making a "long overdue" change in procedure: in the future, "Wild Weasel" antimissile aircraft would accompany F-16 missions over Bosnia (O'Grady 198). Why, then, would the Pentagon approve the release of a movie that portrayed O'Grady's doppelganger Burnett as an insubordinate cowboy who brings about his own misfortune? And why would the Pentagon portray Burnett's commander—an admiral, no less—as rewarding this misconduct? O'Grady himself became so incensed by the film's portrayal that he initiated litigation against Fox for misuse of his name and image (Nason).

As for the reception of the prolonged gruesomeness in *Black Hawk Down,* some upscale liberal publications, which might have been expected to sneer, did not. The *New Yorker*'s David Denby saw it as "exceptionally violent but also truthful to the pain and disorder of battle" while it "achieves the right tone of matter-of-factness, resolution, and defiance" (124). Other elite reviewers, such as Elvis Mitchell at the *New York Times,* scorned the film as "an eye catching misfire" filled with "slathering picture elements" rendered through "video game detachment." Negative criticism of this sort did not prevent the film from earning back its production costs or moving to other venues, where its life was extended through video games and documentaries. In the box office take alone, Internet Movie Data Base (IMDB.com) reports U.S. receipts of $109 million, against estimated costs of $90 million.

BLACK HAWK DOWN: THE VIDEO GAME

Critic Elvis Mitchell correctly viewed the film as a basis for video games, which offer many narrative formats that could have been employed to map the complex world created by book and film. In the manner of the popular *Sims* series, which emphasizes conflict management through deals and compromises, a game about Somalia could have engaged the nation-building challenges to the United Nations and its national partners of India, Italy, the United States, Pakistan, and Malaysia. Or it could have been a strategy game such as Sid Myers's *Civilization*, which calls for the construction of cities and institutions using the background knowledge related to a particular time and place. But just as the film removed the political context that explains the Somalis' hatred of Americans—while retaining the confusion of command inherent in the multilateral peace-enforcing, nation-building mission—Novalogic's *Delta Force: Black Hawk Down* game is just a shooting match. The graphic power of the assorted X-Box, PlayStation, and personal computer platforms is dedicated to first-person-shooter simulations of the killing of Somalis. As Peter Hartlaub, game reviewer for the *San Francisco Chronicle,* put it, "You're the good guy, the armed Somali clansmen are the bad guys, and you slaughter as many as you can without thinking about the consequences" (E1). Unlike popular fantasy games that permit players to change roles—going to the Dark Side with Darth or coming to the Light Side with Obi Wan—this real-world game compels the player to be a U.S. soldier hovering over the battle-scarred, corrugated roofs of Mogadishu's shanties. The throbbing musical sound track creates a catchy backbeat for weapons fire at the smaller, relatively underarmed, and indistinct adversaries seen at a hazy distance. In this morally foreshortened world, the only good Somali is a cowering, captured, or killed Somali.

As much as anything, the video games bring to mind narratives about the conquest of Native Americans. Bowden's book frequently uses the language of the soldiers in referring to Somalia as "pure Indian country" (6). In the American West, settlers, captives, and soldiers told stories of the savages they felt justified in destroying so that settlement could proceed. Without publishing houses, newspapers, stage plays, or comparable cultural instruments of their own, Indians were spoken for only by the rare European who took pity on their losses of territory and life. In a similar fashion, the voices of the Somalis are excluded from this genre. They are just targets. Because the shooter genre has worldwide popularity, speakers of French, German, Italian, Russian, and Spanish—who lack the American revenge motive—can also play the game of killing Somalis.[20] Is disseminating an American perspective through the trigger fingers of game players a more effective way of winning the hearts and minds of the world, whose governments expressed dismay at the military mayhem of 3 October 1993?

HISTORIC DOCUMENTARIES: THE ENLARGING HISTORICAL PERSPECTIVE

Mark Bowden's journalism and the publicity about the movie inspired two documentary films. PBS/Frontline's *Ambush in Mogadishu* moves beyond the limited zone of Operation Irene to explore the policies that led to the violent confrontations and losses, telling a multiperspective story of U.S.-UN involvement that features interviews with policy makers, military leaders, U.S. Rangers, aid workers from NGOs, Somali citizens, and Somali militia. More than the film *Black Hawk Down*, *Ambush* elaborates on the conditions in Somalia, creating a better sense of the squalor and misery that led outsiders to intervene on humanitarian grounds. *The True Story of Black Hawk Down*, shown on the History Channel, is essentially a video presentation of Bowden's book, and like the book, it incorporates many voices and clashing perceptions of the truth.

The PBS program's title reflects the premise that U.S. forces should have anticipated a shoot-down, since the Somalis had seen enough air operations to recognize an opportunity for RPG attacks. Interviews with Somali military tacticians confirm this supposition. Somewhat inexplicably, *Ambush* fails to mention the nighttime RPG shoot-down of a Black Hawk helicopter on 25 September 1993; three U.S. servicemen died in that incident, and their bodies were reportedly flayed and paraded through Mogadishu. As Donatella Lorch reported for the *New York Times* the following day, "Jubilant crowds of Somalis holding pieces of metal and what appeared to be burned flesh danced around the wreckage. Later in the morning, Somalis paraded through the Bakhara market with an object in a white food-aid sack that they claimed to be the torso of an American soldier" (22). Would prudent commanders have contemplated a daring daytime raid that depended on many helicopters circling overhead at low altitude? According to the Levin-Warner Senate report, twelve RPGs had been fired at Black Hawks during TF Ranger's sixth mission in Mogadishu (Ecklund n22).

A recurring theme of *Ambush in Mogadishu* is the changing goals for U.S. involvement in Somalia, which abruptly shifted from protecting humanitarian relief operations to enforcing the peace to counterinsurgency. General Anthony Zinni, director of operations in Somalia in 1992–1993, and Ambassador Robert Oakley were surprised and considered it foolish when they learned that Aideed had been targeted for arrest. Like others close to the center of command, they seemed anxious to distance themselves from the disaster. They were even more surprised when they discovered that former president Jimmy Carter had been authorized by the White House to negotiate with Aideed. But neglected in the documentary is the policy turnabout announced on 28 September, when American military officials declared that they had given up the hunt for Aideed. The Clinton administration announced through a front-page *New York Times* article that Secretary of State Warren Christopher was meeting with UN Secretary-General Boutros-Ghali to stress "the need to move away from pursuing General Aideed and to resuscitate the national reconciliation process." At the same time, the *Times* reported that, according to an "administration official," "Boutros-Ghali remained committed to the capture of General Aideed" (Sciolino A1). This publicized confusion over the center of authority and the goal of policy was not touched on in the documentary.

In addition to this unexplored issue, a major question hanging over the mission is whether it succeeded. In the distant aftermath of the Battle of Mogadishu, it seems that the greatest honor is paid to those who died by calling their loss the price of a mission that achieved its goal. General Garrison was the first to make this assertion when he reported immediately after the battle, "The mission was a success. Targeted individuals were captured and extracted from the target" (Bowden, *Black Hawk Down* 338). In this rendition, since two lieutenants of the Habr Gidr clan targeted by Operation Irene had been brought back along with other top-tier leaders, the raid was successful. But numerous cabinet-level officials and staffers confirmed to journalist Elizabeth Drew that the objective was "to capture Aideed and his top lieutenants" (316). In his interview for *Ambush in Mogadishu*, Specialist Jason Moore (a radio operator) stated, "The call came down that, you know, Elvis—'Elvis has been spotted,' you know, another Elvis sighting." Admiral Howe, General Montgomery, Robert Oakley, and others who were present in Somalia confirmed that Aideed (code-named Elvis) was the objective in interviews with Susan Rosegrant and Michael D. Watkins. Vernon Loeb's extended article in the *Washington Post*, based on interviews with CIA operatives, confirmed that Garrison had been

Revolution Studios/Jerry Bruckheimer Films

The cinematic end to the Battle of Mogadishu: Rangers and Delta Forces, left behind when the armored relief column dashes to safety, run a gauntlet of fire to escape. The film's advisers—participants in the actual battle—call this "Mogadishu Mile" pure Hollywood. In reality, all the troops moved out with the armored column and received constant support from helicopter gunships.

informed that "Aideed might be there" at the target location on 3 October. John Drysdale, a senior adviser to Admiral Howe, confirmed in writing that Aideed was a target (203, 210). Garrison's statement does not exactly contradict these reports, because some of the targeted individuals, if not all of them, were seized. It simply fails to mention a goal that, if acknowledged, would make the mission a tactical failure.

Against the weight of such testimony, it is difficult to find an insider who does *not* believe that Aideed was the objective. Given the importance attached to Aideed as the obstacle to nation building, the great political risks attending the slaughter at the Abdi house and the operational risks of the 3 October raids become comprehensible only if he is the objective. The two-leaders-alone premise sustained by the film—and against the documentaries and the written evidence—reduces the sting of loss felt by those concerned for the troops on the ground. At the same time, it reflects badly on the higher military and civilian leaders in Mogadishu, Tampa, and Washington who ordered such a dangerous mission to achieve such a small result.

LESSONS LEARNED

The *Black Hawk Down* film is a window into history, but like any other, it is an interpretation. As Peter Rollins reminds those who search for truth through cinema, "Filmmakers, in many cases, work very hard at interpreting the past.

So, when we're talking about history vs. film, it's not fact vs. fiction so much as one interpretation vs. another interpretation." The military commentators, from their boots-on-the-ground perspective, would agree. The film succeeds in carrying out its mission: it faithfully represents the ferocity of urban warfare and the courage, loyalty, and professionalism of the members of TF Ranger who are challenged to the extreme. This portrayal of a limited truth is achieved notwithstanding the many factual and technical inaccuracies in the film that were identified by the military commentators. These same technical inaccuracies and broader compromises with truth serve to mask the failures of policy and command that pitched these soldiers into their small, hot corner of hell in the first place. The documentaries do not overcome these limitations by soliciting talking heads who may have something to hide as well as to disclose. It will be a pity if the vector of public understanding takes the low road down the path of the video game rather than the more difficult road of examining the policy weaknesses and tactical errors of American operations in Somalia and seeking precise accountability for these failures. We owe it to our soldiers, and to the people of the nations we might seek to build, to construct a more honest interpretation—assisted, to be sure, by dramatic stories—that urges us to be wiser and more humane in the use of national power.

This hope might not be shared by the high civilian and military officials who greeted the film on opening night. The version they saw opened with a supertitle from T. S. Eliot's *Choruses from "The Rock"*: "All our ignorance brings us nearer to death" (Nolan and Zaillian 1; Schickel 74).[21] The version issued to the public replaced Eliot's truth with a bogus quote from Plato: "Only the dead have seen the end of war."

NOTES

We gratefully acknowledge editorial assistance from Major Frederick B. Harris, Peter Hartlaub, Jess C. Horsley, Robert Silvey, and Lawrence Suid; answers to queries were provided by Philip Strub, special assistant for entertainment–audio visual, Office of the Assistant Secretary of Defense. Archival assistance in the Department of Defense Film Collection at Georgetown was provided by Scott Taylor, manuscripts processor.

1. On the actors' training, see "The Essence of Combat" on disc 2 of *Black Hawk Down;* for Ewan McGregor's remarks, see "Question and Answer Forums: BAFTA" on disc 3.

2. See Woodham-Smith for an account of how the British aristocratic system produced incompetent officers, some of whom failed in battle during the Crimean War, but whose men served them honorably and with valor.

3. The exact dates of this mission were 9 December 1992 to 4 May 1993. Among overviews and chronologies, the most officially authoritative is Hirsch and Oakley.

Robert B. Oakley served as ambassador to Somalia and as special envoy and was closely involved with clan negotiations and coordination between the United Nations and the U.S. military.

4. See Drysdale (vii–xxv) for an overview of internecine complexities in Somalia that existed before Operation Restore Hope.

5. Baumann and coauthors assert that "a brief preparatory warning was given" (118), but Hirsch and Oakley report the UN independent commission's finding that "*no warning was given in advance*" (121n17).

6. In the "Interviews" of *Ambush in Mogadishu*, Mrs. Abshir expresses a more benign view of American mistakes and accuses Oakley of being fooled by the Aideed faction: "The American ambassador was duped by particular groups, who misinformed him and exaggerated the tales that they told him."

7. This point is important because several principals, including General Garrison, commander of TF Ranger, have denied the attempt to capture Aideed on 3 October or at any time after the first week of Operation Gothic Serpent (Karcher 36).

8. Baumann et al. (1–9) contains an excellent summation of many interpretations and accusations.

9. Bowden offers a precise description of his role as screenwriter in Nolan and Zaillian (vii–xv).

10. Throughout the chapter, commentary on the *Black Hawk Down* DVD set is cited by hours, minutes, and seconds.

11. Todd Blackburn, like many other named individuals in the film, is a real person who survived his fall.

12. According to Bowden's book, Blackburn "has not even been to Ranger school" (4). We cannot resolve the discrepancy between the testimony of the officers on the DVD commentary track and Bowden.

13. There is a Norm Hooten in the book, and he is linked to the safety-off cafeteria incident described by Bowden (174); however, Bowden did not interview Hooten. The scaling up of his heroism in the film called for a name change.

14. When Eversmann spoke about his portrayal at St. Thomas University, he denied being "introspective and liberal": "I am probably a little more conservative than somewhere between Ronald Reagan and Attila the Hun" (Connel 2).

15. Kurth's spoken warning is not in the shooting script (Nolan and Zaillian 123).

16. The veterans of the operation emphatically deny this sort of antagonism between Rangers and Deltas.

17. See soldiers' comments on the killing of women and children in *The True Story of Black Hawk Down* (1:04:00).

18. A "C2 bird" is a command and control Black Hawk helicopter that hovers over a battle site. The Pentagon's "Preliminary DoD Notes," written on 8 November 2000, indicate an insistence, contrary to Van Arsdale's understanding, to depict a headquarters controlling the field: "We need to add dialogue to several scenes to indicate that the special operations forces on the ground and in the air had a chain of command and didn't operate independently."

19. The decision to withdraw was actually made in mere days, but Clinton quickly sent reinforcements to cover the withdrawal, which was not complete until 25 March 1994. U.S. General Accounting Office, 1.

20. The game's Web sites <http://www.blackhawkdownthegame.com> and <http://www.novalogic.com> contain links for foreign-language editions.

21. Illustrating the elusiveness of truth, Schickel recalled seeing "All our ignorance brings us closer to death," a citation from George Eliot's *Daniel Deronda*.

WORKS CITED

Ambush in Mogadishu. Prod. and dir. William Cran. PBS/Frontline and WGBH, Boston, 29 Sept. 1998. Video recording. Disc 3 of *Black Hawk Down*. Also available at <http://www.pbs.org/wgbh/pages/frontline/shows/ambush>.

Arnett, Peter. Interview with Osama bin Laden, 20 Mar. 1997. CNN 10 May 1997. <http://news.findlaw.com/hdocs/docs/binladen/binladenintvw-cnn.pdf>.

"Battlefield: Morocco." *The Essence of Combat*. Disc 2 of *Black Hawk Down*.

Baumann, Robert F., and Lawrence A. Yates, with Versalle F. Washington. *My Clan against the World: U.S. and Coalition Forces in Somalia, 1992–1994*. Fort Leavenworth, Kans.: Combat Studies Institute P, 2004. <http://www-cgsc.army.mil/carl/download/csipubs/clan.pdf>.

Black Hawk Down. Prod. Jerry Bruckheimer. Dir. Ridley Scott. Video recording. 3 Disc Deluxe Edition. Columbia TriStar Home Entertainment, 2002–2003.

Bowden, Mark. *Black Hawk Down: A Story of Modern War*. New York: Atlantic Monthly P, 1999.

———. "Narrative Journalism Goes Multimedia." *Nieman Reports* 3 (Fall 2000). <http://www.nieman.harvard.edu/reports/00–3NRfall/Goes-Multimedia.html>.

Connel, Ian. "'Black Hawk' Soldier Shares His Story," *Aquin* (St. Thomas University, St. Paul, Minn.) 4 Mar. 2005: 4. <http://www.stthomas.edu/aquin/030405/00030405.pdf>.

Delta Force: Black Hawk Down. Video game. Novalogic, 2002, 2003 (X-Box, PlayStation 2, PC). Aspyr Media, 2004 (Macintosh).

Denby, David. "Good Fights." *New Yorker* 24 Dec. 2001: 124.

Department of the Army Headquarters. Field Manual 3.06–11. *Combined Arms Operation in Urban Terrain*. 28 Feb. 2002.

———. Field Manual 7–8. *The Infantry Rifle Platoon and Squad*. 22 Apr. 1992.

———. Field Manual 7–10. *The Infantry Rifle Company*. 14 Dec. 1990.

———. Field Manual 71–2. *The Tank and Mechanized Infantry Battalion Task Force*. 27 Sept. 1988.

Department of Defense Instruction No. 5410.16. 26 Jan. 1988. Subject: DoD Assistance to Non-Government, Entertainment-Oriented Motion Picture, Television, and Video Productions. <http://www.js.pentagon.mil/whs/directives/corres/pdf2/i541016p.pdf>.

Drew, Elizabeth. *On the Edge: The Clinton Presidency*. New York: Simon & Schuster, 1994.

Drysdale, John. *Whatever Happened to Somalia?* 1994. London, Piscataway, N.J.: HAAN, 2001.

Ebert, Roger. Rev. of *Black Hawk Down*. 28 Jan. 2002. <http://www.rogerebert.com>.

Ecklund, Marshall V. "Analysis of Gothic Serpent: TF Ranger in Somalia." *Special Warfare* May 2004. <http://www.highbeam.com>.

Hartlaub, Peter. "Delta Force Turns Complex Battle into Boardwalk Shooting Match." *San Francisco Chronicle* 16 Aug. 2005: E1.

Hirsch, John L., and Robert B. Oakley. *Somalia and Operation Restore Hope: Reflections on Peacemaking and Peacekeeping.* Washington, D.C.: U.S. Institute of Peace P, 1995.

Karcher, Timothy. *Understanding the "Victory Disease" from the Little Bighorn to Mogadishu and Beyond.* Fort Leavenworth, Kans.: Combat Studies Institute P, 2004. <http://purl.access.gpo.gov/GPO/LPS58359>.

Kozaryn, Linda D. "Army Declares 'Black Hawk Down' 'Authentic.'" American Forces Information Service 15 Jan. 2001. <http://www.pentagon.mil/news/Jan2002/n01162002_200201161.html>.

Lambeth, Benjamin S. *NATO's Air War for Kosovo: A Strategic and Operational Assessment.* Santa Monica, Calif.: Rand, 2001.

Loeb, Vernon. "After Action Report." *Washington Post* 27 Feb. 2000: W06.

Lorch, Donatella. "Hunted Somali General Lashes Out." *New York Times* 26 Sept. 1993: 22.

Mitchell, Elvis. "Mission of Mercy Goes Bad." *New York Times* 28 Dec. 2001: E3.

Nason, Pat. "U.S. Pilot Downed in Bosnia Sues Hollywood." *UPI International* 21 Aug. 2002.

Nolan, Ken, and Steven Zaillian. *Black Hawk Down: The Shooting Script.* New York: Newmarket P, 2002.

Nordland, Rod. "The Dark Road Ahead." *Newsweek* 12 Apr. 2004: 28.

"O'Grady, Con't." *Defense Daily* 26 Feb. 1996: 280.

O'Grady, Scott. *Return with Honor.* New York: Doubleday, 1995.

Pedersen, Erik. "All the Presidents' Movies." *Hollywood Reporter* 7 Aug. 2003: 2.

"Preliminary DoD Notes on Nov 8, 2000 Version of Black Hawk Down." 6 Dec. 2000. Department of Defense Film Collections/Special Collections. Georgetown U, Washington, D.C.

Ratnesar, Romesh. "Sticking to His Guns." *Time* 7 Apr. 2003.

Rollins, Peter. Interview with Neal Conan. *Talk of the Nation.* NPR 24 Oct. 2004.

Rosegrant, Susan, with Michael D. Watkins. *A "Seamless Transition": U.S. and UN Operations in Somalia, 1992–93.* Boston: John F. Kennedy School/Harvard, 1996.

Schickel, Richard. "An Unsparing Portrait." *Time* 17 Dec. 2001.

Sciolino, Elaine. "Clinton Aides Seek Approval by NATO on Bosnian Air Raids." *New York Times* 8 Feb. 1994: A1.

Seelye, Katharine Q. "When Hollywood's Big Guns Come Right from the Source." *New York Times* 10 June 2002: A1.

"Task Force Ranger Veterans Commentary" (TFRVC). Audio Commentary Option. Disc 1 of *Black Hawk Down.*

The True Story of Black Hawk Down. Line prod. Fran Calderone. Dir. David Keane. History Channel 3 June 2003. Video recording. Disc 2 of *Black Hawk Down.*

U.S. General Accounting Office (GAO). *Peace Operations: U.S. Withdrawal from Somalia.* GAO/NSIAD-94–175. Document B-257228. 9 June 1994.

USAPA [U.S. Army Public Affairs] Guidance for DoD Assistance to Motion Picture "Black Hawk Down." 11 June 2002. Two-page internal memorandum.

"Vice President and Mrs. Cheney's Remarks and Q&A at a Town Hall Meeting in Milwaukee, Wisconsin," 12 Oct. 2004. Office of the Vice President. <http://www.whitehouse.gov/news/releases/2004/10/print/20041012-12.html>.

Woodham-Smith, Cecil B. *The Reason Why.* London: Constable, 1953.

DOCUMENTARY AND THE IRAQ WAR

A New Genre for New Realities

The Vietnam conflict (1959–1975) has been described as America's first televised war, or the first "living-room war." In the ensuing years there was much discussion of the "Vietnam syndrome," the view that a difficult, drawn-out military engagement would be impossible in the new media environment. The Vietnam experience allegedly demonstrated that the American public would not countenance body bags on the nightly news for an extended stretch of time. The current war in Iraq has apparently given the lie to that prophecy. Furthermore, with camcorders on the battlefield and both sides using the Internet, the Iraq war has become the first "digital war." Despite attempts to suppress images of caskets and other representations of dead American soldiers, access to those images is now only a Google search away. The question about war and the public's reaction to cinematic images of it now becomes, does anyone want to look? The answer depends on how compelling the war and the cinematic representations of it are.

In the new digital environment, an interesting genre of cinematic work—with the Iraq war as a focus—is emerging. Indeed, there has been a veritable flood of digital documentaries—Michael Moore's *Fahrenheit 9/11*, HBO's *Baghdad E.R.*, the Sundance Channel's *Occupation: Dreamland*, and A&E's *Combat Diary: The Marines of Lima Company*—as well as independent films such as *Gunner Palace*, the Academy Award–nominated *The War Tapes* and *My Country, My Country*, and interesting low-budget "indies" such as *Battleground: 21 Days on the Empire's Edge* and *Confronting Iraq*. These efforts form a vanguard of work before the inevitable deluge of Hollywood fiction arrives on the scene. *Monsters and Critics.com* reported in March 2006 that six feature films were in development with major directors and stars (Goldberg). A year later, only the rather coolly received *Home of the Brave* (Irwin Winkler, 2006) had appeared, making documentary the most responsive form to date.

Greenhouse Pictures/Subdivision Productions

Widespread use of digital video cameras in Iraq has resulted in photographic records of IED attacks such as this one from *Occupation: Dreamland.*

Just as the American military struggles with lingering doubts about its ability to fight counterinsurgency efforts, media makers face an analogous dilemma. Vietnam-era documentaries and television images have established a template of how to represent modern warfare; that gestalt has influenced the styles and assumptions of the documentaries emerging from Iraq. This chapter examines the first wave of Iraq war digital documentaries (2004–2006) against the existing formula, with an eye toward assessing whether the exigencies of the "digital age" will alter in any substantial way the depiction and understanding of war and thus provide a new media paradigm.

PRELIMINARY CONTEXTS AND CONSTRAINTS

The American documentaries emerging from the Iraq war have operated within certain constraints. The war itself has mutated from the initial "shock and awe" storming of Baghdad and the search for Saddam Hussein to a violent and dangerous occupation. Along the way, the obvious obstacles facing documentarians have been the dangers of gathering images in a combat zone, language and cultural differences, and the distance between front lines and editing suites. Early in the war there were also political constraints; the U.S. Department of Defense sought to influence portrayals of the war by "embedding" reporters, anticipating that the correspondents would bond with frontline soldiers and thus report empathetically on the conduct of the military. (It was hoped that these journalists would not go off on their own to report other war-related conditions, such as the impact of operations on civilians.)

The embedded reporter strategy worked famously in the early months of the war, when television news needed access to the front lines. As the war evolved into an occupation, however, correspondents and cameramen grew less dependent. (Some of the early documentaries reflect a certain freedom of access that reporters had before the insurgency became organized and dangerous.) Recent developments have made travel outside Baghdad's Green Zone so dangerous that reporters seldom venture into the countryside without heavy escorts. John Higgins and Alison Romano estimate that deaths of journalists in Iraq have easily surpassed the total from World War II (20–21), and Sherry Ricchiardi estimates that the total of 700 "embeds" for the 2003 invasion had fallen to 50 or 60 by 2007 (30).

A dramatic example of the danger faced by journalists was presented to a large American television audience with the 27 February 2007 broadcast of *ABC News Special: To Iraq and Back—Bob Woodruff Reports,* which details the extensive trauma and rehabilitation endured by the popular reporter after being wounded by an improvised explosive device (IED). The death of Al-Jazeera reporter Tareq Ayoub, by an American missile, is given considerable screen time in Jehane Noujaim's *Control Room* (2004). Trying to protect journalists is extremely expensive. According to Ricchiardi: "Foreign editors for good reason are reluctant to discuss the specifics of their security strategies or what they pay to protect their staffs. It is no secret that companies like AKE Group Ltd. or Blackwater USA charge around $1,500 a day for each member of a personal security detail" (29).

In the best examples, courage, creativity, and dedication are the operative descriptors for the efforts of the war documentarian. But despite these perils and constraints, a number of documentary films have emerged that explore new techniques and technologies—in effect, creating a new paradigm for how to document America at war.

FAHRENHEIT 9/11

The first major wide-release film with the Iraq war as a subject, Michael Moore's *Fahrenheit 9/11* (2004), easily avoided the limitations of embedded reporting because the director never went to Iraq. He argued that his adversarial celebrity would have made such an effort less than productive. Moore—a master of the compilation documentary—had no compunction about buying file footage from a variety of sources, and the film was delivered in time to fulfill Moore's goal of being an influential factor in the run-up to the November 2004 presidential election.

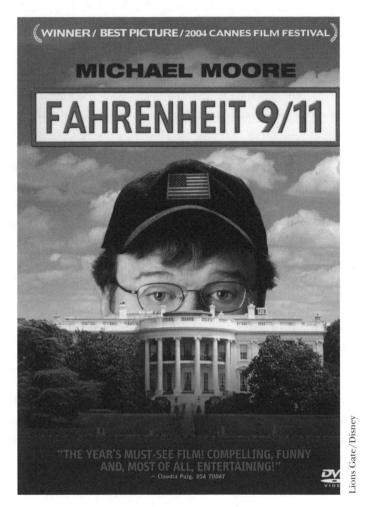

Lions Gate/Disney

Michael Moore's polemical *Fahrenheit 9/11* is the only
documentary with Iraq footage to break into a wide-release
theatrical market.

The title of Moore's film alludes to Ray Bradbury's novel *Fahrenheit 451*
(1953)—the temperature, according to the work of dystopian fiction, at which
books burn in a futuristic totalitarian society. The thesis of Moore's polemical
documentary is that the Bush administration used the attack on the World
Trade Center and the subsequent Iraq war as tools of social control. A strong
subtheme of the film concerns how the U.S. military fought a counterinsurgency war. The documentary techniques Moore employs in the analysis of this
subtheme emulate the documentary styles from the Vietnam era.

Moore has often proclaimed Peter Davis's *Hearts and Minds* (1974) to be one of his favorite films, and it is easy to see its influence throughout *Fahrenheit 9/11* in a variety of narrative devices and arguments; however, there are also some crucial distinctions between the two films. Davis was a veteran CBS news producer with controversial films such as *The Selling of the Pentagon* (1971) and *Hunger in America* (1968) on his résumé. He began *Hearts and Minds* in 1972, a year after the marines were pulled out of Vietnam. It was released in 1974, a year after the last army troops left Vietnam and a year before the collapse of the Saigon government in April 1975. Davis's stated intention for the film was to seek an understanding of the cultural mentality that led to Vietnam, what we did there, and how it changed us. As brilliant as the film was, many lamented that it had not appeared earlier, believing that it might have convinced policy makers to forestall the carnage of the last few years of the war. (More than half the American deaths occurred after 1968, when U.S. leaders began moving toward the strategy of turning the war over to the South Vietnamese. For more on depictions of Vietnam, see chapters 17–19).

Fahrenheit 9/11's appearance one year after military activities commenced in Iraq in some ways answers the question of whether an earlier-released *Hearts and Minds* might have been a significant factor in the Vietnam-era public debate. Moore's film was seen by many people, and there has been much conjecture about its influence on voting in the November 2004 elections. Although it rapidly became dated as a presentation of the Iraq war, its overwhelming commercial success both theatrically and in ancillary markets makes the film's vivid images the only ones encountered by many Americans at home early in the war. There have been reports that the DVD is widely circulated by American troops in Iraq, and Muslim jihadists have referenced or even pirated it for footage. Attempts to discredit the film have been extensive, ranging from Web sites, counterfilms, books, and major magazine articles to screeds from television commentators (Toplin 52–70).

Hearts and Minds encountered its own backlash at the time, most famously Frank Sinatra's attempt to discredit the production at the Academy Awards ceremony, just after Bert Schneider read a letter of congratulation from the North Vietnamese. The incident may have been in the back of Moore's mind at the 2003 Academy Award ceremony when he denounced President George W. Bush to a worldwide audience. More important is the stylistic template that *Hearts and Minds* presented to Moore as he fashioned a response to the Iraq war.

One of the more compelling strategies in the Peter Davis rhetorical armory is his compendium of some of the most disturbing television images from the conflict: the Vietnamese colonel's point-blank shooting of a Vietcong captive, the napalmed Vietnamese girl running down the road naked, American soldiers lighting a peasant's home on fire, George Patton Jr. describing his men to reporters as "a bloody good bunch of killers." Davis also includes footage from World War II films such as *This Is the Army* to give a sense of America's mind-set as it engaged Vietnam. On the "director's cut" DVD voice-over, Davis estimates that the stock footage accounts for 10 percent of the film, an archival component essential to the historical-cultural argument.

Michael Moore edited *Fahrenheit 9/11* before a similar compendium of images had emerged from Iraq. The film predates the now iconic images from the Iraq war: the hooded figure at Abu Ghraib prison, Pfc. Lyndy England grinning in snapshots at the same prison, the four charred American bodies hanging at a Fallujah bridge, and the James Blake Miller "Marlboro Man" photo taken at Fallujah. Moore follows Davis's lead in using Hollywood material, but he plays it for a derisive laugh, such as when key players of the Coalition of the Willing are parodied with black-and-white B-movie footage, or when George W. Bush, Dick Cheney, and Donald Rumsfeld are introduced with music and imagery from the *Bonanza* television series (1959–1973). In a more serious vein is Moore's selection of television news footage for the argument that the 2000 presidential election was a fraud, or his blank screen–live audio depiction of the events of 9/11. (For analyses of depictions of 9/11, see chapters 22 and 23).

In some of the footage purchased by Moore, a grieving Iraqi mother screams at the camera that Americans are murderers, just after her home has been bombed. The scene is reminiscent of Davis's juxtaposing a Vietnamese mother trying to jump into her son's grave with General William Westmoreland saying that the oriental does not put a high value on life. *Hearts and Minds* is exceptional in terms of how many South Vietnamese were interviewed about their disgust with the war, presumably at their peril. Moore confines his representation of Iraqis to the mother, some shots of boys flying a kite, and a wedding party. These few images produced a howl from the Right that Moore failed to represent how horrible life was under Saddam Hussein. (Had he gone to Iraq, more complexity might have emerged, but a reoccurring limitation of American documentaries on *any* war is their ethnocentricity.)

In the shooting plan for *Hearts and Minds*, Davis practiced cinema verité on location in Vietnam. He wanted to get behind the scenes to pick up insight that was unavailable on the nightly news, which gravitated more toward visual drama than nuanced analysis. Most famously, cameraman Richard Pearce was able to persuade two airmen to take him and a sound recordist into a Saigon bordello. The way the airmen spoke to the prostitutes produced a shocking exposé of American racism; the antiwar movement certainly saw the scene as a metaphor for America in Vietnam. Equally flamboyantly, Davis filmed scenes from across America and, in editing the film, crosscut a Massillon, Ohio, football coach haranguing his young charges about their lack of killer instinct against American soldiers in Vietnam. The intention, of course, was to put the aggressive, masculine side of American culture on display and suggest that it was the underpinning of American imperialism.

Fahrenheit 9/11 has its own verité footage. Although edited shortly before revelations about the Abu Ghraib prison scandal of 2004, it shows soldiers humiliating captives. In a poignant scene, with nondiegetic Christmas music on the sound track, soldiers aggressively break into the homes of Iraqi suspects. A tank crew is shown going on patrol listening to Bloodhound Gang's "Fire Water Burn," possibly the source of the film's R rating. Moore carefully buttresses these images with a declaration on the sound track that they are examples of what happens when good kids are sent on a bad mission. Whereas *Hearts and Minds* contributed to the notion that Vietnam veterans were "baby killers," Moore attempts to distance himself and his film from such blanket condemnations.

In deciding who to interview for his film, Davis was clearly biased toward veterans. The only celebrity of the antiwar movement who appears is Daniel Ellsberg, whose background included the Pentagon and the Rand Corporation. Excluded are the strident, nonmilitary voices of the movement such as Jane Fonda, Tom Hayden, the Berrigan brothers, and various officers of Students for a Democratic Society (SDS). Firsthand experience with the war is privileged. In the same fashion, Moore assiduously cultivates disaffected Iraq war veterans both in the film and in his activist work. He features their e-mails and letters on his Web site and published a collection titled *Will They Ever Trust Us Again?* In *Fahrenheit 9/11,* he introduces conscientious objector Raymond Henderson, who in full uniform accompanies Moore on a stunt in Washington, D.C., where they ask congressmen on their way into the Capitol to enlist their children in the armed forces.

In *Hearts and Minds,* some of the most effective antiwar critique comes from veterans such as infantryman Robert Mueller, who was paralyzed by his combat injuries, or pilot Randy Floyd, whose eyes well up with tears when he talks about the human cost of his precision-guided bombs. Davis also has a scene in *Hearts and Minds* in which he visits a factory in New York where returning veterans are fitted for their new prosthetic limbs. Such scenes effectively put the veterans' physical bodies on-screen as a graphic statement of loss.

Moore sought a similar impact by using file footage, which occasioned a lawsuit against Moore, Disney, and NBC. Attempting to illustrate the physical costs to seriously wounded veterans, Moore bought television footage of a double amputee, Sergeant Peter Damon, speaking from a gurney at Walter Reed Army Medical Center. The original NBC story was about new painkillers the army was using, and correspondent Brian Williams noted that the veterans depicted supported the war effort. Moore includes only Damon's specific comments about pain. The crisply edited shot presents a disturbing image, coming right after Congressman Jim McDermott (D-Wash.), a Vietnam veteran, observes: "You know they say they're not leaving any veterans behind, but they're leaving all kinds of veterans behind." Damon was outraged that, through editing, he had become an illustration of McDermott's—and, by extension, Moore's—point that the war had gone sour. The veteran and his wife filed lawsuits totaling $85 million against NBC, Miramax, Lion's Gate, the Weinstein brothers, and Moore, claiming that Damon had been shown in a false light (Reuters). (Earlier, Damon had expressed his displeasure by granting bitter sound bites in two anti-Moore documentaries: *Michael Moore Hates America* [Michael Wilson, 2004] and *Fahrenhype 9/11* [Alan Peterson, 2004].)

Massachusetts judge Stephen Woodlock dismissed the lawsuit in December 2006 on the grounds that Moore's intention was not to establish that Damon was against the war or the Bush administration—the basis of a "false light" suit. Moore's lawyer noted that Damon appears on-screen for only sixteen seconds, but it is doubtful that anyone will convince Peter Damon that he was not ill served in having his image contribute to a film that caused a quarter of a billion dollars to change hands worldwide and became a factor in a presidential election. (As I have written elsewhere, Damon's notoriety and availability for photo ops with figures such as Edward Kennedy, Mitt Romney, and the Boston Red Sox eventually led to his receiving a free handicap-accessible home from the Homes for Veterans organization [Chown, "Bodies and War"].)

Fahrenheit 9/11 angered others besides Peter Damon, as the following three cases demonstrate. Representative Mark Kennedy (R-Minn.) created a controversy by complaining via the *Congressional Record* about Moore's use of a clip showing his quizzical expression when he is asked whether he would have a child of his serve in Iraq. Moore edited out Kennedy's response about where his nephew was serving. A blogger sent out an Internet call that Joanne Duetsch was looking for help in a possible lawsuit against Moore. Duetsch is the woman who walks into the frame and tells Lila Lipscomb that everything is staged; Duetsch claims that Moore edited out the part where she is sympathetic to Lipscomb. There is also the Oregon state police officer who is interviewed about the lack of funding for coastal security. He complained after the premiere that he had no idea his interview was for a Michael Moore polemic.

The broader message of these cases is that war documentaries use human subjects, often American soldiers, as representations or signifiers of diverse points of view on a contested ideological battlefield. America has a set of legal and ethical guidelines that allow subjects in war documentaries a modicum of protection; whether these same protections apply to non-Americans is another question. It is doubtful that the Iraqi subjects in most of the documentaries about the war are being asked to sign release forms—certainly not the detainees at Abu Ghraib, the suspects in house searches, the anguished street-bomb victims, or their grieving relatives. Too often, Iraqis tend to be the "Other" in these documentaries, playing a role analogous to the subjects of ethnographic films going back to *Nanook of the North* (Robert Flaherty, 1925).

Both *Hearts and Minds* and *Fahrenheit 9/11* benefited from a well-funded research staff. Davis produced his film with Bert Schneider, who had Hollywood money behind him going back to *The Monkees* and *Easy Rider* (1967), which led to the creation of his legendary BBS production company. Moore had a $6 million budget from Disney, probably based on the lucrative precedent of *Bowling for Columbine* (2002). Once Disney realized the political ramifications of Moore's documentary, its corporate executives shifted the film to one of its subsidiaries, Lion's Gate Films. Despite the public row with Moore and the Weinstein brothers, Disney still made a handsome profit on *Fahrenheit 9/11;* most sources quote a figure of $220 million at the worldwide box office.

Fahrenheit 9/11, as the first major theatrical release of the Iraq war, can be characterized by both its haste of construction and the anger of its polemic. Given those constraints, it is remarkable that it was so right-on in its predictions of both the quagmire the war would become and that George W. Bush and his cabinet would be reviled in the retrospective analysis of the war's rationale. Moore's epic may look back to Vietnam-era models in its documentary style, but it marks a new milestone in the role of documentary in public policy discourse.

OCCUPATION: DREAMLAND

The subjectivity of perspective in many American documentaries on the Iraq war surfaces in *Occupation: Dreamland* (2005). Two embedded filmmakers, Garrett Scott and Ian Olds, followed a squad of infantrymen of the 82nd Airborne during January 2004. The Vietnam War template here would be Pierre Schoendoerffer's Academy Award–winning *The Anderson Platoon* (1967). Schoendoerffer used the then relatively new cinema verité approach as a way

"Recalls Kubrick's *Full Metal Jacket*, except with real kids."
Adam Sternbergh, New York Magazine

"Unnervingly intimate."
Dennis Lim, Village Voice

Occupation: Dreamland

This is Falluja. Be careful of Falluja.

BEST DOCUMENTARY
Indie Memphis
Film Festival 2005

OFFICIAL SELECTION
SXSW International
Film Festival 2005

OFFICIAL SELECTION
Rotterdam International
Film Festival 2005

AWARD WINNER
Full Frame Documentary
Film Festival 2005

Greenhouse Pictures/Subdivision Productions

Occupation: Dreamland is an early example of the post-MTV generation's familiarity with cinema verité recording techniques.

of revealing the varying attitudes of a platoon of U.S. infantry composed mostly of African Americans and Hispanics and led by Lieutenant Joseph Anderson, a black West Point graduate. If *The Anderson Platoon* seems dated now, it reflects the clumsiness of 16mm sound equipment in a war situation and the limitations on the amount of footage that could be collected in the predigital era. The subjects were probably not familiar with the type of film Schoendoerffer was making, although they would not have been disappointed with the sympathetic final product. (One wonders how they reacted to a French crew.)

Occupation: Dreamland is much more fluid than its Vietnam predecessor. Clearly the soldiers have seen MTV's *Real World* or similar examples of popular culture cinema verité or reality TV: they seem completely comfortable with a camera crew in their sleeping quarters or out on patrol. Several soldiers indulge the filmmakers by wearing wireless microphones. Seemingly average young American males, they appear cool, hip, ironic, sincere, and trusting—apparently not worried that someone will misuse their images in the editing room. One of them is a bodybuilder who does muscle-man poses. The soldiers discuss a magazine and debate whether Cher is "hot." Their sleeping quarters are lined with pinups and pop culture paraphernalia: they have taken their cultural identity with them. They seem to know what they will look like in the eventual film in a way that the grunts of *The Anderson Platoon* could not have foreseen.

As various members of the squad are introduced individually—a technique used at the opening of *The Anderson Platoon*—their diverse perspectives toward the war are quickly apparent, ranging from one cynical soldier who sees it as a war for oil to another who extols Rush Limbaugh. At one point several soldiers begin debating their preferences for Democrats versus Republicans, but then their sergeant walks in and announces, "Hey everybody, we're not going to talk about politics while we are on camera." The filmmakers then cut to individual interviews, where the soldiers are only too glad to elaborate on their political views, which are at variance from official explanations. Significantly, none of the soldiers demonstrates familiarity with the Iraqi culture and the sectarian conflicts that will come to dominate the war.

In the direct interviews, quite a bit of time is spent on the question of why each soldier joined the military. At one extreme, a cynical enlisted man observes, "If you want to join the army, know that you will get f—ed from day one." At the other, a lieutenant comments, "I have faith the government did not send me over here to protect oil." In the middle range are individuals who talk about how they were going nowhere in their civilian lives, and the army gave them direction and purpose. One believes that he would have ended up in prison if not for the army. Another mentions the World Trade Center attacks as he archly but incorrectly observes, "All the hijackers came from Saudi Arabia" (the actual count was fifteen of nineteen). One of them talks about playing in a heavy-metal band in high school and the editor, to illustrate and amuse, cuts to home video footage supplied by the soldier. (Later they are shown watching a video of "Slayer" before going out on a night patrol.)

As is often the case with cinema verité documentaries, by not supplying a controlling voice-over and by allowing participants to express a range of opinions, the filmmaker appears to avoid interpretation. The most pervasive

Documentary often depicts moments of cross-cultural connection, such as this American reservist and Iraqi child in *Occupation: Dreamland.*

American ideology of the war has been to support and appreciate the frontline troops, and *Occupation: Dreamland* respectfully gives a voice to servicemen. Another agenda seems to be motivating the DVD liner notes supplied by author and *Nation* correspondent Christian Parenti, who opines:

> Every war is different. Iraq is not Vietnam. But in some regards *Occupation Dreamland* could be about the work of occupation anywhere at almost anytime because some of the basic tasks and basic humiliations never change. Witness the house searches, the ID checks, the arrests, the quick guerilla attacks, the frustrated response, the muted and confused intelligence, the basic linguistic and cultural alienation between occupiers and occupied. Note how the anxiety and grinding fear of the soldiers transforms into anger. Fallujah could be British-occupied Boston, German-occupied Paris, or French-occupied Algiers.

Perhaps the filmmakers had nothing to do with the packaging of the DVD, but it is doubtful that the soldiers signed their release forms knowing that their service would be compared to the German occupation of Paris (1940–1944).

One of the fascinating aspects of the documentary medium is that, above and beyond the rhetorical power of editing, the images themselves often furnish opportunities for multiple interpretations. A case in point is a vignette surrounding First Lieutenant Matt Bacik, one of the main characters of *Occupation: Dreamland*. He is assigned the task of developing relations with local Iraqis as the platoon goes on a daily patrol. He attempts small talk with various people on the street. Several of the Iraqis are incensed that the Americans arrested a woman the day before, and they demand to speak to the camera; indeed, they look directly into the camera and shout and bluster in agitated fashion. They repeat themselves, and even with the subtitles, their argument is very basic. They have no sense of the cultural etiquette of American television and thus appear to that audience as belligerent hotheads. Their "Otherness" undermines any consideration of why the woman was arrested; no one will investigate it further. Some might see this sequence as a demonstration of how the American military is making an effort to win the hearts and minds of the Iraqis by sending out such an idealistic lieutenant; others might interpret it as a demonstration of the wide cultural chasm between Iraqis and Americans and the military's pathetic attempts to bridge it. Either way, the film is unusual in the amount of time it allows on-the-street Iraqis to voice their complaints.

In the digital age, DVDs now have the capacity to further alter or extend the audience's understanding of a film. *Occupation: Dreamland*'s contribution is to supply raw footage of the full-scale marine assault on Fallujah that occurred in the fall of 2004. This supplemental, barely edited material gives a tragic slant to the squad's positive efforts to relate to the local population—now, it all seems for naught. The DVD extras explain that 47 marines and 1,000 civilians were killed in the fighting. Indeed, the streets once patrolled by the squad are now rubble, and the former city of 300,000 is in a state of catastrophe. The aforementioned essay by Parenti further develops the point that Fallujah may have been the turning point of the war. The film has an eerie moment of foreboding when a soldier talks about his desire to help the Iraqis when he first arrived, but after experiencing violent attacks by insurgents, he no longer cares. He just "wanted to light them up. They don't give a sh–t about us here." The DVD extras relate that this marine is now training army Rangers in the United States. The idealistic lieutenant was wounded in 2005; another participant is in Afghanistan; several others have returned to civilian life. Whereas in *The Anderson Platoon* attention is limited to the fairly uncharismatic soldiers and their business at hand, in the digital age, empathy for the lives documented is stretched beyond the text, often with explicit political intent.

With Patricia Foulkrod's *The Ground Truth* (2006), several of the soldiers featured have since become celebrity speakers at activist gatherings. Likewise, some of Sergeant Peter Damon's activities following *Fahrenheit 9/11* have

"A movingly human and many-sided portrait of the war." –NEW YORK TIMES
"Historically, it's essential viewing." –CHICAGO TRIBUNE

BATTLE GROUND

21 DAYS ON THE EMPIRE'S EDGE

Two filmmakers from the GUERRILLA NEWS NETWORK spent three weeks on the frontlines of the war in Iraq, gathering intelligence, dodging bullets, and capturing the untold stories of what has become the world's most covered and misunderstood conflict.

HOME VISION HVe ENTERTAINMENT

Guerrilla News Network

Low-budget video-making has produced documentaries with countercultural political messages, such as *Battleground: 21 Days on the Empire's Edge.*

been facilitated by his notoriety from that film. The most unusual example of documentary-generated celebrity is Josh Rushing, the American army public relations officer in *Control Room.* After his appearance in the film and his retirement from the army, he was hired by Al-Jazeera as a lead reporter for its English-language edition. A *New York Observer* article trumpeted him as "Ex-Marine Matinee Idol on Al-Jazeera" (Sinderbrand C4–C5). At the other extreme, the ultra-right *Front Page Magazine* acidly commented: "Now this enemy-pandering nimrod, Josh Rushing, is the new face of America to billions of radical Muslims worldwide" (Schlussel). Perhaps it is a measure of our society's need for celebrities that ordinary people snatched from documentaries suddenly become bearers of significance and meaning in the understanding of complex events.

BATTLEGROUND: 21 DAYS ON THE EMPIRE'S EDGE

Guerrilla News Network, as the name implies, is committed to making on-the-fly material that is outside the mainstream. The antecedent in the Vietnam War was the Newsreel collective, which in turn traced its lineage back to activist filmmakers of the 1930s such as the Film and Photo League (Barnouw). Unlike its predecessors, Guerrilla News Network exists in the digital age, with distribution outlets that are much different from those in the days when 16mm film prints were hauled around to college film societies and labor halls; as a result of digital technologies, its documentaries are freer to respond with views from the fringe of political debate. Cheaply produced DVDs and Internet sites such as YouTube and Move.On.org have provided new outlets for activist documentaries. Thus, Guerrilla News Network's production *Battleground: 21 Days on the Empire's Edge* (Stephen Marshall, 2004) foregrounds in its title the view that American involvement in Iraq is for an "empire." With a $10,000 grant, filmmakers Stephen Marshall and Anthony Lappe flew to Jordan and crossed the border into Iraq in October 2003 for three weeks of exploratory filmmaking, apparently with little involvement from the "empire's" army. (As the filmmakers themselves note, their methodology is probably impossible in the Iraq that evolved after 2004.) The resulting three-week snapshot is now interesting mostly as a chronicle of what went wrong.

The film starts on the plane ride into Jordan. By chance, the filmmakers meet "Frank" Farhan, a former anti-Saddam guerrilla who has been living in the United States for thirteen years, out of contact with his family back home. He agrees to take the filmmakers along as he searches for relatives who had written him off as dead. As they cross the border into Iraq, Frank excitedly denounces Saddam to the guards and shows them scars from his torture. The scenes of Frank reuniting with cousins, a brother, and his mother are very moving and provide glimpses of Iraqi culture in an almost ethnographic fashion. For example, the demonstrations of affection between males would be outside the bounds of propriety in the West; the film constructs the Iraqi male as a contrast to American soldiers later in the film.

By traveling with Frank, the filmmakers are able to move deeper into Iraq, beyond the controlled access areas, where they discover an unsettling resentment toward the American presence. Iraqis complain to the camera team about the lack of respect shown to them by American soldiers. The filmmakers meet May Welsh, an American former employee of Al-Jazeera who gives them a tour of Baghdad—including where American jets fired at the offices of the controversial Arab news organization (also detailed in *Control Room*). They meet Raed Jarrar, a popular Iraqi blogger who takes them on a tour of wrecked tanks with depleted uranium polluting the countryside (as shown by the Geiger counter he carries with him). The owner of a fig plantation shows the filmmakers his own site of destruction: after insurgent snipers fired at Americans from the trees, the Americans leveled his entire plantation. These reports suggest a perspective quite different from that of embedded network television journalists.

The Iraqi complaints are juxtaposed with a sequence in which Lieutenant Colonel Nate Sassaman misguidedly attempts to forge cooperation with a local city council near Forward Operating Base Eagle. In camera presence, American officers joke about their lack of training in dealing with the political structure of Arab communities. A scene of Sassaman, a former quarterback at West Point, upbraiding the Iraqi council members about their failure to cooperate with his men suggests just how valuable such training would be.

In one crowded street scene, gunshots are heard just off camera, and people begin to move rapidly. Some American soldiers and Iraqi security forces appear, but it is never explained what is going on, who is shooting, or what the outcome is. Thus, although the title sounds a bit like an action movie, *Battleground* is valuable more for the interesting range of people it displays, not for the vicarious thrills of accompanying soldiers who kick down doors or duck IEDs—the stuff of many of the other "grunt's-eye-view" documentaries. Ending on a philosophical note, the filmmakers give an African American sergeant, Robert Hollis, quite a bit of screen time as he articulates a theory of why Americans are in Iraq. He cynically supplies the word *empire,* and it is quite clear the filmmakers have found a spokesperson for their perspective. In a survey of Operation Iraqi Freedom (OIF) on film, Susan Carruthers notes, "Frequently, soldiers emerge not only as OIF's most trenchant analysts but also its most persuasive critics—sardonic, self aware, scarred" (32). Their persuasiveness is always enhanced in the editing room—in this case, by giving Hollis the last word.

CAMCORDER REALITY: *COMBAT DIARY: THE MARINES OF LIMA COMPANY*

In the post-Vietnam compilation documentary entitled *Dear America* (Bill Couturie, 1987), filmmakers weave together old snapshots that soldiers took with their Kodak Brownies and a sound track of celebrity readings of letters sent home. Although the HBO special won two Emmys, the retrospective is technically unimpressive because of the rather mundane quality of the photos of soldiers lounging around their bases. In contrast, there are thousands of photographically superior camcorders and digital still cameras on the front lines of the Iraq war. The new technology's superior lenses, light sensitivity, capacity for images, and portability ensure that a high-quality visual record is no longer the exclusive province of the professional cameraman.

A&E's *Combat Diary: The Marines of Lima Company* (Michael Epstein, 2006) takes participant video recording in a new direction. Lima Company was a marine reserve unit out of Columbus, Ohio, that in the summer of 2005 took some heavy casualties: 23 of the company's 184 marines (12.5 percent) died during its tour. Filmmaker Epstein learned that many of the marines had their own video cameras and had compiled a significant amount of firsthand footage of both combat missions and barracks life. The soldiers were convinced to share the footage, with the promise that any resulting film would be a commemoration, not an exposé. Epstein shot studio interviews with a number of the marines upon their return to Ohio to intercut with the actual combat footage. The resulting production has many moments of pathos; for example, one young marine, Andre Williams, composed a video greeting to his newborn son. This tender moment is juxtaposed with the revelation that Williams was killed three weeks later.

As a filmmaker, Epstein is certainly sympathetic with the desire to pay tribute to the unit's bravery and sacrifice and to the loss experienced by the tight-knit group. Not surprisingly, the film aired frequently during the 2006 Memorial Day weekend, a national commemorative moment. Significantly, whereas *Dear America* appeared thirteen years after American troops left Saigon, the commemoration in *Combat Diary* is taking place while the outcome of the war is still undecided. Inexpensive and easy-to-use video technology facilitates this commemorative activity, but it also means that such reports are part of an ongoing flow of history rather than a nostalgic encapsulation of its meaning.

THE WAR TAPES

Like *Combat Diary*, Deborah Scranton's *The War Tapes* (2006) relies primarily on camcorder footage supplied by frontline American troops, this time from C Company of the New Hampshire Army Reserve. One important difference is that, in this case, soldiers were preselected to take the cameras along on their year-long tour and were given modest training in camera technique. Scranton

SenArt Films/Scranton/Lacy Films

The War Tapes was constructed from 800 hours of camcorder footage shot by members of C Company of the New Hampshire Army Reserve. Specialist Michael Moriarty was one of three members featured.

was originally approached about being an "embed," but she declined, instead asking ten Guardsmen to send back footage. The film whittled this pool down to three soldiers who appear as identifiable personalities in the final cut: Sergeant Stephen Pink, Specialist Mike Moriarty, and Sergeant Zack Bazzi. They mailed back about eight hundred hours of footage that Steve James (*Hoop Dreams*) spent a year editing. With this project, a different set of philosophical questions emerges.

As the soldiers go out on missions, a critical viewer cannot help but wonder: Are they kicking down that door a little more dramatically because they know their buddy is taping? In an interrogation, are they being more authoritarian for the camera, or less? When a firefight starts, are they in a bit more danger because they are fiddling with a camcorder rather than ducking or lining up a target? Are they more likely to get in harm's way in search of a dramatic sequence? Are they staging events for the camera? More philosophically, at what point does our need to know—even if only to satisfy a simple voyeurism—change the nature of the reality that is being documented for us? Surely a soldier carrying a camcorder into battle for whatever purpose has a different relationship to the experience than a journalistic observer.

These questions having been raised, *The War Tapes* achieves a level of observation of humans in war that is emotionally devastating. There is a harrowing scene in which a young Iraqi girl is run over by an American convoy. Then, the filmmakers follow the troops back home to intimately observe how the resulting post-traumatic stress disorder manifests and reverberates through the soldiers' families. Boundaries of the traditional documentary change. Early in the film one of the videographers questions a sergeant about their mission. He responds, "I'm not supposed to talk to the media." The interviewer responds, "What do you mean? I'm not the media." But of course, he is. The blurred boundaries of participant and observer produce an intimacy that would be unimaginable for a network camera crew. The film was nominated for an Academy Award.

In perhaps the most shocking interview, one of the veterans of Fallujah tells the camera that after a firefight in which his unit killed several insurgents, he noticed a dog eating the flesh of one of the dead enemies, and he did nothing to stop it; in fact, he felt good about it. Scranton then cuts to one of the wives, Randy Moriarty, giving a GI Joe doll to her son. It is one of those ambiguous, open-ended moments that make documentaries so interesting. If the viewer is horrified by the dog-eating-flesh story, GI Joe is a symbol of how we indoctrinate our youth into a warrior culture. If the viewer sees the story as an example of the unpleasant realities of a job that needs to be done, then the GI Joe scene is only a demonstration of how military wives stand behind and support their spouses. Whereas the examination of militarism in the psyche of the American family seems to resonate with some of the concerns of *Hearts and Minds,* the editing of *The War Tapes* is more subtle and ambiguous, demanding an active viewer.

CAMCORDER REALITY: NEW VISUAL PARADIGMS?

The camcorder footage in *Combat Diary* and *The War Tapes* is still subject to the mediation of a professional video editor. The lighting and composition may have a rough edge, but the overall narrative structure and sequencing are far beyond the amateur. It is instructive to compare these works to the less polished, amateur footage that is easily available at YouTube and its growing number of competitors. The material ranges from a simple thirty-second clip of an IED explosion caught by a soldier out on patrol to more carefully edited polemical pieces designed to present pointed commentary. In this arena, documentary representations of the Iraq war are furthest from the Vietnam template and, in effect, offer a new visual paradigm that is more subjective, spontaneous, and unfiltered than previous models.

As an illustration, consider a twenty-megabyte film called "Marines in Iraq and the Regular Mortar Attacks They Face" posted at Filecabi.net in July 2006. It contains a number of interviews with troops and displays evidence of recent mortar attacks on their living quarters. The interview footage is intercut with captured footage from Iraqi insurgents, suggesting that camcorders are plentiful on their side as well. The insurgent video shows them firing mortars and, in one case, executing three prisoners. Reactions to this footage will vary, but the implication seems to be that some of the soldiers on the ground want to put their own spin on video images coming back from Iraq. The producers call themselves "Young Americans Media."

Also on display at Filecabi.net is a piece from GrouchyMedia.com that is designed to strike terror in the hearts of the enemy. The song "Fire Water Burn" (ironically, the same music used in *Fahrenheit 9/11*) overlays a wide range of shots of tanks, jets, and other American technology unleashing "shock and awe" on the Iraqi countryside. It is something that a less artistically minded Leni Riefenstahl—the famous Nazi propagandist—might have done. Another compilation contains images from insurgent propaganda films with about fifteen examples of coalition armored vehicles being hit by IEDs. The impression is that the insurgents do not rig a booby trap without a camera on hand to catch the explosion. Another film at Filecabi.net features American soldiers performing BMX bike stunts in the desert, reminiscent of the water-skiing sequence in *Apocalypse Now*. Nothing comparable to the American worship of leisure time has been observed coming from the insurgent side.

The omnipresence of camcorders in Iraq has other ramifications besides giving American and insurgent soldiers an opportunity for self-representation. The Haditha controversy might not have surfaced without camcorder footage. Iraqi Taher Thabet, a would-be journalist and cofounder of a human rights watch group, heard explosions and shooting on 19 November 2005. The next morning he took a camcorder through several houses and the local morgue and discovered evidence that American soldiers had killed twenty-four Iraqis. Initially, the army reported that fifteen civilians had died as a result of a roadside bomb. When *Time* magazine's Tim McGirk began investigating in January, he was given the camcorder images, which played a big part in the ensuing investigations by both the army and journalists (Duffy, McGirk, and Ghosh). Any conclusion that Haditha does not constitute a contemporary My Lai massacre (1968) must contextualize and explain the camcorder record.

The earlier Abu Ghraib scandal broke in the spring of 2004 and was inflamed by the plethora of still photos taken by American reservists. The images of guards smiling for the camera while they were abusing detainees often had the look of a fraternity hazing, which occasioned a dismissive quip from Rush Limbaugh on his nationally syndicated radio program. Susan Sontag also aroused controversy when she observed in the *New York Times Magazine* that the photos depicted a level of cruelty and triumphalism deeply embedded in American culture. Part of their unsettling quality is the question of why they were taken and what the amateur photographers were attempting to document. Rory Kennedy tried to answer this question by paying some of the guards for interviews for her HBO-produced *Ghosts of Abu Ghraib* (2007); the results were less than definitive. Whatever their intentions, these digital images of prisoner abuse did incalculable damage to American prestige around the world—and in Washington—and they were widely disseminated by enemies through the Internet and propaganda DVDs.

Future historians will debate whether the decision by the Bush administration to demolish Fallujah had something to do with the images of the charred bodies of four American contractors hanging from a bridge. American mainstream news media now seem to be willfully ignoring the frequent Internet release of atrocity footage—captives having their heads sawed off or being punctured by electric drills. Perhaps the emotion they inspire does not need the "oxygen of publicity," to appropriate Prime Minister Margaret Thatcher's rationale for censorship of the BBC's reporting of Irish Republican Army spokespeople during the 1980s.

Regarding the presence of camcorders in Iraq, an officer in charge of training soldiers for deployment related the following story: A friend and former student of his called from a hospital in Iraq just after surviving a highway IED explosion. Despite being wounded, the soldier was quite "jacked up." He excitedly explained a camcorder on his vehicle had been rolling when they were hit, but more importantly, the vehicle behind them also had a camera running. This presented unexplored possibilities. He would now be able to edit the two angles together to show the explosion in all its glory. The same night, just after leaving the hospital, he proudly e-mailed the edited footage to his former trainer.

The officer interpreted the story with the following inflections. The modern army trusts its soldiers to use the Internet, camcorders, and mobile phones as a way to stay connected with loved ones back home. If they have the ability to convey the immediacy of their experience through this technology, it helps the public understand and appreciate their commitment and professionalism. Morale is improved because of the digital connection to supportive loved ones. (This interpretation was offered prior to the May 2007 decision by the Department of Defense to restrict access to YouTube and a list of other popular sites. Concerns about security and bandwidth usage were cited.)

However, as a media scholar, I would interpret the anecdote slightly differently. In 1968 Andy Warhol observed, "In the future everybody will be world famous for 15 minutes." The quip resonated because the modern media have become omnipresent in terms of how people psychologically define themselves and their need for personal recognition in a mass society. That soldiers have the ability to put their exploits on the Internet only hours after an event occurs provides an individual rationale for going to war that is far removed from weapons of mass destruction, the evil of Saddam Hussein, the need to protect oil resources, or the balance of power in the Middle East. It is the grunt's potential fifteen minutes of fame that becomes the goal, and this seems to overwhelm or perhaps disguise any sensible response to the danger that alternates with tedium in a war zone.

French theorist Jean Baudrillard suggests that we live in a hyperreal historical moment in which the signifier has eclipsed the signified, in which "simulations" have obscured our relation to the "real." Put another way, our signs and symbols refer only to the process of discourse itself; they have become "unmoored" from physical or social reality. *Apocalypse Now* (Francis Ford Coppola, 1979) sardonically hints at this stage when the surfer character Lance opines that he prefers 'Nam to Disney Land as he prepares for another drug trip, his own method of dealing with any "horror" that resides in Vietnam. It might seem that, as fiction, *Apocalypse Now* has more license to express the postmodern, performative aspects of identity in a war zone than the reality-bound documentary form. Yet the all-volunteer force that is presently in Iraq grew up on video games, was regularly exposed to the thirty-second "The Few, the Proud, the Marines" ads, and finally saw images of two airplanes deliberately crashing into the World Trade Center replayed ad nauseam on network TV. Should we be surprised that documenting their activities in Iraq with personal camcorders is a way of inserting themselves into a video adventure of their own making? Perhaps this is not revolutionary: Ernest Hemingway participated in World War I because he wanted to have experiences that would be the grist of his modernist writing. It seems that in postmodern Iraq, the camera has eclipsed the pen. The discussion of the next film, *Gunner Palace*, shows how the use of the camera is often informed by the canonized images of war that filmmakers take with them to Iraq.

GUNNER PALACE

Although the Vietnam War documentaries form an interesting stylistic template for assessing films from the Iraq war, there is also an epistemological influence from Vietnam's fiction films. Long before the current filmmakers got to Iraq, they experienced war via Stanley Kubrick's *Full Metal Jacket* (1987), Oliver Stone's *Platoon* (1986), and other feature film critiques of America's experience in Southeast Asia. As a case in point, the aforementioned *Apocalypse Now*'s influence hangs all over Michael Tucker and Petra Epperlein's *Gunner Palace*. This independent film, shot in September 2003 and released in 2004, is unimaginable without Coppola's canonized classic guiding its imagery. Life imitates art, but so do documentary films. (For more on *Platoon*, see chapter 18.)

As documented in his diaristic blog, Tucker, who has a military background, went to Iraq looking to make a film but without a commitment from the military to attach him to any specific unit. Things were relatively quiet at that time, and he found what seemed to be the perfect location. A group of infantrymen was quartered in Uday Hussein's pleasure palace in Adhamiya, an opulently decorated bachelor pad complete with a pool and a private golf range, which befitted his status as Saddam's eldest son. Tucker immediately recognized the possibilities and initiated the proper procedures and clearances to make a cinema verité film about American troops ensconced in this former lap of hedonistic decadence.

In the earliest (1969) draft of *Apocalypse Now*, screenwriter John Milius seized on a metaphor for America's lack of total commitment to modern warfare: Hugh Hefner's playmates tantalizing soldiers in a sexually provocative USO show. In screenplay form, it seemed to be a send-up of the World War II era, when Bob Hope visited the troops with pretty girls and Betty Grable pinups were part of the war's iconography. In the final rendition Coppola takes it further. Helicoptered into the jungle, the girls gyrate provocatively with guns and wear skimpy costumes that mock America's pioneer heritage. That the playmate performance ends with a riot perfectly embodies the debauched collision of Eros and Thanatos that was the counterculture of the 1960s. In Milius's absurdist vision, soldiers want to drop napalm in the morning so they can surf in the afternoon. *Apocalypse Now*'s vision of American preoccupation with sexuality, drugs, and violence against the agrarian peasant nation of Vietnam—essentially the New Left critique—is in the unconscious of many contemporary directors (Chown, *Hollywood Auteur* 123–27).

Soon after American soldiers entered Baghdad, news reports showed images of enlisted men lounging in Saddam Hussein's various living quarters. It had an echo of GIs barging into Hitler's Berchesgarden at the end of World War II, which is highlighted in Stephen Ambrose's *Band of Brothers* (2001). Both these tableaux provide a handy ideological juxtaposition: self-indulgent dictators supplanted by the Everyman agents of democracy. It should have further utility, in that Saddam's material excesses remain anathema to the more fundamentalist representatives of the Islamic culture. The problem with the symbolic economy of a recaptured palace is that those who bivouac there run the risk of sending the message that one dictator has replaced another.

Another memorable aspect of *Apocalypse Now* is the 1960s rock music that seems to make more sense in the context of Vietnam. How can anyone listen to the Doors' "This Is the End" without thinking of the psychedelic opening of the film? *Gunner Palace* goes looking for equivalent music for the Iraq war and comes up with marines doing rap when they are not out on a mission. A *Newsweek* feature on the rappers got them some airplay in the United States (Johnson and Conant). As in the case of Rushing and Damon, mentioned earlier, appearances in Iraq war documentaries seem to offer career advancements for participants.

Tucker and Epperlein's *Gunner Palace* demonstrates how media makers and the soldiers themselves do not approach the Iraq war with an "innocent eye." *Apocalypse Now*, *Full Metal Jacket*, and *Hearts and Minds* form templates and frames of visual reference. In a *Salon.com* piece, Mark Follman writes, "In post-production, Tucker set one nighttime raid to Wagner's 'Ride of the Valkyries,' an inescapable reference to the beach-assault scene in *Apocalypse Now*. Yet he says the soldiers themselves blared 'Valkyries' from their vehicles during psychological operations missions" (3–4). With regard to the first Gulf war, Anthony Swofford's autobiography and the film adaptation *Jarhead* (Sam Mendes, 2005) depict marine trainees singing along to a showing of the helicopter attack scene in *Apocalypse Now* at the moment they get their call to action. Once in Saudi Arabia, Swofford hears a helicopter speaker playing a Doors song and remarks, "That's Vietnam music. . . . Can't we get our own music?"

Vietnam and Iraq present a complex interchange of images and cultural assumptions that are impossible for any analysis to exhaust. Just as policy makers and military leaders continually confront the "Vietnam syndrome" in considering our conduct and future in Iraq, so too are documentaries and other filmic representations beholden to the surreal imagery of the previous war.

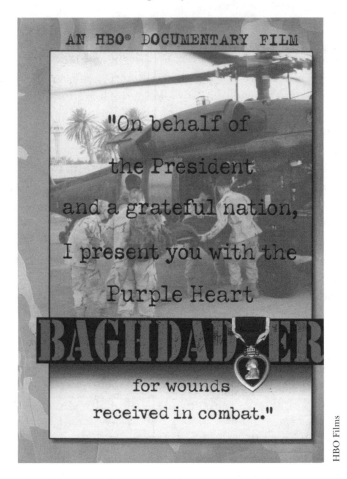

AN HBO® DOCUMENTARY FILM

"On behalf of the President and a grateful nation, I present you with the Purple Heart

BAGHDAD E.R.

for wounds received in combat."

HBO Films

Prior to the broadcast of HBO's *Baghdad E.R.*, the army released a warning that any soldier or relative of a soldier suffering from post-traumatic stress disorder should not view the documentary because of its graphic nature.

BAGHDAD *E.R.*

The film from the Iraq war with the most graphic shock value is probably HBO's *Baghdad E.R.* (2006). Filmmakers Jon Alpert and Matthew O'Neill were given free access to an emergency room in Baghdad for two months and came back with extraordinary footage of doctors attempting to save soldiers and Iraqi civilians choppered in after IED explosions. On view are amputations, a soldier given last rites, doctors moving with speed and professionalism in an attempt to salvage what they can from shattered body parts, and determined soldiers attempting to put on a brave face as they begin to see the existential changes ahead.

The military's response to the presentation has been interesting. Alpert and O'Neill say that they got total cooperation, were transported and housed by the army, and experienced no censorship. With the broadcast imminent, the army released a statement that any soldier potentially suffering from post-traumatic stress disorder or any families connected with soldiers deployed in Iraq should not watch the program because of the anxiety and pain it might arouse. One can only guess at the dilemma the broadcast posed for the military: on the one hand, the depiction is of a professional, caring army doing all it can to ensure the best treatment of its troops; on the other hand, such a broadcast goes against the previous policy of not showing coffins, for fear of the effect on public morale. The problem was nothing new, as a review of World War II cases such as the George Strock *Life* magazine photographs or John Houston's documentary *The Battle of San Pietro* would confirm. (In both cases, World War II commanders demanded suppression of the visual reports.) In defending such censorship, the government usually cites the need to protect soldiers' families; opponents of the policy claim that censorship hides the sacrifice soldiers are making. *Baghdad E.R.* presents graphic footage of the on-the-ground consequences of our military involvement, which has to make some viewers wonder whether the political objectives are worth this kind of suffering.

The filmmakers frame the presentation by placing the following in title cards at the beginning:

> This film is a tribute to the heroism and sacrifice of the soldiers who are the patients and staff of the 86th Combat Support Hospital. The 86th Combat Support Hospital (CSH) is the Army's premier medical facility in Iraq. It is located in Baghdad's Green Zone at a hospital formerly reserved for Saddam Hussein's supporters. Ninety percent of the American soldiers wounded in Iraq survive. This is the highest rate in U.S. History.

Certainly, most viewers will agree with these sentiments about "heroism and sacrifice"; still, framing it as a "tribute" at the outset limits the range of response. Other perspectives might cite this film as strong evidence of the extraordinary waste of life and human potential that is the Iraq war. As an HBO production, it has the potential for wide distribution and impact. If it is a "tribute," then by implication, it turns its attention to something positive. Documentaries should be judged both by what they are about and by what they are not about. This is not a film about torture tactics at detention centers, civilians injured by errant bombings, the prospects of a civil war, soldiers who demonstrate racism toward Iraqis, or the exorbitant financial cost of this war. Instead, under the auspices of the nation's first and most popular cable channel, it is a documentary that attempts to find humanity amidst the horrors of war. Perhaps that is subversive; perhaps that is trying to have it both ways.

The first American injury featured in *Baghdad E.R.* highlights the open-ended quality of the format. A New York National Guardsman is brought in with injuries sustained while distributing candy to Iraqi children. One way to read this scenario is that it demonstrates the evil of an enemy that would attack a soldier engaged in an act of benign public relations. Another interpretation is that it is commentary on the futility of our "hearts and minds" strategy and the ruthless means our enemy is prepared to employ in defeating that strategy. In the diegesis of the film, it is simply another example of how highly professional doctors patch up the soldiers and send them on their way.

The Vietnam antecedent would be *M*A*S*H* (Robert Altman, 1970), without the anarchistic sarcasm and the libertine behavior, but heavy on the competence of heroic doctors. The present-day staff is shown sitting out on the roof enjoying a "cigar night" or having a basketball game, but Trapper John and Hawkeye would find their lack of risqué humor tame. A few of them comment that they hate war, but generally their commentary is guarded. In both *M*A*S*H* and *Baghdad E.R.* the avocation of saving lives is ironically and implicitly contrasted with the larger environment of death and destruction that is war.

A bit of American machismo does emerge. Early in the film, rock music accompanies the introduction of individual members of a Black Hawk helicopter rescue team. The pilot brags that he can fly like Lance Armstrong rides a bike. The statement is followed by quick cuts to each character in a variety of poses. Oddly, these introduced characters barely reappear. Instead, somber scenes in the emergency room predominate, and there is a modest amount of interview footage with another set of subjects. The camera team follows one rescue mission out into the Red Zone, but generally the coverage is restricted to the drama of the emergency room.

HBO, with *Real Time with Bill Maher* and other programming, has clearly staked out a position in the mainstream media as purveyor of some biting criticism of the Bush administration. As a premium cable service, it is relatively free of the Federal Communications Commission restrictions placed on broadcast networks regarding profanity and "fairness." The appeal is to a young, hip, liberal market that constitutes about a 30 percent share of American television households. HBO has a mandate to do what the networks cannot, and it is unimaginable that *Baghdad E.R.* would turn up on CBS, for example, despite the fact that various newsmagazine shows have covered the medical side of the war, such as pieces on the inadequacies of the Walter Reed Army Medical Center that aired in the spring of 2007.

Baghdad E.R.'s presentation, like so much cinema verité, is open-ended and therefore not preachy. Even as it suggests that we have a competent, admirable military, it graphically illustrates the horror of the injuries and the staggering human cost. As with much HBO programming, it seems shrewdly marketed. One looks at the title and cannot help but think that the programming executives at HBO knew that they had something that would hook fans of *E.R.* and the various *CSI* shows and the devotees of graphic hospital reality shows on cable. It seems to look forward to a time when, as with films and television shows about the Vietnam War, there will be a lively market for a historical look backward. In the meantime, it is interesting that none of the copyright holders have challenged Brasschecktv.com's free streaming of *Baghdad E.R.* on a site replete with difficult-to-find antiwar activist pieces. Perhaps this has something to do with Jon Alpert's long career as an advocate for community-based, portapack journalism, outside the auspices of media giants such as HBO.

The films and Internet material surveyed by this chapter constitute a subset of a fairly sizable body of work that is emerging from the Iraq war. The particular works discussed were chosen to illustrate links back to the Vietnam template and forward to the new paradigm of digital representation. Other works ripe for analysis include the Academy Award–nominated *Iraq in Fragments* (James Longley, 2006) and *My Country, My Country* (Laura Poitras, 2006), as well as *The Blood of My Brother* (Andrew Berends, 2006), *The Ground Truth* (Patricia Foulkrod, 2006), *The Prisoner Or: How I Planned to Kill Tony Blair* (Michael Tucker and Petra Epperlein, 2007), *Iraq for Sale: The War Profiteers* (Robert Greenwald, 2006), and many others. Further analysis should explore whether these films collectively appeal only to film cognoscenti or whether they have made inroads to a broader audience.

In assessing the impact of what he calls "grunt documentaries," Tony Grajeda has posed a challenging perspective: "By privileging personal experience over historical awareness, these accounts construct a version of the war in which it becomes impossible to apprehend such atrocities as Haditha, Ramadi, Abu Ghraib." Documentary should have an explanatory power, but if documentary's purview is circumscribed by an ideology of "support the troops" or American triumphalism, then all that has been documented is a patriotic zeitgeist. Grajeda ultimately asks the Iraq documentary genre to "begin the process of questioning why we fight," an allusion to both Frank Capra's World War II series and the 2005 film by Eugene Jarecki (17).

The question of documentary's explanatory power and ability to raise questions about, in this case, militarism brings us back to the two films considered at the outset of this chapter: *Hearts and Minds* and *Fahrenheit 9/11*. They are the most widely seen antiwar documentaries since World War II and also the most controversial—the former coming at the end of a war and the latter at the beginning. With its canonized status as a classic of many Vietnam history classes, it is easy to forget the withering criticism *Hearts and Minds* received at its premiere. Grajeda quotes the attacks that came from both sides of the political spectrum but notes that, in many ways, the film seems validated in hindsight—he cites the Massillon football scene as an example. Likewise, Moore's *Fahrenheit 9/11*, though a box office hit, has been subjected to a barrage of dismissive attacks from all manner of publications and commentators, often because of the director's decision to foreground his own lightning-rod persona. Yet, with a shorter backward glance, was it not Moore who was ahead of the pack in saying that the war could become a quagmire, that the administration was not ready to deal with the casualties coming into Walter Reed, that Halliburton and the contractors would become a scandal, that prisoner maltreatment would become an issue, and that atrocities committed by American troops were a possibility? Critics are fond of labeling the film as propaganda, but its predictions rarely missed the target, and it may have outlined its own template for future documentary investigations of controversial material.

In 1926, when John Grierson coined the term *documentary*, he famously defined it as "the creative treatment of actuality." New technologies, ubiquitous camcorders, and the option of Internet distribution have caused a flood of "actuality" to return to America over uplinks and downlinks. Rather than adding "creativity" to the actuality, perhaps documentarians need to provide a critical insight that helps contextualize and explicate the significance of raw images. If the severed arm that drops to the floor in *Baghdad E.R.* is just an image edited for shock value, then it is nothing more than pornography. If it is part of a larger mosaic of images that helps define the present moment of the American occupation of Iraq, then it is something that should be more widely seen. As with Vietnam, Iraq needs explanation in a visual aesthetic that speaks in the language of its own time.

WORKS CITED

Barnouw, Erik. *Documentary*. New York: Oxford UP, 1993.

Baudrillard, Jean. *Simulacra and Simulation*. Ann Arbor: U of Michigan P, 1994.

Carruthers, Susan L. "Say Cheese! Operation Iraqi Freedom on Film." *Cineaste* 30.1 (2006): 30–36.

Chown, Jeffrey. "Bodies and War: *Fahrenheit 9/11* and *Hearts and Minds.*" Proceedings of 2006 Film and History Conference.

———. *Hollywood Auteur: Francis Coppola.* New York: Praeger, 1988.

Duffy, Michael, Tim McGirk, and Aparisim Ghosh. "The Ghosts of Haditha." *Time* 12 June 2006: 26–35.

Follman, Mark. "Inside *Gunner Palace.*" *Salon.com* 4 Mar. 2005. <http://www.salon .com/ent/feature/2005/03/04/gunner/>.

Goldberg, Andy. "Hollywood Takes on Iraq as Public Opinion Shifts." *Monsters and Critics.com* 24 Mar. 2006. <http://movies.monstersandcritics.com/features/printer _1149826.php>.

Grajeda, Tony. "The Winning and Losing of Hearts and Minds: Vietnam, Iraq, and the Claims of the War Documentary." *Jump Cut* 49 (2007): 1–17.

Higgins, John, and Alison Romano. "Why Journalists Risk Their Lives to Cover Iraq." *Broadcasting and Cable* 136.23 (5 June 2006): 20–21, 34.

Johnson, Scott, and Eve Conant. "Soldier Rap, the Pulse of War." *Newsweek* 13 June 2004. <http://www.msnbc.msn.com/id/8101421/site/newsweek>.

Reuters. "Iraq War Veteran Sues Filmmaker Michael Moore." 2 June 2006. <http://www .abc.net.au/au/news/newsitems/200606/s1653439.htm>.

Ricchiardi, Sherry. "Obstructed." *American Journalism Review* 29.2 (2007): 28–33.

Schlussel, Debbie. "A Marine's Dishonorable Service for Al-Jazeera." *FrontPageMagazine .com* 7 Oct. 2005.

Sinderbrand, Rebecca. "Ex-Marine Matinee Idol on Al-Jazeera." *New York Observer* 26 Mar. 2007: C4–C5.

Sontag, Susan. "Regarding the Torture of Others." *New York Times Magazine* 23 May 2004: 24–29.

Toplin, Robert Brent. *Michael Moore's* Fahrenheit 9/11: *How One Film Divided a Nation.* Lawrence: UP of Kansas, 2006.

JESSICA LYNCH AND THE REGENERATION OF AMERICAN IDENTITY POST 9/11

On 1 April 2003 the broken body of Pfc. Jessica Lynch was recovered by the U.S. military from a hospital in Nasariyah, Iraq, where she lay suffering from injuries incurred in a combat-related Humvee crash. The rescue story quickly took on larger-than-life proportions as the vested interests of the military and the commercial media coalesced around the need for a good story to clarify the moral stakes of the war in Iraq.[1] Within days, the tale of the 507th Main-tenance Unit's blunder into enemy lines had been framed as an "ambush," and Lynch's rescue had become a parable of American innocence lost and regained through the intervention of military might (Schmidt and Loeb A1). Thus sensationalized, the tale was embraced by the American public because it offered, through analogy, a reassuring resolution to the traumatic experience of 11 September 2001.

This chapter examines the Lynch rescue in relation to the ongoing pro-cesses of national regeneration necessitated by the terrorist attacks of 9/11. As Julie Drew has argued, "prevailing narratives of who and what we are, as Americans, took a hit" on 9/11 (71). The process of reconstructing national identity began almost immediately in public discourse following the attacks. Media scholars have shown how breaking news coverage, newspaper editorials, and even advertisements strategically framed the events in ways that made the United States seem to be an innocent victim of a senseless act.[2] Political elites, likewise, decontextualized terrorism, describing it as a "cowardly" act born of "hatred," "jealousy," and "evil," rather than politics (Drew 73). Such rhetoric made "a unified military response" appear to be "the only real alternative to combat future devastation and terror" (Reynolds and Barnett 91). In the process, it also tied national identity and security to notions of masculinity. "Characteristics, actions, and reactions deemed feminine—such as diplomacy, negotiation, and compromise" have been systematically devalued in public discourse since 9/11 in favor of "masculine characteristics of physical strength, punitive response, and violent aggression" (Drew 72). The Lynch rescue dramatically illustrates this process of social reprioritization and provides an occasion for thinking through the consequences of this gendering for U.S. foreign and domestic policy.

By examining documentary and docudramatic representations of the Lynch rescue, including *Saving Private Lynch* (A&E), *Saving POW Lynch* (Discovery), *Primetime's* interview special "Pfc. Jessica Lynch: An American Story" (ABC), and the made-for-TV movie *Saving Jessica Lynch* (NBC), this chapter seeks to illustrate how militarism, masculinity, and national security have become conflated in post-9/11 public discourse and how this fusion has helped legitimate the Bush administration's foreign policy. President George W. Bush has long conceived of the nation as a patriarchal family whose security depends on military strength, but it took 9/11 to convince him that national security could best be pursued through the militarized extension of U.S. hegemony. The goal of this chapter is to illustrate and, hopefully, disrupt the processes of consensus formation sustaining this counterintuitive security policy, for the use of war to achieve peace only spreads insecurity and guarantees the political marginalization of those who fail to embody the ideals of masculinity authorized by security discourse.

GENDER AND NATIONAL SECURITY IN THE (NEO)CONSERVATIVE MIND

Historically, ideas about masculinity have encouraged political elites in the United States to associate security with military strength and to avoid thinking about the physical and emotional consequences of war (Enloe 126). This association has not happened by accident; rather, it is a function of the gendered symbolic system used to interpret U.S. foreign relations. As feminist scholar Carol Cohn has shown, national security discourse depends on a gendered hierarchy of values that privileges "masculine" traits such as rationality, competition, and aggression over "feminine" ones such as emotionality, cooperation, and conciliation ("War, Wimps" 229). As with most binaries, the value of the first term is dependent on the devaluation of the second. The defense analysts Cohn studied, for example, used sexual imagery to police group identity, describing nuclear war as a "pissing contest" ("Sex and Death" 60) and labeling those who questioned the necessity or effects of war as "pussies," "fags," or "women" ("War, Wimps" 235–36). Such derogatory invocations of femininity and homosexuality permit the disavowal of vulnerability, which is necessary to make the work of calculating human destruction psychologically bearable (Cohn, "Sex and Death" 57). However, it also associates militarism with omnipotence and makes war seem like a guarantee of security rather than a threat to it.

This specialized discourse of security has filtered out "to the military, politicians, and the public, and increasingly shapes how we talk and think about war" (Cohn, "War, Wimps" 228). Conservatives in particular (though not exclusively) have favored this view of militarism as the route to security because their value system already conceives of the nation as a patriarchal family requiring masculine protection (Lakoff 65). When the end of the Cold War deprived the United States of a clear rationale for an activist foreign policy, conservatives did not abandon their priorities; rather, they searched for a new rationale. As early as 1992, Paul Wolfowitz, then undersecretary of defense for policy, drafted a defense planning guidance memo advocating the militarized extension of U.S. hegemony as a means of guaranteeing global security. The best defense, he argued, was a good offense (Bacevich 43–44). He and other prominent neoconservatives, including William Kristol, Robert Kagan, Elliott Abrams, Richard Perle, and Donald Rumsfeld, formed a think tank called the Project for the New American Century to press this agenda. They invoked the gendered language of national security to naturalize their positions. For example, they warned that President Clinton's multilateral containment strategy for Iraq left the United States "weak," "helpless," and "dependent" on the goodwill of European allies (Kagan 24; Project for the New American Century A21). They described the United States as a "cowering superpower" and announced that "only violence . . . may recoup the damage that the [British] Labour Party, Bill Clinton, and the Near East Bureau of the State Department have done to America's standing" in the Middle East (Gerecht 29). Weakness, helplessness, dependence, and fear are characteristics associated in U.S. culture with femininity; hence militarized masculinity (violence) is viewed as the only possible antidote to the nation's "feminization." George W. Bush has not only incorporated a number of these individuals into his administration; he has also embraced a number of their ideas.

Even before 9/11, President Bush viewed national identity and security in terms of competing definitions of masculinity. In his first major foreign policy speech, "A Distinctly American Internationalism," he described the Clinton administration's security strategy as promiscuous and, therefore, insufficiently masculine. By "multiplying missions" without regard to the nation's "vital interests," the Clinton administration "squander[ed] American will and drain[ed] American energy." Like sexual potency, Bush implied, military potency is undermined by overuse. Clinton's preference for diplomacy, moreover, made the United States appear "soft." "There are limits to the smiles and scowls of diplomacy," Bush warned, "armies and missiles are not stopped by stiff notes of condemnation. They are held in check by strength and purpose and the promise of swift punishment." Bush offered voters a vision of renewed national vigor guaranteed through Victorian restraint. The United States would "[encourage] stability from a position of strength" but, like a good patriarch, would be "modest" and "humble" about its use of force to conserve that strength. Clearly, Bush had not fully embraced the hegemonic agenda of the neoconservatives prior to 9/11, but he did share their view of security as defined by militarized masculinity. This shared perspective made the transition to an offensive security strategy relatively easy to achieve once terrorist attacks exposed the alleged dangers of national "feminization."

REMASCULINIZATION AS A PUBLIC NECESSITY POST 9/11

Within public discourse, the 9/11 terrorist attacks were depicted in gendered terms that reinforced and extended the Bush administration's extant assumptions about national identity and security. Breaking news coverage of the events set the tone by describing the attacks as "acts of war" directed at an "innocent America" rather than a geopolitically entangled United States. Reporters proclaimed Americans "united" behind the idea that the only "just" response would be violent retribution (Reynolds and Barnett 91). Later news reports and eyewitness accounts described the attacks in terms of a "violation" and emphasized the generalized nature of feelings of fear, vulnerability, and helplessness. Images of men, even soldiers at the Pentagon, screaming, running, and crying were particularly evocative of this sense of violation, for they also violated cultural perceptions of stoic masculinity. This "discursive construction of the polis as far more pervasively feminine than was previously understood" (Drew 72) implicitly corroborated the neoconservative assumption that "weakness is provocative" (Secretary of State Donald Rumsfeld quoted in Bacevich 84). Like the word *violated,* this statement links the terrorist attacks to rape and implies that the United States "got what it deserved" on 9/11 because it dressed improperly; its power was not sufficiently manifest.

The construction of the nation as overly feminized not only encouraged the Bush administration to embrace a military response in this instance; it also facilitated the administration's adoption of the neoconservative strategy for U.S. hegemony. The 2002 "National Security Strategy Statement," a virtual replica of the 1992 Wolfowitz memo (Bacevich 45), left no doubt that the nation's security would be vested in the military and that this remilitarization would also entail a remasculinization of national identity. The document is also exceedingly candid about what this strategy implies for others since the key to securing the homeland is to create military "forces strong enough to dissuade potential adversaries from pursuing a military build-up in hopes of surpassing, or equaling, the power of the United States." In other words, to ensure that U.S. potency cannot be challenged, every other nation must be effectively castrated.

ORIENTALISM AND THE WAR ON TERRORISM

The war on terrorism has provided the ideological framework necessary to depict U.S. hegemonic aspirations as a form of altruistic self-sacrifice undertaken in the name of high ideals: the spread of "freedom, democracy, and free enterprise" and the rescue of "civilization" ("National Security Strategy"). Orientalist assumptions about race and gender structure the opposition between civilization and barbarity in this discourse in ways that preclude the possibility of Arabs and Arab societies acting on their own behalf to secure these freedoms. Instead, action is reserved for the U.S. military, which must save Arab societies from themselves.

Edward Said defines Orientalism as a "style of thought" predicated on the distinction between the West (the Occident) and the East (the Orient). The Orient is both a material space and an imaginary construct whose purpose is to give coherence to the image of the West by serving as "its contrasting image, idea, personality, experience" (Said 2). Specifically, Orientalism seeks to identify the West with civilization by coding the East as barbaric. Again, gender assumptions structure the dichotomy. Orientalism "collaps[es] non-Europeans and women into an undifferentiated field" and understands "the East . . . as the site of passivity and irrationality, awaiting the conquest by the masculine and rational West" (Volpp 154). Western colonization of the Orient has been justified historically through the invocation of "women in need of uplift." Indeed, the project of European empire was virtually defined by "white men saving brown women from brown men" (Spivak 297).

Taking a page from this imperial playbook, the Bush administration has characterized the invasions of Afghanistan and Iraq as rescue missions. Barely a month after the 9/11 attacks, for example, First Lady Laura Bush delivered a presidential radio address elaborating the plight of Afghan women under the Taliban. She proclaimed "the fight against terrorism" to be "a fight for the rights and dignity of women" and implied that the pending invasion was a moral duty that the United States should undertake in the name of "civilized people throughout the world" (L. Bush 250). A similar rhetorical strategy was adopted to legitimate Operation Iraqi Freedom. Even though Iraqi men were the main targets of state violence under Saddam Hussein, President Bush has insistently focused on the rape of women, implying it was common, indiscriminate, and somehow more tragic than the torture of men. In public speeches regarding the invasion, he often invokes torture as a specifically female experience: "every *woman* in Iraq is better off because the rape rooms and torture chambers of Saddam Hussein are forever closed" (G. W. Bush, "Bush's Opening Statement"; emphasis added). This emphasis on women facilitates the Orientalist confusion of the war in Iraq with the war on terrorism, casting Hussein as a terrorist merely for having oppressed and persecuted women.

The manly application of retributive violence will rescue not just Arab women but whole Arab societies, which have been feminized by their leaders. Military dictatorships and theocratic tyrants have left individuals in the Middle East "victims and subjects" rather than "citizens," Bush claims. Therefore, it is the moral duty of the United States, as the leader of the civilized world, to rescue these victims. In the case of Iraq, the whole society was depicted as cowed into passivity and in need of salvation, which may be why U.S. military planners assumed the troops would be greeted as liberators. The gendered discourse of national security, abetted by Orientalist thinking, thus legitimated the invasion as a vital rescue mission undertaken in the name of civilization.

DOMESTICATING FOREIGN POLICY: THE LYNCH DOCUMENTARIES

The conflation of militarism, masculinity, and security reached its apotheosis in media depictions of the rescue of Pfc. Jessica Lynch. Documentaries about the rescue fetishize Lynch's femininity and vulnerability in order to remasculinize a coed military and militarize the identities of civilian men and women in ways that will perpetuate the project of hegemony. Using melodramatic techniques reminiscent of captivity narratives from the colonial era, these documentaries personalize the political and make Lynch's recovery seem to be a matter of family honor. As in most captivity narratives, gender, race, sex, and class assumptions are invoked to police the boundaries of communal identity, excluding those deemed "Other" and justifying the use of violence by coding it as defensive.[3] The documentaries transform Lynch from a soldier at war to a symbol of the American family under attack in order to authorize

Discovery Channel

Symbolic imagery connotes the representatively "American" status of the community of Wirt County, West Virginia.

the U.S. mission in Iraq and elicit popular consent for the ongoing project of U.S. hegemony.

As a small, young, blond, white female from rural America whose visibly broken body renders her completely dependent on the kindness of strangers, Jessica Lynch fits the role of damsel in distress perfectly (Kumar 300). A&E's documentary *Saving Private Lynch* acknowledges as much in its opening monologue: "[her dramatic story] has all the ingredients of a Hollywood movie with its heroes, suspense, the rescue of a young woman in captivity and a bittersweet ending." Rushed to production just eighteen days after the rescue, this documentary follows the paths of the three female soldiers of the 507th Maintenance Unit as they encounter different "fates," but it focuses most intently on Lynch, who is repeatedly referred to as "the blond nineteen-year-old from Palestine, West Virginia." As this description makes clear, Lynch is selected for media stardom over the other candidates—Lori Piestewa, a Hopi Indian from Arizona, and Shoshana Johnson, an African American from Texas—because her race, age, and background identify her with the American heartland and connote the maximum vulnerability.

Both the Lynch biography and the television depictions of her story invoke her roots in West Virginia to create a particular image of the American homeland. Absent Lynch herself, her hometown becomes the center of media attention, evoking "traditional family values." Such values equate national identity with notions of blood and soil and privilege filiation over affiliation in defining citizenship. For example, biographer Rick Bragg writes that Lynch's "kin believe she is alive, in part, because she comes from this place [West Virginia], because she has the right blood in her. . . . Even though she is small and a little prissy, she carries the blood of the mountains—the blood of people who fought and worked and loved here" (15). If Lynch is a pioneering American spirit, this passage implies, her defining qualities are inherited, not learned.

Discovery Channel

Rescue footage provided by the Department of Defense reinforces the image of Lynch as a passive subject in her own story.

A perception of Palestine as uniquely, timelessly, and exclusively American— despite, or perhaps because of, its foreign-sounding name[4]—also pervades the documentaries. For example, *Primetime*'s "Pfc. Jessica Lynch: An American Story" uses frequent aerial shots of the hillsides of Wirt County to connote the tight-knit quality of the community. It also obsessively focuses on the symbols of patriotism displayed in the county—American flags, yellow ribbons, prayer vigils, and support rallies that culminate in the playing of country singer Lee Greenwood's "Proud to Be an American." This exclusive yet reassuring image of national identity conforms to the Bush administration's own conception of the homeland as a vulnerable community in need of militarized protection.

The documentary representations of the ambush and rescue also facilitate the conflation of militarism, masculinity, and security. First, the documentaries fetishize Lynch's femininity and vulnerability so as to reassert traditional gender norms challenged by the presence of women in the military. As Bill Kurtis acknowledges, "The reality of a volunteer army where women are equal partners hits Americans hard" (*Saving Private Lynch*). Lynch's hyperfemininity allays popular anxieties about such gender insubordination. The television documentaries all refer to Lynch's hair color, eye color, stature, and youth because these characteristics make her clearly and safely a "girl." Lynch is also "'rhetorically stripped' of her military identity" (Howard and Prividera 96) by announcers who refer to her as "Jessica" and feature photos of her in civilian, rather than military, clothing: her senior class portrait, a picture of her posing by a tree outside the family home, and, most importantly, shots of her as a begowned Miss Congeniality at the Wirt County Fair. The narratives also take care to explain that Lynch joined the army only to help pay for college, not as a feminist statement. Her dreams for her life are modest and stereotypically feminine: she wants to settle in Wirt County and become a housewife and kindergarten teacher.

In addition to being "small" and "prissy" (Bragg 15), Lynch is utterly in-capacitated by her injuries; she cannot help herself and so must be helped by others. This passivity activates cultural assumptions that portray women as weak and vulnerable while men are strong and protective. The rescue footage pro-vided by the Department of Defense and incorporated into the documentaries reinforces these assumptions by literalizing the classic Hollywood mandate: men act; women appear (Mulvey 62–63). While the camera focuses obsessively on Lynch's face during the evacuation, the shot obscures all but the moving arms and legs of her male rescuers. Her immobility is thus contrasted with their hypermobility. Like a Hollywood starlet, Lynch facilitates the movement of the masculine narrative of war through her passivity. Her *need* for rescue provides the U.S. military with the excuse to exercise its manly might.

Because Lynch embodies the homeland and its values, her personal vulner-ability evokes the nation's vulnerability and makes remilitarization appear the only viable means to achieve security. The documentaries implicitly link the ambush in Nasariyah to the terrorist attacks of 9/11, both of which are imagined as unmotivated crimes perpetrated against innocents. The noncombat status of Lynch's unit is vital to this construction, as is her status as an all-American girl next door. *Primetime* makes the implicit explicit by opening the segment about her captivity with bucolic shots of her family home and the voice-over narration: "West Virginia, terror strikes the Lynch family at home!" ("Pfc. Jessica Lynch"). Recalling the discursive framing of 9/11, this invocation of a vulnerable domestic sphere incites spectators to identify with the need for a militarized security solution. Lynch's status as all-American girl deepens this commitment, for if she is imagined as "everyone's sister or daughter, . . . her enemies [become] ours. In the process of identifying with a soldier, the public [is] invited to consent to the US's goals" in the Middle East and elsewhere (Kumar 304).

Finally, the documentaries aid in the process of consensus formation by exaggerating Lynch's personal vulnerability. They do so in two ways: by specu-lating about the nature of her experience in captivity and by casting her as a fish out of water in Iraq. The documentaries virtually obsess about the danger to women posed by combat duty. Referring to the videos of the five POWs from the 507th Maintenance Unit aired on Al-Jazeera, Bill Kurtis contends, "The sight of women being held is startling to Americans. What seems to worry people most are the accounts of the torture of POWs who were held by Iraqis during the first Persian Gulf War" (*Saving Private Lynch*). This statement is followed almost immediately by references to Colonel Rhonda Cornham, who was molested by an Iraqi soldier during the Gulf War after her helicopter crashed in the desert. Each of the documentaries contains a similar sequence, and all of them mention Cornham's story. None of them mentions the story of Specialist Melissa Rathbun-Nealy, who was also captured during that war but did not suffer sexual abuse (Howard and Prividera).

Such selective attention illustrates how assumptions about female vulnerability are constructed, rather than reflected, by the media. Lacking access to information about Lynch's injuries, the documentaries simply assume that she was violated in captivity. For example, the Discovery Channel's *Saving POW Lynch* claims, "It is unclear whether she sustained her injuries while she desperately fought for her life during the ambush or during her captivity." We now know that her injuries were the result of a Humvee crash, but the suggestion that she was violated lingers nevertheless. Even Diane Sawyer's *Primetime* interview with Lynch, which occurred seven months after the rescue, contains such speculation: "In addition to the wounds that we know about," Sawyer says, "there may have been another wound, so brutal that there's nothing that can reach into her memory and make it real." Sawyer notes that Lynch's army medical file shows she *may* have been sodomized. Although the language of the report is hesitant and contradicted by Lynch's Iraqi doctors, *Primetime* sanctions the rape scenario by ending on Rick Bragg's firm assertion of support for the military version. Such innuendo constructs Lynch as vulnerable and transforms her from American soldier to ordinary woman. It relocates American identity in the private sphere and depicts that sphere as constitutively susceptible to attack, the better to legitimate the perceived need for militarized masculinity.

The documentaries also construct Lynch's vulnerability by depicting her as alienated and alone in Iraq, a stranger in a strange land. As a narrative frame, this motif clarifies the difference between the foreign and the domestic, "them" and "us," and effectively justifies "our" anxieties about "them." The Iraqi landscape is always depicted, for example, as not merely unfamiliar but otherworldly. *Primetime* begins its discussion of the ambush by having Lynch read portions of the following passage from her biography: "It was flat, dull and yellow-brown, except where the water had turned the dust to reddish paste. She got excited when she saw a tree. Trees made sense. She had grown up in the woods, where the solid walls of hardwood had sunk roots deep in the hillsides and kept the ground pulled tight, as it should be, to the planet. All this empty space and loose, shifting sand unsettled her mind and made her feel lost, long before she found out it was true" (Bragg 8). The American homeland, the passage implies, is fixed, familiar, and solid, like a planet "should be," while Iraq is empty, irregular, and inscrutable. Because the treeless, red dust landscape seems more like Mars than Earth, the Iraqis are implicitly likened to aliens. The contrast is heightened by the strategy of intercutting that juxtaposes West Virginia and Iraq to emphasize Lynch's representative Americanness. For instance, *Saving POW Lynch* (Discovery) and *Saving Private Lynch* (A&E) both juxtapose file footage of random, chaotic combat scenes in Iraq with placid pictures of Lynch in civilian clothes. Such intercutting not only distances Lynch from her military identity and heightens the illusion of her victimization but also implies that chaos is the norm in Iraq. The conspicuous absence of shots of Iraqi civilians performing the ordinary tasks of everyday life enhances the impression that violence is endemic to Iraq. In contrast, lavish attention is paid to Lynch's private life and family, their routines, and especially their personal faith.

Melodramatic techniques used to heighten the identification with Lynch further distance the audience from the Iraqis. For example, *Primetime* repeatedly blurs the focus to invoke the "fog of war," suturing the audience into the "ambush" scene and inviting its members to interpret the scene as a terrorist attack. The depiction of the assault on the convoy mimics the chaotic experience of war: fragmented combat sounds and syncopated martial music punctuate a dizzying montage of trucks sticking in sand, Humvees whizzing by, and explosions ripping the air. The sentence fragments that constitute Diane Sawyer's voice-over enhance the perception of urgency by suggesting a paucity of both words and time to describe the barbarism of the Iraqis: "her brutal injuries, the missing hours, what doctors say about a sexual assault." The other documentaries adopt similar strategies, using random combat footage to convey the meaning of "ambush" and addressing the audience directly to facilitate an identification with the experience: "Imagine if your daughter or son were over in Iraq, and you got word that they were taken prisoner of war" (*Saving POW Lynch*). These melodramatic techniques accomplish an astounding reversal of fortune, as the United States becomes the victim of a war it initiated. Moreover, the "ambush" is coded as an attack not just on the 507th Maintenance Unit but on the entire domestic U.S. population and specifically as an invasion of the family home. Thus, preemptive military action is made to seem like a form of self-defense, both necessary and inevitable to ensure the security of the nation and its families.

If Lynch's vulnerability cries out for a heroic rescue, her status as a passive spectator at the event mirrors the status of the television viewer watching the war from the safety of home. The analogy positions audience members to embrace a military identity as a means of preempting their own anxieties about increased globalization and the terrorism it facilitates. All the documentaries

NBC

A flashback highlights the difference between the familiar and familial landscape of West Virginia and the alien and alienating landscape of Iraq in NBC's *Saving Jessica Lynch*.

foreground the first exchange between Lynch and her rescuers and read her willingness to claim a military identity as a sign of her courage. When the U.S. commandos first burst into Lynch's hospital room, they reportedly said, "Jessica Lynch, we are United States soldiers come to take you home." Lynch responded, "I'm an American soldier, too." *Saving Private Lynch* consults several experts in military psychology who all agree that such affirmation "means that she viewed herself, even in her vulnerable state, still as a warrior." In fact, Lynch perceives herself as a survivor, not a hero or a soldier ("Pfc. Jessica Lynch"). Yet her explicit rejection of the hero mantle has failed to register because, in the post-9/11 context, survival has become its own form of heroism (Freda 232). Ordinary Americans, particularly the spouses and children of the victims of 9/11, have been lauded in popular culture merely for carrying on with their lives. President Bush has argued that the best way to defeat terrorism is to "live your lives and hug your children," to go shopping and visit Disney World (G. W. Bush, "Address" 242). The real value of the Lynch rescue for U.S. foreign policy thus lies in its mingling of mundanity and heroism, domestic identity and military identity. Her rescue brings the war home and codes everyone as a potential hero in the fight against terrorism. These documentaries ensure that, like Lynch herself, no one will be left behind in the war on terrorism.

U.S. HEGEMONY AS CIVILIZING MISSION: NBC'S *SAVING JESSICA LYNCH*

The patriarchal assumptions structuring the Lynch rescue narrative also reproduce the Orientalist assumptions used to legitimate U.S. aggression as a defense of civilization against a barbaric Arab Other. The NBC made-for-TV-movie version of Lynch's rescue, *Saving Jessica Lynch,* provides the most elaborate example of this process of Othering, for the construction of Lynch's identity is always relative to the projection of an Iraqi menace. Deepa Kumar argues that the film at least attempts to distinguish between "good" and "bad" Iraqis by incorporating images of Iraqi heroism (309). Unfortunately, "goodness" is still defined by an identification with things American. Thus, the presence of "good brown characters" does not seriously challenge the Orientalist dichotomy of the film or the mission it legitimates. Despite being based on the account of the rescue provided by Mohammed al-Rehaief, the Iraqi lawyer who reported Lynch's whereabouts to the marines, the film is a study in the demonization of Arabs. Its agenda is to affirm a consensual American identity by offering the public a clear and undifferentiated image of the enemy. Both narratively and visually, the film manipulates extant race and gender codes to transform individual Iraqis into an alien mass recognizable as barbaric so that "we" may appear civilized.

Like the documentaries, the movie presents Lynch as an American innocent abroad, lost and alone in a strange environment. The opening credit sequence establishes Lynch's dislocation by fetishizing her race and size. The titles roll over images of a U.S. convoy in inexorable motion with a tiny Lynch (Laura Regan) driving an outsized truck into an infinite horizon. These shots convey a sense that Lynch is already out of place—her social place—before a sandstorm halts the convoy and literally disorients the unit. A conversation between Lynch and her comrades Lori Piestewa (Chrystle Lightening) and Shoshana Johnson (Denise Lee) during the brief rest reinforces this perception by contrasting the self-evidently American Lynch to Piestewa, a Hopi Indian from Tuba City, Arizona. Lynch looks around at the wasteland and sees nothing familiar. Piestewa looks around and says, "You know I grew up on land like this. Joined the army just to get away from it." Lynch insists, "You can't get any further from Arizona than this," but Piestewa replies, "I don't know." Although this exchange might be viewed as a sly critique of U.S. race relations, which have made Indians like Piestewa feel alienated from their native land, the exchange also—and more importantly—affirms Lynch's innocence about such relations as representatively American. Shortly after this exchange, Lynch stares curiously at a group of nomads and camels silhouetted against the desert sky. Intercutting is again used to emphasize the distance between the home Lynch knows and the desert she finds herself in, as the camels fade into shots of verdant West Virginia scenery. A brief montage depicts Lynch's farewell to Palestine and concludes with her father's voice telling her to "remember where you came from" and ordering her to "come home." Home is presented as a place with clear boundaries and stable content. Iraq, in contrast, is represented as inscrutable: its sand-covered roads and invisible berms entrap the military vehicles, and its combatants are indistinguishable from its civilians.

The depiction of Lynch as a naïve traveler is enhanced by the choice to present the ambush from Lynch's perspective using a subjective angle. Lynch becomes the eyes of the audience, and her gaze organizes the sequence into a pseudonarrative whereby the Iraqis fuse into a single menacing entity. When the convoy enters Nasariyah, for example, a point-of-view shot shows Iraqi civilians staring menacingly at the convoy. They talk among themselves, but only in Arabic, which Lynch cannot understand. Since she does not know what they are saying, she assumes it is negative: "So much for the celebrating," she remarks. The Iraqis are generally denied the benefit of a return shot, which means they are objects to be looked at, not subjects capable of returning the gaze. A shot of a mother and her child watching the convoy, for example, slides off the screen before the camera returns to Lynch.

One exception is the man who organizes the ambush. Lynch first sees him riding in the backseat of a passing car. At the point where the vehicles cross, the sequence goes into slow motion, and the two characters lock eyes. A shot-reverse-shot sequence depicts him as powerful enough to return her gaze. Lynch's imperial perspective is effectively undone by his look, and from that point on, Lynch and her compatriots become victims rather than conquerors. When the ambush begins, the man assumes narrative control, striding down the street with an AK-47 on his hip as if challenging the trucks to a duel. Lynch becomes utterly disoriented. She does not fire her weapon or even attempt to; instead, she looks around frantically, trying to find something to fix her gaze on. Her commander even enjoins her to "stay focused," but her eyes register nothing but panic (indeed, Lynch's sole function in this scene is to manifest terror). Her loss of subjectivity is confirmed by her lack of dialogue; during the last hour of the film she has only six brief lines. Thus, she literally becomes "an object about which stories [are] told" (Kumar 310).

The subjective camera portrays the Americans as victims of a brutal and unwarranted Iraqi assault. Swish pans and special effects incorporate the audience into the chaos by mimicking the exchange of gunfire. The Humvee crash is also depicted from the inside, heightening the identification with its military occupants. The Iraqi assailants, meanwhile, are depicted as inhumane zealots. For example, one gleeful Iraqi fires his rifle into the cab of an overturned truck, shouting "Allah, Allah" and waving his gun in the air in triumph. The celebration is captured in slow motion to emphasize its inhumanity. The un-named fedayeen colonel (Navid Negahban) who takes charge of the prisoners after the ambush is the ultimate embodiment of Iraqi cruelty. His power over

NBC

"Bad" Arabs are portrayed as ruthless, brutal, and inhumane. U.S. soldiers are depicted as being subject to their mercy, which seems arbitrary.

the Americans is affirmed by the extreme camera angles used to depict the surrender of Sergeant James Riley (Dak Rashetta). A shaking Riley kneels in the dirt and begins to announce his name, rank, and serial number, according to the Geneva Conventions. As he does so, the camera looks over his shoulder and up at the fedayeen colonel, enhancing the colonel's stature. Riley is then knocked down. The colonel is also depicted from a low angle as he crouches over Lynch's broken body and says, somewhat sarcastically, "Welcome to my country." Lynch immediately blacks out, and a disembodied scream provides the bridge to the next scene. The implication is that the colonel has done something to harm Lynch. Because the colonel and the leader of the ambush are the only Iraqis to achieve individuation at this point, they come to represent all Iraqis. The civilian dress of the ambush leader even implies that ordinary Iraqis are really fedayeen in disguise. Thus, the entire society is demonized for the brutality of Saddam Hussein's specially trained military units. The attempt to convey Lynch's sense of disorientation subjectively, for example, by blacking out when she does and filtering the screen to indicate a drugged state, makes even the doctors and nurses who care for her appear menacing and evil.

The depiction of Mohammed al-Rehaief (Nicholas Guilak) reaffirms, rather than challenges, the Orientalist portrayal of the Iraqi people as an undifferentiated, menacing mass. He is, after all, clearly distinguished from the other Iraqis through his association with American popular culture and family values. His identification with a paternal, militarized masculinity effectively deracializes him, enabling him and his family to be folded into the realm of "civilization." From his first appearance, al-Rehaief is explicitly contrasted with the fedayeen and their barbaric values. When told by a nurse not

NBC

Mohammed al-Rehaief becomes a "good" Arab through his identification with American popular culture and American family values. His reward is to ride off into the sunset in classic John Wayne style.

to go down a particular hallway because the fedayeen "are interrogating an American prisoner of war," al-Rehaief replies, "Do you know what I just saw? I saw them drag my neighbor . . . through the streets. Do you know what her crime was? She waved, waved, at a U.S. Army helicopter, so I know who the fedayeen are." When al-Rehaief does venture down the hallway, he allegedly witnesses Lynch being slapped by one of the interrogators (Lynch and her doctors both claim this incident never occurred). His reaction is paternal: "She's just a girl, a child." Such paternalism identifies him with the Americans, who view their incursion into Iraq as a benevolent mission of salvation, and, like the Americans, he vows to rescue the helpless Lynch. That this reaction is not "Iraqi" is illustrated by his wife's disapproval: "There are millions of her [Lynch's] countrymen marching on our country right now . . . the Americans have made this into a new crusade. They are ruining our country." In response to her political perspective on the war, al-Rehaief invokes the value of kinship: "When I look at that girl, I see our daughter."

Later, al-Rehaief's wife blames his mother for having "poisoned [his] mind with all of those John Wayne movies." His association with American popular culture, and with the militarized masculinity of Wayne, in particular, makes al-Rehaief acceptable as the "star" of what becomes a rescue narrative. His alienation from his Iraqi identity is completed when he goes to find the marines and gets lost in his own land. This disorientation makes him structurally analogous to Lynch, which also makes him worthy of salvation. The film concludes, appropriately enough, with the double rescues of Lynch from Saddam General Hospital and of al-Rehaief and his family from Iraq. The redemption of Lynch thus facilitates the redemption of al-Rehaief, which in turn redeems the U.S. mission. By filtering its narrative through an Orientalist prism, the film characterizes the invasion as a benevolent "civilizing mission" designed to save barbarous Others from themselves.

The invocation of patriarchal race and gender norms in the video re-creations of the rescue of Jessica Lynch enables both the remasculinization of the military and the remilitarization of foreign policy. By foregrounding Lynch's femininity, passivity, and vulnerability, the videos invite Americans to embrace militarized masculinity as the only logical antidote to national insecurity. The videos illustrate how public discourse after 9/11 has reconstructed national identity in ways that naturalize and extend a conservative view of the nation and of national security. By popularizing the conception of the nation as a family in need of masculine providence and protection, such discourse has also made palatable the neoconservative philosophy of security.

It is important to understand how gender assumptions frame notions of security because discursive constructions have consequences. The Bush administration has used public enthusiasm for its conservative foreign policy to push through conservative domestic policies as well. As Drew notes, the administration's "budget priorities and legislative initiatives . . . disproportion-ately target women, children, the poor and citizens of color" (76). Tax cuts, for example, have been enacted at the expense of social welfare programs; federal aid for community assistance has been redirected to "faith-based initiatives," and reproductive rights have been significantly curtailed during Bush's years in office. The situation is even worse for those women "liberated" by the U.S. military in Afghanistan and Iraq. In addition to being virtually excluded from the reconstruction process, they have been targeted by fundamentalist groups struggling with one another and with weaker secular forces for power. In both cases, initial political and social gains have given way to chronic personal in-security and political marginalization.[5]

In Iraq, for example, feminist politicians and political organizations have been excluded from the political process in favor of conservative women's groups willing to subordinate women's rights to national security or Islamic identity. Women have been subjected to kidnapping, rape, and assault and con-fined to their homes or forced to assume the veil to escape being targeted. Basic necessities—food, water, electricity, and health care—are scarce, and education has been disrupted. The situation has become so bad that some Iraqi women now warn their children to behave by shouting, "Quiet, or I'll call democracy" (Zangana). Here is the real danger of continuing to value masculinized tough-ness and militarized hegemony as a means of regenerating national identity and achieving national security. Democracy will become a bogeyman to be

Lynch appears before the House Committee on Oversight and Government Reform, chaired by Henry Waxman (D-Calif.), 24 April 2007.

feared rather than a political ideal to be pursued, and "spreading freedom" will come to look a lot like spreading terror, especially to women.

POSTSCRIPT

On 24 April 2007, four years after her rescue, Jessica Lynch appeared before the House Committee on Oversight and Government Reform to testify about the military's use of her story for propaganda purposes. With grace and aplomb, Lynch once again denied her status as a hero and criticized the administration and the media for substituting "hype" for "truth." "I am still confused as to why they chose to lie and try to make me a legend," she said, "when the real heroics of my fellow soldiers that day were legendary." She went on to celebrate the actions of the soldiers in her unit who stopped to pick up "fellow soldiers in harm's way" and who "actually did fight until the very end." "My hero," she said, "is every American who says 'my country needs me' and answers that call to fight." She concluded by upbraiding the military commanders and the media for underestimating the intelligence of the American public and demeaning the actions of the soldiers in the field by imagining they had to be embellished in order to register as heroic: "The bottom line is the American people are capable of determining their own . . . ideals for heroes, and they don't need to be told elaborate lies. . . . The truth of war is not always easy, but the truth is always more heroic than the hype."[6]

Lynch's testimony was forceful in its condemnation of the military's manipulation of the media for propaganda purposes. Yet her version of the rescue narrative does not differ substantially from the original; it just shifts the locus of heroism from herself to her fellow soldiers. By failing to question the viability of the "hero frame" (she uses the word *hero* seven times during her seven minutes of testimony), Lynch ultimately reinforces the "hype" and makes it more effective because it is less apparently calculated. The center of the war story is still the U.S. soldier, the "noble grunt" who alone is capable of heroism and worthy of empathy (Aufderheide 81). Although no one can blame Lynch for celebrating the heroics of her compatriots, who did in fact show great courage under extreme duress, the use of the hero frame obscures more of the "truth" of war than it reveals. The romanticization of the war hero ultimately depoliticizes the conflict, reducing it to "an emotional drama of embattled individual survival" (Aufderheide 86). Locating the U.S. soldier at the center of the narrative not only marginalizes the other actors in the political drama (diplomatic agents and allies, enemy soldiers, civilian casualties of war, and so forth); it effaces the political context of war entirely. This is not history but melodrama. Such tales are not informative; they are therapeutic (Aufderheide 89). Their purpose is to rehabilitate the U.S. mission in Iraq.

Given the United States' ambiguous motives for invading Iraq, and the ambivalence about continuing the mission four years later, the obsessive focus on the soldier's perspective in documentary and tabloid treatments of the war is not at all surprising. It offers a way of sidestepping moral questions about the necessity, legality, and effects of the war in Iraq. In that sense, it is the logical extension of the practice of media embedding, which, by aligning journalists literally behind the troops, encourages the public to get behind them figuratively. As Tony Grajeda explains, the focus on the "noble grunt" in such coverage, and in the many subsequent documentary treatments of the war in Iraq,[7] creates an "uneven distribution of affect, in which the victimization of 'our boys [and girls]' over there" supplants consideration of the agency of the soldiers in the destruction around them. Indeed, as I have argued, it is the narcissistic focus on the soldier's perspective that enables the U.S. military invasion of Iraq to assume the appearance of an innocent defense (or rescue) of civilization in the first place. This inversion of the real power dynamics (the transformation of an invasion into an ambush) encourages individuals to forget the motives for and effects of U.S. military violence. Thus, the choice to focus on the noble grunt is not politically innocent or lacking in repercussions.

Yet, as the recent hearings into battlefield misinformation illustrate, the political repercussions of the noble-grunt approach are unpredictable.

The reduction of major political events to human-interest stories obviously oversimplifies complex social and political phenomena and, by encouraging cultural amnesia, sets the stage for the future repetition of past mistakes. But focusing on the suffering of the individual soldier in war can backfire as well. When the public perceives that their beloved "heroes" have been mistreated by military and governmental institutions, they can turn against these institutions and their representatives. Political scientist Matthew Baum argues that "soft" coverage of foreign policy crises may even promote isolationism and political apathy among a populace cued by the human-interest frame to interpret events in individualistic terms. The translation of social problems into personal tragedies, he argues, reinforces a belief in the powerlessness of individuals to effect social change (258). The best that can be hoped for in such stories is that the individual will rise above his or her circumstances—or "survive," in the parlance of the noble-grunt tale. The circumstances themselves appear unchangeable, and the idea that institutions or governments can intervene successfully to alter the context of tragedy becomes unthinkable.

Baum's studies document an "inverse relationship between exposure to soft news programming and support for a proactive or multilateral approach to US foreign policy," especially among politically inattentive segments of the population (287). If his studies are correct, then the real danger of the manipulation of stories like Jessica Lynch's is that it will undermine the political will necessary to counter terrorism on a global scale. Tales of heroism obviously tell certain truths about war, but those truths are partial and highly partisan, promoting an uncritical linkage among militarism, masculinity, and national security that nourishes cultural narcissism and leads to self-defeat. A fuller accounting of the effects of the militarization of counterterrorism—on both U.S. soldiers *and* the casualties of U.S. violence—is necessary if the United States hopes to sustain a global coalition willing to address this shared security problem. Hopefully, Representative Henry Waxman's hearings on battlefield misinformation signal the beginning of this difficult but essential process of historical reckoning. The truth of war is not always easy, as Lynch says, but only an honest appraisal of the politics of war can sustain the cooperative relations needed to address the global social problems that inspire acts of terrorism.

NOTES

This essay originally appeared in *Feminist Media Studies* 5.3 (Nov. 2005): 297–310.

1. For an analysis of how this convergence of interests resulted in an exaggerated rescue story, see Kampfner; Ritea; and Sussman.

2. On breaking news coverage, see McDonald and Lawrence and Reynolds and

Barnett. On op-ed pieces, see Lule. On advertising, see Campbell. See also the essays collected in the volumes *Framing Terrorism* (Norris, Kern, and Just) and *Communication and Terrorism* (Greenberg).

3. Melani McAlister and Emily Rosenberg have likewise noted the similarity between the captivity narrative and the Bush administration's rhetorical legitimation of the war in Afghanistan.

4. In a Middle Eastern context, *Palestine* refers to the land now occupied by the countries of Israel and Jordan. On the one hand, the name of the West Virginia town invokes the multicultural character of the nation. It is a reminder of the politics of affiliation that have defined citizenship for most of the nation's history. On the other hand, it invokes the biblical reference to Palestine as the Jewish homeland, which has been used to legitimate Zionist claims to the lands now known as Israel (and to delegitimate the claims of the Arabs living in those territories). Palestine, in this sense, embodies the sense of national identity as a matter of destiny—of blood and soil—rather than political choice. Given the strong support Israel enjoys in the United States, especially among evangelical Christian communities of the type depicted as central to life in Palestine, West Virginia, the latter meaning seems to prevail over the former. Palestine functions, in other words, to naturalize national identity and community as a matter of blood and soil. On support for Israel among evangelical Christians in the United States, see McAlister.

5. For information on the status of both Afghan and Iraqi women's rights post invasion, see the Web site for the international human rights organization MADRE <http://www.madre.org/>.

6. Lynch's testimony can be viewed in its entirety on the CNN Web site <http://www.cnn.com/2007/POLITICS/04/24/tillman.hearing/index.html> or on YouTube <http://www.youtube.com/watch?v=l0OyihqYfF4>.

7. Grajeda analyzes the films *Gunner Palace* (2003) and *Occupation: Dreamland* (2005), but the argument holds for the more recent *War Tapes* (2006) as well. *War Tapes* provides the soldier's view of war, as it was composed using footage shot by soldiers themselves. Reality TV series such as *Profiles from the Front Lines* (ABC) and *Off to War* (Discovery Channel) employ a similar approach, to similar effect. Each of these films or series details the life of a grunt in Afghanistan or Iraq. They "celebrate survival as a form of heroism" and present "cynicism as a form of self-preservation" (Aufderheide 84). They also evacuate the politics of war, even as they permit the cast of soldiers to express a range of political views on the war. In the end, professionalism trumps politics, and war is reduced to a matter of individual perseverance, or "survival."

Works Cited

Aufderheide, Pat. "Good Soldiers." *Seeing through Movies*. Ed. Mark Crispin Miller. New York: Pantheon Books, 1990. 81–111.

Bacevich, Andrew. *American Empire: The Realities and Consequences of U.S. Diplomacy.* Cambridge, Mass.: Harvard UP, 2002.

Baum, Matthew. *Soft News Goes to War: Public Opinion and American Foreign Policy in the New Media Age*. Princeton, N.J.: Princeton UP, 2003.

Bragg, Rick. *I'm a Soldier, Too: The Jessica Lynch Story.* New York: Knopf, 2003.

Bush, George W. "Address to a Joint Session of Congress and the American People (September 20, 2001)." Meyerowitz 241–43.

———. "Bush's Opening Statement: President Opens Third Primetime News Conference with 16-Minute Statement on Iraq Conflict." MSNBC 13 Apr. 2004. <http://msnbc.msn.com/id/4734018/>.

———. "A Distinctly American Internationalism." Speech. 19 Nov. 1999. <http://www.mtholyoke.edu/acad/intrel/ bush/wspeech.htm>.

———. "President Bush Discusses Freedom in Iraq and Middle East: Remarks by the President at the Twentieth Anniversary of the National Endowment for Democracy." Speech. 6 Nov. 2003. <http://www.whitehouse.gov/news/releases/2003/11//20031106–2.html>.

Bush, Laura. "Radio Address on Women in Afghanistan (November 17, 2001)." Meyerowitz 249–50.

Campbell, Christopher. "Commodifying September 11: Advertising, Myth, and Hegemony." Chermak, Bailey, and Brown 47–66.

Chermak, Steven, Frankie Y. Bailey, and Michelle Brown, eds. *Media Representations of September 11.* Westport, Conn.: Praeger, 2003.

Cohn, Carol. "Sex and Death in the Rational World of Defense Intellectuals." *Women on War: An International Anthology of Women's Writings from Antiquity to the Present.* Ed. Daniela Gioseffi. 1987. New York: Feminist Press at City University of New York, 2003. 56–68.

———. "War, Wimps, and Women: Talking Gender and Thinking War." *Gendering War Talk.* Ed. Miriam Cooke and Angela Woollacott. Princeton, N.J.: Princeton UP, 1993. 227–46.

Drew, Julie. "Identity Crisis: Gender, Public Discourse and 9/11." *Women & Language* 27 (2004): 71–78.

Enloe, Cynthia. *The Curious Feminist: Searching for Women in a New Age of Empire.* Berkeley: U of California P, 2004.

Freda, Isabelle. "Survivors in the West Wing: 9/11 and the United States of Emergency." *Film and Television after 9/11.* Ed. Wheeler Winston Dixon. Carbondale: Southern Illinois UP, 2004. 226–46.

Gerecht, Reuel Marc. "A Cowering Superpower." *Weekly Standard* 30 July 2001: 26–29.

Grajeda, Tony. "The Winning and Losing of Hearts and Minds: Vietnam, Iraq, and the Claims of the War Documentary." *Jump Cut* 49 (2007). <http://www.ejumpcut.org/currentissue/Grajeda/text.html>.

Greenberg, Bradley S., ed. *Communication and Terrorism: Public and Media Responses to 9/11.* Cresskill, N.J.: Hampton P, 2002.

Howard, John, and Laura Prividera. "Rescuing Patriarchy or Saving 'Jessica Lynch': The Rhetorical Construction of the American Woman Soldier." *Women & Language* 27.2 (2004): 89–98.

Kagan, Robert. "Saddam's Impending Victory." *Weekly Standard* 2 Feb. 1998: 22–25.

Kampfner, John. "The Truth about Jessica." *Guardian* 15 May 2003. <http://www.guardian.co.uk/Iraq/Story/0,2763,956255,00.html>.

Kumar, Deepa. "War Propaganda and the (Ab)Uses of Women: Media Constructions of the Jessica Lynch Story." *Feminist Media Studies* 4.3 (2004): 297–313.

Lakoff, George. *Moral Politics: How Liberals and Conservatives Think*. 2nd ed. Chicago: U of Chicago P, 2002.

Lule, Jack. "Myth and Terror on the Editorial Page: The *New York Times* Responds to September 11, 2001." *Journal of Mass Communication Quarterly* 79.2 (2002): 275–93.

McAlister, Melani. "A Cultural History of the War without End." Meyerowitz 94–116.

McDonald, Ian, and Regina G. Lawrence. "Filling the 24 × 7 News Hole: Television News Coverage Following September 11." *American Behavioral Scientist* 48.3 (2004): 327–41.

Meyerowitz, Joanne, ed. *History and September 11*. Philadelphia: Temple UP, 2003.

Mulvey, Laura. "Visual Pleasure and Narrative Cinema." *Feminist Film Theory: A Classical Reader*. Ed. Sue Thornham. New York: New York UP, 1999. 58–69.

"National Security Strategy Statement." 2002. <http://www.whitehouse.gov/nsc/nssall.html>.

Norris, Pippa, Montague Kern, and Marion Just, eds. *Framing Terrorism: The News Media, the Government and the Public*. New York: Routledge, 2003.

"Pfc. Jessica Lynch: An American Story." *Primetime*. ABC, 2003.

The Project for the New American Century. "Speaking of Iraq." *New York Times* 27 Jan. 1998: A21.

Reynolds, Amy, and Brooke Barnett. "'America under Attack': CNN's Verbal and Visual Framing of September 11." Chermak, Bailey, and Brown 85–102.

Ritea, Steve. "Jessica Lynch's Story: A Little Too Perfect?" *American Journalism Review* (Aug.–Sept. 2003). <http://www.ajr.org/article_printable.asp? id=3091>

Rosenberg, Emily. "Rescuing Women and Children." Meyerowitz 81–93.

Said, Edward. *Orientalism*. Berkeley: U of California P, 1978.

Saving Jessica Lynch. NBC, 2003.

Saving POW Lynch. Discovery Channel, 2003.

Saving Private Lynch. Perf. Bill Kurtis. A&E, 2003.

Schmidt, Susan, and Vernon Loeb. "She Was Fighting to the Death." *Washington Post* 3 Apr. 2003: A1.

Spivak, Gayatri. "Can the Subaltern Speak?" *Marxism and the Interpretation of Culture*. Ed. Cary Nelson and Lawrence Grossberg. Chicago: U of Illinois P, 1988. 271–313.

Sussman, Peter. "Rescuing Private Lynch—and Rescuing Journalism: The Pressure for a Compelling Story Can Eclipse the Actual News." *Quill* (Nov. 2003).

Volpp, Leti. "The Citizen and the Terrorist." *September 11 in History: A Watershed Moment?* Ed. Mary Dudziak. Durham, N.C.: Duke UP, 2003. 147–62.

Zangana, Haifa. "Quiet, or I'll Call Democracy." *Guardian Unlimited* 22 Dec. 2004. <http://www.guardian.co.uk/comment/story/0,3604,1378411,00.html>.

REPRESENTING THE UNREPRESENTABLE

9/11 on Film and Television

It is surely not a coincidence that French film theorist André Bazin wrote some of his most famous and lasting works about the nature of the cinema during the last calendar year of World War II. Bazin's argument that "photography and the cinema . . . are discoveries that satisfy, once and for all and in its very essence, our obsession with realism" (12) came directly on the heels of a seemingly apocalyptic world war, the vast horrors of which were captured and preserved in various forms of moving and still photography. Bazin's theories about the mechanical nature of the cinema suggest a direct link between the images captured and their objects—a connection that, in his words, "embalms time." In this view, the images of actual catastrophic events, especially moving images, carry a special charge—a remnant of the event itself.

This charge is particularly true of the video images of the terrorist attacks on the World Trade Center on 11 September 2001, an event that ranks among the most documented national traumas in U.S. history. The phrase "It was just like a movie" has been used to describe not only the hyperreal images of the jetliners crashing into the buildings but also the scene on the ground in the aftermath, which some witnesses described as looking just like a movie set teeming with cameras and chaos. The world has seen these images over and over again, from virtually every angle imaginable, played and replayed ad infinitum and, perhaps, ad nauseam. Even the first plane hitting the North Tower, which many thought had gone unrecorded, has serendipitously shown up in three different videos.[1]

All this imagery with which we are so familiar resides in the realm of actuality—recorded footage of the actual event. But what would happen if that event were to be re-created for the camera? What happens to 9/11 imagery, so ubiquitous and so devastatingly familiar, when it is *represented*, rather than

Library of Congress

An American nightmare—the trauma of 9/11.

simply *presented*? In this sense, there is a simple, dichotomous difference between presentation and representation, with the former defined as unaltered documentary footage of an actual occurrence and the latter defined as the re-creation of an event using cinematic means such as special effects, actors, and scripted actions.

For some time, the thought of representing 9/11 imagery was anathema, much like Claude Lanzmann's views about representing the Holocaust. As Lanzmann, the director of *Shoah* (1985), the landmark nine-hour documentary about the Holocaust, put it, the Holocaust is "above all unique in that it erects a ring of fire around itself.... Fiction is a transgression. I deeply believe that there are some things that cannot and should not be represented" (Hartman 84). And, in the days immediately after 9/11, broad sentiment about the representability of the events of that day was similar. The idea of a Hollywood film re-creating those events was unthinkable, even to the point that any film that depicted terrorist violence was deemed suspect.[2] Video footage of the events of 9/11 had, of course, been repeatedly viewed on televisions around the world, but to represent them in a film with special effects and intentional artistry seemed beyond the pale—simply unthinkable. And for almost five years, that remained the case.

The year 2006 witnessed the release of the first two major Hollywood films about 9/11 within a few months of each other: Paul Greengrass's *United 93* and Oliver Stone's *World Trade Center*. *United 93*, the first of the two films to arrive in U.S. theaters (it premiered on 28 April), tells the story of the United Airlines flight that was hijacked but never made it to its intended target (thought to be the White House). The passengers, having learned of the two American Airlines flights that were flown into the World Trade Center, revolted, causing the plane to crash into a field near Shanksville, Pennsylvania, killing all aboard. Greengrass and cinematographer Barry Ackroyd boldly shot the film in the same immediate, handheld style as *Blood Sunday* (2002), Greengrass's film about the 1972 British massacre of Irish civil rights protesters. As filmmaker Greg Marcks notes, "Few filmmakers would have even attempted a cinéma vérité approach to such charged subject matter, let alone succeeded so well" (3). The film takes place in virtual real time, cutting between the events on board United Flight 93 and the commotion on the ground. The film re-creates what might have happened on the flight, based on extensive research that included interviews with the families of all forty passengers killed. Based on these interviews, a dossier was created for each passenger, and these were given to the actors in lieu of a traditional script (Marcks). Roughly half the film takes place inside various air control facilities in New York and Ohio, as well as the Federal Aviation Administration (FAA) command center in Herndon, Virginia, and the Northeast Air Defense Sector base in Rome, New York. In these scenes, nine of the people who were there that day play themselves, including Ben Sliney, an FAA national operations manager whose first day on the job was 9/11.

World Trade Center tells the story of two Port Authority police officers, John McLoughlin (Nicolas Cage) and Will Jimeno (Michael Peña), who were two of only nineteen people to be pulled out of the rubble of the Twin Towers alive. The film depicts with frightening detail what it would have been like to be inside the towers as they came crashing down, although most of the story involves McLoughlin and Jimeno being trapped twenty feet beneath chunks of concrete and twisted metal beams while their families wait to find out whether they are dead or alive. *World Trade Center* also depicts the rescue attempts that began in the immediate aftermath, especially the tireless efforts of marine staff sergeant Dave Karnes (Michael Shannon), who went to Ground Zero independently and was responsible for discovering McLoughlin and Jimeno's whereabouts.

John McLoughlin (Nicholas Cage) and Will Jimeno (Michael Peña) enter the World Trade Center in Oliver Stone's *World Trade Center*.

Much was made about the release of each film. There were anguished protests from New York viewers, who yelled "Too soon!" at the screen during a *United 93* trailer. Also, there was Stone's apparent volte-face in his ideological stance in making a 9/11 film about heroism, family, and loyalty rather than a radical, both-sides exploration of the event, as he infamously mused about at an HBO Films panel a little more than a month after 9/11.

This chapter considers the ramifications of representing 9/11 in Hollywood theatrical feature films versus television documentaries, scores of which have aired repeatedly with little or no controversy over the past five years. For Americans, 9/11 was a historical trauma that has neither the chronological distance of years nor the physical distance of geography to ease the burden of memory. Films that tackle 9/11, whether documentaries or features, must deal first and foremost with that trauma and what it means. Television documentaries have approached 9/11 concretely, either as a harrowing ordeal that must be relived again and again so that it can be mastered or as a historical event the details of which must be deconstructed and therefore understood. Hollywood feature films, in contrast, have focused on reassuring emotional concepts such as heroism and resilience in an attempt to transcend the horrors of that day.

TELEVISION DOCUMENTARIES: THE POWER OF PRESENTING

Because the attacks of 9/11 were broadcast live on all the major television networks and every cable news channel, the event itself and its televisual presentation quickly became inextricably intertwined. For millions of Americans and millions more around the world, as soon as the images of dark smoke billowing out of the impact zone on the ninety-second through ninety-eighth floors of Tower One were broadcast on television, the event and its presentation became one in the same. The fiery explosions as the planes hit the towers and the expanding gray clouds of dust as the mighty structures collapsed became metonyms for the event as a whole, and that connection has persisted ever since.

Television has relived the events of that morning in every conceivable format: documentaries focusing on the experiences of those who lived through the attacks, staged re-creations, detailed structural analyses of why the buildings "pancaked" in progressive collapse. In the years since 9/11, there is no angle that television has not covered. But regardless of the focus, every program returns almost compulsively to the imagery of the towers exploding and collapsing. Normally, it is considered taboo to show actual death on-screen, but documentaries and news outlets have readily showed the towers crashing down, killing thousands of people in the process. The acceptable limits of what can be presented in terms of the violence of that day are rigidly proscribed, however. For instance, all the documentaries that aired on U.S. television shied away from showing those who chose to leap to their deaths actually hitting the ground. Several documentaries, notably the National Geographic Channel's *Inside 9/11* (2005), show detailed images captured with zoom lenses of people leaping—some so close that one can almost make out their facial expressions. But the closest any of them comes to depicting the inevitable end are the sounds of bodies landing in CBS's *9/11*.

The days surrounding the five-year anniversary of 9/11 illustrate the breadth and depth of television coverage. All the network morning news shows dedicated themselves to the five-year anniversary and attendant ceremonies. Cable news channels MSNBC, Fox News, and CNN committed much of their daily coverage to remembering 9/11, and CNN's Web site even posted a continuous feed of its unedited news coverage of the day for those who wanted to relive the televisual experience. Many of the major cable networks, including the History Channel, the National Geographic Channel, and CourtTV, aired new documentaries about 9/11 and its aftermath; Alessandra Stanley of the *New York Times* listed eighteen programs, both new and reruns, as a "sample" of what television would be offering in the days surrounding the five-year anniversary and called 9/11 "the tragedy you can't avoid." The Discovery Channel aired *After 9/11: Rebuilding Lives,* one of many programs focusing on the survivors and how they were affected by the event, as well as *Inside the Twin Towers,* which mixes interviews with those who escaped the burning buildings with staged re-creations of what they experienced. The only program to attract any significant controversy was ABC's two-night docudrama *Path to 9/11* (2006), which re-creates the events leading up to the terrorist attacks from the perspective of government officials, many of whom felt that they were unfairly portrayed.

It is significant that *Path to 9/11* was the only program to sustain notable criticism because, with the exception of *Inside the Twin Towers,* it was the only one to rely entirely on "representing" rather than "presenting." That is, it eschewed the documentary approach and re-created the events surrounding 9/11 in a way familiar to Hollywood feature films based on real-life events: by compressing time, using composite characters, fabricating dialogue, and speculating about why historical figures made the decisions they did. A disclaimer preceding the film admitted as much: "For dramatic and narrative purposes the movie contains fictionalized scenes, composite and representative characters and dialogue, as well as time compression." Following widely reported charges from Clinton administration officials that the miniseries was factually incorrect, some significant edits were made to the version circulated among television critics two weeks prior to its air date, but no amount of editing could change the fundamental fact that *Path to 9/11* is a re-creation. Therein lies the difference between it and most other 9/11 programming, which relied almost entirely on documentary footage and talking-head interviews with survivors and various experts.

The most direct presentation of the events of 11 September is found in the CBS documentary *9/11,* which originally aired six months after its eponymous date and was replayed one night before the fifth anniversary (it had also been available on DVD since September 2002). There was some attendant controversy when the documentary was first announced. Families of 9/11 victims argued that it might exploit the tragedy for ratings and that, at the very least, it was being aired too soon. Most TV critics and pundits praised *9/11,* and even those who questioned the appropriateness of the film before seeing it agreed that it was in no way exploitative, although many still maintained that it was "too soon" (Trigoboff).

In an editorial in *Broadcasting & Cable,* the editors opined that *9/11* was "one of the most affecting pieces of television in memory" ("How to Remember 9/11" 30). Part of the documentary's power is its "accidental" quality. The film exists only because two French filmmakers, brothers Gédéon and Jules Naudet, happened to be making a documentary about a rookie firefighter in Manhattan's Engine 7/Ladder 1 Company. By pure chance, while shooting that documentary, Jules Naudet caught the first plane hitting the North Tower, one of only three video recordings of that event. Their cameras then recorded the firefighters rushing to the World Trade Center and provided the only known footage from inside the lobby of the North Tower from the time the firefighters arrived until the collapse of the South Tower. The film then continues, chronicling the mostly failed rescue efforts in the following weeks and the firefighters' gradual return to some sense of normalcy.

The imagery in *9/11* is the best example of pure presentation in the documentary sense. There is nothing aesthetically pleasing or organized about it; it has the kind of rough, shaky, immediate sense of presence that cuts right through any boundaries between spectator and screen. It is, for most people, the closest they will ever come to experiencing firsthand what it was like to be in close proximity to what would eventually be known as Ground Zero.

Jules Naudet's video footage from inside the North Tower when the South Tower collapsed provides a frighteningly direct experience: the ominous rumble of the faltering building, the overwhelming sense of panic that followed, and the sudden envelopment in the darkness of concrete dust and debris. Both Gédéon and Jules recorded the collapse of the North Tower from the streets outside, and the imagery suggests the experience of being inside a tornado. The footage of the collapsing towers is presented unedited and unadorned; there is no extradiegetic music to heighten the experience, and the film does not cut away from Gédéon and Jules wiping off their dust-streaked lenses or moments when the complete chaos and violence make it impossible to know what is happening. It presents the horrifying events in the most direct terms possible through the camera—something the filmmakers seem to be keenly aware of, at least in retrospect. In his voice-over narration, Jules discusses his thoughts as he walked through the ashen streets following the collapse of the South Tower: "I knew there was nothing I could really do. I mean, I was not a fireman, had absolutely no medical expertise at all. I was just a civilian. But, as a cameraman—yeah, there was something I could do, and it was to look at what was happening. So the cameraman took over, just filmed."

Jules essentially collapses the distinction between his eye and the camera's eye, suggesting that his instincts as a filmmaker brought him to a place of pure presentation—collecting on video direct memories that are unmediated by aesthetic decisions or even thought itself. Later in the film, Jules returns to this mind-set during his footage at the firehouse as the firefighters return, noting, "The cameraman came back. Just filming."

Yet, for all the immediacy of *9/11*, it still bears the hallmarks of a constructed film. It is purposefully edited to create meaning through juxtaposition. It includes footage not shot by the Naudet brothers that allows the film to witness the details of the collapsing towers. There are several points in the film that include nondiegetic musical accompaniment, primarily haunting choral music, that is clearly intended to guide the viewer's emotional experience. The imagery is also interpreted via voice-over narration, much of which comes from those who experienced the event firsthand—Gédéon and Jules and the firefighters. The majority of the voice-over, however, is provided by Jim Hanlon, a firefighter who was a member of Engine 7/Ladder 1 Company but was not working on 11 September.

Nevertheless, even with these markers of constructedness, *9/11* maintains an intensely immediate aura that haunts the film. The presence of the cameras at the moments of collapse is the very definition of presentation that no Hollywood film could ever hope to duplicate, which is quite possibly why it took so long for a feature film to even try.

HOLLYWOOD FILMS: REPRESENTING HEROISM

Despite the prevalence of programs about 9/11 on television, the U.S. feature film industry waited nearly half a decade before it ventured into similar waters, and when it did, its approach to the material was significantly different. While the television documentaries tended to either relive or dissect the events of 9/11—what happened, how it happened, to whom it happened, why it happened—the first two Hollywood feature films, *United 93* and *World Trade Center*, approached 9/11 as a metaphor for coping with national trauma and elided direct reference to the most iconic images of the attacks.

Prior to Vietnam, Hollywood's depiction of America's wars had begun virtually in tandem with the wars themselves, if not before. For example, as soon as President Woodrow Wilson began preparing the United States to enter World War I, Hollywood ceased production of films that reflected the nation's previous antiwar sentiments and began producing films that "project[ed] heroic images of battle" and "incite[d] a fighting spirit" (Rollins 109). Similarly, Hollywood worked with the Office of War Information throughout World War II to produce a steady stream of war films that "played an important role in sustaining morale and optimism" (Fyne 126). Later, as Julian Smith shows in *Looking Away: Hollywood and Vietnam*, Hollywood shied away from dealing directly with Vietnam during the war itself for a number of reasons, including a growing rift between the film industry and the military, a series of aborted projects by well-known directors in the 1960s, and, most important, "a general disinclination to get involved in a brouhaha unless a significant opportunity for profit is involved" (20).

More than any of these reasons, though, Smith argues that Vietnam as a subject was simply too difficult for Hollywood filmmakers to grapple with effectively, especially during the war itself: "Vietnam's disorienting effect on our society, the indeterminate nature of that war we couldn't seem to win or abandon, was reflected in our filmmakers' inability to find an appropriate format for presenting the war to a mass audience" (22). It seemed that 9/11 would be the opposite of Vietnam because, as a clear-cut, Pearl Harbor kind of crisis, it brought the country together in a unified desire to overcome the trauma. Yet 9/11 also posed many of the same problems as Vietnam in terms of cinematic representation, particularly its lack of a fitting conclusion. Any film about 9/11 that did not engage the subsequent invasions of Afghanistan and Iraq (in 2001 and 2003, respectively) would have to end with the World Trade Center and the Pentagon, American symbols of capitalism and military power, in smoking ruins—hardly the stuff of box office gold. In this sense, then, 9/11 was just as "indeterminate" as Vietnam, particularly as popular comparisons of that war and the war in Iraq began to intensify.

A few films prior to 2006 dealt with 9/11, but indirectly. It was like the specter of Vietnam in 1960s films, which Smith describes as going "underground in the movies, tunneling into our subconscious, a true phantom of Hollywood, surfacing in strange places, taking off its mask only briefly" (25). Spike Lee's *25th Hour* (2002) was the first Hollywood production to reference the shadow of 9/11 in its story about an upscale drug dealer's final twenty-four hours of freedom before surrendering himself to a seven-year jail sentence. Lee uses imagery of the gaping hole in the middle of Manhattan where the World Trade Center once stood as an all-encompassing metaphor for both the pain of life and hope for the future. *The Guys* (2003), a feature film based on Anne Nelson's play about a New York City journalist helping a fire captain pay tribute to the men he lost on 9/11, is essentially a drama about 9/11's emotional aftermath, not the event itself (the same can be said of *Rescue Me*, Denis Leary's successful television series on FX about emotionally scarred post-9/11 New York firefighters). *The Guys* had minimal impact on the film-going public, however, because its release was limited to seventeen theaters, where it played a mere three weeks. In *War of the Worlds* (2005), Steven Spielberg takes an even more indirect approach by appropriating 9/11 imagery to give

Photofest

Ben Sliney (playing himself) monitors the chaos as FAA national operations manager in Paul Greengrass's *United 93*.

new resonance to his reinterpretation of H. G. Wells's science fiction classic about alien invasion. The shattered, flaming remains of a downed airplane, with the bodies still strapped into the seats; victims reduced instantly to ash by alien lasers; and teary-eyed family members posting quickly made signs with the pictures of missing loved ones are just a few of the film's most strikingly associative images.

Although *United 93* and *World Trade Center* both deal directly with the events that took place on the morning of 11 September, they largely eschew depictions of the attacks. *World Trade Center* avoids it completely, depicting the attacks from the point of view of the men and women on the ground, which results in little more than a passing shadow before the sound of a crash. *United 93* also takes a point-of-view approach, depicting the crash of American Airlines Flight 11, which hit the North Tower, as a blip that simply disappears from an air traffic controller's computer monitor. This both avoids the need to re-create the explosion via special effects and creates a haunting, metaphoric image: as the indexical sign of the plane suddenly vanishes, so do ninety-two lives, suggesting with terrible power just how quickly life can end. *United 93* does appropriate actual news footage of United Airlines Flight 75 hitting the South Tower, but again, from the point of view of the air traffic controllers and military personnel who were coming to terms with what was happening.

The general eliding of direct visual references to the attacks themselves, and the complete refusal to re-create them using special effects, is crucial because it shifts the focus away from the violence inflicted on the United States by foreign enemies and turns instead to stories of heroism, unity, and resilience that can be used as models for how to endure the unthinkable. *United 93* and *World Trade Center* are not about the attacks of 9/11 so much as how to overcome them.

On the surface, the two films are stridently different. *United 93* is a verité-style account of the doomed United Airlines flight that crashed in a Pennsylvania field and the actions taken by both the aviation industry and the U.S. military on the morning of 9/11; it features a cast of unknown actors, most of whom were drawn from the New York theater scene, as well as several real-life people who were involved in 9/11 playing themselves. In many ways, *United 93* brings to mind the harrowing post–World War II films of Polish director Andrez Wajda, especially *Kanal* (1956), which recounts the failed Warsaw Uprising of 1944 and famously opens with a narrator introducing us to the "heroes of the tragedy" and then telling us ominously, "Watch them closely, for these are the last hours of their lives." The film's power derives from many sources, but none so strong as the knowledge of how it will all turn out. Director Paul Greengrass appears to be less interested in developing suspense than in developing a feeling of unmitigated dread. Yet it is this very sense of dread that is key to the film's underlying message about American unity and resilience.

The film takes place in virtual real time, cutting between the events on board United Flight 93—the only one of the four hijacked planes not to strike its intended target—and the commotion on the ground. As much as 9/11 was a worldwide mediated event, with virtually every second of terror played and replayed on television, Greengrass manages to evoke new horrors by going inside the confusion, showing how the scenario was slowly and belatedly pieced together by those who were in a position to possibly do something about it. There are scenes inside various air control facilities, each of which is a portrait of chaos and frustrating bewilderment. The film is surprisingly blunt in showing how unprepared the designated guardians of the United States—both the military and the aviation industry—were for such an event.

World Trade Center, in contrast, has been described by numerous critics as being more like a Ron Howard than an Oliver Stone film.[3] Stone's previous, often intensely adversarial films about recent U.S. history include *Platoon* (1986), which uses a grunt's-eye view of the Vietnam War to explore the generational divide of the 1960s; *Wall Street* (1987), which is intensely critical of Reagan-era capitalism; *JFK* (1991), which posits a complex web of governmental-military-criminal conspiracies to explain the assassination of John F. Kennedy; and *Natural Born Killers* (1994), which explores the interrelationship between high-profile violent crime and the media. *World Trade Center* is stylistically and ideologically removed from these earlier films, with the death and destruction being carefully restricted to fall within the parameters of a PG-13 rating and the horrors of the day ameliorated through the transcendence of two survivors. The careful curbing of violence in the film is never more evident than in its treatment of the estimated one hundred or more people in the World Trade Center who made the agonizing decision to leap thousands of feet to their deaths rather than be consumed by smoke and flames. This terrible reality is reduced to one quick image of a lone figure falling from the top of one of the towers. The potential power of this image is circumscribed by both the poor special effects used to produce it and the obviousness of its function: much like the classical Hollywood tendency to use an artful trickle of blood to represent severe bodily damage, this lone plummeting figure is an insufficient symbolic stand-in for a grisly reality that resists representation.

World Trade Center is a much more traditional Hollywood production than *United 93*, particularly with its cast of well-known and respectable actors such as Nicolas Cage, Maggie Gyllenhaal, and Maria Bello. The focus of the story is on individuals, particularly John McLoughlin and Will Jimeno, two real-life Port Authority cops who, along with hundreds of other firefighters and rescue workers, went into the burning towers and were buried in them. McLoughlin and Jimeno were in the concourse between the two buildings when the South Tower collapsed, and they were buried twenty feet down in the rubble, badly injured but alive. The film moves back and forth between their physically agonizing experiences immobilized beneath tons of concrete and twisted metal and the emotionally agonizing experiences of their families back home.

Despite their surface differences, *United 93* and *World Trade Center* share a number of characteristics in common. Both films are built around themes of heroism and resilience, although they address these themes with distinctly different attitudes that barely mask an uneasy subtext about helplessness. Both films have simple, uncomplicated titles with a direct, denotative connection to their stories' physical settings, which in turn are crucial signifiers of the entirety of 9/11. Each title is also a metaphor about the American condition post 9/11. *United 93* is the more obvious, with the name of the corporation that owned the doomed airliner conveniently suggesting unity, the ultimate virtue in post-9/11

America. It should come as little surprise that the film's producers opted to go with the title *United 93* rather than the original working title, *Flight 93*.

The title of *World Trade Center* is even more direct in linking story with location, in this case an iconic American landmark that, in the wake of its destruction, is now understood first and foremost as the primary symbol of America's loss on 9/11. The Twin Towers, their functional, modernist design once derided as a blight on the Manhattan skyline when they were first erected in the mid-1970s, were almost immediately replaced in the days following 9/11 with giant beams of light stretching up into the night sky. Although the film focuses on two people trapped beneath the rubble, the title *World Trade Center* stands as both a monument to loss and a metaphor for the powerlessness and inaction the country felt in the immediate aftermath of the attacks.

In one sense, *World Trade Center* derives from a long legacy of American filmmaking about ordinary people surviving against all odds; it is a classic underdog story, fitting neatly into the cherished American ideal of the strength of the individual. John McLoughlin and Will Jimeno survive despite their crushed, broken bodies and their inability to move because they want to reclaim their lives; the terrorists can damage them physically, but not spiritually. Stone evokes these feelings by visualizing McLoughlin and Jimeno's thoughts and memories of American ideals: home, family, religion. At one point McLoughlin imagines his wife literally urging him to survive, while the supportive power of Jimeno's Catholicism finds visual representation in a hallucination of Christ bringing him a bottle of water. It is not incidental that Stone ends the film several years after 9/11, with McLoughlin and Jimeno, their bodies healed after dozens of surgeries, celebrating life with their families at a large picnic. The film fades to black on an image of Jimeno holding aloft the child his wife was pregnant with when he was buried in the rubble, giving the film an appropriately uplifting conclusion: despite the most devastating historical events, life goes on.

World Trade Center also embraces individualism and determination through the character of Dave Karnes, a retired marine staff sergeant who went to Ground Zero independently and was responsible for discovering McLoughlin and Jimeno through his own tenacity and refusal to stop searching. The film aligns Karnes with the same ideals associated with the trapped firemen: religion (he is in a church when he decides to head to New York), family (he calls his sister with instructions on how to relay his whereabouts to the authorities), and patriotism (his commitment to his country transcends his official status as a marine). Karnes is the quintessential American fighting man—stoic, intense, and refusing to give up even when others do. He alleviates the film's otherwise intense feeling of claustrophobia and helplessness, suggesting that Americans

Photofest

The "group" as hero: *United 93*'s passengers prepare to roll.

will always come to the aid of other Americans during times of crisis. Karnes also provides *World Trade Center* with its most blatant political message when he declares that some good men are needed to "avenge" what happened on 9/11. This line of dialogue, though falling neatly in line with Hollywood cinema's long-standing use of righteous vengeance as a narrative device, also clearly suggests a linkage to the subsequent invasions of both Afghanistan and Iraq and contradicts Stone's assertions that *World Trade Center* is an apolitical film.

United 93's depictions of heroism and resilience are significantly more ambivalent than *World Trade Center*'s, especially as embodied by Karnes. This is surprising, given that *United 93* depicts direct action—Americans fighting back against their enemies—while *World Trade Center* focuses on immobility and entrapment. Although the passenger revolt aboard United Flight 93 was the one instance of American retaliation during the attacks of 9/11, *United 93* does not turn it into a call to arms. In fact, many viewers found the film disheartening, especially in comparison to *World Trade Center*. Rabbi Mayer Schiller, a teacher at Yeshiva University High School for Boys, was interviewed after seeing *World Trade Center* and said, "It showed the good that people can do. I feel that life has heroes. It's unlike the one about the plane [*United 93*]—that took you and left you devastated" (Lee 2). Like so many viewers, Schiller was looking for uplifting, uncomplicated representations of heroism, which *United 93* does not provide. Instead, Greengrass takes the same approach that he did in *Bloody Sunday* (2002), which he describes in that film's DVD audio commentary: "It's not treated in this kind of great, heroic way. It just is what it is" (quoted in Marcks 3).

Widely reported in the press, the most memorable statement made by anyone on the morning of 9/11 was a passenger on United Flight 93: Todd Beamer, an Oracle Inc. executive from Hightstown, New Jersey, said to the other passengers right before they made their move against the hijackers, "Are you guys ready? Let's roll." "Let's roll" became a patriotic call to arms in the days and weeks following 9/11, a metonym for collective national sentiments about American heroism and self-sacrifice in the face of unmitigated evil. President George W. Bush even incorporated it into his State of the Union address on 29 January 2002: "For too long our culture has said, 'If it feels good, do it.' Now America is embracing a new ethic and a new creed: 'Let's roll.'" Yet writer-director Greengrass avoids centralizing such sentiments by downplaying the line to the point that it is easy to miss. Instead of showing the passengers as a clear-eyed, nationalistic fighting force, the film presents them as a group of terrified people facing certain death and making a hasty decision to determine their own fate. There is no overstated sense of idealized heroism or national duty but rather the true heroism of combat: the jittery, horrifying sense of one's own death approaching, but being brave enough to tackle it head-on rather than accept it without resistance.

In this sense, *United 93* is explicit in its focus on ordinary Americans. Its collective cast of businessmen, flight attendants, vacationing couples, and other everyday travelers who had no idea what was in store for them when they boarded the plane heightens the Hollywood war film's tendency to focus on soldiers as ordinary men in extraordinary situations. Interestingly, the film focuses less on the individual characters than on the group character, again reifying the significance of the word *united* in the title. The centrality of the group character is contrary to classical Hollywood narrative, which almost uniformly places importance on the individual hero(ine) and how he or she stands out from everyone else. *United 93* is closer in spirit to the group hero as embodied in Soviet silent films such as Sergei Eisenstein's *Battleship Potemkin* (1925); in the chaotic, violent final moments of the film when the passengers revolt, it is all but impossible to pick out individual acts of heroism, thus emphasizing that the event should be understood as a group effort.

All America watched on television and then on the big screen, as depicted in *World Trade Center.*

World Trade Center is much more traditional in its focus on individual characters. John McLoughlin is clearly held up as a man worthy of emulation; strong, proud, and thoroughly professional, he embodies the leadership qualities that America so desperately sought in the days following 9/11 (and some discerned in New York mayor Rudy Giuliani). Even as his strength is compromised by his entrapment beneath the rubble, he is still lionized for his strength of character in simply staying alive and helping his comrade Will Jimeno do the same. As McLoughlin teeters closer and closer to the brink of death, the power of the individual is redistributed, first to Jimeno, who encourages McLoughlin not to let his life slip away, and then to Karnes, who embodies the patriotism and nobility of the American military at its best. In this respect, Karnes is the linchpin character of *World Trade Center,* as he becomes a ready metaphor for the undaunted American spirit in the face of catastrophe. Unlike *United 93,* *World Trade Center*'s focus shifts away from ordinary Americans (McLoughlin and Jimeno, who, though heroic and self-sacrificing, become victims in need of rescue) and onto one extraordinary American.

Although there will surely be more films depicting the events of 11 September 2001 and its aftermath in the years to come, Hollywood has so far been careful in its depiction of this tragedy, eliding the more graphic, disturbing aspects of that morning in favor of real-life stories that can serve as metaphors for how to cope with a national trauma. The television documentaries that have flourished since the event also carefully depict 9/11, albeit with a more direct approach to representation that involves reliving the trauma over and over and over again.

The difficulty of representing such a monumental event so close in time to its occurrence is evident in both *United 93*'s and *World Trade Center*'s elision of the most iconic imagery of 9/11, which at this point still seems to be unrepresentable outside of the documentary genre. And whereas *United 93* is more complex in its depiction of heroism and resilience, *World Trade Center* fits neatly in a long line of Hollywood national fantasies about the triumph of the individual in the face of adversity and the refusal of the United States to back down in the face of aggression. It seems likely that, as the years pass and the distance grows between the here and now and the violence of 9/11, more filmmakers will follow the model of *United 93* and accept the challenge of representing aspects of that day that are less comforting and possibly more disturbing.

NOTES

1. Footage of American Airlines Flight 11 hitting the North Tower was inadvertently captured by three men: French filmmaker Jules Naudet, who was at the intersection of Church and Lispenard streets in Manhattan while filming a group of firefighters checking for a suspected gas leak; Pavel Hlava, a Czech immigrant, who shot his footage while riding in a car just before entering the Brooklyn Battery Tunnel; and German-born artist Wolfgang Staehle, whose show at the Postmasters Gallery, which opened on 6 September 2001, included a live online video stream (updated every four seconds) of Lower Manhattan shot from a Brooklyn window.

2. After 9/11, several major Hollywood studios delayed the release of action and terrorist-themed films such as *Collateral Damage* (2001), which stars Arnold Schwarzenegger as a Los Angeles firefighter avenging the killing of his wife and child, along with nine others, in a terrorist car bombing outside the Colombian consulate in Los Angeles. Yet, at the same time, video stores reported a sharp increase in rentals of similar films such as *Die Hard* (1988) and *The Siege* (1995) (Kakutani).

3. For example, in his review in *Rolling Stone*, Peter Travers laments, "There's little joy in seeing [Oliver Stone] morph into Ron Howard to play it safe at the box office." Similarly, Owen Gleiberman, writing in *Entertainment Weekly*, notes, "*World Trade Center* isn't a great Stone film; it's more like a decent Ron Howard film" (48).

WORKS CITED

Bazin, André. *What Is Cinema?* Trans. Hugh Gray. Berkeley: U of California P, 1967.

Fyne, Robert. "World War II: Features." *The Columbia Companion to American History on Film.* Ed. Peter C. Rollins. New York: Columbia UP, 2003. 125–36.

Gleiberman, Owen. "Heroic Efforts" [Rev. of *World Trade Center*]. *Entertainment Weekly* 11 Aug. 2006: 47–48.

Hartman, Geoffrey. *The Longest Shadow: In the Aftermath of the Holocaust.* New York: Palgrave Macmillan, 2002.

"How to Remember 9/11." *Broadcasting & Cable* 14 Aug. 2006: 30.

Kakutani, Michiko. "Critic's Notebook: The Age of Irony Isn't Over After All; Assertions of Cynicism's Demise Belie History." *New York Times* 7 Oct. 2001: 1E.

Lee, Felicia R. "9/11 on Big Screen, Ambivalence in Audience." *New York Times* 10 Aug. 2006: B2.

Marcks, Greg. "A Credible Witness." *Film Quarterly* 60.1 (2006): 3.

"President Delivers State of the Union Address." Press release. 29 Jan. 2002. <http://www.whitehouse.gov/news/releases/2002/01/20020129–11.html>.

Rollins, Peter C. "World War I." *The Columbia Companion to American History on Film.* Ed. Peter C. Rollins. New York: Columbia UP, 2003. 109–15.

Smith, Julian. *Looking Away: Hollywood and Vietnam.* New York: Charles Scriber's Sons, 1975.

Stanley, Alessandra. "Once Again, the Tragedy You Can't Avoid." *New York Times* 11 Aug. 2005: E1.

Travers, Peter. "*World Trade Center*" [review]. *Rolling Stone* 3 Aug. 2006. <http://www.rollingstone.com/reviews/movie/7667716/review/11077386/world_trade_center>.

Trigoboff, Dan. "*9/11* Not Exploitative." *Broadcasting & Cable* 18 Mar. 2002: 25.

John Shelton Lawrence

FILMOGRAPHY

War filmographies are abundant. The most comprehensive among them induce humility in those who offer yet another. Suid and Haverstick's *Stars and Stripes on Screen* (2005) lists 1,300 feature films and documentaries depicting U.S. military personnel. Shull and Wilt's *Hollywood War Films, 1937–1945* (1996), which used more expansive criteria of theme and reference, lists more than 1,000 films. Then they added 260 war-themed animated cartoons in *Doing Their Bit* (2004). This book's more modest filmography acknowledges these larger ones by providing bibliographical information about them. However, its own entries are limited to films meeting at least one of the following criteria:

- The film receives some analysis in one of this book's chapters; most films appearing in "such as" references are not included.
- The film has received the best picture or best documentary feature Oscar from the Academy of Motion Picture Arts and Sciences (AMPAS).
- The film has been named one of the American Film Institute's (AFI's) 100 Greatest Movies.
- The film has been selected for the ever-growing National Film Registry (NFR) administered by the Library of Congress's National Film Preservation Board.

Using these traits has generated a list of nearly 150 films.

Everyone knows that fans, critics, and scholars argue endlessly about the "best" and the "most historically significant," and the subjectivity of such discussions is surely reflected in official lists. No attempt is made here to offer better judgments or to explain why, for example, *Twelve O'Clock High* (1949) appears in the NFR and *Sands of Iwo Jima* (1949) does not. However, taken together, these lists tell us much about the unstable elements—commerce, popular and critical success, patriotism, and scholarly interest—that give such restless energy to analysis of the war film. Consider that in every year of World War II, best documentary Oscars were given to films that reflected governmental purposes and collaboration. Since the 1960s, however, the most critically and commercially successful documentaries—*The Anderson Platoon* (1967), *Hearts and Minds* (1974), *The Panama Deception* (1992), *The Fog of War* (2003), *Fahrenheit 9/11* (2004)—have shown distanced skepticism or fiercely oppositional, sometimes mocking attitudes toward the U.S. government's military aims. Such a list gives us one more filmographic way to objectively define the differences separating the "Good War" from those that followed.

Some explanation of the tabular information is needed. With regard to production information (the Studio/Distributor column), the film industry has perpetual disputes about credits, particularly when several small organizations collaborate. As distribution rights are sold, the names of small companies are sometimes masked by the much larger companies that merely package titles for resale. In reconciling conflicts about these matters for earlier periods, this filmography relies on AFI's *Catalog of Feature Films, 1893–1970* as its authority. This source is available in many libraries as six printed volumes that detail more than 45,000 films. AFI recently developed its contents for the Internet, available in university libraries and to the public from its Web site, http://www .afi.com. Because of space limitations, the tables usually list only one producing company; this implies no judgment about the relative contribution of other entities.

Subgenre characterizations are limited to two, although the films may be far more complex. The Plot/Theme column aims to concisely describe the topic and narrative structure. Cited reviews in the *New York Times* and *Variety* (the weekly edition) can provide a sense of the initial assessment in national venues. Since both publications issued retrospective volumes and indexes in the pre-electronic era, researchers can continue to access them in research libraries. The *New York Times* Historical (ProQuest) textbase theoretically contains all reviews, but the indexing sometimes frustrates the search for them, leading the dogged researcher back to the bookshelves. *Variety*'s compilation volumes do not contain page numbers but are organized by date. Under Award/Designation, information is limited to the Academy Award (AA) for best picture or best documentary or an equivalent Emmy Award and appearance in the NFR or the AFI 100. Thus blank spaces in the fields for *Black Hawk Down* and *Saving Private Ryan,* for example, conceal the fact that each won dozens of awards from both AMPAS and other organizations. They did not, however, win the best picture

Oscar and are probably too young for the other lists. Information about the wide array of film awards has become increasingly accurate and voluminous at online resources such as the Internet Movie Data Base and Wikipedia. It should also be noted that AMPAS restricted its best documentary award after 1942 to a single best documentary feature.

To conserve space in the tabular listings, the following abbreviations are employed for the film production and distribution companies:

Accuracy in Media	AIM
Columbia Pictures	Columbia
Horizon Pictures	Horizon
Metro-Goldwyn-Mayer	MGM
Miramax Films	Miramax
Paramount Pictures	Paramount
RKO Radio Pictures	RKO
Sony Pictures	Sony
20th Century-Fox Films	20CFox
United Artists	UA
Universal Pictures	Universal
Warner Bros. Pictures	WB

COMPREHENSIVE FILMOGRAPHIES

Davenport, Robert. *The Encyclopedia of War Movies: The Authoritative Guide to Movies about Wars of the Twentieth Century.* New York: Facts on File, 2004. Provides coverage of 800 films, with uneven amounts of information. Includes basic citation and sometimes cast list, plot, and production information.

Eiserman, Frederick A. *War on Film: Military History Education Video Tapes, Motion Pictures, and Related Audiovisual Aids.* Fort Leavenworth, Kans.: U.S. Army Command and General Staff College, 1987. Lists more than 4,500 commercial films, many of them short, classroom-oriented expositions of important events or developments in military history.

Evans, Alun. *Brassey's Guide to War Films.* Dulles, Va.: Potomac Books, 2000. Considers world film production, including date, director, cinematographer, screenplay, and actors, with a brief description and assessment. Includes some images and covers 3,000 films.

Suid, Lawrence H., and Dolores A. Haverstick. *Stars and Stripes on Screen: A Comprehensive Guide to Portrayals of American Military on Film.* Lanham, Md.: Scarecrow Press, 2005. Provides information for 1,000 films in which the U.S. military appears in uniform as well as 100 made-for-TV titles and 175 documentaries. Includes review citations for *New York Times* and *Variety* as well as provocative lists—"25 Best" and "25 Worst."

Wetta, Frank Joseph, and Stephen J. Curley. *Celluloid Wars: A Guide to Film and the American Experience of War.* New York: Greenwood Press, 1992. Explores the relationship between historical experience and cinematic representations.

THE AMERICAN REVOLUTIONARY WAR (1775–1783), THE WARS OF WESTWARD EXPANSION (1775–1890), THE MEXICAN-AMERICAN WAR (1846–1848), AND THE SPANISH-AMERICAN WAR (1898)

Hatch, Thom. *Custer and the Battle of the Little Bighorn: An Encyclopedia of the People, Places, Events, Indian Culture and Customs, Information Sources, Art and Films.* Jefferson, N.C.: McFarland, 2001.

Österberg, Bertil O. *Colonial America on Film and Television: A Filmography.* Jefferson, N.C.: McFarland, 2001.

The Spanish-American War in Motion Pictures. Motion Picture, Broadcasting, and Recorded Sound Division, Library of Congress. <http://memory.loc.gov/ammem/sawhtml/sawhome.html>. Features essays and streaming videos of 68 films—actualities from the United States, Cuba, and the Philippines made by the Edison Manufacturing Co. and the American Mutoscope & Biograph Co.

Imagine Entertainment/Touchstone Pictures

The victorious Mexicans of *The Alamo* (2004) are led by Antonio López de Santa Anna (center, Emilio Echevarría), the "Napoleon of the West," who is presented with epaulettes, gold braid, feather plumes, and caskets of crystal for his dining room.

Year	Title	Director	Studio/ Distributor	Format and Length
1920	*The Last of the Mohicans*	Maurice Tourneur	Maurice Tourneur Productions	Black and white, 6 reels
1924	*America* (chap. 1)	D. W. Griffith	D. W. Griffith/ UA	Black and white, 141 minutes
1935	*Mutiny on the Bounty*	Frank Lloyd	MGM	Black and white, 131 minutes
1939	*Drums Along the Mohawk* (chap. 1)	John Ford	20CFox	Color, 130 minutes
1960	*The Alamo* (chap. 2)	John Wayne	UA	Color, 192 minutes
1990	*Dances with Wolves*	Kevin Costner	Tig Productions/Orion Pictures	Color, 183 minutes
1998	*The U.S.-Mexican War (1846–1848)* (chap. 3)	Ginny Martin	KERA Dallas/PBS	Color, 240 minutes
2000	*The Patriot* (chap. 1)	Roland Emmerich	Columbia	Color, 130 minutes
2004	*The Alamo* (chap. 2)	John Lee Hancock	Buena Vista	Color, 137 minutes

Subgenre	N. Y. Times	Variety	Award/ Desig- nation	Plot/Theme
History/ romance	21 Jan. 1920: 21		NFR	Cooper's tale of British captivity by nefarious French-Indian foes and rescue by sympathetic Indians.
History/ romance	22 Feb. 1924: 20	28 Feb. 1924: 22		Famous incidents with the Minutemen, Battle of Yorktown, and famous personages such as Washington, threaded by romance.
Adventure/ romance	19 Sept. 1935: 19	13 Nov. 1935	AA	Cruel military discipline and its mutinous consequences aboard a British ship (HMS *Bounty*) in eighteenth century; based on 1787 incident.
Adventure	4 Nov. 1939: 11	8 Nov. 1939: 14		Settlers work hard at establishing a frontier and a culture; they wage war with Indians who resist their presence.
History/ romance	27 Oct. 1960: 45	26 Oct. 1960		Defenders are presented as courageous freedom fighters against Mexicans' tyranny; combines military maneuvers, romance, and patriotic speeches.
Adventure/ romance	19 Nov. 1990: C1	12 Nov. 1990: 61	AA, AFI	Union soldier assigned to South Dakota is alone, then merges his fate with Sioux and fights Pawnee, deserting U.S. military.
Documentary				Systematic exposition of the war that describes precursors, conduct of the war itself, and the aftermath.
History/ romance	28 June 2000: E1	19 June 2000: 23		The impetus for independence is underlined when the sadistic British drive a colonial farmer to rebel.
History	26 Mar. 2004: A11	12 Apr. 2004: 36		A more nuanced rendition of the politics, including messy personal lives and logistics, of the Alamo battle.

THE U.S. CIVIL WAR (1861–1865)

Kinnard, Roy. *Blue and Gray on Screen: 80 Years of Civil War Movies*. Secaucus, N.J.: Carol Pub. Group, 1996. Includes stills, posters, quoted reviews, and filmography of silent films from 1903 to 1929.

Reinhart, Mark S. *Abraham Lincoln on Screen: A Filmography of Dramas and Documentaries Including Television, 1903–1998*. Jefferson, N.C.: McFarland, 1999.

Spehr, Paul C. *The Civil War in Motion Pictures: A Bibliography of Films Produced in the United States since 1897*. Washington, D.C.: Library of Congress, 1961.

(Right) Gone with the Wind's (1939) Southern viewpoint is symbolized by the presentation of cruel, race-mixing carpetbaggers who ride comfortably in suits and silks while Confederate veterans painfully stumble home.

Year	Title	Director	Studio/ Distributor	Format and Length
1915	*The Birth of a Nation* (chap. 4)	D. W. Griffith	Epoch	Black and white, 12 reels
1927	*The General*	Buster Keaton	Buster Keaton Productions	Black and white, 8 reels
1939	*Gone with the Wind*	Victor Fleming	David O. Selznick/MGM	Color, 219 minutes
1976	*The Outlaw Josey Wales*	Clint Eastwood	WB	Color, 135 minutes

Selznick International Pictures/MGM

Subgenre	N. Y. Times	Variety	Award/ Desig- nation	Plot/Theme
Epic/ romance	4 Mar. 1915: 9	12 Mar. 1915: 23	AFI, NFR	Civil War and Reconstruction told as a tale of two families, their division, and the dangers posed to all whites by the liberation of slaves.
Adventure/ romance	8 Feb. 1927: 21	9 Feb. 1927: 16	NFR	Southern rail engineer rescues a kidnapped train and becomes a hero to the woman he loves.
Epic/ romance	20 Dec. 1939: 13	20 Dec. 1939: 14	AA, AFI, NFR	Civil War and Reconstruction told as an unhappy love quadrangle that presents a vivid picture of white sacrifice and suffering in the South.
Western/ revenge	5 Aug. 1976: 26	30 June 1976: 20	NFR	Southern soldier who refuses to surrender eventually kills murderous Union troops with Gatling gun and flees from them.

Year	Title	Director	Studio/ Distributor	Format and Length
1989	*Glory*	Edward Zwick	TriStar	Color, 122 minutes
1990	*The Civil War* (chap. 4)	Ken Burns	American Documentaries/ PBS	Color, 680 minutes
2003	*Cold Mountain* (chap. 5)	Anthony Minghella	Miramax	Color, 154 minutes

Subgenre	N. Y. Times	Variety	Award/ Desig- nation	Plot/Theme
Epic	14 Dec. 1989: C15; 15 Dec. 1989: C18	13 Dec. 1989: 30		The story of Massachusetts' black 54th Regiment led by whites into battle at Fort Wagner, near Charleston, S.C.
Documen- tary	25 Sept. 1990: C17	1 Oct. 1990: 89	Emmy	Ironic re-creation of aspirations and failures in the war through pictures, music, talking heads.
Romance/ adventure	25 Dec. 2003: E3	8 Dec. 2003: 50		Story of frustrated love as wound- ed Confederate soldier deserts and then makes Odyssean journey home to the woman he loves.

WORLD WAR I (1914–1918)

Campbell, Craig W. *Reel America and World War I: A Comprehensive Filmography and History of Motion Pictures in the United States, 1914–1920.* Jefferson, N.C.: McFarland, 1985.

Herman, Gerald. 1997. "The Great War Revisioned: A World War I Filmography." *Hollywood's World War I: Motion Picture Images.* Ed. Peter C. Rollins and John E. O'Connor. Bowling Green, Ohio: Bowling Green State UP.

(Right) As German troops march in the streets outside his classroom in *All Quiet on the Western Front* (1930), Professor Kantorek (Arnold Lucy) inspires his students to enlist by promising "a quick war . . . with few losses."

Year	Title	Director	Studio/ Distributor	Format and Length
1921	*The Four Horsemen of the Apocalypse* (chap. 6)	Rex Ingram	Metro Pictures	Black and white, 11 reels
1925	*The Big Parade* (chap. 6)	King Vidor	MGM	Black and white, 12 reels
1926	*What Price Glory?* (chap. 6)	Raoul Walsh	Fox Film	Black and white, 12 reels
1927	*Wings* (chap. 6)	William A. Wellman	Famous Players – Lasky	Black and white, 13 reels

Universal Pictures

Subgenre	N. Y. Times	Variety	Award/ Designation	Plot/Theme
Family drama	7 Mar. 1921: 8	18 Feb. 1921: 40	NFR	Wealthy Argentinian living in Paris leads dissolute life, is caught in adultery with wife of a senator, enlists for the Great War, and is killed on the battlefield by a German relative.
Romance	20 Nov. 1925: 18	11 Nov. 1925: 36	NFR	American wastrel is summoned to war, finds love in France, is wounded, then returns to find the woman he loves.
Romance/ comedy	24 Nov. 1926: 26	1 Dec. 1926: 12		Two sergeants in the marines have adventures and a competitive romance in France but are reconciled.
Romance/ combat	13 Aug. 1927: 10	17 Aug. 1927: 21	AA, NFR	Aviators compete for love; one accidentally kills the other in the air.

Year	Title	Director	Studio/ Distributor	Format and Length
1930	*All Quiet on the Western Front* (chaps. 6, 8)	Lewis Milestone	Universal	Black and white, 140 minutes
1930	*Westfront 1918/ Comrades of 1918* (chap. 8)	G. W. Pabst	Nero Films/ Vereinigte Star	Black and white, 75 minutes (U.S.)
1933	*Cavalcade* (chap. 9)	Frank Lloyd	Fox	Black and white, 110 minutes
1933	*Duck Soup*	Leo McCarey	Paramount	Black and white, 70 minutes
1935	*The President Vanishes* (chap. 9)	William A. Wellman	Walter Wanger Productions/ Paramount	Black and white, 80 minutes
1940	*The Fighting 69th* (chap. 9)	William Keighly	WB	Black and white, 89 minutes
1941	*Sergeant York* (chap. 9)	Howard Hawks	WB	Black and white, 134 minutes
1951	*The African Queen*	John Huston	Horizon/Romulus Films/UA	Color, 103 minutes
1957	*Paths of Glory*	Stanley Kubrick	Brynna Productions	Black and white, 86 minutes
1962	*Lawrence of Arabia*	David Lean	Horizon/Columbia	Color, 220 minutes

Subgenre	*N. Y. Times*	*Variety*	Award/ Desig-nation	Plot/Theme
Combat/ antiwar	30 Apr. 1930: 29	7 May 1930: 21	AA, NFR	Based on notable novel about WWI; German schoolboys develop patriotism, enlist, fight, lose illusions.
Combat/ drama	20 Feb. 1931: 25	25 Feb. 1931		Four Germans disrupt their lives for WWI, fight in trenches, experience domestic betrayal in a film the Nazis were eager to ban.
Family/ antiwar	16 Jan. 1933: 23	10 Jan 1933: 15	AA	Multigenerational British saga of soldiers of imperialism in the early twentieth century and the Great War.
Comedy	23 Nov. 1933: 24	28 Nov. 1933: 20	NFR	Marx brothers skewer European dictatorships with hardly disguised stabs at "Chiccolini."
Drama	8 Dec. 1934: 18	11 Dec. 1934: 19		Fearing a fascist coup and public pressure for war, a pacifist president fakes his own kidnapping.
Combat	27 Jan. 1940: 9	10 Jan. 1940: 14		Arrogant recruit endangers his Irish unit, then redeems himself.
Biopic/ combat	3 July 1941: 15	2 July 1941: 12		Backwoods pacifist becomes deadly killer of Germans.
Adventure/ romance	21 Feb. 1952: 24	26 Dec. 1951: 6	AFI, NFR	Degenerate river captain in Africa and female missionary successfuly attack German munitions.
Combat	26 Dec. 1957: 23	20 Nov. 1957: 6	NFR	French generals waste and even kill their own soldiers.
Adventure/ biopic	17 Dec. 1962: 5	19 Dec. 1962: 6	AA, NFR	Englishman works with desert tribes to fight Turks.

THE SPANISH CIVIL WAR (1936–1939) AND WORLD WAR II (1937–1945)

Kohrs, Deanna, and Sophia McClennen. *Cinergía Filmography of the Spanish Civil War.* <http://www.personal.psu.edu/users/s/a/sam50/cinergia/filmog%20civil%20war.htm>. Lists a dozen films produced in the United States.

Mitchell, Charles P. *The Hitler Filmography: Worldwide Feature Film and Television Miniseries Portrayals, 1940 through 2000.* Jefferson, N.C.: McFarland, 2002.

Royce, Brenda Scott. *Hogan's Heroes: A Comprehensive Reference to the 1965–1971 Television Comedy Series, with Cast Biographies and an Episode Guide.* Jefferson, N.C.: McFarland, 1993.

Shull, Michael S., and David E. Wilt. *Doing Their Bit: Wartime American Animated Short Films, 1939–1945.* 2nd ed. Jefferson, N.C.: McFarland, 2004.

———. *Hollywood War Films, 1937–1945: An Exhaustive Filmography of American Feature-Length Motion Pictures Relating to World War II.* Jefferson, N.C.: McFarland, 1996.

(Right) At sea on Christmas day, the submarine crew in *Destination Tokyo* (1943) fosters a family atmosphere, with Cookie Wainright (Alan Hale Sr.) as Santa Claus.

Year	Title	Director	Studio/ Distributor	Format and Length
1938	*Blockade* (chap. 9)	William Dieterle	Walter Wanger Productions/ United Artists	Black and white, 73 minutes
1938	*Inside Nazi Germany* (chap. 10)	Jack Glenn	March of Time/RKO	Black and white, 16 minutes
1939	*Confessions of a Nazi Spy* (chap. 10)	Anatole Litvak	WB	Black and white, 110 minutes
1939	*Hitler, Beast of Berlin/Beasts of Berlin* (chap. 10)	Sam Newfield	Producers Distributing	Black and white, 87 minutes
1940	*The Great Dictator*	Charles Chaplin	UA	Black and white, 127 minutes
1942	*The Battle of Midway*	John Ford	U.S. Navy/ 20CFox	Color, 18 minutes

Warner Bros.

Subgenre	N. Y. Times	Variety	Award/ Desig- nation	Plot/Theme
Resistance/ espionage	17 June 1938: 25	8 June 1938		Peasant is caught up in romance, resistance during Spanish struggle.
Newsreel	21 Jan 1938: 14		NFR	Anti-German actualities, with mixture of real and fake footage.
Espionage	29 April 1939: 19	3 May 1939		Group of Nazi sympathizers in the United States is exposed by the FBI.
Resistance	20 Nov. 1939: 15	22 Nov. 1939		A German veteran of WWI orga- nizes resistance against Nazis and then escapes.
Comedy/ resistance	16 Oct. 1940: 29	16 Oct. 1940: 16	NFR	Comic treatment of fascist dicta- tors combined with plea for Jews.
Combat documentary			AA	Footage taken at the Battle of Midway.

Year	Title	Director	Studio/ Distributor	Format and Length
1942	*Casablanca*	Michael Curtiz	WB	Black and white, 102 minutes
1942	*Kokoda Front Line*	Ken G. Hall	Australian News and Info	Black and white, 9 minutes
1942	*Moscow Strikes Back*	Ilya Kopalin and Leonid Varmalov	Artkino Pictures/Republic Pictures	Black and white, 55 minutes
1942	*Mrs. Miniver*	William Wyler	MGM	Black and white, 132 minutes
1942	*To Be or Not to Be*	Ernest Lubitsch	Alexander Korda/UA	Black and white, 100 minutes
1942	*Tulips Shall Grow*	George Pal	George Pal/ Paramount	Color, 7 minutes
1942	*Yankee Doodle Dandy*	Michael Curtiz	WB	Black and white, 126 minutes
1942– 1945	*Why We Fight* (chap. 11)	Frank Capra	U.S. Office of War Information	Black and white, 50–80 minutes each
1943	*Desert Victory*	Roy Boulting and David McDonald	RAF, Army Film Unit/British Ministry of Information	Black and white, 62 minutes
1943	*Destination Tokyo*	Delmer Daves	WB	Black and white, 135 minutes
1944	*The Fighting Lady*	Edward Steichen	U.S. Navy/ 20CFox	Color, 61 minutes
1944	*The Memphis Belle*	William Wyler	First MP Unit USAF/Paramount	Color, 45 minutes
1944	*Miracle of Morgan's Creek*	Preston Sturges	Paramount	Black and white, 99 minutes

Subgenre	N. Y. Times	Variety	Award/ Desig- nation	Plot/Theme
Drama	27 Nov. 1942: 27	2 Dec. 1942: 8	AA, AFI, NFR	Noir-style tale of resistance to Nazism in North Africa.
Combat documentary			AA	Scenes of fighting in New Guinea.
Combat documentary	17 June 1942	19 Aug. 1942	AA	Scenes of resistance and counteroffensive against Operation Barbarossa.
Home front/Allies	5 June 1942: 23	13 May 1942	AA	Middle-class family in English village makes sacrifices, faces German air attacks.
Comedy/ resistance	7 Mar. 1942: 13	18 Feb. 1942: 8	NFR	Shakespeare company in Poland outwits Nazis.
Allies			NFR	Allegorical tale about children in the Netherlands oppressed by German occupation.
Biopic/ musical	30 May 1942: 9	3 June 1942: 8	NFR	Tribute to George M. Cohan and "Over There."
Information/orientation for troops	27 April 1943: 13; 15 Nov. 1943: 23		AA, NFR	Newsreels, combat footage, policy analysis combine for stirring troop orientation.
Combat documentary	7 Feb. 1943: X3	31 Mar. 1943	AA	Footage of North African fighting, scenes of tank battles at El Alamein.
Combat	1 Jan. 1944: 9	22 Dec. 1943: 12		Submarine mission gathers weather information in Tokyo Bay.
Combat documentary	14 Jan. 1945: X3	20 Dec. 1944	AA	Combat operations on the *Yorktown* in the Pacific.
Combat documentary	26 Mar. 1944: X3; 14 Apr. 1944: 1; 16 Apr. 1944: 1	22 Mar. 1944	NFR	Bombing mission of German submarine pens.
Comedy	20 Jan. 1944: 15	5 Jan. 1944: 16	NFR	Home-front tale of pregnancy resulting from send-off for serviceman.

Year	Title	Director	Studio/ Distributor	Format and Length
1944	*Tunisian Victory*	Hugh Stewart and Frank Capra	British Service Units/U.S. Army Signal Corps	Black and white, 75 minutes
1945	*San Pietro/The Battle of San Pietro*	John Huston	U.S. Army Pictorial Services	Black and white, 32 minutes
1945	*The True Glory*	Garson Kanin and Carol Reed	British Ministry of Information/ U.S. Office of War Information	Black and white, 87 minutes
1946	*The Best Years of Our Lives* (chap. 12)	William Wyler	Goldwyn Productions	Black and white, 172 minutes
1947	*Design for Death*	Theron Warth and Richard Fleischer	RKO	Black and white, 48 minutes
1949	*Twelve O'Clock High*	Henry King	20CFox	Black and white, 132 minutes
1952–1953	*Victory at Sea*	M. Clay Adams	NBC and U.S. Navy	Color and black and white, 30 minutes each
1953	*From Here to Eternity* (chap 13)	Fred Zinnemann	Columbia	Black and white, 118 minutes
1957	*Bridge on the River Kwai*	David Lean	Horizon/Columbia	Color, 161 minutes
1962	*Black Fox: The Rise of Adolf Hitler*	Louis C. Stoumen	Image Productions	Black and white, 89 minutes
1962	*The Longest Day* (chap. 14)	Darryl Zanuck, Elmo Williams, Andrew Marton	Darryl Zanuck/ 20CFox	Black and white, 180 minutes

Subgenre	N. Y. Times	Variety	Award/ Desig- nation	Plot/Theme
Documentary	25 Feb. 1944: 22			Planning and combat footage of the North African Operation Torch landings of 1942; high-lights U.K.-U.S. unity.
Combat documentary	12 July 1945: 8		NFR	Visceral journey of a rifle squad during Italian campaign.
Combat documentary			AA	U.S.-British collaboration that compiles the footage of some 1,400 combat cameramen.
Drama/ veterans	22 Nov. 1946: 27	27 Nov. 1946: 14	AA, NFR	Poignant tale of veterans' reinte-gration into small-town civilian life.
Documentary	11 June 1948: 27	28 Jan. 1948	AA	Cautionary story of Japanese militarism that uses captured footage.
Combat	25 Jan. 1950: 10	21 Dec. 1949: 8	NFR	U.S. Army air force general rebuilds demoralized bombers through discipline.
Combat	27 Oct. 1952: 35	19 May 1954	Emmy	Attempts to convey comprehen-sive picture of naval operations with emphasis on the Pacific theater.
Drama	6 Aug. 1953: 16	29 July 1953: 6	AA, AFI, NFR	Exposition of the private lives of soldiers stationed at prewar Pearl Harbor.
POW	19 Dec. 1957: 39	20 Nov. 1957: 6	AFI, AA, NFR	The logic of military rules at a Burmese prison camp for U.S. and British soldiers.
Documenta-ry/Parable	30 Apr. 1963: 26	12 Sept. 1962	AA	Use of fables, Mozart, Marlene Dietrich's voice to explain Hitler.
Combat	5 Oct. 1962: 28	3 Oct. 1962: 6		Detailed depiction of the Allies and Germans during the Nor-mandy invasion of 1944.

Year	Title	Director	Studio/ Distributor	Format and Length
1963	*The Victors*	Carl Foreman	Highroad Productions/ Columbia	Black and white, 175 minutes
1965	*The Sound of Music*	Robert Wise	Robert Wise/ 20CFox	Color, 173 minutes
1970	*Patton*	Franklin Schaffner	20CFox	Color, 170 minutes
1980	*The Life and Times of Rosie the Riveter*	Connie Field	Clarity Films	Color and black and white, 65 minutes
1981	*Genocide*	Arnold Schwartzmann	Simon Wiesen-thal Center	Color, 90 minutes
1988	*Hotel Terminus*	Marcel Ophuls	Memory Pic-tures/Samuel Goldwyn	Color, 267 minutes
1993	*Schindler's List*	Steven Spielberg	Amblin Enter-tainment	Color and black and white, 195 minutes
1995	*Anne Frank Remembered*	Jon Blair	Anne Frank House/Sony	Color, 122 minutes
1996	*The English Patient*	Anthony Minghella	Saul Zaentz/Mi-ramax	Color, 162 minutes
1997	*The Long Way Home*	Mark J. Harris	Moriah Films/ Seventh Art	Color and black and white, 110 minutes
1998	*Saving Private Ryan* (chap. 14)	Steven Spielberg	Amblin Enter-tainment	Color, 170 minutes

Subgenre	N. Y. Times	Variety	Award/ Desig- nation	Plot/Theme
Combat	20 Dec. 1963: 21	30 Oct. 1963		Unheroic depiction of war as terrain for cynicism, lust, homesickness, and other frailties in a U.S. rifle squad.
Family biopic/musical	31 Mar. 1965: 34	3 Mar. 1965	AA	Austrian aristocratic family opposed to Nazism sings, escapes.
Combat	5 Feb. 1970: 31	21 Jan. 1970: 18	AA, AFI, NFR	Biopic focusing on the politics of Patton's service in various military theaters.
Documentary	27 Sept. 1980: 13	1 Oct. 1980	NFR	Interviews, newsreels, photo-based exploration of women's home-front roles and connection with feminism.
Documentary	14 Mar 1982: 64		AA	Exposition of the Holocaust, including the liberation of a death camp.
Documentary	30 Aug. 1987: Sun. Mag. 38; 6 Oct. 1988: C25; 24 Dec.1989: 32	25 May 1988: 19	AA	Story of Klaus Barbie, Butcher of Lyon, and how the Allies protected, used him in post-WWII period.
Docudrama/ biopic	12 Dec. 1993: H1	13 Dec. 1993: 36	AA, AFI, NFR	A story within the Holocaust, depicting heroism, Nazism, hope.
Documentary	1 Nov. 1996: B4		AA	Exposition of how Anne Frank hid from Germans; interviews those who helped her hide.
Romance	15 Nov. 1996: B1	11 Nov. 1996: 57	AA	Canadian nurse in North Africa encounters mysterious soldier who arouses her and causes jealousy.
Documentary	9 Sept. 1997: E14	3 Feb. 1997: 44	AA	Exposition of the post-WWII situation of liberated Jews, roles and stances of U.S. military personnel.
Combat docudrama	24 July 1998: E1	20 July 1998: 45-46		D-day invasion of Omaha Beach, with retrieval of a soldier as an objective.

Year	Title	Director	Studio/ Distributor	Format and Length
1998	*The Last Days*	James Moll	Kenn Lipper/ June Beallor/ Alameda	Color and black and white, 87 minutes
2000	*Into the Arms of Strangers*	Mark J. Harris	Sabine Films/ WB	Color, 117 minutes

Subgenre	N. Y. Times	Variety	Award/ Desig- nation	Plot/Theme
Documentary	5 Feb. 1999: E16		AA	Story of liquidation of Hungary's Jews told through interviews with survivors, U.S. Army officers.
Documentary	15 Sept. 2000: 10	11 Sept. 2000: 24	AA	Story of the Kindertransport, in which children were shipped from Germany and Austria prior to WWII to save their lives.

THE KOREAN WAR (1950–1953), THE COLD WAR (1945–1989), NUCLEAR WAR, AND SCIENCE FICTION

Broderick, Mick. *Nuclear Movies: A Critical Analysis and Filmography of International Feature Length Films Dealing with Experimentation, Aliens, Terrorism, Holocaust and Other Disaster Scenarios, 1914–1989.* Jefferson, N.C.: McFarland, 1991. Provides annotated entries for 850 feature-length films produced in thirty-six countries.

Davis, Doug. *Cold War Filmography.* Cold War Science and Technology Studies Program, Carnegie Mellon University. <http://www.cmu.edu/coldwar/film.htm>. Lists narrative films, documentaries, and archival materials.

Lentz, Robert J. *Korean War Filmography: 91 English Language Features through 2000.* Jefferson, N.C.: McFarland, 2003.

Pearson, Glenda. *The Red Scare: A Filmography.* The All Powers Project, University of Washington. <http://www.lib.washington.edu/exhibits/AllPowers/film.html>. Includes lists of films on Cold War themes, including anticommunism, science fiction, anti–House Committee on Un-American Activities, and the "Hollywood Ten."

(Right) In *The Big Lift*'s (1950) reenactment of the Berlin Airlift of 1948–1949, Master Sergeant Hank Kowalski (Paul Douglas) confronts, accuses, and then torments Gunther (Franz Nicklisch), the guard who had punished him in a concentration camp.

Year	Title	Director	Studio/ Distributor	Format and Length
1950	*The Big Lift* (chap. 15)	George Seaton	20CFox	Black and white, 120 minutes
1951	*The Day the Earth Stood Still* (chap. 16)	Robert Wise	20CFox	Black and white, 92 minutes
1951	*Duck and Cover*	Anthony Rizzo	Archer Productions/U.S. Federal Civil Defense Agency	Black and white, 9 minutes
1954	*Night People* (chap. 15)	Nunnally Johnson	20CFox	Color, 93 minutes
1961	*One, Two, Three* (chap. 15)	Billy Wilder	Mirisch/UA	Black and white, 108 minutes

20th Century-Fox

Subgenre	N. Y. Times	Variety	Award/ Desig- nation	Plot/Theme
Drama/ romance	12 Apr. 1950: 27	27 Apr. 1950: 37		The challenge of implementing the Berlin Airlift, combined with local romance for U.S. fliers.
Science fiction	19 Sept. 1951: 37	5 Sept. 1951: 6	NFR	Beings from outer space warn earthlings about self-destruction in an allegorical critique of the Cold War.
Public service	25 Jan. 1952: 7		NFR	Nuclear war training film for children featuring Burt the Turtle, who teaches children how to hide from nuclear blasts.
Leadership/ espionage	13 Mar. 1954: 11	17 Mar. 1954		A colonel in Berlin copes with allies, personalities, betrayals.
Comedy	22 Dec. 1961: 17	29 Nov. 1961		Coca-Cola imperialism in West Berlin is satirized when an executive's daughter takes up with a hippie.

Year	Title	Director	Studio/ Distributor	Format and Length
1962	*The Manchurian Candidate*	John Frankenheimer	UA	Black and white, 126 minutes
1964	*Dr. Strangelove*	Stanley Kubrick	Hawk Films/ Columbia	Black and white, 48 minutes
1966	*The War Game*	Peter Watkins	BBC	Black and white, 48 minutes
1968	*Czechoslovakia 1968*	Robert Fresco and Denis Sanders	U.S. Information Agency	Black and white, 20 minutes
1970	*M*A*S*H*	Robert Altman	Ingo Preminger/ 20CFox	Color, 116 minutes
1996	*Independence Day* (chap. 16)	Roland Emmerich	20CFox	Color, 145 minutes

Subgenre	N. Y. Times	Variety	Award/ Designation	Plot/Theme
POW/ subversive	25 Oct. 1962: 48	17 Oct. 1962	AFI, NFR	Decorated Korean POW is manipulated by red agent mom for assassinations before turning against her.
Comedy	30 Jan. 1964: 24	22 Jan. 1964	AFI, NFR	Insane U.S. Air Force general triggers nuclear war with the Soviet Union.
Docudrama	28 Mar. 1966: 67		AA	Simulated reporting of nuclear war in England resulting from all-out exchange.
Documentary			AA, NFR	Sympathetic story of the Prague Spring, which was crushed by Soviet invasion in 1968.
Comedy/ antiwar	26 Jan. 1970: 26	21 Jan. 1970: 18	AFI, NFR	Pranksters in Korean combat medical unit undermine their clownish superiors.
Science fiction	2 July 1996: C2	1 July 1996: 34		Earth is threatened by aliens and saved by the U.S. military, led by the president.

THE INDOCHINA WARS (1945–1975)

Devine, Jeremy. *Vietnam at 24 Frames a Second: A Critical Analysis of Over 350 Films about the Vietnam War.* Jefferson, N.C.: McFarland, 1995.

Films on the Vietnam War. Wellesley College. <http://www.wellesley.edu/Polisci/wj/vietfilms.html>. An online filmography with annotations and some streaming media.

Malo, Jean-Jacques, and Tony Williams, eds. *Vietnam War Films: Over 600 Feature, Made-for-TV, Pilot, and Short Movies, 1939–1992, from the United States, Vietnam, France, Belgium, Australia, Hong Kong, South Africa, Great Britain, and Other Countries.* Jefferson, N.C.: McFarland, 1994.

Walker, Mark. *Vietnam Veteran Films.* Metuchen, N.J.: Scarecrow Press, 1991.

(Right) In *The Quiet American* (1958), Fowler (Michael Redgrave), a cynical and sexually jealous British journalist, accuses the American (Audie Murphy) of collaborating in terrorist bombings of Saigon.

Year	Title	Director	Studio/ Distributor	Format and Length
1958	*The Quiet American* (chap. 19)	Joseph Mankiewicz	Figaro/UA	Black and white, 120 minutes
1967	*The Anderson Platoon* (chap. 21)	Pierre Schoendoerffer	French Broadcasting Syndicate	Color, 65 minutes
1968	*The Green Berets* (chap. 18)	John Wayne	Batjac Productions	Color, 141 minutes
1974	*Hearts and Minds* (chaps. 17, 21)	Peter Davis	BBS Productions	Color, 112 minutes
1978	*The Boys in Company C* (chap. 18)	Sidney J. Furie	Columbia	Color, 127 minutes
1978	*The Deer Hunter* (chaps. 17, 20)	Michael Cimino	EMI	Color, 182 minutes

Figaro Productions

Subgenre	N. Y. Times	Variety	Award/ Designation	Plot/Theme
Espionage/ romance	6 Feb. 1958: 24	22 Jan. 1958: 6		American idealist in Vietnam promotes a path between colonialism and communism.
Documentary	20 Dec. 1967: 14		AA	French crew tracks a U.S platoon during six weeks of patrols.
Combat	20 June 1968: 49	19 June 1968		Unabashedly pro-U.S. story of fighting the wily foe and educating a liberal journalist.
Documentary/antiwar	23 Mar. 1975: II, 1; 24 Mar. 1975: 38	15 May 1974: 28	AA	Both critics and defenders speak in frames tilted against U.S policy.
Combat	2 Feb. 1978: C15			Tracks the fate of five young marine recruits in Vietnam as they experience demoralization.
Combat/ POW	15 Dec. 1978: III, 5	29 Nov. 1978	AA, AFI, NFR	Story of working-class men and how deeply the war changes their lives.

Year	Title	Director	Studio/ Distributor	Format and Length
1979	*Apocalypse Now* (chaps. 17, 18)	Francis Ford Coppola	UA	Color 152 minutes
1983	*Vietnam: A Television History* (chap. 17)	Richard Ellison (executive producer)	WGBH/PBS	Color, 60 minutes each
1985	*Television's Vietnam: The Real Story* (chap. 17)	Peter Rollins	AIM/Sony	Color, 116 minutes
1986	*Platoon* (chap. 18)	Oliver Stone	Cinema 86/Orion Pictures	Color, 120 minutes
1986	*Television's Vietnam: The Impact of Media* (chap. 17)	Peter Rollins	AIM/Sony	Color, 60 minutes
1987	*Hamburger Hill* (chap. 17)	John Irvin	Paramount	Color, 112 minutes
1987	*Hanoi Hilton* (chap. 17)	Lionel Chetwynd	Globus-Golan	Color, 125 minutes
1989	*Born on the Fourth of July* (chap. 17)	Oliver Stone	Ixtlan	Color, 145 minutes
1994	*Forrest Gump*	Robert Zemeckis	Tisch-Finerman/ Paramount	Black and white and color, 142 minutes
2002	*The Quiet American* (chap. 19)	Phillip Noyce	IMF/Miramax	Color, 101 minutes
2003	*The Fog of War*	Errol Morris	@radical.media/ Sony	Color, 107 minutes

Subgenre	N. Y. Times	Variety	Award/ Desig- nation	Plot/Theme
Combat/ allegory	15 Aug. 1979: III, 15	16 May 1979	AFI, NFR	Surreal journey suggests that war is madness.
Documentary	4 Oct. 1983: A19; 20 Dec. 1983: C19	28 Sept. 1983: 146		Panoramic, interview, and combat footage of causes, results.
Documentary				Counters 1983 PBS series with allegations of leftist bias, dishonesty.
Combat	11 Nov. 1987; H21	3 Dec. 1987: 19	AA	Terrifying battles and bitter feuds within the ranks create an unheroic vision.
Documentary				Focus on Tet Offensive and charges that media turned U.S. victory into defeat.
Combat	28 Aug. 1987: C16	12 Aug. 1987: 12		Ten days of fighting for Hill 937 offer window to home front, media, and casualties.
Docudrama	27 Mar. 1987: C13	25 Mar. 1987: 18		Re-creation of POW courage in suffering, North Vietnamese cruelty.
Biopic	31 Dec. 1989: H9	20 Dec. 1989: 21		His body, paralyzed by shrapnel, Ron Kovic returns home to become an anti–Vietnam War activist.
Fable	6 July 1994: C9	11 July 1994	AA, AFI	Mentally challenged Everyman serves, wins honor in Vietnam.
Espionage/ romance	22 Nov. 2002: E14	9 Sept. 2002		American agent helps align CIA with terror operations to create a "third force."
Documentary	11 Oct. 2003: B9	2 June 2003: B9	AA	Extended interviews with Robert McNamara regarding Vietnam policy.

Post 9/11, the Wars in Iraq (1991 and 2003–), and the U.S. War against Terrorism (2001–)

International Terrorism. Media Resources Center, University of California at Berkeley. <http://www.lib.berkeley.edu/MRC/terrorism.html>. Contains feature films, documentaries, streaming media of panel discussions, and links to government policy statements.

(Right) One of *Jarhead*'s (2005) absurdist moments: a marine unit in Saudi Arabia during the Gulf War plays a staged-for-journalists football game wearing chemical protection suits in the deadly heat.

Year	Title	Director	Studio/ Distributor	Format and Length
1992	*The Panama Deception*	Barbara Trent	Empowerment Project/Tara Releasing	Color, 91 minutes
1998	*Ambush in Moga-dishu* (chap. 20)	William Cran	WGBH-Frontline/PBS	Color, 60 minutes
1999	*One Day in September*	Kevin McDonald	Passion Pictures/Buena Vista	Color and black and white, 94 minutes
2001	*Behind Enemy Lines* (chap. 20)	John Moore	20CFox	Color 106 minutes
2001	*Black Hawk Down* (chap. 20)	Ridley Scott	Revolution Studios/Sony	Color, 144 minutes
2003	*The True Story of Black Hawk Down* (chap. 20)	David Keane	A&E, History Channel	Color, 100 minutes
2003	*Saving Jessica Lynch* (chap. 22)	Peter Markle	NBC	Color, 120 minutes
2003	*Saving POW Lynch* (chap. 22)	Loren Michaelmen	Discovery Channel	Color, 60 minutes

Universal Pictures

Subgenre	*N. Y. Times*	*Variety*	Award/ Designation	Plot/Theme
Documentary	17 June 1993: C18	10 Aug. 1992: 55	AA	Critical analysis of reasons behind U.S. invasion of Panama in 1989 and extent of death among its citizens.
TV documentary	29 Sept. 1998: E6			Analysis of the Battle of Mogadishu by participants, bystanders, policy makers.
Documentary	17 Nov. 2000: E29	11 Sept. 2000: 26	AA	Exposition of 1972 massacre of Israeli athletes in Munich.
Rescue	30 Nov. 2001: E19	26 Nov. 2001: 25		Navy pilot violates mission limits and is shot down but rescued from Serbian pursuers.
Combat/ rescue	26 Dec. 2001: E1	10 Dec. 2001: 31		Special forces in Mogadishu snatch militia leaders and fight their way back to base.
TV documentary	21 Jan. 2002: B3			Analysis of Battle of Mogadishu guided by author Mark Bowden.
TV docudrama		10 Oct. 2003: 38		Re-creation of Pfc. Lynch's capture, hospitalization, and rescue, reflecting Iraqi citizens' help and perspective.
TV docudrama				Docudrama treatment that links Lynch and Rhonda Cornum from earlier Iraq war.

Year	Title	Director	Studio/ Distributor	Format and Length
2003	*Saving Private Lynch* (chap. 22)	Susan Aasen and Caroline Sommers	A&E	Color, 60 minutes
2004	*Battleground: 21 Days on the Empire's Edge* (chap. 21)	Stephen Marshall	Guerrilla News Network	Color, 81 minutes
2004	*Fahrenheit 9/11* (chap. 21)	Michael Moore	Lions Gate Films	Color, 110 minutes
2005	*Confronting Iraq: Conflict and Hope*	Roger Aronoff	Autumn Productions/AIM	Color, 86 minutes
2005	*Jarhead* (chap. 22)	Sam Mendes	Universal	Color, 123 minutes
2006	*Baghdad E.R.* (chap. 21)	Jon Alpert and Matthew O'Neill	HBO	Color, 60 minutes
2006	*United 93* (chap. 23)	Paul Greengrass	Universal	Color, 115 minutes
2006	*The War Tapes* (chap. 21)	Deborah Scranton	SenArt Films	Color, 97 minutes
2006	*World Trade Center* (chap. 23)	Oliver Stone	Paramount	Color, 129 minutes

Subgenre	N. Y. Times	Variety	Award/ Designation	Plot/Theme
TV docu-drama				Docudramatic recounting with journalists, news footage, interviews with POW experts.
Documentary		8 Nov. 2004: 44		A three-week tour of Iraq emphasizing the unofficial views of U.S. soldiers, local citizens, disinterested outsiders.
Documentary	23 June 2004	24 May 2004: 33		Docucollage of complaints against George W. Bush focusing on military cost and competence.
Documentary video				Analysis of causes of Iraq war based on interviews and historical images assigns its beginning to Iran's 1979 revolution and resulting theocracy.
Combat	4 Oct. 2005	31 Oct. 2005: 47		Memoir-based profile of a marine company's personal experiences in the Gulf War.
Documentary	20 May 2006: B7	15 May 2006: 29		Cinema verité record of a field hospital during the counterinsurgency phase of the Iraq war.
Docudrama	28 Apr. 2006: E1	19 Apr. 2006		Reconstruction of struggle between hijackers and passengers that crashed the plane.
Documentary		1 Apr. 2006: 33		The Iraq war filmed by soldiers using digital minicams.
Docudrama	14 Aug. 2006: E2; 21 Sept. 2006: 43	17 Aug. 2006: 18		Dramatization of 9/11 attack highlighting the role of police and fire personnel.

John Shelton Lawrence

BIBLIOGRAPHY

The first war films appeared in the United States during the Spanish-American War (1898). Despite the motion picture's now recognized influence on popular historical perceptions and the patriotic pulse, scholars in the first half of the twentieth century were slow to interpret the territory. An early book was *Look* magazine's 1945 *From Movie Lot to Beachhead: The Motion Picture Goes to War and Prepares for the Future.* It was followed in 1947 by Siegfried Kracauer's much weightier *From Caligari to Hitler: A Psychological History of the German Film;* among other topics, it describes the propagandistic artfulness of Sergei Eisenstein's *October* (1927) and Leni Riefenstahl's *Triumph of the Will* (1935), the latter of which had an impact on Frank Capra's *Why We Fight* series. Scholarship on the war film began to mature only in the 1970s and 1980s. Like the filmography for this book, the sections of the bibliography reflect the chronological periods defined by the represented wars. Readers will notice gaps in the scholarship that reflect Hollywood's own failure to take up certain topics—such as the Mexican-American War (1846–1848) and the U.S. counterinsurgency in the Philippines (1899–1902) that grew out of the Spanish-American War. Such absences are an important fact about the film industry, one that Julian Smith acutely addresses in his book *Looking Away: Hollywood and Vietnam* (1975).

For each historical period, a "Contexts" section lists a few books related to the social and military background and is followed by the "Film Focus" titles. The lists exhibit a bias toward books; however, a few articles are included to compensate for the scarcity of books on certain periods. This bibliography omits books with a predominantly filmographic character, which are listed in the filmography.

GENERAL AND COMPREHENSIVE DISCUSSIONS OF THE WAR FILM

Carnes, Mark C., ed. *Past Imperfect: History According to the Movies*. New York: Holt, 1995. Includes essays on more than twenty war films.

Chambers, John Whiteclay II, ed. *The Oxford Companion to American Military History*. Oxford: Oxford UP, 1999. Has sections on feature films and newsreels and documentaries.

Culbert, David, ed. *Film and Propaganda in America: A Documentary History*. 4 vols. New York: Greenwood, 1990. The series contains a large number of documents from the studios, the U.S. military, and congressional committees.

Eberwein, Robert, ed. *The War Film*. New Brunswick, N.J.: Rutgers UP, 2004. Thirteen essays on genre, gender, race, and history.

Langman, Larry, and David Ebner. *Encyclopedia of American Spy Films*. New York: Garland, 1990. Classifies films by the wars that provide their settings.

Renov, Michael. *Hollywood's Wartime Woman: Representation and Ideology*. Ann Arbor, Mich.: UMI Research P, 1988.

Rollins, Peter C., ed. *The Columbia Companion to American History on Film: How the Movies Have Portrayed the American Past*. New York: Columbia UP, 2003. See pp. 49–136 for ten essays (with bibliographies and filmographies) on wars from the American Revolution to the Vietnam War.

Shane, Russell. *An Analysis of Motion Pictures about War Released by the American Film Industry, 1930–1970*. New York: Arno, 1970.

Suid, Lawrence. *Guts & Glory: The Making of the American Military Image in Film*. 2nd ed. Lexington: UP of Kentucky, 2002. Emphasis on cooperative-antagonistic interplay between the War Department or Pentagon and the film studios.

———. *Sailing on the Silver Screen: Hollywood and the U.S. Navy*. Annapolis, Md.: Naval Institute P, 1996.

Virilio, Paul. *War and Cinema: The Logistics of Perception*. London: Verso, 1989. Develops the theme that film has become a military asset that must be deployed in wartime.

War Movies and War Propaganda. Media Resources Center, University of California at Berkeley. <http://www.lib.berkeley.edu/MRC/Warfilmbib.html>. Lists books organized by war and includes the cinemas of other countries; lists book chapters and journal articles related to war cinema and to individual films.

THE AMERICAN REVOLUTIONARY WAR (1775–1783), THE WARS OF WESTERN EXPANSION (1775–1890), THE MEXICAN-AMERICAN WAR (1846–1848), AND THE SPANISH-AMERICAN WAR (1898)

Contexts

Berkhofer, Robert F., Jr. *The White Man's Indian: Images of the American Indian from Co-*

lumbus to the Present. New York: Knopf, 1978. Contains a section titled "The Western and the Indian in Popular Culture."

Eisenhower, John S. D. *So Far from God: The U.S. War with Mexico, 1846–1848.* Norman: U of Oklahoma P, 2000.

Goldstein, Donald M. *The Spanish-American War: The Story and Photographs.* Dulles, Va.: Prange, 1998.

Greene, Jack P., and J. R. Pole, eds. *The Blackwell Encyclopedia of the American Revolution.* Malden, Mass.: Blackwell, 1999.

Middlekauff, Robert. *The Glorious Cause: The American Revolution, 1763–1789.* Rev. ed. New York: Oxford UP, 2005.

O'Toole, G. J. A. *The Spanish War: An American Epic.* New York: Norton, 1986.

Singletary, Otis. *The Mexican War.* Chicago: U of Chicago P, 1962.

Slotkin, Richard. *The Fatal Environment: The Myth of the Frontier in the Age of Industrialization, 1800–1890.* Middletown, Conn.: Wesleyan UP, 1985.

Trask, David F. *The War with Spain in 1898.* Lincoln: U of Nebraska P, 1981.

Utley, Robert M., and Wilcomb E. Washburn, eds. *The American Heritage History of the Indian Wars.* New York: American Heritage, 1977.

Zimmerman, Warren. *First Great Triumph: How Five Americans Made Their Country a World Power.* New York: Farrar, Straus & Giroux, 2002.

Film Focus

Bataille, Gretchen M., and Charles L. P. Silet, eds. *Images of American Indians in Film: An Annotated Bibliography.* New York: Garland, 1985. Contains a list of 725 films that represent Native Americans.

Bitzer, G. W. *Billy Bitzer: His Story.* New York: Farrar, Straus & Giroux, 1973. See "Filming My First War: 1898," pp. 33–40.

Friar, Ralph E., and Natasha A. Friar. *The Only Good Indian: The Hollywood Gospel.* New York: Drama Book Specialists, 1972.

Kirkpatrick, Jacqueline. *Celluloid Indians: Native Americans and Film.* Lincoln: U of Nebraska P, 1999. Discusses *The Indian Wars* (1914), the films of John Ford, *The Last of the Mohicans* (1993), and other representations of the Native American in warfare.

McCrisken, Trevor B., and Andrew Pepper. *American History and Contemporary Hollywood Film.* New Brunswick, N.J.: Rutgers UP, 2005. Includes treatments of *The Patriot* (2000), *Amistad* (1997), *Glory* (1989), *Ride with the Devil* (1998), and *Cold Mountain* (2003).

Musser, Charles. *Before the Nickelodeon: Edwin S. Porter and the Edison Manufacturing Company.* Berkeley: U of California P, 1991. Contains numerous references to Spanish-American War filmmaking.

Rollins, Peter C., and John E. O'Connor. *Hollywood's Indian: The Portrayal of the Native American in Film.* Expanded ed. Lexington: UP of Kentucky, 2003.

Sarf, Wayne Michael. *God Bless You, Buffalo Bill: A Layman's Guide to History and the Western Film.* Rutherford, N.J.: Fairleigh Dickinson UP, 1983.

Thompson, Frank. The Alamo: *The Illustrated Story of the Epic Film.* New York: Newmarket, 2004.

———. *Alamo Movies*. Plano, Tex.: Wordware, 1991.
Tuska, Jon. *The American West in Film: Critical Approaches to the Western*. Westport, Conn.: Greenwood, 1985.

THE U.S. CIVIL WAR (1861–1865)

Contexts

Culpepper, Marilyn Mayer. *Women of the Civil War South: Personal Accounts from Diaries, Letters, and Postwar Reminiscences*. Jefferson, N.C.: McFarland, 2004.
McPherson, James M. *Battle Cry of Freedom: The Civil War Era*. New York: Oxford UP, 1988.
Pratt, Fletcher. *A Short History of the Civil War: Ordeal by Fire*. New York: Dover, 1997.
Pyron, Darden Asbury. *Southern Daughter: The Life of Margaret Mitchell*. New York: Oxford UP, 1991.

Film Focus

Chadwick, Bruce. *The Reel Civil War: Mythmaking in American Film*. New York: Knopf, 2001. Defines Civil War films as a genre, treating themes, stereotypes, and individual films.
Cullen, Jim. *The Civil War in Popular Culture: A Reusable Past*. Washington, D.C.: Smithsonian Institution P, 1995. Extensive discussion of *Gone with the Wind* (1939) and *Glory* (1989).
Lang, Robert, ed. *The Birth of a Nation: D. W. Griffith, Director*. New Brunswick, N.J.: Rutgers UP, 1994.
Spears, Jack. *The Civil War on the Screen and Other Essays*. South Brunswick, N.J.: Barnes, 1977.
Toplin, Robert Brent, ed. *Ken Burns's* The Civil War*: Historians Respond*. New York: Oxford UP, 1996.
York, Neil Longley. *Fiction as Fact: The Horse Soldiers and Popular Memory*. Kent, Ohio: Kent State UP, 2001.

WORLD WAR I (1914–1918)

Contexts

Fussell, Paul. *The Great War and Modern Memory*. New York: Oxford UP, 1975.
Keegan, John. *The First World War*. New York: Knopf, 1998.
Kennedy, David M. *Over Here: The First World War and American Society*. New York: Oxford UP, 1982.
Winter, J. M. *The Experience of World War I*. New York: Oxford UP, 1989. A well-illustrated reference book with tables, charts, maps, and photographs.

Film Focus

DeBauche, Leslie Midkiff. *Reel Patriotism: The Movies and World War I*. Madison: U of Wisconsin P, 1997.

Dibbets, Karel, and Bert Hogenkamp, eds. *Film and the First World War*. Amsterdam: Amsterdam UP, 1995.

Isenberg, Michael T. *War on Film: The American Cinema and World War I, 1914–1941*. Rutherford, N.J.: Fairleigh Dickinson UP, 1981.

Paris, Michael, ed. *The First World War and Popular Cinema: 1914 to the Present*. New Brunswick, N.J.: Rutgers UP, 2000. Discusses patterns in the cinemas of Australia, Canada, France, Germany, the United States, and others.

Rollins, Peter C., and John E. O'Connor, eds. *Hollywood's World War I: Motion Picture Images*. Bowling Green, Ohio: Bowling Green State UP, 1997.

Ward, Larry Wayne. *The Motion Picture Goes to War: The U.S. Government Film Effort during World War I*. Ann Arbor, Mich.: UMI Research P, 1985.

THE SPANISH CIVIL WAR (1936–1939) AND WORLD WAR II (1937–1945)

Contexts

Campbell, John, ed. *The Experience of World War II*. New York: Oxford UP, 1989. A well-illustrated reference book with tables, charts, maps, and photographs.

Carroll, Peter N. *The Odyssey of the Abraham Lincoln Brigade: Americans in the Spanish Civil War*. Stanford, Calif.: Stanford UP, 1994.

Fussell, Paul. *Wartime: Understanding and Behavior in the Second World War*. New York: Oxford UP, 1989.

Keegan, John. *The Second World War*. New York: Viking Penguin, 1990.

Kennedy, David M. *Freedom from Fear: The American People in Depression and War, 1929–1945*. New York: Oxford UP, 2001.

Rosenstone, Robert A. *Crusade of the Left: The Lincoln Battalion in the Spanish Civil War*. New York: Pegasus, 1969.

Thomas, Hugh. *The Spanish Civil War*. Rev. ed. New York: Harper & Row, 1977.

Film Focus

Baker, M. Joyce. *Images of Women in Film: The War Years, 1941–1945*. Ann Arbor, Mich.: UMI Research P, 1980. Describes the arc of the elevation of women's status, followed by its deflation at war's end.

Basinger, Jeanine. *The World War II Combat Film: Anatomy of a Genre*. Expanded ed. Middletown, Conn.: Wesleyan UP, 2003. This edition has an annotated filmography for World War II and the Korean War and an update covering films of the 1981–2003 period.

Bernstein, Matthew. *Walter Wanger, Hollywood Independent*. Minneapolis: U of Minnesota

P, 2000. Wanger, a studio executive who favored intervention, produced films such as Alfred Hitchcock's *Foreign Correspondent* (1940).

Birdwell, Michael. *Celluloid Soldiers: The Warner Bros. Campaign against Nazism.* New York: New York UP, 2001. Warner Bros. was the first studio to use its films in the cause of intervention and the most consistent in doing so.

Bohn, Thomas W. *An Historical and Descriptive Analysis of the "Why We Fight" Series.* New York: Arno, 1977.

Chambers, John W., and David H. Culbert, eds. *World War II, Film, and History.* New York: Oxford UP, 1996. Studies of individual films and themes, including titles from Japan, Russia, and Germany.

Dick, Bernard F. *The Star-Spangled Screen: The American World War II Film.* Rev. ed. Lexington: UP of Kentucky, 1996.

Doherty, Thomas. *Projections of War: Hollywood, American Culture and World War II.* 2nd ed. New York: Columbia UP, 1998. Examines the interplay of film, culture, and war experience.

Dolan, Edward F. *Hollywood Goes to War.* Twickenham, U.K.: Hamlyn, 1985. Includes many movie stills.

Fielding, Raymond. *The March of Time, 1935–1951.* New York: Oxford UP, 1978.

Fyne, Robert. *The Hollywood Propaganda of World War II.* Lanham, Md.: Scarecrow, 1997.

Graham, Don. *No Name on the Bullet.* New York: Viking, 1989. Biographical study of Audie Murphy, World War II's most decorated hero, and his film career, which included playing himself in *To Hell and Back* (1955).

Kane, Kathryn. *Visions of War: Hollywood Combat Films of World War II.* Ann Arbor, Mich.: UMI Research P, 1982.

Koppes, Clayton R., and Gregory D. Black. *Hollywood Goes to War: How Politics, Profits, and Propaganda Shaped World War II Movies.* New York: Free P, 1987. Recounts the efforts of the Office of War Information to shape the content of studio films to achieve war aims.

Manvell, Roger. *Films and the Second World War.* South Brunswick, N.J.: Barnes, 1974. Well illustrated and cross-cultural; includes a filmography. The author served during World War II in the Films Division of the British Ministry of Information.

McLaughlin, Robert L., and Sally E. Parry. *We'll Always Have the Movies: American Cinema during World War II.* Lexington: UP of Kentucky, 2006. An interpretation that suggests a guiding, faith-inspiring role for war films.

Nornes, Abé Mark. *The Japan/America Film Wars: World War II Propaganda and Its Cultural Contexts.* Chur, Switzerland: Harwood Academic, 1994. A variety of themes and film types are discussed by scholars who describe significant creations within their respective cultures.

Roeder, George H., Jr. *The Censored War: American Visual Experience during World War Two.* New Haven, Conn.: Yale UP, 1993.

Shindler, Colin. *Hollywood Goes to War: Films and American Society, 1939–1952.* London: Routledge & K. Paul, 1979.

Strada, Michael J., and Harold Troper. *Friend or Foe? Russians in American Film and Foreign Policy, 1933–1991.* Lanham, Md.: Scarecrow, 1997.

Valleau, Marjorie A. *The Spanish Civil War in American and European Films.* Ann Arbor, Mich.: UMI Research P, 1982.

Wright, Basil. "Land without Bread and Spanish Earth." *The Documentary Tradition.* Ed. Lewis Jacobs. 2nd ed. New York: Norton, 1979. 146–48.

THE KOREAN WAR (1950–1953), THE COLD WAR (1945–1989), NUCLEAR WAR, AND SCIENCE FICTION

Contexts

Blair, Clay. *The Forgotten War: America in Korea, 1950–1953.* New York: Times Books, 1987.

Brands, H. W. *The Devil We Knew: Americans and the Cold War.* New York: Oxford UP, 1994.

Cold War Bibliography. Yale University. <http://www.library.yale.edu/rsc/history/ColdWar/>. Online links to resources.

Gaddis, John Lewis. *The Cold War: A New History.* New York: Penguin, 2006.

Hastings, Max. *The Korean War.* New York: Simon & Schuster, 1987.

May, Lary, ed. *Recasting America: Culture and Politics in the Age of Cold War.* Chicago: U of Chicago P, 1989.

Whitfield, Stephen J. *The Culture of the Cold War.* 2nd ed. Baltimore: Johns Hopkins UP, 1996.

Film Focus

Dixon, Wheeler W. *Visions of the Apocalypse: Spectacles of Destruction in American Cinema.* London: Wallflower, 2003.

Edwards, Paul M. *A Guide to Films on the Korean War.* Westport, Conn.: Greenwood, 1997. Includes a fifty-page interpretive essay and a filmography.

Evans, Joyce A. *Celluloid Mushroom Clouds: Hollywood and the Atomic Bomb.* Boulder, Colo.: Westview, 1998.

Hendershot, Cindy. *Paranoia, the Bomb, and 1950s Science Fiction Films.* Bowling Green, Ohio: Bowling Green State U Popular P, 1999.

Lipschutz, Ronnie D. *Cold War Fantasies: Film, Fiction, and Foreign Policy.* Lanham, Md.: Rowman & Littlefield, 2001.

Newman, Kim. *Apocalypse Movies: End of the World Cinema.* New York: St. Martin's Griffin, 2000.

Perrine, Toni. *Film and the Nuclear Age: Representing Cultural Anxiety.* New York: Garland, 1998.

Shaheen, Jack G., ed. *Nuclear War Films.* Carbondale: Southern Illinois UP, 1978.

Shapiro, Jerome F. *Atomic Bomb Cinema: The Apocalyptic Imagination on Film.* New York: Routledge, 2002. Essays on feature films, documentaries, and government short films.

Wittebols, James H. *Watching* M*A*S*H, *Watching America: A Social History of the 1972–1983 Television Series.* Jefferson, N.C.: McFarland, 2003.

Young, Charles S. "Missing Action: POW Films, Brainwashing and the Korean War, 1954–1968." *Historical Journal of Film, Radio and Television* 18 (Mar. 1998): 49–74.

THE INDOCHINA WARS (1945–1975)

Contexts

Clark, Gregory, ed. *Quotations of the Vietnam War.* Jefferson, N.C.: McFarland, 2001.

Fitzgerald, Frances. *Fire in the Lake: The Vietnamese and the Americans in Vietnam.* New York: Vintage, 1989.

Kahin, George McTurnan. *Intervention: How America Became Involved in Vietnam.* New York: Knopf, 1986.

Karnow, Stanley. *Vietnam: A History.* New York: Penguin, 1997.

Lewy, Guenter. *America in Vietnam.* New York: Oxford UP, 1978.

Summers, Harry. *Historical Atlas of the Vietnam War.* Boston: Houghton, 1995.

Young, Marilyn Blatt, and Robert Buzzanco, eds. *A Companion to the Vietnam Wars, 1945–1990.* Malden, Mass.: Blackwell, 2002.

Film Focus

Adair, Gilbert. *Vietnam on Film: From* The Green Berets *to* Apocalypse Now. New York: Proteus, 1981.

Anderegg, Michael, ed. *Inventing Vietnam: The War in Film and Television.* Philadelphia: Temple UP, 1991.

Auster, Albert, and Leonard Quart. *How the War Was Remembered: Hollywood and Vietnam.* New York: Praeger, 1988.

Braestrup, Peter. *Big Story: How the U.S. Press and Television Reported and Interpreted the Tet Crisis of 1968 in Vietnam and Washington.* Boulder, Colo.: Westview, 1977.

Dittmar, Linda, and Gene Michaud, eds. *From Hanoi to Hollywood: The Vietnam War in American Film.* New Brunswick, N.J.: Rutgers UP, 1990.

Gilman, Owen W., Jr., and Lorrie Smith. *America Rediscovered: Critical Essays on Literature and Film of the Vietnam War.* New York: Garland, 1990.

Hillstrom, Kevin, and Laurie Collier Hillstrom. *The Vietnam Experience: A Concise Encyclopedia of American Literature, Songs and Film.* Westport, Conn.: Greenwood, 1998. Includes short filmographic and interpretive entries on several dozen films and documentaries.

Jeffords, Susan. *Hard Bodies: Hollywood Masculinity in the Reagan Era.* New Brunswick, N.J.: Rutgers UP, 1994. Extensive treatment of the *Rambo* films.

———. *The Remasculinization of America: Gender and the Vietnam War.* Bloomington: Indiana UP, 1989.

McAskil, John. *Annotated Bibliography of Vietnam War Film Criticism.* Imaginative Representations of the Vietnam War Collection, La Salle University, Philadelphia. <http://www.lasalle.edu/library/vietnam/Bibliographies/home.htm>.

Muse, Eben J. *The Land of Nam: The Vietnam War in American Film.* Lanham, Md.: Scarecrow, 1995.

Smith, Julian. *Looking Away: Hollywood and Vietnam.* New York: Scribner's, 1975.

Taylor, Mark. *The Vietnam War in History, Literature, and Film.* Tuscaloosa: U of Alabama P, 2003. Includes case studies of *The Green Berets* (1968) and several other popular films.

POST 9/11, THE WARS IN IRAQ (1991 AND 2003–), AND THE U.S. WAR AGAINST TERRORISM (2001–)

Contexts

Coll, Steve. *Ghost Wars: The Secret History of the CIA, Afghanistan, and bin Laden, from the Soviet Invasion to September 10, 2001.* New York: Penguin, 2004.

Laquer, Walter. *No End to War: Terrorism in the Twenty-first Century.* New York: Continuum, 2004.

Lewis, Bernard. *The Crisis of Islam: Holy War and Unholy Terror.* New York: Random House, 2004.

Phillips, Kevin. *American Theocracy: The Peril and Politics of Radical Religion, Oil, and Borrowed Money in the 21st Century.* New York: Viking, 2006.

Film Focus

Dixon, Winston Wheeler. *Film and Television after 9/11.* Carbondale: U of Southern Illinois P, 2004.

Valantin, Jean-Michel. *Hollywood, the Pentagon and Washington: The Movies and National Security from World War II to the Present Day.* London: Anthem, 2005.

Weber, Cynthia. *Imagining America at War: Morality, Politics and Film.* London: Routledge, 2006.

CONTRIBUTORS

William S. Bushnell, a lieutenant commander in the U.S. Navy, is a master instructor and associate chair of the English Department at the U.S. Naval Academy, from which he also graduated. His fleet experience includes assignments on USS *McKee* (AS-41) and USS *Kitty Hawk* (CV-63). He previously taught at the Culver Academies, where he was awarded the Major General Delmar T. Spivey Award for excellence in teaching. He teaches and writes on topics in American literature, film studies, and the literature of war. He has published in *Film & History* and is currently working on an article on the film adaptations of Raymond Carver's short stories.

Raymond L. Carroll is professor emeritus at the College of Communication of the University of Alabama. He is senior author of *Electronic Media Programming: Strategies and Decision Making* (McGraw-Hill, 1983).

John Whiteclay Chambers II, distinguished professor of history and former chair of the History Department at Rutgers University in New Brunswick, New Jersey, teaches courses on war and peace in American history and on film and history. He has written or edited a dozen books, several of them prize-winning studies. They include *The Eagle and the Dove: The American Peace Movement and U.S. Foreign Policy, 1900–1922* (2nd ed., Syracuse, 1991); *The Tyranny of Change: America in the Progressive Era, 1890–1920* (2nd rev. ed., Rutgers, 2000); *To Raise an Army: The Draft Comes to Modern America* (Free Press, 1987); *The New Conscientious Objection* (Oxford, 1993); *World War II, Film, and History* (Oxford, 1996); *The Oxford Companion to American Military History* (Oxford, 1999); and *Conflict Resolution and United States History,* 2 vols. (New Jersey Center for Civic and Law-Related Education, 2007). He has received fellowships from the Rockefeller Foundation, the Institute for Advanced Study in Princeton, the University of Rome, and the University of Tokyo.

Jeffrey Chown is a presidential teaching professor in the Department of Communication at Northern Illinois University. He directs the MA program and teaches courses in film aesthetics, documentary theory and practice, and screenwriting. He is the author of *Hollywood Auteur: Francis Coppola* (Praeger, 1988) and has directed a number of documentary films, including *Barbed Wire Pioneers* (1998), *John Peter Altgeld* (2000), and *Lincoln and Black Hawk* (2005), which was screened on WTTW, the Chicago PBS affiliate. He is a recipient of the Illinois Humanities Council's Studs Terkel Humanitarian Service Award.

Gary R. Edgerton is professor and chair of the Department of Communication and Theatre Arts at Old Dominion University in Virginia. He has published eight books and more than seventy essays on a wide assortment of television, film, and culture topics. He received honorable mention (second place) for outstanding scholarly inquiry into American cultural studies for his *Ken Burns's America* (Palgrave, 2001) in the 2001 John G. Cawelti Book Award of the American Culture Association, and he won first place in the textbook category, along with Peter C. Rollins, in the 2001 Ray B. Browne National Book Award of the Popular Culture Association for *Television Histories: Shaping Collective Memory in the Media Age* (UP of Kentucky, 2001). His most recent books are *The Columbia History of American Television* (Columbia UP, 2007) and *The Essential HBO Reader* (UP of Kentucky, 2008), with Jeffrey P. Jones. He is also coeditor of the *Journal of Popular Film and Television*.

Robert Fyne is professor of English at Kean University in New Jersey, where he teaches courses on literature and film. He is active in several international cinema organizations and has presented papers at numerous conferences, with a special emphasis on World War II motion pictures. Some of his essays and reviews have been published in *Christian Century, Alaska Quarterly Review, Film Library Quarterly, Literature/Film Quarterly, France,* and the *Journal of Popular Film and Television*. He is the author of *The Hollywood Propaganda of World War II* (Scarecrow Press, 1994) and is the book review editor for *Film & History*.

Susan A. George, former instructor at the University of California–Berkeley, has taught a range of courses, including advanced classes in media theory, feminist theory, and composition. Focusing on gender construction in science fiction film and television, her work has appeared in the *Journal of Popular Film and Television, Post Script, Science Fiction Research Association Review,* and *Reconstruction: Studies in Contemporary Culture* and in several anthologies, including *Fantastic Odysseys* (Greenwood, 2003), *No Cure for the Future: Disease and Medicine in Science Fiction and Fantasy* (Greenwood, 2002), and *Space and Beyond: The Frontier Myth in Science Fiction* (Greenwood, 2000). She serves as the division head of film and media of the International Conference for the Fantastic in the Arts and was recently asked to join the editorial board of a new academic journal, *Science Fiction Film and Television,* from the University of Liverpool Press.

David Imhoof, associate professor and chair of history at Susquehanna University, Selinsgrove, Pennsylvania, teaches courses on modern German and European history, the Holocaust, and cultural history. He has published articles in *German History* and elsewhere on sharpshooting and sports in Germany between the world wars and is completing a book on culture and political change in the German town of Göttingen during the Weimar Republic and the Third Reich. His next project will be a study of popular music in twentieth-century Germany. He has received fellowships from the German Academic Exchange Service (DAAD), the University of Texas, and Susquehanna University and was twice a fellow at the Max Planck Institute for History in Göttingen.

Michael T. Isenberg, who died in 1994, was an associate professor of history at the U.S. Naval Academy. His publications include *War on Film: The American Cinema of World War I, 1914–1918* (Fairleigh Dickinson UP, 1981); *Puzzles of the Past: An Introduction to Thinking About History* (Texas A&M P, 1985); and *John L. Sullivan and His America* (U of Illinois P, 1988).

James Kendrick is an assistant professor in the Film and Digital Media Division of the Department of Communication Studies at Baylor University, where he teaches classes on film theory and aesthetics, the history of motion pictures, the history of radio and television, and media and society. He has published several book chapters, as well as articles and reviews in such publications as *Velvet Light Trap, Journal of Film and Video, Journal of Popular Film and Television, Film-Philosophy, Kinoeye,* and *Moving Image.* He is also the film and DVD critic for the Web site Qnetwork.com. He is currently working on two books about film violence.

James Latham teaches on contemporary Hollywood and directing for the Semester in Los Angeles Program of the University of Texas at Austin. He also performs research for media and technology companies. Previously, he taught at the University of Arizona and the University of California–Irvine and lectured at the Museum of Modern Art on topics such as film, photography, and graphic art. He has published articles in journals such as *Velvet Light Trap* and *Post Script* and in the books *American Movie Audiences: From the Turn of the Century to the Early Sound Era* (BFI, 1999), *The Cinema, A New Technology for the 20th Century* (Payot, 2004), and *Demnächst in diesem Kino: Grundlagen der Filmwerbung* (Schüren, 2005).

John Shelton Lawrence is professor of philosophy, emeritus, at Morningside College. With Robert Jewett he coauthored *Captain America and the Crusade against Evil* (Eerdmans, 2003) and *The Myth of the American Superhero* (Eerdmans, 2002); the latter received the John Cawelti Award of the American Culture Association as best book of 2002. He provided essays and filmographies for *Hollywood's White House* (UP of Kentucky, 2003), *Hollywood's West* (UP of Kentucky, 2005), and *The Landscape of Hollywood Westerns* (U of Utah P, 2006), as well as this book. An essay on film propaganda coauthored with Marty Knepper appeared in *Representing the Rural* (Wayne State UP, 2006). With Matthew Kapell he coedited *Finding the Force of the Star Wars Franchise: Fans, Merchandise, and Critics* (Peter Lang, 2006). He frequently reviews books for the *Journal of American Culture*.

Lawrence W. Lichty is a professor in the Department of Radio/Television/Film at Northwestern University in Evanston, Illinois. He teaches courses on the history of mass communications, the history of documentary, television-cable programming, media and politics, and documentary production. He was the director of media research for *Vietnam: A Television History,* a thirteen-hour PBS series (1983). He has also been a consultant, historical adviser, or researcher for documentaries on PBS, CBS, A&E, and MSNBC. He is a coauthor of *Ratings Analysis: The Theory and Practice of Audience Research* (3rd ed., Erlbaum, 2006).

Thomas W. Maulucci Jr. is assistant professor of history and international studies at American International College, where he also directs the college's Honors Program. He has written articles about West German foreign policy and Germany's role in the Cold War. He is also the coeditor with Detlef Junker of *GIs in Germany: The History of the American Military Presence,* a forthcoming volume in the German Historical Institute, Washington, D.C., series (Cambridge UP).

John G. McGarrahan has been a member of the New York Bar for more than forty years. He is retired from active practice and now lives in Berkeley, California. His lifelong interest in the military began with a tour of duty in the army as a young man. His particular interest in the movies is the discovery of differences between the Hollywood version of an event and the version that would emerge in a courtroom—where the moviemaker's dramatic license would not be valid. He brings to his viewing of cinema a lawyer's habit of skepticism and thoroughness.

Cynthia J. Miller is a cultural anthropologist specializing in popular culture and urban studies. She is currently scholar-in-residence in the Institute for Liberal Arts and Interdisciplinary Studies at Emerson College in Boston and is a former fellow of the Boston Historical Society. Her writing and photography have appeared in *Film & History, Women's Studies Quarterly, Human Organization, Social Justice, Journal of Popular Film and Television, Contexts: Understanding People in Their Social Worlds, Kansas Quarterly,* and several volumes produced by the International Library of Photography. She was also a contributor to *Hollywood's West: The American Frontier in Film, Television, and History* (UP Kentucky, 2005), *Echoes from the Poisoned Well: Global Memories of Environmental Injustice* (Rowman & Littlefield, 2006), *Heroes and Homefronts* (McFarland, 2008), and *Indian Diaspora: Retrospect and Prospect* (Sage, 2008). She is currently at work on an edited volume, *Too Bold for the Box Office: A Study in Mockumentary* (Wayne State UP), and *The Encyclopedia of B Westerns* (Scarecrow Press).

Robert M. Myers is professor of English at Lock Haven University of Pennsylvania, where he chairs the English Department and teaches courses on American literature. He is the author of *Reluctant Expatriate: The Life of Harold Frederic* (Greenwood, 1995) and has written articles and delivered conference papers on late-nineteenth-century literature. Currently he is working on a book-length study of representations of the Civil War in literature, film, and public monuments.

Martin A. Novelli is dean of humanities, fine arts, and media studies at Ocean County College in Toms River, New Jersey. His teaching interests are the Western film, hard-boiled detective fiction and film, and the literature and films of the Vietnam War.

John E. O'Connor, professor emeritus of history at the New Jersey Institute of Technology, began his career as a historian of the American Revolution and biographer of William Paterson. In 1970, he co-founded, and for twenty years served as editor of the journal *Film & History,* and he is the author or editor of numerous books that relate film and television studies to history. The fullest expression of his methodology can be found in his *Image as Artifact: The Historical Analysis of Film and Television* (Krieger, 1990; updated 2007) and the related two-hour *Image as Artifact Video Compilation* produced by the American Historical Association under a grant from the National Endowment for the Humanities. He has also been honored by the establishment of the American Historical Association's annual John E. O'Connor Award for the best film or television production about history. During the 1960s and 1970s, he and his pacifist wife protested America's involvement in Vietnam. He can be reached at oconnor@njit.edu.

Peter C. Rollins, Regents Professor Emeritus at Oklahoma State University, taught courses in English, film, and popular culture until 2007. He has written numerous articles on the Vietnam War and American culture. He is an award-winning filmmaker and coeditor or editor of *Hollywood's West: The American Frontier in Film, Television, and History* (UP of Kentucky, 2005), *The Columbia Companion to American History on Film* (Columbia UP, 2003), *Hollywood's Indian: The Portrayal of the Native American in Film* (2nd ed., UP of Kentucky, 2003), *Television Histories: Shaping Collective Memory in the Media Age* (UP of Kentucky, 2001), *Hollywood as Historian: American Film in a Cultural Context* (2nd ed., UP of Kentucky, 1989), and *Hollywood's White House: The American Presidency in Film and History* (UP of Kentucky, 2003), two of which were awarded national prizes. He also wrote *Will Rogers: A Bio-Bibliography* (Greenwood, 1982), which was a finalist in a national award competition. He has made several documentaries for television that have appeared on PBS, the Discovery Channel, and WTBS. From 1994 to 2007, he was editor in chief of *Film & History: An Interdisciplinary Journal of Film and Television Studies.* Annually, two popular culture book awards and one national film award are given in his name. During the Vietnam conflict, Rollins served as a Marine infantry platoon commander. He can be reached at RollinsPC@aol.com.

Ian S. Scott is a lecturer in American studies at the University of Manchester in the United Kingdom and is a board member of the Executive Committee of the British Association for American Studies. His most recent books are *In Capra's Shadow: The Life and Career of Robert Riskin* (UP of Kentucky, 2006) and *American Politics in Hollywood Film* (Edinburgh UP, 2000). He has also published articles in numerous journals, including *Film Historia* and the *Journal of American Studies*. His next book, on British filmmakers in the United States, is tentatively titled *From Pinewood to Hollywood*. He is currently writing about the United Nations and Hollywood and is compiling a cinematic comparison of the work of Frank Capra and Leni Riefenstahl.

J. E. Smyth teaches in the Comparative American Studies and History departments at the University of Warwick in the United Kingdom. She is a specialist in classical Hollywood's historical genre. Her articles and reviews have appeared in *Rethinking History, Film Quarterly, European Journal of Native American Studies,* and *Historical Journal of Film, Radio, and Television*. She is the author of *Reconstructing American Historical Cinema from* Cimarron *to* Citizen Kane (UP of Kentucky, 2006).

Stacy Takacs, assistant professor of American studies, teaches courses in American popular culture and media studies at Oklahoma State University. She writes about the intersections of popular and political cultures in the contemporary United States and has published essays on the televisual mediation of topics such as the drug war, immigration, the "new economy," and the war on terrorism in *Cultural Critique, Spectator: Journal of Film and Television Criticism,* and *Cultural Studies*. She also has an article on sit-com representations of the Bush presidency forthcoming in the *Journal of Popular Culture*. She is currently at work on a book-length manuscript tentatively titled *Terror TV,* about the mediation of the war on terrorism in U.S. entertainment programming.

Frank Thompson is an author, film historian, and comedy writer. He has worked in television for more than fifteen years on shows such as *Blind Date* and *The Bachelor.* For a decade he wrote introductions for American Movie Classics hosts, and he has written speeches on the subject of film preservation for Martin Scorsese, Sharon Stone, and Lauren Bacall, among others. Thompson also wrote and directed an AMC special, *The Great Christmas Movies* (1998), and wrote the companion book of the same name (Taylor, 1998). Thompson is the author of nearly forty books, including *William A. Wellman* (Scarecrow, 1983), Tim Burton's Nightmare Before Christmas*: The Film, the Art, the Vision* (Hyperion, 1993), *Robert Wise: A Bio-Bibliography* (Greenwood,

1995), *Lost Films* (Citadel, 1996), *King Arthur* (Hyperion, 2005), and Lost: *Signs of Life* (Hyperion, 2006), an original novel based on ABC's hit series. He has written and produced extensively on the subject of the Alamo.

Robert Brent Toplin is professor of history at the University of North Carolina at Wilmington and has taught courses in recent U.S. history and film and history. He served from 1986 to 2007 as editor of film reviews for the *Journal of American History* and was media editor for *Perspectives,* the newsletter of the American Historical Association. Toplin's books include *History by Hollywood: The Use and Abuse of the American Past* (U of Illinois P, 1996), *Oliver Stone's USA: Film, History, and Controversy* (UP of Kansas, 2000), *Reel History: In Defense of Hollywood* (UP of Kansas, 2002), *Michael Moore's* Fahrenheit 9/11: *How One Film Divided the Nation* (UP of Kansas, 2006), and *Radical Conservatism: The Right's Political Religion* (UP of Kansas, 2006). Toplin has also commented on film for the *New York Times,* the *Washington Post,* and other publications and has spoken frequently about film on National Public Radio and in nationally broadcast television programs on CBS, PBS, the History Channel, and the Turner Classic Movies Channel.

Frank J. Wetta is vice president of academic affairs at Ocean County College, Toms River, New Jersey. He is active in the Society for Military History, having served as chair of the book prize committee and on the society's editorial advisory board. He also chaired the membership committee of the Southern Historical Association. He is the coauthor with Stephen J. Curley of *Celluloid Wars: A Guide to Film and the American Experience of War* (Greenwood, 1992). His other publications include articles coauthored with Martin A. Novelli on the John Ford "Cavalry Trilogy" in *American Nineteenth Century History* and the theme of patriotism in recent American war movies for the *Journal of Military History.* He has also contributed to *Civil War History* and *Southern Studies: An Interdisciplinary Journal of the South.*

James Yates, professor of English and chair of the Department of English, Foreign Language, and Humanities at Northwestern Oklahoma State University, teaches courses in film, composition, and mythology. A member of the faculty since 1990, he has served as Faculty Senate president on several occasions. His published articles include "The Mexican War and the Spanish-American War" in *The Columbia Companion to American History on Film* (Columbia UP, 2003); "William S. Parry, Francis McClintock, and Umberto

Nobile" in *The Encyclopedia of the Arctic* (Routledge, 2005); and "*King Lear* and *Shadowlands*" in *The Encyclopedia of Stage Plays into Film* (Facts on File, 2001). He has also made numerous scholarly presentations on film and history, documentary, film adaptation, David Cronenberg, and Herman Melville. In 2001 he was awarded the John Sheffield Teaching Award, the highest faculty honor at Northwestern OSU.

INDEX

Illustrations are indicated by italicized page numbers. Designations of war film genres are keyed to those used in the filmography.

About the Editors

During the last decade Peter C. Rollins and John E. O'Connor have developed a productive collaboration resulting in six co-edited books, including *Hollywood's World War I: Motion Picture Images* (Popular Press, 1997) and *The West Wing: The American Presidency as Television Drama* (Syracuse UP, 2003). Four of their joint efforts have been published by the University Press of Kentucky: *Hollywood's Indian: The Portrayal of the Native American in Film* (1998), *Hollywood's White House: The American Presidency in Film and History* (2003), *Hollywood's West: The American Frontier in Film, Television, and History* (2005), and *Why We Fought*, the volume at hand.